Anatomy of the
New Testament

A Guide to
Its Structure and Meaning

Robert A. Spivey
THE FLORIDA STATE UNIVERSITY

D. Moody Smith, Jr.
THE DIVINITY SCHOOL, DUKE UNIVERSITY

Anatomy

of the

New

Testament

The Macmillan Company • Collier-Macmillan Limited, London

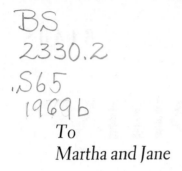

To

Martha and Jane

Preface: The Nature and Purpose of This Book

The problems of writing an introductory book for the study of the New Testament are far greater than the authors imagined when they set their hands to the task several years ago. One can never know too much to write a beginning book. In fact, only the master can confidently stake out the field and make the generalizations that such a book requires. Yet the very immersion in the scholarly disciplines which can produce such mastery tends to reduce radically awareness of what the student or layman knows, or does not know, and the kinds of questions that really interest him. The dilemma is obvious. But must one settle on a choice between a responsible book that does not communicate or an irresponsible one that does? We at least hope not.

Whether we have written a responsible book our colleagues will have to judge. Likewise, our intended readers will know whether we have produced a helpful book. We can only attest that we have tried to produce a book that does not simply repeat what others have done. For the most part introductory books on the Bible approach it from the standpoint of the perspectives, questions, and results of modern Biblical criticism. To a greater or less degree they tend to follow the model of the classical or technical introduction. We have broken radically with that model.

On the assumption that the reader will want to know what the New Testament is about, what its authors intended to say, we have sought to direct his attention to the text of the New Testament itself. In order to help him come to a more than superficial or second-hand understanding, we have dealt extensively with representative texts from the various New Testament books. Working outward from these texts, we have then endeavored to display and illumine the character and movement of the different writings. What has resulted is certainly no comprehensive or even coverage of the New Testament, but a series of dissections or biopsies designed to uncover the nature and structure of the New Testament books and of the collection as a whole. Thus our title, *Anatomy of the New Testament.*

All along the authors have felt the persistent tugging of their scholarly consciences, reminding them of literary and historical questions that they have treated inadequately or not at all. Particularly, standard questions of introduction (authorship, date and place of composition, and so forth) have been dealt with in summary fashion. Sometimes these questions are not crucial; often they are insoluble. In the introductory notes at the beginnings of chapters or at other appropriate places the reader's attention is directed to the existence of such questions. Where there is a consensus on a certain problem, it is stated. Where there is not, the authors briefly give their position and reasons for holding it. In any event, such questions are of little concern to the reader until he has some knowledge of, and involvement in, the content of the New Testament itself. Thus, the sooner he can get to the text the better. He can always return to questions of introduction after he has become aware of their importance for the understanding of the text. Then he will be ready to consult more advanced works on the subject.

It may seem that we stress content too much, even to the extent of belaboring some points about the text which to the professional reader are obvious. Conversely, we may at other points take positions that have been, or are, widely controverted. On such occasions the reader is duly warned that this is the case. Both procedures are at least defensible, if not unexceptionable. In the former case, we think it is scarcely possible to overstress what is in the New Testament or to assume too little advance knowledge on the part of the typical reader. The day when the principal problem of the modern Biblical interpreter was fighting off literalists and fundamentalists is long past. In the case of disputed points, we recognize the danger of leading the novice astray, but we also discern an equal or even greater danger—to leave him with the impression that since the experts disagree, no understanding or interpretation is possible for him. Obviously, there are a number of important difficulties in the interpretation of the New Testament which can not be settled with anything short of a full-scale scholarly monograph. If we seem to the scholarly reader to be short-circuiting them, we are at least aware of what we are doing and why. The scholarly monographs will have to come later. But alas, when and if they should appear, they will not satisfy every reader or produce the ever hoped for, but ultimately unattainable, unanimity of scholarly opinion.

We have written on the assumption that an understanding of a New Testament text can be gained from an analysis of that text and from the larger writing of which it is a part. By this procedure we do not wish to imply that the religious and cultural background is unimportant. Nevertheless, we believe that where such considerations are not indispensable to the understanding of the text, their large-scale introduction will tend to obscure rather than to illuminate the meaning for the uninitiated reader. The same goes for the closely related matter of the meaning of the original Greek. Wherever possible we have simply begun from the text of the Revised Standard Version and sought to explain it without recourse to questions of translation. Although such a course may lead to an imperfect understanding of the New Testament, we believe it can lead to an understanding that will serve the reader well as a beginning point for further study.

The authors thus betray their own belief that the subject matter of the New Testament does not lie beyond the grasp of the lay reader. This implies a certain hermeneutic, which could be stated in terms of literary criticism, but might also be stated in theological terms. It probably also involves certain basal convictions about God and man. We do not, however, ask the reader to share these convictions, only to test the book to see whether it works.

Very likely most authors of books such as this one have some idea of how their works may best be used. We are no exception. After familiarizing himself with the important issues concerning the origin of the book in question by reading the introductory notes, the reader should then look at the brief outline of the entire Biblical document in order to gain some prior conception of what it is about. Then let him read the New Testament book in its entirety, preferably at one sitting. Only now is he adequately prepared to dig into the representative texts with which the book mainly deals. In doing this he will hopefully find the appropriate section of the book a guide and a help in understanding. These interpretative sections, which constitute the greater part of the book, will make little sense unless they are read with the New Testament in hand. That is the intention of the authors.

We wish to acknowledge the source *New Testament Illustrations: The Cambridge Bible Commentary of the New English Bible,* edited by Clifford M. Jones (New York: Cambridge University Press, 1966), for the adaption of the following figures: Time Chart of the New Testament, Diagram of the Synoptic Problem, Map of Galilee, Diagram of the Temple, and Diagram of Jerusalem. Adaption of the end map of the Mediterranean world is courtesy of *The Good News: The New Testament with over 500 Illustrations and Maps* (New York: American Bible Society, 1953). Adaption of the end map of Palestine is courtesy of *The Westminster Historical Atlas to the Bible* (revised), edited by George Ernest Wright and Floyd Vivian Filson. (Copyright, 1945, by the Westminster Press; 1956, by W. L. Jenkins. Adapted by permission.)

We wish to express indebtedness to teachers, colleagues, and students for their stimulation and encouragement in the present undertaking. Above all, we would like to name the three professors under whom we studied together at Yale—Paul Meyer, Paul Minear, and Paul Schubert. We are grateful to Professors Edwin Good of Stanford University and John Bullard of Wofford College, who read much of the manuscript at an earlier stage of its development and offered specific, helpful, and occasionally trenchant, criticism. Naturally, they are not responsible for any of the book's shortcomings.

We also wish to thank Charles E. Smith of Macmillan, editor in the College and Professional Division, and his predecessor, John D. Moore, for their untiring interest in this project. The administrations of The Florida State University and of The Divinity School of Duke University have been generous in furnishing secretarial assistance and other help, for which the authors are grateful.

Our children—Hope, Lee, and Paul; Cynthia, Catherine, David and Allen—have responded with good grace to the stringencies imposed by their fathers' aspirations. Our wives have tolerated our preoccupation with this project over a long period of time. The dedication of the book attests our gratitude for devotion above and beyond the call of duty.

R. A. S.
D. M. S.

Contents

Part II: The Early Church and Paul

List of Maps and Charts

List of Illustrations

TIME-CHART OF THE NEW TESTAMENT*

Significant Pre-New Testament Dates
336-323 B.C.   Conquest and Rule of Alexander the Great
167-164 B.C.   The Maccabean Revolt
63 B.C.   Roman Rule of Palestine Begins

Date	Events	Herods	Governors of Judaea	Roman Emperors	New Testament Writings
10 BC / AD	Birth of Jesus	Herod the Great (37-4 BC)		Augustus (27 BC-AD 14)	
		Archelaus (4 BC-AD 6)			
10		Philip the Tetrarch (4 BC-AD 34)	Coponius (6-9) / Marcus Ambivius (9-12) / Annius Rufus (12-15)		
20		Herod Antipas (4 BC-AD 39)	Valerius Gratus (15-26)	Tiberius (14-37)	
30	Ministry of John the Baptist / Ministry of Jesus / (Crucifixion and Resurrection / Paul's Conversion		Pontius Pilate (26-36)		
40		Herod Agrippa I (37-44)	Marcellus (36-37) / Marullus (37-41)	Caligula (37-41)	
50	Paul's first journey / Council of Jerusalem / Paul's second journey	Herod Agrippa II (50-53)	Cuspius Fadus (44-46) / Tiberius Alexander (46-48) / Cumanus (48-52)	Claudius (41-54)	1&2 Thessalonians
	Paul's third journey		Felix (52-60)		1&2 Corinthians / Galatians / Romans
60	Paul's arrest / Paul's voyage to Rome / Paul's martyrdom		Festus (60-62) / Albinus (62-64) / Gessius Florus (64-66)	Nero (54-68)	Philippians / Colossians / Philemon
70	Destruction of Jerusalem			Galba (68-69) / Otho (69) / Vitellius (69)	Mark
				Vespasian (69-79)	
80				Titus (79-81)	Matthew
90	Council of Jamnia			Domitian (81-96)	Luke / Acts / Revelation
100	(Fall of Jerusalem AD 135)			Nerva (96) / Trajan (98-117)	John

*Chronology is only approximate, especially in regard to dating the books of the New Testament. The dates of the other twelve New Testament books are so uncertain that it is impossible to include them in the time chart.

Introduction

This scene from the Arch of Titus in the Roman Forum celebrates
Titus' capture of Jerusalem in A.D. 70. The victorious Romans bear
triumphantly the sacred objects of the Jerusalem temple, including
the seven-branched lampstand symbolizing the presence of God.
(Courtesy of Jewish Museum.)

1 The Background of the New Testament

The New Testament is the collection of twenty-seven various early Christian writings which for nearly two thousand years has been the distinctive holy scripture of Christianity. With the Old Testament, the

Bible of Judaism, it forms the Christian Bible. Although the New Testament is thus comparable to the Old, there are significant differences. The Old Testament is more than three times the length of the New and was written down over a period of nearly a thousand years, whereas the New Testament was written and composed in a mere fraction of that time.

The New Testament consists of several basic types of writings, usually called books. The four Gospels stand at the beginning and are the best known and probably the most important. They are followed by the Acts of the Apostles, a history of the earliest church; the twenty-one writings usually referred to as epistles; and, finally, Revelation, a book of apocalyptic visions. The twenty-one books styled epistles or letters are themselves of different types. The majority are real letters (for example, the Corinthian letters of Paul and II and III John). Yet quite possibly several are not; at least they may not have been originally composed as letters (for example, Hebrews, James, I Peter, and I John). They have characteristics more appropriate to treatises, sermons, or tracts.

The story of how and why these books were written and at length gathered into the collection we now call the New Testament is a long and complicated one. This book cannot deal at length or in detail with that story but is concerned instead with the meaning of the various New Testament writings. Nevertheless, the interpretation of these documents is not independent of the story of their origin.

The New Testament originated within a particular cultural and historical background. Although it may be possible to understand the New Testament apart from this background, the reader ignores it at the risk of serious misunderstanding. The fact that the New Testament conveys a message to persons who know little or nothing of its background may only mean that clearer understanding will result from better knowledge. Moreover, most people who read the New Testament sympathetically read it as members of the Christian church. As we shall see, the church is perhaps the most important background for understanding the New Testament, for the individual New Testament books were written within and for the earliest church. Moreover, these books, and only these books, were selected, collected, and cherished as holy scripture by the church of the first two Christian centuries. Thus no Christian can read the New Testament without some contact, however remote, with its origin or source. The church tradition in which a person stands may sometimes mislead him as to the meaning of the New Testament writings, yet the church in the broadest sense provides a context in which understanding may begin.

This chapter focuses upon the three principal areas of New Testament background: Palestinian Judaism, the broader Greco-Roman world, and early Christianity. Christianity began with Jesus and his disciples as a movement within Palestinian Judaism, but with his death it quickly spread across the Roman Empire and became a predominantly Gentile religion. In this chapter we shall first survey the history and especially the religious life of Palestinian Judaism in order to understand Jesus in context. Then we shall sketch the religious and political situation of the Greco-Roman world in order to place early Christianity in it. Finally, we shall look more closely at the problems and needs of the developing church so as to answer the question of why the New Testament was composed at all.

The Background in Judaism

Jesus was a Jew. So were his disciples. In fact, the earliest Christians did not think of themselves as members of a new religion separate from Judaism. Yet from the beginning Jesus and his disciples represented something new. It is often said that Christianity began as a revolutionary movement. Such a statement is scarcely correct if it means that Christianity set the style for national, Communist, or racial revolution. But since Christianity proclaimed and embodied a new order of things, in a sense it was and is revolutionary.

No revolutionary movement can be understood apart from its historical background. The primary background of Jesus, early Christianity, and the New Testament is first-century Judaism. Judaism is, of course, one of the world's major religions, as it was in the first Christian century. A remarkable continuity or similarity exists between the Judaism of today and that of the first century, despite the changes that the centuries have wrought. This continuity in itself is a clue to the character of that ancient faith. Both Judaism and Christianity are historical religions. This means more than that they have histories or even a common history. They share a faith in a God who deals with men, individually and collectively, in such a way that his will can be discerned in history. Crucial to both religions is the idea that God *reveals Himself* in history. The holy scriptures of both religions are largely accounts of the past: legends, sagas, and historical narratives. Broadly speaking, they are records of God's historical revelations. The Old Testament is a vast collection of legal, cultic, devotional, and narrative material set in a historical framework. It is the literary product of nearly a thousand years of Israel's history. Although the New Testament is much briefer and covers a much shorter period of time, it too tells of men and events in the conviction that God has wrought wondrous deeds in history that are of utmost importance for the future of humanity. Consciously and deliberately the New Testament writers take up the story of the Old Testament and bring it to a climax.[1] Christianity's origin within Judaism in large measure determined its shape and fundamentally influenced the narrative form that is so important in the New Testament.

Judaism was a religion of revelation, history, and a book. As such, it was a religion steeped in tradition, but this tradition was not an end in itself. Rather it was a means by which Israel identified and understood itself as a distinct and chosen people, the people of the Lord. Moreover, much of the literature of the Old Testament and the oral and written traditions that developed from it were understood as divine directions intended to regulate Israel's response to the Lord's goodness. The most influential law code the western world has known, the Ten Commandments, begins: "I am the Lord your God, who brought you out of the land of Egypt, out of the house of bondage. You shall have no other gods before me." (Exodus 20:2–3.) The statement of what God has done leads to the statement of what the people ought to do in response, forming the basic structure of Old Testament law. The principal preoccupation of the majority of the Jewish leaders in the time of Jesus was the interpretation and fulfillment of that law.

Revelation and history, tradition and law, although immensely important, were not the whole of Judaism. A part of obedience to the law was, in fact, the performance of worship worthy of God. The center of this worship was the temple in Jerusalem, and the heart of the temple was the sacrificial altar and priesthood. Upon the altar the priests offered sacrifice to God, and thus provided a means of mediation or communication. Until its destruction by the Romans in A.D. 70 the temple served as the important focal point of Jewish religious life. Yet Jewish worship was not confined to the temple even in the time of Jesus. There was, of course, private devotion, but beyond this the service of the individual congregation or synagogue was the occasion of a nonsacrificial corporate and public worship. Possibly this form of worship bore a greater resemblance to Protestant Christian worship —certainly to modern synagogue worship—than to the sacrificial worship of ancient Israel at the Jerusalem temple. For most Jews even in Palestine the synagogue was the practical center of worship, whereas the observance

---

[1] The Old Testament had not actually been officially defined in the time of Jesus and earliest Christianity. Yet Jesus himself speaks of "the law and the prophets" (Matt. 5:17) and quotes from the Psalms (Mark 15:34; cf. Psalm 22:1) according to the New Testament. Thus he seems to have known the threefold division of sacred scripture—law, prophets, and writings—that is reflected generally in the New Testament. According to tradition, the Hebrew Old Testament canon was fixed by the rabbis at the Council of Jamnia in about A.D. 90. By and large the Council ratified the then current usage. The limits they set have been followed by most Protestant churches. Catholic churches, following the usage of ancient Greek-speaking Jews and Christians, include the so-called Apocrypha in their Bible. It was a part of the Greek Old Testament, which is the basis for about 80 per cent of the Old Testament quotations in the New.

of the law was the chief means of giving expression to their identity and distinctiveness as Jews.

Another factor played a large role in first century Judaism, namely, the land. The small piece of territory at the eastern end of the Mediterranean Sea, which is variously called the Holy Land, Palestine, or Israel, has been the cause of both hope and frustration for the Jews for over three thousand years. At least from days of the Davidic monarchy the land was regarded as the promise and gift of God to his people. The promise was projected back into the days of the patriarchs Abraham, Isaac, and Jacob, who dwelt in and around the land but did not possess it. Yet Israel believed that God had promised the land to them, and in this faith they occupied and defended it. Israel could never rest easy in the land, however, for, subject to frequent threat and attack, she was only secure when the surrounding more powerful nations were momentarily weak or looking in other directions. In the late eighth century B.C. the territories of all the Israelite tribes save Judah were overrun by the Assyrians, and less than a century and a half later the Babylonians invaded Judea, laid siege to Jerusalem, and overthrew it. The Davidic kingship came to an end, and many of the people were deported into Babylonian captivity. The subsequent history of the land has been a troubled one. For the moment it is sufficient to observe that the modern state of Israel represents the first instance of Jewish control of the land since shortly before the time of Christ, when there was a century of independence under the so-called Maccabean dynasty. Otherwise, since the Babylonian exile the land of Israel has been occupied and ruled by other powers—Persians, Greeks, Romans, Christians, and Moslems. The question of the possession and rulership of the land was quite important in Jesus' day, when the land was occupied by the Romans and ruled by puppet kings and imperial procurators.

A TRAGIC HISTORY

From the Babylonian conquest of Judea in 587 B.C. to the time of Jesus' death the Jews lived under foreign domination, relieved only by a century or so of relative independence under the Hasmonean dynasty just prior to the advent of the Romans in 63 B.C.[2] In the Babylonian conquest numbers of Jews were taken east by their captors to Mesopotamia. Others fled south

---

[2] The concerns of postexilic Israel are reflected in the later Old Testament books and treated directly in Ezra and Nehemiah. The Maccabean period is dealt with in I and II Maccabees. The *Jewish Antiquities,* a continuous history of the Jews to the Roman War by the first century Jewish historian Josephus, is doubtless the most valuable single non-Biblical source. The Greek text and translation are available in The Loeb Classical Library in nine volumes, edited by Ralph Marcus and Allen Wikgren (Cambridge: Harvard University Press, 1926–63).

to Egypt, and the so-called diaspora or dispersion of the Jews began. From this time an increasing number of Jews were to be found living outside their Palestinian homeland.

Shortly after the middle of the sixth century B.C. Babylonian overlordship was replaced by Persian. Jews were allowed to return to their homeland and to begin the restoration of the Jerusalem temple, which had been destroyed by the Babylonians. Although we have an incomplete picture of Jewish life under Persian rule, conditions were certainly much improved. More than two centuries of Persian domination came to an end late in the fourth century before Christ, when Alexander of Macedon and his armies moved east, sweeping everything before them. Alexander overran the Jewish homeland, and over the years he and his successors attempted to introduce Greek culture and customs there, as was their practice in all conquered territories. Alexander was as much a missionary of Greek culture as a conquering general. After his death in 323 B.C. his empire broke up as quickly as it had been formed. But although his successors could not preserve political unity, they were able to continue the process of Hellenization, that is, the spreading of Greek culture.

After the division of Alexander's empire, the Jews found themselves situated between two rival centers of power—the Seleucids, who controlled Mesopotamia and Syria, and the Ptolemies, who ruled Egypt. The geographical setting of Israel as a buffer zone between the two great powers of the Fertile Crescent made the struggle over Palestine inevitable. By and large during the third century, Jewish Palestine was controlled by the Ptolemies with a minimum of interferences in Jewish internal affairs. A similar policy characterized the Seleucids' rule of Palestine after they defeated the Ptolemies in 198 B.C. Following a period of changing rulers, however, Antiochus IV (called Epiphanes because he proclaimed himself to be "God manifest") ascended to the Syrian throne in 175 B.C., and the previous toleration disappeared under a forcible attempt to Hellenize the Jewish people. Heathen altars were erected in the cities of Palestine and even in the temple at Jerusalem. Resistance meant death. A story of the time, perhaps apocryphal, but nevertheless typical, tells of hundreds of loyal Jews hurling themselves to death before a cart bearing a pagan statue of Zeus on the way from the coast to the Jerusalem temple.

In 167 B.C., martyrdom became revolution under the leadership of Mattathias, a village priest, and his five sons. The book of I Maccabees describes the outbreak of open revolt as follows:

> Then the king's officers who were enforcing the apostasy came to the city of Modein to make them offer sacrifice. Many from Israel came to them; and Mattathias and his sons were assembled. Then the king's officers spoke to Mattathias as follows: "You are a leader, honored and great in this city, and supported by sons and brothers. Now be the

first to come and do what the king commands, as all the Gentiles and the men of Judah and those that are left in Jerusalem have done. Then you and your sons will be numbered among the friends of the king, and you and your sons will be honored with silver and gold and many gifts."

But Mattathias answered and said in a loud voice: "Even if all the nations that live under the rule of the king obey him, and have chosen to do his commandments, departing each one from the religion of his fathers, yet I and my sons and my brothers will live by the covenant of our fathers. Far be it from us to desert the law and the ordinances. We will not obey the king's words by turning aside from our religion to the right hand or to the left."

*Antiochus IV (*Epiphanes*—"[God] Manifest") on a Greek coin. The reverse side shows Apollo and bears the words: Basileōs Antiochou— "(coinage) of King Antiochus." (Courtesy of American Numismatic Society.)*

When he had finished speaking these words, a Jew came forward in the sight of all to offer sacrifice upon the altar in Modein, according to the king's command. When Mattathias saw it, he burned with zeal and his heart was stirred. He gave vent to righteous anger; he ran and killed him upon the altar. At the same time he killed the king's officer who was forcing them to sacrifice, and he tore down the altar. Thus he burned with zeal for the law, as Phinehas did against Zimri the son of Salu.

Then Mattathias cried out in the city with a loud voice, saying: "Let every one who is zealous for the law and supports the covenant come out with me!" And he and his sons fled to the hills and left all that they had in the city. (I Maccabees 2:15–28)

One of his sons, Judas, earned the nickname Maccabeus (Hammerer), and this name was applied to the finally successful Maccabean Revolt. Major victories were soon forthcoming. In 165 Judas Maccabeus and his men seized the temple and reclaimed it for Judaism. This victory has ever since been celebrated in the feast of Hannukah (rededication). But it was not until 142 B.C. that the last remnants of the Syrian Hellenizers were driven from Jerusalem.

Although the Maccabean or Hasmonean dynasty was generally welcomed as a blessed relief and the fulfillment of long frustrated expectations, its promise far outstripped its actuality. The propensity of the later Hasmoneans to style themselves kings and high priests, as well as the internecine struggle among them, led to disillusionment. When the Romans arrived on the scene, their general, Pompey, successfully played one Hasmonean claimant against the other. Although some Jews offered fierce resistance, particularly at the temple, the Roman occupation of Palestine and the Holy City could scarcely have been regarded as a disaster by most Jews. For while Roman domination may have been inevitable, the conduct of the later Hasmoneans made it seem initially less distasteful than it might otherwise have been. The Romans allowed the weak Hasmonean Hyrcanus II to hold the office of high priest and ethnarch. But Palestine was now in fact Roman territory, and the power behind the throne was Antipater of Idumea, a master of political intrigue who had helped engineer the Roman *coup* in the first place.

Antipater brought his remarkable career to a culmination by having the Romans declare his son Herod king of the Jews. This Herod ruled effectively, if brutally, from 37 to 4 B.C. and figures prominently in Matthew's story of Jesus' infancy. He is commonly known as Herod the Great, in distinction from the lesser Herods who followed him. During his long and successful rule Herod accepted the necessity of appealing to Jewish religious zeal, at the same time devoting himself to the task of Hellenizing the culture and life of Palestine. He built cities according to the Hellenistic patterns, he constructed stadia, gymnasia, and theaters. Yet he also began to rebuild the temple in a more magnificent style. (Begun in 20 B.C., the reconstruction may not have actually been completed when the Roman War broke out in A.D. 66.) Despite his efforts, the Jews did not love or trust Herod. Nor did he trust them. He executed his Hasmonean wife Mariamne and eventually two of her sons, along with his ambitious and able son Antipater, who had married a Hasmonean princess. Antipater died only five days before Herod.

After the death of Herod, the kingdom was split into three parts and divided among three surviving sons. Philip became tetrarch of the region northeast of the Sea of Galilee, including Iturea and Trachonitis, and reigned over that largely Gentile area from 4 B.C. until A.D. 34. Herod Antipas became ruler of Galilee and Perea and ruled from 4 B.C. until A.D. 39. Archelaus became ruler of Samaria, Judea, and Idumea, but he was deposed after a short reign. Following the deposition of Archelaus in 6 A.D., a Roman procurator was installed as ruler of Judea. The procuratorship remained in effect continuously until the brief reign of Agrippa (37–44) and was resumed thereafter. Pontius Pilate (26–36) was the fifth

Ancient Roman theater capable of seating more than 3,000 people. It stands in Amman, Jordan, on the site of the ancient (63 B.C.) Decapolis city of Philadelphia. (Courtesy of Pan American Airways.)

of these procurators, perhaps one of the worst from the Jewish point of view. He took money from the temple treasury, brought military insignia with the emperor's image into Jerusalem, and ruthlessly destroyed a group of Samaritans who were watching a prophet perform a miracle. It would be an understatement to say that he was not overly sensitive to Jewish religious sensibilities.

But Roman rule was not entirely brutal. The procurator of Judea lived not in Jerusalem but in Caesarea. Although the procurator had final responsibility, much authority was granted to the Sanhedrin, a group of about seventy distinguished Jewish elders—priests, scribes, and laymen. The high priest was the official head of this group and was, as he had been since the Babylonian exile, the most important Jewish governmental figure. In the villages, synagogues served as law courts with scribes as authorities for interpreting and applying the law, or Torah.

11

Jesus was born during the reign of Herod the Great, lived in Galilee under Herod Antipas, and died in Jerusalem during the procuratorship of Pilate and the high priesthood of Caiaphas. Although Jesus was doubtless influenced by the political conditions of the times, there is little evidence that he made any political impact upon them. Possibly he, like his Palestinian followers, opposed the group known as the Zealots, who were plotting military insurrection against Roman rule. Although Jesus spoke frequently of the kingdom of God and aroused hopes that he himself would become king, he evidently did not intend to lead a rebellion (cf. Luke 4:5–8; Matt. 4:7–10; John 6:15). For example, he allowed the payment of taxes to Caesar (Mark 12:13–17 parr.). Yet Jesus, like several others before him, was crucified as a messianic pretender, a claimant to the throne of Israel, and thus a political rebel.

Be that as it may, the influence of the Zealots was increasing in the first half of the century. In Acts 5:35 ff. Gamaliel mentions Theudas, whom the procurator Fadus put to death, and Judas the Galilean, who—despite the contrary statement of Acts—had been put to death in A.D. 6, some three decades previously. Gradually the tension between Roman and Jew heightened. What the Romans regarded as Jewish provocations led to retaliation, which in turn increased the tendency toward polarization of sentiment. More and more Jews became willing to fight and die, convinced that God would vindicate them in their righteous cause. In A.D. 66 war broke out. Although the Jews fought bravely and enjoyed some initial success, they had little chance against Roman power. In 70 the Romans took Jerusalem after a long and grueling siege and laid it waste. A few years later the last Jewish resistance at the fortress of Masada was overwhelmed. Even then the Jewish will to resist was not broken. When word circulated that Emperor Hadrian intended to rebuild Jerusalem as Aelia Capitolina and to erect a temple to Jupiter on the site of the Jewish temple, the Jews rallied around a leader called Bar Cocheba ("Son of the Star"), whom the renowned Rabbi Akiba hailed as the Messiah of Israel. Once more (A.D. 132–135) the Jews fought fiercely, but after a time were subdued. Again God had not vindicated their cause. The Romans went ahead with their building plans and after the new city was complete forbade any Jew to enter it on pain of death. The trend of many centuries reached its logical end. Judaism had become a nation without a homeland.

Because the Jews believed that their land had been given them by the same God who had called them to be his chosen people, not surprisingly they chafed under foreign domination. Indeed, the character of Judaism during the time of Jesus and the early church was much affected by conditions in the Jewish homeland. The attitude of the Zealots, who regarded Roman rule as an affront against God to be removed by violent rebellion, has already been mentioned. During the period of Jesus' activity, however, theirs was not the only, or even the typical, expression of the spirit of

Judaism. Although Jews generally looked for relief from foreign oppression and the restoration of the Davidic monarchy, many were content to wait upon God for the fulfillment of this hope, some thinking that it was near at hand. Certain other Jews had in effect already made their peace with Hellenistic culture and Roman rule and probably did not really yearn for their overthrow. Then, of course, there were large numbers of Jews living outside Palestine for whom political independence was not a burning issue. Indeed, rebellion in the homeland presented the grim and unwelcome possibility of retaliation against Jews elsewhere.

Coin of the Simon Bar Cocheba War (A.D. 132–135). On the first side is a temple with four columns, within which there are a shrine and two scrolls of the law; the inscription reads, "Simon." On the other side are the lulab and ethrog, sacred objects. The inscription reads, "For the liberty of Jerusalem." (Courtesy of American Numismatic Society.)

Moreover, it would be a mistake to view the Judaism of Jesus' time simply in terms of its reaction to an international situation with unfortunate consequences for Jews. Many Jews continued to be primarily concerned with the right understanding of the law and the proper worship of God. The development of various schools of thought continued under Roman rule, and the Romans were willing to tolerate this so long as there was not overt dissension or violence. Postexilic developments had already led to the formation of several schools of religious opinion among the Jews, making for a rather complex situation in the time of Jesus. We must now examine that situation more closely in order to understand why differing positions and parties existed and how their presence shaped the setting in which Christianity appeared.

A PERSISTENT OBEDIENCE

If anything is typical of Judaism it is the law (Hebrew, *torah*). Notwithstanding its human mediation through Moses, the Jew regarded the law as divine revelation. Strictly speaking, the law consists of the five books of Moses—the Pentateuch—which stand at the beginning of the Bible. Obedience to the Torah is, and has been, the paramount obligation of the Jew; it is the way to true righteousness. Because of its central position, practically every major religious group within Judaism can be categorized according to its attitude to the law.

The Pharisees

> The Pharisees . . . are considered the most accurate interpreters of the laws, and hold the position of the leading sect. (Josephus, *The Jewish War*, II, 162)

> The scribes and Pharisees sit on Moses' seat; so practice and observe whatever they tell you, but not what they do; for they preach, but do not practice. (Matt. 23:2 f.)

> But when Paul perceived that one part were Sadducees and the other Pharisees, he cried out in the council, "Brethren, I am a Pharisee, a son of Pharisees; with respect to the hope and the resurrection of the dead I am on trial." (Acts 23:6)

Probably the single most influential and significant religious group within the Jewish community of New Testament times was the Pharisees. The Gospels make clear that they were important during the time of Jesus, and certainly they were predominant after the disastrous conclusion of the Jewish War (A.D. 70). The history of the Pharisees and even the origin of their name is obscure. Very likely they stemmed from the *Hasidim*, or "pious ones," whose ferocious allegiance to the nation and the law gave impetus to the Maccabean revolt. The word *Pharisee* seems to be derived from a Hebrew verb meaning "to separate." If so, it would appropriately designate the Pharisees as those separated or chosen by God for full obedience to the law. Because they understood Judaism primarily as interpretation of and obedience to the law, rather than in terms of nationalistic hopes or temple worship, the Pharisees were well situated to reconstitute and redefine Judaism in the aftermath of the wars with Rome.

In the New Testament the Pharisees are frequently spoken of together with the scribes, and the impression is created that they are closely allied, if not identical groups. The impression is not false, although it must be clarified. The scribes were authoritative custodians and interpreters of the law before the appearance of a distinct group called Pharisees. Moreover, not all Pharisees were scribes. Yet it does not surprise us that the historic task of the scribes was taken up by the Pharisees, whose consuming interest was the interpretation and application of the law to every sphere of life.

They continued and expanded the traditional interpretations of the law, the fruition of which is to be found in the so-called rabbinic literature, a large body of interpretative material from the earlier centuries of our era dealing with every part of the law and with almost every aspect of religious and secular life.[3]

The Sadducees

> But the high priest rose up and all who were with him, that is, the party of the Sadducees, and filled with jealousy they arrested the apostles and put them in the common prison. (Acts 5:17 f.)

A second major group within Judaism, also mentioned in the Gospels, is the Sadducees. As in the case of the Pharisees, their history and the derivation of their name is not entirely clear. Presumably the name is related to the proper name of Zadok, a high priest appointed by Solomon. Whatever the history of the name and of the group, by New Testament times the Sadducees were the priestly aristocracy. In Acts 5:17 the high priest and the Sadducees are linked together and in 4:9 the priests, the captain of the temple, and the Sadducees. The Sadducees seem to have stood in something of the same relation to the priests as the Pharisees to the scribes. Pharisees and Sadducees were thus religious brotherhoods centering upon the authoritative interpretation of the law and the temple worship respectively. As such they represented the chief foci of Jewish faith as it existed prior to A.D. 70. Although the temple and its service of worship had declined in practical importance as the majority of Jews came to live outside the land of Israel, it was nevertheless the symbolic center of Judaism. On the altar sacrifices were offered to God in order for God and man to commune. Men's sins were covered and a right relationship between God and his people restored and maintained. Probably the most graphic example of this priestly function was the yearly ritual of the Day of Atonement, when the high priest alone entered the unapproachable Holy of Holies in the temple and there came, as the representative of the people, into the very presence of the Holy One. On this day his action signified divine favor in that he entered, met, and was not destroyed by the God of Israel.

As custodians of religious tradition and cultic ceremony the Sadducees were somewhat more conservative than the Pharisees. The priests themselves held office by hereditary right. Moreover, the Sadducees represented established wealth and position, factors that tend to make men somewhat conservative. With regard to obedience to the law, they rejected all tradition

---

[3] The basic document of the rabbinic literature is *The Mishnah*, of which the standard English translation is that of H. Danby (London: Oxford University Press, 1933). A valuable introduction to the range of rabbinic literature is the work of C. G. Montefiore and H. Loewe, *A Rabbinic Anthology* (New York: Meridian Books, n.d.).

Jerusalem and the temple area. The domed building is a Moslem shrine, the Dome of the Rock, which stands where the ancient Jerusalem temple was located. (Courtesy of Israel Government Tourist Office.)

and thus the effort of the Pharisees to extend the law's application to every situation in life in a binding way. They accepted only the word of scripture as authoritative. Politically, they were quietists and generally cooperated with the Romans. As members of the establishment it was in their interest to do so. They would have nothing to do with the relatively late doctrine of the resurrection of the dead, but rather adhered to the older and more typically Biblical (Old Testament) view that death is simply the end of significant conscious life. In this they differed from the Pharisees as well as from Jesus and the early Christians.

The Essenes

> The Essenes have a reputation for cultivating peculiar sanctity. Of Jewish birth, they show a greater attachment to each other than do the other sects. They shun pleasures as a vice and regard temperance and the control of the passions as a special virtue. (Josephus, *The Jewish War*, II, 119 f.)

In addition to the Pharisees and Sadducees there existed at the time of Jesus a group called Essenes, whose exact identity and extent are not clear. Two important Jewish writers of the first century, the philosopher Philo and the historian Josephus, speak of them, although they are not mentioned by name in the New Testament. Since World War II, however, our knowledge of Essene or Essene-type groups has been immensely enlarged by the discovery of a monastery and an immense cache of documents at Qumran on the shores of the Dead Sea.[4] The community existed there at the time of Jesus.

The Qumran movement, which probably began during the reign of Alexander Jannaeus (*ca.* 103–76 B.C.), was characterized by a feeling of profound revulsion at the impurity of the temple worship and priesthood and the laxity in the observance of the law. A figure called only the "teacher of righteousness" or the "righteous teacher" was apparently the founder of this group. Unlike the Pharisees and Sadducees, they withdrew from the mainstream of Jewish life, which they regarded as wholly corrupt, and formed monastic communities. Yet this withdrawal had a positive, as well as negative side. It was not only a separation for the sake of the preservation of holiness, but a separation for a positive task and goal. First of all, the members of the community sought to carry out punctiliously the ritual and ethical requirements of the law and thus render a more acceptable obedience to God. This obedience was enforced under a strict discipline, and severe punishment was meted out for even minor infractions:

---

[4] The literature on the scrolls is voluminous, and scroll scholarship has become a profession within Biblical study. Very valuable still are Millar Burrow's two volumes, *The Dead Sea Scrolls* and *More Light on the Dead Sea Scrolls* (New York: Viking Press, 1955 and 1958 respectively). Both volumes contain translations of the major documents discovered up to the time of their publication. A handy collection of the important documents in translation has been made by G. Vermes, *The Dead Sea Scrolls in English* (Baltimore: Penguin Books, 1962).

Cave near Qumran where some of the Dead Sea Scrolls were found. (Courtesy of Israel Information Services.)

One who walks before his neighbor naked when he does not have to do so shall be punished for six months. A man who spits into the midst of the session of the masters shall be punished thirty days. One who brings his hand from beneath his robe when it is torn, so that his nakedness is seen, shall be punished thirty days. One who laughs foolishly, making his voice heard, shall be punished thirty days. One who brings his left hand to gesticulate with it shall be punished ten days.[5]

In addition, they looked toward the future vindication of Israel, or at least of their own community as the remnant of the true Israel. This vindication was expected in the form of an apocalyptic drama, indeed, a conflict, in which the forces of light would overwhelm those of darkness.[6] The victory would never be in doubt, because God was to fight on the side of his elect. Such terms as *light, darkness,* and *elect* highlight the basic character of Qumran thought. Almost everything was seen as a choice between black and white, with no compromise allowed. This point of view,

---

[5] From the *Manual of Discipline,* following Burrows' translation, *Scrolls,* p. 380.

[6] Such an encounter is described in the community document designated *The War of the Sons of Light with the Sons of Darkness* (cf. Burrows, *Scrolls,* pp. 390 ff.; also Vermes, pp. 122 ff.).

often called "dualism," was reflected in the group's extremely rigid attitude toward the law, in its implacable hostility toward those regarded as enemies, and in its view of the coming culmination of history. The triumph of the good people over the bad would result in the elimination of evil from the world.

The Qumraners, or Essenes, as they may perhaps be called, were not purely passive in their hopes and expectations. Rather, they saw themselves, and particularly their separatist existence in the desert, as the fulfillment of the prophecy of Isaiah 40:3 (cf. *Manual of Discipline*, viii). They were in the wilderness preparing the way of the Lord. In this respect there is a striking similarity between the Qumran community and the New Testament church. In the New Testament the same Old Testament passage is found on the lips of John the Baptist, who views his task in a similar way. It is indicative of the fact that both the desert community and Jesus and his disciples lived in an atmosphere of apocalyptic or eschatological expectation. They looked forward to the coming of God. In fact, there were other similarities between the two groups. Both stood apart from prevailing forms of Jewish piety. Both looked to a central leader or founder, whether

Jesus or the teacher of righteousness; in different ways both insisted on a radical interpretation of the law; both formed a community or sect of believers within Judaism. For this reason there has been a great deal of excitement over the Qumran discoveries; they have brought us closer to the origins of Christianity.

Yet there are also significant differences. Christianity insisted upon the essential meaning of the law rather than the letter. Jesus was denounced as a wine-bibber and a friend of publicans and sinners, and his disciples and the other early Christians continued to live among other men. They did not withdraw to themselves. Instead of savoring in advance their own salvation at the expense of nearly everyone else, the Christians went out to preach their good news to mankind at large. Nevertheless, for the purpose of a historical understanding of Jesus, his disciples, and early Christianity, the Qumran documents are quite important. They reveal another Jewish sect of the same period which was engaged in alternately searching the scriptures and the heavens for signs of God's approaching kingdom. For the Christians these hopes and expectations found fulfillment, although not in the way anticipated. For the Qumran community and other Essenes there was only disappointment. The monastery was destroyed by the Romans in the war of A.D. 66–70, and the inhabitants hid their sacred scrolls in nearby caves, where they were accidentally discovered nearly two thousand years later.

AN ABIDING HOPE

Judaism in New Testament times was characterized not only by burdens of the past and earnest efforts to obey the law of God in the present, but by its attitude toward the future. The Qumran discoveries are important evidence of this fact. As we have already noted, most Jews had definite ideas about the future, which were usually tied to the national destiny.

At one end of the spectrum stood those like the men of Qumran who looked for the dramatic intervention of God in history to destroy the wicked and forever establish the righteous Israelites in His favor. At the other stood the Sadducees, whose position of relative security and comfort in relation to the Roman authorities made them little disposed either to sedition or an apocalyptic outlook. The Sadducees looked for no cataclysmic end of history and no resurrection of the dead. In this respect they seem to have been in substantial agreement with the theology of the pre-exilic Israel. Between such extremes stood the Pharisees, who hoped for "the redemption of Israel" (Luke 24:21), but did not expect to initiate it by violent revolution.[7] In this respect they differed from Zealots, the party

---

[7] According to Josephus (*The Jewish War*, II, xvii, 3), Pharisees were among the prominent men who attempted to dissuade the Zealots when they were in the process of launching the rebellion against Rome.

*In the foreground are the walls of the Essene monastery at Khirbet
Qumran; the view is in the direction of the Dead Sea. Not far away
are the caves in which the Dead Sea Scrolls were found. (Courtesy of
Arab Information Center.)*

of rebellion, with whom they were related both in historical origin and in
enthusiasm for the law and for all things Jewish. Although the Pharisees
abjured the kind of active cooperation with Roman authority in which
the Sadducees engaged, they served along with priests and Sadducees on
the Sanhedrin, the highest Jewish court of appeal under Roman rule.
Moreover, they had a history of political involvement during the Maccabean period. Unlike the Essenes, the Pharisees were not monastically
inclined.

It is difficult to say with certainty how the Pharisees expected Israel's
national destiny to be fulfilled. The rabbinic documents, which generally
express a Pharisaic point of view, do not look forward to an *imminent*
apocalyptic drama whereby God would bring ordinary history to an end and
restore the fortunes of Israel. But the rabbinic literature is not necessarily
an accurate guide to Pharisaic expectations during the period of Jesus and
the writing of the New Testament books. It reflects the attitude of Judaism

after the Roman War and the uprising of Bar Cocheba, when disappointed apocalyptic and messianic hope made speculation about such matters unattractive and enthusiasm unlikely. Yet very probably the earlier Pharisees, like the Essenes, cherished apocalyptic and messianic hopes:

> Behold, O Lord, and raise up unto them their king, the son
>   of David,
>   At the same time in which Thou seest, O God, that he
>   may reign over Israel Thy servant.
> And gird him with strength, that he may shatter unrighteous
>   rulers,
>   And that he may purge Jerusalem from nations that trample
>   (her) down to destruction. . . .
> At his rebuke nations shall flee before him,
>   And he shall reprove sinners for the thoughts of their
>   heart.[8]

In the later apocalyptic literature we find a scheme or plan for the culmination of history which was shared by the rabbis. This world or this age was to come to a conclusion with the restoration of Israel's fortunes and the resurrection of her righteous dead, marking the inauguration of the messianic age. After a period of from several hundred to a thousand years, the general resurrection (that is, of all the dead) would take place as a prelude to the final judgment of God. After the Judgment, God would usher in the "age to come," the consummation toward which all history was moving. The existence of similar ideas and expectations, if in less systematized form, in the New Testament shows that they were common currency in the Judaism of Jesus' day.

The Pharisees and others did not espouse apocalyptic and similar ideas solely out of patriotic interests and hopes. The doctrine of the resurrection of the dead provided a lively individual hope and a means of justifying God's ways with men. If, as experience dictated, the righteous servants of God's law suffer in this life, they may expect better things when the dead are raised. The doctrine of the resurrection became the hallmark of the Pharisees (cf. Acts 23:6), so that in time a virtual anathema could be pronounced against those who disbelieved it. Belief in the resurrection appears rarely in the Old Testament, notably in Isaiah 26:19 and Daniel 12:2. Thus it is not surprising that the Sadducees did not feel obliged to

---

[8] The Psalm of Solomon 17, in the Pseudepigrapha, is usually regarded as typical of Pharisaic messianic hope; vss. 23, 24, 27 are quoted above. The passage is cited from R. H. Charles, The *Apocrypha and Pseudepigrapha of the Old Testament*, II (Oxford: Clarendon Press, 1913), p. 649. Psalm 17 is messianic without being clearly apocalyptic. On the positive attitude of Pharisaism to apocalyptic during the New Testament period, cf. W. D. Davies, "Apocalyptic and Pharisaism," *Christian Origins and Judaism* (Philadelphia: Westminster Press, 1962), pp. 19–30.

share it. Nevertheless, the New Testament reports that Jesus (Mark 12:26 f.) as well as Paul (Acts 23:6) believed in the resurrection.

The whole complex of apocalyptic ideas, including the resurrection of the dead, the dualism of good and evil, the distinction between this age and the age to come, and the destruction of evil and the triumph of good in a cataclysmic cosmic upheaval and judgment, cannot be fully explained on the basis of the earlier traditions of Israel, whether historical, prophetic, or cultic. The apocalyptic frame of mind has marked affinities with Persian, particularly Zoroastrian, thought. This is especially true of the dualism, cosmic eschatology, and the last judgment. To what extent they may reflect direct borrowing or even more subtle influences is debatable, although such outside influences cannot simply be discounted, especially in view of the exposure of many Jews to foreign influences in the exile and the diaspora after the sixth century B.C. But the impotence and frustration of the Jews in their homeland doubtless provided the necessary seedbed and impetus for such ideas to develop. In due course this same kind of thinking provided the fertile ground out of which Christianity emerged. For John the Baptist came proclaiming the imminent judgment; Jesus announced the inbreaking of the kingdom of God in power (that is, the age to come); and the early Christians proclaimed that Jesus had risen from the dead and would come again in glory to render judgment (cf. also Daniel 7). Although Jesus surely felt himself to be a son of Abraham, as did the early Christians generally (cf. Gal. 3:29), and consciously stood in the tradition of the law and the prophets, he was the heir of ideas and perspectives that were unknown to the patriarchs, Moses, or Amos. Some of these were perhaps "foreign" in the sense of being non-Israelite. Yet the substance and framework of Jesus' message had deep roots in his people's history and faith. Apart from the glory and the agony of that history Jesus can scarcely be fully understood. In his insistence on obedience to God's will in the present as the key to the future, Jesus exemplifies Israelite faith at its boldest and best.[9] Jesus proposed a radical reinterpretation of both obedience and hope, but in the indissoluble linking of the two he was a true son of Abraham.

Judaism is history, law, tradition, worship, and the land. But perhaps more than anything else Judaism is and always has been a people—a people with a unique sense of identity and purpose, a chosen people, with all the distinctiveness, as well as liabilities, that such a concept implies. As a Jew, Jesus would have been conscious above all of being a member of this people. Likewise, the earliest Christians were Jews and only gradually thought of themselves in any other way.

---

[9] For a sensitive and sympathetic interpretation of Jesus as the embodiment of the Jewish understanding of faith, see Martin Buber, *Two Types of Faith*, trans. N. P. Goldhawk (New York: Macmillan Co., 1951).

The Shrine of the Book, a part of the Israel Museum. This encasement contains the complete scroll of the prophet Isaiah found among the caves of Qumran. (Courtesy of Israel Government Tourist Office.)

The Greco-Roman World

The history, law, and hope of the Jewish people formed the background from which Jesus and early Christianity came forth. Indeed, they provided the ingredients from which the new faith took shape. The pilgrimage and travail of Israel, its scriptures and its expectations, furnished the essential frame of reference for Jesus and his earliest followers. Yet Christian faith soon broke free of Judaism and spread rapidly among the Gentiles throughout the Mediterranean world. In a sense, it became a universal form of Judaism. But how and why did this happen to the sect of Jesus' followers in particular? The answer to this is manifold, although it remains partly a mystery. But some valid reasons can be discerned by observing the conditions in the world into which Christianity spread.

LANGUAGE AND CULTURE

Several hundred years before the beginning of the Christian era, in about the third century B.C, the Hebrew scriptures were translated into Greek. According to the ancient legendary account of the translation in the Epistle of Aristeas, it was done in Egypt for the royal library out of scholarly appreciation for the importance of the books. In all probability, however, the translation was made on the initiative and for the benefit of the Jews themselves, most of whom could no longer read their native tongue, but could read and understand Greek.

Alexander the Great

The Jews had become widely scattered in Egypt and other places as a result of the Exile. They spoke Greek largely because of the remarkable influence of one man, Alexander of Macedon. Probably no single man has ever had a greater impact upon the history, culture, and religion of the world than Alexander. Born in 356 B.C., he succeeded to the throne of his father, Philip of Macedon, in 334. Two years later he set out from his home in Macedonia to begin the conquest of the Persian Empire, which for years had menaced and invaded Greece. In eight years, he and his army swept as far east as the Indus River at the westernmost reaches of India and as far south as Egypt, where only the homesickness of his soldiers halted his advance. Although the Persian Empire and army turned out to be something of a "paper tiger" against the more homogenous and better-disciplined army of Alexander, a superbly effective fighting unit, Alexander's military accomplishment cannot be minimized.

Of greater importance than the sheer military feat, however, was the cultural revolution that it entailed. For Alexander was not only a soldier but also a man of letters and a student of Aristotle. He was eager to establish Greek culture and language in the areas that he conquered, and his success in this respect was remarkable. Alexander seems to have envisioned a genuine cultural mixture throughout the ancient world, with the Hellenic (Greek) element as the common factor everywhere. The seriousness of his intention is exemplified in the fact that he and his soldiers took women of the East as wives. After his conquest he seemed content to remain there, and apparently regarded Babylon as his capital. There, quite unexpectedly, he died of a fever in 323 B.C. at the age of thirty-three, leaving no legal heir capable of succeeding him. His lieutenants struggled for control of his empire and soon managed to pull it apart. Thus the fruit of his military conquests, while immense, proved ephemeral, for his empire dissolved almost as quickly as it had emerged.

Although Alexander did not succeed in establishing a Macedonian empire that would survive his death, his efforts to spread Greek language and culture and to embed them in the life of the East proved highly successful, especially in the cities. He left as his heritage a string of Greek cities across the area of his conquest, outposts of Greek language and culture. Probably the largest and most successful of these was the great Egyptian center of Alexandria, which appropriately bore his name. It was here that a large colony of Jews settled and that the first and most important translation of the Hebrew scriptures into Greek was made.

The Importance of Greek

Without necessarily subscribing to the theory that history is made by great men alone, one can and must grant the singular and outstanding historical importance of Alexander in giving a particular form and character to the world into which Christianity was born. Nothing is more important for human history and culture than language, and nothing promotes communication and understanding like a common language. Among other things, Alexander bequeathed to the Mediterranean world a common language, Greek. It was not the Greek of Plato or Sophocles, but another newer and somewhat simpler dialect known as *koine*, or common, Greek. This Greek became the *lingua franca* of the ancient world three hundred years before the time of Christ, just as Latin became the common language of the intellectual and ecclesiastical world of the Middle Ages and English has become the international language of the post-World War II world. In all probability, however, this Greek penetrated more to lower levels of society than has either Latin or English, for it became the language of common intercourse and commerce, at least in the more highly developed and populated places of the ancient world, as the recently discovered papyri (fragments of everyday correspondence written on papyrus leaves) from Egypt show. People from widely separated areas and with vastly different backgrounds could talk to each other in Greek. Perhaps they could not construct complex Greek sentences with perfect syntax and inflection, but they could make themselves understood. Needless to say, this gift of common speech was of considerable importance in encouraging commerce and other sorts of interchange throughout the Alexandrian world. Indeed, in the centers of Greek culture established by Alexander, conscious attempts were made to promote and spread the manners and customs, especially the athletic games, of Hellenic civilization. The world that Alexander left was one world in a sense that it had never been before. Previously there had been great overarching empires such as the Assyrian, the Persian, and the Egyptian, and certainly various peoples and cultures had interacted, but never before had there been such an attempt to create a common world civilization as was actually and purposefully brought about by Alexander and his successors. This mixture of Hellenic (Greek) and Oriental elements is called the Hellenistic civilization.

The importance of this universal civilization for Judaism and its step-child Christianity can scarcely be overestimated. For Judaism it was at once a threat and a benefit—a threat in that it tended to eliminate just those distinguishing features of life which characterized the Jewish community as such, but a benefit in that it made possible greater extension of the scope and influence of Judaism, especially Greek-speaking Judaism. For Christianity it was an immense boon. Without Alexander the rapid spread of Christianity through the Greco-Roman world might never have taken place. Certainly the Christian message had a power of its own, and its impact cannot be attributed to favorable cultural factors alone. Nevertheless, it is a striking fact that the spread of Christianity in the first centuries occurred principally in those areas which fell under the sway of Alexander's, or at least of Greek, influence.

The New Testament itself was composed entirely in Greek, although the Gospels are in part based on earlier Aramaic sources, either written or oral. Except in Palestine and Syria, and perhaps to some extent even there, the preaching of the gospel was in Greek. In most places of any importance Greek was the language which was spoken and understood by both preacher and hearer. Even in Rome, to which Christianity spread at a very early time, and which we generally associate with the Latin language, Greek was generally spoken and understood. And even Matthew, the Gospel that is most clearly Jewish in character, was first written down not in Aramaic or Hebrew but in Greek. Yet despite the important role that Greek language and culture played in its spread, it would be incorrect simply to call Christianity a Greek religion. Viewed from the standpoint of its origin and original constituents, it is also Oriental and especially Jewish. It is not, therefore, the purely Greek element, but precisely this combination of Greek and Jewish, West and East, which was characteristic of the Hellenistic world.

GOVERNMENT

Alexander created a world but did not live to govern it. That task was finally performed by Rome. It is, of course, true that the limits of Alexander's conquests and those of the Roman Empire at its height were not the same. Alexander's conquests extended farther to the East, whereas the Roman Empire's orbit stretched far beyond Italy to the north and west. Yet in a sense the world of Alexandrian Hellenism and the world of Rome were one world.[10] Through her own conquest of Greece and wholesale appropriation of Greek culture in the second century B.C., Rome fell heir to the legacy of Greece just when she was emerging as the dominant military force and political power of the western world. For a half century before Christ and nearly half a millennium after, the Roman Empire gave to the Mediterranean world a political unity and stability, which, though not unbroken, was about as continuous and dependable

[10] The great classical historian, M. Rostovtzeff, regarded the culture of the Roman Empire as basically Greek. In *A History of the Ancient World:* vol. I, *The Orient and Greece,* trans. J. D. Duff (Oxford: Clarendon Press, n.d.), pp. 281 f., he writes: "The Latin culture of Italy and the West is one branch of the Greek culture of the third and later centuries—not a slavish copy, not an imitation, but an independent national development of Greek ideas, Greek art, and Greek literature in the Latin West, a participation by the West in the city-life of the Hellenic East with all its external characteristics."

as anything so large and varied a segment of the world has known before or since. The marvel is not that the Roman Empire fell—crumbled is the better word—but that it stood so long. At the time of its greatest extent and vitality—that is, during the New Testament period—the Roman Empire stretched from Syria and Palestine to the British Isles. Of western Europe, only Germany and the Scandinavian countries remained outside the Roman orbit, and only Scandinavia completely outside. The southern and westernmost parts of Germany came under Roman domination, as did Austria as far north as the Danube.

The birth and development of Christianity as a world religion came about during the two centuries when Rome was at the zenith of its power. This was the period from 30 B.C., the accession date of Augustus Caesar, to A.D. 180, the year of the death of Marcus Aurelius, the philosopher emperor. In subsequent years the strength and stability of the empire waned, yet for centuries longer it continued to be a power to be reckoned with. Jesus of Nazareth was born during the reign of Augustus, and by the time Marcus Aurelius died the main lines of the New Testament had been established. Also by the end of the period we see in Christian writings the first traces of a confession that we know as the Apostles' Creed. This period, often referred to as the *pax romana* (Peace of Rome), thus saw both the beginning of Christianity and its establishment in what proved to be orthodox form. By the end of the second century the lines for future theological and ecclesiastical development had already been laid down.

The *pax romana* was a favorable time for a movement like Christianity to get under way. There was both absence of war and domestic order. Our present systems of law owe more directly to the Romans than to the Hebrews, and the *pax romana* was a time of lawfulness as well as peace. The Romans administered the empire with firmness, but with a certain sensitivity for the varieties of peoples and customs within their bounds. Local law enforcement and administration were left in the hands of local officials. Where local administration or law enforcement broke down, as in the case of Judea at the time of Jesus, the Romans intervened to make sure that anarchy did not reign. Roman officials were not universally good, as we have already noted. Pontius Pilate, for example, left a great deal to be desired. Yet the Romans themselves removed Pilate from power. Although it is true that Jesus died on a Roman cross and that the church was persecuted by Romans, it is equally true, and probably more important, that early Christianity benefited considerably from the peaceful and lawful conditions of Roman rule which accompanied its beginnings.

Early Christianity profitted also from the network of roads and sea transportation that the Romans had developed and maintained, largely for military purposes. Again, policing of the roads was left to the various provinces and localities as long as they could do the job, but when and

Wilson's Arch is a span of a bridge built across the Tyropoeon Valley in Jerusalem by Herod in 20 B.C. and used during the time of Jesus. (Courtesy of Professor William F. Stinespring, Duke University.)

where conditions demanded, the Roman military intervened to keep roads open for travel and free of bandits and other potential harassments. It would certainly be wrong to imagine that travel in ancient times was as easy as it is today. Yet travel between virtually all parts of the empire was possible, and it was probably easier to go from Jerusalem to Rome in Paul's day than it was to travel from the East Coast to California in this country a little more than a hundred years ago.

Thus favorable conditions of language and culture as well as an orderly government and a workable transportation system favored the spread of the Christian gospel in the Greco-Roman world. They help explain the rapid growth of the church and the ways in which the gospel found expression—not the least of which is the New Testament itself, a collection of books written in Greek, and in many cases written from one Christian or group of Christians to or for another. These documents attest not only a lively faith but also a sense of tangible relationship between one Christian church and another, which was made possible by the conditions of the time. Moreover, they display a concrete sense of mission concerning something called "the world" (Greek, *kosmos*), a concept not unknown previously but given particular point and form by the vision and work of Alexander the Great and the political reality of the Roman Empire.

RELIGION

According to the book of Acts, the apostle Paul began his famous speech to the Athenians by saying, "Men of Athens, I perceive that in every way you are very religious" (17:22). Whether Paul himself spoke in exactly this way is a matter of debate, but the observation attributed to him was certainly true. It was true not only of Athens but of the entire ancient Mediterranean world. The world of New Testament times was a religious world. Christianity did not originate in a time of religious decline. Whatever may have been the general state of culture in the first century A.D., religion did not lack vitality and vigorous manifestations.

A striking characteristic of the religious situation was its variety. This too is represented in Paul's speech, for he mentions the objects of their worship, among which is an altar inscribed to an unknown God, as if the Athenians were taking no chances on omitting, and therefore offending, any deity. People participated in various rites and ceremonies according to law, taste, or desire. The period was also marked by syncretism: various religious traditions merged together or were interpreted in terms of one another.

This toleration does not mean that people by and large did not take religion seriously. If anything, just the opposite was the case. Only from the Christian or Jewish point of view could this toleration of, and participation in, a multiplicity of religious cults be taken as an indication of frivolity. The exclusivism of Judaism and Christianity was itself regarded as odd and even impious in ancient times, and the refusal of Christians and Jews to worship any god other than their own led their neighbors to brand them as atheists. This persistence in worshiping only one God was perhaps the factor that most clearly distinguished Christians and Jews in the ancient world, and it may have had something to do with the fact that of the religions of that civilization only Christianity and Judaism survive today.

The specific manifestations of pagan piety in the Greco-Roman world are far too numerous to discuss fully here. Nevertheless, it will be helpful to notice several basic types of religion that were popular and significant. These include the religion of the Greco-Roman pantheon (a Greek word meaning a temple dedicated to "all the gods"), the worship of the ruler, mystery religions, Gnosticism, and Judaism.

Traditional and Official Religion

At the time of the emergence of Christianity and the writing of the New Testament books, the traditional religion of the Roman Empire was a complex and somewhat amorphous combination of both Greek and Roman elements. Prior to the Christian era there had been a distinctly Roman religious cult involving especially the gods of the hearth and the family, of which the public religion was an extension and enlargement. This state or city cult was presided over first by the king, and later by a pontifical college made up of several prominent men of the realm. Ancient Greek religion of the pre-Christian period seems to have consisted originally of a variety of local deities, each with his holy place. These were later submerged under, or incorporated into, the pantheon of very human gods known to us from Homer, who is the fountainhead of classical mythology. If we think of Greek gods, we generally think of the Homeric pantheon. By the beginning of the Christian period an amalgamation of Greek and Roman deities had taken place. It was taken for granted that the Greek and Roman gods were for the most part actually the same gods, even if they had different names, and an equation of the various gods of the Homeric pantheon with Roman gods had been worked out. For example, the three very prominent Greek gods, Zeus, Hera, and Athena, were identified with the Roman Jupiter, Juno, and Minerva, respectively. Moreover, the purely Greek God Apollo was worshiped on the Palatine Hill in Rome.

By the beginning of the Christian era the traditional piety of Greece and Rome was facing competition from newer religions, especially those of Oriental origin, which were gaining enthusiastic adherents. Moreover, people of some education and intelligence had difficulty taking the myths and stories that were told about the gods seriously, at least as long as they were understood as literal accounts of what actually took place or of the nature of divine reality. Folk of a philosophical bent, especially the Stoics, had been interpreting the myths in an allegorical way for some time.[11] That is, they took them to be narrative representations of philosophical truths, which really had nothing to do with the stories per se and could stand independently of them. Thus the old gods got a new lease on life. For example, Zeus, the head of the Homeric pantheon, could be identified with "the general law, which is right reason, pervading everything . . . the Supreme Head of the universe" (Zeno, *Fragments*, 162, 152).[12] The Stoic monism, according to which God or the logos (Greek for "word" or "reason") pervades the universe much as the soul or animation pervades the body and gives it unity and purpose, was thereby reconciled with a mythology that had quite a different origin and meaning. Especially those

---

[11] W. W. Tarn, *Hellenistic Civilization* (3rd ed. rev. with G. T. Griffith; London: Arnold, 1952), p. 325, points out that Stoicism was the philosophy *par excellence* of the Hellenistic world. Other philosophies there surely were (e.g. Epicureanism, Platonism, Aristotelianism, Skepticism). Nevertheless, the Stoic outlook, especially the Stoic ethic with its responsibility toward the world as well as its inwardness, was predominant.

[12] Cited from C. K. Barrett, *The New Testament Background: Selected Documents* (London: SPCK, 1957), p. 62.

stories of the gods consorting and cavorting with each other in ways that sober men came to regard as shameful were allegorized away, making room for the Stoic ethic, which centered in willing conformity with that reason or logos that governs the universe and the individual. The Stoics themselves, however, were not coldly rationalistic. Philosophy was for them a vital piety, and although this piety was grounded in a philosophical pantheism, its expression often took the form of hymns and prayers to a personal or quasi-personal God, as can be seen from a portion of Cleanthes' famous *Hymn to Zeus:*

> Thou, O Zeus, art praised above all gods; many are thy
> names and thine is all power for ever.
> The beginning of the world was from thee; and with law
> thou rulest over all things.
> Unto thee may all flesh speak; for we are thy offspring.
> Therefore will I raise a hymn unto thee: and will ever
> sing of thy power.

The whole order of the heavens obeyeth thy word: as it
moveth around the earth:
   With little and great lights mixed together: how great
art thou, King above all for ever![13]

The ancient Greco-Roman religion survived not merely in Stoic reinterpretation but also in more naïve popular worship. As such, it remained
the traditional public religion of the Roman Empire, just as its predecessors had been the official cults of old Rome and of the Greek city-states.
We find some indication of its survival in the New Testament. According
to Acts the people of Lystra, in what is now Asia Minor, hailed Paul and
Barnabas as Hermes and Zeus, respectively, upon their performance of a
miracle. Moreover, a temple of Zeus was located near that city (Acts 14:
12 f.). There was in the city of Ephesus a great temple of Artemis (cf. Acts
19:23 ff.), which has been unearthed in modern times by archaeologists,
as have many other temples to the Greco-Roman deities. In addition, the
Roman emperor Augustus, who was ruling at the time Jesus was born,

[13] Cited from Barrett, *The New Testament Background*, p. 62.

Ruins of a fifth-century B.C. *temple to Poseidon, Greek god of the sea, located at Cape Sounion near Athens. (Courtesy of Greek Press and Information Service.)*

made a serious effort to promote the traditional public cult, especially the ancient Roman practices and ceremonies. Upon the death of the high priest, he went so far as to assume that office himself, reviving a custom long fallen into disuse, according to which the kingship and high priesthood were united in one man.

Beginning with Augustus' reign there was an increasing tendency to regard the emperor as a divine figure and to place him among the pantheon of gods to whom worship was due. Although Augustus coyly spurned divine honors during his lifetime they were accorded him upon his death. By the end of the first Christian century, it was no longer a question of ascribing divine honors and worship to deceased emperors. Now such veneration was deemed to be due the living emperor as well. Not surprisingly, this led in due course to a confrontation between the young Christian church and Rome. For Rome insisted upon emperor worship as a pledge of allegiance—or devotion—to the emperor and thus to the empire. It was, in fact, a sort of loyalty oath, but one which Christians could not conscientiously take. Yet when emperor worship is seen against the background of the many gods and many lords of the ancient world (cf. I Cor. 8:5), and when the benefits accruing to mankind from the emperor's rule are recalled, we can understand why the authorities did not regard divine homage as too much to ask of any subject. Moreover, worship of the supreme ruler was not unknown in earlier times. The Romans were doubtless genuinely perplexed to find people who stubbornly refused to participate on religious grounds.

Popular Religion

Although the official religious rites of Greece and Rome were by no means dead at the beginning of the Christian era, they did not represent the principal form of personal piety. Their continued existence, and whatever vitality they had, was probably due largely to the role they played in expressing the political and cultural solidarity of the Roman empire and the Greco-Roman world. No sustained attempt was made to establish public religion to the exclusion of private practices and societies, however, and it is in the latter that the burgeoning variety and strength of religion in later antiquity can be most clearly seen.

Head of Augustus (Gaius Julius Caesar Octavianus), first Roman emperor (27 B.C.–A.D. 14). (Courtesy of Metropolitan Museum of Art, Rogers Fund, 1908.)

Unfortunately, our knowledge of these practices and societies is quite limited, owing in no small measure to the aura of secrecy that surrounded many of them. This is especially true of the so-called *mystery religions*, which were gaining in prominence and popularity at the beginning of the Christian era. The vows of secrecy that the followers of these religions took were meticulously observed. Much of the ancient material on the mysteries comes to us second-hand through Christian and Jewish sources. Consequently, we do not know in detail, or with a high degree of assurance, what they were like.

The most closely guarded secrets of the mystery religions were their rites of initiation, through which the novitiate first received the benefits that the cult deity bestowed. Apparently the candidate somehow re-enacted or saw re-enacted the cult myth—that is, the story about the god or gods on which the cult was based—and thus participated in it. Through participation he received the salvation that was the very reason for the cult's being.

Perhaps the best account of the mystery ritual is found in Apuleius, *The Golden Ass* (xi, 22–26), from which the following description of an Isis initiation is taken:

> Then behold the day approached when as the sacrifice of dedication should be done; and when the sun declined and evening came, there arrived on every coast a great multitude of priests, who according to their ancient order offered me many presents and gifts. Then was all the laity and profane people commanded to depart, and when they had put on my back a new linen robe, the priest took my hand and brought me to the most secret and sacred place of the temple. Thou wouldest peradventure demand, thou studious reader, what was said and done there: verily I would tell thee if it were lawful for me to tell, thou wouldest know if it were convenient for thee to hear; but both thy ears and my tongue should incur the like pain of rash curiosity. Howbeit I will not long torment thy mind, which peradventure is somewhat religious and given to some devotion; listen therefore, and believe it to be true. Thou shalt understand that I approached near unto hell, even to the gates of Proserpine, and after that I was ravished throughout all the elements, I returned to my proper place: about midnight I saw the sun brightly shine, I saw likewise the gods celestial and the gods infernal, before whom I presented myself and worshipped them. Behold now have I told thee, which although thou hast heard, yet it is necessary that thou conceal it; wherefore this only will I tell, which may be declared without offence for the understanding of the profane.[14]

The myth of the cult naturally varied with the different mystery religions. Among others, there were the Eleusinian mysteries of Greece; the cult of Attis and Cybele, originating in Asia Minor; as well as that of Isis and Osiris, which had its origin in Egypt. Most of the cults were probably based upon fertility rites celebrating the return of the growing season. In time, however, the meaning of the cult myth was seen against the background of the life and death of man, so that through initiation into the mysteries a person could assure himself of a happy destiny beyond death. Scholars once confidently asserted that the common factor in the cult myths was the death and resurrection of a deity, in which the initiate participated vicariously through the rites. Thus he rose from the dead with

---

[14] Cited from Barrett, *The New Testament Background*, pp. 98 f.

This Roman sarcophagus (ca. A.D. 220–230) shows Dionysos, the Olympian god who is the giver of the grape and therefore of wine, riding in triumph on a panther and surrounded by a host of figures including the Four Seasons. (Courtesy of Metropolitan Museum of Art. Purchase, 1955, Joseph Pulitzer Bequest.)

the god (cf. Romans 6:1–11). This interpretation has, however, been disputed,[15] and it is a question whether the evidence permits it.

The traditional religions of Greece and Rome, like the religion of Israel, had focused primarily upon the ordering of life in this world, and did not promise the believer a glorious life after death. It is even incorrect to speak of "believers" in connection with them, for these religions were simply accepted as a matter of course and as a part of public and private life. The mysteries, however, appealed to human hopes and fears in the face of death and offered to those who became initiates the promise of eternal life. Perhaps "believer" is not quite the proper word for their adherents, but it is not misleading, for membership in the mysteries presumed a belief in their efficacy and required a conscious act of the will, a decision. Thus the mystery religions had a character decidedly different from the traditional official religions and in some respects not unlike Christianity. They were private, they were oriented around hope and assurance for the future, and they were voluntary. Unlike Judaism and especially Christianity, these new religions generally found increasing official acceptance at Rome. For although they differed decisively from the earlier forms of piety, they did not claim the exclusive loyalty of their adherents. A person could worship Zeus and the emperor and at the same time be an initiate of one or more mysteries. In fact, the official religions and the mysteries were complementary; they applied to different spheres of life, the one to public order and morality, the other to the need for emotional satisfaction and the assurance of the present and ultimate security of one's personal being and destiny. Doubtless the mystery religions were not as

[15] Especially by Günter Wagner, *Pauline Baptism and the Pagan Mysteries*, trans. J. P. Smith (Edinburgh: Oliver & Boyd, 1967).

overtly and thoroughly immoral as the early Christian writers portray them. But with the exception of Mithraism, which was based on the ethical dualism of Zoroastrianism and thus took the struggle of right against wrong quite seriously, none of the mysteries was primarily interested in the problem of morality.

Although the gods of Greece and Rome were not dead, during the New Testament period the mysteries and other religious movements were becoming increasingly popular and the older piety was losing some of its vitality. Christian polemicists at the beginning of the third century reserve their strongest invective for these relatively new cults and thus give good indication that they were by then the chief rivals of Christianity for the religious affections of the people.

At some time after the mystery religions moved into the center of the stage, there appeared another important spiritual phenomenon which was in some ways like them. We say "phenomenon" for it is not quite certain that *Gnosticism* should be called a religion. It was found in various places and in various forms. Until fairly recently most of our knowledge of Gnosticism came from Christian writers of the late second, third, and later centuries, all of whom portray Gnosticism as a Christian heresy, in which a special knowledge (Greek *gnōsis*—hence the name Gnosticism) rather than faith is made the key to salvation. Gnosticism was once regarded as the acute Hellenization of Christianity, a distorted translation of the Christian message into Greek ways of thinking and speaking. Yet recent research and discoveries have shown that Gnosticism is not simply derived from Christianity, and that it owes more to the East, to Syria, Persia, and Babylonia, and perhaps even to Judaism, than to classical Greek culture. (In this respect it is not unlike the mystery religions, many of which came from the Orient.) The exact nature and origin of Gnosticism is still obscure, however, and a matter of controversy among historians of religion.[16]

We can, however, get a fairly clear grasp of the thrust and meaning of Gnosticism. Wherever it appears, in whatever form, it is characterized by an extreme dualism of God and the world. In contrast to the Stoic monism, in which God and the world are essentially related and, indeed, indwell one another, Gnosticism takes God and the world to be separate and incompatible. Far from being the creation of the one God, as in Jewish and Christian thought, the world is at best an excrescence from the divine world, at worst the creation of an anti-god. Its very existence is the antithesis of God's salvation. The mystery religions were primarily moti-

---

[16] As in the case of Qumran, the volume of literature on Gnosticism is immense and is growing constantly. Since the definition of Gnosticism is debated, there is some question as to what bodies of ancient literature are to be understood as Gnostic, and thus there is a lack of agreement on the primary sources.

vated by men's desire to secure their own existence in the face of death. Gnosticism also had this goal in view, but combined with it an abhorence of evil, which was in general identified with this world and its history.

Men live in the world, but at least some of them are not of it. For while human bodies are made of the same substance as the world, there is, or may be, hidden within each one a spark of the divine life. Salvation is then the rescuing of the divine spark from its imprisonment in the material world, and specifically in the flesh. The first and essential step in this salvation is the recognition that one is not at home in this world, that his essential being is related to the divine world and can find its way home.[17]

> Consequently
> if one is a Gnostic, he is from
> above. If he is called,
> he is wont to heed, to respond,
> and to turn to Him who calls
> him, and go upward to Him. And
> he is wont to understand how he is called.
> Being a Gnostic, he is wont to do
> the will of Him who called
> him, is wont to wish to please Him, is wont to
> receive rest. Each one's name is wont
> to become his own.
> He who thus shall know
> is wont to understand whence he came
> and whither he goes.
> He is wont to understand as one
> who, having been drunk, has returned from
> his drunkenness, having returned to be himself
> alone: he has set on their feet
> the things that are his own. (Gospel of Truth, 22:3–20)[18]

Thus the process of salvation in Gnosticism involves, first of all, a sense of profound alienation from the world. One must then find his way out of his imprisonment in this world and into the world above. This can be done only by a special dispensation of knowledge by which the secrets of the way back to one's heavenly home are divulged. In Christian Gnostic

[17] A similar point of view is found in a set of documents known as the Hermetic literature or Hermetica. In their present form, these documents date from about the third century. They are not Christian, although they may have been influenced by Judaism. Whether they ought to be called Gnostic is a debated point. See C. K. Barrett, *The New Testament Background: Selected Documents*, pp. 80–90, for examples from the Hermetica.

[18] Cited from K. Grobel, *The Gospel of Truth: A Valentinian Meditation on the Gospel* (New York: Abingdon Press, 1962).

systems Jesus is the heavenly revealer who awakens man from his stupor in this world, reminds him of his heavenly home, reveals to him the secrets of the way, and perhaps also leads him back. The way back was often conceived as a rather long road, a tortuous climb back through the seven or more heavens, in each of which the Gnostic shed another part of his veil of flesh until his divine essence—the very quintessence of his being—arrived safely home.

This doctrine of salvation had its practical effects upon the life of the Gnostic in the world. He felt himself to be an alien, and, in a sense, already withdrawn from the concerns of ordinary human life. This estrangement sometimes expressed itself in radical withdrawal from the world and its life, that is, asceticism. But it could also result in a free indulgence in sensual pleasure, for since the flesh and the physical world had no significance, what one did with them was of no importance. Whichever course the Gnostic followed, he refused any positive, constructive participation in this human life, which his poor deluded fellowmen held so important.

Early Christianity was deeply engaged with the Gnostic problem throughout the second century, and probably even earlier. We see traces of the conflict in the Johannine literature, Colossians, and the Pastoral Epistles, not to mention the extensive anti-Gnostic literature that appears from the time of Justin Martyr in mid-second century. In addition, a large collection of Gnostic literature going back to the second century (although the actual manuscripts are somewhat later) has recently been uncovered in Nag Hammadi in southern Egypt. It was obviously used by people who considered themselves Christians. Some of the books, such as the Gospel of Truth and the Gospel of Thomas, are apparently Gnostic interpretations of Christianity. Others have little or no explicit connection with anything we can identify with Christianity, except that they were apparently used by this Gnostic Christian church.

The discussion of Gnosticism raises the question of what influence it had on the formation of the Christianity of the New Testament. It has been argued that Gnosticism came into being before the Christian faith and that before it came into contact with Christianity its doctrine already involved a myth about a redeemer who visited men in order to give them the knowledge of life. Some such doctrine is indeed found in the literature of Manichaeism, an Eastern religion post-Christian in origin (third century) and influenced by Christianity. It also appears in Mandaeism, the religion of a small Iranean sect, which still exists and whose origin and antiquity is a matter of keen dispute. The sharpness and vigor of the modern debate is probably not unrelated to the fact that the Mandaean "redeemer-myth" has real similarities to the Christian doctrine of Jesus as the Son of God whom the Father sent into the world, especially as it is set forth in the Gospel of John. Does the Christian doctrine recapitulate an earlier Gnostic myth? Certainly it is not just an imitation of such a myth, even if one existed. The canonical Gospels, which so clearly and intentionally portray the involvement of Jesus in this life and this world, are unprecedented in Gnostic literature. The so-called Gnostic Gospels are quite different from the canonical documents. Granted this, there is still the question of whether any sort of redeemer myth antedates Christianity. Here opinions sharply divide. Although the existence of a pre-Christian redeemer myth is quite doubtful, probably at least the Gnostic perspective or attitude came into contact with Christianity at a very early time.

There were, of course, other manifestations or belief and practice. These we can only note in passing. Many people in the ancient world were fascinated or oppressed by Fate (Greek, *heimarmenē*) or Fortune (Greek, *tychē*). Fortune came to be personalized and venerated as a goddess. The stars were thought to determine the course of men's lives, their fate. As a result, astrology, the "science" dealing with the influence of the stars on life, gained considerable popularity as the key to the secrets of human existence. At the same time, some people relied on magic, invoking on occasion even the names of Yahweh and Jesus. In addition, there were hero cults dedicated to men who had been elevated to the status of gods or demigods. Among these was the healing cult of Asclepius, who claimed many shrines and spas and thousands of devotees willing to ascribe to him miraculous cures no less amazing than those attributed to Jesus in the Gospels.

Diaspora Judaism

In the complex religious picture of the Greco-Roman world, Judaism was a significant factor. Most Jews did not live in Palestine, but in other parts of that world. As previously noted, this diaspora or dispersion of Jews to the far corners of the world began as early as 587 B.C. with the conquest of Judah and the destruction of Jerusalem by the Babylonians. While conditions within the homeland became more difficult during the postexilic period and the number of-Jews increased, the prospects of living outside of Palestine became increasingly attractive.

It is customary and useful to distinguish between the Judaism of the land of Israel and that of the diaspora. Both shared in most of the basic elements of Judaism mentioned at the beginning of this chapter, yet outside Palestine significant changes had taken place, most of which resulted from Hellenization. Even though Hellenization, or accommodation to Greek culture, was practiced by some Jews in Palestine, it occurred to a greater extent among the Jews of the diaspora. Outside Palestine, Judaism of necessity began to take on some of the characteristics of a religion as distinguished from a nation. Nevertheless, the Jews succeeded in maintaining their ethnic identity and a certain separateness in their ways and places of living. Yet Jews mingled to some extent with Gentiles, were inevitably influenced by them, and vice versa. Adjustments to life in a predominantly Gentile world became necessary.

As has already been indicated, one of the most important adjustments was in language. Judaism in the Greco-Roman world was largely Greek-speaking. The fact that the Hebrew scriptures had been translated into Greek and were read and interpreted in that language doubtless influenced the way they were understood. Philo of Alexandria, a contemporary of Jesus and Paul, affords a notable, if perhaps extreme, example of the kinds of changes that could take place. A Jew who never once thought of surrendering that hallmark of Judaism, the law, Philo nevertheless interpreted the Hebrew scriptures in terms of Hellenistic philosophy and piety by using the well-established Greek method of allegorizing. Thus he could wring meanings from Biblical texts of which the original authors would have never dreamed. Eventually, Hellenistic Judaism produced religious books containing ideas that were more Greek than Jewish. For example, one reads of the immortality of the souls of the righteous dead (Wisdom of Solomon 3:1–9), a fundamentally Greek idea, quite foreign to the Hebrew scriptures, although it has since become rather common in Christian thought.

Another adjustment forced on the Jews by the dispersion involved their public worship. Up until the destruction of the temple of Solomon at Jerusalem, the principal form of worship was sacrificial, officially performed at the Jerusalem temple, but sometimes actually carried out elsewhere, much to the disgust of some prophets and other purists. Not surprisingly, after the fall of Jerusalem, the destruction of the temple, the deportations, and the flight of refugees, another form of worship began to gain pre-eminence, the worship of the synagogue, or individual congregation. The synagogue continues to be the focal point of Jewish worship down to the present day. In New Testament times synagogues were sprinkled around the Mediterranean world, as well as in Palestine. The Acts of the Apostles portrays Paul (and by implication other Christian preachers) preaching the gospel in the local synagogue whenever he enters a new town.

The synagogues of the dispersion thus provided a ready-made platform for the early Christian missionaries, who, without necessarily ceasing to regard themselves as Jews, brought the good news of God's new salvation in Jesus the Messiah to the brethren and to others who might by chance listen. Inasmuch as new ideas and terms had already crept into the Hellenistic synagogue from the surrounding pagan culture, it need not surprise us if these appear also in the New Testament. The New Testament writings, at least in their present form, were addressed to a church which had grown up in the midst of the Hellenistic culture of the Roman Empire. The importance of the Greek-speaking Judaism of the dispersion for early Christianity is epitomized in the fact that the New Testament is written in Greek. Moreover, the Old Testament, which is so frequently cited in the New, is more often than not quoted from the Greek version.

Diaspora Judaism also prepared the way for the universal emphasis of the Christian gospel. In fact, the existence of this kind of Judaism helps explain how an historically exclusive community such as Judaism could have produced a missionary religion like Christianity. The Hellenistic synagogue itself did not disdain the missionary enterprise. There is some evidence of a sustained and serious effort to convert Gentiles to Judaism.[19] And not a few Gentiles were attracted by the antiquity and moral seriousness of the Jewish religion. The technical term for the conversion of Gentiles was proselytism, and converts were called proselytes. Even where proselytism was not actively pursued, the situation of the Jews in the midst of an alien and potentially hostile culture demanded they look outward and have a decent respect for public opinion. One sees such an outward-looking perspective in Philo, but perhaps it is even more noticeable in the great first century Jewish historian, Josephus. His extensive *Jewish Antiquities* is an elaborate exposition and explanation of the entire history and faith of his people for a literate Gentile audience. It is at once our best single source for the so-called intertestamental period and a monumental effort to make Jewish history intelligible to the wider world.

First century diaspora Judaism was an important movement in and of itself, but it is of an extraordinary significance for the Christianity of New Testament times. For the modern student it illumines the path that Christianity traversed from its beginnings as a sect of Palestinian Judaism to the status of a world religion.

In summary, the world into which Christianity came was one world by virtue of the universal Hellenistic culture and Roman government, but the religious situation was complex and varied. Within the variety, however, certain trends were developing: the waning of the importance of the older gods and practices, but their continued existence alongside the more recently introduced emperor worship; the emergence of popular philosophy on the one hand, and of religions of personal and otherworldly salvation on the other; widespread disenchantment with the world.

In the midst of such a welter of religions and religious feeling, Christianity must have seemed merely one more strange cult. Indeed, it was at first regarded as yet another manifestation of Jewish superstition.

---

[19] The most recent discussion of the missionary enterprise of Hellenistic Judaism in relation to early Christianity is Dieter Georgi, *Die Gegner des Paulus im 2. Korintherbrief: Studien zur religiösen Propaganda in der Spätantike* ("Wissenschaftliche Monographien zum Alten und Neuen Testament," 11; Neukirchener Verlag, 1964), esp. pp. 83–187.

The fact that its Jewish founder had been crucified as a criminal did not escape the notice of the first Roman historians to mention Christianity. The apostle Paul himself noted the humble origins of most Christians. Of all the religions and religious movements of the ancient world few would have seemed less likely to be the wave of the future than the Christian church. Yet the church succeeded, for people were preoccupied with the search for eternal life and yearned for regeneration, as well as for a sure guide in ordering this life. Christianity's vibrant hope and vigorous ethic spoke to their need. Moreover, the Christian community provided a source of identity and support in a world in which old securities were disappearing.

The Early Church

Palestinian Judaism was the matrix out of which Jesus, his disciples, and the very earliest Christian church sprang, but the Greco-Roman world was the background of the early Christian missionary effort and the extension and development of the church. For the origins of Christianity lay in Judaism, but at a very early point in its history Christianity became a predominantly Gentile religion. The New Testament itself is in considerable measure a testimony to this turning to the Gentiles. It is written in Greek and directed for the most part to churches that already stood apart from Judaism. The more immediate background of the New Testament itself would then seem to be the Greco-Roman world. Yet this is not quite the case; or at least two qualifications must be made. First, when Christians began to separate from the Jewish synagogue, or when Christian missionaries spoke to purely Gentile groups, they did not simply forget their Jewish and Old Testament heritage or leave it behind. (True, some people, such as the second century heretic Marcion, actually did, but their viewpoint is not represented in the New Testament.) Second, the immediate background of the New Testament was the early church itself. The New Testament was not simply written by individuals whose religious sensibilities were shaped by Jewish or Hellenistic culture, or both. The New Testament was written by people who were actively engaged in the life of the Christian communities springing up all around the eastern half of the Mediterranean world.

In studying the New Testament writings themselves we shall attempt to gain some notion of how they reflect and express the church settings in which they were written. It will be helpful, however, to have an overview of the total situation before us.

THE EMERGENCE OF CHRISTIANITY

Jesus' disciples were the nucleus of the earliest Christian church, although they did not constitute themselves as a church during his historical ministry. After his crucifixion and death in Jerusalem the disciples scattered, most of them going back to their northern homeland in Galilee. Only the belief that Jesus had risen from the dead brought them back together in Jerusalem. The Acts of the Apostles portrays the disciples gathered around the temple in the earliest days. At this stage many probably believed that the resurrection of Jesus signified that he would soon return in power and glory to establish God's reign on earth. When time passed and this did not happen, they naturally began to ask themselves why not. The answer was found by and large in what was going on around them —that is, in the preaching of the good news about Jesus and the establishment and spread of the church. God was allowing time, long or short, for this missionary effort to take place. This preaching was at first only in Palestine among Jews, but before long Gentiles were hearing the gospel and seeking admission to the church. This could have happened in the Jewish homeland itself, where there were a number of foreigners, but it was bound to happen with greater frequency as believers circulated among the synagogues and elsewhere in the Greco-Roman world.

One of the first, and certainly the most famous, Christian preachers to seek out Gentile audiences was the apostle Paul. The acute controversy in the church over whether a convert from the Gentile world had, in effect, to become a Jew in order to be a Christian centered largely around his missionary work. We have in the New Testament a number of Paul's letters, and several of them reflect something of this controversy. Paul's letters are the earliest documents in the New Testament, earlier even than the Gospels, and are thus a valuable source of information and understanding concerning how the earliest Christians lived and what they thought. The greater part of the Acts of the Apostles is also about Paul, although it must be used with some caution as a historical source because it was written a generation after its subject had died and manifests certain interests or biases of the author. In addition to the epistles of Paul, the New Testament contains a number of other letters from various times and places which afford valuable insights into the nature of early Christianity. Probably all of them, however, were written after the death of Paul. For the earliest period therefore we are dependent primarily on Paul and the later narration of the apostolic period found in Acts.

As the church spread across the world and became separated in time and space from its point of origin, Christians were faced with a new situation and new problems. Most of the members of the church were now Gentiles, with no first-hand contact with Jesus and the earliest disciples. Moreover, these earliest disciples were now dying away. As long as it was thought that the present age would be short, that history would soon run its course and Jesus would return in the kingdom of his Father, this was no cause for alarm. But as it became more and more evident that the world was not going to disappear either tomorrow or in the near future, the problem of living in the world became an urgent one. Because the Christians looked to Jesus as the author and guide of their life, and because he was now receding rapidly into the past, it became important to make sure that contact with him was not lost. As long as the original disciples lived this contact was secured through them, but as they died, it became necessary to preserve and formulate the church's message about Jesus. Thus in the second generation of the Christian church the Gospels as we have them were composed, Mark's probably being the first. The Gospels are usually thought of as books about Jesus, and so they are, but they were composed as materials that had been kept in the living and corporate memory of the church, and they were composed to serve the needs of that church. That these Gospels have found such a wide and continuous use in the church for nearly two thousand years shows how well they have met that need.

All the books in the New Testament follow the Gospel or letter (epistle) form except two, Acts and Revelation. Though quite different from one another, they both say something about the common outlook and perspective shared by New Testament Christians. Both were probably written toward the end of the first Christian century. Acts looks back over the history of the earliest period and reflects the fact that the church now has the leisure to contemplate its past. It no longer looks for the kingdom tomorrow or the next day. Revelation looks forward toward the last things, interprets events of the present and recent past in the light of the coming end, and mirrors the universal hope in the face of tragic circumstances which has from the beginning characterized the Christian faith. Together Acts and Revelation bespeak the historical character of Christianity, a faith which takes time and history, the present and the future, quite seriously.

THE DEVELOPMENT OF THE CANON

The New Testament is frequently characterized as the expression and deposit of the life and faith of early Christianity. This is true and, indeed, obvious to anyone who has reflected upon the matter. But such a statement does not really explain the New Testament. Although some of the New Testament books are occasional writings—that is, letters or tracts addressed to certain specific situations—by no means all of them are. So not all the individual writings can be viewed as if they were just what we would normally expect from a religious community with many outposts scattered over a broad area. There is something distinctively Christian about them. Or, to put it another way, their existence represents motives and interests that we have come to recognize as distinctively Christian.

The Problem of Authority

Although the letters of Paul are the earliest written communications that have survived from the primitive church, one has only to read the salutation of any of them to learn that they are more than friendly or business letters from one partner in an enterprise to another: "Paul, an apostle of Jesus Christ by the will of God. . . ." Paul addresses his readers as a man commissioned with a task and invested with authority. When he talks of visiting them he asks his readers how they wish him to come, "with a rod, or with love in a spirit of gentleness." When he is challenged, he does not hesitate to speak of the basis of his authority: "Am I not free? Am I not an apostle? Have I not seen Jesus our Lord? Are not you my workmanship in the Lord?" Paul regards the Christians to whom he has preached and the churches that he has founded as his peculiar province and responsibility, given him by God. This is why he writes in such an authoritative way. But why was such authority necessary? This question will concern us later on. For the moment it is sufficient to observe that as an apostle Paul accepts the responsibility of speaking authoritatively to the question of what the gospel is. We have already spoken of Christians preaching the gospel, but what gospel was to be preached? We have used the term *salvation*, but what was meant by it? There were certain widely accepted ideas about how these questions should be answered in the earliest church, but the formulation of precise and accepted answers was the task of earliest Christian theology.

There were several possible answers to the question concerning the nature of the gospel. Some early Christians doubtless thought that it was the good news that Jesus would soon return to establish his kingdom on earth. At least a few evidently felt the prospect of Jesus' imminent return meant this world and its tasks were no longer to be taken seriously. Some probably saw the chief significance of Jesus' coming in what it meant for Israel. He was indeed the Messiah, as God had shown by raising him from the dead. Because Jesus had taught, and his disciples had cherished his teachings even before his death and resurrection, many might have continued to see in his teaching the most important factor. Perhaps others were impressed with his power to heal and cast out demons; there were those in the early church who felt that they were also possessed of such remarkable powers.

Although all these views were represented in early Christianity, in its missionary preaching the church concentrated upon the crucifixion and the resurrection. At first the overwhelming conviction that God had vindicated Jesus by raising him from the dead, and with him the hopes of his followers, must have been predominant. Yet one could scarcely speak of the resurrection without taking account of the death of Jesus. Why did he die, and what did his death accomplish? The question is not unfamiliar to those who have mourned the apparently pointless assassination of important public figures.

The earliest Christians understood Jesus' death in at least two ways. First, it was an event that God in his inscrutable wisdom had ordained. Thus passages from the Old Testament were used to interpret Jesus' death. In the second place, it was a vicarious sacrifice—that is, a sacrifice made on behalf of others, his immediate followers initially, but ultimately all mankind. What appeared to be, and at one level actually was, the tragic work of evil or mistaken men turned out to be an event of far-reaching importance for the salvation of humanity.

In the New Testament Paul appears as the leading exponent and interpreter of the death or, as he puts it, the cross of Jesus. It is the negation of the pride, power, and wisdom of this world, the sign of God's mercy and goodness toward those who are willing to give up any claim on such pride, power, and wisdom and live by faith.

> For since in the wisdom of God, the world did not know God through wisdom, it pleased God through the folly of what we preach to save those who believe. For Jews demand signs and Greeks seek wisdom, but we preach Christ crucified, a stumbling block to Jews and folly to Gentiles, but to those who are called, both Jews and Greeks, Christ the power of God and the wisdom of God. For the foolishness of God is wiser than men, and all the weakness of God is stronger than men. (I Cor. 1:21–25)

Paul's eloquent meditation upon the meaning of the cross sheds light backward on the antecedents of Christianity and forward on the shape of the New Testament and of Christian preaching and theology.

Paul characterizes the Jews as demanding signs and the Greeks as seeking wisdom. Exactly what he means by "signs" and "wisdom" might be the legitimate subject of some debate, but the general significance of what he is saying is clear enough. *Signs* is a term used elsewhere in the New Testament and in the Old of miracles or otherwise tangible and significant deeds. To say that the Jews seek signs may mean that they seek miracles to validate religious claims. In point of fact, Jesus encounters the demand for signs from some of his countrymen. Paul apparently means that the Jews seek some clear indication that the claims made about Jesus by his followers are true. This is the most obvious sense of his statement. But in principle the demand for signs may be taken in a broader sense as referring to all overt manifestations of God's presence or approval. That Paul himself drew this further meaning is not indicated in the immediate context. Nevertheless, the Jewish understanding of history, righteousness, and eschatology could be summed up as a quest for signs. The Jew looked back for signs of God's past favor or judgment of his history. He looked around at his own and his neighbor's conduct to see whether it signified his obedience to the law. He looked forward to the vindication of his obedience and his nation's election in a public intervention of God—that is, the resurrection, the messianic age, and the age to come.

When Paul speaks of the "Greeks" he may mean Gentiles in general, since Greek language and culture were the common coinage of the day. But it is not beside the point to note that the Corinthians, to whom Paul was writing, were Greeks, so the contrast of Jews and Greeks rather than Gentiles in general would have been appropriate in I Corinthians. The important question, however, has to do with the meaning of *wisdom*. There was a tradition of theological and human wisdom in Judaism (cf. the Old Testament books of Proverbs, Job, and Ecclesiastes). But Paul has in mind here a general orientation, and it would be wrong to describe the general orientation of Judaism in terms of wisdom. It is rather the Greek or the pagan who seeks salvation through wisdom or knowledge. This trait is by no means confined to the phenomenon of Gnosticism, although it is perhaps best represented there. There is impressive evidence of the search for salvation through wisdom or knowledge in the Greek philosophical tradition, especially from Socrates down. Apparently the mystery religions presupposed knowledge of the mysteries as necessary for salvation. At a more primitive level one thinks of the knowledge of magical formulations and charms. From the East astrology, the knowledge of the stars, had an impact upon the Greek mind. The statement that the Greeks seek wisdom is true in a variety of senses.

If Jews demand signs and Greeks seek wisdom, what do the two have in common? One might think very little. But over against the cross of Christ the common factor in the demand for signs and the quest for wisdom stands out. Both signs and wisdom put a premium on what is controllable or calculable. The demand for a sign is the demand that one's claim to authority or righteousness be validated publicly in a generally recognized way. The search for wisdom is a search for certainty. Both are in different ways efforts to calculate the divine intention and to control the relation to it so that man's best interest is served. The sign makes the one who receives it the judge of its validity. Wisdom is power in any time and in any relationship. Over against signs and wisdom Paul puts the cross of Christ, which he describes as weakness and foolishness. It is important to remember that he means weakness and foolishness by the world's standards. Yet his contrast does make sense, for the cross upsets all efforts to make the divine reality subject to human calculation and control. It implies the reversal of ordinary standards of evaluation. The one sent from God is crucified and dies, but though he dies, God's will is not thwarted but carried out. By setting the cross over against the religious quests of both the Jew and the Greek, Paul shows how it symbolizes or sums up the essence of the gospel, the Christian kerygma.

Paul's word shows the contrast between the Christian message and the standards and expectations of an unbelieving world. He takes up the theme of the cross, which was given him by history and by the earliest tradition, and develops its theological meaning. Paul thus represents the course that the mainstream of Christian teaching and preaching was to take. His central emphasis on the cross recurs again and again in the New Testament. One finds it in all the Gospels, in the speeches of Acts, in I Peter and in Hebrews. Paul effectively defined the center of the Christian message, that in the cross of Christ God was acting for the salvation of mankind. This emphasis existed and would probably have prevailed without Paul, but Paul immensely deepened and enriched the Christian tradition at its source.

Yet the needs of the church could not be satisfied by simply repeating the message of the cross. From the days of Jesus' public ministry his disciples had remembered and cherished many of the things he said. Alongside the proclamation of the cross there existed a tradition of the sayings of Jesus himself. These were regarded as authoritative words carrying the same weight as the divine revelation of the Old Testament. Although Paul does not dwell upon Jesus' teaching, on the rare occasions when he quotes a word of Jesus he obviously regards it as decisive. Only after Paul's death, however, were the central proclamation of Jesus' death and resurrection and the traditions of his teaching and healing ministry combined, producing the documents we call Gospels. We have then in the Gospels at least two of the main foci of authority in the early church and in the New Testament—the apostolic proclamation of the gospel, centering in the cross, and the word of the Lord himself. We therefore can infer that in the initial stages of the process of the composition of apostolic letters and the transmission of the tradition of Jesus, and in the later stage which saw the combining of the two, there is a single fundamental motivation. That motivation is the desire to say clearly what the Christian message is.

A third important locus of authority in early Christianity was the prophet. Paul speaks of the prophet and ranks him second only to the apostle. The book of Revelation seems to be the work of at least one such prophet. In the Didache, an early work which was not included in the New Testament, we learn that some prophets were beginning to present problems. What was the extent and basis of their authority? Some of them obviously felt empowered to speak in the name of the Lord, as we see in Revelation (cf. esp. 1:17–3:22). Similar prophetic words of the Lord are probably found also in the Gospels. The author of Revelation did not fall out of touch with the reality of the earthly and crucified Lord and surely the evangelists did not. Still, the danger that the prophetic inspiration or imagination would simply run wild was always present, so it became necessary not only to test every spirit (I John 4:1), but to establish definite norms by which the true and the right could be separated from the specious. The writing down of the New Testament books was in part an answer to such needs.

The Collection of the Books

The need to have a norm or rule (Greek, *kanōn*) for faith and life was already at work in the writing of many of the New Testament books. During the period of the formation of the New Testament, as various books were sifted and collected, this need only became more explicit. Some early writings were eliminated because they were not the work of apostles or authors with apostolic connections; others fell into disuse or were considered less profitable, unsound, or even dangerous. Gradually a consensus developed on the need for a canon and on the books to be included in it.

Two approximate dates, the end of the first century and the end of the second, are important for understanding the development of the New Testament. By the end of the first century, or soon thereafter, most of the books now in the New Testament had been written. By the end of the second century the principal books of the New Testament were already recognized as authoritative.

We learn from a number of different sources dating from about the end of the second century that Christians throughout the world were using the same authoritative books. These books now comprise the major portion of the New Testament. They are the four Gospels, the Acts of the Apostles, the thirteen Pauline letters, and at least two of the Catholic or general letters, I Peter and I John. Conspicuous by their absence are the Letter to the Hebrews and the Revelation to John. The apostolic origin of Hebrews was doubted in western Christendom for a long time—it was eventually accepted as the work of Paul. The book of Revelation was suspected in the East, but was eventually accepted as the work of the apostle John. Such omissions are significant, but the really important point is that at least twenty of the twenty-seven books which were eventually to comprise the New Testament were accepted as canonical by about the end of the second century. The Muratorian canon, which lists the books accepted by the Roman church; Irenaeus, representing Gaul and the West; Tertullian, the fiery North African; and Clement, the learned bishop of Alexandria, all testify that by and large the same books were in use. A list of canonical books identical with the twenty-seven accepted by almost all churches does not appear until the latter half of the fourth century, but after A.D. 200 the differences were minor compared with the basic agreement among most Christians.

The history of the New Testament canon from the end of the first century to the end of the second, or from the writing of the individual books until the emergence of an accepted collection at about the end of the second century, is quite obscure. During this time the history of the canon is mainly the history of its two primary parts, the Gospels and the letters of Paul. But concerning the collection of these two sets of documents we actually know little.

Some of the letters of Paul seem to have circulated during his own lifetime and at his direction (see Col. 4:16). How soon after his death an effort was made to collect his letters is uncertain. If, as has been proposed, Ephesians was written as an introduction to a collection of ten of Paul's letters, the collection itself would have to be dated within the first century. This plausible hypothesis cannot, however, be proved, for clear evidence is too slim. It is true that about the middle of the second century Marcion, who espoused doctrines the church condemned as heretical, had a canon consisting of the Gospel of Luke and ten of Paul's letters. Yet this bit of information is not too helpful, for it is uncertain whether Marcion's canon was the first ever to have been put forward or merely an adaptation of a churchly canon. What does seem certain is that between the end of the first century and the middle of the second Paul's letters began to circulate and that they were regarded as fruitful for reading if not holy scripture. Ignatius, the bishop of Antioch (*ca.* 115), mentions "all the letters of Paul" in his own letter to the Ephesian church (12:2) and all of Paul's letters are also spoken of in II Peter 3:16 (written *ca.* 125–150). This indicates that in the early second century his letters were already known as a collection. Moreover, the collection of Ignatius' letters soon after they were written may well have been inspired by the existence of a Pauline collection.[20]

As for the Gospels, we again know little about the circumstances of their collection. Ignatius seems to have known Matthew and perhaps John, but possibly he was principally familiar with oral traditions that have been incorporated into those Gospels. Marcion at mid-second century knew at least Luke. At the same time Justin Martyr, a Samaritan Christian living at Rome, appears to have known our Synoptic Gospels. He probably knew the Gospel of John also, but he betrays a curious reticence in referring to it. His disciple Tatian somewhat later in the second century combined our four canonical Gospels into one unified account of Jesus ministry called the *Diatessaron* (the Greek name indicates that it has been composed out of four other documents). In the last quarter of the second century, Irenaeus wrote at some length about the four Gospels and made a point of the appropriateness and the necessity of four. It is as if he were addressing himself to people who did not think that four were needed. And, in fact, there were those in the early church who questioned the right of the

---

[20] That Ignatius' letters already existed as a collection in the early second century is indicated by Polycarp (died *ca.* 155), Epistle to the Philippians 13:2.

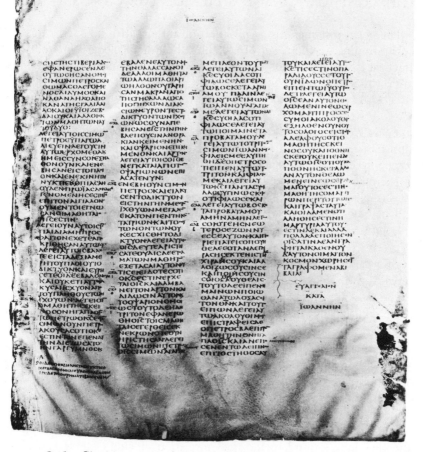

Codex Sinaiticus, one of the great fourth-century manuscripts of the New Testament, discovered by C. Tischendorf at the monastery of St. Catherine on Mt. Sinai in 1859. (Courtesy of American Bible Society and British Museum.)

Fourth Gospel to be regarded as apostolic and authoritative. In all probability, Marcion, whose canon contained only one Gospel, reflects the earlier practice. For in the beginning an individual church, or even a geographical area, would have used only one Gospel. A multigospel canon would have come into use only as the Gospels of various churches were combined. In the process of combination some Gospels doubtless fell by the wayside. In the early Christian writers we catch glimpses of some of these other Gospels, which for one reason or another were rejected in the process of sifting and choosing that led to the formation of what we know as the New Testament.

THE SIGNIFICANCE AND SHAPE OF THE CANON

The New Testament as a collection of authoritative books, a canon of holy scripture, was born out of a combination of theological interests and practical needs. But these interests and needs were not simply imposed from without upon the New Testament books. It is true that the apostle Paul, for example, did not think that he was writing holy scripture when he wrote to the Corinthians or even to the Romans. Yet he was quite consciously asserting his apostolic authority to say what distinctively Christian faith was and what it implied for the life of believers under certain specific circumstances. Similarly, those who preserved the sayings of Jesus may not have thought of themselves as setting up a rival to Moses. Nevertheless, they believed in the sayings of Jesus as faithful guides to the will of God and applied them like holy scripture to the situations that arose in the life of the church. The impulses to establish a canon and thus to provide resources for the guidance and enrichment of the church did not begin with the writing of the last New Testament book, but in some form actually preceded and motivated the writing of many of those books. Thus at the most fundamental level there is a unity in the New Testament.

Of course, the various New Testament books do not all say the same thing. In fact, there are real differences and even some disagreements among them. For the most part, however, the New Testament books show an interest in what is apostolic, authoritative, and original. They attach importance to the earthly life and ministry of Jesus, even if, as in the case of Paul, that interest concentrates mainly upon his death. They regard the death and resurrection of Jesus as the central saving event. They look upon Christ and the church as the fulfillment of Old Testament prophecy, and they look forward to the final revelation of God's power and glory. Moreover, they agree in attaching fundamental importance to the moral life. It is by no means a safe assumption, however, that all early Christians or their literature agreed on these points. Increasing evidence that they did not continually comes to the fore. We shall discover that Paul encountered Christians who thought the gospel was a new legalism or that it meant a license to do anything one pleased. The Pastoral Epistles, II Peter, and Revelation all lash out at supposedly wrong-headed and dangerous ideas held by Christians. The Christian Gnostic texts recently discovered in Egypt reveal an aberrant form of Christianity with ancient roots. Significantly, some words of Jesus in the Synoptic Gospels, especially Matthew, are applied against misguided Christians.

The New Testament as a whole is an effort on the part of the early Christian church to define the faith and indicate its consequences for life. It is intended to lay down certain directions and boundaries, for it is not simply a random or even a representative specimen of opinion. It goes beyond, but does not contradict, the purposes of the individual authors in writing. When we think of the meaning of the New Testament, therefore, we concern ourselves not only with what the authors intended but with the meaning of the canon as a whole.

The shape or structure of the entire New Testament is also a matter of real importance. The order of the books in the New Testament is not, as is sometimes supposed, a chronological one. Nor were they arranged in this order because it was *thought* to be the order of their composition. Rather, it is a logical or theological order. The Gospels appear first, not because they were written first—research has shown that they were not—but because the logic of history and faith gives them priority. They deal with the manifestation of Christ in the flesh, and knowledge of Christ incarnate is necessary if one is to fully grasp the Christian message. Within the canon of the Gospels, the Gospel of John appears last, not because it was written last, although it probably was, but because it represents a longer perspective on the historic Christ and in some ways a profounder view of him. Thus it sums up the other Gospels. After the Gospels comes Acts. Again, Acts is not one of the earlier books of the New Testament, but it purports to deal with the earliest period. Thus it forms a logical introduction to the reading of the epistles (letters), which can only be understood against the background of the history of the early church. After the letters stands the Book of Revelation, very probably not the last New Testament book written but the one that speaks most extensively of the last things. It points the reader to the future, which is the direction in which the whole New Testament bids him look.

In the order of this book we have adopted the basic arrangement of the New Testament with some modifications. Because Jesus as the Christ is the essential subject matter of the New Testament, the Gospels stand at the beginning of the canon. In our treatment of the New Testament, therefore, we have taken up the Gospels first. This is an attempt to take seriously the historical priority of Jesus as well as his theological importance for early Christianity. The Gospels are treated before Jesus, however, in recognition of the fact that our only significant access to knowledge about the historical Jesus is through the Gospels. Because of the consensus of critical opinion that Mark was the first Gospel written, we depart from the order of the New Testament to treat Mark ahead of Matthew. Acts stands immediately after the Gospels in the New Testament presumably because it is the continuation of the story and the necessary background for reading the rest of the books. Accordingly, Acts is treated at the beginning of Part Two, even though it was written later than many of the other documents treated in that part. Paul's letters appear next in the canon and in this treatment. Here and in the case of the post-Pauline letters we have not followed the exact order of the New Testament because it seemed important to show certain aspects of the historical development of the Pauline mission and the New Testament church.

The Johannine literature is treated last. This may seem an odd departure from the usual procedure of generally following the order of the New Testament, but actually it is not. The Gospel according to John stands last among the Gospels and in a sense recapitulates them. The Johannine epistles stand last among the New Testament letters, with the exception of the tiny letter of Jude. The last book in the Bible is the Revelation of John, and appropriately so. Treating the traditionally Johannine books together implies nothing about their authorship. Gospel, epistles, and Revelation are likely written by different authors. But by taking them together and at the end it will be possible to do justice to their positions in the New Testament. At the same time, they represent the various types of literature found in the New Testament and will afford us a kind of summation and review at the conclusion of our study.

Suggestions for Further Reading

Books available in paperback are marked by an asterisk (*). Paperback publishers are indicated only when they differ from the original publisher. Subtitles and series titles have usually been omitted to conserve space.

Primary Sources. The Old and New Testaments are cited according to the Revised Standard Version, as is the Apocrypha of the Old Testament, which is now bound with some editions of the RSV. Josephus' *Jewish* Antiquities *and Jewish War** is conveniently available in orginal Greek and translation in The Loeb Classical Library (Cambridge: Harvard University Press), as are the works of Philo, Eusebius' *Ecclesiastical History,** and the writings of the Apostolic Fathers.* (Josephus' *Jewish War* is in paperback as a Penguin Book. Eusebius' *Ecclesiastical History* and the Apostolic Fathers have been issued in paperback by Baker Book House.)

The only source for the Jewish pseudepigraphal writings (writings under false names accepted as canonical by no Christian or Jewish group) is the massive translation and commentary of R. H. Charles, *The Apocrypha and Pseudepigrapha of the Old Testament,* 2 vols. (Oxford: Clarendon Press, 1913).

The Mishnah, which is the basic collection of material stemming from the earlier Rabbis, has been translated and published by H. Danby (London: Oxford University Press, 1933). The Mishnaic tactate *Aboth* or

Pirke Aboth ("fathers" or "chapters of the fathers") has been translated and published with a selection of ancient Talmudic commentary by Judah Goldin, *The Living Talmud: The Wisdom of the Fathers** (New York: New American Library, 1957).

A recent translation of the Qumran scrolls is G. Vermes, *The Dead Sea Scrolls in English** (Baltimore, Penguin Books, 1962). Still reliable guides to the scrolls are the two volumes of M. Burrows, both of which contain translations of the principal documents, *The Dead Sea Scrolls* (New York: Viking, 1955) and *More Light on the Dead Sea Scrolls* (New York: Viking, 1958). The most convenient collection of translated sources for Jewish religion is S. W. Baron and J. L. Blau (eds.), *Judaism: Postbiblical and Talmudic Period* (New York: Liberal Arts Press, 1954). For Hellenistic religions there is from the same press F. C. Grant (ed.), *Hellenistic Religions: The Age of Syncretism* (1953). For Gnostic sources see R. M. Grant, *Gnosticism* (New York: Harper, 1961). A very valuable collection of translations of sources relevant to the background of the New Testament is C. K. Barrett (ed.), *The New Testament Background: Selected Documents** (London: SPCK, 1957, Harper Torchbook).

Modern Works. Rudolf Bultmann, *Primitive Christianity in its Contemporary Setting,** trans. R. H. Fuller (New York: Meridian Books, 1956), is the best brief survey of the religious and cultural milieu of early Christianity. A treatment oriented more closely about the history of Judaism is Part I of M. S. Enslin, *Christian Beginnings** (New York: Harper, 1938), found in the first volume of the paperback edition. W. Foerster, *From the Exile to Christ: A Historical Introduction to Palestinian Judaism,* trans. G. E. Harris (Philadelphia: Fortress, 1964), treats somewhat more extensively the religious situation of contemporary Judaism. Still the classic on Judaism is G. F. Moore, *Judaism in the First Centuries of the Christian Era,* 3 vols. (Cambridge: Harvard University Press, 1927–30). The works of Burrows on the Qumran scrolls cited above are helpful, as well as F. M. Cross, *The Ancient Library of Qumran and Modern Biblical Studies** (rev. ed.; Garden City, N.Y.: Doubleday, 1961).

For the Hellenistic religious world, F. C. Grant, *Roman Hellenism and the New Testament* (New York: Scribner's, 1962), is valuable, particularly for its extensive, excellent bibliography. On the mystery religions the best readily available work is H. R. Willoughby, *Pagan Regeneration* (Chicago: University of Chicago Press, 1929). Traditional Greek and Roman religion is treated by H. R. Rose, *Religion in Greece and Rome** (New York: Harper, 1959), available only in paperback. For Gnosticism see H. Jonas, *The Gnostic Religion** (rev. ed.; Boston: Beacon Press, 1963), as well as R. McL. Wilson, *Gnosis and the New Testament* (Oxford: Blackwell, 1968).

M. Rostovtzeff, *A History of the Ancient World,** 2 vols., trans. J. D.

Duff (Oxford: Clarendon Press, 1926–30), is available in paperback in volumes entitled *Greece* and *Rome*, from which some of the original material is omitted. Note also W. W. Tarn, *Hellenistic Civilization** (3rd ed. rev. with G. T. Griffith; London: Arnold, 1952; paperback, Meridian Books). The *Cambridge Ancient History*, 12 vols. (Cambridge: Cambridge University Press, 1923–39) is an invaluable reference tool.

For further readings on the early church and its canon, see General Bibliography, IV.

Part I
The
Synoptic
Gospels
and Jesus

Statue of Jesus carrying the cross by Justin Accrombessi, contemporary artist from Ghana. (Courtesy of Spartaco Appetiti.)

2 The Gospel According to Mark: Triumph Through Suffering

Notes on the Gospel of Mark and the Synoptic Problem

The Gospel according to Mark is an anonymous first century Christian writing. The tradition that attributed its authorship to Mark, the interpreter and companion of the apostle Peter, was in all likelihood a second century guess.[1] Indeed all four canonical Gospels were probably first read by early

---

* The brief outline for each New Testament book gives only the basic structure of the writing. Italicized passages will be discussed as representative texts and should not be taken as part of a complete outline.

[1] See the report by the Christian bishop and historian Eusebius (*ca.* A.D. 260–340) concerning the earlier tradition from another bishop, Papias (*ca.* A.D. 150), in *The*

Christian communities as anonymous writings. For the sake of convenience, however, we shall continue to use the customary names to identify the respective Gospels.

Probably Mark is the earliest Gospel. The evidence for this view is derived from a comparison with the other two Gospels that are quite similar, Matthew and Luke. These three Gospels are known as the Synoptic Gospels. ("Synoptic" means that they see together; that is, they present a common view of Jesus' ministry.) One can see and evaluate this evidence with the help of a synopsis of the Gospels, a volume in which the Synoptic Gospels are arranged in three parallel columns for easy comparison. Two striking facts emerge from such a study. (1) The order of events in the narratives of Matthew, Mark, and Luke is frequently the same; but where it is not, Matthew and Luke almost never agree with each other against Mark. (2) A similar observation can be made about the wording of the text. Sometimes it is identical, but where it is not, Matthew and Luke only rarely have the same wording in disagreement with Mark. In both cases, one sees Mark and Matthew agreeing against Luke or Mark and Luke agreeing against Matthew rather frequently. The rarity of agreement of Matthew and Luke against Mark is very significant.

What does this mean? If one finds several factors occurring in the combinations abc, ab, and bc, but never ac, he will observe that b is the common factor. Similarly, if he finds Matthew (a), Mark (b), and Luke (c) agreeing, or Matthew (a) and Mark (b) agreeing, or Mark (b) and Luke (c) agreeing, but never Matthew (a) and Luke (c) agreeing without Mark (b), he will observe that Mark (b) is the common factor. If Mark is the common factor, without which Matthew and Luke rarely agree, then probably Mark was the source of both Matthew and Luke. That is, both Matthew and Luke as they wrote, quite independently of one another, had copies of Mark before them.[2]

There are many cases in which Matthew and Luke have similar or identical sayings of Jesus completely lacking in Mark. The different use and arrangement of this material in Matthew and Luke would seem to indicate that neither copied the other. Probably Matthew and Luke drew upon another common source other than Mark. It no longer exists independently, but is usually called "Q" (German *Quelle*, meaning "source"). In addition Matthew and Luke both had access to special traditions either oral or written.

Ecclesiastical History, III, 39, 14. Papias or his predecessors may have inferred that Mark was the evangelist because of (1) Peter's role as the dominant disciple in the Gospel (fifteen references; see, for example, 1:16–20, 29–31, 35 f.; 3:13–19); (2) the absence of any tradition about direct Petrine authorship of a Gospel; and (3) the knowledge of an association of Mark with Peter in Rome (I Pet. 5:13; cf. Philemon 24; Col. 4:10; II Tim. 4:11).

2 Mark is shorter, cruder, and more difficult to understand than Matthew or Luke. It used to be thought that Mark had condensed the Gospel of Matthew, but Mark contains little of the teachings of Jesus found in Matthew. Would a condenser have omitted the most striking part of Matthew? Where Mark and Matthew report the same incidents, Mark's account is, as a rule, actually longer and more detailed. Would a condenser have lengthened individual stories by adding various details? Such considerations support the view that Mark is our earliest Gospel, not a later condensation. The Gospel of John is very different from the Synoptics and generally thought to be later and relatively independent. For more complete discussion see P. Feine, J. Behm, and W. G. Kümmel, *Introduction to the New Testament*, trans. A. J. Mattill (New York: Abingdon Press, 1966), pp. 33–60. For a different solution, the priority of Matthew,

These insights of source criticism were extended further by the results of form criticism, which went behind the written sources to investigate the period of the oral tradition about Jesus. Form criticism established that even the earliest tradition of Jesus served the church's life; furthermore, this oral tradition circulated in independent units (pericopes), characterized by certain forms or structures. These self-contained units, "pearls" of tradition, were probably first strung together into a connected framework by the anonymous author of Mark. Strictly speaking then the writer of Mark was not an author but a redactor, a shaper of the tradition.

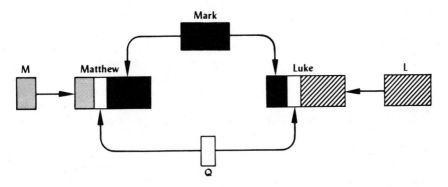

Redaction criticism, the separation of tradition (small independent units of of tradition) from redaction (transitional devices that connect and shape these units), established that, although the Gospels were not created from nothing, the writers used the tradition available to them in creative and constructive ways, partly because the tradition probably contained no outline of the life of Jesus. Each Gospel sought to speak with relevance and power to its own situation, while being faithful to the historical Jesus. The nature of their respective writings is the subject of the following three chapters.

Our method for determining the message of each Gospel consists of four simple steps: (1) Outlining the structure: By determining the anatomy or basic outline (for example, its beginning, climax, and end), we can discern the intention and meaning of the Gospel. (2) Enumerating frequent emphases: These emphases become evident in examining the order and structure of the Gospel; moreover, repeated emphases serve to test any theory of the structure. Interpretation of a writing must take into account dominant emphases. (3) Separating tradition from redaction: By seeing which earlier material is selected and how it has been shaped, we can arrive at probable conclusions about the intention of the author as he selects and redacts the tradition. This primary technique of form criticism is difficult to employ in the case of the Gospel of

---

see W. R. Farmer, *The Synoptic Problem: A Critical Analysis* (New York: Macmillan Co., 1964). For understanding the Synoptic problem the most valuable aid is the *Gospel Parallels: A Synopsis of the First Three Gospels* (adapted from the Huck-Lietzmann Synopsis, 9th edition, 1936; New York: Thomas Nelson & Sons, 1949). This convenient arrangement of the Synoptic material is indispensable for study of the Gospels because it shows the remarkable similarities and differences within the Synoptic tradition which have brought forth the present most generally accepted hypotheses.

Mark because we do not have the sources of tradition which Mark used. (4) Setting forth the historical context: Some historical situations called forth the writing of each Gospel. Out of our knowledge of the historical and religious background we can find an occasion that consistently explains the origin of the particular Gospel in question. In other words, our interpretation must consistently fit some historical situation with the life of the first-century church.

Of course, all four methodological steps mutually inform and correct each other. No neat, simple procedure alleviates the necessity for common sense and imagination as primary ingredients for understanding.

Before turning to Mark's Gospel, we need to have in mind something of the nature of a Gospel. The Greek word for gospel, *euangelion*, means "good news." This word had acquired religious significance in the Roman Empire, chiefly in the cult of the emperor, in which the appearance of the Roman emperor, his accession to the throne, and his decrees were known as glad tidings or gospels. In the New Testament itself, gospel also signifies good news of salvation (see for example, Matt. 11:5; Rom. 1:1; I Cor. 15:1; Mark 1:1). Perhaps the New Testament usage was partly derived from the "good tidings" of freedom from bondage which Isaiah proclaimed to the people of Israel emerging from the Babylonian Exile (see Isaiah 40:9; 52:7; 61:1). Previous usage of *euangelion* implied the oral nature of such news; however, with Mark, Matthew, Luke, John, and the apocryphal Gospels, the Gospel became a distinctive, literary category.* This literary type can be defined negatively. The Gospels are not biographies, for they lack the usual interest in personal character and in the chronological order of Jesus' life. Neither are they myths, tales of the gods, because Jesus of Nazareth, the central figure of the Gospels, was a historical person. Yet elements of both biography (a story of a particular historical man) and myth (a tale of the divine action) are present in the Gospels. Basically the Gospels are religious proclamations based upon historical event.

The writing of the first Gospel was no casual, accidental affair. Up until the time of Mark (or some unknown predecessor), the oral tradition about Jesus and the Hebrew scriptures were authoritative for the early church. Although Papias, a second century Christian bishop, knew of written Gospels, he still preferred the living tradition of the Lord to "the content of books" (Eusebius, EH, III, 39, 3 ff.). In early Christianity the Lord's authority did not stop with his life and death. He was a living Lord; consequently, the tradition was living and developing. When some Christians took the step of writing down, and hence partially fixing, this tradition, it was only because of pressing needs of the church.

One obvious reason for writing Gospels was the death of the apostles, those who had been with Jesus. The church could not afford to lose the tradition of Jesus. Mark probably originated in the mid-sixties when, according to tradition, Paul and Peter, the two great apostles, were martyred.

Other motives were also at work in the writing down of the Gospels. A church facing persecution needed to know the way in which Jesus himself had faced persecution. The early church, furthermore, had to struggle to under-

* In order to distinguish between Gospel as a book (for example, Mark) and gospel as Christian preaching, we shall capitalize the former but not the latter.

stand itself apart from the law, organization, rites, and customs of Judaism. The early church also had to face the problem posed by the delay of the expected parousia (second coming of Jesus) and the end of the world. As the Christian mission expanded into the Gentile world, a further crisis was posed by the problem of how a religion basically Jewish in origin could appeal to the Hellenistic world without losing its identity and distinctiveness.

These, and other needs, were at work in the writing of Gospels. Seemingly these problems could have been handled in some cases without resorting to the Gospel form of literature. Yet the early church looked for direction and guidance basically in the event of Jesus' life, death, and resurrection, so that the Gospel became the most appropriate vehicle for the Christian message. Indeed, our first known Gospel (Mark) originated primarily under the threat of persecution just as Jesus' ministry had taken shape under the threat of danger and death.

We may infer the date and place of Mark's origin from the Gospel itself. In Mark 13 (vss. 2, 14), the destruction of Jerusalem (A.D. 70) is either imminent or has just taken place. An early tradition about this Gospel testifies to its origin in Rome (see Eusebius, EH, VI, 14, 6). Mark was written to a Christian Gentile audience (see Mark 10:12—divorce by women was not possible in Palestine—and 5:41; 7:3 f., 11, 34; 15:22—ignorance of Jewish practices is assumed). Furthermore, events in Rome during the mid-sixties admirably fit Mark's emphasis upon persecution. Such obvious emphases as the suffering of Jesus (8:31; 9:31; 10:33 f.), the centrality of the cross (chaps. 14 and 15), and the necessity for a suffering and serving discipleship (8:34–38; 9:33–50; 10:38–45; 13:9–13) frame Mark's urgent message to a persecuted community. Furthermore, Tacitus, the first century Roman historian, describes persecution of Roman Christians in the mid-sixties by the emperor Nero, who evidently, in order to enlarge his palace complex, started a great fire that burned much of Rome:

> Therefore, to scotch the rumour, Nero substituted as culprits, and punished with the utmost refinements of cruelty, a class of men, loathed for their vices, whom the crowd styled Christians . . . . First, then, the confessed members of the sect were arrested; next, on their disclosures, vast numbers were convicted, not so much on the count of arson as for hatred of the human race. And derision accompanied their end: they were covered with wild beasts' skins and torn to death by dogs; or they were fastened on crosses, and, when daylight failed were burned to serve as lamps by night. (Annals, XV, 44)

Mark's Gospel fits such a situation of persecution in Rome. It was likely written there shortly before the first destruction of Jerusalem by Titus in A.D. 70.

Fuller interpretation of Mark awaits the exegetical sections in this chapter, but a few guidelines will help in reading. Mark is not simply biography or objective history, but rather religious proclamation with historical foundations. The Markan Gospel develops from a tradition about Jesus which circulated in the Christian community prior to his writing this Gospel. Mark does not create his story afresh; however, this Gospel aims to strengthen first-century Roman Christians in the face of persecution.

Prologue: The Spirit and Jesus in the World (1:1–15)

What happens in Jesus' baptism by John?*
How does the episode end and what change has resulted?

Mark's opening verse hardly sounds like an objective biography of Jesus of Nazareth. Not an apology (as in Luke 1:1–4) nor a genealogy of Jesus (as in Matt. 1:1–17), the opening of Mark could scarcely attain a higher note of faith. Jesus Christ is named as though Christ were his last name. His name, however, was Jesus, and Christ is a bestowed title of honor, meaning "anointed one" or "messiah." Any lingering expectation of a neutral history is further dispelled by the final title, "Son of God." The significance of this designation for Mark becomes clearer when at the climactic point of the story Jesus is told by a voice from heaven that he is

Nero, *emperor of Rome* (A.D. *54–68*), *on a Roman coin.* (*Courtesy of American Numismatic Society.*)

the "beloved Son" (vs. 11). The key introductory phrase of the opening verse, however, is probably "the beginning of the gospel." By the prologue's end (vs. 14) the key phrase is "preaching the gospel of God." Something has enabled "the beginning of the gospel" to become "preaching the gospel." This beginning starts, strangely enough, not at the beginning but in the middle of things. Mark begins with the baptism when Jesus was already an adult, instead of with Jesus' birth or an earlier time in Israel's history. Mark did know something about Jesus' earlier life, for later we are informed about Jesus' occupation and family (Mark 6:3). In Mark's view the baptism of Jesus is the crucial initiatory event for Jesus.

The Old Testament prophecy (1:2–3) points toward some kind of fulfillment. Although Mark declares that the prophet Isaiah spoke these words, they are actually a combination of Malachi 3:1, Exodus 23:20, and Isaiah 40:3. This dominance of Isaiah suggests that the prophecy, which on

---

* The questions that precede discussion of each major passage are meant to help the student read the passage with understanding. They are not meant to be exhaustive, but should stimulate reflection upon the passage before the interpretation is studied.

the face of it threatens judgment, should be set within the context of Isaiah's prophecy of hope, reconciliation, good tidings: " 'Comfort, comfort my people,' says your God. . . . 'The glory of the Lord shall be revealed' " (Isaiah 40:1, 5). Mark thus places the threat of judgment within the context of the gospel or good news.

This initial prophecy points toward the future—"shall prepare." Something will happen. By the end of the prologue, the verb tense has shifted, "The time *is fulfilled*, and the kingdom of God *is at hand*" (1:15). Again, we apparently have a pointer to the crucial importance of Jesus' baptism by John.

John the baptizer stands at the center of this next section (1:2–8). John is a wild man; he is in the wilderness; he is a preacher of judgment and repentance. He wears clothes of the wilderness, camel's hair and a leather girdle; he eats food of the wilderness, locusts and wild honey.[3] Although nothing is said to identify John's ministry with that of Jesus, John nevertheless stands at the beginning of the gospel (cf. Acts 1:22, 10:37).

A striking feature of this section is its remarkable emphasis upon repentance for all the people of Judea and Jerusalem, as if a full scale national repentance were taking place. John's decisive act is to baptize the people in the river Jordan. Through this rite of baptism, a cleansing or preparation takes place. Moreover, John declares that this baptism with water would be completed later by one who would baptize with the Spirit. Earlier we read a prophecy about John the baptizer (vss. 2, 3), now John himself prophesies (vss. 7, 8). Just this fact of his prophesying indicates that the Spirit is about to appear. In first century Judaism the Spirit, which was the enabler of prophecy, was thought to have departed Israel with the last prophets (Haggai, Zechariah, and Malachi) and was expected only in the last days.[4] As John clearly points to the approach of another, Jesus, he also foreshadows an irruption of the end time, the time of the active Spirit.

A different mood pervades the next section (vss. 9–13). Whereas previously we had John the baptizer, the crowds, and baptism in the river, now Jesus alone appears. Now the heavens open, the Spirit descends, and a voice from heaven speaks. In other words, we have "cosmic language."[5]

---

[3] Though locusts were eaten during famines in the desert, the diet of John might also symbolize the double nature of the gospel, both judgment and comfort. In the Old Testament, locusts were invariably the agents of destruction and judgment (see, for example, Exodus 10:4; Psalm 105:34; Isaiah 33:4), whereas honey was traditionally the promise of peace and plenty (see, for example, Exodus 3:8; Deuteronomy 6:3; Proverbs 24:13; Ezekiel 3:3).

[4] See the coming of the Spirit in Acts 2:17–22, especially the prophecy from Joel 2:28–32. Also see G. F. Moore, *Judaism*, I (Cambridge: Harvard University Press, 1958), p. 237.

[5] See J. M. Robinson, *The Problem of History in Mark* (SBT, 21; Napierville, Ill.: Allenson, 1957), p. 26. In this chapter we are indebted to Robinson's analysis of the Gospel of Mark. Cf. U. W. Mauser, *Christ in the Wilderness* (SBT, 19; Napierville, Ill.: Allenson, 1963), pp. 77 ff.

The winding Jordan River. (Courtesy of Israel Information Services.)

The decisive action is the baptism of Jesus. At his baptism, the Spirit descends upon him and a voice says, "Thou art my beloved Son. With thee I am well pleased." This utterance combines portions of Psalm 2:7 and Isaiah 42:1. Are these words simply Mark's reporting of appropriate Old Testament prophecy, or did Jesus actually hear a voice from heaven? The Gospel of Mark shows no concern about such a question, for Mark is intent not upon revealing the nature of Jesus' inner experience, but upon proclaiming the occurrence of a cosmic event in which the Son of God is designated. Does this mean that Jesus did not become Son of God until his baptism? Mark again offers no opinion, for the text asserts simply that at this baptism God's Spirit rested upon Jesus, who was declared Son of God.

This title "Son," derived from the Old Testament, was commonly used as a designation for Israel (Exodus 4:22; cf. Jeremiah 31:9 and Hosea 11:1) and for those who especially represented the people of Israel, such as the king or high priest. Obviously "sonship" did not mean biological descendance from God but signified special selection by God for a task. The appropriate response of "sonship," therefore, is obedience to the task. This Hebraic understanding of "sonship" suggests that the voice from heaven revealed to Jesus that God had chosen him for a task. In fact, the unexpected climax of Mark's introduction occurs when the Spirit drives Jesus into the wilderness where he is tempted by Satan (vs. 12). The Spirit did not bring Jesus peace and contentment; instead the Spirit brought conflict with the power of evil, with Satan.

The importance of the Spirit's driving Jesus into the wilderness is underscored when we realize that Jesus was already in the wilderness at his baptism. Why does Mark want to emphasize the wilderness motif?

Both Moses (Exodus 34:28) and Elijah (I Kings 19:8) spent forty days on Mount Sinai; moreover, the people of Israel wandered forty years in the wilderness before they could enter the Promised Land. Thus Jesus' sojourn in the wilderness may anticipate the founding of a new Israel.

The most striking feature of the Markan temptation story is its lack of detail, especially in comparison with the temptation stories in Matthew (4:1–11) and Luke (4:1–13).[6] In the Markan temptation story, Jesus' activity is overshadowed by the supernatural conflict between the Spirit and Satan. The outcome of this conflict, however, has already been anticipated in Jesus' baptism. By Jesus' act of submission to baptism the Spirit has come and with this coming Satan already is being defeated (see 3:23–29; cf. 10:38).

In the successive sections of Mark's introduction, the Spirit is the decisive factor. The Spirit is promised by John the Baptist and is already emerging in his prophecy (1:2–8). During Jesus' baptism (1:9–11), the Spirit descends upon him. In the temptation (1:12–13), the Spirit drives Jesus into conflict and victory over Satan. In the ancient world the Spirit meant divine power (see, for example, Genesis 1:2; Judges 14:6; I Kings 18:12). John the Baptist did not have that power; Jesus did, however, and this power was of such strength that even Satan was defeated. A likely clue to the meaning of Mark's introduction appears in the answer Jesus later gives to the accusation that he is in league with Satan: "But no one can enter a strong man's house and plunder his goods, unless he first binds the strong man; then indeed he may plunder his house" (Mark 3:27). Jesus' baptism and temptation manifest an initial conquest of Satan by the Spirit. Therefore, the way is cleared for Jesus' conflicts with the demons, his religious opponents, and even his disciples. After Jesus' obedient submission to baptism, the Spirit drives him into a conflict that eventually will result in total victory.

The note of future victory resounds in the conclusion of Mark's introduction (vss. 14–15), where instead of "the beginning of the gospel" we now hear of "preaching the gospel of God." Of course, *gospel* itself is good news and carries the notion of victory.[7] After Jesus' baptism and temptation, the preaching of God can take place, because the Spirit has become active in Jesus' obedience. The crucial phrase, "the kingdom of God is at hand" (vs. 15), means neither that victory has fully arrived (realized eschatology) nor that triumph remains wholly future (futuristic eschatology); rather, Mark proclaims that God's ruling presence is now

---

[6] The closest verbal parallel to Mark's story occurs in the Jewish pseudepigraphal Testaments of the Twelve Patriarchs, probably written sometime between 140 and 110 B.C., "And the devil will flee away from you and the wild beasts will fear you, and the angels will come unto you" (Testament of Naphtali 8:4).

[7] For other Markan uses of *gospel*, see 1:1, 15; 8:35; 10:29; 13:10; 14:9. Also see the discussion of its central role in Mark by Leander Keck, "The Introduction to St. Mark's Gospel," *NTS*, 12 (1966), pp. 352–370.

nearer than it was before. This kingdom is *at* hand, not *in* hand. This message, this gospel, rather than Jesus himself, is the object of belief (vs. 15). Thereby Mark concludes his introduction with Jesus' preaching the gospel of God which demands repentance and belief. The introduction has informed the reader that the gospel concerns a victory (the Spirit over Satan) to be won only through conflict (the wilderness) and obedience (the baptism of Jesus). The rest of Mark's Gospel narrates the triumph in conflict which Jesus effects through his exorcisms, debates, and suffering.

The Gospel of Power: Jesus Opposes His Enemies (1:16–8:21)

Now that the Spirit has met Satan in the temptation of Jesus, the public action of Jesus can begin. Jesus came preaching that the kingdom of God is drawing near, yet this kingdom proclamation by its very nature aroused opposition. Forces are at work against the emergence of the kingdom, for the old order does not easily yield.

In the first half of the Gospel of Mark (1:16–8:21), opposition to Jesus comes in the main from two camps—the demons and the Pharisees. Jesus faces the opposition of the demons with exorcism and that of the Pharisees with debate. Thus this first half of Mark centers upon Jesus' miracles and teachings. Indeed, as we shall see, miracles and teachings are mingled within individual units of tradition because both are means for opposing his enemies. The two forms of meeting opposition differ in that the demons recognize Jesus yet do battle against him, whereas the Pharisees, though also utterly antagonistic to Jesus, do not recognize his true identity.

In the second half of Mark (8:22–15:47), the major opposition that Jesus faced was not that of enemies but rather of friends, his disciples. To be sure, the disciples did not put Jesus to death; the chief priests and scribes, along with the Roman authorities, were responsible for his crucifixion. Still, the disciples did oppose Jesus because they failed to understand why he had to suffer and die. Unless we keep in mind the disciples' misunderstanding opposition, the full meaning of Jesus' actions and teachings against the demons and the Pharisees will be missed. The Gospel of Mark shows that the opposition of enemies was met by direct action through exorcisms and debates; however, the opposition of friends required indirect persuasion, even apparent defeat in death.

This preference for persuading rather than compelling the disciples elucidates a major problem in the first half of Mark. After several disclosures of divine healing power, Jesus curiously asks to keep these miracles secret (1:43; 3:12; 5:43). The reader wonders why such deeds should be kept secret until he realizes that Jesus' power had to be a hidden power. He won disciples not simply by naked, brute force, either of deeds or of arguments. Stark power did not convince, did not make a believer, did not get rid of fear. When demons had been exorcized and silenced in debate, the task of making true disciples still remained.

Nevertheless, in this first half of Mark miracles dominate. There are nature miracles, such as stilling the storm (4:35–41; 6:45–52) and feeding the multitudes (6:30–44; 8:1–10); there are healing miracles, such as the healing of the leper (1:40–45) and the raising of the dead girl (5:35–43); and there are miracles of exorcism, the driving out of demons (1:21–28, 5:1–13; see also 1:34, 3:22). These last exorcisms provide a key to understanding the miracles in this Gospel. Mark summarizes the activity of

Galilee, Samaria, Phoenicia, and Syria

Jesus in Galilee as that of preaching and casting out demons (1:39), and Jesus appoints the twelve to do the same tasks (3:14, 15; cf. 6:13). Evidently, for Mark, miracles are understood through exorcisms. They do not constitute a separate class of acts or events.

A crucial question in regard to these actions is whether Jesus performs miracles by Satan or by God (3:20–30). Naturally, in Mark Jesus performs exorcisms with the help of God; anyone who denies this source of Jesus' power (cf. 3:30) must be on the side of Satan. Now that the strong man, Satan, has been bound by the Spirit, Jesus is to plunder the house, to rid the world of demons (3:27). In demon exorcism we are to recognize a transcendent battle taking place in the life of Jesus and his contemporaries. Demons inhabit human beings; they are part of human history. Yet their power comes from beyond, from Satan. Similarly, Jesus exorcises demons from men and teaches men, but claims a power from beyond; for in Mark he is the Son of God, the one upon whom the Spirit descends.

ENCOUNTER WITH THE DEMONS (1:21–45)

What is the primary mission of Jesus?
What is the effect of the healing miracles?

The first exorcism in Mark (1:21–28) follows the calling of disciples and is set within the context of Jesus' teaching in the synagogue on the sabbath. Opposition between the teaching of the scribes and the authority of Jesus characterizes this scene. At first no one truly recognizes Jesus except the demon, who cries out, "I know who you are, the Holy One of God" (1:24; cf. 3:11; 5:7). Perhaps the demon spoke Jesus' true name in order to gain power over him. In the ancient world, knowledge and use of the name gave the speaker magic power.[8] More obviously the demon's recognition of Jesus produces immediate opposition because the demon recognizes that an enemy has appeared ("Have you come to destroy us?"). The result of Jesus' appearance is heightened activity by the demon in the man resulting in his convulsing and crying out. Jesus and the demon had absolutely no communion, only antagonism.

---

[8] A magic word, which automatically causes a desired effect, occurs occasionally in the exorcisms and healings that Jesus performs in Mark (see 5:9, 41; 7:34). Even this usage is, however, quite restrained when compared with the seemingly endless list of magic "names" used by other exorcists at the time of Jesus (see Barrett, *New Testament Background*, pp. 31 ff.). Two memorable Old Testament attempts to gain control through knowledge of the name are Jacob's wrestling with the angel (Genesis 32:29) and Moses at the burning bush (Exodus 3:13). Even today, "magical" use of the name persists in human relationships. For example, in some cultures to be on a first name basis implies friendship and mutual trust, or to know a person's nickname is to know his "secret."

This exorcism implies a "before and after" motif, which occurs explicitly in other miracles of Jesus in Mark (see 6:45–52). Before the exorcism there is opposition, violence, crying out, shouting; after Jesus acts there is silence, victory, and the spread of Jesus' fame. Yet this particular exorcism does not end with a neat resolution of all difficulties. We are perplexed because the by-standers label the exorcism "a new teaching," instead of the expected powerful deed. Indeed the whole encounter seems both an exorcism of an unclean spirit and a debate about the question of authority (see 1:22 and 1:27). Clearly for Mark, Jesus' action and teaching are not finally separable. Moreover, the inconclusive ending of this episode (questioning among themselves) suggests that the exorcism had produced no final victory. Jesus still had to debate with the Pharisees. Thus this episode ends, perhaps ironically, on the note of the spread of Jesus' fame, a fame that will lead, not to apparent success, but to death.

A brief healing episode (1:29–31) and two summary sections (1:32–34; 1:35–39) separate Jesus' first exorcism from the next major healing event (1:40–45). The healing of the disciple Simon's mother-in-law focuses attention upon the disciples who cannot heal. The disciples are impotent, even though she is one of their relatives. Significantly, Jesus' healing enables her to serve; the disciples also have to become servants, though in a different way (see 9:35; 10:35–45; 12:1–11). Therefore, even this brief episode points beyond itself to the necessity for disciples who realize service, a feat that becomes possible only after they allow themselves to be served by Jesus' death (10:45). A summary section of healing and exorcism follows (1:32–34). The people flock to a healer, the healings take place publicly; yet curiously, Jesus "would not permit the demons to speak, because they knew him."

In the following summary section (1:35–39), Jesus retires to a lonely place to pray. In response to the disciples' demands Jesus acknowledges only that he will go to preach in the next towns. The narrative mentions that he continued also "to cast out demons" (vs. 39). Evidently Jesus sees his primary mission as that of preaching (1:14) and the casting out of demons as secondary. Jesus' key action here is praying. On three other occasions in Mark, Jesus prays. Each time the motif of faithful dicipleship is the common thread of the diverse incidents. After the feeding of the five thousand, Jesus prays (6:46); the immediate consequence in his calming appearance to the disciples terrified by the storm. At the healing of the epileptic boy Jesus tells the disciples that they are unable to heal because they have not prayed (9:29). Jesus also prays in the Garden of Gethsemane for strength to accept his impending death, while the disciples sleep (14:32–42). In order to become disciples, they will have to "watch and pray" (14:38). For Mark, Jesus' mission is not primarily healing or exorcising demons; Jesus brings near the kingdom of God to effect *discipleship* rather than cures.

This section's closing episode tells of the healing of a leper by Jesus (1:40–45). No demon appears in this healing miracle; the conversation takes place between Jesus and a man. Here for the first time Jesus is moved with pity, and when the man speaks to Jesus, there seems to be something like the element of faith: "If you will, you can make me clean." In distinction from the exorcism, this healing shows Jesus in touch with the person to be healed, moving more closely within the human realm and eliciting the response of faith. As in the case of the exorcism, the meeting with Jesus produces results; the victim is made well of leprosy and made fit for communion with others. Once again Jesus enjoins silence (cf. vs. 34), but this time he is not obeyed. Although this scene shows Jesus' acting out of compassion and the man's incipient faith, something is still not right. Because the healed man goes "to spread the news," Jesus can no longer move about openly. Instead of righting everything, the healing seems to deter Jesus from his mission of preaching the gospel of God and making true disciples—that is, believers in the gospel (1:15).

In summary, the Markan exorcisms and healings depict one phase of the struggle that erupts with the mission of Jesus. The purely transcendent struggle between the Spirit and Satan adumbrated in the temptation (1:12–13), now takes place at the transcendent-historical level of the "Holy One of God" versus the demons (1:24). As we shall see later, the conflict moves farther within history in the opposition between the rabbi Jesus and the Pharisees and finally between the suffering Son of Man and his disciples. Curiously, although the miracles, the most public deeds of Jesus, arouse the greatest reception (1:28), they also produce inconclusive results in the realization of Jesus' aim of gathering true disciples (cf. 1:16–20).

Jesus' curious demand for silence about the miracles requires an interpretation that makes sense of the Markan intent, for the important question about Jesus' miracles is not whether he healed—undoubtedly he, as well as others, did—but rather what use the early Christians (in this case, Mark) made of this healing tradition. We have in Mark an apparent contradiction: the healing tradition does not convey the crucial aspect of Jesus' ministry, yet much of Mark's Gospel, especially the first half, consists of miracle tradition. Why then does Mark combine this miracle tradition with injunctions to be silent about the miracles (the so-called "messianic secret")? Our suggested answer to this question proceeds from the recognition that for Mark, the basic reality of Jesus consists of his suffering passion on the cross. For the winning of true disciples takes place only through the suffering death of Jesus. Mark neither doubts nor disdains the miracle tradition of Jesus; however, he does set that tradition within the special perspective of Jesus' death.

Mark's Christian contemporaries knew of a "divine man" who performed miracles, whereas stories of Jesus also emphasized his magical powers. In the apocryphal Gospel of Thomas the child Jesus is pictured as a great miracle worker: He makes sparrows of clay; he kills a Pharisee who disturbs a pool Jesus made; he destroys a child who strikes his arm; he stretches a short beam into a longer one to aid Joseph, his carpenter father, and so forth.[9] This popular, one-sided emphasis of the tradition on Jesus as a divine miracle worker is rejected in the Gospel of Mark, not by ignoring that role, but by placing it within the context of Jesus' death and passion. Thus Mark suggests that the fundamental miracle of discipleship comes, not through Jesus' miracle powers, but through his death.

Miraculous signs, though not denied, are insufficient to turn followers of Jesus into genuine disciples. Later in Mark, Jesus replies to the Pharisees who come seeking a sign from heaven, "Why does this generation seek a sign? Truly, I say to you, no sign shall be given to this generation" (8:12). Objective, public signs of power are not the Markan basis of faith.

DEBATE WITH THE PHARISEES (2:15–3:6)

Why do the Pharisees debate with Jesus and his disciples?
How does the outcome of the debates differ from that of the exorcisms?

Communication takes place in many ways. Art persuades indirectly by the moving power of the artistic creation; the viewer is invited to interpret with his total self in order to help bring order out of chaos. Debate persuades by allowing the listener to hear both sides; he then decides whose position is the stronger. Debate, therefore, communicates in conflict, and the Gospel of Mark is an example of such communication by conflict. In Mark, Jesus' teaching takes place primarily in debate, either with the Pharisees, his enemies, or with the disciples, his friends. The debates with the Pharisees and the scribes have parallels with debates in the writings of the rabbis; however, the key for understanding the Markan debates is the exorcisms. Earlier we were puzzled by the peoples' astonishment at Jesus' *teaching* (1:22) when the story related the driving out of an unclean spirit. Mark seems deliberately to commingle healing action and teaching authority so that Jesus' conflicts (demons, Pharisees, and disciples) are all of a piece. The healing of the paralytic (2:1–12) demonstrates that healing action ("Rise, take up your pallet and walk") and authoritative teaching ("Your sins are forgiven") are inextricably interwoven and suggests implicitly that Jesus has to wrestle with the stubbornness of the Pharisees as well as crippling disease.

The prelude for our present section is once again the calling of disciples,

---

[9] On the first century Hellenistic miracle worker, see J. M. Robinson, "The Problem of History in Mark, Reconsidered," *USQR*, 20 (January 1965), pp. 136 f.; on the miracle working Jesus in the Gospel of Thomas, see M. R. James, *The Apocryphal New Testament* (Oxford: Clarendon Press, 1924), pp. 49 ff.

in this case a tax collector named Levi (2:13 f.; cf. 1:16–20).[10] The closely related following episode shows Jesus' eating at table with sinners and tax collectors (2:15–17). Sinners presumably had in some obvious way broken the Mosaic law. Tax collectors were hired by those agents who purchased the right to collect taxes for the Roman government, and in turn were allowed to extract heavy taxes from the Jewish people. Evidently the two groups were social outcasts, yet Jesus and his disciples ate at table with them, thus including them in the group of those who followed Jesus. The scribes and the Pharisees object about Jesus' conduct to the disciples, not to Jesus. Even though not directly addressed, Jesus replies with an answer that silences everyone. He comes to the sick; that is the physician's duty. Jesus' opponents fail to grasp that a new society of disciples, those who follow Jesus, is being formed. The ancient rigid distinctions of clean and unclean, especially the procedure for forgiveness (see vs. 7), are being swept away in the new community that Jesus inaugurates.

The following section (2:18–22) concerning fasting probes this new society further. This time Mark distinguishes not only between Jesus and the Pharisees but also between Jesus' disciples and those of John the Baptist. Surprisingly, John's disciples are in the same camp with the Pharisees. Although the Baptist belongs to the beginning of the gospel (see 1:1–4) and hence cannot be finally grouped with the Pharisees, both John and the Pharisees preach a message of judgment (cf. 1:4) for which fasting is the appropriate ritual. John and the Pharisees differ, however, in that John's disciples fast in expectation of the imminent judgment, whereas the Pharisees fast as part of daily obedience to the law. Jesus, as the bringer of good news, asserts the absurdity of fasting, for his disciples now experience a new reality ("the bridegroom").

The statement implying that they will fast after Jesus' death (2:19b–20) sounds less like a word of Jesus than a word of the early church justifying the later practice of fasting.[11] In the Markan context, however, fasting may refer to the suffering and persecution that the disciples will have to endure. In the second half of Mark, Jesus speaks unequivocally about the necessity of suffering. Indeed, Jesus' words (especially vs. 20) do not allow the reader to forget the impending death. The final words of the episode (2:21 f.) mark an end to the debate and an answer to the conflict over fasting. Everything stresses newness—the bridegroom is present, new

---

[10] Curiously Levi does not appear in the later Markan list of the twelve disciples (3:16–19). Perhaps this omission can be explained by the fact that the tribe of Levi was not numbered among the twelve tribes and was not given part of the land of Israel because it was to function as the Levitical priesthood (cf. Numbers 1:47–54). Thus Levi, like the Levites, is named but not numbered (see D. M. and G. H. Slusser, *The Jesus of Mark's Gospel*, Philadelphia: Westminster Press, 1967, pp. 66 ff.).

[11] See Matthew 6:16–18. Rudolf Bultmann, *The History of the Synoptic Tradition* (New York: Harper & Row, 1963), p. 151, classifies this word as a passion prediction added by the early church.

cloth and new wine are available; fresh skins are needed, for the old cannot determine the new. The old order must make way for the new; real disciples know and act upon this "newness."

The first two episodes of this section stressed the breaking forth of a new society in connection with Jesus; the following two episodes hinge upon unorthodox sabbath activity. Even though the disciples violate the sabbath (2:23–28), the Pharisees now directly debate with Jesus. Jesus answers their charge by quoting scripture, citing the example of David (see I Samuel 21:1–6). His criterion, suggested by the David episode, is apparently that need takes precedence over law. Moreover, the first half of Jesus' final word ("The sabbath was made for man, not man for the sabbath"—vs. 27) also bears out this view, which in isolation sounds quite modern—that is, human considerations take precedence over legalistic ritual. Yet the final clause ("so the Son of man is lord even of the sabbath") indicates that we have in Jesus' saying something more than a general humanitarian principle. The appearance of the Son of Man signifies the beginning of the end time, the irruption of a new age (see pp. 204 ff.; cf. Daniel 7:13 and Mark 13:26). Jesus' disciples can now violate the sabbath because they are beginning to live out of that new time being ushered in with Jesus: the time for joy (vs. 19), the time for wine (vs. 22), and the time for forgiveness of sinners (vs. 17; cf. vs. 10).

The next episode places the debate with the Pharisees in the context of healing (3:1–6). In the synagogue, the stronghold of the Pharisees, Jesus is being watched—the Pharisees are not at first named. The atmosphere is that of a test of Jesus (cf. also 8:11; 10:2; 12:13, 15), similar to his time of testing in the wilderness.

A comparison with the previous exorcism of the unclean spirit (1:21–28) illuminates how debate-conflict is both similar to and yet also different from demon-conflict. Jesus commanded the demon to be silent (1:25). Now, before the healing is performed, his opponents are silent before his question, "Is it lawful on the sabbath to do good or to do harm, to save life or to kill?" After the exorcism, even though there was questioning of his authority, Jesus' fame spread (1:27 f.). After Jesus' sabbath healing his enemies plot to destroy him. A further comparison of this sabbath healing with the previous healing of the leper (1:40–45) is equally striking. There Jesus was "moved with pity" for the helpless man (1:41). Here Jesus, directing his attention to the Pharisees, "looked around at them with anger, grieved at their hardness of heart" (3:5). In both instances Jesus healed; in the debates, however, his miracle served only to intensify the conflict between himself and his enemies.

These enemies are labeled as Pharisees and Herodians. The Herodians may have been followers of Herod Antipas, tetrarch of Galilee and Perea (4 B.C.–A.D. 39) during the life of Jesus. They were probably royalists who hoped for restoration of the united monarchy, as in the time of

Herod the Great (37–4 B.C.).[12] However the Herodians are identified, their presence at this point hints at Jesus' impending suffering and death. The only action specifically attributed to Herod Antipas in Mark is the beheading of John the Baptist (6:14–29; note vs. 29). Every Markan reference to the Herodians or to Herod explicitly or implicitly points to a conflict ending in the death of Jesus (cf. 8:15 and 12:13 with 3:6 and 6:14 ff.). The new is too upsetting to the old; the champions of sabbath observance cannot tolerate the presence of the Son of Man, who is lord even of the sabbath, and so they plot Jesus' death.

The remainder of the first half of Mark may be characterized as a development of what is already implied in the opening scenes of the Gospel. The old order's resistance to Jesus' message and action frees the good news to appeal to new multitudes, even those from Tyre and Sidon lying beyond Palestine (3:7–12). When obviously rejected by the established religious authorities, Jesus inevitably forms the new Israel, founded upon the twelve disciples (3:13–19a). Whoever doubts the authenticity of this new community fails to see the clear manifestations of God's working through Jesus' casting out demons (3:28–30). Moreover, no one can rely upon a guaranteed privilege that reckoned physical descent as assurance of God's favor (3:31–35).

Nothing avails to eliminate the opposition to Jesus by the Jewish leaders. His parables about the breaking in of God's word are closed ciphers to all except the joyful few who really hear Jesus' word about a new society (4:1–20, especially vss. 8 f. and vs. 20).

Even those who hear must receive further private instruction (see 4:33 f.), because Mark has in view the necessity for perseverance to the end (cf. 13:9–13). The hope for such endurance rests in the amazing power that accompanies Jesus ("Who then is this, that even wind and sea obey him?"—4:41). This power protects the disciples from the violent sea (4:35–41) and casts the fearsome unclean spirit Legion into the sea (5:1–13). Oddly, the people beg Jesus to leave their neighborhood because of his demon exorcism. Moreover, instead of the usual command to silence, Jesus urges the restored demoniac to tell his friends about the mercy God has shown (5:14–20). Perhaps the demon's plea not to be sent out of the country (vs. 10) provides the clue to this episode's meaning in Mark, for the tenacity with which Israel held to the land and refused to undergo the new exodus with Jesus would explain both the people's opposition to Jesus' action and the willingness of Jesus, now that the old was destroyed in the sea, to urge the spread of the gospel news of God's mercy.

---

[12] See F. C. Grant, "The Gospel According to Mark," *IB*, VII (New York: Abingdon Press, 1951), p. 683; cf. John Bowman, *The Gospel of Mark: The New Christian Jewish Passover Haggadah* (Leiden: Brill, 1965), pp. 121 f.

This injunction to speak about God's action contrasts all the more with the ending of the following episode, which explicitly enjoins silence (5:21–43). The preceding episode of the demon Legion emphasizes, however, the destruction of the old and the people's fearsome response to that loss. In the present double episode of the raising of Jairus' daughter and the healing of the woman, we have references to two central themes of the second half of Mark: the necessity for faith (vs. 34), and the resurrection from the dead (vs. 41). Although the people still figure in this narrative as they did in the exorcism, the center of attention is beginning to shift more clearly to the response of disciples (see vss. 31, 37, 40). This predominance of the disciples becomes more evident in the following stories: Jesus is rejected by his own people (6:1–6); he appoints the twelve disciples for a mission of healing and exorcism (6:7–13); John the baptizer is beheaded by Herod and given over to his disciples (6:14–29), perhaps in anticipation of the role for which Jesus is beginning to prepare his disciples. The disciples' return from the mission and the miraculous feeding of the multitudes (6:30–44) are to be viewed as a foreshadowing of the Lord's Supper and the death and resurrection of Jesus.

In summary, our brief journey through some of the remaining portions of the first half of Mark (up to 8:21) shows that the debates with the Pharisees are matters of life and death (2:15–3:6). The new reality, especially the new society emerging in Jesus' disciples, represents a freedom toward the law that could not be tolerated within Pharisaism. Consequently, the religious leaders resist; they plan Jesus' death. In a certain sense Jesus opposed the demons more successfully and more easily than the Pharisees. Ironically, the reaction of the Pharisees to Jesus, their rejection and the plotting of his death, become the means for the accomplishment of Jesus' victory in making disciples (8:31; cf. 8:34). For even though the disciples remained close to Jesus throughout the first half of Mark, they had yet to learn the secret of Jesus' power. That came only with the death and resurrection.

The Power of Suffering: Jesus Wins His Disciples (8:22–15:47)

In the second half of the Gospel of Mark, the center of focus is the passion of Jesus. The passion story includes Jesus' decision to go to Jerusalem (10:32–34), the events of the last days in Jerusalem (11:1–14:72), and finally his death on the cross (15:1–47). When we observe that the complete passion story consists of approximately two-fifths of this Gospel, the characterization of Mark as a "passion story with an extended introduction" seems particularly apt.[13] In the first half of Mark, Jesus has dealt with his opponents, the demons and the Pharisees. In the second half, the latter opponents will deal with Jesus. They put him to death by the Roman form of capital punishment—crucifixion. Yet these last chapters do not dwell on the opponents of Jesus. Instead, the disciples and their understanding of Jesus becomes central. The friends of Jesus, the partisans of his cause, wish for signs of glory, triumph, and victory for this man who summoned them to discipleship.

According to Mark, at three crucial moments Jesus predicts the suffering he must undergo: "And he began to teach them that the Son of man must suffer many things, and be rejected by the elders and the chief priests and the scribes, and be killed, and after three days rise again" (8:31; cf. 9:31; 10:33 f.). The disciples' continuing misunderstanding or inability to accept this prediction becomes clear in the Garden of Gethsemane just before the arrest, trial, and crucifixion. They could not watch and pray while Jesus was going through temptation (14:38–41). The terse, seemingly final, verdict on the disciples is pronounced immediately after Jesus' arrest, "And they all forsook him, and fled" (14:50). Indeed, even the closest disciple, Peter, denied Jesus not once, but three times (14:66–72).

The disciples' denial and flight occur because of their unwillingness to acknowledge that their own discipleship must share the same quality as Jesus' suffering. Mark's Gospel speaks not only about the nature of Jesus' messiahship, but also about the nature of discipleship, and the second half implies that there is no victory except through suffering and conflict.

TWO STAGES OF DISCIPLESHIP (8:22–9:9)

Why is Peter's confession rebuked?
How does Jesus answer Peter?

The precise point of transition from the first portion of Mark to the second can be located in the incident at Caesarea Philippi, where Peter confesses Jesus as the Christ (the Messiah) and Jesus answers by declaring that his mission is one of suffering (8:27–33). The preceeding episode, the healing of the blind man at Bethsaida (8:22–26), dramatically symbolizes what follows. This story stands out as the only two-stage healing in the Gospels. When Jesus first heals, the man sees only dimly and men look

---

[13] See Martin Kähler, *The So-called Historical Jesus and the Historic Biblical Christ* (Philadelphia: Fortress Press, 1964), p. 80. Kähler made the remark about the Gospels; its force is most appropriate to Mark.

like trees walking; then Jesus heals again and the blind man sees everything clearly. The unique manner of this healing seems to prefigure the "seeing" of the disciple Peter in the next episode. Peter sees that Jesus is the Christ; however, he does not yet understand the suffering nature of Jesus' messiahship (vs. 32). Peter, like the other disciples, must go through a second stage of "healing" before he can become a true disciple (cf. 8:34 ff.).

The two stages of discipleship receive further confirmation in the material that precedes the healing of the blind man at Bethsaida and the confession of Peter at Caesarea Philippi. After Jesus was rejected in his own country (6:1–6), he turned to his disciples as partners in ministry (6:7–13). Speculation about Jesus' identity led into an account of John's death (6:14–29). The reader, therefore, knows both that John the baptizer is dead and that Jesus and his disciples are continuing their ministry.

The nature of this ministry unfolds in the remaining Markan tradition before Caesarea Philippi. First, the feeding of five thousand occurs (6:30–44). Then Jesus walks on the water and stills a storm to calm the disciples (6:45–52). After a brief summary section (6:53–56), Jesus debates with the Pharisees about the Jewish distinction between clean and unclean. The debate is followed by two miracles, an exorcism of the Syrophoenician woman's daughter and a healing of the deaf and dumb man (7:31–37). In rapid succession, similar events recur as Jesus feeds a multitude of four thousand (8:1–10), debates with the Pharisees (8:11–12), calms the disciples on the water (8:14–21), and finally performs the two-stage healing of the blind man at Bethsaida (8:22–26). Mark's tradition leading up to Peters' confession shows a doubling or duplicating (8:1–26 duplicated 6:30–7:37) of the following events: the feeding of the multitude, an incident on the water, debate, and healing.[14]

Jesus' two feedings of the multitudes provide the clearest instance of this doubling. We observe that this double tradition of the feeding of five thousand (6:30–44) and of four thousand (8:1–10) plays a role in Jesus' conversation with the disciples immediately preceding the healing of the blind man at Bethsaida (8:14–21). The early Christian community, for whom Mark was written, could scarcely read about the loaves, especially the broken pieces, without thinking of the death of Jesus (see Mark 14:22). Furthermore, the twelve and seven baskets also have special significance; for the twelve baskets, like the twelve disciples, correspond to the twelve tribes of Israel. The more enigmatic seven baskets calls to mind that seven is the number for completeness (seventh day, seven seas, seven continents, and in particular, the seven churches of Revelation; see Rev.

---

[14] The Gospel of Luke omits that Markan tradition (8:1–26) that represents a doubling. See also Robinson, *The Problem of History in Mark*, p. 85, and T. A. Burkill, *Mysterious Revelation* (Ithaca, N.Y.: Cornell University Press, 1963), pp. 140–142.

1:4; 1:12; 3:1). Indeed, the early church supplemented the work of the twelve apostles with the appointment of *seven* Hellenistic deacons (Acts 6:1–6). If the twelve represent Israel and the seven represent the Gentiles, we might, therefore, infer that Mark pictures Jesus' mission as an ingathering of both Jew and Gentile by means of the broken body of Jesus. Until the disciples recognize the necessity for suffering and this universal inclusiveness, however, they do not understand discipleship (see 7:24–30). Both the double tradition (6:30–7:37 and 8:1–26) and the two-stage healing at Bethsaida point to these two stages of discipleship in Mark: (1) allegiance to Jesus, and (2) following Jesus in suffering for all people.[15]

Peter's confession of Jesus' identity as the Christ occurs on the way to the villages of Caesarea Philippi, located at the far northern end of Palestine where Hellenistic influence was most prevalent. The location suggests that underneath Jesus' query about his identity may lie the question of whether his ministry should extend beyond the borders of Israel. At any rate, the suggested answers of others (John the Baptist, Elijah, a prophet) are inadequate (cf. 6:14 f.). When Jesus turns the question to the disciples, Peter, speaking for them, answers, "You are the Christ." Jesus then charges them not to tell anyone who he is (8:30). Previous commands of silence concerned his exorcisms and healings; now Jesus commands silence about his identity.

This passage serves as the focal point for what has become known in New Testament research as the problem of the "messianic secret," a term which includes Jesus' commands to keep silent about his miracles (1:34, 44; 3:12; 5:43; 7:36) and his identity (8:27–30; 9:9), his private instructions to the disciples (7:17 f.; 9:39 f.; 10:10), and his private interpretation of parables (4:10 ff., 33 f.).[16] The two most frequent proposals for understanding the "messianic secret" are that (1) Jesus commanded silence in order to keep the uninstructed multitudes from learning about and perverting his nonpolitical messiahship into a political one; or that (2) Jesus actually did not understand himself to be the Messiah, and the secrecy motif is an attempt to explain, from the standpoint of the early church's faith that Jesus was the Messiah, why Jesus was not publicly recognized as such and why the tradition was relatively devoid of messianic claims. Both these solutions can be criticized for their preoccupation with the

---

[15] Support for viewing Jesus' death as freeing him for all people comes from John's Gospel, "Nevertheless I tell you the truth: it is to your advantage that I go away, for if I do not go away, the Counselor will not come to you; but if I go, I will send him to you" (John 16:7). Without Jesus' death, he remains limited as a sign-bringer to the people of Israel in the territory of Judea and Galilee. With his death, the Spirit is loosed through the disciples to complete his mission. Possibly this is why the Markan double-tradition begins with the return of the *apostles* (nowhere else so-called in Mark) from their mission (6:30).

[16] For a succinct discussion of the "messianic secret" literature, see Kümmel, *Introduction to the New Testament*, pp. 66 f. The classic treatment is still that of William Wrede, *Das Messiasgeheimnis in den Evangelien* (Göttingen: Vandenhoeck & Ruprecht, 1901).

question of whether Jesus thought that he was the Messiah. It seems doubtful that Mark was interested in this particular historical problem because in the Gospel the question is not whether Jesus was Messiah, but why he was the kind of Messiah he was.

Within the Gospel itself the "messianic secret" focuses the reader's attention on the question of the nature of Jesus' messiahship and consequently upon the nature of Christian discipleship. The disciples, including Peter, misunderstood the role of Jesus as the Christ. As the Son of Man (the apocalyptic, heavenly figure) Jesus must suffer many things and be killed, and after three days rise (vs. 31). Peter's rebuke of Jesus leads to Jesus' rebuke of Peter (vss. 32 f.). The disciples' expectation of a miracle-working Messiah who delivers his followers from all unpleasantness into great reward (cf. 10:32–45) is rejected. The "messianic secret" restrains and tones down the miracle tradition of Jesus precisely because the reader is being forced to acknowledge and accept Jesus' suffering.[17]

The subsequent section on discipleship (8:34–9:1), spoken not only to the disciples but also to the multitudes, characterizes the following of Jesus as fellowship in service and suffering. The disciples, in becoming followers of Jesus, have taken the first step; however, they have not yet realized the full implications of discipleship. Victory can be realized only in conflict. Just as the Spirit fought Satan, and just as Jesus opposed demons and Pharisees, so too the disciples must continue to struggle until the end which, according to Mark, cannot be far off: "There are some standing here who will not taste death before they see the kingdom of God come with power" (9:1, cf. Mark 13:24–37). Nowhere does Jesus himself connect the coming kingdom with his title, Christ. In Mark at least, Jesus is not to be understood primarily as the political messiah, the expected restorer of Israel.[18] The most frequent Markan designation for Jesus is the Son of Man. As Son of Man he exercises freedom over the law (2:10, 28), goes to his suffering and death (8:31 and *passim*), and will come again as eschatological judge (8:38; 13:26; 14:62).

This section (8:34–9:1) focuses upon the nature of discipleship rather than the identity of the one whom the disciples follow. Not until the following episode, the transfiguration scene (9:2–9), does Mark finally answer the question of Jesus' identity. The transition (9:1) to this incident raises the question of when the kingdom of God will come in power. The usual answer—Jesus' expectation of the immediate end of the world—fails to take account of Mark's having been written several decades after Jesus' death when the end of the world had not yet occurred (cf. 13:32 ff.). For Mark, the time of the kingdom's coming was less important than the time

---

17 See Hans Conzelmann, "Jesus Christus," *RGG*, III, pp. 632 f.

18 See 8:29; 13:21 f.; 14:61; 15:32. Mark of course does not deny the appropriateness of this title when properly used (cf. 1:1; 9:41; 12:35–37).

of its coming in power (cf. Matt. 16:28 and Luke 9:27). The transfiguration story addresses the question of the kingdom's coming in power.

Jesus, with three disciples, climbs a high mountain where he is transfigured. His clothes become glistening white, like that of the angels; moreover, even Moses and Elijah appear to speak with him. According to Israel's tradition, Moses gave the law from a mountain (Exodus 19:16 ff.) and Elijah prophesied from a mountain (I Kings 19:9 ff.). Thus Jesus converses with the two men representing Israel's heritage of the law and the prophets. Again the disciples misunderstand (vs. 6), not realizing that the coming of Jesus in some way fulfills the law and the prophets, for Jesus alone remains (vs. 8).

The climactic statement of the transfiguration scene, made by the voice from the cloud ("This is my beloved Son; listen to him"—vs. 7), alludes to the kingly tradition of Israel (cf. Psalm 2:7). If any other Old Testament figure were worthy of this distinguished company on the mountain, it would be David, the king of ancient Israel (cf. 2:25; 10:47 f.; 12:35 ff.). Possibly his exclusion prevents any political misunderstanding about the role of Jesus. At any rate, the voice announces to the disciples that Jesus is the eschatological king of Israel, the true final king. Jesus is Son of God with kingly power. At another crucial revelation of Jesus' identity in Mark, similar words are spoken (1:11). Mark's opening, "The beginning of the gospel of Jesus Christ, the *Son of God*" (1:1), has already coupled this designation with Jesus.

Such kingly power has to be viewed, however, in the context of the injunction "listen to him" (vs. 7). In the following section (9:9–13), Jesus not only charges the disciples to be silent, but explicitly links his power with both John's suffering ("Elijah has come"—vs. 13) and his own (vs. 12). The final Markan designation of Jesus as Son of God occurs at the cross (15:39). Jesus' kingly power fulfills the law and the prophets by enduring suffering. A definite scheme thus appears: at the baptism, Jesus is declared Son of God by a voice from heaven. At the transfiguration, Jesus is announced as Son of God by a voice from the cloud to the three major disciples. At the cross, Jesus is proclaimed Son of God by a Gentile centurion. By implication, the kingdom comes with power when the Son of God's suffering is acknowledged and accepted by Jesus' disciples.

FAITH TO PRODUCE HEALING (9:14–32)

How does the attitude of the father contrast with that of the disciples?

From this point to the end of the Gospel, the disciples are often in the foreground (see especially 9:33–41; 10:23–31; 13:1 ff.) and always in the background. The present episode illustrates how the Markan tradition

probably combines two stories, the one showing how a father's faith enables healing of his son and the other drawing a contrast between the master's ability and the disciples' inability to heal,[19] in order to present an example of genuine faith for the disciples. They are unable to heal because they do not yet understand the nature of true belief (cf. 9:32).

The argumentative disciples form a contrast with the beseeching father. He cries out, "I believe; help my unbelief!" (vs. 24), thereby demonstrating that all things are possible to the believer (vs. 23). The disciples cannot heal because they do not pray (vs. 29). Earlier we observed that prayer was characteristic of Jesus' life style (1:35; 6:46). Later the ability to pray seems almost equivalent to the act of faith. "Therefore I tell you, whatever you ask in prayer, believe that you receive it, and you will" (11:24; cf. 11:22–26). The necessity for prayer becomes evident in the major Markan prayer episode, Jesus in the Garden of Gethsemane (14:32–42). The disciples are to wait while Jesus prays (vs. 32), but they are also warned to pray (vs. 38). Jesus prays that suffering (the cup) might pass from him; however, he asks that God's will, not his own, be done. The disciples cannot heal, because they neither pray nor believe; they do not accept Jesus' death. The necessity for such an acceptance is made explicit at the close of this healing episode (9:30–32). Again, Jesus predicts future conflict, but the disciples "did not understand the saying, and they were afraid to ask him" (vs. 32).

Fear dominates the disciples (cf. 4:40; 5:15; 9:6, 32; 10:32; 16:8). Perhaps this indicates that Mark's Gospel was written to a church undergoing persecution, as was suggested earlier. According to Mark, this fear can be overcome by faith (vs. 23). The worst the disciples had to fear from persecution was death. In the healing of the epileptic boy, however, even the verdict, "He is dead" (vs. 26), proves false because of the father's faith. Moreover, although Jesus, as the Son of Man, will be killed, "after three days he will rise" (vs. 31). If the disciples truly follow Jesus, then they too will go through persecution into victory.

For the time being, however, the disciples are afraid. Out of their fear and lack of faith they dispute about greatness (9:34), deter nondisciples from casting out demons (vs. 38), and in general unsuccessfully try to avoid persecution (vs. 50). They have still to understand that Jesus' messiahship rejects "bread and circuses" and demands discipleship of service (vs. 41) to one another (vs. 50).

After Jesus goes into Judea (10:1), the Markan narrative moves inevitably toward Jesus' death. Before we consider one final passage (15:33–47) as representative of the passion of Jesus, we need briefly to characterize

[19] Note that the boy's condition is described twice (9:17 and 9:21 f.) and that the convulsions take place twice (9:20 and 9:26). Cf. Vincent Taylor, *The Gospel According to St. Mark* (New York: Macmillan Co. 1955), pp. 395 f., and Bultmann, *History of the Synoptic Tradition*, pp. 211 f.

"Christ Cleansing the Temple" by the Spanish artist El Greco (1541–1614). *(Courtesy of National Gallery of Art, Washington, D.C., Samuel H. Kress Collection.)*

the four major emphases that dominate this long block of tradition (10:1–15:32): (1) Jesus' proclaims fulfillment of the old religious tradition of Israel with a new reality. (2) The disciples, though retaining their allegiance to Jesus, eventually desert and reject him. (3) In spite of the disciples' apparent failure, victory will be theirs. (4) Jesus' death not only takes place without resistance, but is understood in faith as divine necessity. Although these Markan emphases are interrelated, such a classification should provide a better understanding of the movement and major motifs of Mark.

Fulfillment of the old. The Pharisees try to trap Jesus by raising the question of divorce (10:2–12), but Jesus declares that the will of God is communicated through the scripture rather than being identical with the scripture. A man who obeys the law goes away sorrowful because his allegiance rests finally with himself rather than God (10:17–22). Jesus triumphantly enters Jerusalem, the holy city of Israel, but only to cleanse the holy temple (11:1–19). Indeed, Jesus cannot accept the crowd's accolades ("Blessed be the kingdom of our father David that is coming!" —11:9) because Christ is not the Son of David (12:35–37) in a political sense. The kingdom that Jesus announces brings the end of history (chap.

13) rather than the restoration of Israel's kingdom. The religious leaders of Israel reject this new society and its leader to their damnation (12:1–12) because they quibble about taxes (12:13–17) and resurrection (12:18–27) and ignore God's coming near.

Desertion by the disciples. The disciples continue to follow Jesus; however, they question his "hard" sayings (10:23–31) and they follow only in fear, not faith (10:32). Just before Jesus' trial they all flee (14:50). Moreover, Mark underscores that fact with the little tale of the young follower of Jesus who flees away naked (14:51–52). The most crushing rejection of Jesus occurs in Peter's denial (14:66–72), especially tragic when viewed against Jesus' prediction and Peter's protest (14:26–31).

Victory through failure. The disciples are, however, the closest followers of Jesus, and in spite of their desertion, Jesus will still come to them in Galilee after his death. In fact, the Last Supper anticipates such a reunion (14:12–28). The disciples may confidently look forward to that victorious reunion because Jesus shows mercy even to little children (10:13–16); because the God who can do all things is at work (10:23–31); because the one thing necessary is a recognition of need (10:46–52; cf. 9:23) and a letting go of self (12:41–44)—that is, a response of faith (11:20–26).

Necessity for Jesus' death. The disciples' paralyzing fear in the face of persecution (see 13:9, 19) cannot be taken as final, for Jesus' death by crucifixion is the way in which God's victory can be achieved for them (10:32–45). This death not only is predicted by Jesus, but also is prepared for by the anointing with costly ointment (14:1–9) and is celebrated in the Last Supper (14:12–25). It occurs at the instigation of one of the disciples (14:10 f.). Although Jesus himself prays that his death may be avoided, he accepts the cross as God's will (14:32–42). In the scenes immediately before and during the crucifixion Jesus' innocence is apparent (14:53–65, 15:1–15) and his behavior is exemplary (15:16–32). Thereby Mark shows the injustice of the human agents in Jesus' death and the perfect submission of Jesus to a death that ultimately triumphs through God's will.

THE PASSION OF JESUS (15:33–47)

What is the mood of Jesus' last words?
How do the people respond to Jesus' death?

The Markan account of Jesus' crucifixion ostensibly depicts an action accomplished by his opponents. Jesus himself remains passive. Pilate's question as to whether he is the king of the Jews is answered enigmatically (15:1–5). He makes no plea for his life before the crowd when Barabbas is released (15:6–15). He does not protest the scourging (15:16–20). Someone else carries his cross. Furthermore, he does not even acknowledge

Part of the Via Dolorosa, the traditional way through which Jesus carried his cross to Golgotha. (Courtesy of Israel Government Tourist Office.)

those who mock his helplessness on the cross (15:21–32). The one action of Jesus upon which Mark centers is the loud cry in the Aramaic language (note its retention) from the cross, "My God, my God, why hast thou forsaken me?" (15:34; cf. Psalm 22:1). The meaning of this cry can only be understood from the context. The setting for Jesus' death is somber. At noon darkness comes over the whole land for three hours before he dies (vs. 33). Although normally it took at least twelve hours for someone to die by crucifixion, Jesus died after only six hours. At the critical moment, Jesus shouts this cry of apparent despair. Someone rushes to give him vinegar while others mockingly ask whether Elijah will come to help. Then he "uttered a loud cry, and breathed his last" (vs. 37). From the reading of the text, we observe that Jesus gave two loud cries just before his death. Perhaps "My God, my God, why hast thou forsaken me?" was a later addition spelling out what the "loud cry" was.[20] If that were so, then Mark, or the tradition lying behind Mark, added these words for a specific reason. Whatever the answer to the question of the cry's origin, clearly this shout is the Markan key to Jesus' death.

Traditionally these words (vs. 34) have been considered the "cry of dereliction," the cry of despair at abandonment by God. Yet these words

[20] See Bultmann, *History of the Synoptic Tradition*, p. 313; but cf. Taylor, *The Gospel According to Mark*, p. 594.

Jesus' crucifixion by a contemporary African sculptor, E. G. Isacco. (Courtesy of Spartaco Appetiti.)

may be a cry of victory, for they duplicate the opening words of Psalm 22, which begins in despair but ends on a note of triumph: "All the ends of the earth shall remember and turn to the Lord; and all the families of the nations shall worship before him. For dominion belongs to the Lord, and he rules over the nations" (Psalm 22:27 f.). Furthermore, one commentator maintains, "In no case did this cry express a doubting sense of abandonment, for to quote from the Bible is always a proof of faith."[21] This reasoning, however, does not remove the element of despair and suffering. Clearly the Psalmist suffers, and Jesus suffers; Mark intends for the reader to perceive Jesus' sense of despair, even to the point of being seemingly abandoned by God. Thus Jesus' last fearful word in Mark maintains tension to the very end. No premature miracle rescues Jesus from this final struggle with God himself (cf. 14:36).

The preceding crucifixion scene (15:29–32) stresses the Markan perception of the necessity for suffering. Here Jesus is mocked because he cannot save himself, although he has claimed to save others. The mockers ironically make Mark's point. Suffering cannot be avoided for Jesus, the disciples, and Mark's persecuted church, because thereby others can be saved.

In addition, Mark claims for Jesus and the church victory in suffering. The mockery over his boast of destroying and rebuilding the temple in three days (15:29 f.) is answered by the tearing apart of the temple curtain

---

[21] Martin Dibelius, *From Tradition to Gospel* (New York: Charles Scribner's Sons, 1935), p. 194; cf. Ernest Best, *The Temptation and the Passion: The Markan Soteriology* (SNTS, 2; Cambridge: Cambridge University Press, 1965), p. 100.

at Jesus' death (vs. 38). Mark proclaims that Jesus' death and resurrection affect the temple. A curtain that limits access to God is rent asunder, for Jesus' death extends God's exclusive relation with Israel to all men.

Fittingly the Gentile centurion confesses Jesus as "Son of God" (vs. 39). This extension of God's salvation to everyone answers the mocking of those waiting for Elijah to take Jesus down. God has come down to open the temple. The principal actor in the passion is neither Jesus nor the people and officials, but God. In suffering, God is acting to effect triumph. We might have anticipated this conclusion. Even when Jesus cried out in despair (vs. 34), his cry was addressed to God; Jesus was praying. In Mark, prayer or faith makes all things possible, even victory in the face of apparent defeat (cf. 14:34 f.; 9:29; 11:24).

Mark depicts three responses to Jesus' death: those of the centurion, (vs. 39), the women (vss. 40 f.), and Joseph of Arimathea (vss. 42–47). The most important of these is that of the centurion (cf. 1:1, 11; 9:7).[22] Unlike the disciples who were earlier afraid (4:40; 6:50; 10:32), the centurion boldly confesses Jesus as the Son of God. This affirmation of Jesus occurs directly after Jesus' death. Possibly the centurion was impressed with the manner in which Jesus died, but the Markan text fails to mention any such impression. What we do know is that "Son of God" is a key Markan designation of Jesus (1:1). At the baptism such Sonship involved obedience to God (1:11); at the transfiguration such Sonship announced the kingly power of Jesus (9:7); and now at the crucifixion the centurion proclaims the kingship of God's Son precisely at Jesus' death. Thereby Mark manifests Jesus' suffering messiahship and the way of discipleship.

The women confirm that Jesus is dead, for since the disciples have all fled, they are the only ones left. In addition, however, the Galilean women make peculiarly good Markan witnesses of Jesus' death. We are told that they "followed him, and ministered to him" (vs. 41). Of course, "following" is another way of saying discipleship (cf. esp. 1:17), and their "ministering" picks up Jesus' emphasis upon "service" (the same Greek word): "For the Son of man also came not to be *served* but to *serve*, and to give his life as a ransom for many" (10:45). Furthermore, Jesus charged his disciples, "If anyone would be first, he must be last of all and *servant* of all" (9:35). These women are the first followers of Jesus to see his death, witness his burial, and hear the resurrection report. They also were

---

[22] There are three possible translations of the centurion's affirmation of Jesus: (1) "Truly this was *the* Son of God." (2) "Truly this man was *a* Son of God." (3) "Truly this man was a *son* of God." (Cf. Luke 23:47 and see Taylor, *The Gospel According to St. Mark*, pp. 497 f.). The first translation represents a specifically Christian affirmation of Jesus as the Son of God. The second declares Jesus to be a divine being come to earth, like other divine saviors who appeared in Hellenistic religions. The third proclaims Jesus a righteous man who, because of his faithfulness, is acclaimed a child of God. The Greek grammatical construction permits any of the three, but the context demands the first.

apparently the first followers to accept Jesus' way of service. The way of discipleship receives further explication in the action of Joseph of Arimathea, a respected member of the Jewish council (vs. 43). In contrast to the "real" disciples, he has courage (cf. 14:50). Furthermore, he seeks the kingdom of God, whereas the disciples appear to be seeking their own welfare (cf. 10:35-45).

The passion story ends with conclusive evidence of the death of Jesus. Pilate learns from the centurion that Jesus is dead. The body is laid and sealed in the tomb. Yet already in the centurion, the women, and Joseph of Arimathea, something new is being born.

Epilogue: The Future Victory (16:1–8)

How is the piety of the women treated in Mark?
What is its significance?

After Jesus' death the Christian reader expects a happy ending: resurrection and glorious triumph. The note of victory is in fact present in Mark's epilogue, but it is restrained. Among the Gospels, only Mark fails to record an appearance of Jesus to the women or disciples.[23] The only evidence contradicting the natural assumption that the death is final is the empty-tomb story, which in itself is ambiguous. The absence of Jesus' body does not necessarily imply his resurrection (cf. Matt. 28:13–15).

These opening verses (1–4) set the atmosphere for the incident. The women are going to perform a pious deed, to anoint the body of Jesus. Evidently burial was hasty and they could not anoint the body on the holy sabbath. At the first opportunity ("early in the morning"), they go to the tomb. Being pious rather than practical, they have not thought about the problem of rolling away the stone. They have come to honor the dead Jesus, but their plans are upset. Mark portrays a young man sitting in the open tomb, who, from his apparel, must be an angel, a messenger from God. Naturally the women are quite amazed, but the angel chides them for their perplexity (vs. 6a). Earlier encounters with Jesus evoked similar awe and amazement from the crowds (1:27; 9:15), the Pharisees (12:17), and the disciples (10:24). This response, however, falls short of the required act of faith. Amazement and awe at Jesus' numinous, divine quality are not enough. Neither is the reaction of fear (16:8) an adequate response

---

[23] Our interpretation of Mark's ending omits Mark 16:9–20 because this passage is doubtless a later addition to the text. See Taylor, *The Gospel According to St. Mark*, p. 610.

to Jesus, whether on the part of Jesus' opponents (11:18) or his disciples (4:40; 9:6, 32). Fear occurs when the terrible possibilities of death and persecution come to the forefront. The classic passage, which links both amazement and fear, occurs at the first explicit reference to Jesus' unalterable movement toward Jerusalem: "And they were on the road, going up to Jerusalem, and Jesus was walking ahead of them; and they were amazed, and those who followed were afraid" (10:32).[24] True discipleship consists of more than awe at the numinous or fear at the realities of human finitude. Something more, a response of faith, of belief in victory through suffering, is meant by Mark (cf. 4:40; 10:52; 11:22).

The women, disciples, and Peter are promised that something more will occur. Jesus will go before them into Galilee (16:7). Of course, they have no guarantee other than the angel's word (cf. 14:28) that he will appear in Galilee. The precise reason for the choice of Galilee is not certain. Perhaps the disciples are to meet Jesus in Galilee, rather than Jerusalem, in order to gather forces for the Gentile mission. The precise meaning of the promise is also unclear. Perhaps the disciples are to wait the second coming of Christ, the parousia, when God's kingdom will fully come (cf. chap. 13).[25] More likely, they will await a resurrection appearance of Jesus ("there you will see him"; cf. 14:28). Whatever the exact meaning, the promise stresses the future. Everything has not yet happened; a future victory awaits. The Markan story of Jesus does not promise to deliver the church from persecution, even though in Jesus' life and death a first victory has been won. Satan was bound, demons were exorcized, opponents were defeated in debate, disciples were gathered. Moreover, the future promises a second, complete victory. But the future can still only be assured through faith. In the present the church faces strife and persecution.

Mark's concluding words ("for they were afraid") corroborate this interpretation. Some scholars challenge this ending, even though manuscript evidence decisively supports it, because it sounds like a half sentence.[26] Nevertheless, the present ending of Mark fits the Gospel. The women are left with fear, the normal and ever-present fear of a church undergoing persecution in the mid-sixties at Rome. Of course, Mark wishes to encourage endurance, faith, and prayer in spite of fear, but the Gospel does not command faith at the last instance. Instead, Mark's whole Gospel implies the need for faith in a final victory, because an initial triumph

---

[24] Cf. Robinson, *The Problem of History in Mark*, pp. 68–78.

[25] See the elaborate Galilee hypothesis of Willi Marxsen, *Der Evangelist Markus: Studien zur Redaktionsgeschichte des Evangeliums*, 2nd ed. (Göttingen: Vandenhoeck & Ruprecht, 1959), who also sees the Markan situation as one of persecution.

[26] In addition, the end of a manuscript, especially a papyrus scroll, could easily be lost. Inferior manuscripts do provide a more satisfying ending to Mark (cf. 16:9–20); however, as far as we can tell Matthew and Luke, who used Mark, appear to know only our version of Mark (16:1–8). Their respective resurrection appearance stories have no parallels to Mark's longer ending (16:9–20). Cf. note 23.

through suffering has occurred in Jesus. Mark is realistic enough to acknowledge fear and Christian enough to proclaim the breaking of fear's power through faith in a future victory promised by the suffering and resurrected Jesus.

In summary of our Markan interpretation, let us briefly review the results of our four-step methodology:

In *structure* this Gospel presents a series of conflicts between Jesus, allied with God's Spirit (1:1–15), and opponents at various levels: Satan, demons, Pharisees, and finally disciples. The major Markan watershed is Peter's confession at Caesarea Philippi (8:22 ff.); from this point attention shifts to Jesus' relationship with his disciples. The first half of Mark shows Jesus' victorious movement toward apparent success both in miracle and debate, whereas in the second half he moves toward apparent failure in death and the disciples' misunderstanding.

We have found five *emphases* that are basic: the miracles of Jesus, his passion, the "messianic secret," the call to discipleship, and the confession of Jesus as Son of God. Our interpretation reconciles the apparent contradiction of the first two emphases (the "strong Jesus" of miracles versus the "weak Jesus" of death) through the third emphasis, which calls attention also to Jesus' use of persuasion in making true disciples (the fourth emphasis). Mark took over the miracle tradition of Jesus and set it within the perspective of Jesus' passion, for the creation of the disciples' faith could occur only if Jesus abandoned miracles at his death in order to allow God to work.

The "messianic secret" motif occurs precisely at those points where the tradition was most likely to be understood to represent Jesus as a divine man with power to avoid any difficulty. In effect, Mark opposed such an attitude about Jesus and the life of discipleship. The fifth and final Markan emphasis supports this reading of Mark: The declaration of Jesus' Sonship at the baptism and at the transfiguration is finally affirmed at Jesus' death.[27] Jesus is Son of God in death, but not because of any miracle working power.

Although we do not have the Markan sources of tradition from which to study his *redaction* of that material, we can see that such motifs as the "messianic secret" and the predictions of Jesus' suffering death and resurrection occur in the transitional sections of the Markan Gospel. Moreover, we may safely assume that Mark selected and arranged the tradition in order to accomplish his purposes; notice the dominance of miracle tradition in the first half and the passion story in the second half. Relative to Matthew and Luke, Mark used little teaching material of Jesus. Mark

---

[27] Note how the occurrences of "Son of God" confirm the Markan structure: 1:1, 11; 9:7; and 15:39.

obviously wished to stress the passion story even though some apocryphal Gospels omit this tradition.

The Markan *situation* requires the bolstering of the church undergoing persecution, probably at Rome in the mid-sixties. Jesus Christ, the Son of God, had himself gone through persecution and no escape had been offered him. Jesus triumphed through his suffering and the same victory is promised to the faithful disciple, "For whoever would save his life will lose it; and whoever loses his life for my sake and the gospel's will save it" (8:35).

Suggestions for Further Reading

The Synoptic Gospels. Probably the classic work on the problem of Synoptic relations and sources is B. H. Streeter, *The Four Gospels: A Study of Origins* (rev. ed.; London: Macmillan, 1930). The arguments for the priority of Mark, its use by Matthew and Luke, their use of a common sayings source "Q", and their use of distinctive sources "M" and "L" are all stated here. A discussion of further advances in the study of Gospel origins, especially form criticism, is V. Taylor, *The Formation of the Gospel Tradition* (2nd ed.; London: Macmillan, 1935). Also useful is F. C. Grant (ed.), *Form Criticism* (New York: Harper, 1962), containing essays by R. Bultmann and K. Kundsin. Both pioneering studies in form criticism are now in English: Bultmann, *History of the Synoptic Tradition*, trans. J. Marsh (New York: Harper, 1963) and M. Dibelius, *From Tradition to Gospel** (New York: Scribner's, n.d.). A valuable general book on the Gospels is F. C. Grant, *The Gospels: Their Origin and Growth* (New York: Harper, 1957). F. C. Beare, *The Earliest Records of Jesus* (New York: Harper, 1957), affords useful commentary on the Synoptic Gospels, following Huck-Lietzmann, which in turn is followed by the RSV *Gospel Parallels*.

The Gospel According to Mark. Commentaries in series named in the General Bibliography, III, are not all mentioned individually at the ends of chapters. Commentaries on the Greek text are not listed.

The commentary by S. E. Johnson in the Harper Series (1960) is reliable. Another up-to-date commentary is D. E. Nineham, *The Gospel of St. Mark** (Baltimore: Penguin Books, 1963). Other works on Mark that are recent and helpful include: R. H. Lightfoot, *The Gospel Message of St. Mark** (Oxford: Oxford University Press, 1950), J. M. Robinson, *The Problem of History in Mark* (SBT, 21; Naperville, Ill.: Allenson,

1957); T. A. Burkill, *Mysterious Revelation: An Examination of the Philosophy of St. Mark's Gospel* (Ithaca, N.Y.: Cornell University Press, 1963; and E. Best, *The Temptation and the Passion: The Markan Soteriology* (SNTS Monograph Series, 2; Cambridge: Cambridge University Press, 1965).

3 The Gospel According to Matthew: A Christian Manual

NOTES ON THE GOSPEL OF MATTHEW

Like the Gospel of Mark, Matthew contains direct reference neither to its author nor place of origin. The earliest indication of either is a report from Papias (ca. A.D. 130):

> Matthew compiled the reports in the Hebrew language, and each one interpreted them as best he could (Eusebius, *EH*, III, 39, 16).[1]

This information about the Gospel's origin is of little value. Not only is the statement unclear; it is in all probability erroneous. Because this Gospel is based upon Mark and the Q sayings source, it is extremely unlikely that it was written by Matthew, a disciple and eyewitness (cf. Mark 3:18 parr.). Furthermore, our Gospel according to Matthew is written in Greek, not Hebrew.

This Gospel was probably at first anonymous. Papias, or his predecessors, probably attributed authorship to Matthew, one of the twelve disciples, because only this Gospel distinguishes Matthew as a tax collector (10:3; cf. Mark 3:18) and changes the incident of the tax collector (who is Levi in Mark 2:14) into a story about Matthew (Matt. 9:9). We do not know the reason for this change other than to give some prominence to Matthew.

The author was familiar with Jewish Christianity and wrote to a Greek-speaking audience. Possibly he was a Christian scribe, similar to the Jewish scribes of the law (see 13:52).[2] The author or authors of Matthew took over and expanded the Markan framework by adding two types of material, sayings common also to Luke (Q source) and special Matthean tradition, which came from oral tradition or, less likely, from a written source or sources. Matthew used so much sayings material that narrative tends to be dominated by discourse. The Jesus of Matthew is at least as much a teacher as an actor. Our five-part outline of Matthew (excluding the Introduction, 1:1–2:23, and Conclusion, 26:2–28:20) reflects the evangelist's own intention. The end of each major discourse section is clearly marked by an editorial conclusion (see 7:28 f.; 11:1; 13:53; 19:1 f.; 26:1 f.).

The place of origin of Matthew's Gospel is generally thought to be Syria, probably the city of Antioch. The oldest witness to this Gospel is Ignatius, bishop of Antioch (A.D. 110–115). In all probability, Matthew could not have been written until after A.D. 70, for its addition to the parable of the marriage feast ("The king was angry, and he sent his troops and destroyed those murderers and burned their city"—22:7; cf. Luke 14:21) apparently refers to the destruction of Jerusalem in that year. Since Mark was probably composed shortly before Jerusalem's fall, some time would likely have

[1] See Kümmel, *Introduction to the New Testament*, pp. 43 f. Eusebius also earlier wrote, "Matthew, having first preached to the Hebrews, when he was about to go to others, compensated for the loss of his presence . . . by delivering to them in writing his Gospel in their native language" (*EH*, III, 24).

[2] See Krister Stendahl, *The School of St. Matthew and Its Use of the Old Testament* (Lund: C.W. K. Gleerup, 1954); cf. Gottfried Schille, "Das Evangelium des Matthäus als Katechismus," *NTS*, 4 (1957–58), pp. 101–114.

elapsed before Mark's authority became sufficient for the anonymous author of Matthew to use it as a primary source. Consequently, a date of about A.D. 80–100 seems likely. Indeed, the obvious tension between the Christianity of Matthew and the Judaism of the Pharisees (cf. Matt. 23) also suggests a date after the Roman annihilation of the temple in A.D. 70. At this time Judaism retrenched in the face of the threat of possible extinction and began to develop a rabbinic, Pharisaic uniformity heretofore unknown. Sectarian movements within the faith, such as Jewish Christianity, were read out of the then-developing normative Judaism.[3]

Clearly this Gospel is more systematic and more intricately organized than Mark. It emphasizes fulfillment of prophecy, Jesus as teacher, and the place of the law and final judgment within the Christian congregation. These broad interests suggest a churchly Gospel written to give direction to the community as it faced problems pertaining to organization, separation from Judaism, and disappointed eschatological hopes. Matthew serves the church, and probably for that reason the church placed it first in the New Testament canon.

Introduction: The Christian Way (1:1–2:23)

Matthew's Gospel begins with two chapters of his special tradition. This tradition seems to be largely legendary: a genealogical list of Jesus' ancestors; a story of Jesus' birth; exotic wise men from the East, their encounter with Herod and worship of the baby Jesus; the flight to Egypt; the slaying of the innocent children; and the return to Nazareth. These matters may seem preliminary to the real work of Jesus, which for Mark began at Jesus' baptism and ended at the crucifixion. But these "Christmas stories" bear the heart of Matthew's message, his good news.

RADICAL OBEDIENCE (1:18–25)

Why does this story of Jesus' birth center upon the response of Joseph?

The immediately preceding genealogy (1:1–17) helps in understanding the birth story. At first glance, this list of Jesus' ancestors looks rather

---

[3] G. D. Kilpatrick, *The Origins of the Gospel According to St. Matthew* (Oxford: Clarendon Press, 1946), p. 109, cites the Birkath ha-Minim, a Pharisaic benediction from *ca.* A.D. 85, which reads as follows: "For the excommunicate let there be no hope and the arrogant government do thou swiftly uproot in our days; and may the Christians and the heretics suddenly be laid low and not be inscribed with the righteous. Blessed art thou, O Lord, who humblest the arrogant." See W. D. Davies, *The Sermon on the Mount* (Cambridge: University Press, 1966), pp. 83–90.

unpromising for determining Matthew's intent and purpose. We do notice that the genealogy is divided into three sets of generations of fourteen each—from Abraham to David, from David to the Babylonian deportation, and from Babylon to the Christ (vs. 17). Abraham is the father of the Jewish people, for Israel's God is the God of Abraham, Jacob, and Isaac (see Gen. 12:1–3; cf. Matt. 3:9; 22:32). The Christ who climaxes this genealogy fulfills the hope of Israel; therefore, the age of fulfillment is dawning with the birth of the expected Messiah. This Christ is also descended from David, the great king in Israel's history. Indeed, the Lord promised through the prophet Nathan that David's offspring would be established in a kingdom forever (II Samuel 7:12–17). Thus Jesus Christ will fulfill Israel's hopes prefigured in Abraham and David (see 1:1). Yet the Babylonian Exile, the next major division in the genealogy, meant disaster for Israel's hope of establishing a political kingdom in which God's rule would triumph. Perhaps for Matthew the deportation raises the question of whether fulfillment of Israel's hopes will take a form other than that of a Davidic political kingdom.

The inclusion of women in the genealogy suggests a possibility of the unexpected; the Christ who comes may not correspond to the image of the Messiah for whom Israel was waiting. In the ancient world, descent was traced through the male; yet five women intrude into the genealogy: Tamar (vs. 3), Rahab and Ruth (vs. 5), the wife of Uriah (vs. 6), and Mary (vs. 16).[4] Moreover, these are quite unusual women. Tamar disguised herself as a harlot in order to seduce her father-in-law Judah so that she could bear children, Perez and Zerah (Genesis 38). Rahab, the harlot of Jericho, saved Joshua's two spies and consequently preserved her own life when the walls of Jericho fell (Joshua 2, 6). Ruth, the Moabitess who was loyal to her Hebrew mother-in-law, gained her future husband Boaz one night during the grain festival (Ruth 3). And the wife of Uriah is none other than that Bathsheba who bathed in the right place during "the spring of the year" and thus became the wife of David (II Samuel 11–12). Likely each of these women was a foreigner. Yet in spite of this and their questionable moral actions, God acted through each of them.

Within this setting, Matthew's story of Jesus' birth takes place, with the genealogy strongly suggesting that Jesus' ancestry includes not only the men (especially Abraham and David) but also the women, Tamar, Rahab, Ruth, Bathsheba, and finally Mary. Clearly our story (vss. 18–25) centers

---

[4] According to one view, Matthew's genealogy serves to prove that Jesus was the Messiah because he was descended from Abraham and especially David. Yet Joseph does not, according to the following verses, father Jesus even though the genealogy would have to be traced through him in order to function as proof. This tradition might have originally (apart from 1:18–25) proved the Davidic descent of Jesus and therefore his messiahship, but in the Matthean context, descent from David through Joseph cannot be maintained. Cf. Sherman Johnson, "The Gospel According to St. Matthew," *IB*, VII (New York: Abingdon Press, 1951), pp. 252 f.

on Joseph's response to the pregnancy of his betrothed Mary. Though Matthew explicitly talks about a virgin birth (vss. 18, 20, 23, 25), the story focuses not upon wonder at the virgin Mary, but rather on how Joseph will react to the dilemma posed by the question of whether she is pregnant from unfaithfulness or the power of God.[5] Not only is the question posed within the birth story itself but also by the preceding section. Inclusion of the women in Matthew's genealogy raises the question of how God works to achieve his purposes, and at the culmination of the birth story Joseph must decide whether Mary's pregnancy is God's action.

Joseph at first thinks that he has been wronged by Mary. "Being a just man" he decides to divorce her quietly (vs. 19). According to Jewish law, a man could do one of two things. He could bring his betrothed to public trial where conviction of infidelity might carry the penalty of death by stoning, or he could divorce his betrothed privately. Engagement, like marriage, could only be severed by divorce. Joseph generously opts for the latter course. At this moment, however, the angel intrudes and through a dream Joseph learns about a higher righteousness (see, for example, 3:15; 5:20; 6:33). He hears that this conception is from the Holy Spirit, the agent of God's activity on earth; furthermore, this son of Mary will "save the people from their sins" (vs. 21)—people like Tamar, Rahab, Ruth, and Bathsheba (cf. 9:1–13; 26:28).

The theme of Jesus as the savior of his people is developed in the following quotation from Isaiah 7:14 (vss. 22 f.). Whether these words are from the angel or the narrator, the virgin birth of Jesus fulfills the Old Testament and signifies Emmanuel ("God is with us"). This linking of Jesus as saviour from sins and Jesus as sign of God's presence also occurs near the opening of the Matthean miracle section (8:1 ff.). There another quotation from the prophet Isaiah ("He took our infirmities and bore our diseases" —53:4; Matt. 8:17) affirms Jesus as the bringer of forgiveness and the presence of God (cf. Matt. 9:1–7). Still another, subsequent statement of Jesus sounds like a promise of Emmanuel, "For where two or three are gathered in my name, there am I in the midst of them" (18:20). It is immediately followed by Jesus' declaration of the necessity for limitless forgiveness (18:21 f.), for Matthew understands Jesus' coming as bringing both forgiveness and God's presence (see Mark 2:7). At a time in which God was feared, dreaded, or thought to be removed from the affairs of Israel, Matthew announces God's presence, because through Jesus forgiveness can now be given and received (Matt. 6:14 f.).

This good news does not imply that Matthew understands the Christian

---

[5] H. J. Held, "Matthew as Interpreter of the Miracle Stories," *Tradition and Interpretation in Matthew* (Philadelphia: Westminster Press, 1963), pp. 238 f., maintains that this story is the composition of the evangelist himself and suggests that the usage of catch phrases, such as taking a wife (1:20, 24), bearing a son (1:21, 23, 25), and calling his name (1:21, 23, 25), are evidences of the evangelist's work.

gospel to be the end of human responsibility, for the heart of this story is Joseph's response. Joseph forgives; Joseph accepts the presence of God, when it draws near to him in a dream. The text simply states that when he "woke from sleep, he did as the angel of the Lord commanded him; he took his wife" (vs. 24). Joseph obeyed; he practiced a higher righteousness.

From one end of Matthew to the other, beginning in this opening scene and ending with the last words of Jesus to the disciples (28:20), the theme of obedience recurs repeatedly. We will meet this theme again and again (see 5:17–20; 7:15–27; 21:28–32). Such obedience is not, however, a meritorious work. Radical obedience occurs in God's forgiveness and presence (again, see 28:20). Therefore, Joseph is no hero but rather one who responds to God's initiative in Jesus' birth.

THE NEW ISRAEL (2:13–15)

Why does Herod seek to destroy the child Jesus?

The second chapter of Matthew's introduction has little direct connection with the first. The first half of chapter two is dominated by the "wise men from the East," and the entire chapter is organized around a series of geographical places: the East, Jerusalem, Bethlehem, Egypt, and finally Nazareth.

The wise men and their reaction to the birth of Jesus compose the initial scene (vss. 1–18). Perhaps they are Zoroastrian priests or Babylonian astrologers, but without doubt they are Gentiles. Whereas Joseph showed the reaction of a loyal, just Jew to the birth of Jesus, now we see the response of wise Gentiles (28:19). They have come to worship him as they would a king or a god (2:2, 8, 11; cf. 14:33; 28:17). Their reaction to Jesus' birth contrasts with that of Herod, the political king, who can think of Jesus only as a threat to his rule. And with some reason, for the unusual star's appearance serves as a sign of a crucial event; the old age, typified by Herod's kingdom, yields to the new, manifested in the birth of Jesus.[6]

At the mid-point of this chapter a small unit of tradition (vss. 13–15) discloses Matthew's intent. After the wise men have left, an angel of the Lord again appears to Joseph. This time he is told to flee to Egypt, and again Joseph obeys (vs. 14). In the opening two chapters Joseph consistently obeys, and by his response to the dream revelations the story moves forward.

---

[6] "Just so on the birth-night of Alexander, Magi prophesied from a brilliant constellation that the destroyer of Asia was born."—W. C. Allen, *A Critical and Exegetical Commentary on the Gospel According to St. Matthew* (ICC; New York: Charles Scribner's Sons, 1907), p. 12. Cf. Ignatius' explanation of the Bethlehem star in his letter to the Ephesians 19:2.

All this occurred in order "to fulfill what the Lord had spoken by the prophet, 'Out of Egypt have I called my son'" (vs. 15; cf. Hosea 11:1). Originally this verse recalled Israel's being brought out of Egypt. Now "my son" refers not to Israel, but to Jesus. Thus Matthew suggests that Jesus and the disciples who follow him are the new Israel.

Chapter two, furthermore, contains tradition suggesting that Jesus is to be understood as a new Moses. Moses lived in Egypt before leading the people to the promised land; Jesus also fled to Egypt before coming to Nazareth. The Hebrew male children were killed at the birth of Moses; the

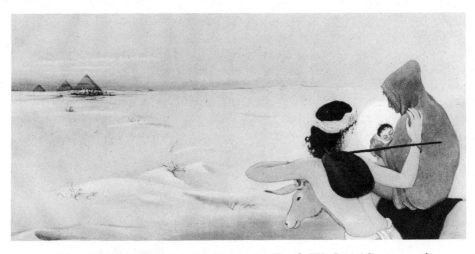

The flight into Egypt by Indian artist Frank Wesley. (Courtesy of Spartaco Appetiti.)

Bethlehem male children were killed at the birth of Jesus (2:16–19; cf. Exodus 1:15–2:10). Yet the text seems to imply something more than a Moses-Jesus typology. Jesus is not a new Moses, but a new Israel. The Old Testament equated God's Son with the people, not Moses (Exodus 4:22). The Moses analogy is present within Matthew;[7] however, the text primarily proclaims the formation of a new Israel. In the new people of God Jesus is front and center. In Judaism Moses never occupied the exalted position of Jesus. Whereas Moses was honored and respected, Jesus is worshiped (2:11; 28:17).

In his own demonic way Herod recognizes the breaking in of a new era. He unsuccessfully tries to kill the new "king" (vss. 16 ff.). Fittingly, the chapter ends with Jesus in Nazareth (vs. 23). From this point, the focus of the narrative narrows, and a particular history replaces the prophetic, eschatological overview of the introduction. Whether the first two Matthean chapters contain any history in the sense of observed and reported events is debatable. They do, however, proclaim Matthew's understanding of the new Christian way. This way of radical obedience becomes possible with the appearance of Jesus, who both is and brings into existence the new Israel.

In summary, the significant geographical references of chapter two are as follows. The East comes to Jerusalem, but the true "King of the Jews" (vs. 2) is worshiped beyond Jerusalem in Bethlehem (see Micah 5:2). A divine messenger intervenes so that Joseph obediently flees with the child

---

[7] The "forty days and nights" of fasting in the wilderness temptation (4:2) picks up the "forty days and nights" Moses also fasted when he wrote the commandments from God (Exodus 34:28). In the six antitheses (5:21–48) Jesus elaborates the commandments of Moses; indeed, the entire Sermon is from the Mount (cf. Exodus 19:2 f.). Finally, the five-part structure of Matthew (see the initial outline) parallels the Pentateuch, the five books of Moses. See B. W. Bacon, *Studies in Matthew* (New York: Henry Holt, 1930).

The present-day city of Bethlehem. (Courtesy of Pan American Airways.)

to Egypt. At the death of Herod, they return to Nazareth, where Jesus will begin his ministry. Thereby the history of salvation (represented by Jerusalem) moves with universal history (the East, Egypt) into the everyday (Nazareth). Moreover, the journey from the distant illustrious past (the genealogy) to the concrete present (the birth of Jesus) has been effected in the obedient response of Joseph (the Jew) and the worshiping response of the wise men (the Gentiles).

The Higher Righteousness (3:1–7:29)

This section, like the four other major Matthean sections, consists of narrative and discourse. The narrative includes the baptism, temptation, preaching, and calling of disciples by Jesus (3:1–4:25). The discourse is the Sermon on the Mount (5:1–7:29). By this arrangement, Matthew uses the discourse of Jesus in order to interpret the narrative, which he has basically taken over from Mark. Our interpretation of this overall section, as a depiction of "higher righteousness," is borne out by a comparison of treatments of John the Baptist.

Both Matthew and Luke record John the Baptist's reaction to some people who come out to be baptized by him (3:7–10; cf. Luke 3:7–9—Q source). According to Luke, John's scathing attack is directed against the multitudes because they are not bearing fruit that befits repentance. Matthew characteristically has John the Baptist assault the Pharisees and Sadducees, although in the time of Jesus they were the groups most likely to show obedience. Thus through his presentation of the incident, Matthew stresses that even the Pharisees are not bearing good fruit. Therefore, they are liable to judgment, and their claim to descent from Abraham will be of no avail against final judgment (vss. 9 f.). A higher righteousness is demanded.

This discussion of the necessity of bearing fruit receives further explanation in the discourse of the Sermon on the Mount: "So, every sound tree bears good fruit, but the bad tree bears evil fruit (7:17; cf. 7:18–20). Matthew prefaces this statement with an attack upon false prophets who appear in sheep's clothing, pretending to be righteous (7:15 f.). These false prophets rely upon their record of prophesying and casting out demons in the face of God's judgment (7:21–23). But such activity is of no avail unless they produce fruits—that is, deeds of righteousness, such as loving the enemy (5:44), not being angry with one's brother (5:22), praying without hypocrisy (6:5), not judging (7:1), and so on. Although the Matthean words of Jesus clearly define the higher righteousness (5:20) that Jesus demands, hearing is not enough; doing is indispensable (7:24). Therefore, Matthew moves from an emphasis on redefining righteousness to the necessity for practicing it. Higher righteousness is more than knowledge; it consists also of doing.

FULFILLING RIGHTEOUSNESS (3:13–17)

Why does Jesus accept baptism by John the Baptist?

Jesus' first act in the Gospel of Matthew occurs in connection with his baptism. In Mark, Jesus did not really act at the baptism; rather he was acted upon by John the Baptist. Consequently, Jesus' first action in Mark was the calling of the disciples. Matthew, however, shows Jesus' acting during this baptism by John.

Before turning to our specific passage (3:13–17), we must set this baptism story in context. In comparing the Matthean baptism story with that of Mark (Mark 1:9–11), we note four distinct characteristics of Matthew which illumine his intention: (1) the preaching of John the

Baptist and Jesus are identical; (2) Jesus explicitly decides to be baptized; (3) his baptism fulfills all righteousness; and (4) the voice from heaven speaks to John the Baptist rather than to Jesus.

According to Matthew, both John the Baptist and Jesus proclaim "Repent, for the kingdom of heaven is at hand" (3:2; 4:17).[8] Such identical messages show clearly that Matthew does not reject the close relationship of John and Jesus. Yet Matthew also makes clear that John the Baptist's message is prophecy, "Prepare the way of the Lord, make his paths straight" (3:3; Isaiah 40:3), whereas Jesus' coming is fulfillment, "The people who sat in darkness have seen a great light, and for those who sat in the region and shadow of death light has dawned" (4:16; Isaiah 9:1 f.). There is no polemic against John the Baptist.[9] We have already seen that John the Baptist's injunction to bear good fruit (3:10) is supported and elaborated by Jesus at the close of the Sermon on the Mount (7:16). Moreover, Matthew's Jesus, unlike Mark's, decides to leave Galilee in order to be baptized by John (vs. 13). What seemingly just happened to Jesus in Mark (1:9) occurs in Matthew because of Jesus' decision and action (cf. vs. 14).

John's protest about the inappropriateness of his baptizing Jesus is answered by the first words of Jesus in Matthew, "Let it be so now; for thus it is fitting for us to fulfill all righteousness" (vs. 15). This answer, appearing only in Matthew, explains why the sinless Jesus needed a baptism for repentance. Such an apologetic motif occurs in accounts of Jesus' baptism in noncanonical Gospels.[10] Jesus' reply may also be understood as asserting his acceptance of a requirement for the whole nation in order to establish an identity between himself and his people. Both explanations make Jesus' baptism into a routine of going through the motions. But in

---

[8] Matthew's preference for "kingdom of heaven" rather than "kingdom of God" probably reflects his reluctance to use the name God. Such reluctance is characteristic of Judaism and may further support the Jewish Christian origin of Matthew. See the opening preaching of Jesus in Mark, "The time is fulfilled, and the kingdom of God is at hand; repent, and believe in the gospel" (1:15). Cf. Allen, *The Gospel According to St. Matthew*, pp. lxvii–lxxi.

[9] The story of Jesus' baptism by John is, therefore, not to be read basically as polemic against John the Baptist and his followers. Followers of John the Baptist continued as a sect within Judaism throughout the first Christian centuries. Acts reports that Paul encountered some disciples of John at Ephesus, who were distinguished from Jesus' followers in that their baptism did not include the gift of the Holy Spirit (Acts 19:1–7). The Mandaean religious movement, which still exists in Iran, holds John the Baptist in high esteem and may have originated from a Baptist sect. See C. H. Dodd, *The Interpretation of the Fourth Gospel* (Cambridge: Cambridge University Press, 1953), pp. 115–130.

[10] In the Gospel according to the Ebionites, John asked Jesus to baptize him *after* the voice spoke from heaven. The Gospel according to the Hebrews reports the following dialogue, "Behold, the Lord's mother and his brother said to him: 'John the Baptist baptizes for the remission of sins; let us go and be baptized by him.' But he (Jesus) said to them: 'In what have I sinned, that I should go and be baptized by him?'" —James, *The Apocryphal New Testament*, pp. 9 and 6. See Johnson, *IB*, VII, p. 268.

Matthew Jesus himself initiates the action and says that this baptism is "to fulfill all righteousness" (cf. 5:17), a central Matthean theme. Consequently, we need to look more carefully into Jesus' reply.

In the first place, Matthew uniformly uses righteousness to mean that conduct which is in agreement with God's will and well pleasing to him. It is rightness of life before God.[11] This term will be considered more fully in the following section. In anticipation, however, we may say that Matthew does not speak about righteousness as a preliminary step toward the kingdom of heaven but rather as the very substance of this kingdom (see 5:6, 10, 20; 6:33).

Second, the fulfilling of all righteousness should be understood in the context of the preceding verses (3:11 f.), where John declared that he himself only baptized with water for repentance, but that after him would come one who would baptize with "the Holy Spirit and with fire." The Holy Spirit, of course, signifies the presence of God (see 1:18), and fire depicts judgment, as the context implies ("unquenchable fire"). The coming of Jesus, then, is the sign both of God's presence (cf. 1:23) and his judgment. The relationship between the two was already anticipated in John the Baptist's previous speech (3:7–10). Judgment comes to whoever does not bear fruit. But, as this passage makes clear (3:13–17), God's presence now makes it possible to bear fruit because the Holy Spirit has come with Jesus. Jesus willingly undergoes baptism, for because of the Spirit's presence he can now be obedient (bear fruit) and fulfill all righteousness, being well pleasing to God (vs. 17).

The unexpected plural in Jesus' answer to John, "thus it is fitting for *us* to fulfill all righteousness," must in this context refer to Jesus and John the Baptist. John the Baptist also is obedient ("he consented"—vs. 15). Jesus obeyed in his decision to come from Galilee to be baptized and John the Baptist acted to complete Jesus' obedience. With their fulfillment of all righteousness, the Spirit of God appears visually to Jesus and aurally to John the Baptist (in Mark 1:11 the voice spoke to Jesus).

This interpretation of the story of Jesus' baptism is supported by the following temptation story (4:1–11). The beloved Son of God, announced in the baptism, now acts as the Son in response to each temptation. "If you are the Son of God" (vss. 3, 6) does not really imply that Jesus might not be the Son of God. The baptism (3:17) left no doubt that Jesus was the Son of God. The only doubt concerns the nature of the Sonship, whether Jesus will act in obedience to God or on his own authority. Just as obedience characterized his baptism, so the temptations show the Son of God acting in accordance with the will of God (vss. 4, 7, 10).

After the temptation, Jesus first goes to territory close to the Gentiles

---

[11] Gerhard Barth, "Matthew's Understanding of the Law," *Tradition and Interpretation in Matthew* (Philadelphia: Westminster Press, 1963), pp. 138 f.

(4:12–16) where he begins to preach (vs. 17) and immediately calls disciples (vss. 18–22). These disciples respond by following him (vss. 20, 22). A brief summary section of healings (vss. 23–25; cf. Mark 1:21–3:11) shows how he attracts crowds from everywhere and leads into the first discourse, the Sermon on the Mount.

TEACHING RIGHTEOUSNESS (5:17–20)

What is Jesus' attitude toward the law and the prophets?
What is the righteousness which exceeds that of the scribes and Pharisees?

The Sermon on the Mount (chaps. 5–7) has been acclaimed as the heart and center of Christian faith. In Matthew, this is the first and most important discourse of the Gospel. In all probability, the Sermon was not spoken by Jesus on one occasion, for much of the same material is scattered throughout the Gospel of Luke (see, for example, the Sermon on the Plain, Luke 6:17–49 and 12:22–34).[12] Hence the arrangement of the tradition probably reflects Matthean interests and concerns.

Two preliminary observations about the staging will serve to characterize this discourse. First, Jesus appears as a rabbi, a teacher (5:2). This initial depiction of Jesus contrasts with that of Mark where Jesus initially appeared as a miracle worker and healer (Mark 1:21 ff.). Second, the Sermon is delivered from the Mount. Two other crucial events, the transfiguration scene (17:1 ff.) and the final word to the disciples (28:16 ff.), occur on a mountain in the Gospel of Matthew. The delivery of the Sermon from the mountain is deliberately reminiscent of Moses' receiving the law on the mountain in the wilderness (Exodus 19). According to Matthew, a new teaching comes from the mountain—a righteousness higher than that delivered by Moses.

In addition, two further observations about the content of the Sermon show its intention and meaning. First, it begins with a series of nine beatitudes or blessings (5:3–12), which describe the condition of those for whom Jesus' message is good news—"the poor in spirit," "those who mourn," and "the meek" (5:3–5).[13] These conditions are not requirements,

[12] The significance of the Sermon on the Mount for Matthew is illustrated by the fact that his passion story picks up motifs already prepared for in the Sermon. For example, in Gethsemane Jesus prays word for word the third petition of the Lord's Prayer (26:42; cf. 6:10). Jesus also advocates peace in the confrontation at his arrest (26:52; cf. 5:39). Moreover, Jesus never relaxes the commandments; he is innocent and righteous (27:4, 19, 24; cf. 5:19). Jesus refuses to reply to the high priests' request for an oath (26:63; cf. 5:34). All these instances are Matthean additions not found in the Markan text. See G. Barth, *Tradition and Interpretation in Matthew*, pp. 144–146.

[13] Even the last six "beatitudes" (5:6–12), which might be taken as ethical requirements, are still within the setting of unconditional blessing. Any "merit" goes back to the astonishing generosity of God.

for Matthew declares the unmerited grace of God in present blessing and promises future participation in the kingdom of heaven to those who have need. Thus the opening of the Sermon on the Mount stresses God's favor rather than his demand. Second, the Sermon on the Mount ends with a clear call to obedience (7:15–29): "You will know them by their fruits" (7:16). Entrance into the kingdom of heaven will reward whoever "does the will of my Father who is in heaven" (7:21); the wise man hears Jesus' words and does them (7:24). Hence the grace of God does not make obedience unnecessary.

We now turn to the word of Jesus about the law and prophets (5:17–20), which appears only in Matthew. In the first three verses Jesus declares his complete acceptance of the law and the prophets. Nothing will pass away from the law until all is accomplished. No one may relax one of these commandments or teach anyone else to do so. This complete acceptance of the law is difficult to understand in view of later criticism of the law. The final verse demanding a "higher righteousness" (vs. 20) already hints at criticism but other passages are more explicit. John the Baptist is identified with the law and the prophets, yet he who is least in the kingdom of heaven is greater than he (11:11–15). Moreover, Matthew follows Mark in Jesus' criticism of the law's distinction between clean and unclean: "Hear and understand: not what goes into the mouth defiles a man, but what comes out of the mouth, this defiles a man" (15:10; cf. Mark 7:14). But Jesus' first words on the law (vss. 17–19) make clear that Jesus is no antinomian (that is, one who disavows the law). He expects nothing less than fulfillment of the law. Although Matthew does contain a torrid diatribe against the scribes and Pharisees (chap. 23), this criticism is directed toward their failure to practice and observe the law (23:3) and their hypocrisy (23:13, 23, 25, and so on).

In another passage, however (22:34–40; cf. Mark 12:28–34), Jesus discusses the nature of the law and the prophets and generalizes that the first and great commandment is love of God, and the second love of neighbor. *All* the law and the prophets depend on these commandments (vs. 40). This conclusion, which appears only in Matthew, suggests that the "higher righteousness" that Jesus teaches consists of a primary relation with God and a secondary relation with other men. This view of higher righteousness helps explain the castigation of the scribes and Pharisees that follows (chap. 23). As we noted, they are chastised because they do not observe the law and are hypocrites. Yet by any "normal" measure the scribes and Pharisees were the most observant group within Israel, during both the time of Jesus and of Matthew. Only by the extraordinary norm of the love of God and the love of man, which nevertheless is derived from the law and the prophets, could they be denounced.

We have already encountered the verb "to fulfill" in Matthew. At the baptism Jesus and John the Baptist fulfilled all righteousness (3:15), primarily by their respective acts of obedience. Here in the Sermon, "he who does them and teaches them shall be called great in the kingdom of heaven" (vs. 19b). Jesus fulfills the law and the prophets not only in deed, but also in teaching. The Gospel of Matthew understands the congregation of followers of Christ as founded not only upon Jesus' action but also upon his teaching. Jesus' closing words in the Gospel reiterate this theme, "Go therefore and make disciples of all nations . . . teaching them to observe all that I have commanded you" (28:19 f.).

The key to Jesus' teaching about fulfillment of the law and the prophets lies, of course, in the enigmatic last verse of this passage (vs. 20), where Jesus calls for more righteousness than that of the scribes and Pharisees. The rest of the Sermon seeks to teach this higher righteousness, which first becomes explicit in the "antitheses" of the Sermon on the Mount.

The six antitheses (5:21–48) are so designated because of the antithetical form in which they are cast, "You have heard it said . . . but I say to you." These antitheses seem to indicate that Jesus pays attention to a person's intention as well as his actual deed. His words would therefore advise the hearer to root out evil thoughts so that evil actions will not follow. We might observe that such good advice is easier to hear than to heed. It is sometimes difficult to refrain from killing, committing adultery, and hating one's neighbor; it is almost impossible to keep from anger, lust, and hate of one's enemy. These words are not, however, a counsel of despair, for the extremely radical nature of their demand elicits from the hearer the recognition that these are more than human commands. The antitheses set forth the will and presence of God. The commandments are transparent so that God shines through them. Indeed the Sermon's opening beatitudes already indicated the present blessing of God. Moreover, Jesus' following teaching emphasizes the availability of God in prayer (6:5–15) and everyday life (6:25–34). Therefore, the final, seemingly impossible requirement, "You, therefore, must be perfect as your heavenly Father is perfect" (5:48), is Jesus' call to align onself with the perfection or righteousness of God, which God not only requires but also manifests. With the demand for the higher righteousness comes the gift of God's grace. Indeed, for Matthew the teaching of "higher righteousness" takes place only after Jesus and John at the baptism have in obedience fulfilled all righteousness.

Matthew develops the entire Sermon under the implied rubrics of love of God and love of neighbor as the fulfillment of the law and the prophets (cf. 7:11 f.). The antitheses call for an unlimited concern for the neighbor (vss. 21–48; see also 7:1–5), whereas the remaining sections of the Sermon point to the one gracious source of life. What is impossible apart from God becomes a promise in his presence (6:33). To return to an opening generalization, the Sermon on the Mount begins with the promise of blessings (5:1–12) and ends with the demand for obedience (7:24–27). This tension characterizes the Jewish Christianity of Matthew, and is actually typical of the New Testament as a whole. God's grace enables man to obey; it does not nullify human responsibility.

True Discipleship (8:1–11:1)

In the first major section of the Gospel, Jesus appeared as Messiah of the word (chaps. 3–7), but in the second major section he appears as Messiah of the deed. Matthew has brought together ten miracle narratives (chaps. 8–9),[14] accounts of Jesus' deeds, which lead naturally into the missionary discourse (chap. 10) that describes the deeds required in discipleship. Just as Jesus' words in the Sermon on the Mount anticipated action (7:21), so Jesus' deeds in his miracles anticipate righteous acts from the disciples (10:42).

This movement from Jesus' miracles to the disciples' working is reflected in Matthew's three-fold division of the miracle section. The first part (8:2–17) portrays Jesus as bearing the infirmities and diseases of all people—the leper, the centurion's servant, the disciple's mother-in-law. At its close Jesus fulfills the prophet Isaiah's word, "He took our infirmities and bore our diseases" (8:17; cf. Isaiah 53:4). The middle and dominant division (8:18–9:17) places the disciples at the center of action. The initial episode (8:18–22) shows a concern about "following." Next the plight of the perishing disciples (8:23–27) is overcome in the power of Jesus' exorcism of the two demoniacs (9:28–34) and the healing forgiveness of the paralytic (9:1–8). After these miracles Jesus immediately calls the disciple Matthew, who is a tax collector (9:9–13). Therefore, Jesus' disciples rejoice rather than fasting like John's disciples (9:14–17). In distinction from the previous division's emphasis on the disciples, the third and final part of the miracle section (9:18–38) concerns faith. Indeed, Matthew has reduced the narration about the raising of the daughter and the healing of the woman with the hemorrhage (9:18–26) to a bare minimum to emphasize the essential point of the father's faith. The same is true of Matthew's treatment of the healing of the two blind men (9:27–31); moreover, faith is implicitly the subject of the final healing of the dumb demoniac (9:32–34). Without faith there is no miracle.

---

[14] The ten miracles correspond to the following Mishnah tradition (a collection of rabbinic tradition, *ca.* A.D. 200). "Ten wonders were wrought for our fathers in Egypt and ten at sea. . . . Ten wonders were wrought for our fathers in the temple" (Aboth 5:4–5). Cf. Johnson, *IB*, VII, p. 336.

In summary, Matthew's miracle section portrays a compassionate healer, drawing out disciples who believe in working with God rather than the prince of demons (9:34). Thus Jesus draws out faithful disciples who will continue his own work. In other words, he calls for faithful disciples to join with him in the labor of sharing the suffering of people.[15] Confirmation of our view that Matthew intends to define discipleship in this section (chaps. 8–10) is found in the transitional sentences. Only Matthew says, "When he came down from the mountain, great crowds *followed* him" (8:1; cf. Mark 1:39 f.). "Following"—that is, discipleship—is actually the theme of the Matthean miracle section. The missionary discourse (chap. 10), which immediately follows the miracles, links the twelve disciples directly with the acts that Jesus has just performed: "And he called to him his twelve disciples and gave them authority over unclean spirits, to cast them out, and to heal every disease and every infirmity" (10:1; cf. 6:7). Finally, the closing transitional sentence of this section reads, "And when Jesus had finished instructing his *twelve disciples*, he went on from there to teach and preach in their cities" (11:1).

LITTLE FAITH (8:23–27)

Why does Jesus rebuke the disciples as men of little faith?

This miracle story, which recounts Jesus' stilling of the storm, appears in all three Synoptic Gospels (cf. Mark 4:35–41, Luke 8:22–24). Matthew alone inserts this incident following a discussion of discipleship (8:18–22). Moreover, only Matthew says that when Jesus got into the boat, "his disciples *followed* him" (vs. 23).[16] Clearly, the Matthean episode remains a nature miracle—contrast the great storm at the beginning (vs. 24) and the great calm at the end (vs. 26). The decisive occurrence, however, is Jesus' word to the disciples, "Why are you afraid, O men of little faith?" (vs. 26).

Four Matthean changes from the Markan account underscore his emphasis on faith and discipleship: (1) Some dramatic details of the storm —for example, the beating of the waves—are omitted by Matthew, for they are unnecessary to his point. (2) In Mark the disciples speak normally to Jesus, "Teacher, do you not care if we perish?" (4:38), but in

---

15 See Held, *Tradition and Interpretation in Matthew*, pp. 165 ff.

16 Indeed the two preceding sayings about discipleship—"the Son of man has nowhere to lay his head" (8:20) and "leave the dead to bury their own dead" (8:21 f.) —may provide the outline for the missionary discourse. The first half (10:5–23) has to do with the necessity of the disciples' being on the move (nowhere to lay their heads) and the second half (10:24–42) stresses the radical decision called for by discipleship, a decision that may result in bursting family bonds (vss. 35 ff.).

Matthew the disciples pray to Jesus, "Save, Lord, we are perishing."[17] For Matthew the threat of perishing was not confined to Jesus' first disciples, but includes the contemporary congregation of "little faith." (3) Matthew reverses the Markan order of events. In Mark, Jesus first rebukes the wind and the sea and then asks the question about their faith (4:39 f.); in Matthew after being aroused, Jesus first questions their discipleship, then calms the storm. The question of faith is made prior. (4) In Mark, Jesus asks "Why are you afraid? Have you no faith?" (4:40). Perhaps Matthew intends to soften the rebuke by having Jesus say that the disciples have a "little faith" (vs. 26). This is understandable if he sees the church represented in the disciples. Yet Matthew does not intend to detract from the seriousness of the question addressed to the disciples. Indeed, throughout Matthew a key theme is the "little faith" of the disciples (cf. especially 14:31; 16:8; 17:20). Their trouble lies not in their lack of profession of allegiance to Jesus ("Save, Lord"—vs. 25) but in their inability to act on the basis of that devotion. "Not everyone who says to me, 'Lord, Lord,' shall enter the kingdom of heaven, but he who does the will of my Father who is in heaven" (7:21).[18] These disciples understand Jesus, but they do not obey by acting with confidence. In this light the episode's conclusion (vs. 27) makes sense. The disciples marvel "that even winds and sea obey him." True disciples of more than "little faith" would also obey. Probably it is no coincidence that the next story of the Gadarene demoniacs (8:28–34) narrates how the demons obeyed Jesus and "perished in the waters" (vs. 32). If disciples would obey Jesus, they would be saved from perishing in the sea (cf. vs. 25).

A RELATION OF RECEIVING AND GIVING (10:34–42)

How does the disciple "find" his life?

The composition and character of Matthew's missionary discourse (chap. 10) discourages the notion that this tradition is simply the report of Jesus' instructions to his twelve disciples. This discourse concerning the nature of true discipleship is primarily intended for the disciples in the congregation of Matthew's time. This is evident in the changes Matthew has made in his Markan tradition (cf. Mark 6:7–13). First, Matthew has no report of Jesus' disciples' actually carrying out the mission that he gave them, even though his Markan source contained the statement that "they

---

[17] The Greek term for "Lord" cannot be translated here simply as a title of respect, such as "Sir." In each Matthean occurrence, this term is associated with majesty (cf. 7:21; 8:2, 8; 14:28; 16:22, and so on.). See G. Bornkamm, "The Stilling of the Storm in Matthew," *Tradition and Interpretation in Matthew*, p. 55.

[18] See G. Barth, *Tradition and Interpretation in Matthew*, pp. 119–121.

went out and preached that men should repent . . ." (Mark 6:12 f.; cf. Matt. 10:14 f.). For Matthew, this missionary task was delivered to the church that came into existence with the death and resurrection of Jesus (28:19 f.). Second, Matthew inserts a passage from Jesus' apocalyptic discourse concerning the future end of the world (Mark 13:9–13) into Jesus' missionary discourse (Matt. 10:17–25), which is intended to instruct the church for its present task. According to Matthew these words are spoken by Jesus to the church for application to the time between Jesus' resurrection and his parousia; thus Matthew changes an apocalyptic warning into churchly instructions.

Matthew's editing or redaction does not mean that he has no regard for tradition, that he changes it at will or creates it anew. Indeed, his respect for the tradition extends to inclusion of two sayings with which Matthew does not agree; the disciples are to go only to the lost sheep of Israel (10:5) and they "will not have gone through all the towns of Israel before the Son of man comes" (10:23). These words clearly reflect an earlier stage of the tradition that Matthew has included in order to frame them within his more comprehensive understanding of discipleship, which extends to both Israel and the Gentiles.[19]

The picture of discipleship in the missionary discourse falls into three parts: the answer to persecution is confession and endurance (10:5–23); the disciple is unequivocally joined to the master (10:24–33); and separation from natural ties leads into a receiving and giving of a rewarding fellowship (10:34–42). Our passage for examination (10:32–42) seems to offer good advice; namely, associate with disciples, members of the congregation, and separate from outsiders, even if that means a radical family break.

One key to Matthew's fuller intent in this passage is his addition of "for my sake" (vs. 39). In Luke the saying reads, "Whoever seeks to gain his life will lose it, but whoever loses his life will preserve it" (Luke 17:33).[20] Matthew's addition makes clear that discipleship is a relationship to Jesus. Therefore, the greatest potential barriers to discipleship are conflicting relationships, even family ties (vss. 35–37). Indeed, the second part of the missionary discourse emphatically stressed that discipleship is a relation with the master or teacher (10:24 f.). Thus the closing words on discipleship (vss. 40–42) are not simply ethical commands about performing acts of charity, but rather they speak about receiving of persons, and of Christ himself, in a new relation. "He who receives you receives

19 Note how Matthew adds the phrase, "and the Gentiles" (10:18; cf. Mark 13:9). Also note emphasis upon Gentiles in 2:1 ff.; 8:5–18; 12:18–21; 15:22–28; 24:14; and 28:19.
20 The probability is that Matthew adds rather than that Luke omits this phrase; Luke would hardly minimize the role of Jesus.

me, and he who receives me receives him who sent me" (10:40; cf. 10:32 f.).

The question at issue for Matthew concerns the nature of Christian discipleship, whether it is a goal or ideal for which the disciple strives or a relation within which the disciple lives. A similar question might be asked of the conclusion to the antitheses in the Sermon on the Mount, "You, therefore, must be perfect, as your heavenly Father is perfect" (5:48). Is perfection a goal for which the disciple strives, or is perfection a way in which both the disciple and the Father are working?

Matthew deliberately talks about discipleship in terms of receiving (vs. 40) and giving (vs. 42), in terms of relation. This terminology is explained in Matthew's parable of the great judgment (25:31–46), which elaborates the giving of a "cup of cold water" (vs. 42, cf. 25:35; see pages 126 f.). Matthew understands discipleship to consist of realizing the presence of a relation, both with Jesus, the Lord of the congregation, and with the "little ones," the neighbor in need (cf. 18:1–6, see pages 122 f.).[21] Thereby, Matthew frees the disciples from self-righteousness while still demanding obedience from them. The disciples know that whatever giving they may accomplish originates in their relation with the teacher and master. It is a gift. From Jesus' presence comes the power for discipleship that enables them to separate from the normal world and to become a part of the world of giving and receiving, a world of mercy (cf. 8:17; 9:13, 36; 10:31, 42).

In this treatment of discipleship Matthew has shown Jesus as the Messiah in deed, whose miracles alleviate suffering humanity. In turn, the disciples respond with obedient deeds. They realize true discipleship in so far as they acknowledge Jesus' lordship and follow him, performing acts of mercy toward their fellowman.

The Kingdom of Heaven (11:2–13:52)

Were Matthew presenting a historical narrative in the usual sense, we might expect information in this section about what happened to the disciples after they responded to Jesus' missionary imperative (chap. 10). Instead, this section details further activity of Jesus and the reaction, both positive and negative, which he elicits. First, a series of passages deals with

---

[21] Matthew subordinates the reception of a prophet or a righteous man to that of giving to the "little ones" (vss. 4 f.). Later he indicates that disciples are greater than prophets and righteous men (13:17).

the relationship of John the Baptist and Jesus (11:2–19); next, the cities that rejected Jesus are chastised (11:20–24); blessing is then pronounced upon those who accept the yoke of Jesus (11:25–30); and controversy with the Pharisees involving a series of miracles follows (chap. 12). The section ends with a series of parables initially addressed to the crowds, but adapted by Matthew for the disciples (chap. 13).

The key to this section lies not so much in the order of events, as in the way Matthew has brought his own special interests into these events. Four emphases stand out: (1) The section is devoted overall to the question of the nature of the kingdom of heaven. The opening incident raises the Christological question, "Are you he who is to come, or shall we look for another?" (11:3). However, Jesus' answer and the ensuing discussion transform the Christological question into an eschatological one, the nature of the kingdom of heaven. Though John the Baptist is greater than anybody else born of woman, "yet he who is least in the kingdom of heaven is greater than he" (11:11). Moreover, in a later debate with the Pharisees about whether Jesus casts out demons by God or Beelzebul, the climactic answer again focuses on the kingdom: "But if it is by the Spirit of God that I cast out demons, then the kingdom of God has come upon you" (12:28). Finally, the discourse of this section is throughout an unveiling of the "secrets of the kingdom of heaven" (13:11). The seven kingdom parables with which this section ends show that, for Matthew, understanding of Jesus as the Christ comes through understanding Jesus' proclamation about the kingdom of heaven.

(2) Not unexpectedly, this kingdom of heaven is a kingdom of mercy. Jesus answers John the Baptist's disciples by enumerating deeds of mercy that he performed (11:5; cf. Luke 7:22). Furthermore, Jesus' demand for discipleship is a yoke that is gentle and restful, because Jesus himself is gentle and lowly in heart (11:28–30, only in Matthew). Sabbath observance is understood within the context of mercy (12:7 f.; cf. 9:13 and Hosea 6:6). Indeed, Jesus' parable of the sower proclaims God's abundant mercy; the sower generously sows seed everywhere without distinction, and the seed on good soil bears grain prodigiously (13:3–8).

(3) The kingdom of heaven is, however, not mercy only; judgment also occurs. Chorazin, Bethsaida, and Capernaum will be brought down on the day of judgment because they rejected the words of mercy (11:20–24). Jesus' opponents, especially the Pharisees, will be brought to account on the day of judgment because they have not borne the good fruit—that is, acts of mercy (12:33–37). Indeed, this present generation is an evil one (12:45, only in Matthew). Finally, at the close of the age "all causes of sin and all evildoers" will be gathered out of the kingdom and thrown "into the furnace of fire; there men will weep and gnash their teeth" (13:42; cf. 8:12; 13:50; 22:13; and so on).

(4) Jesus' disciples are ones who will realize the true nature of the kingdom of heaven. Those who have been gathered to Jesus learn that the kingdom is both mercy and judgment. They are the "babes" who learn that this yoke is easy (11:25–29). They are the true family of Jesus. Matthew alone records Jesus' saying that the disciples are his mother and brothers (12:49; cf. Mark 3:34). Matthew also directs the final six kingdom parables to the disciples, for they are the ones who know the secrets of the kingdom (13:10–17). Indeed, Matthew omits Mark's castigation of the disciples, "Do you not understand this parable? How then will you understand all the parables?" (Mark 4:13). In Matthew the opposite point is true—the disciples do understand; therefore, when Jesus asks them, "Have you understood all this?" (13:51), the only possible answer is "Yes." This general understanding of Matthew's kingdom section is supported by the next two passages that we shall examine.

A KINGDOM OF MERCY (12:9–14)

What criterion does Jesus give for sabbath observance?

The healing of the man with the withered hand (cf. Mark 3:1–6), like the earlier Matthean miracle stories, subordinates miraculous action to Jesus' message. The crucial question is not whether Jesus will heal, but whether it is lawful to heal on the sabbath (vs. 10). In the Markan version, Jesus himself, rather than his opponents, asked this question, and his very question settled the matter, for "they were silent" (Mark 3:4). Matthew, on the other hand, gives attention to Jesus' answer.

Before looking at this answer, we need to note the context. In Mark this healing was set alongside a parallel story, the gathering of grain on the sabbath (12:1–8; cf. Mark 2:23–28). Matthew, however, adds a conclusive word about sabbath observance by citing the prophet Hosea, "I desire mercy, and not sacrifice" (12:7; 9:13; Hosea 6:6). This affirmation—mercy controls sabbath observance—prepares for Jesus' answer in the next sabbath healing about the man with the withered hand. Even though Matthew has followed Mark's order, his insertion of this prophetic word alters the meaning of the events.

Jesus replies to the question of his opponents about the legality of healing on the sabbath (vs. 10) by asking a question about what they would do if a sheep fell into a pit on the sabbath (vs. 11, cf. Luke 14:5). The answer (vs. 12a) and its implications are obvious. Jesus then gives a rule for the congregation, "So it is lawful to do good on the sabbath" (vs. 12b). In Matthew, Jesus does not advocate doing away with sabbath observance

(24:20 implies sabbath observance); yet sabbath keeping does not set aside the necessity of doing good—that is, mercy.[22]

Sabbath observance is a subordinate obligation within a kingdom of mercy. In one sense, this may be a relaxing of the commandments (cf. 5:19), but in another sense, the practice of mercy means a deepening and fulfilling of the law and the prophets. Clearly the doing of mercy does not mean a sentimentalizing or softening of the kingdom's rigor. Matthew makes this evident in the final parable in this section on the kingdom.

A KINGDOM OF JUDGMENT (13:47–52)

When is the time for judgment?

In effect, the proclamation of a kingdom of mercy separates those who hear—that is, the disciples—from those who reject this good news of mercy. Normally such separation serves as an excuse for self-congratulation. Indeed we would expect something like this from disciples to whom Jesus addresses these words, "To you it has been given to know the secrets of the kingdom of heaven, but to them it has not been given" (13:11). The favored position of the disciples could easily lead to that self-righteousness which Matthew condemns in the Pharisees (cf. 23:5–8, 27 f.). To discourage any such complacency Matthew ends the section on the kingdom with this parable of judgment (vss. 47–52).

The judgment motif recurs frequently throughout the Gospel of Matthew. The Sermon on the Mount closed with a threat of judgment against those who heard Jesus' words and did not do them (7:21–27). Jesus even pronounced judgment on those cities that did not receive his works or mercy (11:20–24). Moreover, the fifth and final major section of Matthew deals with this very theme of judgment (see esp. 25:31–46). Matthew's stress falls, however, not upon judgment for those outside the church, but upon the judgment awaiting the disciples.

In a preceding parable, the weeds of the field (13:24–30), the interpretation (13:36–43) made plain that judgment cannot take place in the present (13:29; cf. 7:1); it will be a future act of the Son of Man at the close of the age (13:41). In the present no one can tell who are the good and who are the bad disciples. The church and the disciples are a mixed

---

[22] In a related passage the Pharisees ask Jesus about the great commandment in the law, and Jesus' reply stresses love of God and love of neighbor (22:34–40). Here Matthew defines more precisely how sabbath observance is controlled by the "love principle." Matthew also advocates mercy in the parable of the great judgment (25:31–46). Another relevant passage occurs in the Sermon on the Mount where "doing good" is defined as "whatever you wish that men would do to you, do so to them" (7:11 f.)— the well-known "Golden Rule."

group, not a pure elect who have already secured salvation. Matthew's version of the parable of the marriage feast (22:1–14; cf. Luke 14:16–24) precisely illustrates this message. Some people, those who are not disciples, reject the king's gracious invitation to the marriage feast (22:3). Yet among the many who do accept are the bad as well as the good (22:10). One who accepted lacked a wedding garment. Therefore, when the king came, he caused him to be bound hand and foot and cast into the outer darkness where "men will weep and gnash their teeth" (22:13; cf. 13:42, 50). This clearly implies that although the disciples have responded to the present mercy, they will still have to face the final judgment. The church is no place for complacency.

Matthew ends this section on the kingdom with the question "Have you understood all this?" (13:51). The disciples answer in the affirmative. Matthew then concludes, "Therefore every scribe who has been trained for the kingdom of heaven is like a householder who brings out of his treasure what is new and what is old" (vs. 52). In view of previous discussion, the new refers to the kingdom of mercy, new in comparison with Pharisaic insistence on strict sabbath observance (cf. 12:12b); the old refers to the kingdom of judgment, the old expectation of judgment under the criterion of obedience to the will of God (cf. 12:50). Therefore, the scribe trains for the kingdom by accepting the new mercy and by carrying out the old obedience. Matthew speaks to the church in the time between the resurrection and the parousia, a time of mercy and judgment. The disciples have no security other than the gracious presence of Christ (cf. 10:40; 28:20). They are to work between the times so that at the future judgment they will be found merciful. Matthew thus prepares for the subject matter of his next section, the church.

The Forgiving Church (13:53–19:2)

In Matthew's preceding section, the kingdom of heaven was characterized as an eschatological reality, already present in mercy and expected in judgment. In this section, stress falls upon the church, the community of disciples existing between the resurrection and the parousia, those who are closely identified with the mercy motif of the kingdom of heaven. Moreover, in the fifth and final Matthean section (19:3–26:1), we find that even the church will have to face the future judgment. Thus the emphases of the final two sections confirm our interpretation of Matthew's treatment of the kingdom of heaven.

As in every other section of Matthew, here also narrative is dominated by discourse. What Jesus teaches controls his own actions and those of his opponents and disciples. The concluding discourse (17:22–19:1) centers upon the nature and authority of the church. Fittingly, then, the climactic action of the narrative (13:53–17:21) is Jesus' establishment of Peter as the rock upon which the church is built (16:17–19). We receive clues as to the intention of this section simply by observing the heightened role of Peter. For example, Matthew takes over Mark's story of Jesus' walking on the water (14:22–33; Mark 6:45–52) and, instead of using it as an occasion to illustrate the disciples' misunderstanding (Mark 6:51 f.), shows Peter's amazing, albeit faltering, courage in trying to walk on the water. When he sinks from fear, Peter cries out with a Christological confession, "Lord, save me" (14:30).[23] Partly because of Peter's action, at the end of the story the other disciples worship Jesus and confess, "Truly, you are the Son of God" (14:33). Other instances of Peter's increased prominence include his role in the temple tax incident (17:24–27; cf. also 15:15 and 17:4) and his reception of Jesus' congregational rule demanding forgiveness (18:21 f.).

This increased emphasis upon Peter is matched by a more prominent role for the disciples throughout this section. Perhaps the clearest evidence is Matthew's treatment of the two feedings of the multitudes. In the feeding of the five thousand (14:13–21; cf. Mark 6:30–44) Matthew omits the question in which the disciples misunderstand Jesus (Mark 6:37). In Matthew the disciples immediately understand, but they doubt their ability to supply bread for the multitudes: "We have only five loaves here and two fish" (14:17). Moreover, in Matthew the disciples actually fetch the food (14:18). Finally only Matthew depicts the disciples' duplication of Jesus' action in distributing the loaves to the crowds (vs. 19b, cf. Mark 6:41). Similarly, in the feeding of the four thousand (15:32–39, cf. Mark 8:1–10) the disciples again immediately understand their task; they are concerned only about their ability to accomplish it (vs. 33; cf. Mark 8:4). Once more the disciples actually give the bread to the people in imitation of Jesus (vs. 36; cf. Mark 8:6). In addition, Matthew omits distribution of the fish to the crowds (Mark 8:7), thereby bringing his account closer to the actual celebration of the Lord's Supper in the church's life. By implication, the disciples are ministers of the church. Through Matthew's use of the tradition, these events in the life of Jesus are in the process of becoming events in the life of the church.

The conclusion is inescapable. By using the framework of Mark (Mark 6:14–9:32), by abbreviating it and adding other material, especially that not found in other Gospels, Matthew has turned this section into a discussion about the church. On the surface we have here a series of incidents:

---

[23] This section's stress on the Christological foundation of the church is evident in the exalted titles for Jesus: "Lord" (15:22; 16:22; 17:4, 15), "Son of God" (14:33; 16:16), "Son of Man" (16:13, 27 f.) and "Son of David" (15:22). These are all Matthew's additions.

the death of John the Baptist, the two feedings, the healing of the Canaanite woman, controversy with the Pharisees and the Sadducees, the confession by Peter, the transfiguration, and an extended teaching section. But such a surface view does not do justice to the careful way in which Matthew illuminates the nature of the community brought into being by the life, death, and resurrection of Jesus and charged to act with disciplined forgiveness until his coming again.

PETER AS THE ROCK (16:13–23)

To whom are the keys of the kingdom given?
Why is Peter castigated by Jesus?

Only in Matthew does Jesus actually accept Peter's confession at Caesarea Philippi, for in Mark Jesus seems to reject it (cf. Mark 8:27–33, see pp. 80 ff.). Indeed the source of Peter's insight is said by Jesus to be none other than "my Father who is in heaven" (16:17). Furthermore, Peter has the keys to the kingdom: whatever he binds and looses (that is, his solemn decisions in matters of discipline) will be upheld on the judgment day (vs. 19; cf. 18:18).[24]

In spite of this seeming praise of Peter, after Jesus' announcement that he must suffer (vs. 21), Peter and Jesus engage in controversy (vss. 22 f.). Perhaps Matthew is simply following the Markan text so that Peter's difficulty with Jesus should be overlooked; however, this explanation is not sustained by closer scrutiny of the text. Matthew could have omitted the rebuke by Peter and the retort of Jesus as Luke did (Luke 9:18–22). Moreover, Matthew not only includes the rebuke by Peter, but he increases Peter's opposition to Jesus' suffering by adding Peter's words, "God forbid, Lord! This shall never happen to you" (vs. 22). At one moment in Matthew Peter is literally praised to the heavens and the next moment he is thrust into the company of Satan (vs. 23).

Matthew's tension between praise and blame for Peter is deliberate. He wishes to say that though the church has accepted Jesus as the Lord

[24] Our interpretation of this celebrated passage stresses the founding of the church through Peter rather than the founding of the episcopacy through Peter. Without going into the much-debated question of 16:17–19's authenticity, we contend that Matthew speaks here not so much of the primacy of Peter but of the primacy of the church (cf. esp. 18:17–18). Peter represents the disciples and the disciples in turn represent the church. Further exegesis of the passage supports this contention. For a brief valuable discussion of the question of authenticity, see F. W. Beare, *The Earliest Records of Jesus* (New York: Abingdon Press, 1962), pp. 137–139. See also K. L. Schmidt, "The Church," *Bible Key Words*, trans. and ed. J. R. Coates (New York: Harper & Row, 1951), pp. 35–50, and Oscar Cullmann, *Peter: Disciple-Apostle-Martyr*, trans. F. V. Filson (New York: Meridian, 1958), pp. 155–238.

and the Son of the living God and has thereby been granted the authority to bind and loose on earth, individual Christians, like the disciple Peter, have to accept Jesus' suffering. Even the disciple Peter is not spared suffering. Christians must imitate Christ. Even though the church has the authority to bind and to loose, disciples cannot avoid Christ's way. Thus Matthew's earlier identification of Christ with the role of the suffering servant (12:18–21) takes on new meaning, for the disciples must also become suffering servants (cf. 5:10–12).

The inescapability of suffering as a disciple is now depicted in Jesus' definition of discipleship as taking up one's cross and following him (16:24–28). To his Markan source (cf. Mark 8:34–9:1) Matthew adds that when the Son of Man comes in glory, "he will repay every man for what he has done" (vs. 27). Matthew's emphasis on obedience implies that though the church exists between the resurrection and the second coming, with great power to bind and to loose, every disciple is still accountable to the Judge for what he has done. This demand for obedience avoids self-righteousness or complacency in the church. Peter is pronounced blessed, but his blessedness, along with that of all disciples, will have to endure and be judged.

To sum up this episode, confession of Christ leads to the founding of a church whose authority is binding. The disciples, however, must individually do the will of God in order to prepare for the future judgment. The nature of the church that has been founded becomes transparent in the following discourse.

DISCIPLINE IN COMMUNITY (18:15–22)

How is the church to exercise discipline?

Just as Peter's confession of the Christ was not simply an occasion for praise and rejoicing, so too Matthew's depiction of the disciples' liberation from the Pharisaic law (15:1–20; 16:1–12) does not mean the creation of a community without discipline. Matthew's concluding discourse for the church (17:22–19:2) asserts that the Christian disciple comes under discipline of the churchly community. The incident of the temple tax (17:24–27), which serves as a transition to the discourse, illustrates the point. In this distinctively Matthean scene that follows a prediction of suffering (17:22), Jesus and Simon Peter discuss whether the temple tax should be paid. Although "the sons are free" (17:26), Jesus orders the paying of the tax in order not to give offense (17:24–27). The members of the church possess freedom, yet freedom is restricted by the necessities of a community (cf. I Cor. 10:23 f.).

Our present passage (18:15–22), in agreement with what precedes, indicates that it may be necessary for the church to exclude people in exercising its authority to bind on earth (18:18). But this power of excommunication does not exist for the purpose of condemning people, for the church acts under rules (vss. 15 f.) and always in forgiveness (vss. 21 f.). This concern for the individual Christian is indicated by the talk about "children" (18:3) and "little ones" (18:5, 10, 14). These "little ones" are to be received, not because they are actual children or even weaker members of the congregation, but rather because they are the disciples, the members of the congregation. Just as Matthew characterized the disciples by "little faith" (see 8:23–27), so the "little ones" are Christian disciples who journey from the privilege of forgiveness (18:10–14) to deeds of obedience (18:5–9). Indeed, these same little ones are blessed in the beatitudes. They are poor in spirit, mourning, meek (5:3–5); they yearn after righteousness, mercy, purity in heart, peace, knowing that they are blessed (5:6–12).[25] Matthew sets the discipline of the church in the context of God's grace. Even the community that exercises discipline consists of "little ones" who are in constant need of mercy (18:14).

Finally, the passage containing the most rigorous word of discipline in Matthew ("Let him be to you as a Gentile and tax collector"—vs. 17b) closes with the most definite promise of Christ's presence ("For where two or three are gathered in my name, there am I in the midst of them" —vs. 20). The church exists, then, not only with authority to bind and to loose, but also in the authority of the gracious presence of Christ. Consequently the church's most characteristic activity is that of worship (2:2, 8, 11; 8:2; 9:18; 14:33; 20:20; 28:9, 17). Such worship, adoration of the Lord, allows the church to bind or loose in a distinctively Christian way, the way of forgiveness. Therefore, Matthew concludes his exhortation for discipline in the church community with a word of Jesus about the radical necessity to forgive (18:21 f.) and with a long parable (only in Matthew) about the necessity to punish the wicked servant who does not forgive (18:23–35).

The church community is founded upon the confession of Jesus as the Christ. In its exercise of authority for judgment and discipline the constant limiting factor is Jesus' demand for forgiveness (cf. 6:14 f.). Matthew's congregation of believers is the forgiving church.

Judgment: Doing God's Will (19:3–26:1)

Matthew's discussion of the church as the forgiving community leads into this section: the church facing the last judgment. The judgment theme is found in Jesus' apocalyptic pronouncement (chap. 24), especially the

[25] See G. Barth, *Tradition and Interpretation in Matthew*, pp. 121–125.

command of watchfulness for the coming end (24:36–51), and his parables of the wise and foolish maidens, the talents, and the great judgment (chap. 25). The church, which exists in the blessedness of forgiveness, also has to live under the threat of judgment. Therefore, the disciples are called to do God's will in the face of judgment.

Although again Matthew is dependent upon Mark's framework (Mark 10–13), his use of Q and his special M tradition and his shaping of all the material have made this section into a manual on how the church meets judgment by doing the will of God. For example, the opening unit of tradition, the debate with the Pharisees about divorce (19:3–12; cf. Mark 10:1–12), places a discussion about doing the will of God in the proper Jewish-Christian context of the law. Several other episodes also concern interpretation of the law: the rich young man (19:16–30), paying taxes to Caesar (22:15–22), the resurrection question (22:23–33), the great commandment question (22:34–40), and the "woes" against the scribes and Pharisees (chap. 23, especially 23:23 f.). According to Matthew, in order to do the will of God one must properly understand the nature of the law.

Matthew's strongest stress finally lies in a direction other than that of debating about the fine points of the law. Matthew is concerned about discerning the will of God in the law and, most important, obeying it. In Jesus' divorce discussion with the Pharisees, Matthew has apparently softened the radical prohibition against divorce (cf. Mark 10:10–12) by allowing divorce on the grounds of unchastity (19:9, cf. 5:32). Yet in the very next episode Matthew shows a demand for obedience to the law more stringent than that of his Markan source, for the young man must be perfect (19:21; cf. Mark 10:21).[26] The will of God cannot be equated either with a stricter or more lenient interpretation of the Jewish law. The one thing necessary for the doing of God's will is the very presence of God, "With men this is impossible, but *with God* all things are possible" (19:26).

Matthew's concept of reward for doing God's will is distinct from the idea of reward as so much merit accumulated through following the formula of the law. Instead, Matthew proclaims that there are no degrees of reward; the only, and even final reward (25:41–46) is God's presence, already anticipated in the doing of God's will. For example, Jesus answers the disciples' question about reward (19:27–30) with the parable of the laborers in the vineyard (20:1–16; only in Matthew), which points out

---

[26] The suggestion that Matthew commends two levels of morality, one for real Christians and another for halfway Christians, is not defensible. In the Sermon on the Mount the injunction to "be perfect" (5:48) is for all disciples—that is, all Christians. See G. Barth, *Tradition and Interpretation in Matthew*, p. 99, and cf. W. D. Davies, *The Setting of the Sermon on the Mount* (Cambridge: Cambridge University Press, 1964), pp. 95, 209–215.

that no one grumbles in the joy of God's generosity (see vs. 15). Moreover, those who · reject Jesus' authority, notably the Pharisees (see especially chaps. 21 and 22), do not bear fruit (21:19) or, if they do, they keep it for themselves (21:33–44); therefore, they cannot escape judgment. The narrative portion of this entire section (19:3–23:39) ends appropriately, then, with the chastisement of the Pharisees. Their discernment of the law and their obedience were for their own justification instead of the doing of God's will. Thus at the judgment they will be condemned.

A final indication of this section's preoccupation with judgment is the narrative setting in the territory of Judea and the city of Jerusalem (see 19:1; 21:1, 10; 24:1). At Jerusalem the condemnation of Jesus takes place, but that judgment ultimately turns against Jesus' enemies and for his disciples if they continue to do God's will. Jesus' second coming as the Son of Man will determine whether disciples are sheep or goats, accepted or rejected (25:31 ff.). The test for discipleship is the same one Jesus had to pass: the doing of God's will, not one's own (26:39). The passages selected for further examination confirm this understanding of Matthew's view of judgment.

BELIEVING DOERS OF THE LAW (21:28–44)

Is promising to do the law enough?
Is producing the fruits enough?

The parable of the two sons has to do with the authority of Jesus and, in the last analysis, the authority of the church. The preceding incident (21:23–27) closed with Jesus' saying that he would not tell them by what authority he was acting; Note how this parable is related to the previous episode by the reintroduction of John the Baptist (vs. 32; cf. vs. 25).

In the parable itself the son who first said he would not go, but then did, actually did the will of the father. This means that mere words claiming authority (cf. vs. 30) are without value; Jesus' authority can only be understood in terms of whether association with him produces actual obedience. Further, Jesus' opponents, the chief priests and elders, who turn out to be Pharisees (21:45), are condemned because even though they saw John's righteousness they did not believe him (vs. 32). This "higher righteousness" requires both an actual obedience and belief. The nature of such belief becomes clearer in the following parable.

In the parable of the wicked tenants (21:33–46; cf. Mark 12:1–12) the owner sends his servants and his son "to get his fruit" (vs. 34), all to no avail. The climax *will* occur when the unfaithful tenants are put to death and the vineyard is delivered to other tenants "who will give him the fruits in their seasons" (vs. 41; cf. Mark 12:9). Matthew's conclusion to the parable, which is not in his Markan source, states that the kingdom "will be taken away from you and given to a nation producing the fruits of it" (vs. 43; cf. Mark 12:11). The trouble with the wicked tenants was not their failure to produce fruit (cf. 21:19), but their refusal to acknowledge the rightful owner of the fruit. The Pharisees do not believe; they try to justify themselves by their obedience rather than acknowledging the gracious God. In good Jewish fashion Matthew underscores the necessity for obedience; but additionally he asserts the need for belief in the giver of all obedience—God through Christ (cf. 21:42). Only thereby will the church be delivered from self-righteous, possessive obedience. The authority of Jesus lies in his enabling of obedience that does not separate the believer from God (5:17).

DOING MERCY WITHOUT CALCULATION (25:31–46)

What is the unexpected development in the parable?

The parable of the great judgment indicates that judgment will come. Whether Matthew expected it in the immediate future is debatable. In the apocalyptic discourse the gospel has to be "preached throughout the whole world, as a testimony to all nations; and then the end will come" (24:14; cf. Mark 13:10). Clearly there will be judgment, and even disciples will have to be ready lest they be condemned to "weep and gnash their teeth" (24:51; 25:30).

The parable of the talents (25:14–30; cf. Luke 19:12–27), which immediately precedes, gives a framework for viewing judgment. The prospect of judgment may be met in one of two ways: paralysis caused by great anxiety over the severity of the judge, or responsible action through trust in the judge's generosity. The servant who knows the master to be hard and therefore makes no effort is condemned (25:24 ff.); the good servant who responsibly accepts the bounty of the master enters into full joy (25:21, 23).

The great judgment parable tells about the shepherd who will separate the sheep from the goats. The standard of separation is simply whether the one judged has performed acts of mercy for his fellowman (25:35 f.). The element of surprise of this parable is that neither the righteous nor the unrighteous realized that their deeds of mercy were acts performed (or not performed) for the Lord (vss. 37 ff.). The climactic word of Jesus, "Truly, I say to you, as you did it to one of the least of these my brethren, you did it to me" (vs. 40), alludes to the fact that he who truly does God's will acts because of having already been shown mercy in Christ (cf. 25:20, 22). What he does not realize is that this same mercy is also present for the neighbor, and that service to others is service to Christ (cf. 7:21–

*The Last Judgment with Christ separating the sheep from the goats.
Part of an early fourth-century Christian sarcophagus. (Courtesy of
Metropolitan Museum of Art, Rogers Fund, 1924.)*

23). Therefore, the true disciple shows mercy to others without calculation, without thinking that his deed will somehow cause God's judgment
upon him to be more favorable. Such noncalculation grows out of a relation with Christ in which anxiety is diminished and the disciple responds
to whatever human need is at hand, especially to his neighbor (10:40–42).

Those who show mercy act without calculation, without thought that
thereby they will insure their future blessedness. They are merciful because
they have been shown mercy; moreover, their deeds for the neighbor are
deeds for Christ, who is present in the least of the brethren. Thus Matthew
pictures the church in the time between the first and second comings. The
church's role of obedience in that time has been most clearly anticipated
in the final death and resurrection of Jesus, Lord of the congregation, who
serves as the paradigm for the Christian life.

Conclusion: Obedience and Resurrection; Lord and Congregation (26:2–28:20)

Matthew opens this concluding section with a clear indication that what
happens in Jesus' passion occurs at the bidding of God. The passive voice
("will be delivered up to be crucified," 26:2; see also 26:18) represents the
divine action. The action both of Jesus and the other characters is determined by a power not their own. For example, the woman who anoints
Jesus' head with the expensive ointment (26:6–13) prepares his body for
burial even though her action would ordinarily be understood as the expression of a woman's sentiment or as an anointment of kingship (see
27:11, 29, 37, 42). Ironically, however, her anointing for death is also an
anointing of the future Lord of the congregation, resurrected from death.
The power of resurrection over death is also evident in the supernatural
events surrounding Jesus' death: the earth shook, rocks were split, saints
were raised from the dead and appeared to many in the holy city (27:
51–54; cf. Mark 15:38 f.). Moreover, Matthew hints at the victory of the

resurrection by reminding the reader that Jesus is the Son of God (27:40, 43; only Matthew). Matthew alone adds the detail that Jesus, had he wished, could have prevented his arrest by summoning twelve legions of angels from his Father (26:53).

Matthew subtly transforms the Markan passion story so that the element of Jesus' suffering, which cannot be removed completely, is modified into Jesus' obedience and becomes a paradigm for disciples. Insofar as Jesus acts or speaks in the passion, he voluntarily accepts his death; he obeys God's will. He could have called legions of angels, but "how then should the scriptures be fulfilled?" (26:54, 56; cf. Mark 14:48–50). Matthew adds to Mark's account of Jesus' accepting the cross ("nevertheless, not as I will, but as thou wilt"—26:39, cf. Mark 14:36) a reinforcing word of obedience, "My Father, if this cannot pass unless I drink it, thy will be done" (26:42). Thereby, Matthew shows that in his passion Jesus fulfills the "higher righteousness" he set forth in the Sermon on the Mount (6:20; cf. 7:24); Jesus acts as the one who fulfills "all righteousness" (3:15).[27] The Jesus of Matthew not only demands obedience, he enacts obedience because this Jesus has come not to abolish but to fulfill the law (5:17–20). Therefore, Jesus' resurrection and establishment as Lord of the congregation are based upon faithful obedience to God.

In the ending of Matthew (28:16–20) the resurrected Jesus charges the disciples—that is, the Christian congregation—with the task of teaching all nations to observe what he has commanded (28:20). Such observance is now possible because Jesus has obeyed: at death the bruised reed did not break; he brought judgment to victory (12:20). Even in the passion story where attention focuses upon Jesus, Matthew hints, by shaping the tradition, that Jesus' fulfillment of all righteousness will enable the disciples to imitate his obedience. At the preparation for the passover, Jesus instructs his disciples what to say when they meet the owner of the Passover meal site:

> "The Teacher says, My time is at hand; I will keep the passover at your house with my disciples." And the disciples did as Jesus had directed them, and they prepared the passover (26:18 f.).

> "The Teacher says, Where is my guest room, where I am to eat the passover with my disciples? And he will show you a large upper room furnished and ready; there prepare for us." And the disciples set out and went to the city, and found it as he had told them; and they prepared the passover (Mark 14:14–16).

---

[27] G. Barth, *Tradition and Interpretation in Matthew*, pp. 143 ff., also points out how Jesus' silence (esp. 26:63) is interpreted by Matthew as fulfillment of Jesus' word against swearing in the Sermon on the Mount (5:33–37). In Matthew, therefore, the "swearing" denial of Peter (26:69–75) becomes all the more telling as a sign of disobedience.

Whereas Mark's account concentrates upon the miraculous predictive power of Jesus, Matthew emphasizes first the obedient submission of Jesus and then the disciples' obedience to the command of Jesus (cf. 1:24). Matthew adds the detail that Joseph of Arimathea was also "a disciple of Jesus" (27:57; cf. Mark 15:43). Therefore, Joseph's burial of Jesus stands as another pointer to the obedience that Jesus effects in his disciples. Our final two incidents also illustrate Jesus' obedient majesty, which results in the obedience of his disciples.

RIGHTEOUS BLOOD (27:24-26)

Who is to blame for Jesus' crucifixion?

This incident, inserted into the Markan Barabbas episode (Mark 15: 6–15), is usually interpreted as an attempt to exonerate the Roman government, especially Pilate, and to blame the Jews for the death of Jesus. "His blood be on us and on our children!" (vs. 25) is a *locus classicus* for anti-Semitism. Yet this entire passage (except for vs. 26; cf. Mark 15:15) appears only in Matthew, and we have good reason to doubt any charge of anti-Semitism against Matthew. True, Matthew does attack the Jewish leaders, especially the Pharisees (chap. 23); however, from his opening emphasis on Abraham (1:1) to the more pointed pro-Jewish statement that Jesus comes only for the lost sheep of Israel (10:6; 15:24), Matthew seeks to show that the new way is a fulfillment, rather than an annulment, of Israel (5:17–20). Therefore, in studying this passage, we ought not to be easily satisfied with an anti-Semitic interpretation.

Another Matthean insertion into the Markan Barabbas tradition precedes our present passage and reports a message to Pilate from his wife, "Have nothing to do with that righteous man, for I have suffered much over him today in a dream" (27:19; cf. Mark 15:10 f.). Apparently Pilate takes her advice because he washes his hands saying, "I am innocent of this man's blood; see to it yourselves" (vs. 24b.). Some reliable manuscripts have the variant reading, "I am innocent of this man's righteous blood." Whether "righteous blood" is the original reading, the context definitely declares that the condemned criminal Jesus is righteous because he obeys God's will. Ironically, then, Pilate's attempt to disassociate himself from the entire event is not only morally impossible, but also makes him the one person completely unaffected by the righteous one's death. On the other hand, when "all the people answered, 'His blood be on us and on our children!'" (vs. 25), that word becomes an explicit statement of involvement. It is also an implicit promise of forgiveness. Further perusal of Matthew's passion story gives substance to this latter point.

Blood figured prominently in a previous passion episode. At the Last Supper (26:26–29; cf. Mark 14:22–25), Jesus spoke the following words over the giving of the cup: "Drink of it, all of you; for this is my blood of the covenant, which is poured out for many for the forgiveness of sins" (vs. 28). Only Matthew explicitly links the blood of Jesus both with all the people (that is, "many"), and with forgiveness of sins. The cry of "all the people" (27:25) may be intended by Matthew to bring all sinners under the forgiveness effected through Jesus' death.[28]

Further support for this interpretation comes from Matthew's careful use of "the people" within the rest of the passion story. Every reference to "people" shows them on the side of Jesus. The plotters of Jesus' death fear to kill him during the feast "lest there be a tumult among the people" (26:5). The guardians of the tomb fear that something will happen to convince the people that Jesus has been raised from the dead (27:64; 28:13). We might have anticipated this usage because the birth of Jesus, indeed his very name, meant for Matthew that "he will save his *people from their sins*" (1:21).

Thus we conclude that Matthew's special passage (27:24–26), which seems to bespeak a negative judgment, belongs with Matthew's proclamation that Jesus' death fulfills all righteousness (3:15) and brings forgiveness to all.[29] Therefore, Jesus' yoke is easy, not hard (11:28–30), for he came "even as the Son of man not to be served but to serve, and to give his life as a ransom for many" (20:28; cf. 12:18–21, 23:10 f.). The special Matthean way is that of faithful obedience thereby fulfilling the law. Jesus goes to his death on behalf of sinners; moreover, his obedience is incorporated into the life of the church in the final message of the resurrected Lord.

THE LORD'S COMMAND (28:16–20)

What is the task of the disciples?

The resurrected Jesus' final appearance is treated concisely. It occurs in Galilee (26:32; 28:7) at a mountain (5:1; 15:29; 17:1). The disciples' reaction to this climactic moment is described briefly: "they worshiped him (see 2:2; 18:26; 28:9); but some doubted" (vs. 17). This report of doubt strikes the reader as inappropriate, especially since the disciples have just worshiped Jesus. In other resurrection appearances doubt also occurs, but in those instances some further action of Jesus overcomes the doubt

---

[28] Another special Matthean passion tradition, the repentance and death of Judas (27:3–10), also speaks of "innocent blood" (a few manuscripts have "righteous blood"). Moreover, Judas' returning the money results in the purchase of the potter's field where strangers are buried. Does Matthew's insertion imply that forgiveness is available for whoever repents (yet Judas hangs himself)?

[29] Barabbas, the notorious prisoner, is *released* immediately after all the people ask that Jesus' blood be upon them and their children—27:26.

(Luke 24:41; Mark 16:14; John 20:25). Here the expression of doubt is simply followed by the word of Jesus. As the disciples make no further response we can only conclude that Jesus' word overcomes the doubt. We shall discover in looking more closely at this passage that doubt is finally to be vanquished in the disciples' obedience. Consequently, these closing words imply a task to which the disciples are committed. In effect, Matthew is saying that as impressive as were the first resurrection appearances, they were not enough—doubt still remained. The victory over doubt will come finally through obedience to Jesus' subsequent word.

Before exhorting the disciples to action, the resurrected Jesus declares,

"The Resurrection" (ca. 1509–15) painted by M. Grünewald as one wing of the Isenheim Altarpiece. (Courtesy of Marburg-Art Reference Bureau.)

"All authority in heaven and on earth has been given to me" (vs. 18). Jesus' authoritative announcement has an implicit reference to the cosmic enthronement of the apocalyptic Son of Man depicted in Daniel: "And to him was given dominion and glory and kingdom, that all peoples, nations and languages should serve him; his dominion is an everlasting dominion, which shall not pass away, and his kingdom one that shall not be destroyed" (7:14). The combination of authority, dominion, and extension to all nations makes this passage relevant to Jesus' word.[30] Jesus' authority in heaven and on earth exists until "the close of the age," that is, while the church exists. Previously, Matthew dealt with the subject of authority as an aspect of Jesus' earthly activity: he taught with authority (7:28 f.), he healed with authority (8:9), he forgave with authority (9:6, 8). Now the resurrected Jesus is put in touch with this world; his authority is expressed precisely through the disciples' earthly task of making obedient disciples. The new thing about this authority is that with Jesus' resurrection it is extended to include all the nations.[31]

Matthew, furthermore, does not allow the resurrected Jesus to become a heavenly Lord issuing new revelations that will inevitably split the church between the specially blessed recipients of a new, more authoritative heavenly message (cf. I Cor. 12:1 ff.) and the unblessed rank and file. Such a possibility is excluded by the resurrected Jesus' word to the disciples: "teaching them to observe all things that I *have commanded* you" (vs. 20a; cf. 24:34 f.). The resurrected Lord's words are rooted, not in heavenly visions or revelations, but in words already spoken by the earthly Jesus. Yet Matthew does not allow the authority of the resurrected Jesus to rest simply with Jesus' activity on earth. The disciples, in the presence of the Resurrected One, will extend his authority to all nations. Consequently, the church's mission extends beyond those who claim election simply because of membership in the chosen people Israel (3:9; 21:33–43; cf. II Cor. 11:15–29).

Matthew's distillation of the resurrected Jesus' authority to the simple command to make disciples, baptize, and teach obedience (28:19, 20a) may contain another subtle warning in addition to those against the notions of a chosen people or a continuing revelation. In the spurious ending of Mark's resurrection account (16:9–20), Jesus gave a commission to his disciples that included preaching, baptizing, and performing charismatic acts of healing, exorcism, and speaking in tongues.[32] On the surface, these

[30] G. Barth, *Tradition and Interpretation in Matthew*, p. 133.

[31] G. Bornkamm, "Der Auferstandene und der Irdische," *Zeit und Geschichte*, ed. E. Dinkler (Tübingen: J. C. B. Mohr, 1964), pp. 174 f. If worldwide mission begins only after Jesus' death and resurrection, this may account for Matthew's omission of the report about the sending out of the twelve, even though Jesus does give them instructions for their missionary journey (10:1–11:1).

[32] Although Mark 16:9–20 is a spurious ending (see p. 91), it may well represent tendencies at work in early tradition of the church.

phenomena seem much more impressive as evidence for the authority of Jesus and his disciples than Matthew's simple obedience. However, Matthew has already prepared the reader for this "reduction" in authority because he denied that such manifestations were proof of faith and obedience (7:21–23). In addition, Matthew declared that false prophets would arise in the church because "most men's love will grow cold" (24:12; cf. Mark 13:13). True discipleship will be demonstrated not in ecstatic, marvelous activity, but rather in obedience. More than ever the disciples are called to obey the words Jesus commanded. What at first appeared to be simply a call to missionary endeavor on closer inspection turns out to be a call for discipleship that embraces obedience.

Looking now more directly at the imperative from the resurrected Jesus (vss. 19, 20a), we find that the task is divided into three stages: making disciples, baptizing them, and teaching them to observe all that Jesus has commanded. Matthew definitely emphasizes the first and the third, for he sees the church as the community of discipleship (13:52; 16:13–20; 27:57), which consists of lowliness, readiness for suffering, and above all obedience (10:40–42; 16:24–27; 18:1–6; 22:11–14). The esteem in which Matthew holds discipleship is illustrated by the fact that he recognizes only one level of church membership. In first century Judaism the ambitious disciple hoped one day to become the teacher or rabbi. But in Matthew, Jesus says to his disciples, "But you are not to be called rabbi, for you have one teacher, and you are all brethren" (23:8; only in Matthew). Although Matthew never has the disciples address Jesus with the title teacher or rabbi (instead their more customary form of address is "Lord"), there can be little doubt that the final words to the disciples establish once and for all that the Lord of the congregation is, in the last analysis, the only Rabbi or Teacher.[33]

In this light the second task of the disciples, that of baptizing, must be subordinate to the first and third. Perhaps Matthew has adopted an earlier tradition which included an appearance of Jesus to the disciples in Galilee and a final commission with a command to baptize (again cf. Mark 16:9–20; also Luke 24:44–53). Matthew does not deny that tradition, but he imparts it with his own emphasis that making disciples means teaching them to observe all that Jesus has commanded. This command signifies that the decisive task of the church will be a worldwide missionary effort that has as its distinctive mark the quality of obedient discipleship.

The Gospel according to Matthew has thus come full circle. The initial emphasis on the radical obedience of Joseph (1:24) has now been expanded through the body of the Gospel to spell out the way of righteousness (3:15; 5:6, 20; 6:33) that is fulfilled in obedience (7:21; 21:28–32; 25:31–46). The disciples are to observe all that Jesus has commanded. Yet

---

33 G. Bornkamm, *Zeit und Geschichte*, pp. 182 f.

this radical demand becomes possible because in Jesus, his mission and message, God has come near (1:23; 18:20). Above all, the way of right- eousness was fulfilled by the action of Jesus, particularly in his obedient submission to death (20:26–28). Therefore, the final word of the resur- rected Jesus assures the disciples that the Lord of the congregation both is and will be present until the close of the age. Between the resurrection and the final judgment, the presence of the resurrected Lord enables obedi- ent mercy and guards against false reliance upon unaided human resources. The continuing presence of Jesus with the congregation, moreover, means that these final words are not a farewell from Jesus. As long as the con- gregation continues, the resurrected Jesus lives and abides in the obedience of his disciples to his teaching.

In summary, our investigations show overwhelming evidence that the Gospel of Matthew is an interpretation of the tradition of Jesus based upon Mark's Gospel, the Q collection of sayings, and the oral tradition. Matthew's interpretive procedure does not, however, mean that he did not stand in the service of the tradition of Jesus which he received. He remains faithful to it. Both Matthew and Luke combine the predom- inantly narrative Gospel of Mark with the predominantly discourse collec- tion of Jesus-sayings known as Q. Thereby these Gospels serve as a check against any inclination within the early Hellenistic Christian community toward making the Christian faith into a kind of mystery religion domi- nated by the pattern of a dying and rising god. In effect, Matthew and Luke are saying that Christian faith involves a particular teaching.

This protection of the Christian faith is especially clear in Matthew. This Gospel's stress on the words that Jesus spoke binds the Christian revelation to the historical Jesus, one whose past words and action demand and promise obedience. The Christian congregation, therefore, knows its unity and origin in the historical Jesus. Even though Matthew undoubtedly contains words of Jesus that were never spoken by him (ironically 28:18– 20 probably belong in this category),[34] its principal function in bringing together the narrative and the discourse traditions is to limit in principle the revelation of Christian faith to Jesus of Nazareth. Matthew and the other canonical Gospels thereby preserved the peculiar glory and offense of Christian faith, the "scandal of particularity." A particular man at a particular time and place is claimed as the revelation of the creating and judging God of the universe.

We can now review generally our use of four approaches in under- standing Matthew's Gospel:

[34] See F. W. Beare, "Sayings of the Risen Jesus in the Synoptic Tradition: An In- quiry into Their Origin and Significance," *Christian History and Interpretation: Studies Presented to John Knox*, ed. W. R. Farmer, C. F. D. Moule, R. R. Niebuhr (Cam- bridge: Cambridge University Press, 1967), pp. 161–166.

The *structure* of Matthew is clear cut. The Introduction (1:1–2:23; see the outline at the beginning of the chapter) sets the tone for the main body of Matthew. The coming of Jesus establishes a new and more radical obedience (Joseph); moreover, this obedience takes place within the "new Israel," where Jew and Gentile (wise men) worship together. Matthew then proceeds to divide the Gospel into five major sections consisting of narrative-discourse, reminiscent of the five authoritative books of Moses. Book One (3:1–7:29) depicts the "higher righteousness" both effected (the baptism) and demanded (Sermon on the Mount) by Jesus. Book Two (8:1–11:1) previews the life of discipleship by showing that the real miracle of Jesus is turning men of "little faith" into disciples, dependent on what they have received and charged with the necessity of giving. Book Three (11:2–13:52) puts earthly activity into the perspective of the kingdom of heaven. Present mercy stands within the context of future judgment; the followers of Christ are to train for this future event. Book Four (13:53–19:2) sets this present mercy into the context of the forgiving church, where the basis for discipline and exclusion becomes the unwillingness to practice forgiveness. Book Five (19:3–26:1) appropriately concludes with the expectation of future judgment on the basis of deeds, not promises. Furthermore, the doers of mercy are those who live in faith without thought of reward. The Conclusion (26:2–28:20) reports Jesus' obedient submission to death and God's response, which is the resurrection. Finally, the Risen Lord commissions the disciples, both Jew and Gentile, to obey and to teach obedience, knowing that he abides with them till the close of the age.

Matthew's carefully worked out structure already indicates this Gospel's *major emphases*. We may now bring them together under three headings: the Christian way, its source, and its community. Matthew advocates a higher righteousness, which is the Christian way. This higher righteousness enables and requires a radical obedience, and the spelling out of this obedience becomes clearer in Matthew's treatment of the law. Nowhere does he claim that the law has been abolished; on the contrary, the law is affirmed. Yet Matthew singles out for emphasis: the love of God and the love of man, which cannot be neglected through preoccupation with carrying out details of the law. Thereby Matthew seeks to make the will of God present and alive.

The second major emphasis is upon the source of higher righteousness, the Lord Jesus Christ. In one sense the Jesus of Matthew is a more majestic figure than the Jesus of Mark. Matthew tends to abbreviate Mark's miracle stories and consequently makes them even more inexplicable as human events. Yet this abbreviation is the primary means for expressing the dominance of Jesus' teaching. Even in the miracle acts, Jesus is a teacher, an extraordinary, first-century rabbi. This teaching makes Jesus an authoritative, majestic figure. The Jesus of Matthew, however, is also a lowly and obedient figure. He fulfills the scripture by becoming the suffering servant who not only teaches obedience to disciples, but actually performs it. The mighty Lord goes to his death in obedient lowliness, thereby fulfilling the way of higher righteousness.

The third and final emphasis follows from the preceding ones: the higher righteousness fulfilled in Christ must be realized in the congregation. This community of Christ-followers learns that the present is determined by the mercy of God's presence, even for the sinner. The beatitudes proclaim God's love for the poor in spirit, the meek. The congregation knows itself as the "little ones," who obediently await the final judgment in the presence of Christ.

Our total interpretation has depended upon observation of Matthew's *redaction* of the tradition. Among other things, redaction criticism shows that Matthew's treatment of the disciples is significantly less harsh than that of his predecessor Mark. Indeed, one commentator maintains that "Matthew . . . strongly idealized the disciples by expunging reproof or reference to their failures."[35] Yet our study suggests that Matthew has a more realistic view of the disciples' actual behavior than Mark. Matthew recognizes that the disciples do "understand" Jesus; after all, they followed him. Nevertheless, they were still of "little faith" because they had not yet acted in obedience. According to Matthew, they could not obey until Jesus completed his own obedience through death and resurrection.

The general *situation* that produced the Gospel of Matthew is in many ways implicit in the document itself. In the first place, Matthew does not reflect a church that observed the Jewish law and still stood within Judaism. Although the law is kept, such observance is motivated by consideration for Jewish Christians who still have scruples for the minutiae of the law (cf. 17:26 f.). Here Matthew and Paul stand together, for Paul memorably formulates a similar position, " 'All things are lawful for me,' but not all things are helpful" (I Cor. 6:12; 10:23). Freedom is not license. Moreover, the congregation of Matthew already understands itself as opposed to Judaism (not to Israel and the Old Testament), for Judaism in Matthew's understanding has already become Pharisaism (see 3:7; 5:20; 9:34; chap. 23).

Second, the eschatology of Matthew cannot be classified as "apocalyptic."[36] Matthew's church did not cherish the belief that the end of the world was just around the corner and that people should gird themselves by extreme piety and ethical effort for the imminent encounter with God. True, Matthew emphasized the coming of the final day (chap. 24; cf. also 4:17; 26:28), yet he also spoke about a time of waiting for the church. For Matthew the church's time was truly significant (see 24:6, 36 ff.,

---

[35] Kümmel, *Introduction to the New Testament*, p. 76.

[36] For a characterization of Matthew's transmuted apocalypticism, see Wayne Rollins, *The Gospels: Portraits of Christ* (Philadelphia: Westminster Press, 1963), pp. 49–75.

42 ff.). Indeed, the close of Matthew (28:16–20) would make no sense if the evangelist held an extreme, futurist eschatology.

Matthew strikes out in more than one direction. On the one hand, as we have seen, he attacked Pharisaic Judaism's misleading interpretation of the law. On the other, Matthew attacked a Christianity that was developing without regard for its roots in Israel and the Old Testament into an unrestrained and undisciplined spiritualism. This Jewish-Christian Gospel understood Christian faith to be firmly rooted in the historical Jesus. While rejecting Pharisaism, Matthew opposed the teaching of Jesus to any lack of moral responsibility. Matthew called his congregation to the obedience that Jesus had both commanded in his teaching and fulfilled in his passion.

It is evident from Matthew that his church is a community both Jewish and Christian. Standing within this community Matthew maintains the Jewish themes of righteousness and obedience to the law; but he sets them within the context of faith in Jesus Christ, in whom they are fulfilled. Because of God's action through Christ and his continuing presence with the congregation, the end of Christian faith is not at all unlike the way. Thus, the kingdom of heaven is both present and future. Therefore, Matthew's Gospel mirrors not only the "life of Christ," but also the life of the Christian community, a life that evades both the lawlessness of some Hellenistic religiosity and the self-righteousness of some Judaic piety.

Suggestions for Further Reading

Two recent and reliable commentaries are F. V. Filson in the Harper series (1960) and J. C. Fenton, *The Gospel of St. Matthew** (Baltimore: Penguin Books, 1963). Other worthwhile and recent books include: G. D. Kilpatrick, *The Origins of the Gospel according to St. Matthew* Oxford: Clarendon Press, 1946); K. Stendahl, *The School of St. Matthew and Its Use of the Old Testament* [Philadelphia: Fortress, 1968 (reissue)]; E. P. Blair, *Jesus in the Gospel of Matthew* (New York: Abingdon, 1960); G. Bornkamm, G. Barth, and H. J. Held, *Tradition and Interpretation in Matthew*, trans. P. Scott (London: SCM, 1963); W. D. Davies, *The Sermon on the Mount** (Cambridge: University Press, 1966) an abridgment of the author's longer and more technical work, *The Setting of the Sermon on the Mount*, published by the same press in 1964.

4 The Gospel According to Luke: A Christian Apology

NOTES ON THE GOSPEL OF LUKE

The earliest tradition about the Gospel of Luke, from the Muratorian Canon,[1] gives one reliable bit of information: both the Gospel According to Luke and the Acts of the Apostles were written by the same author. This view is supported by the opening verses of each book, in both cases dedications to a certain Theophilus, and by Acts' reference to a "first book" (1:1). The two books definitely display a kinship in style and emphasis. Yet neither Luke nor

---

[1] A catalog of New Testament writings originating in Rome about A.D. 200. For the text see Edgar Hennecke, *New Testament Apocrypha*, I, ed. W. Schneemelcher and trans. R. McL. Wilson (Philadelphia: Westminster Press, 1963), pp. 43–44.

Acts makes a direct claim about the author's identity. Luke-Acts is an anonymous two-volume work.

To be accepted by the church at the end of the second century, a Gospel had to be able to claim apostolic authority. Mark rests upon the authority of one great apostle, Peter, and Luke rests upon the authority of another great apostle, Paul. In his letters, Paul mentions as a companion, "Luke, the beloved physician" (Col. 4:14; Philemon 24; II Tim. 4:11). Furthermore, this same Luke is supposed to be a companion on Paul's missionary journeys (see pp. 260 ff.).

Some doubt attaches to the relationship to Paul, but two things may be said with some certainty about the author of the Gospel According to Luke. First, he was more consciously an author than the writers of Mark and Matthew. The preface (1:1–4) makes explicit the literary aim of the Gospel: it is dedicated to Theophilus and speaks knowingly of previous works. Second, the author of Luke was a Gentile Christian, who knew little about the geography of Palestine, probably spoke Greek as his native tongue, and, in general, minimized controversy with the Pharisees that so dominates Matthew and, in part, Mark.

Luke is not, however, an example of modern historical writing. It is a Gospel, religious writing. Although Luke used the Gospel of Mark, as did Matthew, he used his source more critically. Whereas Matthew took over practically all of Mark, Luke used about half. Like Matthew, Luke used the sayings source, Q. In addition, a considerable body of tradition, found only in Luke, makes up the special Lukan tradition.

As in the case of other Synoptic Gospels, the dating of Luke is difficult and precarious. Although Jesus' prophecy about the coming judgment of Jerusalem still appears (Luke 13:34 f.), Luke seems to know about the actual destruction of Jerusalem (cf. Luke 21:20 and 19:43 f.). The earliest date for Luke would therefore have to be sometime after Jerusalem's fall in A.D. 70. Since the introduction of Acts mentions Luke as "the first book," the latest date for Luke would have to be sometime before the final version of Acts. The letters of Paul were written in the middle of the first century but were not assembled until the end of the first century. It is unlikely, in view of the disparity between Acts' picture of Paul and the Paul of his own letters, that the author of Luke-Acts knew the Pauline letters. Therefore, a date sometime before the end of the first century is suggested for the writing of Luke-Acts. From the preface (1:1–4), Luke apparently belongs to the third stage of the Christian tradition; he speaks of eyewitnesses, collectors, and his own composition. If that is the case, then a date only shortly before the turn of the century would be appropriate. Probably Luke-Acts was written sometime between A.D. 80 and 100. Little is known about the geographical origin of Luke other than that it was probably not written in Palestine.

The exact occasion for the writing of Luke is unknown; however, his more general purpose may be fixed by taking account of the fact that Luke is the only Gospel continued by a sequel, the Acts of the Apostles. The rest of this chapter and chapter six will examine the purpose more closely; however, we may anticipate our study by suggesting that Luke presents a view of the history of salvation extending from the time of Israel through the life of Jesus and continuing in the history of the church. The good news for Israel is extended through Jesus to all people.

Preface: A Time for True Remembering (1:1-4)

What is Luke's intention in writing his Gospel?

In the first four verses Luke makes the reader conscious of the predecessors of his own account, using a literary device not found in the other Gospels, yet common in the writings of antiquity. That the style of the preface was a literary convention can be seen from a comparison of the opening sentences of Luke and Acts with the prefaces of the first century Jewish historian Josephus. His *Against Apion*, Book I, opens:

> In my history of our Antiquities, most excellent Epaphroditus, I have, I think, made sufficiently clear to any who may peruse that work the extreme antiquity of our Jewish race, the purity of the original stock and the manner in which it established itself in the country which we occupy today. . . . Since, however, I observe that a considerable number of persons . . . discredit the statements in my history concerning our antiquity, . . . I consider it my duty to devote a brief treatise to all these points, in order at once to convict our detractors of malignity and deliberate falsehood, to correct the ignorance of others, and to instruct all who desire to know the truth concerning the antiquity of our race.

Book II begins in this way:

> In the first volume of this work, my most esteemed Epaphroditus, I demonstrated the antiquity of our race, corroborating my statements by the writings of the Phoenicians, Chaldeans, and Egyptians. . . . I also challenged the statements of Manetho, Chaeremon, and some others. I shall now proceed to refute the rest of the authors who have attacked us.[2]

The very fact that Luke followed the prevailing literary fashion of his day indicates part of his purpose—to make his Gospel acceptable to the literate man. Yet the preface suggests an intent more definite and a more wide-ranging purpose.

With the admission that many others have undertaken to compile a

[2] E. J. Goodspeed, *An Introduction to the New Testament* (Chicago: University of Chicago Press, 1937), pp. 190 f.

narrative about the things that he will relate, Luke obviously gives up any claim to originality. Nor does he claim a divine revelation superseding all other previous accounts. Yet the opening verses unmistakably give the impression that he means to set things right in this Gospel. Though there have been other compilers and eye witnesses and ministers of the word, Luke purposes to write a better, truer Gospel than anything yet presented. This prefatory statement alone excludes the notion that each writer worked independently of all preceding tradition. In all probability among Luke's many sources are Mark, the Q source, and special Lukan tradition.

One difficult question in connection with Luke's preface is the meaning of the "things which have been accomplished among us" (vs. 1). The "among us" refers naturally to the Christian community, but the reference to "the things" is uncertain. Since Luke is the only Gospel to continue its story beyond Jesus' resurrection into the story of the early apostles, he may refer both to the life of Jesus and the early church.[3] There can be little question that Luke does speak about "the things" of Jesus; however, his inclusion of the early church in "the things" at this point is doubtful. Eye-witnesses and ministers of the word delivered the tradition of Jesus, not the tradition of the apostles. Therefore, in spite of Luke's high evaluation of the apostolic church, he first is concerned about the decisive events of Jesus. Even the preface to Acts confirms this view, "I have dealt with all that Jesus began to do and teach" (Acts 1:1). Jesus' time is crucial for Luke's Gospel.

Luke's historical situation emerges in the statement of his relation to his predecessors (vs. 2). In all, there are three stages of the gospel tradition: The first stage of eyewitnesses consists of those who have been with Jesus most intimately; for example, the twelve apostles (6:12 f.; cf. Mark 3:13 f.). Later we learn that apostles are those eyewitnesses who were with Jesus from the baptism to the ascension (cf. Acts 1:21–26). The second group, ministers of the word, pass on the eyewitness tradition by preaching. Although in Acts ministers of the word are first of all the apostles themselves, there are other ministers, such as Stephen and Philip, who preach the word. The final stage, in which Luke himself stands is that of the compilers of the tradition. With the advantage of hindsight the compiler is able to see what is most important and worthy of being preserved. Though Luke stands within that third phase, he intends to surpass all the rest. By "following all things closely" (vs. 3), he is able to give both an orderly and truthful account of the life, death, and resurrection of Jesus (vs. 4).

Not only does Luke consider his compilation of the tradition more adequate than that of his predecessors, but also he considers this third stage the most advantageous perspective. This high regard for the third phase recalls his developmental view of the Gospel itself (see the initial outline).

[3] See S. M. Gilmour, "The Gospel According to St. Luke," *IB,* VIII (New York: Abingdon Press, 1952), p. 27.

In the first stage Jesus gathers witnesses to himself in Galilee (3:1–9:50), and in the second he is on the way to Jerusalem (9:51–19:27). At the third stage, the passion and resurrection of Jesus take place (19:28–24:53), so that the Gospel's plan of Jesus becomes clear. Luke's certainty of getting to the truth about Jesus from his viewpoint in the third stage of the tradition sounds like the confident final interpretation that Jesus himself gives at the close of Luke's Gospel (see 24:45 ff.). Luke appears to assume that his later perspective is more comprehensive and truthful than that even of eyewitnesses, although the latter are certainly indispensable.

Luke stresses that he is going to write an "orderly account" (vs. 3). This cannot mean he is going to arrange his account differently, for Luke generally follows Mark's order. Probably Luke refers to his general scheme for placing Jesus within the history of salvation so that Jesus fulfills the story of Israel and initiates the story of the church. Luke's overall order serves to convince the reader both of the antiquity and of the enduring truth of Jesus' mission and message. This larger perspective is intimately related to Luke's three-fold development within the Gospel itself.

Luke emerges as an author who is quite aware of what he is doing. Perhaps the "Theophilus" to whom he addresses his work (vs. 3) is an actual person: an esteemed Roman official or an eminent citizen, or perhaps the name "friend of God," as translated, stands for the religious reader who as a "God-fearer" is interested in Christianity.[4] Whoever Theophilus may have been, he was certainly someone who had a preliminary knowledge of the Christian faith and was willing to read both the story of Jesus and that of the early church. He represents all who wished to know the truth about these things (literally "words"—vs. 4).

Luke's preface suggests his purpose. Luke, a man of the church, seeks to write the Gospel of Jesus which serves as the foundation for the church. Up until his time, oral tradition of Jesus (and that of the apostolic church) had been received somewhat uncritically. Now Luke, after having carefully studied this tradition seeks to set a framework for its total meaning and to establish its truth. Luke writes for the Christian faith an *apology* in the classical sense—that is, a *defense* that spells out and explains the truth and the basis of Christian faith.

Luke understands himself as living at a time in which true remembering needs to take place.[5] He wishes to recover and reformulate the roots of Christian faith so that the certainty and continuity of Christian faith

---

[4] See Alfred Plummer, *A Critical and Exegetical Commentary on the Gospel According to St. Luke* (ICC; New York: Charles Scribner's Sons, 1914) p. 5.

[5] In studying immigration to the United States, Marcus Hansen graphically formulated what he termed the "principle of third-generation interest" in the following formula, "What the son wishes to forget, the grandson wishes to remember" [Will Herberg; *Protestant-Catholic-Jew* (rev. ed.; Garden City, N.Y.: Doubleday, 1960), p. 30]. Similarly Luke wishes to remember the roots of the church both in Israel and in the historical Jesus.

from the beginning up to the present can be established: from Israel through Jesus to the church. Implied within this positive purpose is Luke's intention that his reader be guarded from error or heresy—which is another way of saying the reader must hear the whole Christian tradition, not just part of it.

Introduction: A Universal Story (1:5–2:52)

The first two chapters of the Gospel according to Luke are primarily concerned with the birth stories of John the Baptist and Jesus of Nazareth. This tradition is not contained in the other Synoptic Gospels. According to one view, since these stories play an insignificant role in the rest of Luke's Gospel, they should be ignored in its interpretation.[6] But would Luke have begun his Gospel with two chapters reflecting little of his own special understanding of the Christian message? There is abundant evidence that the motifs of these opening chapters are consistent with the rest of the Gospel and help to illuminate its intention. A sustained look at two passages from this section will support this contention. At this point we can do no more than hint at some motifs that emerge in the introduction.

Of course, not every detail of the opening section is relevant for later exegesis. A number of persons mentioned here do not appear elsewhere; a list of them would include Zechariah, Gabriel, Elizabeth, Joseph (apart from Luke 3:23 and 4:22), the shepherds, Simeon, and Anna.[7] However, the absence of these names in the body of the Gospel does not prove that Luke may not have said something here that he continues to say throughout his work. Continuity involves more than repetition of names.

This Gospel opens with a priest named Zechariah in the temple at Jerusalem (1:5 ff.), a city important to Luke. Like none of the other Gospels, Luke's begins in Jerusalem. In the central journey section Jerusalem is the destination (9:51). Furthermore, Jesus' resurrection appearances occur in Jerusalem and its vicinity, rather than Galilee as in the other Synoptics (24:6; cf. 24:13, 18, 33). Finally, the disciples wait in Jerusalem until the Holy Spirit manifests itself so that they may witness to the rest of the world (see Acts 1:4, 8). Note also Luke's later emphasis on the temple (cf. 2:22 ff.), as shown in the fact that the first Christians

---

[6] See Hans Conzelmann, *The Theology of St. Luke,* trans. G. Buswell (New York: Harper & Row, 1960), pp. 118, 172.

[7] See P. S. Minear, "Luke's Use of the Birth Stories," *Studies in Luke-Acts,* ed. L. E. Keck and J. L. Martyn (New York: Abingdon Press, 1966), p. 127.

View of present-day Jerusalem. (Courtesy of Israel Government Tourist Office.)

worship in the temple (Acts 2:46). In addition, in his last days Jesus takes over the temple (19:47; 21:37 f.; 24:53).

Another prominent emphasis of Luke's opening chapter is the twofold nature of witness. The birth of Jesus is coupled with the birth of John. A revelation occurs to Mary, the mother of Jesus; a revelation is also given to Zechariah, husband of Elizabeth, mother of John the Baptist. Both Simeon (2:22 ff.) and the prophetess Anna (2:36 ff.) testify to Jesus. Luke also carefully sets the story within the context of world history: "In the days of Herod" (1:5), "In the sixth month" (1:26), "In those days a decree went out from Caesar Augustus" (2:1; cf. 3:1). Luke emphasizes the role of women and the humble: Elizabeth and Mary are front and center; the shepherds come and worship Jesus (2:8 ff.; cf. 1:53, 6:20, 7:22). A romantic idyllic quality pervades this section where salvation emerges among humble folk, women exult in childbirth, and shepherds come to worship a babe born in a manger.

A final motif is the subordination of John the Baptist to Jesus. John is the forerunner, Jesus is the fulfillment (1:45). The babe in Elizabeth's womb leaps at the meeting with Mary, mother of Jesus (1:39–45). John is "prophet of the Most High" (1:76); Jesus is the "Son of the Most High" (1:32). The two are not, however, set over against one another but are in continuity. John the Baptist belongs to the time of Jesus as a witness and a prophet (cf. 1:80 with 2:40, 52; also see 3:4 ff.). The primary meaning of the introduction may be seen in the following two episodes.

The announcement of Jesus' birth to the shepherds by a contemporary Chinese artist, Lu Hung Nien. (Courtesy of Spartaco Appetiti.)

TWOFOLD WITNESS TO JESUS (2:22–40)

How do Simeon and Anna receive Jesus in the temple?

The Simeon episode reveals Jesus' parents as law-abiding adherents of the Jewish faith (cf. 2:39). After Jesus' circumcision on the eighth day (2:21), attention turns to the purification of the mother, which according to Jewish law took place on the thirty-third day after circumcision or the fortieth day after birth (see Leviticus 12:2–8). Strangely, this story depicts the parents as bringing the child Jesus "to do for him according to the custom of the law" (vs. 27). But purification is for the mother, not the child. Perhaps Luke is unfamiliar with Jewish practices, or it may be that we have in the Gospel of Luke something more than simply a reliable historical account of Jesus' life. Even when the mother's purification is taking place, attention remains on Jeusu.

The scene presents a contrast between the old man Simeon, who has been patiently waiting for the consolation of Israel, and the child Jesus. Upon seeing Jesus, he exclaims, "Lord, now lettest thou thy servant depart in peace" (2:29–32). The astonishment of Jesus' father and mother at Simeon's words (2:33) is itself surprising, for they already knew that Jesus was to be a messianic figure (cf. 1:32 ff.; 2:13 ff.). But Simeon's speech does contain one item of new information, for Jesus' coming is "a light for revelation to the Gentiles" (vs. 32). Jewish parents would understandably be surprised, especially since the news comes from a devout fellow Israelite (cf. vss. 34 f.). Even this point is not entirely novel, however, for Simeon's speech goes back to Isaiah the prophet (cf. 52:10; 42:6; 49:6). Still the principal point of this episode (under the Spirit's guidance; cf. vss. 25, 26, 27), and of the entire introduction, is that Jesus is for all people, even Gentiles.[8] He is meant for old and young, for women like Mary and Elizabeth, and for priests and shepherds.

In the final part of this episode Jesus is meant not only for the righteous and devout Simeon, but also for the old prophetess Anna (2:36–38). Again Luke's twofold witness appears: An old man and an old woman praise Jesus. Anna's piety is also exemplary (vs. 37). Her actions are similar to those of the early Christians who also went to the temple in order to worship and pray (cf. Acts 2:46–3:1). Furthermore, what she anticipates —"the redemption of Jerusalem" (vs. 38)—is effected in the early church by the life of Jesus (cf. 19:28–24:53, especially 24:21). Antiquity, represented by the old woman and the old man, prophesies the new salvation to result from the coming of Jesus and calls attention to that redemption's ancient roots in Israel.

INITIAL VICTORY IN THE TEMPLE (2:41–52)

What is the outcome of Jesus' first action in Luke?

The one boyhood story of Jesus contained in any of the canonical Gospels shows Jesus in the temple.[9] This Lukan emphasis was already apparent in the initial scene with Zechariah and the preceding encounters

---

[8] Appropriately, the message about Gentiles occurs in the temple, where symbols of exclusion abound. Its outer court allowed the presence of Gentiles and women, but the inner court was reserved only for male Jews in good standing. The Holy of Holies within the temple could be entered only once a year and then only by the high priest. See William Stinespring, "Temple, Jerusalem," *IDB*, IV (New York: Abingdon Press, 1962), pp. 534–560.

[9] The apocryphal Gospels contain numerous stories of the infancy of Jesus, sometimes grotesque and occasionally downright distasteful; see Hennecke-Schneemelcher, *New Testament Apocrypha*, I, pp. 363–417.

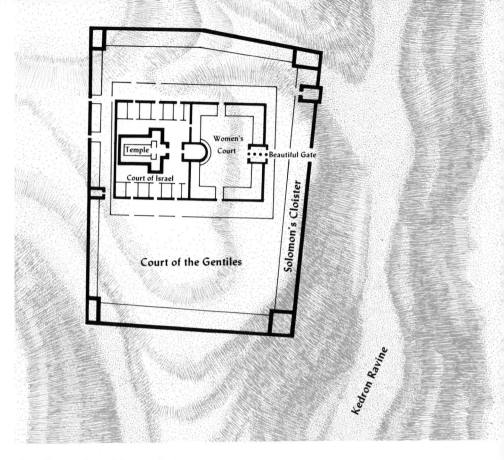

Labels within the diagram:
Women's Court
Temple
Beautiful Gate
Court of Israel
Solomon's Cloister
Court of the Gentiles
Kedron Ravine

Herod's temple and its precincts.

with Simeon and Anna. Now Jesus' first real action is a triumphant demonstration before the rabbis in the temple. When his parents question him, he replies, "Did you not know that I must be in my Father's house?" (2:49). The temple is Jesus' inheritance because he fulfills the hope of Israel.

This conversation actually takes place with Jesus' mother rather than his father. She speaks (2:48); moreover, "his mother kept all these things in her heart" (2:51). Throughout the introduction, Mary has the central role to the neglect of his father Joseph. In the purification episode, Simeon speaks to Mary (2:34). In fact, Mary is mentioned twelve times in the opening two chapters. Clearly, she is the one unifying character in these chapters. Yet in the rest of the Gospel she is not particularly important and is even rebuked (8:19 ff.). The fact that her womb bore Jesus and that her breasts were sucked by him is declared insignificant in comparison with those "who hear the word of God and keep it" (11:27 f.; only in Luke). Luke's emphasis upon Mary does not particularly stress the virgin birth; the passages themselves concentrate on a series of wonders

rather than one particular miracle.[10] The consistent flow of marvels underlines the fact that "with God, nothing will be impossible" (1:37). In that
context, the reason for Mary's centrality may be that she is a *woman*.
With God, nothing is impossible—not even a woman as the one human
being most responsible for Jesus' coming. This possibility is stronger when
seen against the background of Judaism, a preeminently masculine religion.
Judaism's stress upon circumcision (cf. 1:59 and 2:21), a male ritual, seems
to be subordinated to the purification of Mary (2:22 ff.). This may be
another of Luke's ways of saying that Jesus comes for all people, male and
female (cf. Gal. 3:28).

The essential point of the birth stories, around which Luke's introduction
is built, is the stress on the overwhelming power of God. Luke uses the
miraculous birth of Jesus (Luke 1–2) to introduce Jesus' life in the same
way as he uses the miraculous birth of the church (Acts 1–2) to introduce
the church's mission. The outpouring of the Spirit upon various people at
Jesus' birth is matched in Acts by the Spirit's descending upon apostles
and disciples. The close of the introduction anticipates further developments (2:52). This verse duplicates an earlier one (2:40). Further manifestations of God through the Spirit are thereby foreshadowed, for what
was begun by the Spirit (cf. 1:14; 1:35; 1:41; 1:67; 2:25; 2:26) is now to
be accomplished in the ministry of Jesus.

Until this point in the narrative, the main actor has been God, working
through the Holy Spirit. This suggests another reason why Mary remains
at the introduction's center. She, like all women, represents passivity, the
ability to wait and to receive (cf. 1:38). In Luke's opening section, the
main characters do not do anything; God does it for them. Fittingly,
throughout most of the story, Zechariah cannot speak. The characters
function to receive the Spirit, the power of God's acting in Jesus' birth.
Only with the final episode, Jesus in the temple, does a person act with
authority. And this action serves as the transition to Luke's first major
section, which concerns Jesus' gathering of witnesses in Galilee for the
journey to Jerusalem and the temple.

Gathering Witnesses in Galilee (3:1–9:50)

Thus far the source of Luke's material has been his special tradition,
but from this point (3:1) the major source is the Gospel of Mark. A
segment of Luke, found also in Matthew but not in Mark, is probably
derived from the Q source. We would be on relatively shaky ground in

---

[10] See Minear, *Studies in Luke-Acts*, p. 129.

trying to deduce the aims and purposes of Luke from his use of this source, simply because we do not possess Q. We shall therefore largely confine our separation of tradition and redaction to Luke's use of the Markan source. In addition, we shall continue to assume that the special Lukan material reveals something of the purpose of this Gospel.

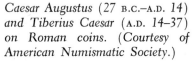

Caesar Augustus (27 B.C.–A.D. 14) and Tiberius Caesar (A.D. 14–37) on Roman coins. (Courtesy of American Numismatic Society.)

Luke locates the beginning of Jesus' ministry in two spheres, that of world history (3:1; see also 2:1) and that of God's word. This word is preached by John, the son of Zechariah (Luke 3:2 ff.). Curiously, John the Baptist seems to be handled rather carelessly by Luke. For example, whereas Matthew carefully showed that Jesus was baptized by John in order to fulfill righteousness (Matt. 3:13 ff.), Luke does not make clear to the reader that Jesus was even baptized by John (cf. 3:20 f.). That could be Luke's way of minimizing his role, although John the Baptist preaches exactly the same message of repentance and forgiveness (3:3) which becomes the heart of Jesus' own proclamation (see Luke 15; 24:47 and pp. 157 ff.).

The only special Lukan material concerning John is not particularly striking (3:10–14). John speaks about a familiar theme, "all flesh shall see the salvation of God" (3:6; only in Luke). As the opening birth stories already indicated, this Gospel does show a high regard for John (cf. 7:28). John the Baptist belongs to the old Israel (16:16), though he is the one who points ahead to the new time of Jesus (3:16).[11] Within the three stages of salvation history the Baptist belongs to the time of Israel. This scheme may explain why only Luke shows John in prison before Jesus is baptized or begins his ministry (3:18–21).

Characteristic Lukan emphases abound in this first major section. Jesus is a universal savior: the genealogy goes from Jesus back to Adam, the first man (3:38), but not to Abraham (Matt. 1:1 f.). Jesus is an exemplar of piety: whenever a crisis arises, he is at prayer (5:16; 6:12; 9:18, 28 f.). Moreover, the Spirit descends upon Jesus while he is praying almost as if the Spirit were summoned by prayer rather than by the baptism (3:21; cf. Mark 1:9 f.). The Gospel of Luke apparently seeks to establish the

[11] See Conzelmann, *The Theology of St. Luke,* pp. 20 ff.

practice of prayer as a basis for the continuing life of the church. Emphasis upon the church's contemporary situation may be reflected in Luke's omission of Mark's summary of Jesus' preaching, "The time is fulfilled, and the kingdom of God is at hand; repent, and believe in the gospel" (Mark 1:15). Although Luke also mentions the kingdom in this section, Jesus rarely preaches the kingdom as if it were imminent (see 4:43 and 8:1; cf. 9:27). This loss of a sense for the imminent coming of the kingdom is related to his greater emphasis on the church.

This section narrates Jesus' gathering of disciples in Galilee. Many people flock to him (4:15, 42; 5:1, 15); some are in opposition (5:30; 6:2) and remain only in the crowd (6:17; 7:11); but he gathers the disciples (5:1–11). Indeed, from the disciples, he calls the twelve together whom he "named apostles" (6:13; cf. Mark 3:14). Here in Jesus' own territory there is the gathering of those who will be witnesses to carry on his work after his death. The continuing importance of women is shown by their inclusion alongside the twelve as part of Jesus' retinue (8:2 f.). Later, they too, along with the twelve, will be witnesses. "The women who had come with him *from Galilee* followed, and saw the tomb, and how his body was laid; then they returned, and prepared spices and ointments" (23:55 f.; see 23:49). At Jesus' ascension, two men address the disciples as "men of Galilee" (Acts 1:11). Luke seeks to establish certainty of witness: someone had accompanied Jesus all the time, from his baptism until the day when he was taken up (see Acts 1:21 f.).

THE OFFENSE OF JESUS' PREACHING (4:16–30)

Why do the people of Nazareth become angry with Jesus?

In Mark Jesus' first act after the baptism and temptation is to call disciples (Mark 1:16–20); in Luke his first act after these events is to preach in his home synagogue at Nazareth. This episode's special importance is indicated not only by its position at the beginning of Jesus' public ministry but also by Luke's uncharacteristic departure from the Markan order. In this instance, he has shifted the incident for his own purposes (cf. Mark 6:1–6).

Jesus appears as a pious Jew: "He went to the synagogue, as his custom was, on the sabbath day" (vs. 16). He then reads from the prophet Isaiah,[12] whose message from the Old Testament (Isaiah 61:1–2; 58:6) proclaims the end time; the Spirit acts, good news is preached to the poor, and a new age has dawned. After finishing, Jesus says, "Today, this scripture has

---

[12] Worship in a Palestinian synagogue consisted of the recitation of the Shema, a prayer, a fixed lection or reading of the law, a free lection from the prophets, an explanation, an application of one or both scriptural passages, and a blessing by the priest, or a prayer by a layman; see Gilmour, *IB*, VIII, p. 89.

View of present-day Nazareth. (Courtesy of Israel Government Tourist Office.)

been fulfilled in your hearing" (vs. 21; only in Luke). In other words, salvation has appeared with Jesus. He has come to preach good news to the poor, to release the captive, and to proclaim the arrival of the good news. The kingdom is not merely imminent; it has arrived.

The reception given to Jesus' announcement by the people of Nazareth is rather surprising. Luke's account suggests that they accept Jesus as the one who brings salvation (vs. 22). In Luke's source (Mark 6:1-6), the people immediately took offense at Jesus' claim to authority. In Luke, "Is not this Joseph's son?" (vs. 22), seems to proceed from surprise rather than anger (cf. Mark 6:3). But Jesus is finally rejected, not because he claims authority, but because he extends salvation to the wrong people.

Evidently, Jesus thinks they want him to perform miracles as he has done in Capernaum (vs. 23; although Luke has not yet reported any miracles). Jesus rejects their request by talking about miracles in the Old Testament which the prophets Elijah and Elisha performed, not for the people of Israel, but for foreigners. At this news, the audience's anger is aroused. Jesus' proclamation is going beyond Israel to the Gentiles. They drive him out of the city and almost kill him, but he escapes (vss. 29 f.).

We might now expect Jesus to leave Palestine in order to preach to

151

Gentiles. Luke, however, stands under the authority of tradition, and there is no record in the Synoptic tradition of Jesus' going outside Israel. For Luke the matter is solved, for Jesus' saying will be fulfilled in the church's mission. Acts makes clear that the Gentiles do hear the word (cf. Acts 11:18; 22:21; 28:28).

Incidents following this opening scene further reveal Luke's intention. What Jesus has done in Nazareth, he now proceeds to do in Capernaum (4:31 ff.). He refused to perform a miracle at Nazareth, but in this synagogue and on this sabbath, he heals. The point may be to show Jesus' sovereignty (cf. 4:31 f., 41); more likely Jesus now heals because he is on his way toward his goal. When the people try to hold him, he says, "I must preach the good news of the kingdom of God to the other cities also; for I was sent for this purpose" (4:43). Precisely because this preaching to other cities cannot be done by Jesus alone, the necessary conclusion to the opening Nazareth scene is the calling of disciples. When all is said and done by Jesus, these disciples will be the instruments for spreading the message beyond Israel to the cities of the Gentiles.

A comparison between the calling of disciples in Luke (5:1–11) and in Mark (1:16–20) shows that Luke alone includes a miracle, that of the great catch of fish.[13] Stress is laid, however, upon the consequence of the miracle, Simon Peter's confession of sin, "Depart from me, for I am a sinful man, O Lord" (vs. 8). After this repentance, Simon Peter and those with him become fishers of men or true disciples. Similar action as a condition for being called as witnesses is evidenced in the episode with Levi (5:27–32). The Pharisees and their scribes call the disciples, "tax collectors and sinners" (5:30). Jesus agrees, "I have not come to call the righteous, but sinners to repentance" (5:32).

Another example of the Lukan repentance motif is contained in the story of the woman "who was a sinner" (7:36–50). Although this story has some affinities with Mark (14:3–9), its present form has, nevertheless, a distinctly Lukan cast. In Luke, the sinful woman who shows great love to Jesus serves as the occasion for a parable by Jesus which stresses that someone who has been forgiven then loves (7:43). Yet the actual incident first mentions the woman's love, then Jesus' forgiveness (cf. 7:47 f.). Perhaps the confusion about which comes first, repentance[14] or forgiveness, is intentional. Repentance and forgiveness are both necessary and cannot readily be distinguished by a logical or chronological priority (see 3:3). Repentance, the response of man, occurs with forgiveness, the action of

---

[13] Luke's call of Simon at this point in the narrative makes Jesus' previous healing of Simon's mother-in-law (4:38 f.) seem out of place (cf. Mark 1:29–31). Perhaps this change of the Markan order is also a device to show the importance of miracles in bringing disciples. Cf. John 21:4–8.

[14] That her love is an expression of repentance is clear from the story: she is a sinner, she weeps, she kisses the feet of Jesus.

Ruins of an ancient synagogue at Capernaum, built in the second or third century after Christ. (Courtesy of Israel Information Services.)

God. The essential point, however, has to do with quantity, not sequence, for her great love and God's great forgiveness contrast with the petty formality of the Pharisees.

Jesus' presence elicits two kinds of response, either rejection by those who cling to the old righteousness of Israel or repentance by those who accept his promise of salvation. Those who repent become witnessing disciples to the forgiveness that Jesus brings.

SURE WITNESS TO THE WORD (8:1–21)

How does the parable of the sower relate to the word of God?

In the introduction of this passage, a number of witnesses are gathered around Jesus, the twelve and the women (8:1–3). At its close, the mother and brothers of Jesus, who come to see him, are told by Jesus, "My mother and my brothers are those who hear the word of God and do it" (8:21). This sequence is designed by Luke to demonstrate that true disciples not only hear Jesus' word, but also go out to become preachers of this word (cf. 8:15; see 1:2; Acts 6:1–7).

In comparing this section with its parallels in Mark (4:1–34; 3:31–35), two major differences are evident: first, Luke shifts the position of the discussion about the true mother and brothers of Jesus so that it now follows, instead of precedes, the parable of the sower; second, Luke has only one parable (Luke 8:4; cf. Mark 4:2). Both changes reflect Luke's concentration upon the theme of the word of God. For example, in Luke's interpretation of the parable of the sower Jesus says, "Now the parable is this: The seed is the word of God. . . ." (8:11; cf. Mark 4:13 f.).

Luke's version of the parable of the sower (8:4–8) unfolds much as in Mark (4:1–9) except that Mark emphasized response to Jesus' teaching in parables, whereas Luke stresses response to Jesus' message of the word of God. By a series of slight changes Luke transforms the passage into an exhortation for careful and sure witness. Such phrases as "the seed is the word of God" (8:11; cf. Mark 4:13), "then the devil comes and takes away the word from their hearts that they may not believe and be saved" (8:12b; cf. Mark 4:15), and "they are those who, hearing the word, hold it fast in an honest and good heart, and bring forth fruit with patience" (8:15; cf. Mark 4:20) show Luke's intention to depict the importance of hearing and holding to the word of God.

Further emphasis upon the time of the church may be suggested by Luke's inclusion of "the devil" in Jesus' interpretation (8:12b; cf. Mark 4:15). According to Luke's temptation story, the devil left Jesus to return at an opportune time (4:13; cf. Mark 1:13; Matt. 4:11). In Luke this satanic figure does not begin to act again until Jesus' last days (22:3, 31) and he continues during the early days of the church (Acts 5:3; 10:38; 13:10; 26:18).[15] The time between Jesus' temptation and passion is for Luke an ideal time of the kingdom of God (cf. 10:18; 11:20). In that idyllic period a foundation was laid so that in later conflict disciples who had truly heard would continue steadfastly preaching the word. Consequently, the saying about not hiding the lamp (8:16) refers in Luke to those who hear the word and patiently bring forth fruitful witness (8:15; cf. Mark 4:20). Gathering sure disciples in Galilee assures the faithful continuation of the word of God into the time of the church.

The next episodes in Luke, following basically the order of Mark, are a series of miracles: the miracle of calming the waves (8:22–25); the driving out of the demons at Gerasenes (8:26–39); the healing of the woman with the flow of blood (8:43–48); and the raising of the dead daughter (8:40–42, 49–56). This series culminates when Jesus "called the

---

15 W. C. Robinson, Jr., "On Preaching the Word of God (Luke 8:4–21)," *Studies in Luke-Acts*, pp. 132 f.

twelve together and gave them power and authority over all demons and to cure diseases, and he sent them out to preach the kingdom of God and to heal" (9:1–2). The witnesses are gathered, are convinced, and even Herod begins to wonder (9:7–9). The crowds are filled, for after the feeding of the five thousand "twelve baskets of broken pieces" are left over (9:10–17). Only then are the disciples asked to affirm that Jesus is the Christ of God (9:18–20).

The conclusion of the first part of Luke, "the gathering of witnesses in Galilee," begins a discussion of Jesus' identity, and especially of the necessity of his suffering (9:21–27; 43b–45). At the close of this first major section instead of Mark's "he that is not against *us* is for *us*" (Mark 9:40), Luke's Jesus says, "he that is not against *you* is for *you*" (9:50). These are clearly instructions for the early church.

Witness to the Word on the Journey to Jerusalem (9:51–19:27)

The closing incidents of Luke's first major section indicated the necessity for Jesus' suffering in Jerusalem rather than Galilee (9:31). The Galilean witnesses gathered by Jesus must journey with him to Jerusalem. But Luke's second major section, which narrates the journey, seems much longer than the short distance (about sixty miles) and the brief time (about three days) that it would take to travel from Galilee to Jerusalem. Though Jesus is on the way to Jerusalem all this time, he seems to make little progress (see 9:51; 10:1, 38; 13:22, 33; 17:11; 19:11).

Luke's reason for such an extensive account of the journey is not simply an interest in geographical matters, for it is difficult to answer questions about Jesus' itinerary from Galilee to Jerusalem on the basis of the information in the text. For example, we are uncertain whether he went through Samaria, which separates Galilee from Jerusalem (cf. 9:53). Luke does make clear, as the journey progresses, that certain people are present with Jesus throughout the trip. Continuity in witness to the work and word of Jesus is thereby assured (cf. 23:49).

The opening verse is a key for this section, "When the days drew near for him to be received up, he set his face to go to Jerusalem" (9:51; only in Luke). Jesus goes to Jerusalem because, "I must go on my way today and tomorrow and the day following; for it cannot be that a prophet should perish away from Jerusalem" (13:33; only in Luke). As prophet to Israel, Jesus goes to die at Jerusalem, the capital of Israel. The journey turns out to be instruction in the purpose and meaning of Jesus' death.

A comparison of the structure of Luke's Gospel with that of the Acts of the Apostles reveals a striking similarity that helps to illuminate the reason for the journey. In Acts the order is: first, the Spirit's appearance in Jerusalem; second, journeys of missionaries, especially Paul; third, Paul's arrest and trial ending in Rome. In Luke the order is: first, gathering of witnesses in Galilee; second, the journey to Jerusalem accompanied by preaching the word; third, Jesus' arrest, trial, crucifixion, and resurrection in Jerusalem. Together Luke-Acts shows a continuity of witness stretching from Galilee to Rome; the journey motif emphasizes an orderly, gradual development of the new faith.

Luke stresses a theme of witness throughout this section in two senses: (1) a witness *observes* something; (2) a witness *testifies* to something. The first two episodes (9:51–56 and 9:57–62; mainly special Lukan material) indicate the necessity of following Jesus closely—that is, of observing. The mission of the seventy (10:1–17) implies that the twelve remained with Jesus even during the sending out of the seventy (10:1; note "others"); moreover, the disciples are singled out, "Then turning to the disciples he said privately, 'Blessed are the eyes which see what you see!' " (10:23; cf. Matt. 13:16). Other passages point out that disciples are always with Jesus so that his journey has been faithfully observed.[16] By the end of this section the emphasis includes not only faithful observation but also faithful testifying to what has been observed (cf. 19:11–27). This distinction between "eyewitnesses and ministers of the word" (1:2) is the basis for Luke's understanding of witness.

An explicit example of "ministers of the word" is the mission of the seventy (10:1–17). However, we find out little regarding the mission and message of such "ministers" except that they proclaim, "The kingdom of God has come near" (vss. 9, 11). Perhaps we learn something about the kingdom's immediacy in Jesus' parable of the good Samaritan, which proclaims that one must *be* a neighbor instead of trying self-righteously to identify the neighbor (10:25–37).

This entire teaching section is, however, a depiction of Jesus' telling the disciples about the word of God. They are shown that women matter, especially the one who sits attentively at Jesus' feet. (See also the story of Mary and Martha, 10:38–42.) Prayer is part of Jesus' life and those with him (11:1 ff.). The kingdom of God becomes present whenever Jesus casts out demons (11:20). Physical closeness to Jesus guarantees nothing by itself; the blessed are "those who hear the word of God and keep it" (11:27 f.). True disciples cannot be satisfied with the old rules of piety (11:37–12:3). Riches are clearly a barrier to hearing the word that Jesus proclaims (12:13–34; cf. 14:33; 16:11, 14, 19–31; 18:22–30; 19:1–10). Watchfulness and faithfulness are demanded over a long period of time

---

[16] 11:1; 12:1, 22, 41; 16:1; 17:1, 5, 22; 19:28–40. See C. H. Talbert, *Luke and the Gnostics: An Examination of the Lucan Purpose* (New York: Abingdon Press, 1966), pp. 24 ff. Note how these verses belong to the editorial passages of Luke.

(12:41–49) and repentance is necessary now (13:1–9). Jesus' ministry must continue for a long period of time (13:10–35); furthermore, the end of the world is not in sight (17:20 ff.). The Messianic banquet with Jesus will include great multitudes, the unexpected (14:13), the Gentiles (14:23; cf. 17:18 and 10:33); but not all will enter (14:25–35). The following special Lukan material from the journey gives the heart of Jesus' instructions: repentance and forgiveness.[17]

JESUS' WORD ABOUT THE PRESENT (15:1–32)

What is the common emphasis of all three parables?

Jesus' words, "He who has ears to hear, let him hear" (14:35), are a transition to the statement: "Now the tax collectors and sinners were all drawing near to him" (15:1). In the center of the journey section, Luke inserts three parables, of which only the parable of the lost sheep occurs outside Luke (cf. Matt. 18:12–14). They clarify and extend Jesus' word, which the disciples are to transmit to others. The Pharisees and the scribes are irritated by Jesus' association with sinners (vs. 2). In contrast, the parables emphasize joy and openness to all (cf. 15:7, 10, 32), a prominent motif throughout Luke (cf., for example, 1:14, 44; 2:10; 6:23).

The first two parables pose a problem of interpretation, for the general conclusions of each speak of a sinner's repenting (15:7, 10), yet such repentance is hardly exemplified in the parables themselves. A lost sheep or a lost coin does not repent. The usual explanation is that the general conclusions anticipate and more properly belong to the third parable, that of the prodigal son. Moreover, this last parable contains the key passage concerning repentance, for the prodigal son repented—"when he came to himself . . ." (15:17). From that moment the parable moves toward the happy ending (vs. 24). According to this viewpoint, we might suppose that Luke emphasizes the forgiveness of God less than the necessity for the sinner's repentance (note the polemic against the Pharisees—vs. 2). Lukan theology would then insist primarily upon man's need for repentance rather than God's action in forgiveness (see vss. 7 and 10).[18]

If, however, Luke wishes to stress the repentance of man in contrast with the forgiveness of God, he has made a poor selection from the tradition of Jesus' teaching. An *opposite* conclusion could be drawn: Luke's very purpose in using the two introductory parables is to prevent an incorrect reading of the parable of the prodigal son in terms of repentance. The first

---

[17] Further elaboration of the repentance-forgiveness motif is given in these distinctively Lukan sayings: the word from the cross (23:34), the action-word on the cross (23:39–43); and the charge to resurrection witnesses (24:47).

[18] Relevant texts for supporting the repentance motif are 13:5; 14:33; 16:30; 17:3 f.; 19:1 ff. See Plummer, *Gospel According to St. Luke*, p. 371.

Shepherd and sheep in the Judean hills near Jerusalem. (Courtesy of Pan American Airways.)

two parables unmistakably emphasize the initiative of the one who seeks out the lost. Whether this is Jesus or God is not crucial—probably both are intended—for the decisive announcement is that salvation is present (see 4:21; 10:13; 11:20; 17:20; 18:30; 19:9). Luke is addressing the charge made against Jesus that he eats with sinners (vs. 2), and he claims that precisely the avowed sinner recognizes what is happening and, unlike the Pharisees and scribes, receives the forgiveness of God. We can now look more closely at the familiar parable of the prodigal son.

A more appropriate title for this story would be the parable of the prodigal's father. The parable runs smoothly and understandably through the son's realization that he would be better off as one of his father's hired servants (vss. 17 f.), at which point he returns home confessing himself a sinner. The surprise of the story is the way in which the father receives him. Instead of greeting him with self-righteousness ("I told you so") and a demand that he demonstrate his "repentance," the father runs

158

out to embrace him and gives orders to bring the best robe, the ring, shoes, and the fatted calf. He will have a feast for his son. There is joy and merriment for one who was lost and is now found (vs. 24).[19]

To prevent our missing the point, the elder son is introduced. He is angry; he cannot understand his father's joyful reception, much as the Pharisees and scribes cannot understand Jesus' action. But the father exclaims, "Son, you are always with me, and all that is mine is yours. It was fitting to make merry and be glad, for this your brother was dead, and is alive; he was lost, and is found" (vs. 32). The problem with the elder brother is his failure to recognize the joy and salvation that is already present. He needs to repent and to accept the good news of God's forgiveness (15:7, 10, 25–32). Only then is God's word truly heard.

These same themes of forgiveness and repentance recur in the remaining portions of the journey. The rich man tries too late to repent (16:19 ff.), and the poor man Lazarus cannot help him. Unexpectedly, some do repent because the kingdom is in their midst (17:11–21). He who hears Jesus' word is one who impetuously keeps knocking at the door (18:1 ff.) and admits that he is a sinner in need of God's mercy (18:9 ff.). Things are unhappy for those who are self-satisfied (18:18–23), yet whoever calls on the mercy of Jesus will see (18:35–43). Even a rich chief tax collector will be saved because he sees himself as a sinner (19:1–10). The word Jesus proclaims during this journey effects salvation; those who are close to him will testify to what they have heard and seen, "Today salvation has come to this house, since he also is a son of Abraham" (19:9).

At times, Luke seems to be saying that salvation has arrived, Jesus has already brought it. But Luke knows that there is more to come: the long history of the church will be unfolded by men acting under the Spirit of God. Though Jesus' final days in Jerusalem are coming, Luke does not think that nothing else remains to be done. Hence he closes this journey section with the parable of the pounds.

JESUS' WORD ABOUT THE FUTURE (19:11–27)

What mistake does the "wicked servant" make?

In Jesus salvation is present (see 10:18; 11:20; 17:20). Yet how does the presence of salvation in him relate to the coming kingdom of God? The opening of the parable of the pounds does not suggest the expectation

---

[19] In Buddhist literature there is a similar parable which speaks of a son who also wastes his inheritance and returns home. This father, however, makes the son do penance for a number of years in order to prove that he is truly repentant and worthy of being received back as his son. See R. Otto, *India's Religion of Grace and Christianity*, trans. J. H. Foster (London: SCM Press, 1930), pp. 136 ff.

of an imminent kingdom (19:11; cf. 21:8 and Acts 1:6 ff.). Seemingly, present salvation and future kingdom are distinguished in the thought of Luke, and the kingdom is in the indefinite future.[20]

In the parable of the pounds, the nobleman goes into a *far country* to receive kingly power (cf. Matt. 25:14–30), a hint that in Luke's eschatology the king will return again only after a long journey. Some citizens do not want him to be king; they resist by sending an embassy to oppose him. The surprise of the parable is that when he returns, he condemns the one who in fear of him as a severe judge had simply hidden the gift away. Concentration upon God's future severity misses the point. Even though the king does deal severely with his enemies at the end (vs. 27), the one who makes use of the gift of salvation (that is, continues his witness to a forgiving God over a long period of time) need not fear.

Throughout this section Jesus' word brings forgiveness for whoever will receive it—sinners, people in the highways and hedges, a prodigal son, or foreigners. But if they do not see and testify to it, then judgment will come. A joyful present and a threatening future are proclaimed as they journey to Jerusalem. Now Luke brings Jesus into Jerusalem, the place where he must die and be resurrected.

III. The True Israel Through the Passion and Resurrection (19:28–24:53)

In the third and final section of the Gospel of Luke, two distinctive motifs emerge: first, Jesus triumphs in the temple; second, Jesus' innocence is established. The temple motif is not new in Luke.[21] Now, however, he reiterates his emphasis more insistently. Jesus is teaching daily in the temple (19:47; 20:1; 21:37 ff.; 22:53); even after the resurrection the disciples return to the temple to bless God continually (24:53). Moreover, the apocalyptic discourse takes place in the temple rather than on the Mount of Olives as in Mark and Matthew (21:5–28; cf. Mark 13:1 ff. and

[20] One famous passage suggests, however, that the kingdom is already present, "Behold, the kingdom of God is in the midst of you" (17:20 f.; only in Luke). Evidently Luke means that the key to the future kingdom is already present in the word and action of Jesus, which bring forgiveness and effect repentance. The kingdom itself will not come until the disciples shall have gone throughout the world with this word of forgiveness and repentance (24:47). Indeed, Luke follows this kingdom saying (17:20 f.) with caution against assuming that the kingdom's Son of Man has already come (17:22 ff.). See Conzelmann, *The Theology of St. Luke*, pp. 120–125.

[21] See the introductory section, especially 2:41–52. The order of temptations in the Gospel of Luke may reflect Luke's temple emphasis. In Luke 4:1–13, Jesus' temptation to throw himself off the temple's pinnacle is the last temptation (unlike the parallel in Matthew 4:1–11), perhaps to signal the temple scene as the climactic one.

Matt. 24:1 ff.). Why then does Luke so emphasize Jesus' frequenting of the temple?

In the Acts of the Apostles the earliest church is also centered in the temple (cf. Acts 2:46; 3:1 ff.; 5:20). Apparently Jesus establishes himself in the temple in order that the early church may also operate from this base. Thereby Luke seeks to show how the new faith in Jesus is the true Israel and the authentic extension of the dominant religious institution of Israel.[22] Luke's apology consequently assures both Jewish and Gentile believers of the antiquity and continuity of the new faith. The disciples, who return to the temple immediately after the resurrection appearances in order to bless God and to await the power of the Spirit (24:53), are neither a band of fanatics expecting the end of the world nor political revolutionaries against the Roman empire. This latter emphasis becomes most explicit in the book of Acts (see pp. 274 ff.), but already in the Gospel the truth and innocence of Christian faith is demonstrated in Jesus.

The second major motif of this passion and resurrection section is the trial and death of the *innocent* Jesus. A special Lukan detail illustrates this emphasis: at Jesus' trial before Pilate, the elders of the people accuse Jesus of having forbidden the giving of tribute to Caesar (23:1–5; cf. Mark 15:1–5), but an earlier debate about Jesus' authority absolutely established the falsity of this charge (20:19–26). In Mark, Pilate, the Roman procurator, finds Jesus not guilty on only one occasion (15:14), but in Luke this verdict of innocence occurs three times (cf. 23:4, 14–16, 22). Luke alone records the incident of Herod's declaring Jesus innocent (23:6 ff.). Furthermore, in Luke the centurion at the cross says, "Certainly, this man was innocent" (23:47); in Mark he said, "Truly this man was the Son of God" (15:39; cf. Matt. 27:54). The subtle way in which Luke opposes Jesus to Barabbas suggests that Jesus was definitely not an insurrectionist like Barabbas (cf. Luke 23:19, 25 with Mark 15:7). Jesus' climactic word from the cross establishes his innocence, "Father, forgive them for they know not what they do" (23:34; only in Luke). Luke further underlines Jesus' innocence as one of the thieves from the cross—who would doubt the word of a dying man?—says, "We are receiving the due reward of our deeds; but this man has done nothing wrong" (23:41; only in Luke). This major theme receives further and unqualified substantiation in Acts, "This Jesus . . . you crucified and killed by the hands of *lawless* men" (Acts 2:23; cf. Acts 8:32 ff. and 17:30).

The innocent Jesus is falsely accused, tried, and executed. Instead of concentrating upon the guilt of those responsible for this miscarriage of justice, Luke focuses upon Jesus' triumph even under adversity. At the cross Jesus' general word of forgiveness (23:34) and his forgiveness of the

---

[22] Another view of this temple motif suggests that Luke intends thereby to show that Christianity is a legitimate, nonsubversive extension of Judaism; see B. S. Easton, *Early Christianity: The Purposes of Acts and Other Papers*, ed. F. C. Grant (Greenwich, Conn.: Seabury Press, 1954), pp. 33–114.

repentant thief (23:39–43) show that guilt need not be overwhelming. Finally, this passion is the working out of God's plan ("This Jesus, delivered up according to the definite plan and foreknowledge of God"— Acts 2:23; cf. 3:18 and Luke 22:22). Jesus dies a martyr's death prefiguring the martyrdom of others in the early church, especially Stephen and James (cf. Acts 7:54–8:3; 9:1; 12:1 ff.). But through all these events God's word of "repentance and forgiveness of sins" is being preached to all nations (24:47), and his plan thus fulfilled.

THE TRUE INHERITORS (20:9–19)

To whom will the vineyard be given?

In focusing upon the passion events up to and including Jesus' death and resurrection, Luke is obviously in company with the other Synoptic Gospels. In the parable of the wicked tenants Luke shows his understanding of the reason for Jesus' death and resurrection. This parable is an incisive commentary upon Jesus' death and its result.

In the preceding passage (19:47–20:8) Jesus' authority for teaching daily in the temple has been challenged by the chief priests and the scribes. Comparing the opening of the parable with its Markan source (Luke 20:9; cf. Mark 12:1; Matt. 21:33), we are struck by Luke's distinction between the people *to* whom this parable is spoken and the chief priests and the scribes *against* whom it is spoken (cf. 20:19). In Mark's version (12:1–12), the parable is clearly polemical against the chief priests, scribes, and elders because they have rejected God's servants, the prophets and even the "beloved son" (Mark 12:6, see pp. 86 f.). The identity of the Markan "others" who will receive the vineyard is indefinite, although the reader may surmise that they are the Gentiles (Mark 13:10; cf. also Matt. 21:43).[23]

In Luke, however, this parable is addressed not to Jesus' opponents, but to the people, who "hung upon his words" (19:48). Furthermore, the people protest strongly the destruction of the former tenants and the giving of the vineyard to others: "When they heard this, they said, 'God forbid!'" (20:16b; only in Luke). This protest serves, however, to allow Jesus to restate his conclusion (vss. 17 f.) and to imply that the people do finally accept Jesus' word because the leaders acknowledge that the people are on Jesus' side (vs. 19).

Throughout this section Luke consistently portrays the people as being sympathetic to Jesus. They are the ones who praise God (18:43); they

---

[23] Joachim Jeremias, *The Parables of Jesus*, rev. ed., trans. S. H. Hooke (New York: Charles Scribner's Sons, 1962), p. 76, suggests that "others" refers to the "poor." The leaders of the people reject the gospel; therefore, Jesus offers it to the poor.

listen in the temple (19:48, 21:38); they observe Jesus' defeat of the authorities (20:26). They stand by, instead of mocking, at the crucifixion (23:35). Within Jewish tradition reference to "the people" carries with it the connotation of God's chosen people, the people of Israel.[24] Consequently the alignment of the people with Jesus implies that Jesus' word is finally accepted by Israel.

In the book of Acts, Luke clarifies the identity of these "others." They are the true inheritors, for they are "the men of Israel" and the Gentiles who hear the preaching (cf. Acts 2:22; 3:12; 13:16, 46–48). The last speech of Paul, at the conclusion of Acts, confirms that the Gentiles have become the true people of God, because the old Israel has rejected the preaching (Acts 28:26–28). However, Luke clearly shows in the parable that the people are on Jesus' side so that "others," the inheritors, include both Jew and Gentile. In Luke, a parable concerning the rejection of Jesus becomes also a parable stressing the true inheritors, those who *hear*.

Luke does emphasize rejection in this parable and in his own special way. Jesus' explanation of the reason for the tenants' destruction reads as follows in Mark:

> Have you not read this scripture:
>   The very stone which the builders rejected
>   has become the head of the corner;
>   this was the Lord's doing,
>   and it is marvelous in our eyes?
>   (Mark 12:10 f.; cf. Psalm 118:22 f.)

In Luke the element of praise (last two lines) is omitted and another condemnation is added (20:18; cf. Isaiah 8:14 f.). Thereby Luke emphasizes the judgment that occurs for those who do not truly understand or interpret the scripture. They cannot tell the true from the false Israel. This necessity for rightly interpreting the scripture is the subject of our final Lukan passage.

FULFILLING THE SCRIPTURE (24:13–35)

How does Jesus try to clear up misunderstanding?
What enables the men to recognize Jesus?

Before turning to this climactic event on the road to Emmaus, we need to observe the way in which Luke prepares for this scene. Throughout the passion, especially after the parable of the wicked tenants, two themes

---

[24] See *"laos"* in Kittel, *TDNT*, IV, pp. 29–57, and especially Luke 2:32 and Acts 26:17, 23. Cf. Acts 4:10; 28:26 f.

mutually reinforce each other: (1) these events necessarily happened; (2) they were closely and surely witnessed.

Definite things must happen before the end can come (Luke 21:12) in order to fulfill scripture (21:22; 22:37; especially 24:25–27, 32). These things are done at the bidding of God, who alone is in command of the situation (see 21:18, a Lukan addition picking up 12:7). God's direction of the events is implicitly claimed by the assurance that these things happen in order to fulfill scripture: "Was it not necessary that the Christ should suffer these things and enter into his glory?" (24:26; cf. 22:15 f.).

Not only must these things happen, but they also have to be observed by the disciples, especially the apostles. For after Jesus is gone, "this will be a time for you to bear testimony" (21:13; cf. Mark 13:10; see especially Luke 24:48). To insure this witness the apostles, disciples, and women of Galilee are constant companions of Jesus. It is especially important for the apostles to be with Jesus (22:14; cf. Mark 14:17). We learn in Acts that an apostle is one who "beginning from the baptism of John until the day when he was taken up from us" was constantly with Jesus (Acts 1:21–26). The apostles continue with Jesus in his trials (22:28); they follow Jesus to the Mount of Olives (22:39; cf. Mark 14:26), and even when they fall asleep, it was "for sorrow" (22:45; cf. Mark 14:37). Luke omits Mark's statement, "And they all forsook him and fled" (14:50). At the crucifixion, "all his acquaintances and the women who had followed him from Galilee stood at a distance and saw these things" (23:49; cf. Mark 15:40 f.). Luke insists that ministers of the word based their testimony on eyewitness reports. They observed in order that the truth about these things might be known (see Luke 1:1–4).

The story of the empty tomb, which precedes the road to Emmaus story, bears out these preliminary observations (24:1–12, cf. Mark 16:1–8). Two men greet the women instead of a single young man (cf. Mark 16:5). This twofold witness guarantees authenticity (see pp. 145 ff.). Luke also subtly changes what had been a prediction of Jesus' resurrection appearances in Galilee into a statement about what Jesus said while he was in Galilee (24:6; cf. Mark 16:7). This change brings his text into harmony with Luke's view that the resurrection appearances were in Jerusalem (cf. Matt. 28:16). Luke's Gospel shows a clear, straight-forward development: beginning in Galilee, extending to Jerusalem, and from there to the rest of the world (24:47). Moreover, Luke's story of the empty tomb points ahead to the confirmatory appearances to the disciples, for when the apostles hear the report from the women, "these words seemed to them an idle tale, and they did not believe them" (24:11).[25] Luke's stress upon both continuity and certainty required more than an account by excited

---

[25] In Luke the empty tomb narrative is subordinate to Jesus' appearance on the road to Emmaus. See Paul Schubert, "The Structure and Significance of Luke 24," *Neutestamentliche Studien für Rudolf Bultmann* (ZNW, Beiheft 21; Berlin: Topelmann, 1952), p. 172.

women. Full recognition of the resurrected Jesus occurs only on the road to Emmaus (24:13 ff.).[26]

The followers of Jesus are on the road to Emmaus, where they meet the risen Christ. This meeting takes place "on the road," perhaps in keeping with the journey motif of Luke; for this encounter will prepare the disciples for their preaching throughout the Roman world. Furthermore, we hear twice in this episode about "the things that have happened" (24:14, 18); indeed, Jesus asks, "What things?" (24:19). These lines recall the Gospel's introduction, for this was to be a narrative about "the things which have been accomplished among us" (1:1; cf. 1:4).[27]

The puzzling thing about this story is the initial nonrecognition of Jesus by the men. Perhaps they were kept from recognizing him because God willed it thus (vs. 16). Yet why did God want to keep them from recognizing Jesus? Probably they failed to recognize him because of their preoccupation with the tragic events of the preceding days (vss. 19–21). Jesus proceeds to interpret the scriptures to show that the Christ did have to suffer in order to enter into his glory (vss. 26 f.). Jesus' role in God's plan was that of a suffering servant (see 22:37; Isaiah 53:12). Even this disclosure, however, does not enable them to recognize Jesus, although later they recall, "Did not our hearts burn within us while he talked to us on the road, while he opened to us the scriptures?" (vs. 32).

The crucial moment of recognition comes only during the meal: "Their eyes were opened and they recognized him; and he vanished out of their sight" (vs. 31). Later their report confirms that the decisive act was "the breaking of the bread" (vs. 35). There are at least two immediate possibilities for understanding the significance of the "breaking of bread": (1) Jesus performed a familiar act which they had often observed; therefore, they recognized him; (2) the "breaking of bread" was a sacramental communal act of worship in the early church (Acts 2:42, 46), and Luke thereby implies that the believer knows the resurrected Jesus primarily in the sacrament of the church. Neither view is wholly satisfying. The first ignores the fact that Jesus must have done other familiar things on the way, and the second presupposes a strong sacramental emphasis not otherwise present in Luke.

A different interpretation takes its cue from the act of eating. In the following story (24:36–43), even though Jesus appeals directly to the disciples and tells them to look at his hands and feet, they still "disbelieved for joy" (vs. 41). Only after he has eaten does he speak his farewell address.

---

[26] Although this story appears only in Luke, caution should be exercised in attributing it to him. An argument against its Lukan authorship is that the two disciples who encounter Jesus are not apostles (24:33). Indeed, they are unknown in the rest of the Gospel tradition.

[27] This relationship is weakened by the fact that the Greek is not identical in 1:1, 4; 24:14, 18. But interpretation does not depend upon an identity of wording; in both instances the passages reflect the intention of the entire Gospel.

"Supper at Emmaus" by Rembrandt (1606–1669). (*Courtesy of Alinari-Art Reference Bureau.*)

Again, eating seems to be crucial for full recognition. The closest previous reference to eating was the last supper with the apostles (22:14–19), at which Jesus said, "I have earnestly desired to eat this passover with you before I suffer; for I tell you I shall not eat until it is fulfilled in the kingdom of God" (vss. 15 f.; only in Luke). Evidently, Jesus will not eat until suffering is accomplished. That he now eats with the disciples indicates that his suffering has been completed and that he is now raised to glory. Therefore, in Luke the scripture interpretation emphasizes the necessity for suffering (24:26 f.), and the eating with the disciples (24:30, 35, 42 f.) emphasizes that the suffering is accomplished and the glory of Jesus has begun. With that sure foundation, the church can now receive its charge from the risen Christ.

Jesus' final words to the disciples suggest the plausibility of this interpretation (24:44–49). The redemption of Israel is effected by Jesus' suffering, which fulfills scripture (vss. 45 f.). Repentance and forgiveness of sins are to be preached beginning from Jerusalem and extending to all the world (vs. 47). The witnesses who have observed and who will now testify await only the coming of the Spirit (vss. 48 f.; cf. Acts 1:8).

Because Jesus' word and deed is now accomplished and because his followers can continue the witness, the new Israel returns to the temple with joy and with Jesus' blessing (24:50–53).

166

In summary, the purpose of the Gospel of Luke, like that of Mark and Matthew, is religious proclamation and reflection more than historical reporting. This characterization does not mean that there is no history recorded in Luke. Of all the Gospel writers Luke is the most consciously interested in preserving the truth about the life of Jesus. But for him, as for most so-called "historians" in the first century, truth is not equated with historical data. Luke intended for his reader to see the life of Jesus through a proper perspective, that of the third generation. He wrote so that careful observation and a comprehensive outlook would be available to the church of his day.

As a convenient means of reviewing results, we shall now break down our presentation under our four stages for understanding a Gospel:

The *structure* of Luke is distinctive. Only Luke follows his Gospel on Jesus with a second volume on the early church. In itself this structure indicates Luke's interest not only in Jesus, but also in the church which he originated. A long-range perspective on the life of Jesus is also suggested by the preface, where Luke writes of three stages of the tradition: eye-witnesses, ministers of the word, and writing of the Gospel.

In Luke's introduction Simeon, a man of Israel who has long awaited salvation, is finally rewarded by Jesus' appearance to him in the temple. Toward the close of his life Jesus frequents the temple and, in effect, triumphs in this central religious institution of Israel. After Jesus' death and resurrection the disciples return to the temple in order to wait for the coming of the Spirit, which will empower their preaching of repentance and forgiveness to all people. Their testimony to Jesus' message is certain because they have observed its beginning from Galilee to Jerusalem.

This overall view of Luke is confirmed by the threefold division of the Gospel itself: gathering witnesses in Galilee (3:1–9:50), witness to the word on the journey to Jerusalem (9:51–19:27), and the establishment of the true Israel through the passion and resurrection (19:28–24:53). These main divisions show how the old is incorporated into the new. Israel is on a journey through the Old Testament culminating in the life of Jesus and moving into the early church. Luke's structure is devised to insure that the journey has been closely recorded and presented in the correct order.

The frequent *emphases* of Luke confirm our proposed structure for the Gospel. A classification of emphases, though somewhat artificial, does help to clarify major points of Luke's stress. These include: the new faith as the true Israel, the history of salvation's expansion to include world history, and the necessity for accurate and continuous witness.

Luke affirms that the new religion is the true Israel. What happened to Jesus occurred according to the word of God, known through the Old Testament. For example, Jesus' first public act is to preach fulfillment of the prophet Isaiah in the synagogue at Nazareth (4:16 ff.). Moreover, at the resurrection appearances Jesus interprets his suffering as a fulfillment of scriptures (24:27, 44). A further emphasis supporting the theme of "the true Israel" is the centrality accorded the temple and Jerusalem. The Gospel opens with Zechariah in the temple in Jerusalem; at the introduction's close, Jesus is placed in Jerusalem in the temple. The journey section of the Gospel moves toward Jerusalem, "he set his face to go to Jerusalem" (9:51; cf. 13:33). The passion centers primarily on Jesus' teaching in the temple (19:47 f.). In addition, the Gospel closes with the disciples' return to the temple in Jerusalem (24:52 f.). This elaborate picture of Jesus in the temple and in Jerusalem implies that Jesus embodies the true Israel and that his followers are the authentic people of God.

The second major emphasis of Luke is that the true Israel aims to embrace the whole world. For Luke, the world outside Israel is not an adversary, but a mission field: Luke-Acts progresses from Galilee to Jerusalem and on to Rome. Furthermore, Luke records traces of world history (2:1; 3:1; also Acts 24:27) in order to keep this final goal in mind. Involvement with the world occurs by God's acting in the Spirit through the person of Jesus (Luke) and eyewitnesses and ministers of the word (Acts) to bring "truth" to all people (Luke 24:47 and Acts 2:38 f.). Luke's Christianity is universalistic: Simeon speaks about salvation "to the Gentiles" (2:32); Jesus' genealogy goes back to Adam (3:38); and Jesus' opening preaching speaks favorably of Gentiles (4:24–29). Of course, the second volume shows the extension of the new religion beyond the confines of the old Israel (Acts 10:1–11:18). Furthermore, this Gospel speaks about women (Mary and Elizabeth, chaps. 1–2; Mary and Martha, 10:38 ff.; and so on) and includes the poor and humble (2:8–20; 4:18; 6:20 *passim*). The new religion is subversive neither to Israel nor the Roman government. Jesus is innocent of the charges brought against him. This theme is developed at greater length in Acts in connection with the early Church.

The final major Lukan emphasis is witness (1:2), which consists of accurate observation (eyewitnesses) and truthful testifying (ministers of the word). Apostles, disciples, and women accompanied Jesus throughout his ministry; they in turn became, or were followed by, preachers who declared Jesus' own themes of repentance and forgiveness (Luke 15; 24:47; Acts 2:38). Forgiveness begins with the divine initiative, irrespective of human action; Jesus' actions embody this forgiveness in the present (7:48). Yet forgiveness elicits a human response of repentance. Whoever receives the forgiveness or mercy of God acts without anxiety for the future coming of God's judgment (cf. 19:1–10). In Jesus salvation becomes available (4:21; cf. 23:43); therefore, the ministers and preachers of the early church testify to what God has done in Jesus and continues to do for the committed (Acts 4:31 f.).

These things are presented as sure because all were predicted and foretold in the scriptures. The witness of Jesus began and ended with correct interpretation of the scripture. Jesus' conviction and crucifixion were a monumental mistake, according to Luke (23:14); at the same time Jesus was the suffering servant of Isaiah for all people (22:37). Jesus was finally recognized after his resurrection in that the disciples came to acknowledge his role of suffering (24:26, 46). As witnesses they were to preach the "good news" (2:10; 3:18; 4:18; 7:22; 16:16) of forgiveness and repentance.

Luke's *redaction* of the tradition has been consistently used as a key in the establishment of Luke's emphases. Luke's shaping of Mark—for example—in the parables of the sower (8:4–21) and the wicked tenants (20:9–18), disclosed his emphasis on the word of God (8:11) and the true Israel (20:9).

There have been many attempts to identify precisely the *historical situation* of Luke, none of them unexceptionable. Our interpretation, instead of precisely locating the historical situation in which Luke was written, views the Gospel generally as an apology. It was not designed primarily to convert the unbeliever, but it speaks principally to Christians and "almost" Christians, showing the continuity and certainty of the Christian faith. According to Luke, the journey of Christian faith is made in joy and victory. The life and work of the church at Luke's time is authentic, according to the scriptures, because the true Israel is emerging and because the world is slowly and surely being Christianized. The forgiving Jesus is presented as standing both as the fulfillment of the old and the sure originator of the new. The witnesses have not been arbitrarily chosen; they were prepared for their task, and their present successes show the sweep and power of the new way.

Luke's Gospel has something of the romance about it. There are women, there are journeys and quests, there are successful adventures. At the end of the Gospel the disciples are in the temple blessing God and waiting for the Spirit's coming with power for the mission. At the end of Acts of the Apostle Paul is preaching in Rome and things will turn out well. Luke idealizes the story, perhaps, but he thereby testifies to the faith and history of Jesus and the early church. What was founded by Jesus, observed by the apostles, and proclaimed by them will continue without faltering until all have come into the kingdom of God and the fellowship of the Lord Jesus Christ "quite openly and unhindered" (Acts 28:31).

Suggestions for Further Reading

Worthwhile commentaries include A. R. C. Leaney in the Harper series (1958); G. B. Caird, *The Gospel of St. Luke** (Baltimore: Penguin Books, 1963); and B. S. Easton, *The Gospel according to St. Luke* (New

York: Scribner's, 1926). The most important single study of the theology of Luke-Acts is H. Conzelmann, *The Theology of St. Luke,* trans. G. Buswell (London: Faber and Faber, 1960). A valuable summary of scholarship is C. K. Barrett, *Luke the Historian in Recent Study* (London: Epworth Press, 1961). An important collection of articles on the work of Luke, L. E. Keck and J. L. Martyn (eds.), *Studies in Luke-Acts* (New York: Abingdon, 1966), honors Professor Paul Schubert. Old, but still pertinent, H. J. Cadbury, *The Making of Luke-Acts* (New York: Macmillan, 1927), marked out the direction that the following generation of scholarship would take. Most recently H. Flender, *St. Luke: Theologian of Redemptive History,* trans. R. H. and I. Fuller (Philadelphia: Fortress, 1967), has taken issue with Conzelmann at a number of points.

5 Jesus
The Messiah:
A Portrait

Introduction: The Tradition About Jesus
    A. Kerygma, Gospels, and Jesus of Nazareth
    B. The Basic Tradition of Jesus
  I. The Healing Messiah
          Matthew 8:17*
    A. Miracles in the First Century
    B. Miracles in the Synoptic Gospels
      1. The Eschatological Context
          Luke 7:18–23; Matthew 12:28; Mark 8:11 f.
      2. Three Types of Miracles
          Mark 1:40–45; 6:30–44; 4:35–41; 5:21–43
      3. Miracles and Faith
          Mark 6:5 f.; 14:36
    C. Miracles in the Twentieth Century
 II. The Teaching Messiah
    A. The Proclamation of the Kingdom of God
      1. The Kingdom as Present and Future
          Matthew 12:28; Luke 17:20 f.; Mark 1:14 f.;
          Matthew 6:10
      2. Jesus and Apocalypticism
          Mark 13; Luke 17:20 f.
      3. The Kingdom and the Parables
          Matthew 13

*Passages for special attention

Introduction: The Tradition About Jesus

To write a "life of Jesus" is impossible. We cannot accurately understand or portray Jesus' chronological and psychological development. The reason for this state of affairs is readily apparent, for the nature of the sources for Jesus' life does not permit this kind of historical reconstruction.

Sources for the historical Jesus outside the Synoptic Gospels are extremely meager. Perhaps the most important non-Christian passage comes from the *Annals* of the Roman historian, Tacitus (early second century), who reports the false accusation by Nero that Christians were responsible for the disastrous fire in Rome (A.D. 64). Another probable Roman reference to Jesus occurs in the biography of the Emperor Claudius by Suetonius (second century), "He [Claudius] expelled from Rome the Jews who, under the influence of Chrestos, did not cease to agitate" (XXV, 4). The first century Jewish historian, Josephus, recounted Jewish history during the period of Jesus' life, but, although he described the Essenes and John the Baptist in some detail, Jesus is barely mentioned. When the Christian embellishments of the text are cleared away, Josephus refers only to "James, the brother of Jesus who was called the Christ" (*Jewish Antiquities*, 9:1). Polemical references to Jesus in the Jewish Talmud contain little independent tradition about Jesus.[1] Although no early non-Christian source questions the historical existence of Jesus, at the same time the literature takes little notice of him.

Quantitatively more extensive sources for the historical Jesus are the apocryphal Gospels. These Gospels, which did not become part of the Christian New Testament canon, can be divided into two basic types. Jewish-Christian Gospels provide additional stories about Jesus, especially his hidden childhood. Much of this material, like the infancy Gospel of Thomas and the Gospel of Peter, helped satisfy pious curiosity and served to entertain the faithful. Gnostic Gospels, like the Gospel of Phillip and the Nag Hammadi Gospel of Thomas, present a secret teaching of Jesus which elaborates a way higher than that given in the common Gospel tradition.[2] Although the apocryphal Gospels offer much additional teaching and narrative material, they are fundamentally valueless for reconstructing the historical Jesus. The Jewish-Christian Gospels are characterized by a grotesque appeal to vulgar taste and are obviously fictitious. The Gnostic Gospels are marked by an esoteric wisdom that renders Jesus' message and mission unintelligible save to the initiated few.

Another source for the historical Jesus is the so-called *agrapha*, sayings attributed to Jesus and preserved outside the canonical Gospels—for example, the word of Jesus handed down by Acts, "It is more blessed to give than to receive" (20:35).[3] Although some of these sayings may be authentic, they are relatively few and do not greatly affect understanding of the historical Jesus.

Astonishingly little tradition about Jesus occurs in the literature of the New Testament apart from the Gospels. On two occasions Paul refers to the tradition of the Lord which he had received (I Cor. 11:23–26; 15:3 f.; cf. 7:10, 12, 25). These Pauline exceptions prove the rule: little tradition of Jesus exists in the latter half of the New Testament.[4]

---

[1] For a listing and discussion of these references, see Maurice Goguel, *Jesus and the Origins of Christianity*, I, trans. Olive Wyon (New York: Harper & Row, 1960), pp. 70–104, and Joseph Klausner, *Jesus of Nazareth*, trans. Herbert Danby (Boston: Beacon Press, 1964), pp. 17–62.

[2] For the text of the apocryphal Gospels, excepting the Gnostic Gospels of Nag Hammadi, see M. R. James, *The Apocryphal New Testament*. For a discussion of all apocryphal Gospels, their origin and purpose, see Hennecke-Schneemelcher, *New Testament Apocrypha*, I.

[3] See Joachim Jeremias, *The Unknown Sayings of Jesus*, trans. R. H. Fuller (London: SPCK, 1957).

[4] Our exclusion of the Gospel of John from the tradition to be used for understanding the historical Jesus derives from three basic observations: (1) the striking dissimilarity

The principal sources for knowing the historical Jesus are the Synoptic Gospels, but they do not include the information necessary for a biography. In previous chapters, we have learned that the Synoptics have only secondary chronological, psychological, and factual interest. Yet their concern for proclamation of good news took the form of telling the story of Jesus. Although we cannot know every detail about his life, these Gospels do give sufficient material to portray the historical Jesus with some certainty.

In this chapter we will attempt to reconstruct one portrait of Jesus of Nazareth which emerges out of the three Synoptic portraits. Our justification for this procedure lies not only in contemporary historical interest in Jesus, but also in inclusion of, not one, but three Gospel portraits in the New Testament. The three Synoptics invite an encounter once again with the historical Jesus of Nazareth.

KERYGMA, GOSPELS, AND JESUS OF NAZARETH

At the beginning of the church was the kerygma (preaching). In the introductory chapter we characterized kerygma as the word of the cross, the message about what God had done through Jesus' death and resurrection. According to the early Christian kerygma the event of death and resurrection was both the act of Jesus of Nazareth and the act of God.[5]

In one sense the kerygma announced that Jesus now had to be viewed in light of the resurrection. Faith believed that the one who died a criminal's death was also raised by God, "Let all the house of Israel therefore know assuredly that God has made him both Lord and Christ, this Jesus whom you crucified" (Acts 2:36). Hearers of this message did not first think of the historical Jesus, for believers were primarily conscious of the power of God's new life. This kerygma's power did not, however, rest in new knowledge or wisdom but rather in an event—the death and resurrection of Jesus.

The kerygma's concentration upon event is the seed from which the Gospels originated, for the Gospels are based upon the kerygma. Although

---

between the Synoptic portrait of Jesus and that of the Fourth Gospel; (2) the difficulty of identifying and assessing the sources of John's Gospel; and (3) the highly theological nature of the material of this Gospel. This negative judgment concerning the historical usefulness of the Fourth Gospel in no way minimizes the significance of this Gospel within the Christian canon.

[5] See C. H. Dodd's *The Apostolic Preaching and Its Developments* (New York: Harper & Row, 1951), especially pp. 7–35; Oscar Cullmann, *Christ and Time: The Primitive Christian Conception of Time and History*, trans. F. V. Filson (Philadelphia: Westminster Press, 1950), especially pp. 121–130; Rudolf Bultmann, *Theology of the New Testament*, I, trans. K. Grobel (New York: Charles Scribner's Sons, 1954), especially pp. 42–53.

we will not use the Fourth Gospel as a source for the historical Jesus, the words with which this Gospel closes are also applicable to the Synoptics, "These (things) are written that you may believe that Jesus is the Christ, the Son of God, and that believing you may have life in his name" (John 20:31). This also was the purpose of the kerygma. Even the tradition of Jesus that came to the Gospel writers from oral tradition and written sources was already, down to individual units, shaped by the kerygma. In fact, early Christians remembered the tradition of Jesus only because they were convinced that God had acted for them in this man, especially in his death and resurrection.

Yet no matter how much the Gospels may have been indebted to the kerygma, they were also history. The Gospels show that Christian faith is not based upon myth. The early Christians believed that the source of life and faith within their community was ultimately God, but the means of God's action was Jesus of Nazareth. From our reading of the Synoptic Gospels, it has become evident that the writers show loyalty to the tradition of Jesus, at the same time exercising freedom toward it. This freedom was a natural corollary of the early community's conviction that Jesus was not dead but had been raised to live and speak as their Lord. Their loyalty to the tradition reflected their conviction that the risen Christ was always also the historical Jesus.

THE BASIC TRADITION OF JESUS

Although the Gospels do not always record the exact deeds and words of Jesus, they do portray the historical Jesus as well as the Christ of faith. In our treatment of the tradition of Jesus, we will make use of the following guidelines in trying to identify the truly historical materials: (1) A solid *core* of authentic tradition about Jesus can be identified "when there are no grounds either for deriving a tradition from Judaism or for ascribing it to primitive Christianity, and especially when Jewish Christianity has mitigated or modified the received tradition, as . . . too bold for its taste."[6] (2) By working with broad cross sections of the tradition, such as Jesus' teaching about the kingdom, his interpretation of the law, his miracle deeds, his crucifixion, and so on,[7] we seek to form a *coherent* portrait of the one historical figure who stimulated this varied tradition. Once a coherent core picture begins to take shape, other tradition of similar emphasis and intent may be added to fill out our portrait of Jesus.

[6] Ernst Käsemann, "The Problem of the Historical Jesus," *Essays on New Testament Themes,* trans. W. J. Montague (SBT, 41; Napierville, Ill.: Allenson, 1964), p. 37.

[7] See N. A. Dahl, "The Problem of the Historical Jesus," *Kerygma and History,* trans. and ed. C. E. Braaten and R. A. Harrisville (New York: Abingdon, 1962), pp. 138–171, esp. 153 f.

Our coherent picture is neither a collection of facts about Jesus nor an interpretation of him. We are neither so empirical that we want only the facts nor so idealistic that we want only the meaning of Jesus. Yet we do acknowledge that the basic tradition of Jesus does include facts. Not all facts we might desire are included, such as details of Jesus' physical appearance, educational background, home environment, and so on. There are, however, factual materials basic to the Synoptic Gospels which have to do with the *miracles* of Jesus, his *teaching*, and his *death*.

The existence of these three separate strands of the basic tradition raises the question of their interrelationship. A coherent picture of Jesus must somehow show how the three major tradition areas unite in one historical figure. How, for example, does the powerful Jesus who performs miracles relate to the Jesus who is powerless to prevent his own death?

The basic tradition of Jesus includes not only facts, but meaning. The early Christians did not feel free to read any meaning into Jesus. They saw his deeds, words, and death in the light of the commonly held conviction that he was the Messiah. Therefore, in our presentation, we speak of the healing Messiah, the teaching Messiah, and the suffering Messiah.[8] The Synoptic Gospels unanimously and unequivocally see all three main aspects of Jesus' mission and message as messianic, and our reconstruction takes this into account. The reconstruction of such a portrait does not, however, prove that Jesus was the Messiah; it only makes this messianic claim comprehensible in terms of tradition.

In this chapter we do not contradict, but continue to depend upon the three portraits of Jesus that appeared in the Synoptic Gospels. They in turn complement rather than contradict one another, for each evangelist looked at Jesus from a different perspective. They were concerned less about exactness in detail than about being true to Jesus in their respective portraits. Something of the same freedom and loyalty should accompany our study of the basic tradition of Jesus.

The Healing Messiah

The most characteristic miracles in the Synoptics are Jesus' healings, including the exorcism of demons, which Mark especially emphasizes. After reporting three healings by Jesus, Matthew summarizes the meaning of Jesus' miracles as follows, "This was to fulfill what was spoken by the prophet Isaiah, 'He took our infirmities and bore our diseases'" (Matt.

[8] For this typology we are indebted to Paul Meyer, Professor of New Testament at Colgate-Rochester Divinity School. He is not, of course, responsible for our elaboration.

8:17; cf. Isaiah 53:4). Similarly, when John the Baptist's disciples ask Jesus whether he is the one to come or whether they should look for another, Jesus replies, "Go and tell John what you have seen and heard: the blind receive their sight, the lame walk, lepers are cleansed, and the deaf hear, the dead are raised up, the poor have good news preached to them. And blessed is he who takes no offense at me" (Luke 7:22 f.; see Matt. 11:4–6; cf. Isaiah 29:18 f., 35:5 f., 61:1). The miracles are done by Jesus in order to heal, to bring health. Therefore, in our presentation the miracle Jesus is designated as the healing Messiah. He both ministers to the needs of people and in the evangelists' view he fulfills the Old Testament's expectation of messianic activity.

Miracle stories comprise a large part of each of the Gospels. Nearly one-third of the Gospel of Mark is devoted to healings. Matthew and Luke report practically all the Markan miracles and add others. Approximately thirty-five miracles are reported in the Synoptics. In Peter's first speech to the Gentiles, no mention is made of Jesus' teaching, but the good news includes "how God anointed Jesus of Nazareth with the Holy Spirit and with power; how he went about doing good and healing all that were oppressed by the devil" (Acts 10:38). Even the Jewish Talmud acknowledges that Jesus healed, but dismisses his work as that of a sorcerer.[9] Contemporary stress on Jesus' teachings has to reckon with the unequivocal Synoptic evidence that one of Jesus' principal activities was healing.

In the Synoptic Gospels, however, Jesus' miracles are not used as powerful signs to prove his messiahship; in fact, Mark seems deliberately to combat this tendency within the tradition (see pp. 82 ff.). When the crowds gathered around Jesus after many healings, his friends "went out to seize him, for they said, 'He is beside himself.' And the scribes who came down from Jerusalem said, 'He is possessed by Beelzebub, and by the prince of demons he casts out demons'" (Mark 3:21 f.). Thus healing miracles could be the work of God or of the devil; they do not prove messiahship. Indeed, according to one major New Testament strain Jesus' power is not in mighty words, but in his crucifixion and death. Christ crucified is "to those who are called, both Jews and Greeks . . . the *power* of God and the wisdom of God" (I Cor. 1:24). Moreover, to desire miracles as proof of Jesus' messiahship would be to seek after signs (cf. I Cor. 1:22). When the Pharisees come to Jesus asking for a sign, he replies, "An evil and adulterous generation seeks for a sign; but no sign shall be given to it except the sign of the prophet Jonah" (Matt. 12:39; see Mark 8:12).

Before looking more closely at miracles in the Synoptic Gospels, we need to understand the first century's view of miracles so that the Synoptic tradition is set within its environment. This, in turn, will set the stage for our final section when we look at miracles from the modern perspective.

---

[9] See Klausner, *Jesus of Nazareth*, pp. 27 f.

MIRACLES IN THE FIRST CENTURY

How did the ancient world view miracles?
Were there other miracle workers?

In the first century, indeed in the New Testament itself, Jesus is not the only miracle worker. Simon the Magician is said to have done great wonders and amazed people by his magic. Moreover, he tried to buy the Spirit from the apostles and was refused because according to Peter the gift of God could not be obtained with money (Acts 8:9–24). Simon desired the Spirit because the disciples performed signs and great miracles (Acts 5:12). The apostle Paul himself performed wonders (II Cor. 12:12). Even the rabbis, who were known primarily as teachers, performed miracles. Onias, the Circlemaker, a rabbi in the first century B.C., is reported to have made it rain for Israel neither too fiercely nor too gently, but in moderattion. A famous miracle worker in Greek literature was Apollonius of Tyana, a Pythagorean philosopher who lived during most of the first Christian century.[10] He is reported to have miraculously exorcised a demon from a young man who later became a philosopher and a miracle worker himself.

Within this context the miracles of Jesus are not quite so unusual. In fact, some early Christians felt constrained to enlarge the miracle activity of Jesus beyond what is reported in the Synoptics. Consequently, in the apocryphal Gospels bigger and better miracles are attributed to Jesus. According to the infancy Gospel of Thomas, Jesus reportedly fetches water for his mother with a garment instead of a pitcher. When the carpenter Joseph discovers that one of the boards for a bed is too short, then his son Jesus corrects the situation by stretching the board to the proper length. In the Gospel of James, Jesus makes twelve clay birds that become real birds after he claps his hands. When a young boy disturbs a pool of water in which Jesus is playing, Jesus withers him as if he were a tree.[11] Under the influence of popular piety Jesus became a real magician. Miracle stories served both to entertain the pious and to support their belief that Jesus was the Christ, the Son of God.

This brief glance at miracles in the ancient world makes us aware of the different "miracle world" of the Synoptic Gospels. We might inquire, however, whether the tendency to make Jesus a bigger and better miracle worker was not already at work in the oral tradition that circulated before the Synoptic Gospels were written. We will be interested to see whether the Synoptic Gospels furthered or checked the tendency toward the miraculous.

---

[10] C. K. Barrett, *The New Testament Background: Selected Documents*, pp. 150 f., 76–79.

[11] See James, *The Apocryphal New Testament*, pp. 63, 49 f.

MIRACLES IN THE SYNOPTIC GOSPELS

In what context do miracles occur in the Synoptic Gospels?
Why does Jesus resist the demand for miracles?
What are the types of miracles? Do they share anything in common?
What is the relation between faith and miracles?

The Synoptic Gospels do not contain the word *miracle*. Miracle is a modern term that, according to Webster, describes an occurrence contrary to known scientific laws. Because the evangelists wrote at a time in which there was no commonly accepted concept of "known scientific laws," they understood miracles as powers, wonders, mighty words, signs. These strange, remarkable happenings caused people to be amazed and terrified, and to wonder whether these occurrences were the power of God (the good) or of Satan (the evil). Remembering this, we may nevertheless, for convenience's sake, speak about miracles in the Synoptic Gospels. The term roughly corresponds to the reported events.

To understand miracles in Jesus' ministry in the Synoptics, we must first take account of the view of the world and history in which they are set, then attempt to classify the miracles according to type, and finally explore the relation of miracles to faith.

The Eschatological Context

The proclamation of the kingdom of God dominates the preaching and teaching of Jesus. We have already noted that John the Baptist's disciples inquired of Jesus whether he was the expected one (Luke 7:18–23; Matt. 11:2–6). This scene implies a question about whether the kingdom of God is already present or approaching, for the kingdom and the messiah were closely related in Jewish apocalyptic thought. In fact, Jesus answers the implied question about the kingdom rather than the direct messianic one, as he points to what is happening in miracles, healings, and the preaching of good news to the poor (Luke 7:22 f.). These occurrences fulfill the Old Testament prophecy (Isaiah 29:18 f.; 35:5 f.; 61:1), as Luke makes quite clear. When Jesus speaks at the Nazareth synagogue, he proclaims that the promises of the scriptures—release of the captives, sight to the blind, good news to the poor, release for the oppressed—are fulfilled that day in him (Luke 4:16–21). In short, Jesus' miracles are signs that the eschatological kingdom of God is breaking in.

This linking of Jesus' activity and the present irruption of the kingdom is found elsewhere in the Synoptic Gospels. According to first century Jewish thought, the activity of the Spirit of God ceased with the close of prophecy and would reappear on earth only at the end time.[12] Now, through the teaching and healing of Jesus, the Spirit of God is said to be manifested. Jesus says, "But if it is by the Spirit of God that I cast out demons, then the kingdom of God has come upon you" (Matt. 12:28; cf. Luke 11:20). When the seventy are sent on a mission, their healing of the sick is to be accompanied by the words, "The kingdom of God has come near to you" (Luke 10:9). When Jesus and his disciples heal, the defeat of Satan and the reign of God begin.

The breaking in of the kingdom of God in the miracle activity of Jesus is not, however, the kingdom's final realization.[13] The miracles signify an inaugurated kingdom, not a completed one. This setting of Jesus' miracles within the context of "inaugurated eschatology" has at least three implications: (1) The nature of the irrupting kingdom defines the meaning of the miracles rather than the reverse; the kingdom's promise includes and extends beyond physical healing, as the exorcisms already suggest. (2) The miracles point to the working of God rather than the status of Jesus. God's kingdom, not the rule of Jesus, is inaugurated. (3) These miracles or wonders are ambiguous and can be viewed as either the work of God or of Satan.

Modern man's first and last questions about the miracles, "Did they happen?" and "How did they occur?" start from a different perspective from that of the New Testament. Consequently, modern "Christian" historical critics, embarrassed by the miracles, often try to rationalize them. For example, Jesus' feeding of the five thousand is explained as a sharing of food prompted by a young boy's display of generosity. When the people saw his willingness to share his meager lunch, they also brought out their loaves and shared with others. Jesus' walking on the water was a product of the disciples' delusion, for Jesus was only walking close to the shore. Or perhaps Jesus' healings were accomplished through his exceptional knowledge of the nervous system and of medicines.[14] This modern, reductionistic explanation of miracles reflects a too-simple notion of historical events. Tyrannized by a cause-and-effect relationship, the critic assumes that every effect must have a comparable cause and that his task is to locate precisely the cause, just as people still, for example, talk naively about the "three causes" of the French Revolution. But this treatment oversimplifies the origins of Christian faith in the event of Jesus, for the New Testament

[12] See G. W. H. Lampe, "Holy Spirit," *IDB*, II, pp. 626–638; cf. also Acts 2:17–21 and Joel 2:28–32.

[13] Cf. the proponent of "realized eschatology," C. H. Dodd: "Miracles in the Gospel," *ET*, 44 (1932–33), pp. 504–509; Dodd, *The Parables of the Kingdom*, rev. ed. (New York: Charles Scribner's Sons, 1961); and Norman Perrin, *The Kingdom of God in the Teaching of Jesus* (Philadelphia: Westminster Press, 1963), pp. 58–74.

[14] See Albert Schweitzer, *The Quest of the Historical Jesus*, trans. W. Montgomery (3rd ed.; London: Adam & Charles Black, 1954), p. 52, who describes the efforts of the nineteenth century rationalist, Heinrich Paulus, to rid the Gospels of miracles.

miracles claim that an extraordinary time, that of the irrupting kingdom of God, accompanied Jesus' healings. The so-called historian's question, Did Jesus perform miracles? pales into insignificance beside the Synoptics' question, Was the kingdom being inaugurated in Jesus' miracles? To trivialize that question by rationalizing miracles does injustice to the claim of the Gospels.

A fairer basis for putting the question of whether Jesus performed miracles is to note more closely the intention of Jesus' miracles. Did Jesus heal as a magician for whom the world was bedeviled (thus Jesus subscribed to a metaphysical dualism of God and Satan as the two warring powers) or did he heal as one who knew the human heart with its demonic power and took possession of this heart for the God whom he declared present?[15] According to the latter view, Jesus upsets the ancient world's notion that demons cause evil; for Jesus thrusts man into the naked situation of being, by his own response, for or against God, not fate or the devil. Moreover, Jesus shatters the ancient distinction between the sacred and the profane (Mark 7:14–23) in that God's coming near means that God can be met at any place or at any time. In his healings Jesus faces man with God, frees him from control by the devil, and offers him the possibility of ministering to his fellow man in the Spirit of God. The consideration of the intention of Jesus' miracles does not solve the question of whether he actually performed them, but it places the question in the proper perspective.

Our interpretation of Jesus' intention receives support from the Synoptic tradition. Jesus refuses to use the miracles as signs to validate himself (Mark 8:11 f.; Matt. 12:39); not even Jesus can become a divine man. Similarly the temptation stories point to the presence of God, rather than to Jesus. In Mark (1:9–13) the Spirit does not separate Jesus from the world but drives him closer to it. In the other temptation accounts (Matt. 4:1–11; Luke 4:1–13) Jesus says in effect that God's will, not Satan's, matters. The healings bear witness to the kingdom's appearance, and to this extraordinary presence of God Jesus consistently and continually points in his message. God's coming, Jesus believes, touches everything, even Jesus' own death, so that Jesus cannot perform a miracle in order to save himself.

Three Types of Miracles

Now that we have discerned the framework of the proclamation of the kingdom in which the miracles occur, we turn for a closer look at the actual miracle stories themselves. The Synoptic Gospels contain basically four types: exorcisms, healings, resuscitations, and nature miracles. The first

---

[15] See Käsemann, *Essays on New Testament Themes*, pp. 39 f. Cf. elaboration of the contemporary meaning of Jesus' exorcisms by Harvey Cox, *The Secular City* (New York: Macmillan Co., 1965), pp. 149–154.

three have to do with changes in human subjects whereas the fourth involves changes in inanimate matter. Generally speaking, the exorcisms pertain to what we would call mental disorders and the healings to physical diseases. For our purposes they both can be treated under one heading—healings; therefore we are left with three major types of miracles: healings, nature miracles, and resuscitations.

An example of *healings*—the healing of the leper (Mark 1:40–45; cf. Matt. 8:1–4 and Luke 5:12–16)—illustrates why both exorcisms and physical healings belong together. Jesus' anger (1:43) is directed neither against the physical disease nor against the leper (note Jesus' compassion, vs. 41), but toward the demon that inhabits him. We may make several generalizations on the basis of this story. First of all, although the initiative for the healing comes partly from the leper himself, Jesus' presence breaks down fateful resignation to his illness (cf. Mark 2:4 f.; and so on). A new power is breaking through the old barrier dividing the clean from the unclean (cf. Leviticus 13:45). Second, this healing does not prove Jesus' messiahship, for Jesus acts simply out of compassion. Moreover, Jesus uses the ordinary channels for certification of a healing, sending the man to the priest. This is apparently done, not in order to establish the miraculous deed, but to emphasize the new "clean" existence God offers him. Third, Jesus commands the healed man to silence about the miracle. Whether this order comes from Mark or Jesus himself, its effect is to subordinate the role of Jesus' healing to his primary proclamation of the nearness of the kingdom of God.

The question of whether the miracle occurred may be illumined by the fact that the "leprosy" spoken of need not have been the incurable disease called by that name. Moreover, similar miracles have been attributed to others.[16] Nevertheless, such considerations are not decisive. There is an overall impression of authenticity, however, that stems from the fact that the miracle does not call attention to itself. The restraint in detail bespeaks its probable historicity. It is pointless, though, to offer scientific or psychological explanations of what happened; for although these are not ruled out in principle, they are purely speculation in light of the silence of the text about most matters of detail.

Two examples of *nature miracles* are the feeding of the five thousand (Mark 6:30–44; cf. Matt. 14:13–21 and Luke 9:10–17) and the stilling of the storm (Mark 4:35–41; cf. Matt. 8:18–27 and Luke 8:22–25). Both of these miracle stories were previously discussed; the feeding in our study of Mark (see pp. 81 f.) and the storm stilling in connection with Matthew (see pp. 112 f.). In comparing the three Synoptic accounts of the feeding

---

[16] See Rudolf Bultmann, *History of the Synoptic Tradition*, pp. 218–244. Also F. W. Beare, *The Earliest Records of Jesus: A Companion to the Synopsis of the First Three Gospels by Albert Huck* (New York: Abingdon Press, 1962), pp. 72–74.

"Christ with the Sick Around Him, Receiving Little Children" by Rembrandt (1606–1669). (Courtesy of Metropolitan Museum of Art, bequest of Mrs. H. O. Havemeyer, 1929.)

of the five thousand, we note a certain freedom in detail regarding the occasion of the miracle. They do agree, however, that Jesus is surrounded by hungry throngs at a place where food is not accessible. We cannot find a setting for an earlier, nonmiraculous version of the story; the central point is that of a miracle feeding, possibly with Eucharistic overtones.[17] It is absurd to explain this story as some kind of picnic in which Jesus and his disciples encourage the people to generosity. Yet when this is said, the question of whether such an incredible miracle took place remains still unanswered. The form of this story clearly reflects the Eucharistic practice of the early church (see Mark 6:41). Therefore, the miracle may be a postresurrection story, based upon the Christians' experience in the Lord's Supper that the living Christ feeds the hungry multitudes.[18] Such a conjecture is supported by the fact that this nature miracle does concentrate more upon the person and action of Jesus than do most other miracle stories. This emphasis on Jesus may reflect a concern of the early church more than the attitude of the historical Jesus. But again, the compassion upon the multitudes is what we would expect of Jesus of Nazareth. The essence of the story agrees with our evolving picture of the historical Jesus. The form, however, reflects the interests of the early church. Therefore,

[17] See Beare, *The Earliest Records of Jesus*, pp. 126 f.
[18] See Bultmann, *History of the Synoptic Tradition*, p. 230; cf. II Kings 4:42–44.

183

The Jordan River flowing into the Sea of Galilee from the north. (Courtesy of Israel Government Tourist Office.)

the historical critic is justified in questioning the historical probability of this miraculous feeding even apart from considerations of whether the event could have happened.

The stilling of the storm on the Sea of Galilee also belongs in the category of nature miracles (Mark 4:35–41 parr.). Its present form may obscure an earlier story about the exorcism of a storm demon (4:39; cf. 1:25). As it now reads, however, it demonstrates Jesus' authority over nature and challenges the disciples' lack of faith (4:40 f.). Moreover, this action by Jesus seems to embody that salvation ascribed to God in the Old Testament: "Who dost still the roaring of the seas, the roaring of their waves, the tumult of the peoples" (Psalm 65:7; cf. 89:9).[19] The entire miracle story makes Jesus the object of religious awe. Probably we have here a Christological confession, occasioned not by an incident out of Jesus' life but by the total impact of Jesus, particularly his death and resurrection. Although an actual historical kernel, such as Jesus' calm during a storm, may have originated the story, its present form centers exclusively on belief in Jesus and thus reflects the attitude of the postresurrection church.

[19] See Beare, *The Earliest Records of Jesus*, p. 121; cf. also Psalm 106:9, 107:23–32. Bultmann, *History of the Synoptic Tradition*, pp. 234 f., denies the relevance of the Psalm parallels.

An example of *resuscitations* is the story of the raising of Jairus' daughter (Mark 5:21–43; cf. Matt. 9:18–26 and Luke 8:40–56).[20] It is strangely interrupted by an account of the healing of the woman with the hemorrhage (Mark 5:25–34 parr.). Yet this break in the story of the resuscitation is not accidental, for the interlude illustrates the power of believing (cf. 5:36). The striking thing about the healing of the woman with the hemorrhage is its occurrence without Jesus' being aware of her presence. Consequently, Jesus cannot possibly intend the miracle (see 5:28–30). If the miracle happens without Jesus' intent, then in a sense the miracle happened to Jesus as well as the woman. This healing of the woman makes the point that belief in Jesus is actually faith in the power that works through Jesus rather than in Jesus himself (5:30, 34).

This understanding of belief is then taken up in the raising of Jairus' daughter (5:36). Jesus' raising of the dead girl might rest upon an actual incident in which he aroused a girl who was in a coma (cf. vss. 35 f., 39). As it now stands, however, it raises the question of whether belief in God goes so far as to affirm the victory of Jesus over death. Thus the story of Jesus' raising of Jairus' daughter possibly uses an actual incident of healing to affirm a central matter of faith, God's power to raise the dead.

Miracles and Faith

A consistent theme of all three types of miracle story is the response of faith, but what is the relation between faith and miracles? In the Gospel of Mark faith appears only in connection with miracles, but at the same time no one truly believes until after Jesus' death (14:50; cf. 15:39). One possible answer to the question of why the miracles did not produce lasting faith is that they were not miraculous enough; enduring faith could only result after the great miracle of Jesus' resurrection. But this suggestion ignores the obvious fact that many people believed Jesus' life ended with his death; not everyone believed in the resurrection. Moreover, the resurrection is not portrayed as a public event of the same order as the miracles.

Another view of the relation between faith and miracles maintains that faith is the triggering mechanism that produces miracles. God is always ready to perform miracles; consequently, if a person has faith, miracles occur. Support from the Synoptic Gospels for this understanding is found especially in such statements as, "And he (Jesus) could do no mighty work there, except that he laid his hands upon a few sick people and healed them. And he marveled because of their unbelief" (Mark 6:5 f.; cf. Matt. 13:58). Furthermore, Jesus replies to the woman with the hemorrhage, "Daughter, your faith has made you well; go in peace and be healed of your disease" (Mark 5:34 parr.). The disciples' astonishment at the

---

[20] Only two other resuscitations are reported by the Gospels, the raising of the widow of Nain's son (Luke 7:11–17) and of Lazarus (John 11:1–44). For parallels, see Bultmann, *History of the Synoptic Tradition*, pp. 233 f.

withered fig tree prompts Jesus to say, "Have faith in God. Truly, I say to you, whoever says to this mountain, 'Be taken up and cast into the sea,' and does not doubt in his heart, but believes that what he says will come to pass, it will be done for him" (Mark 11:22 f. and Matt. 21:21; cf. I Cor. 13:2).

Yet before we conclude that faith produces whatever the believer wishes, we should remember that according to the Gospels even Jesus did not have his own way. The temptation stories set the tempo for Jesus' entire life in that he denies his natural impulses. Moreover, in Gethsemane Jesus prays, "Abba, Father, all things are possible to thee, remove this cup from me; yet not what I will, but what thou wilt" (Mark 14:36 parr.). Because the cup was not removed, we can only conclude that faith is not an automatic device for accomplishing the will of Jesus or of the believer. Faith's ultimate object is God and His will. In the Gospels, faith means that man trusts, accepts, and responds affirmatively to the coming of God. If in some instances faith appears as the condition for a miracle, the reader ought not to conclude that this represents the fundamental understanding of faith in the Gospels, or even in the ministry of Jesus. The faith that Jesus demands is belief in the good news of his announcement of the coming of God and His kingdom. Everything else depends on such faith (Mark 1:15; 8:34–38; Matt. 12:28, and so on).

In essence, the question of whether Jesus did miracles becomes the question of whether God acted in Jesus, especially to raise him from the dead. This question cannot be answered apart from belief; no prior miracle establishes belief and belief cannot prove that the miracles happened. Nevertheless, faith makes the New Testament miracles comprehensible, although it cannot verify them. According to the Gospels a miracle produces change, for the believer "repents" and becomes a new person who lives out of the wonder performed for him. In later times no one would have thought twice about Jesus if such lasting change had not taken place. Undoubtedly Jesus did perform "miracles": the sick were healed, the people were terrified and amazed at his actions (see Mark 1:27; 2:12; 9:15). Yet these extraordinary acts were ambiguous and did not prove that Jesus was the Messiah. Some people saw this as the work of the devil; others saw and did not believe (cf. Mark 3:22). These events, like many at that time and many since, aroused temporary wonder, amazement, and faith. But in themselves, the miracles did not produce that faith which changed "sinners" into persons who radically obeyed, trusted God instead of themselves, forgave their enemies, and so on. Once Jesus did miracles, but was he somehow the once for all act of God? The miraculous acts of Jesus make faith comprehensible and they are comprehensible through faith, but they do not compel faith. Affirmation of God's presence in the activity of Jesus requires more than knowledge; the demand is for belief, trust, and risk.

MIRACLES IN THE TWENTIETH CENTURY

How does the modern world view miracles?
Does our "scientific" view reflect all of reality?
What is the central question of Jesus' miracles?
Do miracles happen?

In order to understand miracles we need a clearer view about the nature of miracle language.[21] Miracle language describes events that are awesomely significant for the people to whom these events occur. In fact, they are so significant that these people are usually willing to commit themselves to a changed understanding of life, themselves, and other people. We have all seen or heard about such people who have been "miraculously" saved from a disease or an accident and consequently began to live quite differently.

To express this extraordinary event, many people speak about miracle as a "breach of scientific, natural law." Taken literally, however, such language has little significance because scientific laws are always being broken. The scientific process runs something like this: out of observation and experiment a law is formed, then with more testing it is found to be inadequate, so the law is broken, reformulated; then it is again found to be inadequate, broken, reformulated again, and so forth. We need to keep in mind that scientists themselves realize that the models or laws that the scientific process constructs are only aids toward understanding reality. They are impersonal oversimplifications that are useful in a pragmatic way but are not determinative of reality. To mistake these "scientific, natural laws" for reality itself pushes the observer into a flat "scientific" (actually unscientific) view of the world in which all complexity and mystery are abolished for the sake of simple solutions.

What happens in miracles is that the impersonal world comes alive; something happens to some person that is extraordinarily significant and could not have been expected under normal conditions. No doubt scientific language can be used to describe a miracle. For example, a man survives a severe heart attack that normally would have been fatal. The personal background of this man, the work of the physicians, and his psychological desire to live can be accurately described; however, for him and possibly for others, this scientific language does not suffice. Some mysterious "more" was at work for which his only appropriate language is that of a miracle. The full story is not told by the impersonal language of scientific law.

Turning back to the New Testament miracles, we find that this under-

[21] See I. T. Ramsey, *Religious Language* (New York: Macmillan Co., 1957), pp. 167–174.

standing of miracle language does not fit with the explanation that the feeding of the five thousand was a display of generosity. Such an interpretation reduces the miracle to scientifically comprehensible language. But such language does not tell the full story. Miracle stories convey mystery; they speak about extraordinary events, situations in which things are more than they seem. Miracle stories claim that a power is at work which is personal concern—that is, the will of God, which declares itself personal at a point where it is not expected. The point of miracle stories is not scientific explanation; their point is beyond all such explanation.

It has been thought possible to reconcile Biblical miracles with a modern view of the world by assigning them to those areas of experience that have not yet been explored or explained by science. Thus all conflict with the sciences is avoided. But the increase of scientific knowledge threatens radically to reduce such areas, and thus the scope of the miraculous activity of God. Conversely, it is possible to regard all events as miraculous because they stem from God. This notion is usually associated with pantheism (from the Greek words *pan*, "all," and *theos*, "God"; God is all). The first option views miracle as an event contrary to nature and reduces God's activity to peripheral, occasional interventions. The second option of pantheism asserts God's activity in every event and hence renders man's role in the world insignificant. Yet neither of these viewpoints corresponds with the Biblical perspective, and each threatens to dissolve miracles, either into remote and barely conceivable possibilities or into everyday occurrences.

According to the Gospels, Jesus' miracles were real, specific, and discernable events. Yet they occurred in an atmosphere of eschatological expectation and faith. When wrenched from this context, they look like the works of a magician or a sorcerer. In his own time and in the earliest church the question of miracle could not be separated from faith in Jesus' preaching and power, both of which had to do with the dawning kingdom of God. Faith could not, and cannot, prove the miracles happened; faith provides the context in which their meaning can be discussed. Apart from their eschatological context, Jesus' miracles, if they are not rejected outright, must be viewed as occult phenomena with certain parallels in ancient and modern times. If, however, one believes that the new age was really dawning in Jesus, a basis is provided for understanding the miracles.

Did the miracles then occur? Do miracles occur? A book such as this can give no final answer. Apologists use the argument that Christians faced the lions of Nero, forgave their enemies, started a movement which spread over the Western world and became one of the major world religions, and so on. But at the same time, one can also argue that this same religious movement has caused untold strife, religious wars, nationalism, extreme individualism, and brutal imperialism. No empirical evidence exists to prove faith or that miracles did and do happen.

The Teaching Messiah

For popular Christianity Jesus has always been the teacher. Ernest Renan, who wrote probably the most popular life of Jesus, depicts him as a young rabbi whose "sweet theology of love won Him all hearts. His preaching was gentle and mild, full of nature and the fragrance of the country. . . . [He was] a winsome teacher who offered forgiveness to all on the sole condition of loving him."[22] This sentimental Jesus, the teacher of goodness and love, has won friends and influenced people down through the ages. Yet the partial distortion of this portrayal was evident even to Renan, who was forced by the tradition of Jesus to maintain that at a later stage in his life Jesus became a transcendent revolutionary; his simple love was unable to convince the hard hearts of the Jewish leaders. However, the sweet appeal of the loving, tender Jesus pales against the power, compassion, and awe that accompany the actual teaching of Jesus.

Our portrait of the healing Messiah has already pointed to the urgency with which Jesus taught and acted. He proclaimed the irruption of the kingdom of God. How far this message was dominated by the conviction that the end of the world was imminent is debatable, but that Jesus' teaching reflected an eschatological hope is undeniable. Jesus rejected the Jewish expectation of a historical, messianic king who as God's representative would destroy all the enemies of Israel and establish the political rule of Israel in a bright new epoch of history. Instead Jesus shared the equally Jewish apocalyptic expectation of the establishment of God's kingdom through a series of completely supernatural events including: "The coming of a pre-existent Son of Man, a general resurrection, a final Judgment, the breaking-down of the barriers between earth and heaven. In this expectation God does not transform the world and usher in the final epoch of history. He suddenly puts an end to the world and to history."[23] Jesus' miracles were harbingers of that cataclysmic, earth-shaking irruption of the kingdom.

Tributes to Jesus as the greatest teacher mankind has ever known and characterizations of his message as "one of the most wonderful collections of ethical teaching in the world"[24] miss the major point. Even the important ideas of the Fatherhood of God and the brotherhood of man do

[22] Schweitzer, *The Quest of the Historical Jesus*, p. 185, paraphrases and quotes from Renan's *The Life of Jesus* (New York: Albert & Charles Boni, 1936).

[23] See Norman Perrin, *The Kingdom of God in the Teaching of Jesus*, p. 113; cf. Rudolf Bultmann, *Jesus and the Word*, trans. L. P. Smith and E. H. Lantero (New York: Charles Scribner's Sons, 1958), pp. 35–38.

[24] Klausner, *Jesus of Nazareth*, p. 381; cf. T. W. Manson, *The Teaching of Jesus* (Cambridge: Cambridge University Press, 1955), p. 285.

not take account of the eschatological core of Jesus' teaching.[25] Since Schweitzer's monumental *The Quest of the Historical Jesus* no one can talk about the teaching of Jesus without dealing first with the center of Jesus' teaching, his eschatological preaching. Of course, that eschatology, with its expectation of an imminent end of the world, can raise problems for the modern mind. For example, can Jesus' teachings still be valid today in view of the fact that the end did not come immediately? If Jesus were wrong about one thing, he could be wrong about many things. Our efforts to understand the teaching of Jesus cannot be governed, however, by a desire to assure the immediate relevancy of his words.

THE PROCLAMATION OF THE KINGDOM OF GOD

Does Jesus proclaim the immediate end of the world?
Is the kingdom this worldly or other worldly?
How is the kingdom effected, by God's action, man's action, or both?
Is the kingdom present, future, or both?
What is the relation of Jesus' kingdom proclamation and his ethical message?

The message of Jesus centers upon the kingdom of God, "Now after John was arrested, Jesus came into Galilee, preaching the gospel of God, and saying, 'The time is fulfilled, and the kingdom of God is at hand; repent, and believe in the gospel' " (Mark 1:14 f.; Matt. 4:17). After the scribe applauds Jesus' summary of the law in the twin commandments of love of God and neighbor, Jesus says to him, "You are not far from the kingdom of God" (Mark 12:34). In the beatitudes Jesus says, "Blessed are you poor, for yours is the kingdom of God" (Luke 6:20; Matt. 5:3). Concerning John the Baptist, Jesus says, "Truly, I say to you, among those born of women there has risen no one greater than John the Baptist; yet he who is least in the kingdom of heaven is greater than he" (Matt. 11:11; Luke 7:28). In one petition of the Lord's Prayer Jesus prays, "Thy kingdom come. Thy will be done, on earth as it is in heaven" (Matt. 6:10; cf. Luke 11:2). Jesus' exorcisms show the coming of the kingdom, "But if it is by the Spirit of God that I cast out demons, then the kingdom of God has come upon you" (Matt. 12:28; Luke 11:20). Jesus' proclamation is pregnant with the kingdom of God. This centrality is indisputable; yet the meaning of Jesus' kingdom proclamation is debatable.

Two major questions concerning Jesus' concept of the kingdom have occupied scholarship since the beginning of the century: First, did Jesus

---

[25] Cf. Adolf Harnack, *What Is Christianity?*, trans. T. B. Saunders (New York: Harper & Row, 1957), p. 68.

stress the present kingdom, the future kingdom, or some combination of the two? Second, was Jesus' teaching oriented toward an apocalyptic kingdom to be brought about by God or an ethical kingdom to be realized by man's response? Although the questions are related, we shall reserve the latter for treatment under Jesus' radical demand. In considering the former question, we shall group the varied sayings according to present or future orientation in order to reach tentative conclusions about Jesus' temporal emphasis. As a check upon our findings, we shall briefly investigate seven kingdom parables (Matthew 13). Then we shall be able to say more precisely how Jesus' kingdom proclamation is oriented to the present and future.[26]

The Kingdom as Present and Future

Altogether the three Synoptic Gospels contain approximately 114 references to the kingdom of God. This contrasts with 34 references in the rest of the New Testament, including the Gospel of John. As we would expect, the Gospels of Matthew and Luke, which embody the bulk of Jesus' teachings, contain more references than Mark (54 in Matthew, 41 in Luke, 19 in Mark).

Clearly the kingdom of God is said to be already present in some sense in Jesus' mission and message. Several important passages refer to Jesus' activity as indicative of the kingdom's presence. Jesus says that his exorcisms by the Spirit of God show that "the kingdom of God has come upon you" (Matt. 12:28; cf. Luke 11:20). As we can be reasonably certain that Jesus did perform exorcisms (see pp. 181 f.), it is highly probable that he himself is responsible for relating the exorcisms to the kingdom's presence. On another occasion in which Jesus is asked by the Pharisees when the kingdom is coming, he replies, "The kingdom of God is not coming with signs to be observed; nor will they say, 'Lo, here it is!' or 'There!' for behold, the kingdom of God is in the midst of you" (Luke 17:20 f.).[27] Evidently the present already contains what the Pharisees seek in the future. After the seventy go out upon their mission and find that they also can conquer demons, Jesus says to them, "I saw Satan fall like lightning from heaven" (Luke 10:18). Satan's defeat marks the beginning of the end time (cf. Rev. 20:1–3).

[26] For valuable, recent discussions of Jesus' proclamation of the kingdom of God, see Perrin, *The Kingdom of God in the Teaching of Jesus* and Gösta Lundström, *The Kingdom of God in the Teaching of Jesus*, trans. J. Bulman (Richmond: John Knox Press, 1963); also R. H. Hiers, "Eschatology and Methodology," *JBL*, 85 (1966), pp. 170–184.

[27] The final phrase "in the midst of you" may be translated "within you." See W. G. Kümmel, *Promise and Fulfillment* (SBT, 23; London: SCM Press, 1957), pp. 33 f., and Perrin, *The Kingdom of God in the Teaching of Jesus*, pp. 174–178. For a recent affirmative argument as to the authenticity of this saying, see R. J. Sneed, *The Kingdom's Coming: Luke 17:20–21* (Ann Arbor, Mich.: University Microfilms, 1962).

These passages raise questions of interpretation. Moreover, there are relatively few instances in which the presence of the kingdom seems to be unequivocally stated. The presence of the kingdom is also placed in question by sayings of Jesus in which the kingdom is clearly placed in the future. For example, according to the summary of Jesus' teaching which was quoted initially (Mark 1:14 f. parr.), the kingdom is "at hand" —that is, has not yet arrived. It is nearer than before (around the corner) but not yet present. In spite of these sayings, however, Jesus' kingdom message is not oriented only to the future. This point is confirmed by the parables, but already Jesus' exorcism of demons and his miracle working power suffice to indicate the present irruption of the kingdom.[28]

The kingdom of God in the message of Jesus is also future, however, and the evidence for this futuristic emphasis is quite overwhelming. The previously cited summary statements of Jesus' preaching (Mark 1:14 f.; Matt. 4:17) declare the kingdom to be future, though imminent. The prayer Jesus gives to his disciples contains a petition for the future coming of the kingdom (Matt. 6:10; Luke 11:2). After the confession of Peter at Caesarea Philippi, Jesus instructs the disciples, "Truly, I say to you, there are some standing here who will not taste death before they see the kingdom of God come with power" (Mark 9:1; Matt. 16:28, Luke 9:27). At the Last Supper, Jesus says to the disciples, "Truly, I say to you, I shall not drink again of the fruit of the vine until that day when I drink it new in the kingdom of God" (Mark 14:25; Matt. 26:29; Luke 22:18). Jesus speaks frequently about entering and receiving the kingdom of God. Such sayings also fit the concept of a future or coming kingdom (Matt. 5:20; 7:21; 18:3; 19:23; 25:34; Mark 9:47; 10:15; 15:43; Luke 9:62; 12:32; 18:17).

If, as seems reasonable, we can associate with the kingdom other references to the coming of the end time, such as the coming of the Son of Man, the tribulations of the end day, the coming of the judgment, then we have an abundance of indirect evidence that Jesus understood the kingdom as future. The apocalyptic discourse (Mark 13; cf. Matt. 24 and Luke 21) again and again speaks of the impending future tribulation that ushers in the rule of God. Although it contains much material that probably did not originate with Jesus, it would scarcely have obtained its present form had he not proclaimed the future, coming kingdom of God.

One surprising thing about the apocalyptic discourse is the near neglect of the concept of the kingdom. It is mentioned only once in Mark, and only twice in the other Synoptics. One saying does deal explicitly with the imminent coming of the kingdom, "When you see these things taking

---

[28] See Kümmel, *Promise and Fulfillment*, pp. 105–40, for a summary of evidence that Jesus understands the kingdom as already present; cf. also Perrin, *The Kingdom of God in the Teaching of Jesus*, pp. 74–78.

place, you know that the kingdom of God is near" (Luke 21:31). Here, however, Luke has evidently modified a word of Jesus which was originally spoken about the Son of man (cf. Mark 13:29). The other saying does not necessarily support the idea of a future coming of the kingdom: "And this gospel of the kingdom will be preached throughout the whole world, as a testimony to all nations; and then the end will come" (Matt. 24:14). In this saying the kingdom is identified with the gospel and partly disassociated from the end. If this were a genuine word from Jesus, then Jesus would have preached the kingdom as a preparation for the end and therefore a present possibility. Yet Mark's silence at this point and the neat way in which this saying fits into Matthew's program for the disciples (Matt. 28:16–20) render it suspect. We can only conclude on the basis of individual sayings and related apocalyptic references in the teaching of Jesus that he himself proclaimed the kingdom as future.[29]

Jesus and Apocalypticism

In the tradition of the Synoptic Gospels Jesus proclaims the kingdom as both present and future. It is frequently said, and rightly so, that Jesus must be understood against the background of Jewish apocalyptic thought. Yet Jesus is no ordinary apocalyptic thinker. Two marks characterize apocalyptic teaching but only the first of them is fully shared by Jesus. First, apocalypticism looks toward a future consummation of history which God will command. Second, this event is set in a dualistic framework and occurs as the final climax of an overall "plan" for history. Jewish apocalyptic literature, which developed during the period between the Maccabean uprising and the final destruction of Jerusalem (167 B.C. to A.D. 135), embodied the fundamental hope that "the succession of world powers, Babylonian, Median, Persian, Seleucid Greek, [and Roman] would be brought to an end by an act of God in history whereby God himself will take the dominion into his own hands."[30] This view reflects pessimism about any possibility of man's extricating himself from the present evil situation. The powers of Satan, represented by the foreign powers dominating the Jewish people, had won the upper hand. The only hope was the advent of God's new age, in which the old powers would be annihilated and his reign established. This world view deals in dualistic contrasts: good and bad, new and old, God and Satan. In its perspective on history and God's plan it presumes that the world has become progressively more evil, descending from an initial paradise to the present hell

---

[29] For evidence supporting the idea of the future kingdom, see Perrin, *The Kingdom of God and the Teaching of Jesus*, pp. 79–84; also Hiers, *JBL*, 85 (1966), pp. 182–184. For a different categorization of the kingdom sayings see J. L. Price, *Interpreting the New Testament* (New York: Holt, Rinehart & Winston, 1961), pp. 235–239.

[30] Perrin, *The Kingdom of God in the Teaching of Jesus*, p. 53, is presenting the view of F. C. Burkitt.

on earth. This evil, instigated by men and God's adversary Satan, is especially rampant against God's elect in the last days.[31] But God's plan, visible only to the discerning elect, calls for a final intervention in which all will be reversed, so that the oppressed will triumph and the rulers will be destroyed. Therefore, apocalypticism calls for repentance in face of the terrible judgment of the imminent end.

Jesus is related to this apocalyptic world view, but not close enough to warrant labelling him an apocalypticist. John the Baptist, the angry preacher of judgment (see Matt. 3:1–12), deserves that title more than Jesus does, and the book of Revelation with its fantastic imagery of the end time has quite appropriately been called the Apocalypse (see Rev. 21:1–8). Jesus is an eschatological teacher who proclaims the imminent end (Mark 1:15 par.; Matt. 8:11 f. par.). Yet Jesus proclaims neither knowledge of the plan of God nor a pessimistic, dualistic rejection of this world. Jesus rejects the favorite apocalyptic sport of looking for signs and speculating about the exact time for the end: "Why does this generation seek a sign? Truly, I say to you, no sign shall be given to this generation" (Mark 8:12; cf. Matt. 16:4; Luke 11:29). Even in the so-called "apocalyptic discourse," which is largely the product of a later time, Jesus refuses to speculate (Mark 13:32). When the Pharisees ask Jesus about the time of the kingdom's coming, Jesus replies that the kingdom is not coming "with signs to be observed," for it is already in their midst (Luke 17:20 f.). John the Baptist's disciples inquire whether Jesus is the sign that the apocalyptic end time has arrived (Matt. 11:2–6; Luke 7:18–23). Jesus' only answer is to describe what he is doing. Even though Jesus' acts of preaching and healing are good news, they are hardly the dreadful, cataclysmic signs of the end of the world.

Jesus is an eschatological, but not an apocalyptic, teacher. In his healings and exorcisms, the power of God is already at work. Jesus claims that the kingdom is inaugurated in his ministry, it is in the process of being realized; but it has not yet fully come, for its completion is still future. That was the secret of Jesus' message about the kingdom,[32] and his parables bear this out.

The Kingdom and the Parables

In our discussion of Jesus' proclamation of the kingdom we have thus far deliberately ignored the numerous kingdom parables. The parables are usually linked to Jesus' message about the kingdom by the introductory

[31] See Daniel 7:2–8, the book of Revelation, and the "War of the Children of Light against the Children of Darkness," which depicts the final eschatological battle. Cf. T. H. Gaster, *The Dead Sea Scriptures* (Garden City, N.Y.: Doubleday & Co., 1956), pp. 275–306.

[32] Cf. Martin Dibelius, *Jesus*, trans. C. B. Hedrick and F. C. Grant (Philadelphia: Westminster Press, 1949), pp. 76–88, where a similar view is elaborated with a somewhat different conclusion. For Dibelius the work of Jesus is not the presence of the kingdom but the *sign* of the kingdom.

phrase, "the kingdom is like," or its equivalent. The connection of the parables and the kingdom message becomes further established when we recognize that they were spoken to concrete, historical situations in the life of Jesus and are not intended to convey general truths.[33] It is not too much to say that if Jesus taught anything, he proclaimed the irruption of the kingdom of God and that if he taught in any form, he spoke in parables.

In view of the tradition's linking of the parables with the kingdom teaching, we may expect that the parables will be invaluable guides in understanding the intention of Jesus' eschatology. Moreover, their use in regard to Jesus' kingdom message promotes greater clarity about Jesus' actual message, for we can separate tradition and redaction in the parables with relative confidence, and thus come close to the historical Jesus.[34]

Before looking directly at selected parables, we need to understand something of the nature of a parable. To begin with, the parables of Jesus have accumulated redactional additions during the course of their oral and written transmission. This material was added in order to make the parables meaningful to later situations. One way the early church made Jesus' parables applicable was by allegorizing, giving them new meaning by making each point of the parable refer to some Christian truth.[35] In Matthew the interpretations of the parables of the sower (13:18–23) and of the weeds in the field (13:36–43) are examples of such allegorization. But this sort of interpretation is not true to the original intent of the parables. Jesus was not a Christian, and Jesus' parables were not designed to fit already given patterns of meaning. Jesus spoke parables in order to drive home a specific point by way of an analogy drawn from the everyday world. The parables do not allow the hearer to remain aloof but involve and surprise him. They are not stories told to illustrate general truths; they are sharp words with implied directives for concrete situations.[36]

In the Gospel of Mark, parables are spoken in order that the "mystery" of the kingdom of God may be hidden from those outside, but later revealed to the disciples (Mark 4:10–13). To suggest, however, that Jesus spoke in parables so that his hearers would not understand and in another way to his disciples so that they would understand falsifies the intent both of the tradition and of Jesus. Yet this interpretation does contain an element of truth about Jesus' parables, for the hearer who resists does indeed

---

[33] Jeremias, *Parables of Jesus*, especially pp. 115 ff., ably supports this view of the parables. A most perceptive view of the relation of the parables and the kingdom message is elaborated by D. O. Via, Jr.: "The parables offer some help in interpreting Jesus' eschatology at the conceptual level, but more importantly, they are an independent and richer expression of the *intention* of his explicit eschatology" (*The Parables: Their Literary and Existential Dimension*, Philadelphia: Fortress Press, 1967, p. 205).

[34] See Jeremias, *The Parables of Jesus*, pp. 113 f.

[35] See the discussion of allegory and parable in Via, *The Parables*, pp. 4–10.

[36] Cf. A. Jülicher's position as described in Jeremias, *The Parables of Jesus*, p. 19.

find the parables enigmatic and puzzling. The parables, in other words, are self-evident only to the eyes of faith.

The parables include the everyday but also the unexpected. In interpreting the parables, attention must focus not upon the particulars, but upon the total impact of the story. By contrast, allegory allows the particulars to dominate by referring each element to some previously known framework of meaning. The parable does not relate first or primarily to something beyond the parable itself. The many elements of the parable are a whole, and it is impossible to translate the parable into other terms. Any generalization about a parable is always secondary. Consequently in our interpretation of certain parables we need to keep in mind that genuine understanding occurs simply in reading and hearing the parables. The directive, the stimulus to action or to repentance, that they imply, is clear enough in most parables. We need only ask about the view of the kingdom that they imply or assume.

The first parable for consideration is that of the sower (Matt. 13:3-8; cf. Mark 4:3-8 and Luke 8:5-8). It requires some knowledge of Jesus' time and place in order to be understood. First, the harvest image was already connected with the eschatological notion of the end of the world; the end time was the harvest time (cf. Isaiah 9:3; Psalm 126:6). Second, the yield of grain (13:8) was excessively large; a ten-fold yield would have been a good harvest, and a yield of seven and a half an average one.[37]

Turning now to the meaning of the parable of the sower and assuming that this parable was spoken by Jesus, we may dispense with the interpretation (13:18-23), for it is quite difficult to imagine that this allegory tells what the parable meant. For example, the identification of the birds with "the evil one" is artificial and would have been unlikely to occur to Jesus' listeners. The parable points quite simply to activity taking place in the present: seed being sown, but much seed being lost. Jesus speaks this parable about the sower not to encourage endurance from people already committed to him (cf. vs. 21), but to declare what is happening in their midst and what its magnificent results will be. Even now the sowing is taking place; moreover, the future harvest will be beyond imagination. Undoubtedly the parable's movement portrays in everyday, yet unexpected, language Jesus' proclamation of the kingdom. The present is for Jesus the time of the hidden coming of the kingdom; the future will witness an unbelievable consummation of that kingdom. Salvation is not only future but already present in a hidden way.[38]

The second parable, the weeds in the field (Matt. 13:24-30), also has an allegorical interpretation, which is clearly secondary and does not belong

---

[37] See Jeremias, *The Parables of Jesus*, p. 150.
[38] *Ibid.*, pp. 77-79, 149-151; Jeremias classifies this under Jesus' preaching of "great assurance" of salvation.

Present-day ploughing in Galilee, not unlike that in the time of Jesus. (Courtesy of Israel Government Tourist Office.)

to Jesus' message (13:36–43). According to the interpretation, Jesus warns against false security by depicting vividly the punishment and reward of the last judgment. But this interpretation obscures the surprising point of the story.

Again we have a parable of the harvest. This time, instead of announcing a magnificent future yield and thereby claiming hidden significance for the present sowing, the parable depicts the future as a time of judgment, a process of separation (vs. 30). But the present is a time when judgment cannot be exercised (vs. 29). Actually the weight of the parable falls on the latter point. Final judgment belongs to God, not to man. (cf. Matt. 7:1 and Luke 15). Any attempt to bring judgment into the present misses the point of Jesus' proclaiming the kingdom as inaugurated (cf. Matt. 13:44 ff. and Mark 2:18 ff.), but not realized.

The following twin parables, the parable of the mustard seed (Matt. 13:31 f.; cf. Mark 4:30–32 and Luke 13:18 f.) and the parable of the leaven (Matt. 13:33; cf. Luke 13:20 f.) also speak about present and future. Note that exaggeration has occurred in the Matthean and Lukan accounts, for in actuality the mustard seed only becomes a large shrub,

197

about nine feet in height, rather than a tree.[39] Also the specified measures of meal is a huge quantity of flour for a housewife, approximately fifty pounds (cf. Gen. 18:6). Many modern interpreters view these parables as depicting the growth of the kingdom of God, which starts small but through the course of years grows through human effort until it encompasses the whole world. But this interpretation misses both the eschatological urgency of Jesus' message and the thrust of the images themselves. Jesus uses the tiny and insignificant mustard seed and leaven in order to surprise the hearer with the tremendous results: the tree that shelters the birds and enough dough for a housewife to feed 150 people. These are parables not of growth, but of contrast. Jesus contrasts the small, present beginning with the great result to come in the future. The process of growth is nowhere mentioned so that the "how" of this great result remains a mystery.

The twin parables of the treasure (Matt. 13:44) and the pearl (Matt. 13:45 f.) further elaborate man's present response to the kingdom.[40] No calculation is involved; the finder of the treasure and the finder of the pearl have only one thing on their minds—the grace of the find that overshadows everything else. To interpret the parables as demands by Jesus for complete self-surrender turns the parables upside down. The finders do not understand themselves as surrendering everything but as gaining the one essential thing, the treasure or the pearl. In one instance, the treasure is found accidentally by a laborer in the field; in the other, the merchant finds the pearl after a great search. But in both cases, everything is forgotten in the joy of finding the treasure and the pearl.

These two parables, which deal with present response to the kingdom, are followed by the parable of the net and the fish, a parable relating to the future (Matt. 13:47–50). Jesus' original parable probably consisted simply of the image of throwing the net and gathering and sorting the good and bad fish (vss. 47–48), but Matthew's redactional addition (vss. 49–50; cf. Matt. 8:12; 13:42; 22:13) correctly interprets this parable in light of the final judgment. The future orientation becomes evident when this parable is seen together with the parable of the weeds and the wheat (13:24–30); for the latter's secondary point was that judgment could and would take place in the future.

In summary, Jesus' parables, like his kingdom message, stress both the present and the future: a small beginning now is to be consummated fully in the future. This present beginning is a time for great joy. Whoever seeks to control the future by immediate judgment loses the future reward. Whoever discerns the present activity of God will be astonished at the final results.

---

[39] Jeremias, *The Parables of Jesus*, p. 31, suggests that the tree imagery heightens the eschatological flavor of the parable and reflects Daniel 4:17.

[40] See Jeremias, *The Parables of Jesus*, pp. 32 f., 198 ff.

Our use of "religious" language in order to interpret the parables must not lose sight of the fact that not a single parable anywhere mentions God or uses any "religious" language. Thus Jesus talks about eschatology and God in everyday language. According to Jesus, therefore, the meeting with the unexpected, with God, always occurs within the world.

We may now make certain negative conclusions about the kingdom of God in the proclamation of Jesus: First, Jesus did not mean by the kingdom of God primarily a political territory or social order under God's rule.[41] In Jesus' message God's "kingship" (a possible translation of the Aramaic and the Greek) was of a different order from society's normal structures of government.[42] Second, Jesus was not an apocalyptic fanatic. His proclamation of the kingdom was eschatological, but not marked by the usual imagery and extravagances of the apocalyptic.[43] The refusal of signs, the lack of description about the future kingdom of God, the absence of a strict dualism, and the omission of any complex plan of God meant that Jesus' kingdom message was certainly not apocalyptic in any conventional sense. Third and finally, Jesus never viewed the kingdom of God as a slowly evolving movement within history which could be brought about by mankind's adhering to the principles of his own ethics.[44]

To these negative conclusions, we may now add certain positive comments about Jesus' kingdom teaching. Eschatology was dominant; God's activity, not man's, was foremost in his conception of the coming kingdom. The kingdom was both present and future, yet its futurity was not described in lurid apocalyptic imagery any more than its presence was conceived as a purely inner or spiritual reality. The kingdom involved both the action of God and the response of man. The present hidden reality of the kingdom challenged the disciple to accept it now, and thus enabled him joyfully to anticipate the future. God was the primary actor: divine initiative came forth in the history of Jesus and would encompass the world at the future consummation. Jesus' eschatological message proclaimed an "already" and a "not yet." Already in Jesus the kingdom is inaugurated, but not yet has the kingdom fully come.

An illuminating analogy to describe the tension between present and future in Jesus' eschatological message is suggested by Oscar Cullmann, contemporary New Testament scholar. Using a metaphor from World War II, he compares the present breaking in of the kingdom to D-Day, the day when the Allied troops successfully invaded Europe and in effect won the war. Although months passed before the war was over and though

---

[41] R. R. Niebuhr ("Religion within Limits," *Harvard Divinity Bulletin*, New Series, I, No. 2, 1968, p. 2) speaks of "God-ruling."

[42] S. G. F. Brandon, *Jesus and the Zealots* (Manchester: University Press, 1967), does see a political interest in Jesus.

[43] See R. Bultmann, *Jesus and the Word*, pp. 150 ff.

[44] See Price, *Interpreting the New Testament*, p. 239.

the Allied troops suffered losses in ensuing days, the establishment of that beachhead in Europe was the assurance of final victory. Similarly, Jesus' proclamation and action was the decisive beachhead for the kingdom of God. Although the opposition might at times seem to be winning, the final victory was already inaugurated or in process. The D-Day analogy suggests that Christ stands close to the end time instead of at the mid-point; therefore, the analogy becomes even more appropriate in illuminating the tension of present and future in Jesus' kingdom proclamation. With Jesus the end time has broken into history; no long continuing battle is envisioned.[45]

Three major questions about Jesus' kingdom proclamation yet remain. What is the relationship between the eschatological and the ethical messages of Jesus? Is the kingdom's inauguration to be located in the word or deed of Jesus? How does Jesus' death relate to his proclaiming of the kingdom? The last two questions carry us beyond the eschatological teaching of Jesus into the question of his "messianic consciousness" and his role as "suffering Messiah"; however, we need to keep them in mind in order to get a full picture of Jesus' kingdom message and to recognize that no part of the historical Jesus remains untouched by the kingdom proclamation.

THE RADICAL DEMAND OF THE KINGDOM

How does Jesus' kingdom proclamation fit with his radical demand?
Does Jesus proclaim an impossible ethic in the "antitheses"?
What is Jesus' view of the law?

Scholarly debate has centered about whether the kingdom was future or present. Much of this discussion, however, boils down to the rather simple question of whether Jesus was primarily an apocalyptic prophet or an ethical teacher. The majority of interpreters have chosen the latter alternative, sometimes in order to free Jesus from dogma—that is, to free the real humanitarian, ethical teaching of Jesus from centuries of dogma's incrustation—and sometimes to free Jesus for dogma—that is, to demonstrate that the founder of Christianity was not an apocalyptic fanatic who had wrongly predicted the imminent end of the world. As long as the question was framed as a simple alternative, "apocalyptic prophet or ethical teacher," the modern mind most often favored the ethical teacher. But if one or the other must be chosen, Jesus was actually closer to being an apocalyptic prophet. As we have seen, however, the heart of Jesus' message was an eschatological proclamation of a kingdom *both* present *and* future. It included God's action and the necessity for man's response to

---

[45] See Cullmann, *Christ and Time*, pp. 71 f., 83 f.

it. Yet how does the good news of the inauguration of God's kingdom relate to the ethical demand of Jesus? Is the urgency of the demand undercut by the proclamation of salvation? We will now deal directly with these important questions.

The Demand of the Sermon on the Mount

The most concentrated expression of Jesus' radical statement of the will of God occurs in the Sermon on the Mount (Matt. 5–7). The higher righteousness (5:20) is defined by prohibitions against anger (5:22), the lustful look (5:28), divorce (5:32), and swearing (5:34). Jesus also commands nonresistance to evil (5:39) and love for one's enemies (5:44). All this reaches a stunning climax: "You, therefore, must be perfect, as your heavenly Father is perfect" (5:48).

These words of Jesus (5:21–48), called the "antitheses" because they are set over against the law of Moses, are so radical that they could hardly be inventions of the early church. Further words, such as the prohibitions against anxiety (6:25), the command not to judge (7:1), and the injunction to do the will of the Father (7:21), strike the reader as extraordinarily demanding. Basically, they must be from Jesus.[46] Consequently, our question concerning Jesus' words of radical demand is not their authenticity but their meaning, especially their relation to his kingdom proclamation. Is Jesus' radical demand a righteousness *for* the kingdom or *of* the kingdom? Does this call for obedience to the will of God lay down conditions *for* entrance into the kingdom or does it show those deeds which signify the presence *of* the kingdom? If the former, then the kingdom truly is future; if the latter, then the kingdom may be both present and future.

There have been a number of proposed solutions to the problem of the relation of Jesus' teaching in the Sermon to his preaching about the coming kingdom. Most emphasize ethics at the expense of eschatology or vice versa. In some cases eschatology has been virtually ignored, and Jesus' teaching interpreted as a counsel of perfection for an elite group (that is, a monastic order). A popular Protestant interpretation has viewed the ethical injunctions as impossible to fulfill and therefore really intended to evoke despair and repentance.

Our basic understanding of the Sermon has already been elaborated in the treatment of Matthew (see pp. 108 ff.). Obviously, some material in Matthew 5–7 comes from the evangelist or his tradition, rather than Jesus. Nevertheless, even unauthentic words may capture the authentic Jesus. Moreover, Matthew's construction of the Sermon begins in eschato-

---

[46] Their radical character can hardly be ascribed to Matthew or the transmission of his tradition because this Gospel and its tradition show a conservative, and at times almost Judaizing, treatment of the tradition: Jesus fulfills the law and the prophets (5:17). See Davies, *The Setting of the Sermon on the Mount*, especially pp. 105–108, 412–414; cf. Käsemann, *Essays on New Testament Themes*, pp. 37 f.

logical promise and ends with eschatological demand.[47] No hint at all is given in the Sermon that anything less is required than obedience to the demands of Jesus. On the other hand, we do not read that this obedience is to take place through the unaided effort of the hearer of Jesus' words. The truth of this observation may be seen from several perspectives. First, the opening beatitudes may be understood to mean that God loves those who eagerly receive what is graciously occurring in the present. In addition, the blessing of God as present eschatological action effects higher righteousness, greater obedience. Second, although this new reality means a deeper regard for the life of man with man (Matt. 5:21–48), still this new life, according to Jesus, is built on the relationship that the Father has already established with man (5:48). Third, barriers to the relationship of man and God—hypocrisy, prayer for show, anxiety about one's own destiny—have to be eradicated (see Matt. 6). Seeking first the kingdom and righteousness of the Father enables man to find freedom and enjoyment in the present. Fourth, the future belongs to God (7:1; cf. 7:7). God's grace accompanies Jesus' command, yet whoever encounters the grace of God must still bear good fruit (7:19) and face God in the future judgment (7:24–27).

Matthew correctly understands the relation of eschatology and ethics in Jesus' teachings: reward is not just some future prize for good deeds accomplished in the present, for reward belongs already to the right relationship with God. Present blessing and obedience simply become expanded and enlarged in the future. Jesus' proclamation of the kingdom seeks to bring a response from his hearers, a response defined as doing the will of God. Thus the righteousness that Jesus demands is no righteousness for the kingdom, not even the proper attitude with which to unlock the kingdom. Instead Jesus demands the righteousness *of* the kingdom. To be sure, this kingdom is only partially present, inaugurated, but the power of the kingdom is already at work. A close reading of the Sermon reveals that Jesus speaks as one convinced that the kingdom is breaking into the present and will be consummated both as the act of God and the response of man in the future.

Jesus and the Law

Indirect support for the unity of Jesus' kingdom preaching and ethical teaching may be seen in the fact that Jesus' words, especially in the Sermon on the Mount, express a freedom toward the law only possible for one convinced that the eschatological time was beginning. In the "antitheses" Jesus opposes his understanding of the law to that of Moses, even though no ordinary rabbi would dare assume that kind of authority. His "but *I*

---

[47] This order does not basically differ from that of Luke's considerably more condensed version (Luke 6:20–49).

say unto you" implies that for him the present is a time of radical reinterpretation of the old law. This reinterpretation, characterized by the command to love one's enemies and by prohibitions against lust, anger, and swearing, is rooted in the dawning of the kingdom of God. Nowhere else does Jesus' daring become more evident than in his abolition of the law's crucial distinction between clean and unclean: "Hear me, all of you, and understand: there is nothing outside a man which by going into him can defile him; but the things which come out of a man are what defile him" (Mark 7:14 f.; cf. Matt. 15:1–20). With God's coming near, distinctions of the sacred and the profane, the clean and the unclean, are no longer valid. Jesus' message compels men to seek and to do the will of God in the law—in view of the coming kingdom—rather than quibble over insignificant minutiae (cf. Matt. 23:23 f.).

The solution, therefore, to the problem of eschatology and ethics in Jesus' message entails a recognition that the kingdom is both present and future. The kingdom is present in blessing; therefore, no one can afford to spend time in calculating the end of time. God is present; therefore, man has to respond, to hear, and to obey today. Yet the kingdom is also future. Final judgment can be exercised by no one other than God himself. The urgency of Jesus' demand derives not from the law as a thing of the past, but from the onset of the kingdom or rule of God, a prospect that dominates the future.

THE RELATIONSHIP OF JESUS TO HIS MESSAGE

What does Jesus think of his own person and work?
Does Jesus use any messianic title for himself?
Why does Jesus call disciples to follow him?
Why do the authorities execute Jesus?

The center of Jesus' message is the proclamation of the inaugurated kingdom of God. The person of Jesus himself does not stand at the center of his message. Jesus points to God, not himself. Yet it would be misleading to leave the matter there. The relationship of Jesus to his proclamation of the kingdom is an important question raised by the tradition of Jesus itself.

The New Testament unequivocally maintains that the identity of Jesus is related to his work. When the New Testament speaks about the person of Jesus, it is nearly always in connection with his work.[48] In other words, the question, "Who was he?" leads to another question, "What did he

---

[48] See Oscar Cullmann, *The Christology of the New Testament,* trans. S. C. Guthrie and C. A. M. Hall (Philadelphia: Westminster Press, 1959), pp. 3 ff.

do?" Eschatology, rather than Christology, is the center of Jesus' proclamation. Throughout the Gospels Jesus talks about God and his kingdom rather than himself. His message is not about his own person but about God's rule. Neither do the Gospels show much interest in Jesus' personality or self-consciousness, for they are concerned with his mission and message.

The Question of Jesus' Messianic Consciousness

A logical beginning place for understanding Jesus' view of himself is the various Christological titles used either by Jesus or his contemporaries. The major titles are Son of God, Savior, Lord, Messiah, Son of Man, suffering servant of God, and prophet.[49] We need to investigate which ones of these titles Jesus actually used.

Two basic types of messianic hope dominated first-century Israel. The first type was the hope for a political Messiah, usually expected to be an heir of King David, and perhaps Son of God (see Psalm 2:7). He was to overthrow the political enemies of Israel, establish the chosen people in a new and perfect reign of David, and inaugurate the kingdom of God. Of Jesus' actions the entry into Jerusalem (Mark 11:1–10 parr.) and the subsequent overthrow of the money changers in the temple (Mark 11:11–19 parr.) are most susceptible to political interpretation. Although Jesus here appears in the role of political revolutionary, at least at one point the tradition clearly denies his linkage with David, "How can the scribes say that the Christ is the son of David?" (Mark 12:35, but cf. Rom. 1:3). Significant evidence for Jesus' political messiahship is the fact that he was undoubtedly executed as a messianic pretender, a political threat to the Roman government. At the trial Pilate asks him, "Are you the king of the Jews?" (Mark 15:2), and the inscription over the cross describing the charge against him read "King of the Jews" (Mark 15:26; cf. 15:18, 32). Nevertheless, the total impression of the tradition works against viewing Jesus as a messianic political figure. At the temptation the devil is rebuked when he offers Jesus political power (Matt. 4:8–10 par.); moreover, Jesus not only denies that he is seeking to establish an earthly kingdom (Mark 10:42–44), but he also offers no resistance at his arrest, trial, and death (Mark 14:48 f.). If Jesus was arrested and executed as a politically subversive messianic pretender, this only shows how thoroughly his opponents misunderstood or misused him (see especially the discussion of Mark, pp. 86 f.).

The second major type of first-century Jewish messianic expectation was apocalyptic. It looked forward to an end of history in which God would effect the perfect, supernatural kingdom without any human aid. As we

---

[49] See the discussion of these Christological titles in Cullmann's *The Christology of the New Testament*. He also includes "the word," "high priest," and Jesus as "God." Cf. R. H. Fuller, *The Foundations of New Testament Christology* (New York: Charles Scribner's Sons, 1965), especially pp. 102–141.

have already seen, Jesus' eschatological message fits more comfortably into this world view than that of political messianism. Of the many messianic titles of the New Testament, the "prophet" and "Son of Man" are most at home within this atmosphere of urgent expectation of God's final, cataclysmic act. No doubt John the Baptist functions as a prophet announcing the imminent approach of the last days (Matt. 11:9; Mark 1:2–8), and Jesus was named prophet by some of his contemporaries (Matt. 14:5; 21:11). Yet Jesus uses the designation prophet of himself only once (Mark 6:4 parr.), and then only to quote a proverbial saying. The situation is quite different with the "Son of Man" title, which appears frequently in Jesus' speech as a self-designation. Moreover, according

Entry of Jesus into Jerusalem by the contemporary Chinese artist Luca Cheng. (Courtesy of Spartaco Appetiti.)

to the Synoptics no one else used this title as a designation for Jesus. In fact, it is rarely used by anyone else in the entire New Testament. Consequently, "Son of Man" appears to be the title by which Jesus designated and understood himself.

The title, "Son of Man," originated in late Jewish apocalypticism, where the Son of Man was a mythical, transcendent, supernatural figure associated with the final cataclysmic end of the world.. He was to come with clouds of heaven and to be given everlasting kingdom and dominion over all people (cf. Dan. 7:13 f.). Though in Daniel the Son of Man was probably identified with the remnant people of Israel, he later became a definite messianic figure. Thus it is extremely doubtful that the title originally designated the humility of Jesus.[50]

In the apocalyptic literature of late Judaism (Enoch 48:2 ff.; 72; IV Ezra 13) the coming of the Son of Man signifies the demise of the old era and the beginning of the new. He was to be the judge of the world who would gather his elect around him. Such a figure corresponds precisely to the concept of the Son of Man reflected in many sayings attributed to Jesus. Moreover, any consideration of these Son of Man sayings must take into account the facts that this title is rarely used as a designation for Jesus beyond the Synoptic Gospels[51] and that within the Synoptic Gospels only Jesus himself ever speaks about the Son of Man. Nowhere does the narrative name Jesus as the Son of Man and nowhere does anyone call him the Son of Man. Our conclusion, therefore, is that Jesus actually used the Son of Man title and the crucial question is how he used it.[52]

The Son of Man sayings in the Synoptic Gospels can be classified under three types: (1) those that speak of a future, glorious Son of Man; (2) those that speak of the present suffering Son of Man; and (3) those that speak of an earthly Son of Man.

Mark records that after Peter's confession at Caesarea Philippi, Jesus says, "For whoever is ashamed of me and of my words in this adulterous and sinful generation, of him will the Son of man also be ashamed, when he comes in the glory of his Father with the holy angels" (8:38; cf. Luke

---

[50] In Ezekiel (2:1, *passim*) and the Psalms (8:4; 80:17), "Son of Man" is used more as a form of address rather than a title; see Cullmann, *Christology of the New Testament*, p. 138.

[51] Exceptions are the Gospel of John 1:51; 3:14; 5:27; 6:27; Acts 7:56; Rev. 1:13. See Bornkamm, *Jesus of Nazareth*, pp. 175 ff.

[52] An imposing array of scholarship is now appearing which flatly denies that Jesus used the title "Son of Man" in any way; see the excellent summary in Norman Perrin, *Rediscovering the Teaching of Jesus* (New York: Harper & Row, 1967), pp. 259 f. Perrin's book probably appeared too late to mention the massive study by Frederick Borsch, *The Son of Man in Myth and History* (Philadelphia: Westminster Press, 1967), which supports our conclusion. See also H. E. Tödt, *The Son of Man in the Synoptic Tradition*, trans. D. M. Barton (Philadelphia: Westminster Press, 1965).

9:26 and Matt. 16:27). Here is the *future, glorious Son of Man*. The apocalyptic discourse of Mark 13 (parr. in Matt. and Luke) brings out details of the Son of Man's coming—how he will "send out the angels, and gather his elect from the four winds, from the ends of the earth to the ends of heaven" (Mark 13:26 parr.). The nature of the relationship between Jesus and this Son of Man remains unclear, although the fact of a relationship is clearly asserted, "And I tell you, every one who acknowledges me before men, the Son of man also will acknowledge before the angels of God" (Luke 12:8 f.; cf. Matt. 10:32 f.). In the apocalyptic Son of Man sayings Jesus never explicitly says that he is the Son of Man.[53]

The sayings concerning the present, *suffering Son of Man* are more stereotyped than the first category. They teach "that the Son of man must suffer many things, and be rejected by the elders and the chief priests and the scribes, and be killed, and after three days rise again" (Mark 8:31 parr.).[54] The most crucial saying of this type speaks explictly of Jesus' redemptive mission, "For the Son of Man also came not to be served but to serve, and to give his life as a ransom for many" (Mark 10:45 par.; cf. Luke 22:27).

A less clearly defined type deals with the *earthly activity of Jesus as Son of Man*, apart from his suffering. In this role Jesus has authority to forgive sins (Mark 2:10 parr.) and is lord of the sabbath (Mark 2:27 f. parr.). The earthly Son of Man is accused of being a glutton, a drunkard, a friend of tax collectors and sinners (Matt. 11:18 f.; Luke 7:33 f.), and, as Son of Man, Jesus has nowhere to lay his head (Matt. 8:20, Luke 9:58).[55]

How then are we to understand the Son of Man sayings and the relationship among the three types of sayings? Are they all authentic words of Jesus, or have some sayings originated in the early church? For example, what is the origin of the belief that Jesus will come in the parousia as the glorious, powerful Son of Man? Was this hope originated by Jesus or the early church? How is it possible to relate the suffering Son of Man and the future glorious Son of Man, especially when Jesus talks of the latter as if he were someone other than himself?

One ingenious way of understanding the varied uses of "Son of Man" by Jesus suggests that the title functioned as a kind of nickname. Any traditional title for Jesus, such as "Christ" (Messiah) or "Son of God," would have allowed Jesus' disciples to pigeonhole him, to put his message and person into some preconceived messianic expectation. Therefore, Jesus chose the enigmatic title, "Son of Man," which both arrested the attention of Jesus' disciples and left them puzzled as to the nature of his

[53] For other apocalyptic Son of Man sayings, cf. Luke 12:40; 17:22–30; 18:8; 21:36; Matt. 13:41–43; 19:28; 24:29–44; 25:31 ff.
[54] See also Mark 9:9 par.; Mark 9:31, cf. Matt. 17:22 f. and Luke 9:44; Mark 10: 33 f. parr.; Mark 14:21 par.; Mark 14:41, cf. Matt. 26:45 and Luke 22:48.
[55] Cf. also Luke 11:29 f. (Matt. 12:40); Matt. 13:36 ff.; and Luke 19:10.

activity and word. Only after Jesus' death and resurrection did the disciples understand. Jesus used the obscure and puzzling nickname, "Son of Man," in order to express the paradox that the one whom they awaited in a future glorious coming was the same one who suffered, died, and was raised from the dead.[56]

A similar understanding of the relationship of the three types of "Son of Man" sayings takes its clue from the saying: "For the Son of Man also came not to be served but to serve, and to give his life as a ransom for many" (Mark 10:45; Matt. 20:28). The future, glorious Son of Man has to act in the present as the suffering servant (see Isaiah 53). Jesus realizes that his suffering and death are necessary in order to bring forgiveness for mankind. Otherwise the future, glorious coming in power and judgment as Son of Man would only bring condemnation to a hopeless mankind. Thus Jesus' messianic consciousness uniquely combines two originally separate and distinct messianic expectations, the suffering servant and the Son of Man.[57]

This interpretation of Jesus' messianic consciousness finds a place for all three strands of the Son of Man tradition: Jesus understands his first earthly activity as that of announcing the kingdom and enacting suffering for redemption of sins, and his future activity of glory will follow upon its successful completion. This explanation, however, is called into question by the difficult fact that the expression, "servant of God," occurs only once in the Synoptic Gospels (Matt. 12:18), and this instance looks like Matthean redaction (cf. 12:18 ff.). Another possible implicit reference to the suffering servant occurs again in the Matthean editorial conclusion of a group of miracle stories (Matt. 8:17). Although the early church undoubtedly read Jesus' death in light of the suffering servant of Isaiah (see Mark 10:45 par. "his life as a ransom for many," and Mark 14:24 par. "blood poured out for many"), no convincing evidence has emerged that Jesus saw his role as that of the suffering servant.[58] If Jesus saw himself under any messianic title, it was "Son of Man." It is therefore scarcely right to interpret this title in the light of suffering servant when it is not at all obvious that Jesus thought of himself as the servant.

Our own interpretation of Jesus' use of the "Son of Man" title can be clarified by three critical observations: First, in the apocalyptic Son of

---

[56] See Ramsey, *Religious Language*, pp. 159–167.

[57] See Cullmann, *Christology of the New Testament*, pp. 51–82, 164, and 317 f. Other numerous supporters of this understanding of Jesus' consciousness include William Manson, *Jesus the Messiah* (Philadelphia: Westminster Press, 1946); Vincent Taylor, *Jesus and His Sacrifice* (New York: St. Martins Press, 1953); J. Jeremias and W. Zimmerli, *The Servant of God* (SBT, 20; London: SCM, 1961); and J. W. Bowman, *The Intention of Jesus* (Philadelphia: Westminster Press, 1943).

[58] See also Acts 3:13, 26; 4:25–30, Rom. 4:25, I Peter 2:21–25. Cf. M. D. Hooker *Jesus and the Servant* (London: SPCK, 1959); and Eduard Schweizer, *Lordship and Discipleship* (SBT, 28; London: SCM Press, 1960), pp. 50 f.

Man sayings, Jesus speaks of the Son of Man as someone other than himself. Second, the suffering Son of Man sayings, with their very explicit reference to Jesus' having to suffer, die, and be raised on the third day, seem to be the early church's confession put into Jesus' mouth. (We have to reckon with the creative handling of the tradition by the early church.) Third, the miscellaneous type of saying probably reflects the early church's assumption that Jesus referred to himself as the Son of Man. Under that assumption the reporters of the Jesus tradition quite naturally and easily substituted "Son of Man" for an original "I" (for example, Matt. 10:32 f.; cf. Luke 12:8 and Mark 8:38 par.).[59]

The apocalyptic Son of Man sayings recommend themselves most highly as the words of the historical Jesus because they do not represent any later Christian interest, for in them Jesus does not speak of himself as the Son of Man. His proclamation of a coming Son of Man also fits well into his conception of the coming kingdom. Moreover, if only this type were original with Jesus, then it is possible to understand how the other two types of Son of Man sayings arose. The early church identified the expected Son of Man with Jesus. Therefore, it felt no compunction about both substituting "Son of Man" in sayings of Jesus which originally had the simple "I" (the third type) and creating sayings that explained the central mission of Jesus, his death and resurrection (the second type), as the destiny of the Son of Man.

Earlier we maintained that Jesus' eschatological message was both present and future oriented. Yet our conclusion regarding the Son of Man sayings stresses the future glorious coming and apparently leaves no room for Jesus' having understood the kingdom as already being "inaugurated" in the present. These same future-oriented words, however, also stress the significance of the present, "And I tell you, every one who acknowledges me before men, the Son of man also will acknowledge before the angels of God; but he who denies me before men will be denied before the angels of God" (Luke 12:8 f.; cf. Matt. 10:32 f.).[60] This and similar apocalyptic Son of Man sayings confirm what we have already discovered about the message of the historical Jesus: (1) Though pointing to an eschatological future, wild apocalyptic detail is noticeably lacking. (2) Warning and promise (tension of present and future) are characteristically combined. (3) The sayings call for a response to Jesus, his message and his action. (4) This response does not, however, center on Jesus' understanding of himself, but rather on the crisis of salvation and new life for his hearers. Those who respond to Jesus in the present are preparing salvation

---

[59] Cf. also Matt. 16:13 and Mark 8:27 and Bornkamm, *Jesus of Nazareth*, p. 230.

[60] See also Mark 8:38 (Luke 9:26); Matt. 24:44 (Luke 12:40; Luke 17:22 f.; Matt. 24:26 f.); Matt. 24:37–39 (Luke 17:26 f.); Luke 11:30 (Matt. 12:40). Tödt, *The Son of Man in the Synoptic Tradition*, p. 344, carefully argues for the authenticity of these Son of Man sayings.

for the future. Jesus understood his present activity of proclaiming the kingdom and calling for radical obedience to the will of God as decisive for the future consummation of the kingdom.

Do we then imply that Jesus did not claim to be the Son of Man and therefore made no messianic claim? If so, we seem to be running counter to the explicit evidence of the New Testament. Three passages seem to prove that Jesus thought of himself as the Messiah—the confession of Peter at Caesarea Philippi, John the Baptist's question to Jesus, and Jesus' answer to the high priest at the trial.

Each of these incidents is often taken to mean that Jesus claimed to be the Messiah. Yet close examination shows that this is not clearly the case. In the Markan account of the confession at Caesarea Philippi (8:27–33), Peter does say that Jesus is the Messiah; however, it is by no means clear that Jesus accepts the title.[61] When John the Baptist sends emissaries to Jesus to determine whether he is the One to come, the Messiah, Jesus does not give a direct answer. Although Jesus' response is usually taken as affirmative, Jesus points only to his activity and does not claim or accept any title (Matt. 11:2–6). In the trial scene Jesus answers the high priest's question about messiahship positively (Mark 14:62), but the historicity of this exchange is at least questionable. Moreover, the Matthean and Lukan versions of the incident do not contain this clear, affirmative answer, and the original text of Mark may not have either.[62] In view of the unanimous testimony of the New Testament writers that Jesus was the Christ, it is very striking that the Synoptic writers so seldom portray him as making, or even accepting, messianic claims. Whether Jesus thought of himself in messianic terms is a difficult question to decide. It is clear enough, however, that he did not measure the response to his message and action by the titles that hearers might confer upon him. Rather the true response came about when men saw in his mission and message the advent of God's kingdom. Allegiance to Jesus or honoring him with messianic titles meant nothing unless a new reality, a new way of life, resulted for those whom Jesus encountered.

What, then, was Jesus' understanding of himself? Though he offered no Christological blueprint, he certainly reflected upon his own role in the mission upon which he embarked. Jesus' "self-concept" becomes clear in his reply to the inquiry of John the Baptist's disciples, "And blessed is he who takes no offense at me" (Matt. 11:6; Luke 7:23). In context, Jesus says that he asks nothing more than acknowledgment of the miracles that are occurring and the good news that is being proclaimed. In other words,

---

[61] See R. H. Fuller, *The Mission and Achievement of Jesus* (SBT 12; London: SCM Press, 1963), pp. 109 f.; and Cullmann, *The Christology of the New Testament*, pp. 120–125.

[62] See Bultmann, *History of the Synoptic Tradition*, pp. 269–271; also Borsch, *The Son of Man in Myth and Tradition*, pp. 391–394.

the center of Jesus' message is the eschatological salvation being offered the hearer.[63]

Jesus' Call to Discipleship

Jesus gathered disciples (Mark 1:16–20) crying out, "Follow *me* and *I* will make you become fishers of men" (Mark 1:17; Matt. 4:19; cf. Luke 5:10). He summoned Levi, the tax collector, with a curt, "Follow me" (Mark 2:14; Luke 5:27 f.; cf. Matt. 9:9). Jesus speaks, men drop what they are doing and follow then or not at all (cf. Luke 9:59–62).

The Synoptic Gospels report that the Pharisees had disciples (Matt. 22:16), as did the later rabbis and John the Baptist (cf. Mark 2:18 parr.). Yet despite certain analogies with other leaders and teachers, Jesus stands out as one who called disciples with an unprecedented authority. Indeed such authority already implies something like a messianic claim: "Nothing like this is to be found except in connection with the would-be messiahs, Judas and Theudas, and with John the Baptist, who was however regarded by his disciples as a messianic figure."[64] Our assessment of the evidence has made us hesitate until now to speak of any direct, explicit messianic claim by Jesus. We are not, however, thereby committed to the position that Jesus retreated from any assumption of authority. That there ever existed a gentle Jesus, meek and mild, is highly improbable. In order to form a coherent portrait we must bear in mind the authoritative claim that is at least implicit in Jesus' teaching, healing, and suffering. Probably this claim comes to clearest expression in Jesus' calling of disciples.

Jesus called disciples to a close, personal relationship with himself (Mark 1:17; 2:14). The source of that authoritative action lay in Jesus' proclamation of the dawning of the kingdom (Mark 1:15), for this sense of God's immediate presence gave impetus to the call. Henceforth, the disciples had a new allegiance; the old had to be left behind, whether vocation (fishing, tax collecting), possessions (Mark 10:17–31 parr.), or sacred obligations (Matt. 8:22 par.). Discipleship promised no easy way. On the one hand, the disciples were called to proclaim the kingdom and to heal the sick (Mark 6:7–13; cf. Matt. 10:1–11:1, Luke 9:1–6, 10:1–12), and on the other hand they were to follow Jesus into service and suffering (Mark 10:32–45 parr.). Nevertheless, the relation to Jesus promised a blessed future for whoever, without shame, remained close to him (Mark 8:38; cf. Matt. 16:27 and Luke 9:26).

---

[63] This point receives support in Mark 8:38, where instead of enjoining a positive "acknowledgment," Jesus commands a negative "not being ashamed"; and in Matthew's parable of the great judgment (25:31–46), where the meeting with the Son of Man evokes a judgment based not upon confession of Jesus, but rather upon whether the disciple loves the neighbor. In addition, Jesus nowhere identifies himself with the Son of Man in this parable.

[64] Schweizer, *Lordship and Discipleship*, p. 14.

Jesus' call to discipleship was not an autonomous act on his part. Rather it resulted from his proclamation of the inbreaking kingdom of God, and the understanding of God's radical demand which that message involved. Jesus rejected the temptations of worldly security symbolized by the miracle of bread, the possession of the temple, and the rulership of all kingdoms (Matt. 4:1–11; Luke 4:1–13). Similarly Jesus called disciples away from their security to the business of following him. Only those who followed would truly know Jesus and recognize that his confidence rested not in himself but in the God who beckoned him to proclaim the kingdom, heal the sick, and risk his life in Jerusalem.

Jesus' call brought men into the rule of God, but they would have to follow Jesus before they could be permanently assured of that kingdom. Yet the disciple was not left to survive or perish on his own. He was truly a follower, and benefited from the work of the one who had led. The call to discipleship was a challenge and a demand. Yet Jesus asked his disciples to do nothing that he himself was unwilling to do, and he promised God's ultimate protection to those who came after him.

The Authority of Jesus

For the sake of clarity the evidence for Jesus' implicit authority may be divided into four groupings:

(1) That Jesus *acted* with authority in the exorcisms and healings as well as in the calling of disciples has already become apparent. Of first importance is the fact that these acts were all the more authoritative by virtue of their having been done in the context of Jesus' proclamation about the dawning kingdom of God.

(2) Jesus indirectly *claimed* an unprecedented immediate relationship with God. An indication of this close relationship was Jesus' use of *abba*, the child's intimate, everyday word for father, to address God. This way of speaking to God was so daring that the Synoptics record only one instance of it, in the Garden of Gethsemane, where Jesus prayed, "Abba, Father, all things are possible to thee; remove this cup from me; yet not what I will, but what thou wilt" (Mark 14:36; cf. Rom. 8:15, Gal. 4:6). No parallel for such intimate familiarity with God is known from first-century Judaism.[65] A second indication of such an intimate relationship was Jesus' remarkable use of *amen* to introduce a pronouncement. Ordinarily *amen*, meaning "so be it," was a liturgical response. In Jesus' usage, however, it is a solemn assurance, like the swearing of an oath.[66] Thus in effect, Jesus' style of teaching claimed an authority unprecedented among first-century rabbis and teachers.

(3) Jesus authoritatively grants *forgiveness* to all sorts of people. The

[65] See R. Kittel, "Abba," *TDNT*, I, pp. 3 f.
[66] The RSV translates the Greek *amēn* with "truly." See Matt. 5:18; Mark 3:28; Luke 23:43; and Käsemann, *Essays on New Testament Themes*, pp. 41 f.

forgiveness of God was, of course, nothing new to Judaism, but Jesus proclaimed a more radical forgiveness. For him all men were basically in need of forgiveness because no one could merit God's favor. But beyond this, Jesus is reported to have himself spoken a word of forgiveness over sinners (Mark 2:5; Luke 7:48; 23:34). In so doing he assumed a unique position of authority (Mark 2:7). Although proclaiming the kingdom of God, both in terms of judgment and forgiveness, Jesus spoke primarily in terms of the latter, "I came not to call the righteous, but sinners" (Mark 2:17 parr.; Luke 7:36–50; 18:9–14).

(4) The final evidence for Jesus' assumption of authority is his *radical interpretation of the law*. Jesus was and remained a Jew in his obedience to the law, as the Gospel tradition attests. Yet Jesus radically reinterpreted the law in at least three particular respects: First, he denied that impurity could invade a man from external sources (Mark 7:1–23 par.). Such an extreme qualification of the ancient world's distinction between clean and unclean constituted an attack upon the law's cultic structure, whether or not Jesus acknowledged it. Second, Jesus set his own authority over against that of Moses, especially in the antitheses of the Sermon on the Mount (Matt. 5:21–48). The antitheses ("But I say to you . . .") followed traditional rabbinic form. But a rabbi opposed his teaching to other rabbis whereas Jesus opposed his teaching to that of Moses. This authoritative claim exceeded the bounds of piety. Third, Jesus set scripture over against scripture and by so doing assumed authority over the written word of scripture (Mark 10:2–12; cf. Matt. 19:3–12). Although scribes developed oral interpretation of the scriptures, their interpretation did not set one passage over against another and claim that one scripture was less authoritative because it represented a concession to human weakness.

How could Jesus assume such authority? The probable explanation proceeds from the central proclamation of Jesus concerning the irruption of the kingdom of God. This emergent rule of God rendered all other authority provisional and transitory. The preaching of the inaugurated kingdom gave to Jesus' message a fresh, almost revolutionary, quality that inevitably offended those who respected traditional authority.

Healings were occurring; disciples were being called; forgiveness was being offered; a new community of "forgiven sinners" was being formed; and the law was being radically reinterpreted. Something new was appearing in many forms. But Jesus' treatment of the law was very likely the primary cause for opposition to him. Jesus had, probably unknowingly, touched the nerve of first century Judaism. Eventually the separation of his followers ("Christians") from the old religious community resulted. Understandably, the leaders of Judaism rejected Jesus and his authority; their opposition led to his being handed over to be crucified by the Roman government as a politically dangerous revolutionary. To this last dramatic chapter of Jesus' ministry we now turn.

The Suffering Messiah

Our efforts to reconstruct the historical Jesus have been guided by the principle of coherence. According to the tradition, Jesus of Nazareth was a man who healed, taught, and suffered a criminal's death. Our portrait of him must include these three elements in a coherent, understandable way or else historical criticism is unable to make sense of the tradition. The necessity for coherence becomes a problem when we now turn to the final element in the historical Jesus tradition, the death of Jesus. Why was Jesus crucified? Was his death simply the tragic end of a man who had gone about doing good, both in deed and word? How was it possible that one who had performed miracles could die in such weakness? How could one who evidently attracted such crowds of followers have been completely deserted at the last days?

Already some indications of answers to these questions have become apparent. The Teaching Messiah turned out to be something more than an instructor in good works, piety, and universal kindness. At the center of Jesus' teaching was the kingdom proclamation. As herald of the kingdom, Jesus claimed an authority which startled and astounded some and

Judaea, the Dead Sea, and Idumaea.

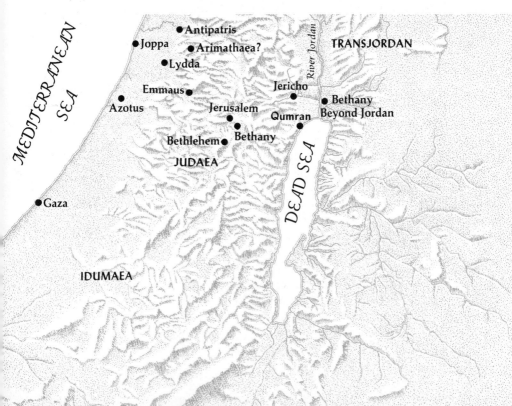

threatened others. The challenge of Jesus' authoritative message and activity met resistance that finally culminated in his death.

We have already observed that the Healing Messiah possessed authority. But without faith in the power of God, healing did not take place. Moreover, the healings that Jesus effected demonstrated not his rulership but his service to God and others. The Gospel of Matthew aptly and succinctly characterized the miraculous healing power of Jesus with the passage from Isaiah, "He took our infirmities and bore our diseases" (Matt. 8:17). Surprisingly, just that passage could be applied to the death of Jesus (Matt. 26:28; cf. Rom. 5:8 and John 3:16). Perhaps the powerful miracle-working Jesus and the crucified Jesus complement, rather than contradict, each other.

We have also come to recognize Jesus' limited use of power by the way in which the miracle tradition is treated in both Mark and Matthew. The heightened miracle tradition in the first half of Mark did not succeed in producing true discipleship. The disciples become truly faithful only after Jesus' death and resurrection. In Matthew, condensation of the Markan miracle tradition focused attention upon the word of Jesus rather than upon his miracle power. Each Gospel affirms that Jesus worked miracles, yet each Gospel sets the miraculous within the framework of a ministry that concludes with Jesus' crucifixion. Jesus' power did not deliver him from that apparently ignominious end. Jesus' words and works led unerringly to his death. Thus, it is correct to say that the Gospels are "passion narratives with extended introductions."

THE PASSION AND DEATH OF JESUS

Why does Jesus go to Jerusalem?
Who are the chief actors in the passion narrative?
Does Jesus will his death?

Before looking more closely at the passion narrative, we need to reckon with possible reasons for Jesus' final fatal journey to Jerusalem. Although the Fourth Gospel records several trips to Jerusalem, the Synoptic Gospels give the impression that Jesus journeyed from Galilee to Jerusalem only at the close of his ministry.[67] This journey occupies a central place in the Gospels. As we discovered, Luke made that journey the crucial middle section of his Gospel (Luke 9:51–19:27), even though the distance

---

[67] Our interpretation of Mark has already shown the difficulty of accepting the Markan outline as a reliable chronological guide to Jesus' ministry. We can be certain of little more than that Jesus' mission began with his baptism and ended with his crucifixion. See Kümmel, *Introduction to the New Testament*, pp. 63 f., and F. C. Grant, *The Gospels: Their Origin and Growth* (New York: Harper & Row, 1957), pp. 83–86.

between Galilee and Jerusalem was less than one hundred miles. Mark's tradition describes the journey to Jerusalem as a decisive and awesome step, "And they were on the road, going up to Jerusalem, and Jesus was walking ahead of them; and they were amazed, and those who followed were afraid" (Mark 10:32; cf. Matt. 20:17 and Luke 18:31).

Some New Testament interpreters take at face value the Markan view that Jesus went to Jerusalem to die. For example, it is maintained that a new conviction dawned upon Jesus at Caesarea Philippi: "The [apocalyptic] tribulation, so far as Jesus is concerned, is now connected with an historic event: he will go to Jerusalem, there to suffer death at the hands of the authorities. He must suffer for others . . . that the kingdom might come."[68] This hypothesis not only takes Mark (8:31) at face value, but assumes that Jesus had an apocalyptic mind set. As we have seen, both aspects of the hypothesis are subject to serious question. Moreover, so far as we can tell from the Synoptic Gospels themselves, Jesus did not act in Jerusalem as if he were carrying out a preconceived plan to die. The hypothesis rests in part upon the view that Jesus took upon himself the role of the suffering servant of Isaiah 53: "For the Son of man also came not to be served but to serve, and to give his life as a ransom for many" (Mark 10:45). Our previous discussion suggested that this saying more likely reflects the faith of the early church than the consciousness of Jesus.

The reasons for Jesus' journey to Jerusalem can be discussed when we look at the incidents that reportedly took place in Jerusalem. As an alternative working hypothesis we suggest that Jesus went to Jerusalem in order to preach the coming kingdom of God, for no person who had a message for Israel could fail to take it to the capital city. In Jerusalem Jesus sought a final decision about the irrupting kingdom.[69] In the carrying out of this mission Jesus could hardly have been blind to the possibility that his own death might result (cf. Luke 13:33). That he consciously sought his death, however, is improbable. Jesus' kingdom proclamation does not center upon his own role, and the traditions of the kingdom and the coming Son of Man say nothing explicitly about his intention to die. Moreover, the view that Jesus sought to bring in the kingdom through his suffering lacks support of the Gospels themselves.

The Events of Jesus' Passion and Death

Unlike other traditions in the Synoptics, the passion story, beginning with the entry into Jerusalem (Mark 11:1; Matt. 21:1; Luke 19:28), constitutes a full, detailed narrative covering a period of days. Moreover, we get the impression that we are being told the facts without embellishment and without obvious intrusion of faith considerations. The opponents

---

[68] Schweitzer, *The Quest of the Historical Jesus*, pp. 386 f.
[69] See Bornkamm, *Jesus of Nazareth*, pp. 154 f.

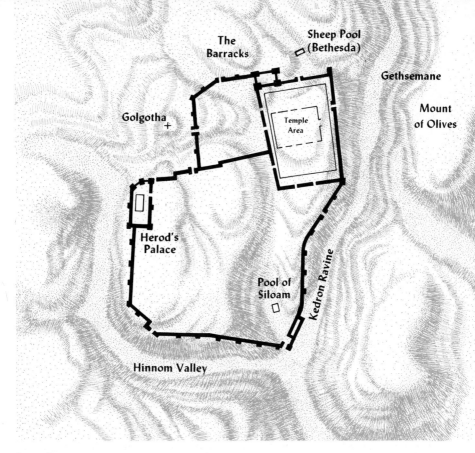

Jerusalem.

of Jesus have the upper hand, and Jesus dies. The impression of accuracy is heightened by the remarkable agreement of the Synoptic Gospels in sequence of events and in details, an agreement considerably greater than in the earlier portions of the Gospels. This becomes even more pronounced with the arrest, trial, and crucifixion of Jesus; even the Fourth Gospel (John 18–19) seems but another voice in the Synoptic chorus.

The major episodes of the passion story in their general order are: the triumphal entry into Jerusalem (Mark 11:1–10); the cleansing of the temple (Mark 11:15–19); the controversies about authority (Mark 11:27–33; 12:1–12, 13–17, 18–27, 28–34); the apocalyptic discourse (Mark 13); the anointing of Jesus (Mark 14:3–9); the last supper (Mark 14:12–25); Jesus in the Garden of Gethsemane (Mark 14:32–42); Jesus' arrest and trial (Mark 14:43–65); the release of Barabbas (Mark 15:6–15); and finally the crucifixion and burial of Jesus (Mark 15:16–47). Without going into extensive detail in regard to these individual episodes, we suggest that the narrative leads naturally to the following reconstruction of Jesus' activity and reception in Jerusalem.

217

Entry of Jesus into Jerusalem. Sculpture from a lintel over a doorway near Massa Carrara, Italy (ca. 1175.) (Courtesy of Metropolitan Museum of Art. Purchase, 1962. The Cloisters Collection.)

Jesus' triumphal entry into Jerusalem was open to dangerous misinterpretation. The acclamation of the crowds, "Blessed is the kingdom of our father David that is coming!" (Mark 11:10; cf. Matt. 21:9, Luke 19:38), designated him as a political king who would restore the fortunes of Israel by leading a revolution to overthrow Roman domination. Consequently, Jesus' first action after entering Jerusalem was well suited to squash any such political misunderstanding. Jesus cleansed Israel's temple, and thus attacked, not Rome, but the center of Israel's piety in Jerusalem. Perhaps Jesus' attack was motivated as much by the exclusivism of the temple as it was by "business" in the holy place (Mark 11:15–17; cf. Isaiah 56:7 and Jeremiah 7:11). In all probability, Jesus went there to proclaim the coming kingdom (cf. Malachi 3:1), but the temple's corruption provoked him into hostility against its custodians. Understandably, the religious leaders reacted violently to this action (Mark 11:18); at the trial they accused him of having come to destroy the temple (Mark 14:57 f.; cf. 13:2).

Accordingly, the controversy of the passion story centers more upon the question of what authority Jesus possessed to do these things than upon the specifically messianic question (Mark 11:28). The opponents of Jesus tried to fit him into the category of a political revolutionary (cf. Mark 12:13–17) and to engage him in theological disputes (cf. the resurrection question in Mark 12:18–27 and the query about the first commandment in Mark 12:28–34). But Jesus continued to threaten their security by proclaiming the immediacy of God's rule (Mark 12:17, 27, 34), which demanded the response of the whole person (cf. the poor widow in Mark 12:41–44). Jesus preached the dawning kingship of God rather than a political, spiritual, or moral ideology. That emphasis becomes most evident in the passion story's apocalyptic discourse; for the final days are unmistakably to be the triumphant coming of God's kingly rule and the world's judgment (note especially Mark 13:24–26 and 32 f.). Even though the apocalyptic discourse is in part probably not from Jesus, its message in the passion story authentically elaborates the last message of Jesus.

It is uncertain whether the Last Supper that Jesus shared with his disciples was a Jewish Passover meal.[70] In any event, the setting makes clear that the meal was eschatological, "Truly, I say to you, I shall not drink again of the fruit of the vine until that day when I drink it new in the kingdom of God" (Mark 14:25). This word of Jesus[71] indicates that by this time he knew that his death was imminent. His overwhelming conviction about the immediacy of the reign of God had aroused opposition, which now sought his death. The proleptic anointing of Jesus' body for burial (Mark 14:3–9) and his betrayal by Judas (Mark 14:10–21) point to the impending death. Ordinary piety had been offended. Moreover, Jesus' kingdom proclamation made him vulnerable to misrepresentation as a political revolutionary. Ironically, the very reason for Judas' betrayal may have been his disappointed realization that Jesus was not going to lead an armed revolt against Rome.

In the Garden of Gethsemane Jesus prayed that he might escape death if he would not thereby betray God's rule and will (Mark 14:36; cf. 8:35). After Gethsemane Jesus was alone, deserted even by his closest disciples (Mark 14:37, 40; see esp. Peter's denial, 14:66–72). The Gethsemane story may not be the report of an eyewitness—who was there?—yet it makes sense of the last hours of Jesus. In substance if not in detail, it is an accurate portrait.

The trial scene raises some difficult historical questions[72]; our subsequent conclusions, therefore, must remain conjectural. In the confrontation between Jesus and his judges, whether Jewish or Roman (Mark 14:53–65; 15:1–5), Jesus emerged as the victor. Although the authorities, including the Jewish high priest, condemned Jesus because he claimed to be the Messiah, no record exists of any Jewish court ever condemning anyone as a messianic pretender. Perhaps the Jewish trial before the Sanhedrin was invented by the early church as anti-Semitic polemic, especially in view of the fact that Jesus was undoubtedly killed, not by the Jewish form of capital punishment, stoning (cf. Acts 5:26, 7:58 f.), but by Roman crucifixion. Probably Jesus was first condemned by the Jewish authorities and then delivered to the Romans as a messianic pretender in order to mask the basic reason for his execution.

The Nature of the Passion Tradition

At this point we may profitably reflect about the overall nature of the passion tradition. This series of connected incidents makes sense, and the events absorb our interest purely as story. Few pious or theological interpretations interrupt the flow of the action. Later Christian doctrines on

---

[70] See Dibelius, *Jesus*, pp. 128–132. Also cf. J. Jeremias, *The Eucharistic Words of Jesus*, trans. A. Ehrhardt (Oxford: Basil Blackwell, 1955), especially pp. 1–60.

[71] Bornkamm, *Jesus of Nazareth*, p. 160, argues that it is authentic.

[72] See Bornkamm, *Jesus of Nazareth*, p. 163. For a different account, cf. Paul Winter, *On the Trial of Jesus* (Berlin: Walter de Gruyter, 1961).

the death of Jesus are not the specific focus of attention. Yet the passion story cannot be read simply as a neutral detached account of the last days of Jesus in Jerusalem.

In the study of the three Synoptic Gospels we have already become aware of some disagreement about details in the passion story. For example, Jesus' word of forgiveness from the cross in Luke (23:34) leaves quite a different impression from his final agonizing cry in Mark (15:34; Matt. 27:46). Yet obviously the various passion stories tell of the same event, the death of a Jewish religious figure in first-century Palestine, and they tell the story in much the same everyday terms. But in all the accounts another, stranger dimension is visible. The conviction that somehow God is at work

View of Jerusalem with the Garden of Gethsemane in the center and the Mount of Olives in the background. (Courtesy of Pan American Airways.)

in the very death of Jesus governs the telling of the story. Yet the reader does not look away from the incidents in order to grasp this dimension and understand their meaning. Rather the events contain their own meaning, their own depth dimension, which is conveyed within the story but is not identical with it. Jesus died and his death clarified who he was.

Two further observations about the passion story support our contention that it seeks to communicate the divine action in terms of the everyday. First, the major events are seen as the fulfillment of sacred scripture. This is especially evident in the crucifixion scene where parts of the narrative correspond closely to Psalm 22 (Mark 15:24, 29, 34; cf. Psalm 22:18, 7, 1 respectively).[73] In earlier scenes allusions to the Old Testament are also numerous. When Jesus enters Jerusalem, he apparently fulfills the prophecy of Zechariah 9:9: "Rejoice greatly, O daughter of Zion: Shout aloud, O daughter of Jerusalem: Lo, your king comes to you; triumphant and victorious is he, humble and riding on an ass, on a colt the foal of an ass" (cf. Mark 11:1–10). The cleansing of the temple fulfills the prophecies of Isaiah 56:7 and of Jeremiah 7:11 (cf. Mark 11:11–18). These Old Testament allusions are not intended to prove that Jesus was the Messiah so much as to confirm the belief that within these everyday events God was at work in extraordinary and atypical ways.

Second, the Synoptic Gospels do not dwell on the physical suffering of Jesus in the crucifixion. Although the reader is made aware that this form of execution was terrifying (cf. the scourging, Mark 15:15; the striking, 15:19; the offering of the drug, 15:23; the loud cry, 15:34, 37), the enormous possibilities for exploiting detailed description of torture in order to win human sympathy are not realized. The Roman author, Cicero (106–43 B.C.) called crucifixion "that cruel and disgusting penalty."[74] Since death by crucifixion represented one of the highest achievements of the torturer's art, we might surmise that the lack of emphasis on physical suffering in the Gospels was due to pious considerations or delicate concern for readers, but the point probably lies elsewhere. The purely human sphere of torturous agony and sympathetic response is minimized because Jesus' crucifixion was regarded as primarily the saving activity of God rather than the ordeal of a righteous martyr. Jesus is not portrayed as a hero or martyr in the modern, or ancient, sense.

The Nature of Jesus' Death in the Tradition
In the death of Jesus the passion story reaches its climax. Our conclusions concerning the earliest Christian convictions about the nature of that

---

[73] See also Mark 15:36 (Psalm 69:21); Mark 15:19 (Isaiah 50:6); Mark 15:28, note relegation to alternate reading in RSV (Isaiah 53:12); Mark 15:43 ff. (Isaiah 53:9), and so forth.

[74] *Against Verres* V, 64. Cf. the further description quoted by Goguel in *Jesus and the Origins of Christianity*, II, pp. 534 f.

Arab girl on a donkey in Palestine. (Courtesy of Israel Government Tourist Office.)

death may be gathered up in four pointed statements: (1) The real actor in the passion story was God. (2) God willed the death of Jesus. (3) That death was willed in order that men might be set free. (4) Jesus willed his own death by his life.

Though the death of Jesus occurred because of the enmity of conventional piety and political complicity, the *real actor in the passion was God*, not man. During the course of events the will of the characters was subject to the will of God. This is reflected in Mark's emphasis upon the necessity of Jesus' death and the events associated with it (cf. Mark 8:31; 14:31). Further confirmation of the "divine necessity" for Jesus' death comes from one of the primary verbs used in the passion story, *paradidōmi* (see Mark 13:9, 11, 12; 14:10; 15:1, 10, 15). This Greek verb can be translated "to betray," "to hand over," or "to deliver." In Mark, Jesus predicted, "Behold, we are going up to Jerusalem; and the Son of Man will be *delivered* to the chief priests and the scribes, and they will condemn him to death, and *deliver* him to the Gentiles; and they will mock him, and spit upon him, and scourge him, and kill him; and after three days he will rise" (10:33 f.). Next Judas (representing the disciples?) delivered Jesus into the hands of the Jewish authorities (Mark 14:10 f., 18, 21, 41 f.), and the Jewish authorities in turn delivered Jesus into the hands of Pilate (Mark 15:1, 10). Finally Pilate delivered Jesus to be crucified (Mark 15:15). In the passion story, this inexorable deliverance of Jesus to death is a token of the power of God at work behind the events.

The action that God willed was the death of Jesus. God did not directly

222

reveal this information to Jesus' contemporaries. This statement reflects the conviction of faith that the death of Jesus was, under the circumstances, the will of God. In the two direct Old Testament quotes that refer to the impending death, Jesus says to his opponents, "Have you not read this scripture, 'The very stone which the builders rejected has become the head of the corner; this was the Lord's doing, and it is marvelous in our eyes'?" (Mark 12:10 f.; cf. Psalm 118:22 f.), and to the disciples, "You will all fall away; for it is written, 'I will strike the shepherd, and the sheep will be scattered.' But after I am raised up, I will go before you to Galilee" (Mark 14:27 f.; cf. Zechariah 13:7). Both quotations are intended to imply that the death of Jesus occurred at God's bidding. Moreover, in the Gethsemane prayer Jesus asked that the cup of suffering be taken away from him *unless* his death be God's will (Mark 14:36).

The reason that God wills Jesus' death has nothing to do with divine wrath; quite the opposite, for *Jesus died in order that the guilty might go free*. This is aptly illustrated in the Barabbas episode (Mark 15:6–15). At this point in the story all notion of a trial has been abandoned, and the one amnesty possible at the festival is the center of attention. When the crowd demands the death of Jesus instead of Barabbas, the revolutionary and murderer, Pilate asks, "Why, what evil has he done?" (vs. 14). The same question dominates the reader, for Jesus had done nothing to deserve their enmity. Barabbas was guilty; Jesus was innocent. The crowd's verdict was completely wrong. Why, then, should God assent to injustice and will the death of Jesus? Jesus, who was finally crucified by the Romans as an insurrectionist, dies in order that the real revolutionary might go free. This is the meaning of Jesus' death, for the death of the innocent one allows the guilty to go free. Ironically, this point becomes explicit at the crucifixion in the scoffing of the bystanders and the chief priests as they demand that Jesus miraculously descend from the cross (Mark 15:29 f.): "He saved others; he cannot save himself" (Mark 15:31). Of course Jesus could not come down from the cross because he would thereby disobey the will of God and annul his mission and message, the bringing of life and freedom to sinners (cf. Mark 2:17 and 14:41). Jesus could do no miracle precisely because the miracle of God's coming near in forgiveness rather than judgment was taking place. Within the everyday occurrence of a Roman execution occurred the salvation of mankind—so the Christian faith claims (Rom. 5:8; cf. John 3:16, Mark 10:45, I Peter 3:18, and the like).

Jesus willed his own death by his life. We have already observed that the view that Jesus saw himself as the suffering servant of Isaiah, whose death was a means of reconciling God with man, is at least doubtful. Also Jesus probably did not enter Jerusalem with the express intention of dying, but rather to proclaim the coming kingdom of God. But if Jesus' death were not understandable as the outcome of his life, then there would be no reason why the Christian faith should be tied to this historical person's death. Why not anyone's death? Or, why any death at all?

It is our contention that Jesus willed his own death by his life. This way of stating the matter is deliberate. In effect, we are simply saying that Jesus' death climaxed and actualized his proclamation of the irruption of the kingdom of God. Jesus' radical sense of the nearness of God, his consequent break with the usual standards of righteousness, his association with sinners, and his radical criticism of the law aroused a reaction that caused his death. To be sure, Jesus did not go about his mission in Jerusalem blindly. He knew that his message and action had set in motion forces that might cause his death, but he did not seek it.

Jesus does express his intention to die in sayings ascribed to him in Mark, but these are likely the church's later interpretation of the meaning of his death as God's act. The interpretation is made definitive by putting it on Jesus' lips. Although it is difficult to regard such sayings as historically authentic, they nevertheless portray faithfully the way in which Jesus' death is related to his life. It makes a difference to historical interpretation and to Christian faith that Jesus was not accidentally run down by a chariot. He died during a Jewish passover on a Roman cross.

Although we have so far concentrated upon his death, Jesus' full identity was only seen in the light of the resurrection. But our reading of the

Crucifixion of Jesus by a contemporary West Pacific artist, A. Papuasia. (Courtesy of Spartaco Appetiti.)

Gospels confirms that the resurrection cannot be separated from the death. For Christian faith, the passion and resurrection are one story. Whether the early Christians were right, whether the story was true, still remains a matter of faith. Certainly Jesus died on a cross, that much is virtually indisputable. Yet whether that cross was really the salvation event depends upon whether the resurrection report is believed. Without the cross the resurrection is meaningless, but without the resurrection the cross remains only a tragedy.

THE RESURRECTION OF JESUS OF NAZARETH

Can the resurrection tradition be separated from the death of Jesus?
Does historical criticism establish the resurrection?
What are the agreements and disagreements in the resurrection stories?
What is the nature of the resurrection for Jesus? For the disciples?
Why does Jesus appear only to believers?
How does modern man appropriate the resurrection?

According to the New Testament, the resurrection is central for faith: "If Christ has not been raised, then our preaching is in vain and your faith is in vain" (I Cor. 15:14; cf. 15:17). Without the resurrection there would have been no Gospels, no history of the apostles, no letters, no vision of the future, and no church. Reportedly, "Michelangelo once broke out in indignant protest against his fellow-artists because they were forever depicting Christ in his death on the Cross. 'Paint him instead,' he cried, 'the Lord of life; paint him with his kingly feet planted on the stone that held him in the tomb'."[75] The origin of New Testament faith is the victory over death realized in Jesus of Nazareth.

When we talk about the resurrection of Jesus we cannot lose sight of the obvious fact that it is resurrection from the dead. Death and resurrection belong together in the New Testament tradition. Who Jesus was is answered by what he did in his life and death and by what was done for him in his being raised from the dead—"Was it not necessary that the Christ should suffer these things and enter into his glory?" (Luke 24:26).

Although the "modern mind" might find congenial the view that the resurrection stories are simply interpretations of Jesus' true identity as the one sent by God and have nothing to do with an actual event, the nature of the resurrection tradition will not allow this easy conclusion. This tradition does not read like a mythological tale. Its realistic quality allows for and demands historical investigation. To maintain that the event of Jesus'

[75] Hugh Anderson, *Jesus and Christian Origins: a Commentary on Modern Viewpoints* (New York: Oxford, 1964), p. 185.

resurrection is removed from historical investigation denies the factual claim of the early Christian faith. On the other hand, to maintain that historical investigation can decide about the resurrection denies the uniqueness and mystery of the event. Whether the resurrection of Jesus occurred is a question "for the answering of which evidence is relevant, but the evidence might all be believed without the question itself being answered in the affirmative."[76]

The question of whether the resurrection of Jesus occurred is similar to the question of whether General Douglas MacArthur really loved his country, or whether Romeo or Juliet truly loved each other, or whether the saving of another person's life was an act of genuine heroism. The evidence concerning love and heroism is all relevant, but no amount of evidence gives a final answer to the question; for someone may still raise objections by looking at the facts from a different perspective. In the same way historical criticism cannot establish the resurrection of Jesus but the work of historical criticism is relevant to the problem.

Keeping in mind, then, the centrality of the resurrection in the New Testament tradition, its inseparable relation to Jesus' death, and the important, but not decisive, role of historical criticism in investigating the resurrection, we turn to the nature of the resurrection tradition. In due course, we shall return to the problem of the nature of the resurrection itself.

The Nature of the Resurrection Tradition

The major New Testament sources of the resurrection tradition are I Corinthians 15:3–8, Mark 16:1–8, Matthew 28:1–20, Luke 24:1–53, and John 20:1–21:25. They present a bewildering array of material. The resurrection tradition presents a problem because of the variety, and even disagreements, in these reports. Our first task is to understand the discrepancies and similarities within the resurrection tradition. Next we will look at the two major types of resurrection tradition—the empty tomb reports and the accounts of resurrection appearances. Only then can we classify the traditions as to their various emphases and attempt a preliminary understanding of the nature of the resurrection.

Discrepancies within the New Testament resurrection traditions are obvious. According to Paul's tradition (I Cor. 15:3–8) the first appearance is to Peter, then to the twelve, and so on. In the Synoptic Gospels no appearance to Peter is directly reported (cf. Luke 24:34). In Mark and Matthew, only the women visit the tomb of Jesus. Luke adds that Peter then follows alone. In John's Gospel, Mary visits the tomb; then Peter and the beloved disciple follow. In Mark and Matthew, Jesus appears to the

---

[76] Ramsey, *Religious Language*, p. 149. Cf. Bornkamm, *Jesus of Nazareth*, p. 180 and P. M. Van Buren, *The Secular Meaning of the Gospels: Based on an Analysis of Its Language* (New York: Macmillan Co., 1963), p. 128.

disciples in Galilee; in Luke and John he appears in Jerusalem. Paul's tradition reports resurrection appearances to the five hundred and to James; the Gospels make no mention of any such event. Mark and Matthew do not report Jesus' eating with his disciples; Luke and John do. According to Luke, Jesus vanishes from the sight of two disciples on the road to Emmaus. Moreover, both Luke and John hand on the tradition that Jesus passed through closed doors. Such obvious discrepancies and variety raise questions about the nature of the resurrection tradition. Does a substantial historical core exist, or are these reports fantastic flights of the Christian imagination?

Paul's resurrection tradition (I Cor. 15:3–8) lists a number of eyewitnesses to the appearances of the resurrected Christ. This tradition does not claim that the witnesses saw the resurrection itself—that is, the emergence of Jesus from the tomb or his resuscitation, but rather that they saw the resurrected Christ. Paul, however, admits that he was untimely born (vs. 8), that is, his resurrection appearance was unusually late. Paul's tradition places the initiative for the appearances not with those to whom the risen Christ appeared, but with the Resurrected One himself. Moreover, the resurrection is said to have taken place "on the third day" (vs. 4). Although this time reference was probably not meant to be exact, it stresses that the resurrection occurred shortly after Jesus died.[77] The phrase, "in accordance with the scripture" (vs. 3), declares that what happened in Jesus was not the death and resurrection of just any man but of one who fulfilled the promise of God to Israel. The tradition also makes it quite explicit that he who was raised and appeared to his followers and Paul is the same Jesus who died and was buried. The Christ of faith is linked by this resurrection tradition to the historical Jesus.

In Mark (16:1–8) no resurrection appearance is reported. Instead there is the story of the empty tomb, in which the young man announces that Jesus has risen and will appear to the disciples in Galilee. Again, the initiative is with Jesus. This resurrection tradition is characterized by the women's awe at finding the tomb empty (vss. 5, 6, 8). They came piously to pay homage to the dead body, but the crucified Jesus departed ahead of them.

Matthew's tradition (28:1–20) enlarges that of Mark. His story of the empty tomb includes a resurrection appearance to the women (vs. 9), which is followed by an appearance to the disciples in Galilee (vss. 16–20). Here the dominant mood is that of joy and worship. In contrast to this response, we read that the Jews have made elaborate precautions to prevent the theft of Jesus' body (27:62–66; 28:11–15). The resurrected Jesus' speaks to his disciples about their future tasks and affirms his identity with

---

[77] See Anderson, *Jesus and Christian Origins*, p. 214. We are indebted in this discussion of the resurrection tradition to his analysis (*ibid.*, pp. 211–237).

the historical Jesus (". . . teaching them to observe all that I have commanded you" vs. 20; see pp. 130 ff.).

Luke (24:1–53) contains the most elaborate tradition of the resurrection in the Synoptic Gospels. The empty tomb is subordinated to the resurrection appearances, for, as Luke puts it, "these words seemed to them an idle tale, and they did not believe them" (vs. 11). In the road to Emmaus story (vss. 13–35), the two disciples do not recognize Jesus by his physical appearance. They only know him when he, taking the initiative, explains the scriptural basis for his death and resurrection and performs the familiar act of blessing, breaking, and giving the bread. "Then they told what had happened on the road, and how he was known to them in the breaking of the bread" (vs. 35). Jesus then eats with his disciples in order to show that he is not a disembodied spirit (vss. 36–43), even though he has just been reported to have vanished and appeared again in the same context (cf. vss. 31 and 36). Like Matthew, Luke includes Jesus' final instruction to his disciples, which reiterates Luke's message of Jesus: "Repentance and forgiveness of sins should be preached in his name to all nations, beginning from Jerusalem" (vs. 47). Luke's resurrection account ends with Jesus' departure (vss. 50–53; cf. Acts 1:9–11). In Luke as in the other accounts, something happens because of the Resurrected One's initiative. Furthermore, it is again made clear that the risen Jesus could not be known apart from his historical life and death. More directly than in Matthew the task of the church is explained and handed over to the disciples. In fact, they must now perform that task without the aid of the resurrected Jesus.

In John's Gospel account (John 20:1–21:25) Mary Magdalene comes alone to the tomb; Peter and the other disciples follow later. Then Mary, like the disciples on the road to Emmaus, receives an appearance of the risen Christ whom she only recognizes after he speaks her name. Curiously, she is told not to hold him (vs. 17), for he has still to ascend to the Father. Before departing to the Father, however, Jesus gives the disciples the Holy Spirit, after having demonstrated that he is the same Jesus who has been crucified. This point is underscored in the appearance of Christ to Thomas. The Johannine resurrection appearances, like those of Luke, are reported to have occurred in Jerusalem. The appendix of John also includes an appearance in Galilee (chap. 21; cf. Matt. 28:16–20) in which Jesus eats fish to show that he is no spirit or vision. Moreover, he identifies himself with reference to his earthly mission, commanding Simon Peter to feed his sheep (cf. John 13:34).

The traditions we have surveyed present two problems centering about the relation between the empty tomb stories and the appearance narratives and the character of the resurrection appearances themselves.

The empty tomb story appears in all four Gospels, although it is not mentioned by Paul in his report of the resurrection appearances. The most probable inference is that the empty tomb story was later than the reports of appearances. Its inclusion in all the Gospels is probably to be attributed to their dependence on Mark. This conclusion rests in part upon evidence within the resurrection stories themselves that the tradition of the empty tomb was not initially known (see Matt. 27:51–54 and Luke 23:43). There are also innumerable parallels to the empty tomb story in the history of religions.[78] Moreover, we need to keep in mind that the empty tomb was an ambiguous witness to the resurrection. It attests the absence of the body, but not necessarily the reality or presence of the risen Jesus. Not illogically the Talmud reports that the body of Jesus was stolen. Apparently against just such a rumor Matthew elaborated a defense (28:11–15). Probably the empty tomb story reflects the deliberation of faith about what actually happened to Jesus' body, for according to the best New Testament evidence the early disciples were convinced of Jesus' resurrection, not by the empty tomb, but by the appearances. These appearances of the risen Christ attest most accurately the nature of the resurrection tradition. In effect the disciples exclaimed, "He appeared to me!" Their faith had been broken by Jesus' death and they had fled. Yet something had happened at the resurrection, something not of their own initiative, but of the One who acted through the crucified Jesus—the God who raised him from the dead.

The problem of the character of the resurrection appearances is summed up in the question of whether they were physical or spiritual. The traditions are unanimous in saying that the resurrection was both physical and spiritual. Jesus ate with the disciples, they could see and touch the marks of the nails; but he could go through closed doors and vanish out of their sight. Paul claimed that the appearance to him was of the same nature as the appearances to Peter, the twelve, and so on (see Acts 9:1–9; 22:4–11; 26:9–18), but how could that be a physical appearance? Indeed, in the same chapter of I Corinthians, he describes the resurrected body as a spiritual, not a physical, body and says that flesh and blood (that is, a physical resurrection) cannot inherit the kingdom of God (I Cor. 15:50; cf. 15:35–58). Paul knew, like the evangelists, that he was talking about a mystery which no "either . . . or," either physical or spiritual, could solve. The decisive emphasis in all accounts is that the one who appeared was the same Jesus who had also died and been buried. Faith believed that the risen Jesus was no figment of the imagination; the historical Jesus had been raised from the dead. Therefore, the disciples knew that death had been conquered. Exactly how it was conquered remained a mystery, but that it was conquered, of this Paul was as certain as were the evangelists. "Thanks be to God, who gives us the victory through our Lord Jesus Christ" (I Cor. 15:57).

In summary, the varied resurrection traditions point to some basic

[78] See E. Bickermann, "Das leere Grab," ZNW, 23 (1924), pp. 281–292.

assumptions about the resurrection. The death of Jesus had left the disciples in confusion (Luke 24:4) or fear for their lives (Mark 14:50). At Jesus' death, he was completely alone, forsaken by all of them (however, cf. John 16:32). But at the resurrection, the disciples were changed and made new. This transformation is implicit in the various traditions. It was not of their own doing; they attributed it to the resurrected Jesus who had appeared to them. Jesus' resurrection was not a product of faith. Rather, the resurrection had forced itself upon them, sometimes unwanted and always unexpected. And the resurrected one who appeared was always that Jesus whom they had known in his life and death.

The Nature of the Resurrection

The most pressing and immediate question about the resurrection of Jesus is whether or in what sense it was a real occurrence. Although differences exist among the resurrection traditions, the accounts unanimously agree that the one who died and was buried was also raised and appeared to a number of eyewitnesses. We can be reasonably certain that something happened, but we are less certain about exactly what happened. As even our sources acknowledge that the resurrection is a unique event, analogous occurrrences cannot be adduced to support its actuality.

The difficulty of knowing exactly what happened may be illustrated by a recent effort to prove that the empty tomb actually occurred.[79] The basic premise of the argument is that historical criticism assumes that a cause must be at least equal to the effect. The early church would not have claimed the actuality of the empty tomb if someone could have checked the tomb and found Jesus' body there. We may therefore assume that the tomb was empty for any who wished to see. The only answer to the question of what caused the empty tomb, other than the resurrection of Jesus, would be that the disciples stole Jesus' body. But would the disciples risk their lives for a deception? To believe, moreover, that the empty tomb was a fraud involves believing that the rise and growth of the early church occurred in spite of the fact that everything was based upon a hoax. It can also be argued that the disciples had no reason to expect only Jesus' resurrection. Jesus talked about a general resurrection, not his individual resurrection. If cause for the belief in Jesus' resurrection is to be found neither in the teaching of Jesus nor in a deception about the empty tomb, then it must be found in the risen Jesus himself. Thus the resurrection of Jesus is demonstrated by the historical-critical method.

Apart from the questionable premise that a historical cause has to be at least equal to its effect, the notion that the empty tomb could be

[79] See D. P. Fuller, "The Resurrection of Jesus and the Historical Method," *JBR*, 34 (January, 1966), pp. 18–24. Cf. H. von Campenhausen, *Der Ablauf der Osterereignisse und das leere Grab* ("Sitzungsberichte der Heidelberger Akademie der Wissenschaften"; Heidelberg: Carl Winter Universitäts Verlag, 1958).

checked presupposes that the empty tomb tradition arose immediately after Jesus' death. But we have already suggested that this tradition was a later addition in elaboration of the resurrection story. The prospects of defending the resurrection of Jesus against unbelief by means of historical arguments are, therefore, not promising. Even if it could be proved that the corpse of Jesus had been resuscitated, that would not necessarily prove the reality of the resurrection as Christian faith understands it. The Gospels themselves report other instances of people raised from the dead: the widow of Nain (Luke 7:11–17), the daughter of Jairus (Mark 5:21–24, 35–43), and Lazarus (John 11:1–44). Yet no one, not even the early Christians, claimed these resurrections from the dead were *the* decisive eschatological acts of God. It was furthermore assumed that these people could, and would, die (John 12:9 ff.).

If the resurrection was a historical occurrence, it was, according to the New Testament, one that could be separated neither from Jesus' death nor from the act of faith. The resurrection was not a separate event beside the death of Jesus. It preserved, and was based upon, knowledge of that event. We have already noted that the tradition continually stressed that the resurrection had fully occurred only when the risen one was identified and recognized as the crucified Jesus of Nazareth. Furthermore, resurrection faith pointed to something new. Easter was the beginning of Christian faith. Not until Easter did the disciples have the Spirit and power, for not until Easter was the identity of Jesus as the reigning Christ manifest. Yet Easter was rooted in Jesus' life and death. Thus with some justification the Christian era is dated from the birth, rather than the resurrection, of Jesus.

What precisely did the resurrection mean for the earliest Christians? It meant, in summary, that despite appearances, even Jesus' crucifixion, God had not abandoned him. Moreover, the message of Jesus, which had centered on the proclamation of the kingdom, could now be presented in a new form in which the action of God was seen to have taken place already. A new dimension was added to Jesus' proclamation. The message about the irrupting presence of God became concrete in his death and resurrection. Finally, something happened both to Jesus and the disciples at the resurrection. In new faith and confidence they were able to recommit themselves and remain his disciples. The resurrection was an answer to death, for the resurrection cannot be viewed otherwise than from the perspective of death. In the Gospels resurrection occurred only after the agony and seeming finality of Jesus' passion and death. Yet for the disciples Jesus' resurrection anticipated and overcame the threat represented by their own deaths (cf. Rom. 6).

We have perhaps succeeded in demonstrating the truth of our earlier statement. What the resurrection is and what it means cannot be confirmed by historical investigation, even if that investigation could vindicate all the apparent factual claims that the New Testament makes. At stake is the truth of the Christian faith's claim that God was in Christ. To believe in the resurrection is to believe that this is in a unique sense true. Not to believe in the resurrection is to reject that claim, even if one honors Jesus as a very great religious leader and martyr. The New Testament witnesses insist that the resurrection was real and not an illusion. Yet they never separate resurrection and faith, as if the resurrection could have been experienced and analysed apart from faith. Faith accompanies every resurrection report of which we have any record.

For Christians after the first generation, believing in the resurrection has meant believing the reports and records of the witnesses. Yet Christians have not usually been content to think that faith in the resurrection, faith in Christ, is nothing other than the ability or willingness to believe what one is told—that is, credulity. New Testament writers like Paul and John, to whom we shall turn in Part Two, addressed readers who had not seen the resurrected Lord and by and large did not expect to see him. For them and others the preaching of the good news, worship in the church, and the presence of the Holy Spirit in the community and with the individual surrounded and supported the word of the witnesses. Although the report of the witnesses was considered necessary, the believer in the church gained his own access to Christ through other means as well. Thus in the Gospel of John the resurrected Jesus blesses those who have not seen and yet believe, immediately after having demonstrated to Thomas the reality of his risen body (John 20:26–29). Thereby he assures later Christians that their faith may be as surely grounded as that of the first witnesses. Jesus proclaimed the coming of God's new world, the kingdom of God. In the resurrection the earliest Christians perceived that this reality of which he spoke was actually coming to be. In the church they found a new community to receive this reality and proclaim it to the whole world. In the Spirit they found confirmation that their faith was based neither on illusion nor on an isolated occult phenomenon, but upon the will and action of God.

Our fundamental working assumptions in this chapter have been two: (1) Although the Synoptic Gospels are kerygmatic documents, they have not deliberately perverted or falsified the object of their attention, Jesus of Nazareth. (2) By working with three major areas of the tradition of Jesus —the healing, teaching, and suffering material—it is possible to understand the nature of each and their unity in the one historical figure Jesus. Thus the criterion of coherence was crucial for our portrait of Jesus.[80] We have

[80] For an illuminating discussion of major portraits of the historical Jesus, see the comparison of Edwyn Hoskyns and Noel Davey's *The Riddle of the New Testament* (London: Faber and Faber, 1947), with Bultmann's *Jesus and the Word* by Paul Meyer, "The Problem of the Messianic Self-Consciousness of Jesus," *Novum Testamentum,* 4 (1960), pp. 113–131; also the comparison of T. W. Manson's *The Teach-*

sought to represent the mystery of Jesus of Nazareth, a unique historical person. In the consequent portrait, we have consistently attempted to understand the continuity, rather than identity, between the mission and message of Jesus and the church's message about Jesus.

Jesus performed miracles of healing, out of compassion rather than for power. Jesus proclaimed the irrupting rule of God, without claiming to know the future or making man's response insignificant. Jesus demanded forgiveness of enemies, fellowship with sinners, radical obedience to the heart of the law, and announced God's blessing to the poor, the repentant, the believing, and the merciful. Jesus called disciples and followers, without promise of immediate reward but with a command to service. Jesus went to Jerusalem to proclaim the kingdom, and neither sought nor rejected the death that came. Jesus spoke, acted, and died. According to the faith of the church, God raised him from the dead.

Suggestions for Further Reading

Many popular books about Jesus, especially lives of Jesus, are really historical novels that rely upon the imaginations—more or less disciplined —of the authors. Virtually all the reliable information about Jesus that survives is found in the canonical Gospels. The so-called apocryphal Gospels add little but pious legend, if not fantasy, to what we already know. The best source for these is W. Schneemelcher (ed.), *New Testament Apocrypha*, originally edited by E. Hennecke and now edited in English translation by R. McL. Wilson (London: Lutterworth, 1963), Vol I. (Vol. II contains other early writings.) There is also the handy one-volume *Apocryphal New Testament*, ed. M. R. James (Oxford: Clarendon Press, 1924).

Probably the most widely used general work on Jesus' ministry nowadays is G. Bornkamm, *Jesus of Nazareth*, trans. I and F. McLuskey with J. M. Robinson (New York: Harper, 1960). The history of nineteenth century attempts to write a life of Jesus is brilliantly recounted by A. Schweitzer, *The Quest of the Historical Jesus,** trans. W. Montgomery (New York: Macmillan, 1954), who was among the first to establish the eschatological character of Jesus' teaching. More recent critical efforts to recover the Jesus of History are assessed by J. M. Robinson, *A New Quest of the Historical Jesus* (SBT, 25; Naperville, Ill.: Allenson, 1959), and H. Ander-

---

ing of Jesus with Bornkamm's *Jesus of Nazareth* by Anderson, *Jesus and Christian Origins*, pp. 149–184; and the comparison of Jeremias with Bultmann by J. L. Martyn, "Attitudes Ancient and Modern toward Tradition about Jesus," *USQR*, 23 (1968), pp. 129–145.

son, *Jesus and Christian Origins* (New York: Oxford University Press, 1964). Also valuable is Anderson, *Jesus** (Englewood Cliffs, N.J.: Prentice-Hall, 1967), a collection of excerpts from important works on Jesus. E. W. Saunders has recently published a worthwhile textbook on Jesus, *Jesus in the Gospels* (Englewood Cliffs, N.J.: Prentice-Hall, 1967).

Among other important modern works on Jesus are the following: R. Bultmann, *Jesus and the Word,** trans. L. P. Smith and E. H. Lantero (New York: Scribner's, 1934), M. Dibelius, *Jesus,* trans. C. B. Hedrick and F. C. Grant (Philadelphia: Westminster, 1949); M. Goguel, *The Life of Jesus,** trans. O. Wyon (New York: Macmillan, 1933), available as a Harper Torchbook paperback in 2 vols.; and V. Taylor, *The Life and Ministry of Jesus** (New York: Abingdon, 1955). The volume by Bultmann embodies the results of Bultmann's form-critical methodology. Somewhat more conservative historically is the form-critical approach of Dibelius and his interpretation of Jesus. Written from a more liberal theological point of view, Goguel's work is still more conservative in its historical results. Goguel is more confident of being able to establish the facts of Jesus' ministry than are Bultmann and Dibelius. The same may be said of Taylor's somewhat shorter work.

On the teaching of Jesus, one may still consult with profit T. W. Manson, *The Teaching of Jesus,** 2nd ed. (Cambridge: University Press, 1935), and the more recent work of N. Perrin, *Rediscovering the Teaching of Jesus* (New York: Harper, 1967). J. Jeremias has produced a classic work in *The Parables of Jesus,** trans. S. H. Hooke, (rev. ed.; New York: Scribner's, 1963).

The eschatological outlook of Jesus is a principal subject of Schweitzer's work mentioned above. Also important is A. Wilder, *Eschatology and Ethics in the Teaching of Jesus* (rev. ed.; New York: Harper, 1950). A good history of recent discussion of the problem is provided by N. Perrin, *The Kingdom of God in the Teaching of Jesus* (Philadelphia, Westminster, 1963).

On the question of Jesus' own understanding of his role there is a variety of scholarly opinion. Schweitzer forcefully argued that Jesus thought of himself as the coming Messiah and that every move of his ministry was dictated by his concept of his role in the eschatological drama. He was in part reacting to the view of W. Wrede, who thought that Jesus did not regard himself as the Messiah. Wrede's view was developed in a work published in German shortly after the turn of the century entitled *The Messianic Secret in the Gospels.* Only recently Wrede's work has been announced for translation, but as this book went to press it had not appeared. Bultmann in several works, especially *Theology of the New Testament,** Vol. I, trans. K. Grobel (New York: Scribner's, 1951), pp. 26 ff., strongly espoused Wrede's view. More conservative is W. Manson, *Jesus the Messiah* (London: Hodder and Stoughton, 1943). In support of Bultmann's view that Jesus also did not identify himself explicitly as the Son of Man is H. Tödt, *The Son of Man in the Synoptic Tradition,* trans. D. M. Barton (Philadelphia: Westminster, 1965). The relationship of Jesus to political activity in Palestine is explored by S. G. F. Brandon, *Jesus and the Zealots* (Manchester: University Press, 1967).

The miracles of Jesus are treated by A. Richardson, *The Miracle Stories of the Gospels* (New York: Harper, n.d.) and R. H. Fuller, *Interpreting the Miracles* (Philadelphia: Westminster, 1963), both of whom deal principally with their theological meaning and interpretation. Helpful discussions of the problem of miracles per se appear in C. F. D. Moule (ed.), *Miracles: Cambridge Studies in their Philosophy and History* (London: Mowbray, 1965), and in T. A. Burkill, *Mysterious Revelation* (Ithaca, N.Y.: Cornell University Press, 1963), pp. 41–61. For a historical survey of the problem in ancient times, see S. J. Case, *Experience with the Supernatural in Early Christian Times* (New York: Century, 1929); also R. M. Grant, *Miracle and Natural Law in Greco-Roman and Early Christian Thought* (Amsterdam: North Holland, 1952).

The trial and death of Jesus, a difficult problem for the historian, has been treated by J. Knox, *The Death of Jesus: The Cross in New Testament History and Faith* (New York: Abingdon, 1958), and P. Winter, *On the Trial of Jesus* (Berlin, Walter de Gruyter, 1961).

Part II
The Early Church and Paul

"Crucifixion" by the German painter M. Grünewald (completed 1511) is part of the Isenheim Altarpiece. The figures, other than Jesus, are Mary, the disciple John, Mary Magdalene, and John the Baptist. The latter repeats John 3:30; the letters INRI above the cross are the initial Latin letters of the inscription, "Jesus of Nazareth, King of the Jews." (Courtesy of Marburg-Art Reference Bureau.)

6 The Acts of the Apostles: The Missionary Community's Advance

NOTES ON THE ACTS OF THE APOSTLES

Acts was written by Luke, the author of the Gospel, probably within the last two decades of the first century A.D. *The book ends with Paul debating and*

239

preaching while under arrest in Rome. We are not told about his ultimate fate. Paul arrived in Rome about 60 A.D. and, according to the last statement of Acts (28:30 f.), remained there two years. Yet it is not likely that Acts was written immediately thereafter. We know that Luke used Mark as a source for his own Gospel, which was written before Acts (cf. Acts 1:1), and that Mark itself was not composed until about A.D. 65 or later. Moreover, there are strong hints (cf. Acts 20:22–25, 38) that Luke actually knew of Paul's death, even though he did not report it.

Luke used the Gospel according to Mark and probably two other sources in composing his account of the ministry of Jesus, and he may have had written sources for the book of Acts. The detailed account of Paul's journeys in chapters 13–28 is probably based on some kind of record of Paul's travels. In addition to this itinerary, Luke knew some traditional stories from the earliest days of the church (for example, 3:1–10; 5:1–11). Whether he had any traditions or records of the speeches he records is another question, which will have to be considered as we examine some of the speeches. Judging from the practice of ancient historians, he likely wrote these speeches with considerable fredom, impressing them not only with his own literary style, but also with his thought. Particularly in chapters 1–2, Luke has skillfully tied the narrative together with summary statements (for example, 2:43–47), in which he speaks in general terms of the activities of the early church.

Like the Gospels, Acts is a narrative, a story, and may profitably be read as such. Yet Acts is more than just a story, even as the Gospels are. In and through the story the author's understanding of the meaning and truth of the Christian faith can be perceived. In our approach to Acts we shall assume that it is not primarily the story that needs to be explained, except where Luke may refer to strange customs or places. What most needs explanation is the understanding of the gospel that lies behind the story and is expressed in it.

Introduction: A New Beginning (1:1–2:47)

The first two chapters of Acts are basic. They lay out and define the themes and principal concerns that are fundamental to the rest of the work. For this reason it is necessary to examine them carefully. Numerous questions may be raised as one studies these chapters, all of which are refinements of the basic question about what Luke, the author, was trying to say or to accomplish.

JESUS' DEPARTURE (1:1–11)

What task does the departing Jesus give to the disciples?

The first two verses of the Acts of the Apostles hark back to Luke's earlier work, which is also addressed to Theophilus. There can be little doubt that by "the first book," the author means the Gospel. The brief description: "all that Jesus began to do and teach, until the day when he was taken up," corresponds to the content of the Gospel. The "many proofs" of the resurrected Christ (Acts 1:3) are found in the final chapter of Luke (24:36 ff.; perhaps in 24:44 ff.). Even without such clear indications, however, there would be strong reasons for supposing that the two books are by the same author, for they are written in the same style and from the same general point of view.

Despite the obvious points of contact, there are discrepancies and outright inconsistencies between the resurrection accounts of Luke 24 and what we find in Acts 1. Nothing is said about forty days of resurrection appearances in the Gospel, nor is there any mention of the kingdom of God in all of Luke 24 (cf. Acts 1:3). The command to stay in Jerusalem (1:4) appears also in Luke 24:49, but the word of Jesus about the baptism of John and baptism by the Holy Spirit (1:4–5) is found neither in Luke 24 nor anywhere else in the Gospel. Is Luke simply careless? Probably the explanation lies rather in a difference of emphasis and purpose.

Luke's own purposes and interests come to light in the next section (vss. 6–11, especially 6–8). The hope that the two disciples on the road to Emmaus had already voiced (Luke 24:21) is now put in the form of a question: "Lord, will you at this time restore the kingdom to Israel?" The disciples seem to be asking whether Jesus will now fulfill the traditional hopes of the Jewish nation with the inauguration of the kingdom of God on earth. Jesus does not answer directly. Instead he replies that it is not for them to know the times and seasons that the Father has fixed by his own authority (cf. Mark 13:32). In other words, these matters are not their primary concern. Such hopes as they have will be fulfilled in God's own way at the time of His choosing. Thus the disciples' expectations are effectively put off.

The reason for this is given in the very next verse: "But you shall receive power when the Holy Spirit has come upon you; and you shall be my witnesses in Jerusalem and in Judea and Samaria and to the end of the earth." The time of the kingdom is not yet, because the gospel must first be preached throughout the world. The witnesses to Jesus have a mission to perform. The coming of the Spirit has already been mentioned (1:5), now its specifically missionary function is spelled out. The Spirit empowers the disciples for their mission, which is described in stages: Jerusalem, Judea, Samaria and the end of the earth (vs. 8). These stages correspond to the plan of the book of Acts, in which the mission of the church unfolds by degrees: first in Jerusalem and the environs, then Samaria, then Syria, Asia Minor, Greece, and finally Rome. With Paul's preaching of the gospel in Rome the book of Acts comes to an end. This commissioning of the disciples for a worldwide mission is in close agreement with Luke 24:47, where the risen Jesus tells them that re-

Christ giving the law to the apostles. A relief marble fragment from the second half of the fourth century. (Courtesy of Metropolitan Museum of Art, Beata M. Brummer, 1948, in memory of Joseph Brummer.)

pentance and forgiveness are to be preached in his name to all nations, beginning from Jerusalem.

Luke's description of the ascension of Jesus (vss. 9–11) has become the model for its conception and artistic representation in the church. But the ascension is portrayed in this way only in Acts. Even in the Gospel of Luke it is described much more enigmatically (24:51). Here Luke carefully reconstructs the scene in order to drive home a point. The ascension is now viewed not from the standpoint of Jesus, but of the waiting disciples. Jesus indeed ascends to heaven and will return in like manner. The disciples ("men of Galilee"), however, are not to stand looking up into heaven in expectation of him, for they have already been given a task. They can perform it with the assurance that their ultimate hopes and expectations will not be disappointed, for Jesus will return in God's good time. But the interval gains a special significance; it is the period of the church and its mission. To that work the disciples' and the reader's attention is directed.

Luke utilized his knowledge of the earliest days of the Christian movement in interesting and important ways. He knew that the question of when the kingdom was coming or when Jesus would return perplexed many Christians. From the Gospels it is clear that Jesus proclaimed the near advent of the kingdom, and we can see from Paul's letters that this expectation was very much alive in the earliest church. By the time Luke wrote, however, the kingdom had not yet appeared and Jesus had not returned. Why not? Luke's answer is that God ordained between Jesus' earthly ministry and the day of his return a time in which the gospel was to be preached to all mankind. Paul, the apostle to the Gentiles in the latter half of Acts, evidently shared this same view because he declares to the church at Rome that he will visit them on the way to preaching the gospel throughout the world (Rom. 16:17 ff.).

242

ESTABLISHING THE APOSTOLIC WITNESS (1:12–26)

Why is the selection of the twelfth apostle so important?

From vss. 12–14 we learn that the disciples returned from the Mount of Olives, where the ascension apparently took place,[1] and gathered in an upper room in Jerusalem. The list of disciples present agrees with that found in Luke 6:14–16 with one notable exception. Judas Iscariot, the betrayer of Jesus, is missing (cf. vss. 16–22).[2] What became of him? It is curious that Peter should have to answer this question for his fellow disciples and companions. Presumably they were in as good position as he to know what had occurred. Moreover, these folk would have surely known who Judas was, so why was it necessary for Peter to identify him so thoroughly? Vss. 18–19 underscore the difficulty, for here Peter translates *Akeldama*, which would certainly not have been necessary for his Aramaic-speaking hearers, and refers to "their language," as if his hearers spoke a language different from that of the inhabitants of Jerusalem. This cannot have been the case. Verses 18 and 19 have to be understood as a notation addressed to the reader. With good reason these verses appear in parentheses in the RSV. We should recall, however, that in the Greek text the words were not set apart. This shows that the author evidently felt no obligation to distinguish clearly between Peter's words to his hearers and his own message for his readers. Probably he would not have considered such a distinction nearly so important as we would. Thus, as one reads Luke's account, he may well ask to whom the speeches of the chief characters are directed and to what extent they are means by which Luke sets before his *reader* the meaning of the events that are unfolding. To understand the speeches one must always ask what role they play in the unfolding of the book of Acts.

The Old Testament quotations (vs. 20; cf. Psalms 69:25 and 109:8) form not only the culmination of the first half of Peter's speech, but also the transition to the second part (vs. 21–22) in which he sets forth a course of action. A replacement for the disqualified and defunct Judas, must be chosen: "His office let another take." Furthermore, the replace-

---

[1] According to Luke 24:50 f. the ascension took place at or near Bethany. The seeming contradiction suggests that Luke may have mistakenly taken Olivet and Bethany to be the same place; cf. K. Lake and H. J. Cadbury, eds., *The Beginnings of Christianity*, V: *Additional Notes to the Commentary* (New York: Macmillan Co., 1933), p. 475.

[2] Notice that the Acts description of Judas' death differs from that given in Matthew 27:3–10, except that in both cases the name of the place where he died is the Field of Blood. Perhaps the fact that Luke preserves the Aramaic name whereas Matthew's version appears to be based upon the Old Testament quotation indicates that Luke's version is the older. (Matthew purports to quote Jeremiah, but the exact passage cannot to be found; cf. Zechariah 11:12–13.)

ment must have a specific qualification; he must have accompanied Jesus and his disciples during his ministry up to the time of his ascension. He may then become a witness, with the apostles, to the resurrection. In the selection of the new apostle (vss. 23–26) two men are put forward by the group, but the widest latitude is left for God (or Jesus, depending on whom is here meant by "Lord") to make the final choice. The new man is to be no less an apostolic figure than the eleven original disciples.

Luke is careful to show that the number of the original twelve apostles was again filled out before the beginning of the church's missionary activity. (The word *apostle* comes from the Greek *apostolos,* which is in turn related to the verb *apostellein,* "to send out"; the apostles are literally "men sent out.") The concept of *twelve* apostles probably originates with the *twelve* tribes of Israel (cf. the saying of Jesus in Matt. 19:28 and Luke 22:30). It is likely that Luke was aware of this connection with the Old Testament and the Israelite nation, since for him the church, led by the apostles, was the new Israel. Yet Luke, like Paul, seems more interested in the close relation between apostleship and the resurrection of Jesus (Acts 1:22; cf. I Cor. 9:1: "Am I not an apostle? Have I not seen Jesus our Lord?"; also 15:8, where Paul explicitly relates the appearance of the risen Jesus and his apostleship). Unlike Luke, however, Paul did not believe that having been a disciple of Jesus was an indispensable qualification of an apostle. Indeed, Paul seems to have distinguished between the twelve and the apostles in I Cor. 15:5, 7. He evidently regarded the twelve as apostles, but did not limit apostleship to them. Nevertheless, precisely this identification of apostles with the twelve disciples of Jesus has informed the Christian understanding of "apostle" and "apostleship" down through the centuries. The church has come to share Luke's view that there can be, and is, no doubt about the existence and competence of a complete and fully qualified group of twelve apostles identical with the inner circle of Jesus' disciples.

After Matthias is selected he plays no role in the story—nor do many of the twelve. In fact, the twelve were not the only early witnesses to the gospel of Jesus Christ. Not even in Acts do they play the predominant role in preaching the gospel. For only Peter appears as a real flesh and blood figure. But Luke, who has written to Theophilus in the first place so that he may know the truth of the things of which he has been informed (Luke 1:4), uses the concept of the twelve to assure the reader of the legitimacy, historical accuracy, and therefore the truth of the Christian message.

In chapter one Luke has done two principal things. First, he has explained the meaning of Jesus' departure and of the indefinite period before his return. Second, through his treatment of the reconstitution of the twelve apostles he has shown that real contact still exists between Jesus and his disciples on earth. The apostles guarantee this, for they have firm connections with Jesus of Nazareth, of whose resurrection and life they are witnesses. Luke can now turn his attention to the description and exposition of the earliest missionary preaching of the Christian church.

SPIRIT, GOSPEL, AND CHURCH (2:1–47)

How does the coming of the Spirit fulfill the Old Testament prophecy?
What does Peter's preaching stress?

Chapter two falls into two main parts, vss. 1–13, which describe the descent of the Holy Spirit upon the disciples and the reaction of the bystanders, and vss. 14–43, an account of the earliest missionary preaching by Peter. The remainder of the chapter (vss. 43–47) gives a brief general description of the life of the Jerusalem church.

The day of Pentecost comes on the fiftieth day after the sabbath of the Passover, according to the Jewish calendar. This would be the forty-ninth day after the resurrection and, according to the Lukan chronology, a little over a week after the ascension of Jesus.[3] (Jesus' resurrection appearances continued over a period of forty days.) In the Gospel of John, however, the Holy Spirit comes, not at Pentecost and after the ascension of Jesus, but directly from the risen Jesus himself (John 20:21–23). Indeed, the ascension is not described at all in John. Luke evidently separates into chronological sequence events or experiences that were not so divided in the memories of other early Christians (that is, the resurrection of Jesus, the ascension, and the bestowal of the Holy Spirit).

Luke clearly regarded the coming of the Holy Spirit (cf. vss. 1–4) as a miraculous event. Yet we should not assume that Luke attached primary importance to such signs as the wind and fire. For him the most marvelous thing was the inspiration of the apostles and their speaking in tongues. Only highly unusual accompanying circumstances could do justice to this remarkable event. The rushing of the wind and the tongues "as of fire" are subordinate to the main miracle of inspired speech.

That Luke is describing a genuine experience of early Christianity need not be doubted. We learn also from Paul that the gift of the Spirit was associated with speaking in tongues (I Cor. 14). Be that as it may, Paul assumes that this speaking in tongues (*glōssalalia*) is unintelligible to the hearer, as indeed it generally is when practiced by Christians today, whether in a Pentecostal sect in the mountains of North Carolina or in an Episcopal student group in an Ivy League university. Precisely the authentic note of this first part of the story calls into question the interpretation of the

---

[3] According to Acts 1:3 Jesus continued to appear to his disciples for forty days after the resurrection. Note the close connection of the Christian celebrations of Good Friday, Easter, and Pentecost with the Jewish feasts of Passover and Pentecost.

nature of glossalalia (cf. vss. 6–8), where it is understood as a speaking in the various native languages of the people who are gathered in Jerusalem. In Luke's view, a miracle of translation has occurred. That, however, is not what speaking in tongues was in early Christianity according to the earlier Pauline account. The description of the circumstances under which the multitude came together and the course of events as a whole also betray Luke's own perspectives and interests. When the disciples are gathered in one place, the Spirit descends and they immediately begin proclaiming "the mighty works of God" (vs. 11) in all the languages of those Jews who have come from far and wide to dwell in Jerusalem, presumably for the feast of Pentecost. These people hear the commotion and come together. Some inquire sincerely as to what all this means (vs. 12). Others understandably attribute the uproar to new wine (vs. 13). Luke provides as auspicious an occasion and hearing as possible for Peter's sermon or speech. Accordingly, the audience, although Jewish, is thoroughly cosmopolitan and representative of the eastern half of the Mediterranean world, the mission field of early Christianity (vss. 8–11). To this great congregation Peter addresses himself, standing with the eleven (vs. 14) to emphasize the authoritative character of his speech. The speech is not only Spirit-inspired but also apostolic.

Although Pentecost is often celebrated as the birthday of the Christian church, Luke may not have understood these events in this way. In a sense, the church is already present in the disciples of Jesus and in the apostolate of the twelve, established before Pentecost. What Pentecost clearly represents is the descent of the Holy Spirit upon the church. This empowers it for witness and mission, the preaching of the word, which is the gospel of Jesus Christ. This evangelical preaching is represented initially and definitively in the speech of Peter (2:14–42), the first Christian missionary sermon.

After Peter first explains that the Christians are not drunk (vs. 14–16), he declares that their speaking fulfills what was spoken by the Old Testament prophet Joel. There then follows the long quotation from the book of Joel (2:28–32), which is a description and prediction of what will happen in the days when God restores the fortunes of Judah and Jerusalem (Joel 3:1). Not only will there be the standard apocalyptic signs (vss. 19–20), but also the pouring out of God's Spirit (vss. 17–18), which results in visions, dreams, and especially prophecy. Apparently Luke understands the speaking in tongues of the apostles and their companions as this prophecy of which Joel spoke.

Significantly, the first Christian preaching is represented as beginning with an appeal to the Old Testament. This is typical of the New Testament as a whole, for the Christian gospel is understood as the fulfillment of an ancient promise. Jesus Christ is the culmination of what God has been doing from creation on in the history of Israel. So even the gift of the

Spirit and the speaking in tongues is set forth as fulfillment of Old Testament prophecy. By use of Old Testament prophecy the Christian preachers and writers did not necessarily imply, however, that the prophets themselves possessed a kind of clairvoyance (although something like this is, in fact, attributed to David in 2:29–31). The Christians, as this very text states, believed themselves to be possessed of prophetic power and authority. Thus they were able to perceive and declare the fulfillment of the prophetic words that the men of the Old Testament, so to speak, cast out ahead of them. The early Christian preachers, therefore, implicitly claimed a better understanding of Old Testament texts than their human authors.

The prophetic word (vss. 17–21) was doubtless understood to concern both the present manifestation of the Spirit and the forthcoming signs of the end, as well as the appeal of the Christian preaching for conversion in the light of these startling occurrences (vs. 21). Before this appeal could be made, however, its specifically Christian basis had to be set forth, for Peter has so far only said that the time for fulfillment of the Old Testament prophecies and of God's promises to his people has come. The distinctly Christian proclamation appears in vss. 22–24. Most surprising, however, is the brevity of the reference to Jesus' ministry (vs. 22). Jesus himself is not presented as the acting subject. Rather he is the means or agent through whom God acts. This is true even of his miracles. The divine purpose at work in the crucifixion is made quite clear (vs. 23), and the same purpose is also discerned in the resurrection (vs. 24) as the Old Testament proof from prophecy (vss. 25–28) shows. The author recognizes that the words of the Psalm (16:8–11) were generally believed to have been spoken by David about himself, but he maintains (vss. 29–31) that they were actually meant to apply to Jesus.

Only after the Old Testament proof is the disciples' witness to the resurrection mentioned (vs. 32), but even then it is passed over rather briefly. Emphasis falls rather upon the ascension of Christ to heaven (vs. 33), again confirmed by the Old Testament (vss. 34 f.; from Psalm 110:1), and upon the gift of the Spirit. Apparently, Peter does not draw too sharp a distinction between the raising of Jesus from the dead and his ascension (or exaltation) to heaven. In Luke's own mind, however, the distinction is very clear. Jesus is first raised from the dead; then after forty days he ascends into heaven. Luke's view is probably a later development.

The speech reaches its pinnacle and conclusion in vs. 36. Once again God is the subject who acts upon Jesus. Here Jesus becomes, or at least is recognized as, "Lord and Christ" only with the resurrection and exaltation. This point of view is rather uncommon in the New Testament, for Jesus is usually regarded as having been the Messiah during his earthly ministry. Yet just because this verse does not conform to the common conception, and because it would scarcely have been set forth at a time

Crucifixion of Jesus by a contemporary Brazilian sculptor, A. Solimoes. (Courtesy of Spartaco Appetiti.)

when that conception was widespread, it may well present a primitive point of view. Certainly the crucifixion and resurrection were pivotal points in primitive Christian experience and faith. Whether the disciples only recognized Jesus of Nazareth as the Messiah after Good Friday and Easter is a real question. Mark, the earliest Gospel, apparently understood that Jesus was the Messiah during his earthly ministry. Yet a really valid pre-resurrection recognition of Jesus as Messiah on the part of the disciples is missing in Mark.

Peter's appeal for conversion and repentance follows naturally (vss. 37–42). As he has already indicated ("Let all the house of Israel therefore know. . . ."—vs. 36) and as the situation demands, it is still addressed to Jews. Yet there is already a hint that it will not be limited to them (see vs. 39). The hearers are called upon to repent and to be baptized, and the gift of the Spirit is promised.

No explanation is given here or anywhere else in the New Testament of why believers had to be baptized. According to every indication, baptism was practiced from the very beginning, yet we do not know precisely why or how it became the ritual of initiation into the Christian community. Paul, whose letters are the earliest New Testament writings, simply mentions baptism as a matter of course, as if it were a long-accepted practice. Acts mentions some disciples, presumably Christians, who knew only the baptism of John the Baptist and had not received the Holy Spirit (19:1-17). In the Gospels and the missionary speeches of Acts, John's baptism marks the beginning of Jesus' own ministry, and John's baptism in water is contrasted with Christ's baptism in the Holy Spirit. All of this suggests that Christian baptism is somehow rooted in the baptism of John. Yet baptism may have been practiced by Christians quite apart from the influence of John, inasmuch as the Jewish community baptized new converts, as well as circumcising them. The Qumran community also practiced baptism or lustrations (washings), but their rite was repeatable, whereas early Christian baptism—or at least the form with which we are familiar— was a once-for-all ceremony. At any rate the appeal to repent and be baptized takes us back as far as we can go in the history of Christian preaching and practice.

Whereas the practice of baptism was universal, the call to repentance has a particularly Lukan ring. Of course, Luke was not the first to set forth a relation between baptism and repentance or to describe conversion in terms of repentance. The understanding of repentance as the essential element of Christian conversion is, however, quite characteristic of Luke. Although repentance and forgiveness were already possible for the Jew (cf. Psalm 51), Luke believed that God's forgiveness and the possibility of repentance were made known in an unprecedented way in the coming of Jesus. Baptism "in the name of Jesus Christ" (2:38) was the symbolic expression of repentance and the acceptance of God's forgiveness. The act itself implies a washing away of sin.

At the end of Peter's speech and the account of the conversions, Luke presents a glimpse of the life of the early Jerusalem church. Such general summaries were probably composed by Luke without the help of older accounts. They recur frequently in Acts and usually reflect such knowledge of the early church as could be gathered by the author from the traditional stories that he narrates. For example, the reference to common ownership (vss. 44 f.) is probably a generalization based upon the stories of Barnabas and Ananias and Sapphira (4:36 f.; 5:1-6). The signs and wonders, as well as the "fear" (vs. 43), are exemplified in such miracle stories as 3:1-10, 9:32-35, and 9:36-43. The general favor that the Christians found among the people (2:47) is also mentioned in 4:21 and 5:33-39, quite possibly traditional material. Such matters as the great number of converts, the breaking of bread, and attendance in the temple are included in the summary without the direct support of traditional stories. This is not to say that Luke simply manufactured them. Doubtless he believed he had a right to describe these activities and attribute them to the early church on the basis of what he knew of Jesus and the disciples, and of what he knew of the church of his own day. Of course, we cannot be sure that Luke did not possess more detailed information from earlier days which did not come to him in the form of traditional narratives. Yet we have already noted that Luke did not hesitate to set forth the ascension and the bestowal of the Spirit in distinct and different ways, apparently supplying details as needed.

Nevertheless, Luke has some basis for these details. That large numbers of people were converted at the beginning would have seemed only natural to him in view of the size and influence of the Jerusalem church, which, however, disappeared before the destruction of Jerusalem (A.D. 70) and perhaps twenty years before Luke wrote. The common meals might have been suggested not only by the sacrament of the Lord's Supper and the story of the Last Supper (Luke 22:14–27), but also by the traditions about the resurrection of Jesus in which he eats with his disciples (Luke 24:35, 42 f.; John 21:1–14). Attendance in the temple might be deduced from the location of the miracle story of 3:1–10 or from the account of the vow that Paul took (21:17–26). It is, however, still probable that Luke mentions some things simply because they are important to him. The immediate success of the Christian witness at the very heart of Judaism, the constant presence of Christians around the temple, the table fellowship and piety of Christians all represent typical Lukan motifs. Especially significant is the emphasis on Christianity's acceptance and prominence in the Holy City of Judaism, for in Luke's view the church is the new, and true, Israel.

Thus Luke's conception of the piety and life of the early Christian church appears in 2:42–47. On the one hand, the reader must remember that it is not an uninformed conception. On the other, he must understand how Luke's procedure differs from the modern historian's in that Luke was willing to sacrifice accuracy in historical narrative for the sake of the truth of the message that he was trying to convey. Moreover, the material out of which he composed chapters 1–12 was not extensive. The rich resources of his Gospel afforded relatively little information that he was able to sort out and use in Acts. He had only a collection of various stories and anecdotes, which he was able to weave together into a surprisingly smooth and coherent narrative. Yet there is a sense in which Luke knew enough to tell the story that he wanted to tell and to achieve his own goals. The opening chapters of Acts are a good example of this fact. Here Luke accounts for the departure of the risen Jesus from his disciples, the reason that he has not yet returned, the existence and mission of the church, and the foundation of that church upon the apostolic witness. Then he proceeds to report the bestowal of the Spirit upon the disciples and to give an extended example of the preaching of the apostolic church, followed by a brief characterization of its life. This preaching (that is, Peter's speech) contains the elements essential for

Christian preaching in any age: the announcement and demonstration of the fulfillment of scripture, the centrality of the crucifixion and resurrection, a characterization of the historic ministry of Jesus, the announcement of the coming of the Spirit, and an appeal for repentance and conversion, which naturally includes the offer of forgiveness. To answer the question of whether Luke fulfilled his purpose, one only has to reflect upon how it is just these elements that have remained the hallmarks of Christian evangelical proclamation. It is, of course, true that Luke may have drawn upon older materials in composing these speeches, and that a certain uniformity in Christian preaching might have been expected because of the character of the Christ event itself. Nevertheless, Luke must have played a formative role in the development of Christian preaching. We can hardly deny his skill, influence, and perception of what the later church would regard as sound insight and doctrine.

The Growth of the Church and Its Witness (3:1–12:25; 15:1–41)

Now that we have seen in this introduction the way the author of Acts works and have some conception of his interests and goals, it is possible to read the remainder of the first section of the book (chap. 3–12) with more understanding.

IN JERUSALEM AND BEYOND (3:1–9:43)

What are the reasons for the stoning of Stephen?

Chapters 3–5 portray the power manifest in the preaching and healing activity of the apostles in Jerusalem. The stories found there are not told simply for their own sake, for they show important aspects of the church's life and mission about which Luke wants his readers to know. They depict the Christians preaching and healing in Jerusalem, especially in the vicinity of the temple, the center of the Jewish religion. The location is significant, for Luke wants his reader to understand that Christianity emerged out of the very heart of Judaism and is the true expression of the ancient faith in the new time. The refusal of the apostles to be silent, even when officials warn or punish them (see, for example, 4:29 and 5:29), shows how strong was the sense of mission in the very earliest Christian congregation. Yet in chapters 3–5 the mission is confined to Judaism and indeed to the city of Jerusalem.

In chapters 6–7, however, the basis is laid for the extension of the witness. Chapter 6 describes the "murmuring" of the Hellenists against the Hebrews because their widows had been overlooked in the daily distribution, which must have been the church's way of looking out for its poor and disadvantaged (6:1). Who are these Hellenists and Hebrews? It is clear that they are Christians. Beyond that, absolute certainty is not possible. Probably by "Hebrews" is meant Aramaic-speaking Christians. In that case "Hellenists" means Greek-speaking Christians (note the Greek names, vs. 5) although, as soon becomes apparent, they are distinguished by factors other than language. Apparently the seven Hellenists who were appointed to serve tables and to see that their widows were not slighted did not stick strictly to their jobs. Luke's narrative makes this fact clear, although he himself does not remark upon it.

Stephen first appears not as a waiter, or even an administrator, but as a wonder-worker and especially a debater, incurring the hostility of the Jews (6:8–15). The charges made against him (vss. 11, 13 f.) are quite important, for to the extent that they are true, they indicate a sharp break on the part of some Christians with the institutions of Judaism. The accusation about destroying the temple (vs. 14) has a familiar ring, for according to Mark 14:58 it was first leveled at Jesus himself (cf. Mark 13:2; 15:29 and John 2:19). Insofar as Stephen questioned the validity of the law, he stood with the apostle Paul and later Hellenistic Christianity against Judaism and the Jewish or Judaizing Christians. Whatever Stephen's views, he held them with great tenacity. If anyone had hoped that Stephen's appearance before the Council (the Jewish Sanhedrin) would exonerate him of the suspicions and charges against him, his hopes would certainly have been cruelly dashed by the speech that Stephen chose to make.

The speech (7:1–53) is almost surely the composition of Luke himself. It does not answer the question of the high priest (6:15), and the Council probably would not have endured such a long, largely superfluous, and, from their point of view, defamatory speech in answer to so simple a question. The speech contains an extensive statement of the theological position of Stephen, which is by implication that of the Hellenists. Although it does not deal with the charges made against Stephen, it sheds some light on how such charges may have arisen, for Stephen denounces the past disobedience of the Israelite people, questions the necessity of the temple (vss. 47 ff.), and concludes with a strong denunciation of the betrayal and murder of Jesus. The final reference to the law (vs. 53) is almost an afterthought.

The reaction of Stephen's hearers to such a speech was predictable. The account is embellished with details of his subsequent death, traditionally the first Christian martyrdom. There is an additional bit of information about a young man named Saul, who held the coats of those who were stoning him (vss. 58 ff.). This Saul is the man who, under his Roman name of Paul, became the great Christian apostle to the Gentiles. Around him the later half of the book of Acts revolves. We know from Paul's own letters (especially Gal. 1:11–24) that he was a persecutor of the church before he himself became a Christian, and it is certainly not impossible that he could have been in Jerusalem and present on this occasion. That he was, however, is almost too coincidental. For in that case Stephen, the first Christian critic of Judaism, would have been martyred in the presence of the one who was to become the decisive figure in Christianity's separation from Judaism. Yet history has witnessed strange ironies.

The conversion of Saul might have then been recounted immediately by an author less resourceful than Luke, but he is too subtle for that. He mentions Paul's further devastation of the church (8:3), but the bulk of chapter 8 describes the missionary harvest reaped as a result of the persecution that broke out on the heels of Stephen's martyrdom. Philip makes converts in Samaria (cf. Acts 1:8) and on the road south from Jerusalem to Gaza, where he converts an Ethiopian eunuch to Christianity and baptizes him on the spot. Others also went out from Jerusalem preaching the word (8:4), but Luke tells us only of the instances involving Philip. Probably this is another indication of the relative sparseness of the tradition upon which Luke drew. Yet his statement of 8:4 (cf. 11:19–21) very likely conveys exactly what happened in this first demonstration of the famous maxim: the blood of the martyrs is the seed of the church.

Since, according to Luke's account, the gospel has now spread outside Jerusalem into Judea, Samaria, and Galilee, the territory of ancient Israel, we are prepared for the next step, the evangelization of the Gentiles. But first the apostle to the Gentiles must appear at the center of the stage. So we are next told of Paul's conversion (chap. 9). Probably this is the best attested event in the entire New Testament. There are no less than three accounts in the book of Acts (cf. also chaps. 22 and 26). In addition, there is the account from Paul's own hand in Galatians (1:11–17), as well as other allusions to the event in his letters (for example, I Cor. 9:1; 15:8).

With the appearance of Paul, we reach a point in the narrative at which it is possible to check the accuracy of the Acts account and also to learn something more about the methods and intentions of Luke as an author. The comparison of Acts with the evidence of Paul's letters is a complex and difficult task, and one that we shall not undertake in detail. Nevertheless, the consensus of scholarship allows us to adopt the general principle that where Acts contradicts or cannot be made to fit what Paul says, the critical reader must prefer Paul. He provides first-hand information, whereas Acts is secondary. Moreover, Acts does not report some things we would like to know about Paul—to name the most obvious, whether he ever left Rome after his initial imprisonment and, if so, where he went and how his career and life finally came to an end.

Luke's primary purpose in writing, however, was not that of a contemporary historian or journalist. He was not much interested in the variety and complexity of events and phenomena that constituted early Christianity. Reporting accurately everything that happened would not have accomplished his purpose. He wished to tell the story of how Christianity spread in such a way that it would not only inform the reader, but also edify the church and bring it to a better understanding of the ways in which God had accomplished his purpose in its history. Thus, in describing the expansion of Christianity, Luke concentrates on Paul, the imposing missionary figure of the previous generation about whom he has some information and concerning whom he can presuppose familiarity on the part of at least the Christian reader. In the last great portion of Acts, which sees Paul move from Antioch to Rome, many details and whole areas of the mission and expansion of Christianity are necessarily ignored.

MISSION TO THE GENTILES (10:1–11:18; 15:1–41)

Peter is portrayed by Luke as the founder of the mission to the Gentiles and the representative of the "liberal" position that the gospel can be preached to those outside the bounds of organized Judaism, presumably without their first, or ever, becoming members of the Jewish congregation. Thus, Peter's position seems close to that of the apostle Paul, who struggled so valiantly for the principle that Peter establishes with relatively little effort. If Peter actually secured so large a victory at the outset, however, we might wonder why Paul had so much difficulty over the matter. Moreover, Paul himself had something less than admiration for Peter, whose tolerant conduct among Gentiles was at first just what we would expect on the basis of the Acts passage, but who later seems to have reversed his field (cf. Gal. 2:11 ff.). In the light of Paul's struggle and his description of Peter's conduct in Galatians, we might ask whether Peter actually won a victory as a result of this incident, or whether he himself was as fully committed to the mission to the Gentiles as the Acts passage would lead us to believe. In fact, Acts itself indicates that the question about the status and obligations of Gentile converts did not die easily. It is the chief subject matter of chapter 15, and in chapter 21 Paul is arrested for the last time in an incident growing out of this question and controversy.

The Cornelius Incident (10:1–11:18)
How is the mission to the Gentiles effected?
Why is there detailed repetition of the events?

We come now to the lengthy account of the conversion of Cornelius and the subsequent discussion of its meaning. This grouping of narrative and discourse materials is quite complicated. The complexity stems in some measure from the editorial work of Luke, who has woven together older traditional material. The long account can, of course, simply be read as an interesting story, without asking what purpose Luke might have had in incorporating it at this point in his narrative. But that is the most important question. Furthermore, one should ask why so much of the story, especially the reports of visions, is repetitious.

First of all, the vision of Cornelius at Caesarea instructs him to summon Peter from Joppa (10:1–8). Even while his emissaries are on the way, Peter in turn has a vision (10:9–16). Cornelius' men then explain to Peter the purpose of their mission and bring him with them to Caesarea (10:17–19). After Cornelius has explained the details of his vision (10:30–33), Peter delivers what amounts to a missionary sermon, the Holy Spirit descends upon those standing about, and Peter commands that they be baptized. When Peter returns to Jerusalem he is criticized by the circumcision party for going to uncircumcised men and eating with them. So Peter, in order to justify his actions, recounts the entire course of events (11:1–18). Upon hearing this, his critics' mouths are stopped. Indeed, they glorify in God and fall fully into line with the position which Peter has espoused.

Although the vision (10:1–8) does not require detailed explanation, it is worth observing that Cornelius was a Roman officer and thus a representative of the power and prestige of the empire. He is also described as "a devout man who feared God" (vs. 2), which may mean that he was a Gentile associate of a Jewish synagogue, who had not formally become a Jew. That he was still a Gentile is clear from the subsequent narrative and discussion of his conversion to Christianity.

Significantly, Cornelius' approach to Peter is made at the direction of an angel. The angel comes at the ninth hour (3:00 P.M.) while Cornelius is at prayer, and Cornelius sees him clearly. There can be no mistaking the divine origin of the instruction to be delivered. Of the character or appearance of the angel we are told nothing; this is of no importance to Luke; he is interested only in the origin and authority of the message, symbolized by the angel. In Acts several such messages are delivered in visions—also an indication of divine authorization. For example, in the very next stage of the narrative Peter sees another vision while standing on the housetop at midday, as the emissaries from Cornelius approach the city of Joppa.

The meaning of Peter's vision (10:9–16) is not so obvious as that of Cornelius. In fact, Peter is said to be puzzled about it (vs. 17). In itself the vision seems to indicate that all animals may be eaten without regard for Jewish custom and law. There is little reason for Peter to be perplexed about this, except in view of the approaching mission from Cornelius, about which, of course, he as yet knows nothing. Luke and the reader know about it, however. Therefore, the perplexity at this point is really more appropriate to the reader than to Peter—a sure sign that Luke has his reader in mind. Peter's perplexity disappears by the time he reaches Cornelius at Caesarea (vss. 28 f.). In the meantime the Spirit has instructed him to go with the three men who have come from Cornelius, for the Spirit has sent them. Peter goes with them to the house of Cornelius, who has already gathered his close friends and family for what he obviously expects will be an important occasion. This is underscored by the way in which he greets Peter (vs. 25). Peter's response is like that of Paul and Barnabas in a similar situation (14:15). Only at this point do we discover that Peter has now understood the meaning of the vision of the rooftop at Joppa: "God has shown me that I should not call any man common or unclean" (vs. 28). The vision evidently had to do primarily with the status of men rather than of animals. This interpretation of the vision becomes possible only in the light of the events that follow it. A new meaning is given to the vision different from the one that had seemed obvious, but had left Peter "perplexed." Its real meaning is that God is no respecter of persons.

This point is not, however, immediately developed. Instead, we hear Cornelius describe his vision to Peter (10:30–33). So, Peter first tells Cornelius his vision, or at least its meaning; then Cornelius tells Peter his. Luke would not have recounted all this had it not suited his purpose; for even if his report is strictly historical, there must have been some reason for him to give such an overly complete account. He could have simply reported that Cornelius recounted to Peter his vision and all that had happened in connection with it. Probably the clue to Luke's procedure is found in vs. 33: "Now therefore we are all here present in the sight of God, to hear *all that you have been commanded by the Lord.*" Luke is concerned to show that the initiator of all these events is not man, but God. No one acts until he is moved to do so by the divine initiative and Cornelius anticipates nothing else from Peter but what he has been commanded of God. The abundance of visions and reports of visions emphasizes that what is taking place is something other than the natural course of events or the working out of a human scheme to evangelize the Gentiles. Thus the break with the past in the offering of the gospel to the Gentiles comes about by the will and action of God himself, who gives explicit guidance and direction to the major participants in this drama.

Now that all has been properly prepared, Peter delivers his sermon (10:34–43). It has a great deal in common with the other missionary speeches of Acts. The initial statement, however, applies specifically to the present unprecedented situation (vs. 34 f.), making clear that God is favorably disposed toward what is about to happen. In addition, the tenor of the speech sets it somewhat apart from similar pronouncements. Peter, after his opening remarks, introduces the main body of his speech, the Christian kerygma, with the phrase "you know," thus making his presentation of the gospel a kind of review of matters with which his audience is already familiar. Apparently they have not been converted up to this point because the time has not been right. In the latter part of the speech (vss. 39 ff.) emphasis falls on the crucifixion and resurrection of Jesus and on the authority of the witnesses and their obligation to proclaim the gospel of forgiveness of sins in Jesus' name to all (vs. 42). This implies that Peter's own proclamation to these Gentiles is fully justified.

Before Peter can make the characteristic appeal for repentance and conversion (cf. 2:37–42), the Holy Spirit descends upon his hearers (vs. 44), who promptly begin speaking in tongues (vs. 46). All this is witnessed by Jewish Christians (vs. 45), who are amazed that God should give his Spirit even to Gentiles. That these people, Gentiles though they may be, should be baptized is now a foregone conclusion (vss. 47 f.). The Jewish Christians are in no position to object, inasmuch as they themselves have observed the manifestation of the Spirit. That the Spirit should be given before baptism could only be taken as an unmistakable sign of the will of God in the matter.

Peter now returns to Jerusalem, where he encounters the criticism of the circumcision party (11:1 ff.) and in response to them explains fully what happened. Again Luke is not content simply to say that Peter gave an explanation, but gives a full account of it. We now get the second rendition of Peter's vision (vss. 4–10) and the third of Cornelius' (vss. 13–15). As repetition is not necessary for the simple narration of the story, it is apparently a technique by which Luke drives home the significance of the events he is recounting. In fact, the whole point of Luke's narrative really comes to focus-in Peter's somewhat repetitious response to his critics. Only here does the sense of the preceding narrative finally become entirely clear: God wills the conversion of worthy Gentiles to Christianity. Although it is not obvious from the question (vs. 3) that this is what the Jewish Christians are challenging, their final concession (vs. 18) indicates that for Luke precisely this question is settled by the conversion of Cornelius.

A closer examination of certain details of the text confirms this observation. In 11:14 Cornelius' account of his vision is expanded to include as its central point the expectation that Peter will preach the gospel to him and his household. This expectation was not expressed in the earlier accounts (cf. 10:33 and 10:3–6). In Peter's report of his own sermon (11:15), the Holy Spirit no longer falls upon the Gentiles toward the conclusion of his epoch, but at the beginning—a further indication of the divine initiative. The descent of the Spirit is then likened to Pentecost (chap. 2). This is a new dispensation of the Spirit of God in fulfillment of Jesus' own promise (11:16; cf. 1:5), and Peter draws its full implications for the missionary practice of the church: "If then God gave the same gift to them as he gave to us when we believed in the Lord Jesus Christ, who was I that I could withstand God?" (vs. 17). Peter had no idea of preaching to Gentiles. Rather the Gentile mission originated in a discrete and epoch-making revelation by God of his purposes for the church and the gospel. This interpretation of the meaning and significance of the conversion of Cornelius and its aftermath is borne out in Luke's report of the Jerusalem Council.

The Jerusalem Council (15:1–41)[4]
What is the basis for the council's decision about the Gentiles?

The question of whether non-Jewish converts to Christianity had to be circumcised in accordance with the Jewish law was never raised in chapter 11. We were left with the impression that they were not circumcised and that the Jewish Christians were satisfied that God intended the conversion of the Gentiles without their having also to become Jews. Yet at the beginning of chapter 15 a group from Judea who insist that circumcision is necessary for salvation arrives in Antioch. Apparently they are representatives of the converted Pharisees in Jerusalem (15:5), who also demand that Gentile Christians be circumcised. This is probably the same group who caused trouble for Peter after he had converted Cornelius (cf. 11:2). Their interest in preserving the Jewish character of Christianity is also in agreement with the attitude of the multitude of Jewish Christians in Jerusalem who are later described as zealous for the law and suspicious of Paul (21:20 f.).

Despite the fact that Paul and Barnabas were the principal parties to the dispute, they do not do the talking when the apostles and elders come together to deliberate in Acts 15. They give an account of their activities (vs. 12) as if they had been called on the carpet, but Peter and James, the brother of the Lord, make the crucial speeches. Peter's speech (vss. 7–11) is a defense of the Gentile mission on the basis of the Cornelius incident (cf. vss. 7–9), and thoroughly supports our interpretation of the significance of that incident. Cornelius' name is not mentioned, but the

---

[4] The relation of the council of chapter 15 to the meeting between Paul and the leaders of the Jerusalem church described in the second chapter of Paul's letter to the Galatians is a problem that has long tantalized and puzzled scholars. Cf. Kümmel, *Introduction to the New Testament*, pp. 195–97.

reference is crystal-clear, for the important thing is not the persons involved but the manifestation of the divine will. God is from beginning to end the actor; even Peter is only his agent. He established the Gentile mission independently of Judaism by sending his Spirit upon the Gentiles (cf. 10:45–47) and, making no distinction, cleansing their hearts by faith (cf. 10:43). Thus to reject the establishment of this mission by requiring adherence to the Jewish law is tantamount to putting God himself on trial. Peter's speech ends with a ringing declaration of salvation by grace (vs. 11). His position, as it is here set forth, is not far from that of the apostle Paul. Yet it is not exactly Paul's position, for the great apostle to the Gentiles did not maintain that the law was too heavy a yoke to bear. In other respects, however, this speech of Peter is a better specimen of Pauline theology—taking the epistles to be the norm of what is Pauline —than any speech attributed to Paul in the book of Acts. In a sense, Paul does not need to make a speech at this point, for Peter has made it for him.

When Peter's speech has ended and after Paul and Barnabas inform the assembly of the "signs and wonders which God had done through them among the Gentiles" (15:12), presumably referring to the conversions to Christianity made on their recently completed missionary journey (cf. chaps. 13 and 14), James speaks. Harking back to Peter's speech and thus to the Cornelius incident, which is described as "how God first visited the Gentiles to take out of them a people for his name," James' speech shows once again how crucial for Luke was that incident in the establishment of the Gentile mission. James grounds the Gentile mission on the prophetic words of Amos, Jeremiah, and Isaiah, and then proceeds to give his own judgment on the matter at hand. It is, for the most part, a fairly liberal one. According to Paul's letters, however, James appears to have been more cautious about the Gentile mission, if not downright hostile to it (cf. Gal. 2:12). Even in Acts James puts some restrictions on the freedom he is willing to grant Gentile Christians, although he limits these to the Noachian commandments (so-called because they were thought to have been in effect since the time of Noah), which the rabbis regarded as obligatory for all men. Thus he appears as the representative of a somewhat more conservative point of view than that of Paul, Barnabas, and even Peter. This fact, however, is neither emphasized nor explicitly noted.

It is apparently on James' initiative that the council of apostles and elders acts. After adopting his recommendation, they publish it in the form of a letter, which is sent back to Antioch by Judas, called Barsabbas, and Silas, who accompany Paul and Barnabas (vss. 22–29). After they reach Antioch we hear nothing further of this apostolic decree. In fact, after 16:4 it is not mentioned in Acts, and Paul never refers to it in his letters. It should be noted that the decree itself does not speak directly to the original question of circumcision, although since its stipulations do not include circumcision, it must be considered to represent a victory for proponents of the Gentile mission. So at the conclusion of the council the question of the Gentile mission is settled. Moreover, in the council's deliberations it has become clear that it was really settled by the conversion of Cornelius—that is, before the Gentile mission had actually begun.

Christianity's Triumphal March (13:1–28:31)

In this latter portion of his work Luke narrates the movement of Christianity from the East to the West, from Antioch in Syria to Rome. The book ends with Paul under custody in that city, but with great latitude and freedom to preach the gospel. Probably this brings us down to about A.D. 60, several years before Paul's death in the Emperor Nero's persecution of Christians and a decade before the liquidation of the Jewish rebellion. Luke wrote his Gospel after that rebellion and, if anything, the book of Acts was composed still later (Acts 1:1). That he did not continue his narrative to include these events shows that his primary purpose was not to recount fully the history of Christianity down to his own day, but to give a selective account of the pivotal events through what seemed to him to be the crucial period of Christian origins—which indeed it was. By this movement to Rome Christianity was to become a primarily western religion. This does not mean that in essence it is an expression of a Western spirit, but that its greatest expansion and development, intellectual and institutional, was not in the Oriental land of its birth but in the Occident.

Luke makes the transition from Jerusalem to the West seem natural and normal. He skillfully dovetails the two major portions of his account so that the coming mission to the Gentiles is prefigured by the conversions of Cornelius and of Paul and by the speech of Stephen. In fact, the descent of the Spirit and the preaching of Peter at Pentecost before the representatives of many lands already points ahead to the wider missionary effort. After the scene shifts away from Jerusalem, we are kept aware of the authority and vitality of the Jerusalem church, and of the contact between that church and the Gentile mission. The church's work and geographical distribution may become diverse, but its origin, loyalty, mission, and purpose are one. This conviction Luke shares with other New Testament writers, but he expresses it in a unique and effective way.

The Gentile mission falls into several sections defined by Paul's various activities:

(1) First missionary journey: Cyprus and Asia Minor (13:1–14:28).
(2) Jerusalem Council (15:1–35).

(3) Second missionary journey: entry into Greece (15:36–18:22).
(4) Third missionary journey: Ephesus and Greece (18:23–21:14).
(5) Paul in Jerusalem: arrest and imprisonment (21:15–23:30).
(6) Caesarean imprisonment (23:31–26:32).
(7) Journey to Rome (27:1–28:31).

Note how this half of Acts shows the movement of the witness to the gospel across the world. The above outline makes this movement unmistakably clear by repeated reference to Paul's journeys. The concentration on missionary journeys in Acts typifies the perspective of the author. The gospel is on the move.

THE UNIVERSAL MISSION (13:1–21:14)

Has the mission to the Gentiles become the mission of Paul?

In chapters 13 and 14 we find the first description of missionary activity beyond Palestine and Syria. (This was not the first such effort, however; cf. 11:19–20) Paul and Barnabas are commissioned, not by the Jerusalem church, but by the church at Antioch (13:1–3), and sent off under its auspices. This church had been founded by those fleeing Jerusalem during the persecution of the Hellenists. It is perhaps understandable that the Jerusalem church may have had some reservations about its activities and that the Antiochene Christians may have harbored some resentment toward the mother church. After all, the Jewish Christians had been able to remain in Jerusalem after the founders of the Antioch church had been driven out, presumably because of their views about Judaism.

The most important incident of chapter 13 is the sermon of Paul (13: 17–41) in the Jewish synagogue at Pisidian Antioch. Throughout Acts and until the end of his missionary labors in Rome, Paul is portrayed as appealing first to the Jews in every city he visits. Although such a procedure fits almost too well with Luke's conviction about the positive relation of Christianity to Israel, the Hellenistic Jewish synagogue doubtless did provide an almost indispensable foothold for the earliest Christian preaching. In keeping with the setting, Paul's sermon is an address by an Israelite to Israelites, although some Gentile God-fearers are also present (vs. 16). It is designed to portray Jesus, the son of David, as the culmination of their history of salvation, the One promised by God. In proof of this Paul calls upon the Old Testament to show how the ancient prophecies are now fulfilled in him, especially in his resurrection. Many of the Jews believe (vs. 43), but some do not, and, characteristically, the nonbelievers work systematically to undermine him (vs. 45). This moves Paul and Barnabas to condemn these recalcitrant Jews and to turn forth-

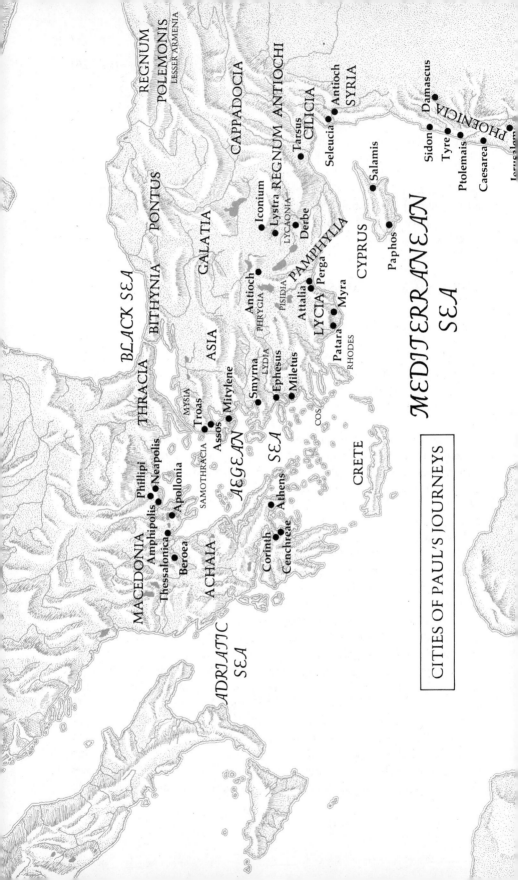

REGNUM
POLEMONIS
LESSER ARMENIA

CAPPADOCIA

REGNUM ANTIOCHI

Antioch
SYRIA

Damascus

Tarsus
CILICIA

Seleucia

PHOENICIA

Sidon
Tyre
Ptolemais
Caesarea

Iconium
Lystra
LYCAONIA
Derbe

Salamis

CYPRUS

Paphos

BLACK SEA

PONTUS

GALATIA

Antioch
PHRYGIA
PISIDIA
Attalia
Perga
PAMPHYLIA

LYCIA

Myra

Patara
RHODES

MEDITERRANEAN
SEA

BITHYNIA

ASIA

Smyrna
LYDIA
Ephesus
Miletus

THRACIA

MYSIA
Troas
Assos
Mitylene

COS

AEGEAN SEA

CRETE

SAMOTHRACIA

Philippi
Neapolis
Amphipolis
Apollonia
Thessalonica
Beroea

MACEDONIA

ACHAIA

Corinth
Athens
Cenchreae

ADRIATIC
SEA

CITIES OF PAUL'S JOURNEYS

with to the Gentiles, still quoting the Old Testament (Isaiah 49:6) to justify their action (13:44–47).

In 14:15–18 Paul and Barnabas are at Lystra making their first address to a purely pagan audience. This speech has less in common with the sermon of chapter 13 and the earlier missionary speeches than with Paul's address to the Athenians on Mars Hill. At the end of chapter 14 Paul and Barnabas return to Antioch, where some question has been raised by the Judean Christians about their preaching the gospel to the Gentiles. We have already seen how this question was settled in favor of Paul and Barnabas at the Jerusalem Council. Yet a similar or related question is raised against Paul again in chapter 21.

At the end of the Jerusalem Council (chap. 15) and after a sharp dispute over John Mark, Paul and Barnabas separate. Paul returns to the scene of their earlier missionary activity, taking Silas with him (15:36–41). Thence he heads west and, reaching Troas, sees the famous vision (16:9) that leads him to extend his missionary effort to Europe. Europe here means Macedonia and Greece, which was henceforth, with Ephesus, the chief focus of his missionary activity until his imprisonment and subsequent journey to Rome. His chief missionary accomplishments were in the Greek cities of Philippi (chap. 16), Thessalonica (17:1–9), and Corinth (chap. 18) and in the Asian city of Ephesus (chap. 19). Luke, however, gives an extended account of the relatively brief visit of Paul to Athens.

Paul's Speech in Athens (17:16–34)
How does Paul seek to make contact with his hearers?

As a missionary station Athens is certainly not typical—Paul's efforts there seem to have borne little fruit. However, Luke's account of his visit occupies a prominent place and includes the longest rendition in Acts of a sermon before an entirely Gentile audience. Obviously, Luke regards Paul's stay in Athens as an important event. Therefore, we need to understand its significance for him.

Luke's brief description of the character of Athens and the Athenians shows that he has some awareness of the nature as well as of the importance of the city.[5] Yet he reports that Paul was not at all impressed by Athens, but was instead shocked by the profusion of idols he found there. Paul apparently took the sculpture of Athens to be of religious

---

[5] The Athens of Paul's time was not large, however, even by ancient standards. Haenchen, *Die Apostelgeschichte* ("Kritisch-exegetischer Kommentar über das Neue Testament," 3. Abt. 12. Aufl.; Göttingen: Vandenhoeck & Ruprecht, 1959), p. 454, puts the total number of citizens (not total population) at about 5,000. Haenchen's commentary, hopefully soon to appear in English translation, has been invaluable in the preparation of this chapter.

rather than aesthetic significance, and therefore regarded it as idolatrous (vs. 16). His displeasure led him to engage in debate, not only in the synagogue, as had previously been his custom, but even in the public market place (vs. 17). Luke does not explicitly tell us, but this is presumably the same market place where centuries before Socrates engaged his fellow Athenians in discussions. Perhaps Luke is aware of a certain parallel here, even though he does not mention Socrates' name, for we read that Paul is accused of preaching "foreign divinities" (vs. 18). The Greek *Xenōn daimoniōn* could as well be translated "of strange demons" and thus corresponds closely to that *daimōn* which led Socrates to raise those simple, pointed, and troublesome questions that at length roused the ire of his fellow Athenians and led to his execution as an atheist.[6]

Paul's lack of appreciation of Athenian culture is no greater than the Athenians' misunderstanding of him, as his encounter with the Stoic and Epicurean philosophers shows (vs. 18). The epithet that some of them apply to him, "babbler," means literally "cock-sparrow." It was a term of derision for a person who, without real understanding, picks up ideas from here and there, as the sparrow picks up seed, and passes them off as his own. That this estimate of Paul is an off-hand judgment based on no genuine understanding of him may be inferred from the fact that the philosophers take Jesus and the resurrection to be two gods. (This is not quite as absurd a misunderstanding as it may seem, since the Greek word *anastasis*, resurrection, is feminine in gender, and pagan gods frequently had goddesses as consorts.) In the light of this beginning, the Athenians' desire to hear Paul's teaching in greater detail is difficult to understand, but Luke makes clear that it only stems from their insatiable curiosity about anything new (vss. 20 f.).

Paul was taken to the Areopagus (vs. 19) by the Athenians, and there he made his speech. At the time of Paul a court was held on the Areopagus—the name means Mars Hill—which is a small promontory west of the more famous Acropolis. Although it has sometimes been suggested that Paul was himself taken there to be tried, this is nowhere explicitly stated (although the verb "took hold of" in vs. 19 could imply arrest). Moreover, the whole affair does not read like a legal proceeding. Rather, Paul is put on display, almost as if he were some kind of freak, by a crowd of intellectual dilletantes.

Paul's initial remark (vs. 22) is probably not to be taken in a negative or sarcastic sense. Rather, as the following verses show, it is the point of

---

[6] *Daimōn* has more the meaning of "good spirit" than of "demon" as the latter is usually understood. The accusation against Socrates was two-fold: (1) corruption of the young; (2) neglect of the traditional gods and the recognition of new and strange deities (*daimonia*).

contact with the pagan audience which Paul hopes to follow up and develop in his delivery of the Christian message. This becomes clear in vs. 23, where Paul concedes that this "unknown god" is worshipped in a valid, if inadequate, way by the Athenians. The time has now come, however, for the unknown God to be revealed in the Christian preaching. A right understanding of this God will mean the recognition of the erroneous character of the pagan worship that has heretofore been offered (vss. 24 f.). This point of view is not, of course, unique to Christianity. It is also Jewish, and this part of Paul's speech may owe something to earlier Jewish missionary propaganda. Furthermore, although the idolatry and polytheism described here may have been practiced and taken seriously by many people in the ancient world, the cultured Greek would have also shared something of Paul's attitude. In fact, whether verses 24 ff. owe more to Judaism and the Old Testament or to Stoic philosophy is a good question.

The concepts (vss. 26 ff. especially) actually fit better into the Stoic view of the cosmos than into the Biblical-Jewish conception of the history of salvation. For verse 26 has to do with the characteristic Stoic ideas of the providence of God and verses 27 and 28 with his immanence or presence in the world. Moreover, just at the point at which we might have expected a quotation from the Old Testament, Paul quotes the Greek poet Aratus (vs. 28).[7] To such an extent does Paul accommodate his message to what is familiar and acceptable to his Greek hearers. When seen in the light of verse 29, verses 26–28 support the assertions of verses 24 and 25 and thus drive home the argument against idolatry. Although verses 26–28 are now frequently cited as Biblical proof of the brotherhood of man under God, in this context they are probably not intended primarily to set forth that idea. Rather, they are an argument from the evidence of the existence of God in man and nature to a conclusion concerning the nature of God and the proper knowledge and worship of him. God orders the world and men (vs. 26) in such a way that they should be disposed to seek him (vs. 27), and he so indwells his creation that this seeking is by no means vain (vs. 27 f.). Indeed, as the quotation from Aratus shows, the idea of immanence is understood to imply that mankind already has a close relationship to God: "For we are indeed his offspring." Probably Luke takes this to mean that man is God's creature, in line with the Old Testament and Hebraic point of view and not in the sense of kinship which the poet originally intended. Nevertheless, creaturehood here already implies the possibility of knowing God and having access to him.

---

[7] *Phaenomena*, 6; cf. Cleanthes, *Hymn to Zeus*, 4. Only the last of the two quotations marked in the RSV has been positively identified. "In him we live and move and have our being" has sometimes been attributed to Epimenides, but it may not be a quotation at all.

Only in verses 30 and 31 does Paul turn from these arguments from natural theology, which many Hellenistic Jews or even pagans might have found perfectly congenial, to the distinctly Christian message. The whole history of paganism down to the moment in which Paul speaks is described simply as "times of ignorance" that God has overlooked (vs. 30). The pagan world will presumably incur no guilt as a result, provided it now repents. Curiously enough, no mention at all is made of the ministry and crucifixion of Jesus in this preaching of repentance; only the coming judgment is invoked, and only in connection with it is Jesus

The Parthenon, celebrated temple of Athena, built in the fifth-century B.C. on the Acropolis at Athens. (Courtesy of Greek Press and Information Service.)

mentioned. Even then Paul does not explicitly name him, but only alludes to him as the man whom God has appointed to judge the world, giving assurance of this "to all men by raising him from the dead." At the mention of the resurrection of the dead, Paul is interrupted; some hearers become contemptuous—the late Jewish and Christian notion of resurrection is foreign to them—but others remain curious (vs. 32). Paul departs (vs. 33), and although we have the impression that his preaching to the Athenians was something less than a success, he does succeed in making a few converts to the faith (vs. 34).

The Character of Paul's Speech
What is the relation of Gentile piety to Christian faith in the speech?

The speech is notable on several counts. First, it differs from the missionary speeches of chapters 1–13 in its total lack of reference to the Old Testament and the history of Israel. Second, it is remarkably dissimilar to the genuine letters of Paul. Third, it has certain affinities, as we shall see, with the speech ascribed to Paul and Barnabas in 14:15–18. Finally, this is one of the rare places in the New Testament in which a positive, though highly qualified, estimate of pagan piety and culture is expressed or implied and a natural theology is set forth. Each of these points demands further comment.

We have already noticed that at just the point we would have expected Paul to refer to the Hebrew scriptures (Old Testament) he quotes a pagan poet. The Old Testament would have been of little use in confirming the truth of the Christian message before a non-Jewish audience who did not accept its authority in the first place. The appeal to this purely Gentile audience had to be made on the basis of arguments from Hellenistic natural theology and Greek literature. This does not mean that the use of the Hebrew scriptures in Christian preaching was regarded either by Paul or Luke as a purely apologetic device. There is ample reason to suppose that both regarded it as revelation in and of itself. Yet the non-Jewish hearer might be brought to assent on other grounds. In the other instance of a missionary sermon before a non-Jewish audience, the brief speech of Paul and Barnabas (14:15–18), there is no reference or allusion to the Hebrew scriptures or the narrative of salvation history. It may be that in recounting the speeches to Gentile audiences in this way Luke is following a common procedure, or is influenced by a common practice of the Hellenistic Christian mission in his own day.[8] As far as we know, Paul did not limit his use of the scriptures to situations in which he was addressing Christians of Jewish background.

This observation leads directly to our second point. Even a casual reading of the first three chapters of the Epistle to the Romans reveals that Paul's attitude toward the pagan world was not that portrayed in the Areopagus speech. Whereas in this speech pagan piety and the possibility of a natural theology is the point of contact and, in fact, the basis of his preaching, in Romans practically the reverse is true. In Romans, the knowledge of God is indeed possible because of creation and the natural order, but the possibility of such knowledge is not the basis of Christian

---

[8] Ulrich Wilckens, *Die Missionsreden der Apostelgeschichte: Form und traditionsgeschichtliche Untersuchungen* ("Wissenshaftliche Monographien zum Alten und Neuen Testament": Neukirchener Verlag, 1961), p. 99, suggests that Luke employed a pattern of heathen missionary preaching attested by I Thess. 1:9–10 and Heb. 5:11–6:2.

preaching. Rather it is grounds for condemnation because it does not lead to a proper response to God (1:18–23). In Acts the hearers are credited with worshipping God without knowing him; in Romans man is charged with knowing God but not worshipping him. Whereas in Acts 17:30 the past prior to the preaching of the gospel is simply a period of ignorance for which no blame is placed, in Romans the history of man is the history of sin. Further, when the salvation event is announced in Acts 17:31, Paul speaks primarily of the coming judgment, with a backward look at the resurrection. In Romans 3:21 ff. the salvation event is described in terms of the cross. Admittedly Paul's speech is interrupted, but we have the impression that with the mention of the resurrection and judgment he has said all he needs to say. Thus in almost every important respect Paul's Areopagus speech seems to be the antithesis of the theology of Paul in Romans. This naturally raises the question of whether this speech is Paul's or whether Luke has put into Paul's mouth what he considers to be an appropriate and typical missionary sermon to Gentiles. In order to ascribe the speech to Paul, one must suspect that after this occasion Paul gave up this apologetic approach. That is, after an unsuccessful attempt to make contact with pagan culture in the preaching of the gospel, he took a more hostile stance toward the world. Yet there is little indication in all the genuine Pauline letters that the apostle himself ever espoused such a theological position as we find in the Acts speech. It is much easier historically to understand the Areopagus speech as the composition of Luke. This, of course, does not mean that Paul did not visit Athens and preach there (cf. I Thess. 3:1).

Modern standards of historical reporting were unknown to Luke. Ancient historians sometimes used a speech by a leading figure as a literary device to convey something to their readers which they thought was important for an understanding of persons or situations.[9] Such a procedure was understood by the literate reader and not considered dishonest or fraudulent. This need not seem strange to us. In popular historical and biographical works material attributed to historical personages is often partially, if not wholly, the composition of the author.[10] We agree tacitly that the author's task is not simply to sift and collect such fragments as can be

[9] Cf. M. Dibelius, "The Speeches in Acts and Ancient Historiography," *Studies in the Acts of the Apostles,* ed. H. Greeven and trans. M. Long (London: SCM, 1956), pp. 138–91, esp. 138–40, and H. J. Cadbury, *The Making of Luke-Acts* (New York: Macmillan Co., 1927), pp. 184–93.

[10] Reports of conversations are bound to be at most approximations, and sometimes simply products of the author's conception of what would have been appropriate. For example, in the preface to *PT 109: John F. Kennedy in World War II* (New York: McGraw-Hill, 1961), p. 14, Robert J. Donovan writes: "The conversations are, *of course,* recreated, but in roughly the words the participants remember using" (italics mine).

remembered, but to create in the minds of his reader a total picture that corresponds as nearly as possible to what actually occurred. Moreover, for the Biblical writer, what actually occurred could not be equated with what the modern tape-recorder and camera might pick up, but rather included the totality of the historical situation in all its meaning and significance for the church and the church's faith. So, even had Luke possessed a transcript of Paul's Areopagus sermon, in the light of the subsequent course of events he might have seen fit not to use it.

We observed earlier that Luke seems to be presenting what he considers a typical missionary sermon to Gentiles. Now we are able to support this observation further by our third point, namely, that the Areopagus speech has its closest affinities with the speech of Paul and Barnabas to a pagan audience at Lystra (14:15-18). The Lystra speech manifests certain specific points of agreement with the Areopagus address. Especially striking are the concept of divine creation (vs. 15), the notion that God has tolerated the idolatry of the Gentiles in times past (vss. 15 f.), and the belief that the beneficent natural processes attest a divine author (vs. 17). Except for the lack of direct reference to Christ, the Lystra speech is quite similar to the one at Athens. And like the latter, it is dissimilar to the speeches of chapters 1–13 and unlike the theology of the Pauline epistles.

We thus arrive at our fourth point. Both the Athens speech and the Lystra speech are most unlike the Pauline theology and the rest of the New Testament in their ascription of a positive and significant role to a natural knowledge of God, a knowledge both possible and extant apart from the Jewish and Christian traditions. They are also unique in regarding the history of mankind prior to the coming of Christ and the preaching of the gospel as ignorance rather than sin. The revelation in Christ is not, first of all, the revelation of God's wrath (cf. Rom. 1:18) and of human sinfulness, but of a coming judgment and the necessity of repentance (Acts 17:30 f.) and forgiveness. Thus, for Luke the human predicament is not quite so desperate as for Paul, and pagan culture and piety are allowed to play a positive preparatory role for the appearance of the gospel.

The idea of a valid general revelation apart from Israel and the Old Testament, although rare in the New Testament, was taken up and developed by Christian apologists and theologians of the second and third centuries and has persisted among Christians down to our own day. For Luke, the entire world and its history provide the scope for the Christian mission and message. Its roots are to be found not only in the history of Israel, but also in the general history of man and his culture. Luke's Gospel traces the genealogy of Christ back to Adam, and in Acts the necessary presuppositions of Christian preaching are found in a popular philosophic view of God and the world, as well as in the Old Testament.

FROM JERUSALEM TO ROME (21:15–28:31)

What is the result of Paul's arrest and trials?

Chapters 21–28 are devoted entirely to the fortunes of Paul from his last visit to Jerusalem until his arrival as a prisoner in Rome. From the point at which Paul is arrested near the temple in Jerusalem (21:33) to

Roman statue at Caesarea, the residence of the Roman procurators in Judea. (Courtesy of Israel Information Services.)

the end of the book he is a Roman prisoner, and it is probable that he, like Jesus, died at the hands of the Romans. Paul is at first held for a couple of days in Jerusalem. Then he is transferred to Caesarea, the site of the Roman governor's headquarters (chaps. 24–26), and finally, on the basis of his own appeal to Caesar, he is sent to Rome (chaps. 27–28). There the story simply ends, with Paul a prisoner in Rome, albeit with certain freedoms and privileges. As we take leave of him he is still "preaching the kingdom of God and teaching about the Lord Jesus Christ quite openly and unhindered" (28:31).

The larger part of chapters 22–28, with the exception of the sea voyage to Rome (chap. 27), is devoted to extensive descriptions of Paul's defense of himself before the representatives of Judaism and Rome. It is as if the prophecy of 9:15 were being literally fulfilled: "He is a chosen instrument of mine to carry my name before the Gentiles and kings and the sons of Israel." Luke describes Paul's hearings and speeches in considerable detail. Paul's conversion, reported in full in chapter 9, is repeated with some variations in chapters 22 and 26. In the course of many scenes and speeches several themes are often reiterated. Paul has not betrayed Judaism; rather, he understands his whole mission to pertain directly to the fulfillment of the hope of Israel. Paul's mission to the Gentiles is not simply his own idea, but the direct result of divine causation and directive. Thus Paul's conversion is always closely linked to his commission to preach to the Gentiles—as it is by Paul himself (Gal. 1:15 ff.). Paul's innocence of any crime is established with certainty. The various hints, statements, and indications tending to exonerate Paul are well summarized in the conversation between Agrippa and Festus reported at the end of chapter 26, where it is agreed that Paul could have been released had not he appealed to Caesar. Yet the fact that he must stand before Caesar (27:24) is not finally a tragedy, although it has tragic overtones (for example, 20:22–25, 38), but the culmination of the triumphant spread of Christianity across the known world and the high point of Acts. Although Paul's imprisonment and journey to Rome might be regarded by some as the result of the work of evil men or the quirk of a cruel fate, for Luke they are nothing other than the fulfillment of the will of God.

The *structure* of the Acts of the Apostles must be considered along with the Gospel. At the same time the division between Gospel and Acts is more than a convenient literary device. It marks a major division in Luke's theology and perception of history. His three-fold division of the history of salvation can be discerned from the shape and structure of his writing. The Old Testament (cf. Luke 1:5–2:51 especially) constitutes the first part of a story of salvation that finds its culmination in the coming of Jesus as the Christ (Gospel). But this fulfillment was not limited to the historic appearance of Jesus of Nazareth; it embraced also the existence and mission of his church (Acts). As in Luke 4, Old Testament prophecies find fulfillment in Jesus, so in Acts 2 other such prophecies are said to be fulfilled in the descent of the Spirit and the witness of the church. The final chapter of the story is not, however, the appearance of the church.

The church continues to look forward to a culmination of history when Jesus will return to hold judgment and establish God's reign (1:11; 3: 19–21). Luke envisages a drama beginning with creation, ending with an eschatological redemption, and within this framework passing through three distinct phases: a preparatory phase, which is the period of Israel and her prophetic message; a central phase, which is the fulfillment of this prophecy in the earthly mission of Jesus; and a final phase, which is the mission of the church, likewise a fulfillment of ancient prophecy. Luke's distinct theological outlook thus allowed him to add the book of Acts to his account of the ministry of Jesus. He viewed this book, not as a postscript, but as an account of the continuing activity of God through his apostles in a distinct stage of the history of salvation.

The basic structure of Acts itself is quite simple. After the ascension, the election of Matthias, and the inaugural preaching of the gospel by Peter, which take place in or around Jerusalem, there are two principal divisions, the one dealing with the establishment and growth of the church within Palestine (chaps. 3–12), and the other with the expansion of the church to the Gentile world (the remainder of the book). Even as the journey of Jesus to Jerusalem forms the central part of the Gospel, so the missionary journeys of Paul are the central portion of Acts. Just as the last part of the Gospel deals with the arrest, trial and death of Jesus, so the last seven chapters of Acts narrate the arrest of Paul, his trials, and the eventual journey to Rome. The motifs of journeying and witnessing thus predominate in Acts as in Luke's Gospel.

The *emphases* of Acts are intricately bound to its structure, and intimately related to those of the Gospel. In fact, the same emphases—Christianity as the new Israel, worldwide expansion, and the importance of witnessing—are developed somewhat further in Acts. In the Gospel, Luke is tied to the tradition of Jesus, which he cannot radically change, but in Acts he can with a relatively free hand tell the story of the church's advance so as to bring out its inner truth.

Luke was deeply convinced that Judaism should have become Christianity, and, as it had not, that the promises to Israel were being fulfilled through Christ in the church. Thus the new faith is the proper and genuine continuation and fulfillment of the old. The many quotations from the Old Testament and allusions and references to it are a clear indication of this. The speech of Peter (chap. 2) and Paul's initial missionary sermon (chap. 13), delivered in the synagogue in Pisidian Antioch, are strikingly similar in their Biblical orientation. Both bristle with Old Testament quotations and references. The speech of Stephen (chap. 7) is concerned almost exclusively with the interpretation of the history of Israel. Its effect is to show that the Jewish nation is not, and for a long time has not been, an obedient people and the legitimate heir of the covenant promises of the God of Israel. In fact, the culmination of Paul's ministry in Rome (recounted in chap. 28) is his application of the famous Isaiah 6:9–10 passage to those Jews who had not believed his preaching (vss. 25–28). Israel has forfeited its inheritance to the Gentiles by rejecting the gospel, and the young Christian church has now become the true Israel. This understanding of the relation of the church to Israel is, as we have already seen, incorporated into the three-fold structure of salvation history.

Acts is often called "the first church history," and in a sense it is. Yet insofar as it is a history at all, it is history of a very special kind. It has been written from a definite theological perspective with certain purposes in view. When all allowances are made for Luke's motivations and interests, however, it is apparent that a major part of his purpose in Acts is to tell an interesting and, for the most part, happy story. He describes the establishment of Christianity and its progress across the Greco-Roman world during the apostolic age. The scope of the gospel is universal, and it will not be denied. Although we hear of persecutions and martyrdoms in the course of this story, the story-teller's attitude remains confident and optimistic throughout, and the narrative is brought to an end on a positive note (28:30 f.). The gospel knows no obstacle too great and no enemy too powerful to stand in the way of its successful march from Jerusalem to Rome. The universal emphsis, which is subtly conveyed in Luke's Gospel, becomes the principal subject matter of Acts.

Even as Luke told the story of the gospel's advance, he was conscious of the increasing weight of evidence that the Jewish people, and especially official Judaism, were not accepting the Christian message. Could this mean that the church was not, after all, the true Israel? No, for Luke held that the failure of the greater part of the Jewish people to accept the gospel by no means discredited it. The ignorance and hostility that brought Jesus to the cross was also manifest against Paul in the same Jerusalem in which Jesus was crucified, a city that did not know "the things that make for peace" (Luke 19:41). Luke knew that Jerusalem had been destroyed by the Romans in the war of A.D. 66–70 and interpreted this as recompense for the city's hardness of heart (Luke 19:41–44; 20:9–18; 21:20–24). Every opportunity is given the Jewish people to believe in the gospel, up to and including the final chapter of Acts, but despite persistent efforts they do not. Although Jews are represented as accepting the message of the earliest preachers in Jerusalem and in the synagogues of Gentile lands, Luke was well aware that relatively few Jews had been converted and that Christianity already had become a predominantly Gentile religion.[11]

The centrality of Luke's emphasis upon the universality of the Gospel implies an emphasis on witnessing. Again, what is handled somewhat indirectly in the Gospel becomes a major theme of Acts. As the interpreta-

---

[11] This fact is also reflected in his Gospel, 4:16–30. Jesus begins his ministry with a clear indication that he is to be rejected by the Jews and accepted by Gentiles.

tion of Acts 1 made clear, Luke's first concern was to show that in the apostolic group, the twelve, a firm basis for the witness to Jesus had been established. Matthias, who was elected to the twelve to replace Judas, qualified by virtue of intimate and longtime knowledge of Jesus. Having been a witness of Jesus he was qualified to bear witness. If Luke emphasizes the universality of the gospel, he does so by telling of the apostles and others witnessing. Their witnessing encounters persecution, as we had already been led to expect by the Gospel. Indeed, the witness (Greek, *martyr*) may even become a martyr, as in the case of Stephen, not to mention Peter, Paul, and others who are arrested and otherwise harassed.[12] Although Luke takes full account of such dangers, he does not dwell upon them, for he is fully convinced that such opposition fails utterly to impede the spread of the gospel and the growth of the church.

In connection with the reporting of such opposition and persecution, however, Luke does have another important interest. He wants to show that Christianity is not a subversive movement. One only has to note that in contact with Roman or other authority, Christianity is exonerated of any suspicion of illegal practices. The classical example is perhaps the statement about Paul which Agrippa made to Festus, the Roman procurator: "This man could have been set free if he had not appealed to Caesar" (26:32). Christians are not arrested because the authorities have seen them commit a crime, but because they have become involved in some incident as a result of the accusations or actions of either Jews or Gentiles. The only Christian martyrs we hear of in Acts are victims of the Jews. That Luke should have had some interest in showing Christians innocent of any crimes against the state is thoroughly understandable. After all, Jesus had been crucified by the Roman authorities, whatever role the Jewish leaders may have played, and this fact was apparently widely known.[13] Thus, from the outset Christianity stood under the suspicion of being a subversive movement, and this suspicion could only have been heightened by the refusal of Christians to participate in the worship of the Roman emperor. Luke intends to show that the suspicion is groundless.

The method of *redaction criticism*, which can be so profitably applied to the Gospel, yields less fruit in Acts. The reason for this, of course, is that we can identify the major sources of the Gospel (Mark and Q) with some certainty, whereas it is quite difficult to separate tradition from redaction in Acts. Nevertheless, the assumption that sources and traditions of some sort lie behind Acts is probably warranted. Evidence of the author's

---

12 The tradition of Paul's martyrdom is found only in extracanonical documents: I Clement 5:7; Acts of Paul, x; Eusebius, *EH*, II, 22. The supposed site of Paul's martyrdom is commemorated by the ancient church St. Paul Outside the Walls in Rome. The present structure was rebuilt in modern times after fire destroyed the fourth century building. According to tradition, Peter also was martyred at Rome (see f.n. 16 below).

13 Tacitus, *Annals*, xv, 44 and Baraitha *Sanhedrin*, 43a, to cite noteworthy examples from the well-known Roman historian and an early Rabbinic tractate.

editing can surely be found in the summary reports and transitions, and it is likely that the speeches in their present form are largely his composition. The material of Acts is well permeated with Luke's own point of view, which can usually be identified with some confidence.

Rather than tread an interesting but uncertain path in search of the precise *historical occasion or situation* of Acts, we are again content with the general position taken on the Gospel. Luke-Acts is an apologetic history set in a theological framework and addressed to the educated reader; it was probably written in the last two decades of the first century. If the author writes for the general reader, the needs and purposes of the church are nevertheless always in the forefront of his attention. In all probability the author expected his work to be useful within the church as well as for apologetic or missionary purposes.

That Luke wrote with the church and her interests in mind is immediately apparent when we inquire about the value of Acts as a historical source. Viewed as historical writing, Acts will scarcely win laurels for its neutrality or objectivity. Yet in some respects the author shows unusual historical insight.

His picture of the westward movement of Christianity from Jerusalem to Rome is not only historically perceptive, but almost prophetic. In addition, Luke doubtless does give us, within his schematic presentation, a great deal of information about what went on in the early church. A comparison with Paul reveals that although Acts contains some inaccuracies, it is in touch with actual historical events. It is not a pure fabrication spun out of the fertile theological imagination of the author, as much as that imagination may have shaped the telling of the story.[14] Still, important qualifications must be made. Luke apparently did not know a great many things about the origin of Christianity which we may infer from other documents, and he seems to have omitted deliberately some things that did not accord with his understanding of the essence of apostolic Christianity.

For example, Luke does not tell us how Christianity reached Rome. We know from 28:14 ff. that Christians were already in Rome when Paul arrived; Paul's letter to the Romans also makes it clear that Christians were there before him. Yet Luke tells us nothing about how the gospel was brought there.[15] In fact, after chapter 12, we only hear of the missionary activity of Paul and those associated with him, for Luke uses Paul to personify the entire Gentile mission. Doubtless Paul was a very important apostolic figure. Yet our present-day estimate of his importance as *the*

---

[14] That Acts has a solid historical foundation in the times that it portrays is shown by H. J. Cadbury, *The Book of Acts in History* (New York: Harper & Row, 1955).

[15] Presumably Christianity also reached Egypt at a rather early date, but we learn nothing about this from Acts. Nor do we learn anything about any expansion of Christianity to the East. In fact, we are told nothing very specific of the founding of the church in Antioch (11:9), probably the most important early Christian center outside Jerusalem.

apostle to the Gentiles may be somewhat exaggerated as a result of his pre-eminence in Luke's narrative.

The prominence given Paul reminds us that we learn little from Acts about the activities of the twelve. With the exception of Peter they are all shadowy figures. True, John accompanies Peter in the early chapters, but he is at best a silent partner. The martyrdom of James is mentioned in chapter 12, but we are told neither the reasons for it nor the conditions under which it took place. There is, of course, a list of the eleven apostles (Act 1:13), but we hear little about what happened to the group individually or as a whole.[16] Probably Luke concentrates on Paul at least partly because he has information about him and says little about the twelve because he lacks it. But in other cases his treatment strongly indicates other factors were at work in the selection of material.

Luke does not report accurately or fully on the state of mind of early Christianity. It is clear from the large amount of apocalyptic material preserved in the sayings of Jesus that the earliest church, or a substantial portion of it, expected the imminent return of Jesus and the establishment of the kingdom of God (cf. Matt. 10:23; I Cor. 16:22). The continuing vitality of this expectation of the Lord's return and the end of this world order may be seen in the Revelation to John, probably written toward the end of the first century during the persecution of Christians under the emperor Domitian. As Luke plays down the element of urgent expectancy in the preaching of Jesus in the Gospel, so in Acts there is no longer great excitement or anticipation that the return of Jesus may soon take place. We have already seen how in the ascension scene any such expectation of an imminent return is excluded. The very fact that Luke wrote his second book presupposes the continuation of world history and the church into the third generation after Christ and takes for granted their continued existence for an indefinite period.

Again, a comparison of Acts and Paul on the point of the relation of Jewish and Gentile Christianity leads us to suspect that Luke does not quite reveal everything there is to tell. Paul's letters indicate that there was considerable disagreement and even hostility toward his Gentile mission on the part of some of the more conservative members of the Jerusalem community, who believed that Judaism was, so to speak, the prerequisite for Christianity. Luke does not avoid this issue completely. As we have

---

[16] Later legend connects individual apostles with Christianity in various lands; for example, John with Ephesus and Thomas with India. Although it cannot be said that all these legends lack any factual basis, it is impossible to establish a case for their historicity because of the uncertain origin of the tradition on which they are based. As much as we might like to know what happened to these followers of Jesus, we search Acts in vain for any substantial traces of their whereabouts and activity. The ancient Roman Catholic tradition maintains that Peter was the founder and the first bishop of the church at Rome, although this claim has been widely disputed by Protestant scholars. Recently Cullmann, in his book *Peter: Disciple—Apostle—Martyr*, has accepted as probable the claim that Peter was at least martyred in Rome.

noticed, the question of the gospel and the Gentiles is raised throughout the book of Acts, although the sharp edge of the controversy is consistently dulled. In every instance (cf. chaps. 11, 15, 21) the problem is amicably settled without harsh words or bitterness. Yet it keeps recurring. We wonder why until we read Paul's letters and realize that early Christianity, like other dynamic and revolutionary movements, had its share of internal dissension and strife. How much Luke knew of the extent of these controversies is hard to say. Surely he should have known a great deal had he actually been the companion of Paul. In any case, he portrayed the life of the early church and the development of the Christian mission as if it were more harmonious and free of disagreement and friction than it actually was.

Although as a historical document Acts leaves something to be desired when judged by contemporary standards, it contains much valuable information and insight. It can profitably be studied for the light it sheds on its own generation as well as on the earlier period. Nevertheless, we have not studied Acts merely, or even primarily, to obtain an accurate or complete picture of early church history. Our approach to Acts has sought to find out the questions and issues that occupied the center of Luke's thought by studying the way he has composed his work. Here as in the Gospel it has been necessary to observe the structure and movement of the book, its recurring emphases, the indications of the author's editing, and the factors in his own time and place that motivated him to write as he did.[17] As a result, our estimate of the capacities of Luke and his accomplishments has certainly not been diminished, but rather enhanced. His two-volume work stands as perhaps the greatest literary and historical accomplishment of the New Testament period.

Suggestions for Further Reading

A worthwhile commentary on the English text of Acts is that of C. S. C. Williams in the Harper series (1957). For works on the history of earliest Christianity, see General Bibliography, IV. Consult the "Suggestions for Further Reading" under chapter 4 for works on Luke-Acts.

In addition, the following books deal principally with Acts. M. Dibelius,

---

[17] For this perspective and interest we are indebted to a number of German and American works; for example, Cadbury, *The Making of Luke-Acts*; Dibelius, *Studies in the Acts of the Apostles*; Haenchen, *Die Apostelgeschichte*; Paul Schubert, "The Structure and Significance of Luke 24," *Neutestamentliche Studien für Rudolf Bultmann* ("Beihefte zur ZNW," 21; 2. Aufl.; Berlin: Töpelmann, 1957), pp. 165–86; Philipp Vielhaur, "On the 'Paulinism' of Acts," *Studies in Luke-Acts: Essays presented in Honor of Paul Schubert* (New York: Abingdon Press, 1966), pp. 33–50.

Studies in the Acts of the Apostles, ed. H. Greeven and trans. M. Ling (New York: Scribner's, 1956), is a collection of pioneering essays on the literary analysis and interpretation of Acts written over a period of decades by the well-known German scholar. On the historical basis of Acts, H. Cadbury, *The Book of Acts in History* (New York: Harper, 1955), is informative. F. J. Foakes-Jackson and K. Lake (eds.), *The Beginnings of Christianity*, 5 vols. (London: Macmillan, 1920–33), is still a landmark of scholarship; the work is now being reissued (Grand Rapids, Michigan: Baker Book House). A responsible and up-to-date study book is L. E. Keck, *Mandate to Witness: Studies in the Book of Acts** (Valley Forge, Pa.: Judson Press, 1964).

7 Paul: Apostle and Man of Faith

NOTES ON PAUL'S CAREER

The Acts of the Apostles give a clear picture of the nature and scope of Paul's missionary career. Nevertheless, difficulties arise when one attempts to reconcile Acts' description of Paul and his message with Paul's own letters. It is possible, however, to make an approximate correlation of the Acts account of Paul's career with the letters, to bring his life and work into relation with the main events of the epoch in which he lived, and thus to construct a tentative Pauline chronology. On the basis of an ancient inscription found at Delphi in Greece, Gallio's proconsulship in Corinth may be dated about A.D. 51–52. According to the Acts report, while Paul was in Corinth for eighteen months on his second missionary journey (15:36–18:21) he was arrested and

---

[1] This heading is suggested by the book of the same title by Archibald Hunter (rev. ed.; Philadelphia: Westminster Press, 1961).

280

brought before this same Gallio (18:12 ff.). Thus we can arrive at an approximate date for Paul's first visit to Corinth, which is the surest fixed point of Pauline chronology. We may confidently place Paul's career in the middle third of the first century. Probably he was converted in the early 30's and died in the early 60's. Within this period there is less certainty about the exact dating of events.[2]

More of the New Testament has been ascribed to Paul than to any other author. The Pauline authorship of Hebrews is universally rejected among critical scholars, however, and that of the Pastorals (I and II Timothy and Titus) generally so, with Colossians and II Thessalonians as well as Ephesians sometimes considered doubtful. Therefore, Luke now seems to have been the most prolific New Testament author. Yet slightly more than one-half of Luke's total work is about Jesus and therefore embodies much pre-Lukan tradition. Of the rest more than one-half is about Paul. That so much later literature was ascribed to Paul and that his chief rival for literary productivity devoted a great part of his second work to a description of his career are accurate indications of the significance of the man. Paul was not only the most important missionary of the first Christian generation, but also its most productive literary figure. Moreover, he was a notable organizer, man of affairs, and thinker. We would know a good deal about him if we had only the book of Acts, in which he plays so large a role. Fortunately, we also have at least some of his letters, which reflect not only his activities and thought, but also his own personality.

It is impossible to do full justice to Paul in a treatment such as this. Yet we may attempt an accurate representation of the character of the man and his work. In this chapter passages from Galatians, I Corinthians, and I Thessalonians will be examined in order to show Paul's relationship to his predecessors and to the already emerging Christian tradition. Then two different, but not unrelated, problems in the life of the Pauline churches will be examined by a close look at other texts from Galatians and I Corinthians. Hopefully, the manner in which important theological and ethical issues emerge from these practical situations will become clear. Finally, texts from Philippians and Colossians will show graphically what kinds of problems beset Paul in the world and in the church as he sought to fulfill his calling and commission as apostle, churchman, and faithful servant. In chapter eight a comprehensive view of Paul's theological thought will be sought through an examination and interpretation of Romans.

---

[2] The chronology adopted in our table (see xx) is widely accepted, but John Knox has rejected it in his *Chapters in a Life of Paul* (New York: Abingdon Press, 1950), especially pp. 85 ff. He argues that the evangelistic activity of Paul described in Acts possibly began as early as A.D. 37 and that his arrest in Jerusalem occurred in A.D. 53 or 54. He thus dates I and II Thessalonians *ca.* A.D. 40, I and II Corinthians in 51–53, and Romans in 53 or 54. Recently John Hurd, *The Origin of I Corinthians* (New York: Seabury Press, 1965), pp. 19–41, has also questioned this consensus chronology. Such attacks upon the chronology usually involve skepticism about equating the second visit of Paul to Jerusalem (Gal. 2) with the Jerusalem Council described in Acts 15, which occurred during Paul's third visit to Jerusalem according to the Acts account.

Paul and His Predecessors

Outlines and Notes on Galatians and I Corinthians appear in the subsequent sections, where portions of these books are dealt with for their own sake. In this section the relevant passages are to be read for the light they shed on Paul's personal history and attitudes. A brief note on the Thessalonian letters, which are not studied later, also appears in this section.

APOSTLE BY GOD'S REVELATION (Gal. 1:1–2:10)

Why does Paul seek to establish his independence of human authority? Has Paul's apostleship, or his right to preach, been challenged?

At this point we are not interested in identifying the precise occasion of the Jerusalem meetings of Paul and the other apostles referred to in this section. Instead, we want to understand Paul's own attitude toward his predecessors and his estimate of where he stood in relation to them. Fundamental to Paul's perspective is the aside at the beginning of Galatians. He is an apostle, "not from men nor through man, but through Jesus Christ and God the Father, who raised him from the dead" (1:1). Clearly and unequivocally Paul grounds his apostleship, and therefore his right to preach to the Gentiles, upon the call of God in Jesus Christ. It is not finally or fundamentally dependent on any human approval. He is not an apostle because some other apostles have instituted or ordained him as such. Therefore, he is not dependent for the source and authority of his gospel upon any human institution or agency.

All of this amounts to quite a radical claim; Paul makes no humble or self-effacing presentation of his own role and status. At the same time nothing could be clearer than Paul's theological reasons for asserting his independent and apostolic authority. These are already obvious in vss. 3–5, and the problem that has called forth Paul's drastic assertion of his divine right appears in vss. 6–9. What is crucial here is not Paul's self-esteem or status, but rather the validity of the gospel as he has preached it in Galatia and elsewhere. It is the one true and saving message, beside which there cannot be rival or competing versions. Paul calls down the sternest *anathema* (the Greek term for "curse") upon anyone who preaches a gospel contrary to his own—not because it is his gospel, but because it is God's. If he had proclaimed his own religious ideas to the Galatians, he would have been but one among many purveyors of perversion. This all sounds frightfully inflexible and dogmatic—and so it is. Yet it is not the dogmatic expression of an opinion, but the confession of one who feels himself moved by a God who has called and directed him. Thus Paul's understanding of his commissioning as an apostle and his insistence

Saint Paul, a plaque from thirteenth-century France. (Courtesy of Bulloz-Art Reference Bureau.)

upon the validity of his message go hand in hand. Each apart from the other becomes untenable. Paul's claim of apostolic authority would be empty apart from the power and truth of his message. Conversely, the truth of the message is guaranteed by Paul's apostolic commission, which comes directly from the Lord.

Apparently Paul's vigorous assertion of his authority and his gospel was evoked by intruders in the Galatian church who sought to discredit Paul's gospel as something less than the whole truth by calling in question his apostolic legitimacy, and therefore his God-given authorization. In 3:1–5:12 Paul argues against the version of the gospel preached by these people, who certainly thought of themselves as Christians (and better Christians than Paul). From this central section of the letter it is clear that the intruders sought to introduce circumcision and obedience to the Jewish law as requirements for membership in the Christian community. To them Paul's gospel must have seemed the broad and easy path that leads to destruction rather than the hard and narrow one that leads to life (cf. Matt. 7:13 f.). Very likely they suspected Paul of making the gospel easy by dispensing with circumcision and the law. They called him a man-pleaser (1:10), one who has softened the requirements of the gospel. In attempting to institute what they regarded as their superior version, they must have claimed that Paul's apostolic status was inferior to their own (or to those apostles whom they purported to represent) because he had received his gospel from men. Paul does not tell us directly, but his violent and repeated rejection of the idea that he is dependent on some human authority (1:1, 10, 11 ff.) makes it highly probable this was the case.

The justification of Paul's contention that his gospel is from God is the claim that he received it by revelation, and the proof of this claim can only be the recitation of his own history, into which this revelation has broken. Thus we find in 1:13–17 Paul's striking combination of personal reminiscence and the confession of God's initiative and activity in his life. This is the only description of the so-called conversion which we have directly from Paul. Significantly, he does not call it his "conversion" at all, although it might be so understood from the standpoint of the psychology of religion. He speaks instead of God's foreordination and call (vs. 15) and of the revelation of the Son of God to him in order that he might preach the gospel to the Gentiles. Paul does not focus upon his "religious experience" but upon the revelation of God which he discerns in his own personal history (cf. Jeremiah 1). Indeed, he regards the decisive moment of this history to be the manifestation of the risen Lord to him (cf. I Cor. 15:8).

The scope of God's action and purpose is not, however, limited to the single event of this revelation and call. The remainder of the narrative (1:18–2:10) is principally intended to show that none of Paul's subsequent actions calls in question the certainty or adequacy of the commission that he received in the first instance directly from God. He does not immediately thereafter seek human confirmation or assurance. Only after three years does he first go to Jerusalem, the seat of the original Christian community (vs. 18), in order to see Cephas (Peter). When after fourteen years he makes another trip, he is guided by revelation. Let no one think he has been summoned by his superiors! Did he circumcise Titus (2:4) in order to placate anyone? He did not consider the possibility for an instant (2:5).[3] Moreover, he showed no special deference to the reputed pillars of the Jerusalem church (2:6, 9), and on good theological grounds (vs. 6).[4] Indeed, he did not hesitate to reproach Peter himself, when the latter was not straightforward about the truth of the gospel (vss. 11 ff.).

Yet, although Paul forthrightly asserts his apostolic commission and independence of human authorization, he firmly believes that the gospel did not originate with him, but with God, and that it is not given to him alone but to the church. Thus, although he insists upon his independence of those who were apostles before him (1:17), he is most eager to show that these same apostles approved his preaching of the gospel (2:7–10). In fact, he candidly says that he put his gospel before them for their approval, as if everything depended upon that (2:2).

Paul's assertion of his independence and his concern for apostolic approval may seem contradictory, but they are not really. Paul is not concerned to say that his gospel is novel or unique, but to affirm God's initiative in revealing it to him and commissioning him to preach it to the uncircumcised (2:7), that is, to Gentiles (cf. 1:16). Paul does not, in other words, put himself forward as the second founder of Christianity, the one and only man to whom the true meaning of Christ's coming has been revealed. For despite the claims for his own commission and authority, which he is not in the least embarrassed to make, Paul wishes only to show that his gospel is the same gospel with which the church has been entrusted. The uniqueness of his commissioning lies in the fact that God has made him apostle to the Gentiles. Paul does not even put forward his central doctrine of justification by grace through faith as an original insight, but as an elementary deduction from the gospel itself, and one that anyone should have been able to make. Thus he can upbraid Peter for his dissimulation (2:11 ff.) rather than his ignorance.

Paul was a charismatic figure and an original thinker, yet he did not wish to set himself above, but only alongside, those who were apostles before him. Although not dependent on them, he actively sought their approval. For Paul was a churchman and was concerned for the unity of

---

[3] Paul here denies that Timothy was circumcised at all (not that his circumcision took place because of outside pressure), as has been shown by E. D. Burton, *A Critical and Exegetical Commentary on the Epistle to the Galatians* (ICC; Edinburgh: Clark, 1921), pp. 75 ff.

[4] The pillars are, of course, James, Cephas, and John (2:9). John is presumably the Son of Zebedee, who also appears in the stories of Acts 3–5. James is not the brother of John, but the brother of Jesus himself (1:19). Cephas (literally, "Rock") is the original Aramaic name of Peter. The fact that in Galatians 2:9 James is mentioned first (cf. 1:18 f.) may be an indication of the pre-eminence that by this time he already enjoyed in the Jerusalem church.

the church. He enthusiastically agreed to make a collection in his mission field for the poor in the Jerusalem church (2:10; cf. I Cor. 16:1–4; II Cor. 8, 9; Rom. 15:25–29). This act was more than charity. It was a visible and tangible expression of the oneness of the churches he had founded with the church at Jerusalem and, by implication, of the unity of the gospel.

THE RECEIVED TRADITION (I Cor. 15:1–8)

Did Paul receive the gospel from human hands or by divine revelation? Why does Paul cite the tradition that he has received?

Paul claims to have received the gospel and the commission to preach it to the Gentiles by divine revelation. Does this mean that the content of the gospel, the facts about Jesus' life, and especially his crucifixion and resurrection, were given to him quite apart from any human action or agent? Such a claim would present obvious difficulties, and Paul apparently does not wish to imply that all his knowledge came as a sudden revelation. In Galatians, Paul stated that he had been a persecutor of the Christian church (cf. Acts 9). Doubtless he did not persecute a movement about which he knew nothing. The very fact that Paul vigorously opposed the primitive Christian church indicates that he knew something about it. Moreover, in II Corinthians 5:16 he speaks of having once regarded Christ from a human point of view (Greek, *kata sarka*, literally "according to the flesh"). This phrase probably refers to Paul's distorted perception of Christ prior to his conversion.

Paul was baptized (Acts 9:18). At that time he presumably made a confession of faith in Jesus as the Messiah, a confession that had perhaps already attained the status of a traditional liturgical formula. We may also assume that he received some further instruction in faith, although we can say little or nothing about its exact nature. Paul did in fact at some time receive a traditional interpretation of the gospel. In I Corinthians he writes: "For I delivered to you as of first importance, what I also received" (15:3). He then proceeds to proclaim the essential elements of the early Christian preaching. Clearly vss. 3–5 contain common affirmations of the New Testament that cannot be attributed to Paul or to his influence.[5] Also when Paul refers to what he has received (after having first spoken of what the Corinthians have received) he seems to be using terminology associated with the passing on of tradition. ("Tradition" itself means a process of passing on from one person or generation to another.)

---

[5] At least this much can now be said in the wake of C. H. Dodd's important study of *The Apostolic Preaching and its Developments* and the discussion of the questions it raised. Cf. Hunter, *Paul and His Predecessors*, pp. 15–23, and M. Dibelius, *From Tradition to Gospel*, pp. 16–22.

How much of the material in I Corinthians 15:3–8 is traditional is a matter of debate. Surely Paul himself adds to the list of resurrection appearances the one that he himself witnessed. Most certainly traditional are the affirmations that Christ died for our sins and that this happened according to the Hebrew scriptures, that he was buried, that he was raised on the third day according to the scriptures, and that he appeared to Cephas (Luke 24:34) and to the twelve (Luke 24:36 ff.; Matt. 28:16 ff.; John 20:19, cf. vs. 24).

If Paul received and used such traditional material, does this belie his claim that he did not receive the gospel from human hands (Gal. 1:12)? The Greek word for "receive," *paralambanō,* is the same word Paul uses in I Corinthians 15:1, 3 to refer to what he has received from tradition, which he significantly describes as "of first importance" (cf. 11:23). In the light of I Corinthians how can Paul baldly claim (Gal. 1:12) that the gospel came to him through no human mediation, but through a revelation of Jesus Christ? The solution may be that Paul is simply inconsistent, but inconsistency on such an important point would have been a serious matter. More likely, Paul distinguished between the revelation of the gospel and the appropriation of common kerygmatic or credal formulations. The use of such formulations does not call in question Paul's claim that he first was confronted by and believed the gospel, not because of human preaching, but because of a revelation of Jesus Christ (I Cor. 9:1; 15:8). Paul is interested in affirming not the uniqueness of his gospel but the uniqueness of God's revelation of it to him. Paul's willingness to submit his gospel to the pillars in Jerusalem and his desire to demonstrate his essential agreement and unity with the Jerusalem church show that he does not espouse an individualism independent of tradition and disdainful of its forebears. The crucial point for Paul is that apart from the divine initiative in his life he would have had no gospel and no apostolic status. For both he owes everything to God. By the canons of human behavior and expectation he should have gone on disbelieving the gospel and persecuting the church. But by God's action toward him, an action ordained from before his birth (Gal. 1:15), he was turned around and set upon a new course. He was made an apostle of the gospel that he had once persecuted. Such an astounding reversal of his life Paul can attribute only to God.

As has been noted, the revelation of God's son (Gal. 1:16) was given to Paul as an appearance of the risen Christ. Paul's belief that he had seen the risen Lord (cf. I Cor. 9:1; 15:8) was the ground of his claim to be an apostle independent of any human authority. The apostles of the primitive church were apparently those who could claim a commission from the Lord himself, and such a commission was usually tied to a resurrection appearance (cf. John 20:21; Acts 1:8; Matt. 28:16 ff.). Thus, through God's action in Jesus Christ, and specifically through Christ's appearance to him, Paul has "received grace and apostleship to bring about obedience to the faith for the sake of his name among all the nations" (Rom. 1:5). Nevertheless, Paul stands within, not above, the church. To prove his claim to divine revelation he shows that his gospel is the same as that of the other apostles. Furthermore, he is quite willing to concede that the specific content of this gospel is something given him by tradition.

THE WORD OF THE LORD (I Cor. 11:23–26; I Thess. 4:13–18)

Why did the church preserve the word of Jesus in I Corinthians?
Does the I Thessalonians passage correspond to apocalyptic passages in the Gospels?

NOTES ON THE THESSALONIAN LETTERS*

The two Thessalonian letters are probably the earliest surviving letters of the apostle Paul, here joined in writing by Silvanus and Timothy. Emphasis falls on the necessity for a sober, moral life. The Christian should continue to work hard while awaiting the imminent return of Jesus. Anxiety about his failure to return before the death of some brethren (I Thess. 4:13) as well as overzealous willingness to believe that he had already come back (II Thess. 2:1 ff.) played a role in prompting Paul to write. The immediate occasion of I Thessalonians is described in 2:17–3:10 (cf. Acts 17:10–15; 18:5.) I Thessalonians 3:11 ff. seems to contradict Acts 17:14 f., but 3:6 corresponds to Acts 18:5, which would point to Corinth as the point of origin for the letters. If so, they would have been written during the second missionary journey, probably in A.D. 50 or 51.

Pauline authorship of II Thessalonians is subject to some doubt. Its relationship to I Thessalonians is unclear and the apocalyptic mythology of 2:1–12 is unlike anything else we find in Paul. The emphasis upon the genuineness and authority of the letter (cf. 2:1; 3:14 f., 17) suggests that the author protests too much and thus arouses suspicion. Yet the supposition of pseudonymity (that is, that the author only writes under Paul's name) does not immediately and completely clarify the situation and interpretation of the letter.

The fact that Paul speaks of his relationship to Jesus Christ raises the question of how it is mediated. The answer is, first of all, through the manifestation of the risen Lord at Damascus, and second, through tradition. That much is already clear. In admonishing the Corinthians about their table fellowship (I Cor. 11:17–34), however, Paul also invokes what he has received (*paralambanō*) from the Lord and delivered (*paradidōmi*) to them (I Cor. 11:23–26). The terminology of vs. 23 is exactly the same as that of 15:3. In addition, the words of the Lord that Paul gives are substantially the same as Jesus' words of institution found in Matthew

---

* For notes on the Corinthian correspondence see pages 297 ff.

16:26–28; Mark 14:22–24; and Luke 22:19–20. As it is unlikely that Paul received these words directly from the Lord either on the Damascus road or anywhere else, we must suppose that he is here giving a tradition that he has received in the church, but a tradition which the church traces back to the Lord himself. Moreover, the close parallel with the Synoptic accounts demonstrates conclusively the traditional character of this material. The life-situation that made necessary the preservation of such words of the Lord as are found in 11:23–26 is clear. It is the continuing worship of the church, which in celebrating the Lord's Supper looks back to the earthly ministry and death of Jesus, and forward to his return (II Cor. 11:26).

Another instance of the quotation of Jesus' words is probably to be found in I Thessalonians 4:15 ff., although here matters are not so clear as in I Corinthians 11. What Paul says in vss. 15 ff. he clearly presents on the authority of the Lord—that is, Jesus—and presumably on the basis of a traditional saying ("by the word of the Lord"). The problems are that we have no obviously parallel tradition in the Synoptic Gospels (although Matt. 24:31 is similar to 4:16) and that if Paul is giving a traditional word of the Lord (beginning in 4:15), it is not clear where he considers it to end. Perhaps with verse 17; but perhaps only verse 16 is based directly on such a traditional word of Jesus. Yet despite the fact that certainty or even clarity on some points is impossible, two things are beyond question. First, Paul draws directly or indirectly upon a traditional word of Jesus, and in a way calculated to culminate and conclude the discussion. Second, Paul manifests a knowledge of the apocalyptic element in the tradition of Jesus' teaching, which is prominent in the last discourse with his disciples (Mark 13 parr.) and present elsewhere in the Synoptic Gospels. Probably Jesus and certainly Paul believed they were living in the final days or years of the present age. Mark summarizes Jesus' teaching with the words, "The time is fulfilled and the kingdom of God is at hand" (1:15), and Paul can pray with the author of the Revelation to John (Rev. 22:20), "Our Lord, come!" (I Cor. 16:22). In reading Paul it should not be forgotten that he lived in a time of eager expectancy, and with other Christians looked forward to the imminent return of Jesus.

In these two instances and several others (especially I Cor. 7:10 and 9:14) Paul relies upon a word of the Lord. In addition, he reveals some knowledge of Jesus' ministry elsewhere (Gal. 1:19; 2:9; 3:1; 4:4; I Cor. 2:2; 15:4 ff.; Rom. 1:3). Still Paul's letters contain disappointingly little information about the life and teaching of Jesus. We find him preoccupied with the question of the meaning of the crucifixion and resurrection of Jesus Christ, with eschatology, and with the history of salvation. When Paul is read in and for himself and not from the standpoint of the Gospels, it is apparent that he does not seek to expound the meaning of the event of Christ by reference to the specific historical details of Jesus' life. It is easy to forget this, because it is customary and natural to read the Gospels before Paul and, so to speak, assume them as we read his letters. But the Gospels as we have them developed only after Paul and thus cannot form the background and source of Paul's theological reflections. There is no longer any way of knowing how much Paul knew of the tradition about Jesus. Aside from the allusions to Jesus' life and the rare instances where he explicitly cites a word of the Lord, there are several places where Paul seems to hark back to such a saying (Rom. 12:14; 13:9; 14:14; II Cor. 13:1). But one can rarely be certain whether Paul actually had a saying of Jesus in mind or was only drawing upon a common Jewish or Christian ethical tradition. Living when he did, having visited Jerusalem many times, if indeed he was not educated there (Acts 22:3),[6] Paul had ample opportunity to become acquainted with those who had known Jesus. In fact, in Galatians he mentions his personal acquaintance with James, the brother of the Lord, as well as Peter and John. Why did he not take the trouble to learn more about Jesus? Or, if he did, why does he not clearly and explicitly tell us in his letters? It can always be argued that, after all, we have no specimens of the apostle's actual preaching and that perhaps in his oral delivery of the gospel he spoke more extensively of the ministry of Jesus. Yet, we have in Romans an extensive presentation of his theological thought which is strangely silent on this score. This comparative silence still needs to be fully explained.

On the other hand, before it was discovered that the Gospels were composed later than Paul's letters and cannot be presupposed in the interpretation of them, the letters were read against the background of the Gospels and little or no incongruity was discerned. In fact, most people continue to read them in that way today. Despite many differences of terminology, conceptuality, and emphasis, it is clear that they both have to do with the same person.

Faith, Freedom, and Love: The Gospel

Paul never wrote in abstract theological language, and he probably did not think in those terms. Yet he has with good reason been called the founder of Christian theology.[7] His thought arises out of real, concrete situations, and so far as we know, it is expressed in letters addressed to

---

[6] W. C. Van Unnik, *Tarsus or Jerusalem? The City of Paul's Youth*, trans. G. Ogg (London: Epworth, 1962), argues that Paul was reared and grew up in Jerusalem.
[7] Bultmann, *Theology of the New Testament*, I, p. 187.

such situations—usually for the purpose of improving them. A Paul separated from his world or church would be a cut-flower substitute for the man and his message. So one must study Paul in the context that was so important to him. Yet Paul had a keen sensitivity for important and profound issues underlying specific human situations and the relevance of the gospel to them. In such questions as whether Galatian Christians should allow themselves to be circumcised or whether Corinthian Christians should eat meat that had been offered to idols, Paul discerned theological and ethical issues that he deemed to be of great importance. In this the verdict of the history of Christianity has confirmed his judgment.

FAITH AND FREEDOM (Gal. 2:11–21)

Why is circumcision crucial in this discussion?
Why does Paul vigorously oppose "works of the law"?

NOTES ON GALATIANS

The Galatian letter was written to combat the influence in the Galatian churches of so-called Judaizers—that is, people who insisted that Christians be circumcised and keep the law. The exact location of these churches is in doubt. According to the South Galatia theory, they were to be found in the region of Pisidian Antioch, Lystra, and Derbe, which Paul evangelized on his first missionary journey (Acts 13 and 14). According to the North Galatia theory, they were located farther north in the ethnic region called Galatia after its inhabitants; this is probably the area referred to in Acts 16:6 and 18:23. Supporters of the North Galatia theory stress the fact that Paul repeatedly refers to his readers as Galatians, which he would have scarcely done had he been addressing merely the inhabitants of the Roman province.

Apparently because he was so angry about the course of events in the Galatian churches, Paul omitted the usual formal thanksgiving immediately following the salutation at the beginning of the letter (cf. Rom. 1:8–15; I Cor. 1:4–9). Galatians is the only extant Pauline letter in which such an omission occurs.

Galatians has sometimes been considered the earliest of Paul's letters. This is just possible if the South Galatia theory is accepted, in which case Galatians could have been written from Antioch after the first missionary journey. Galatians 2:1–10 seems to deal with the same Jerusalem Council described in Acts 15 and could have been written soon thereafter. But the Greek *to proteron* in Galatians 4:13 probably means "the first time" (RSV, "at first"), implying not one, but two previous visits. This would necessarily date Galatians after Acts 16:6, and we would thus already be in the second missionary journey and the period of the Thessalonian correspondence. Moreover, if the North Galatia theory is accepted and two previous visits to Galatia must be posited, then the letter cannot be earlier than the third missionary journey, for the *two visits would be those noted in Acts 16:6 and 18:23. This would probably put it in the period of Paul's Ephesian ministry (Acts 19), as indicated on the chronological table. Moreover, such a dating is supported by the many affinities with I and II Corinthians and Romans, which are much more striking than similarities to the early Thessalonian letters.*

OUTLINE OF GALATIANS
    Introduction or Salutation (1:1–5)
       I. Paul's Defense (1:6–2:21)
         A. Paul's Charge Against the Galatians (1:6–9)
         B. Autobiographical Section (1:10–2:10)
         C. Justification by Faith (2:11–21)
      II. Law and Faith (3:1–4:31)
         A. Appeal to the Galatians (3:1–5)
         B. The History of Salvation (3:6–4:11)
         C. Personal Reminiscences and Appeal (4:12–20)
         D. The Allegory of the Two Women (4:21–31)
      III. Freedom and Spirit (5:1–6:10)
         A. Freedom versus Circumcision (5:1–12)
         B. Living by the Spirit (5:13–6:10)
    Conclusion (6:11–18)

With scarcely a break in stride Paul moves from the autobiographical section of Galatians (see pp. 282–286) to a discussion of the principal problem facing the Galatian church. The two are, of course, intimately related. Paul's long apology is not merely self-justification, much less self-glorification. He must establish his apostolic authority as given by God and approved by his fellow apostles in order to defend the validity of the gospel he preaches. He therefore attacks those who call it in question, add to it, or subtract from it, since they undercut the work that God intends to do through Jesus Christ. At the same time Paul reiterates his own view of what the gospel essentially is.

That Paul had already been vigorously defending his own preaching and probably had to do so recurrently becomes apparent in 2:11 ff. Presumably the incident with Peter had occurred some time before. Obviously Peter, Paul, Barnabas, and other Jewish Christians had been enjoying table fellowship among the Gentile Christians until some representatives from James appeared on the scene (2:11–13). They, and perhaps James also, represented the "circumcision party," a powerful group of Jewish Christians, probably based in Jerusalem, who regarded circumcision as a necessity for Christians as well as Jews. Apparently for them, as for Paul, "circumcision" implied the obligation to keep the Jewish law and therefore entailed far more than the rite itself. To the mind of the Judaizers there was no such thing as Christian faith in distinction from Judaism. They seem to have regarded themselves as Jews who had recognized Jesus as the Jewish Messiah. Probably they looked for his imminent return (as did Paul, I Thess. 4:13 ff.) and the establishment of the kingdom or reign of God in a radically transformed world (cf. Rev. 21:1–8). It was probably in Christian circles such as these that important elements of the tradition about Jesus and his teaching were preserved. This same circumcision party had evidently made inroads into the Galatian church, occasioning Paul's letter. As one begins reading the letter it is not immediately obvious that this has happened. Paul argues in a more general manner about the place of the law. Yet it is clear from such passages as 5:1 ff. and 6:11 ff. that the controversy in Galatia focused on the question of circumcision, and appropriately so, for, as Paul says (5:3), the whole Jewish legal system was bound up with this rite. It had become the fitting symbol of the problem of whether Christians must be held accountable to the Jewish law.

The appearance of the circumcision party in Antioch doubtless intimidated the Jewish Christians who had previously been exercising their freedom in Christ in disregard of Jewish restrictions against eating with Gentiles.[8] We know that Peter was not immune to intimidation (recall his three-fold denial of Jesus in the courtyard of the high priest). When he succumbed, Barnabas and the rest understandably followed suit. Possibly the separation of Paul and Barnabas recounted in Acts 15:36–41 really resulted from Barnabas' behavior on this occasion. Paul's reproach to Peter (2:14 ff.) has understandably been something of an embarrassment to later Christian interpreters. It surely shows Peter in a bad light vis-à-vis Paul, although admittedly we have only Paul's version of the story.

Paul's reproach to Peter is based not on his own interpretation of the gospel, but on what he plainly believes is the understanding of the gospel which Peter also accepts. The right understanding of the gospel is at stake. The simple statement that Peter and the others "were not straightforward about the truth of the gospel" (vs. 14) and the use of "we" (vss. 15–17) show that Paul was not trying to convince Peter of the truth of his own position, but recalling him to an agreement about the gospel which they had shared. That this was more than merely intellectual assent is borne out by the fact (vs. 14) that Peter himself had been living like a Gentile. Whether Peter and company later began trying to force Gentiles to live like Jews, or only made this a prerequisite of continued table fellowship is uncertain. In any event the net result was apparently the same. Gentiles were forced to submit to Jewish regulations in order to participate in the life of the church on an equal footing. For Paul this was unthinkable, despite the fact that he and Peter were by birth Jews (vs. 15), and not Gentile sinners. (The reference to Gentiles as "sinners" may well be

---

[8] By eating with Gentiles the Jew inevitably exposed himself to the possibility of contamination by violating the Jewish laws concerning food and drink (cf. Leviticus 11).

an element injected into the discussion by the Judaizers in refusing to have anything to do with the uncircumcised and literally lawless Gentiles.) Why was it unthinkable? Not because it was unnecessary or impolite. Rather, because Paul and Peter knew that a man is not justified (that is, judged acceptable to God) on the basis of "works of the law" but by faith in Christ. At least Paul knew it, and he felt that Peter should.

From verse 16 on it is clear that Paul does not entertain the possibility of two modes of salvation—one by the law, the other by faith in Christ. He is not just saying that one must choose one way or the other, although that is indeed necessary. In actuality there is only one way, since no one will be justified by works of the law. The important thing for Paul is that a new and viable access to God has been opened by his Son just when other avenues had shown themselves to be blind alleys. And precisely from the standpoint of faith their futility became apparent. This conviction lies at the heart of the gospel.

If for the moment we use the somewhat anachronistic term "Christianity," which Paul never uses, we may say that for Paul Christianity is faith in Christ. On the other hand, faith in Christ makes possible the concept "Christianity" as something new and distinct. For apart from the insistence that faith alone, not works of the law, justifies (that is, makes one righteous before God), Christianity does not clearly distinguish itself from Judaism—as the Jewish Christians apparently did not. To believe that a particular person was the Messiah (Greek, *Christos*) was possible *within* Judaism. The Messiah, or Christ, would then be understood within the framework of Jewish messianism and eschatology. Paul's understanding of the essential meaning of the gospel of Jesus Christ goes beyond this, however. For to say, as he does, that Jesus Christ alone is the crucial factor in the determination of a man's destiny breaks through the categories of Jewish messianic expectation and makes the Jewish legal requirements of no avail in the quest for salvation. Man cannot make himself righteous before God by his obedience to the many specific injunctions of the law. He can only accept this righteousness as something given to him (cf. Rom. 3:21 ff.). This was certainly radical doctrine, and it is no wonder that some Christians with a Jewish background found it intolerable. Yet Paul sees clearly (Gal. 2:21) that it is an either-or matter. Either Christ is sufficient or he is not, and if one sets up other criteria for participation in the Christian church instead of, or alongside, faith in Christ he is undercutting the Christian conviction and confession. In effect, Paul not only points unerringly to the distinctively Christian confession, but at the same time lays down the fundamental criterion for Christian community. Thus he can say in relation to Jew and Greek, slave and free, male and female: "You are all one in Christ Jesus" (3:28). There is no room for invidious human distinctions or discrimination within the church of Christ.

In verse 17 an objection is met. It had probably been raised by the circumcision party against the doctrine of justification by faith and its corollaries of freedom from the law and uninhibited free association among Jewish and uncircumcised Gentile Christians. In endeavoring to be justified by Christ and giving up adherence to the Jewish law, have the Antiochene Jewish Christians become sinners like Gentiles (cf. 2:15) and made Christ an agent of sin? Certainly not, says Paul. But does Paul deny that they have become sinners, or that Christ has become an agent of sin? Certainly the latter, and probably only the latter. In the opening chapters of Romans Paul argues that all men, whether they claim to keep the law or not, are really sinners apart from the grace of God in Christ. Thus it should not surprise us here if he should concede that men "become sinners" in seeking to be justified by Christ. Of course, it may by no means be inferred that those who seek to be justified by the law thereby escape the onus of sin. They simply do not understand their condition.

The real sin or transgression would be to go backward, to submit again to the law after having escaped its grasp. This is the meaning of verse 18, as verse 19 shows. Paul has died to the law that he might live to God. Paul's dying to the law and his dying with Christ seems to be the same thing. He necessarily dies to the law that he may live to God and that Christ may live in him. And Paul can now describe his own life as Christ's living in him. Christ's living in him is not, however, an esoteric mystical experience, but faith: "The life I now live in the flesh I live by faith in the Son of God, who loved me and gave himself for me" (vs. 20). Paul ends this description of his encounter with Peter—somewhere along the way his focus seems to have shifted from the debate with Peter to the problem of the Galatian churches—with a succinct statement of his tight theological logic. Justification does not come through the law, or else Christ died to no purpose (2:21). If one insists on observance of the law as a prerequisite to salvation, he implies that faith in Christ is not enough, and that the law supplies what is lacking. For Paul, who understands the gospel to be absolutely Christo-centric, this is an intolerable suggestion.

We have been using the word "justification" up to this point as if its meaning were obvious, but this cannot be taken for granted. Justification means, in the first place, righteousness. That is to say, there is only one Greek word, *dikaiosyne*, which is sometimes translated righteousness, sometimes justification, depending on which English word seems more appropriate in a given context. With respect to God, righteousness refers to that quality or relationship in his dealings with the world and especially his people through which he shows himself to be a righteous God, a God who rightfully and with right performs the role and the function appropriate to him. The righteousness of God takes on concrete meaning in the Old Testament covenant relationship between God and Israel, through which in fulfilling his part of the covenant God shows himself to be a righteous God. With respect to man, righteousness means primarily standing in the right before God. This idea too takes concrete shape in the Bible in relation to the Old Testament idea of the covenant. In fulfilling the role appropriate to him in the covenant relationship man may expect to be accounted righteous before God. Thus for the Jew, the fulfilling of the covenant is obedience to the law, the obligation his forefathers accepted at Mt. Sinai.

Paul's concept of righteousness lies within the sphere of Israelite and Jewish thought. Thus he can carry on a discussion with the Jew about how man may be, or may be accounted, righteous before God—that is, how he may be justified. Paul, out of his own Jewish background, understands that in Judaism this righteousness is sought through "the works of the law." His Christian faith, however, revolves about the conviction that in Jesus Christ God offers man the status of being righteous, and, indeed, puts him in the right, prior to and apart from his own efforts to justify himself. This is what Paul means by grace. Righteousness before God cannot be earned, it can only be accepted in faith. To attempt to earn it is both impossible in and of itself, and a rejection of the good news (gospel) that God has given it freely. This is what the heated discussion of Galatians is all about. Paul see in the effort of the Judaizers to impose circumcision and the law upon the newly formed church the rejection of the very thing that distinguishes the gospel and is essential to it. Chapters 3 and 4 are devoted to explaining in some detail, and in language and concepts that are not always clear to the modern reader, why this is so. Chapters 5 and 6 draw the practical consequences.

In chapter 3 Paul sets about to show the secondary role of the law, not only in the light of the coming of the Messiah, but also in the history of Israel, and therefore in the plan and purpose of God. Abraham, the father of Israel, is not a man under law, but a man under promise and the prime example of faith (3:6–18; cf. Rom. 4). The law was given by God and fulfills a real, if secondary and temporary, role in the history of salvation (3:16–19). Yet there is no justification, no righteousness, that is to say, no salvation by the law (3:21). Its role is a negative and restraining one. In turning to the law after faith has already come (3:23), the Galatians are falling out of the realm of the Spirit and back into that of the flesh (3:3). Now that they have been brought out from under the confinement of the law and subjection to the elemental spirits of the universe (cf. 3:23; 4:3, 9) and come into their own as heirs of Abraham, why should they remain in bondage? Paul's obvious chagrin and perplexity (4:12–20) stem from his fear that the Galatians are reversing the direction of the history of salvation in moving from grace to law after already having come all the way in the other direction. The allegorical scriptural interpretation (4:21–31) is therefore intended to underscore the status of the Christian as already a child of the promise and therefore a free man.

The new status of the Christian is made plain in 5:1 ff.: "For freedom Christ has set us free; stand fast therefore, and do not submit again to a yoke of slavery." Paul now lays out the practical implications of his theological position, and at the same time comes to terms with the specific and immediate problem in the church of Galatia. Should Christians accept circumcision? Paul reiterates in 5:2 the principle already enunciated in 2:21. Here circumcision stands in place of law, since, as we noted previously, the rite of circumcision as the expression of membership in the Jewish community already implies the law. Paul makes crystal clear that to accept circumcision means to obligate oneself to the keeping of the whole law and to cut oneself off from the grace of Christ (vss. 3 f.). Yet circumcision is not in itself bad (vs. 6; cf. 6:11–16, especially 15). Those who are already circumcised have nothing to fear (cf. I Cor. 7:18 f.). Rather, the desire to have circumcision, to have this or any mark of religious distinction or accomplishment after one already has Christ, is blameworthy, for it is a movement away from grace to the law and away from the Spirit to the flesh (3:3; 5:4; 6:12). Paul regards such a retrogression as incredible and perverse. He understands the Christian as that man who through God's graciousness in Jesus Christ has been freed from sin and the law to live by the Spirit in faith and hope (5:5). He is no longer under bondage, for he has been set free (5:1), or he has been called to freedom (5:13). From his shoulders has been lifted the oppressive burden of the "law of sin and death" (Rom. 8:2). He can really live. He can be his own man.

Yet his freedom is not absolute. That is, it is not freedom without responsibility. But the Christian no longer experiences responsibility as a burden, for he no longer lives under the law in order to earn his own salvation. He is not a slave to the law. At the same time the law continues to be the valid expression of the will of God (Gal. 5:14), and gives ethical content and direction for the new life in Christ under God. The freedom for which Christ sets man free is not anarchy or freedom to do as one pleases. Paul can, in fact, describe this freedom as faith working through love (5:6). He states the character and purpose of freedom most aptly and succinctly: "For you were called to freedom, brethren; only do not use your freedom as an opportunity for the flesh, but through love be servants of one another" (5:13).

LOVE—THE EXPRESSION OF FAITH AND THE RESPONSIBILITY OF FREEDOM (I Cor. 8:1–13)

What limit is set upon eating meat offered to idols? Why?

NOTES ON THE CORINTHIAN LETTERS

The letters to the church Paul founded in the Greek city of Corinth were written from Ephesus in Asia (I Corinthians) and perhaps from Macedonia (II Corinthians) in the mid-fifties of the first century, probably during Paul's third missionary journey (see chronology, p. xx). I Corinthians was written before II Corinthians. This is clear not only from their order in the New Testament, but from their content. II Corinthians presupposes a much deteriorated relationship between the Corinthian church and Paul, whose once-acknowledged status as apostle is now being challenged. In I Corinthians Paul was able to speak authoritatively, without much suggestion that the church's acknowledgement of his apostolic authority was a major question (although the problem does emerge in chap. 9).

I Corinthians was at least the third letter in the correspondence between Paul and Corinth. Paul had already written the Corinthians previously (cf. 5:9), and they him (7:1). Neither of these letters survived. Much of the latter part of I Corinthians (from 7:1 on) is devoted to answering questions raised by the Corinthians. Chapters 1–4 deal with problems in the Corinthian church reported by Chloe's people (1:11). Chapters 5 and 6 are concerned with moral problems Paul has learned about from some undesignated source. It is sometimes suggested that I Corinthians is a composite of several letters, but the original unity of the document is defended by most scholars.[9]

A much stronger case can be made for the composite character of II Corinthians. In its present position, 6:14–7:1 interrupts the flow of thought. Perhaps it is a fragment of a previous letter (cf. I Cor. 5:9). Also, chapters 10–13 introduce a harsh and jarring note at the end of II Corinthians which does not seem appropriate and does not fit well with what precedes. This section may be a separate letter, or a fragment thereof, perhaps that letter referred to by Paul in II Corinthians 7:8 as one that had grieved the Corinthians. In addition, both chapters 8 and 9 deal with the collection Paul was making for the Jerusalem church, but from somewhat different perspectives. In 9:1 Paul appears to be introducing the subject anew. This may indicate that they are separate notes or belong to different letters. If one accepts this critical analysis of the Corinthian letters, he may reconstruct the correspondence between Paul and Corinth as follows:

(1) Paul's "previous letter" (cf. I Cor. 5:9).
(2) A letter from the Corinthian church to Paul raising certain questions (cf. I Cor. 7:1).
(3) This letter and the visit of Chloe's people (I Cor. 1:11) evoke a response from Paul—namely, the writing of I Corinthians.
(4) Paul learns of continued opposition in Corinth.
(5) Paul's second visit to Corinth, which evidently was neither pleasant nor successful. (Cf. I Cor. 16:5 f., which indicates that Paul planned another visit to Corinth; II Cor. 12:14 and 13:1, in which he anticipates a third, thus implying that he had made a second; II Cor. 1:23 and 2:1, in which he refers to a previous painful visit and his cancellation of a subsequent visit for fear it would likewise be unpleasant.)
(6) Paul's "angry letter," written as an aftermath of that visit (cf. II Cor. 7:8): II Corinthians 10–13.
(7) Paul's meeting in Macedonia with Titus (cf. II Cor. 7:6 f.), who brings news of developments in Corinth favoring Paul.

---

[9] For scholars espousing this position, see Hurd, *The Origin of I Corinthians*, p. 45.

(8) Resulting "joyful letter" of Paul: II Corinthians 1–8.
(9) Subsequent collection note?: II Corinthians 9.
(10) Eventual third visit to Corinth (cf. Rom. 15:25–29; Acts 20:2 ff.).

The preceding reconstruction is hypothetical, although not without substantial supporting evidence. Nevertheless, some scholars still regard II Corinthians as a single letter and reject the separation of stages 6–9 above.[10]

OUTLINE OF I CORINTHIANS
>Introduction: Salutation and Thanksgiving (1:1–9)
>>I. Division in the Church (1:10–4:21)
>>>A. The Corinthian Situation (1:10–17)
>>>B. Paul's Own Practice and Example (1:18–3:4)
>>>C. Paul and Apollos as Servants (3:5–4:7)
>>>D. Admonition to the Corinthians (4:8–21)
>>II. Immorality in the Church (5:1–6:20)
>>>A. Sexual Immorality (5:1–13)
>>>B. Christians in Court Against One Another (6:1–11)
>>>C. Uses of the Body (6:12–20)
>>III. The Corinthians' Questions (7:1–15:58)
>>>A. Church Discipline (7:1–10:33; esp. 8:1–13)
>>>B. Church Worship and Order, Spiritual Gifts (11:1–14:39)
>>>C. The Resurrection (15:1–58)
>>Conclusion: The Collection and Other Church Business (16:1–24)

In Corinth Paul faced a situation quite different from Galatia. The problem there was not legalism but, if anything, just the opposite—libertinism.

In I Corinthians 1–4 Paul is concerned with factionalism in the Corinthian church. Behind this problem, however, there lurks the question about the very character of Christian faith and life. Paul argues passionately that the Christian gospel is different from any worldly wisdom (chaps. 1, 2). At its heart is the word of the cross, the crucified Lord, folly to the Greeks and scandal to the Jews. This word shakes old confidences, and offers new possibilities of life. Throughout this letter, however, there are indications that the Corinthians, or some people in the Corinthian church, take a different view of the matter. Some of them think that Christian faith centers in a priviledged knowledge (Greek *gnōsis*), beside which questions of ethics are of strictly secondary importance (cf. chap. 8). Therefore, various practical ethical problems have arisen that demand resolution, at least in Paul's view. A man is living with his father's wife, presumably not his own mother, however (chap. 5); Christians are in-

[10] Most recently, W. G. Kümmel, in his revision of the Feine-Behm *Introduction to the New Testament*, pp. 214 f.

volved in law suits against one another (6:1–8); apparently some have not given up sexual intercourse with prostitutes (6:12–20). The existence of what Paul considers immorality in the church is understandable, because at least some of the Corinthian Christians had led immoral lives before their conversion (6:9–11). Moreover, the non-Jewish background of many would not predispose them to understand the Christian faith in ethical terms.

Over and above these morally dubious situations, of which Paul had evidently been informed by Chloe's people (cf. 1:11; 16:17), the Corinthians raised a number of knotty problems in a letter to Paul (cf. 7:1). The first of these concerns marriage and relations between men and women, a question of almost unfailing interest in every place and age. In chapter 7 Paul offers his wisdom on the subject. From the Lord, Paul has the prohibition against divorce which we find also in the Synoptic Gospels (7:10 f.; cf. Mark 10:2–9, parr.). Beyond that he is more or less on his own (I Cor. 7:12), and he obviously exercises some freedom in interpreting Jesus' words (7:15 f.). Paul's advice in this chapter will not commend itself to modern men and women, inside the church or out. The contemporary minister or priest will scarcely counsel a couple contemplating engagement that although total continence is preferable, it is better to marry than to burn (7:9). Yet it is worth observing that, though Paul has a definite preference for the ascetic life (7:1, 6 f.), he grants the legitimacy of the married state and definitely discourages celibacy within marriage (7:1–5), as well as undue suppression of strong sexual instincts (7:9). One very important factor in Paul's attitude, which is usually not taken into consideration by the general reader, is the anticipation of an imminent crisis culminating in the return of Jesus and the end of world history as we know it (7:29–31; cf. 16:22; I Thess. 4:13–18; Rom. 13:11 f.). In view of this, marriage and the assumption of family responsibility were scarcely things to be sought. Paul does not, however, oppose marriage, even under these conditions. On the other hand, it is doubtless true that Paul's own ascetic bent has contributed heavily to the high premium placed upon celibacy in Christianity, which has so often manifested itself in the denigration of the physical, especially the sexual, dimension of life, and which has by and large prevented the church from assigning a thoroughly positive role to sexual life. But we should not too quickly blame Paul for this. There is in the history of religion considerable evidence of man's uneasiness about what to do with his sexual instincts, an uneasiness that manifests itself on the one hand in religious asceticism and celibacy, on the other in licentiousness and cultic prostitution.

The subsequent brief chapter (8) dealing with the question of what to do about meat offered to idols is even better than the interesting chapter on women for grasping the fundamental character of Paul's problems at Corinth. On the face of it this may seem doubtful, inasmuch as the prob-

Hades carrying off Persephone, the daughter of Zeus and queen of the underworld. From a fourth-century B.C. *Apulian vase. (Courtesy of Metropolitan Museum of Art. Gift of Miss Matilda W. Bruce, 1907.)*

lem of sex is very much alive in Western culture, whereas the number of persons who either offer meat to idols or worry about the problem of whether or not to eat such meat is microscopic. But a sympathetic reading reveals that far more is involved than the resolution of a practical problem faced by Christians in the ancient world. A fundamental theological and ethical question is raised.

Nevertheless, we should begin by attempting to understand the specific problem. Christians living in a pagan world, among associates, relatives, and friends who were not Christian, were frequently placed in the position of having to eat or refuse to eat meat that had been offered to idols. Even if Christians avoided feasts in the temples of pagan gods, as Paul sternly admonishes them to do (I Cor. 10:14–22), they could not entirely escape the problem. For in the ancient world, much of the meat sold in the markets had also been offered to idols, even if in a most perfunctory way. That is, the slaughtering of animals was frequently accompanied by a quasi-religious rite or token sacrifice. So closely related were slaughter and sacrifice that the verb *hiereuein* (to sacrifice, slay) could be used not only

Ruins of the ancient Temple of Apollo (sixth century b.c.) at Corinth, capital of the Roman province of Achaia. (Courtesy of Greek Press and Information Service.)

to mean "offer a sacrifice" but also simply "to slaughter."[11] So the Greek stem *hier-*, which basically denotes the holy, becomes itself associated with the slaughter of animals for eating. Thus although Paul's instructions to the Corinthians seem to assume that some meat had not been offered to idols, it is at the same time clear that the Christian could scarcely have avoided the problem of whether to eat meat that had been so offered. It would sooner or later have been thrust upon him unless he withdrew from the world, an alternative that Paul does not recommend (I Cor. 5:9 f.).

If we compare the way in which Paul approaches this problem with the way he approached the question of table fellowship in Galatians 2, he seems at first glance to be taking a contradictory position. Remember that in Galatians 2 Paul attacked Peter for withdrawing from table fellowship with Gentile Christians because of the arrival of Jewish Christians from Jerusalem to whom this was offensive. Paul there seems to regard the matter of clean and unclean foods, so important to the Jew, as of no significance. More important, he is not concerned to avoid offending the

[11] Cf. J. Weiss, *Der erste Korintherbrief* ("Kritisch-exegetischer Kommentar über das Neue Testament," 5. abt., 9. Aufl.; Göttingen: Vandenhoeck & Ruprecht, 1910), pp. 210 ff.

302

Jew or Jewish Christian. Therefore we may be surprised to discover that in I Corinthians 8 Paul admonishes Christians who have knowledge not to eat meat known to have been offered to idols. This admonition, however, has an entirely different basis. The Christian refuses to eat meat offered to idols out of respect for the weaker brother (that is, another Christian; cf. 8:7, 11), who may thereby be led into eating the meat, thinking it really has some special potency or sanctity because it has been offered to idols. Or, alternatively, he may believe that he has incurred real guilt before God for eating the idol meat. Either way, the stronger brother offends against his fellow because of his knowledge. He knows that the idol has no real existence (vs. 4) and that there is only one God who has any authority over the Christian and to whom he owes allegiance and one Lord Jesus Christ. Knowing the essential meaninglessness and powerlessness of the pagan gods and worship,[12] the Christian can eat meat without any concern about whether it has been offered to idols. This is, of course, far different from actually participating in a pagan cultic meal, which is quite impossible for the Christian (cf. 10:14–22).

Paul grants that the Christian who has such knowledge may buy and eat meat without raising the question of whether it has been offered to an idol or to a pagan god—indeed, he defends his own right to do so (10:29b–30)—but he does not consider this an unrestricted privilege. It must be exercised with due regard toward one's Christian brother. Thus knowledge must be restricted by love. Love takes precedence over knowledge whenever the two come into conflict. The man with knowledge has no inalienable right to exercise that knowledge at the expense of his fellow. At the same time, however, he does not have to submit to needless scruples except in a concrete instance in which his eating meat offered to idols might actually lure another Christian back into idolatry. In this connection it is important to observe that Paul has transcended any point of view that regards cultic food per se as having the power to condemn (or save; cf. 10:1–13). Sin is no longer the violation of ritual observance or taboo, but breaking faith, betrayal of one's convictions. The concept of sin is interiorized in this respect, which is not to say that it is spiritualized so as to have nothing to do with one's actions. Sin is still offense against God (I Cor. 6:12–20) and neighbor (8; 10:23 ff.). Eating or drinking things offered to idols may be of no significance to the man who knows this to be so, but it may be disastrous for the man who does not. The former therefore must care for the ignorance of his brother. He may not flaunt

---

[12] Paul does not necessarily deny that other gods and lords exist (vs. 5), but only that they have any significance for the Christian. Paul, of course, would have denied that there were other gods and lords of equal power and authority with the one God and Father of Jesus Christ. That other worldly and supernatural powers hold sway over the heathen Paul need not deny. Indeed, he seems to assume their existence (cf. our discussion of Colossians).

Jesus and the disciples at the Last Supper by the contemporary Indian painter A. De Fonseca. (Courtesy of Spartaco Appetiti.)

his knowledge. So, the act itself no longer definies sin, but rather the effect it has on one's neighbor.

Paul was aware of the potential danger of knowledge in a way that the Corinthians were not. He therefore makes it clear at the outset (8:1–3) that knowledge alone is a questionable gift. Some Corinthians were evidently so smitten with their newly found knowledge and consequent freedom that they identified knowledge and freedom with the essence of Christian existence.

At the beginning of this discussion Paul puts love and knowledge in proper perspective (8:1 f.). Paul will go so far as to agree with the Corinthians that "all of us possess knowledge." But he immediately issues a warning: Knowledge, especially that knowledge that knows that it knows, and by implication takes pride in the fact, is a potential menace. The contrast between such knowledge and love is graphically put. Knowledge puffs up; love builds up. Obviously, to be puffed up is a bad thing. (The same word meaning literally "to be puffed up" is translated "arrogant" in 5:2 in the RSV—an accurate translation, which unfortunately loses the connection with chap. 8.) To be built up on the other hand is highly desirable. The term implies inner and outer strengthening of the church and the individual (cf. 3:10–15). The priority of love over knowledge is driven home most memorably in I Corinthians 13, the famous chapter on love. At the beginning of this hymn in praise of love Paul accords it a place above prophecy, knowledge, and faith (13:2). Again in 13:8, 9 he comes back to the theme of the superiority of love over knowledge. There is nothing wrong with knowledge per se, but in this world and this life it must give place to faith, hope, and love. Perfect knowledge will characterize the life to come, but in the present age the Christian must not make knowledge his primary concern (13:12 f.). All this confirms that the key to I Corinthians 8 is the supremacy of love over knowledge, not the impropriety of giving offence.

There is, then, no real inconsistency between Paul's attack upon Peter for withdrawing from table fellowship with Gentiles and what he writes the Corinthians. In Galatians the gospel is being called in question by the behavior of Peter and his followers; therefore, right understanding of the gospel takes precedence over any possible offence caused to "Judaizers" who continue in table fellowship with Gentile Christians. The deeper offence against the Gentile Christians was no mere breach of social amenities, but a breach of faith against the gospel. There could be no question of the Gentile Christians meeting Jewish standards so as not to offend the circumcision party. In both cases (I Cor. 8 and Gal. 2), a vital dimension of the gospel is at stake. In Galatians the gospel is threatened by the reimposition of legalism implied by Peter's action; in Corinth the gospel is threatened by those who understand it as a special knowledge and freedom rather than a new relation to God and to their fellow men. The tendency of the Corinthians to interpret Christian freedom as freedom to do as they pleased without respect to their relations to others, which are inseparable from their relation to Jesus Christ (I Cor. 6:12–20), verges in the direction of genuine lawlessness—that is, anarchy. Paul stands as firmly against this as against the reintroduction of the law as the means of justification.

The character of the problems Paul faced in Corinth and his attitude toward them may be accurately assessed on the basis of I Corinthians 8. Thereafter, as before, Paul deals for the most part with specific problems. Chapter 9 is a defense of his apostleship and his conduct. In chapter 10 he returns to the question of food offered to idols in the light of the danger of a return to idolatry. In chapter 11 there begins a discussion of matters pertaining to the church, which continues through chapter 14. Chapters 11 and 14 deal with worship and the Spirit; 12 is the well-known description of the church as the Body of Christ; 13 is the chapter on love. In chapter 15 Paul takes up the defense of the bodily resurrection of the dead, a doctrine that has at least been questioned, and perhaps denied, in Corinth. This would accord with the attitude of the Corinthians, who fancied that they possessed superior knowledge. Against them Paul contends that to deny the bodily resurrection is to deny the resurrection of Jesus as well. Yet in the face of incredulity about the concept of the resurrection as the resuscitation of so many corpses (a concept hardly more acceptable today than it was then), Paul maintains a distinction between the present physical body and the future resurrection body, which is a spiritual body. Chapter 16, devoted to personal and business matters, includes Paul's plans for a collection for the Jerusalem church and his intention of visiting Corinth from Ephesus, whence I Corinthians was doubtless written (vs. 8).

Whether the letters or letter under the name II Corinthians was written to combat the same problems found in I Corinthians is doubtful. In II Corinthians the question of Paul's own apostolic authority predominates.

Some interlopers have challenged Paul personally and gained the allegiance of a part of the Corinthian church. In this situation, more like that of Galatians than I Corinthians, Paul felt the reins slipping out of his hands as he was attacked by outsiders. It has often been thought that the opponents who entered the Corinthian church were the same Judaizers whom Paul opposed in Galatia, and there is some basis for this view (especially II Cor. 11:22). Yet circumcision and the law are not discussed in II Corinthians, so the character of the opposition—whoever the opponents may have been—was apparently somewhat different. One receives the impression that the specific questions and problems that engaged Paul in I Corinthians had, by the time of II Corinthians, paled into insignificance as new threats appeared. But there is probably some continuity between the two situations. For it is altogether likely that the intruders in the Corinthian church, with their pretensions and claims and their attack upon Paul (chaps. 10, 11), would have had considerable appeal for the Corinthian Christians who were already, as Paul put it, puffed up with knowledge. Whatever their doctrine, they seem to have taken delight in just the sort of self-glorification that Paul attacked in I Corinthians. If this were the case, the rather irritated and injured attitude of Paul in II Corinthians becomes all the more understandable.

Hardship, Heresy, and God's Grace

Notes on the "Captivity Epistles": Philippians, Colossians, Philemon, and Ephesians

Both Philippians and Colossians, along with the brief personal letter to Philemon, were written from prison (Phil. 1:12–18; Col. 4:10; Philem. 1, 23). Ephesians also purports to be a prison epistle (3:1; 4:1), but in all probability this is a part of a garb of pseudonymity by which apostolic authorship is claimed for the work of a second generation Paulinist. Philemon and Colossians are closely related by many personal references (for example, the slave Onesimus in Philem. 10 and Col. 4:9; Epaphras in Philem. 23 and Col. 1:7; 4:12) and by common destination (Colossae). They were apparently dispatched at the same time, possibly by the same bearers (Col. 4:7–9). Philippians, on the other hand, stands somewhat apart.

Although the evidence of the so-called prison epistles is not unambiguous, tradition has it that they were written from Rome during the two-year imprisonment of Paul recounted in Acts 28—that is, about A.D. 59–61. We know, however, that Paul was in prison at other times in other places (cf. II Cor. 11:23): in Caesarea (Acts 24–26), Philippi (Acts 16:19–40), and possibly Ephesus (I Cor. 15:32; cf. Acts 19:28–41). It is, therefore, not impossible that one or more of the captivity epistles was written from elsewhere. This position

The Roman Forum with the Arch of Titus and the Colosseum in the background. Just to the left of this picture is the site of Mamertime Prison where tradition asserts that Paul and Peter were prisoners. (Courtesy of Robert Spivey.)

has been argued with vigor and some cogency by several scholars. Still, there is no compelling alternative to the long-standing view that the captivity letters (excluding Ephesians) were written in Rome toward the end of Paul's ministry. As a matter of fact, such general considerations as the character of the Colossian heresy and Paul's reminiscent frame of mind in Philippians suggest a late date for these letters and therefore point in the direction of a Roman origin. We shall proceed on the assumption that these are the last extant letters of Paul, probably written from Rome. (The pseudonymous Pastoral Epistles will be dealt with in Chapter 9.)

The captivity or prison epistles bring out aspects of Paul's character and work which we see only intermittently in his other letters. In Philippians he looks back over a long and arduous ministry with at least the intuition that it is now drawing to a close. Such resentment as he has toward his enemies and the enemies of the gospel—Paul never distinguished between them—is now overshadowed by his feelings of appreciation for the church that has supported him in bad times as well as good.

In the little letter called Philemon, Paul writes on behalf of Onesimus, a Christian slave, to his Christian master Philemon, urging compassion and forebearance upon him. The same conciliatory spirit that pervades the greater part of Philippians is found also in Philemon.

Colossians is another matter. Here Paul seems to be writing to exhort, encourage, and warn a church that is endangered by the encroachment of a heretical teaching. The exact nature of this heresy is somewhat obscure, but it

307

involved the incorporation of Christ into an already established hierarchy of heavenly powers or divine beings. Paul's response is not to deny their existence, but to say that Christ ranks far above them. Although Paul obviously felt that important matters were at stake, he did not respond to the Colossian challenge with the almost bitter invective that we find in Galatians and II Corinthians. To this extent Colossians shares something of a common stance with the other prison letters.

Moreover, Colossians, like Philippians and Philemon, reflects both Paul's concentration upon his own task as an apostle and his reliance upon the grace of God. With the end perhaps in view (cf. Phil. 1:21 ff.), Paul never ceases to take seriously the task of caring for the churches which falls to him as an apostle of Christ, whether this task requires an expression of gratitude, a plea for personal reconciliation, or a sustained theological argument, as in Colossians. At the same time, we find in Paul, paradoxically perhaps, an utter reliance upon God's grace. This can be seen in Paul's theological argument in Colossians, as well as in his quiet reflection upon his own lot in Philippians.

HARDSHIP (Phil. 1:12–26)

What is Paul's attitude toward his own misfortune?

NOTES ON PHILIPPIANS

The possibility exists that the question of place and date of origin needs to be stated in the plural, since Philippians, a loosely structured document (see outline), may be a composite of three Pauline letters or fragments.[13] If so, the segments would be (1) 1:1–3:1; (2) 3:2–4:1; (3) 4:10–20, with the distribution of 4:2–9 and 21–3 uncertain. A recent commentator suggests Rome as the place of origin of the first and third letters or fragments (during the captivity described in Acts 28) and leaves the time and place of origin of the second undecided.[14] Although this partitioning of Philippians is commended by breaks in the structure and flow of thought, it is not impossible that these irregularities stem from Paul himself and that the letter is an original unity. In any event, our text (1:12–26) was probably written from Rome during Paul's imprisonment there. By contrast, there is no uncertainty about the Philippian destination of the letter (1:1; 4:15), unless perhaps chapter 3 as a separate letter or fragment was not originally intended for Philippi. According to the Acts account (16:11–40), with which Philippians 4:15 seems to agree, Philippi was Paul's first mission stop on his initial journey into Macedonia and Greece.

OUTLINE OF PHILIPPIANS

Introduction: Salutation and Thanksgiving (1:1–11)
I. Personal and Theological Communication (1:12–3:1)

[13] H. Köster, "The Purpose of the Polemic of a Pauline Fragment (Philippians iii)," *NTS*, 8(1962), p. 317, especially n. 1 for the relevant literature.
[14] Cf. F. W. Beare, *A Commentary on the Epistle to the Philippians* ("Harper's New Testament Commentaries"; New York: Harper & Row, 1959), pp. 4 f., 101.

The most striking thing about this passage is the spirit and enthusiasm that Paul displays. He is in prison (vss. 7, 13) in Rome on account of his preaching of the gospel (vs. 13). (A narrative account of his arrest and imprisonment is found in Acts 21–28.) Despite his unfortunate circumstances, Paul is despondent neither over himself nor his cause. Far from having impeded his work and the advance of the gospel, his opponents have done just the opposite (vs. 12), for by his very imprisonment Paul bears witness to Christ (vs. 13). In addition, and contrary to what might ordinarily have been expected, Paul's coworkers have been emboldened rather than intimidated by the treatment accorded the apostle to the Gentiles. Do these attitudes merely bespeak the foolhardiness, if not the foolishness, of the Christian community? In their adversity are these people so far removed from reality that even misfortune seems to be fortunate and genuine threats to their existence are not taken with due seriousness? Such an assessment is always possible, and doubtless many of Paul's contemporaries outside the church would have agreed with it.

Yet the attitude to which Paul gives utterance is at least no casual or passing foolishness, but a fundamental tenet of his faith. It is an aspect of the foolishness of God, which is the gospel of the crucified Messiah. (I Cor. 1:18–25). "My grace is sufficient for you," the Lord, the exalted Christ had said to Paul, "for my power is made prefect in weakness" (II Cor. 12:9). Paul actually believed that "God chose what is foolish in the world to shame the wise . . . what is weak in the world to shame the strong . . . what is low and despised in the world, even things that are not, to bring to nothing things that are, so that no human being might boast in the presence of God" (I Cor. 1:27–29). His ultimate ground for believing this was the cross of Jesus, in which the humiliation of God's Son becomes the demonstration not only of his love, but of his power. Likewise for the apostle and the whole church, humiliation and even suffering may be expected to redound to God's glory in the spreading of the gospel. For through such unlikely means the church bears unmistakable and effective witness to its crucified Lord. Paul not only can confess this as a matter of faith; he sees it actually coming about: through the suffering and hardship of the disciple, the cause of the gospel is being advanced. This is a token of God's grace.

Paul was not engaged in daydreaming, as is revealed by his realistic assessment of the motivations of his colleagues in preaching (1:15–18). We know that Paul was not everywhere welcome, even among Christians in his own churches. Therefore it should not be surprising that his appearance among Roman Christians aroused not only love but also envy and rivalry. Paul was not modest about the importance of his own role in the apostolic preaching and suffered from no sense of personal inadequacy in comparison with his colleagues (Rom. 15:17; I Cor. 15:10; II Cor. 11:5, 21 ff.). He was doubtless capable of arousing antagonisms. In all probability, therefore, he is presenting a true picture in verses 15–18.

Paul was able to rise above petty jealousies not merely because of superior personal or moral character but on the basis of theological insight. The proclamation of the word of the gospel, not the personalities (cf. I Cor. 3) or even the motivations of the preachers, was for him primary. The gospel had a validity and an effect independent of the one who conveyed it. Paul did not think the motivation and moral character of the preacher was unimportant, but he would not grant that the validity and effectiveness of the gospel was dependent upon them. Thus, in spite of the intention of some rivals to harass him, presumably by making more converts than he could while he languished in jail, Paul was able to rejoice, for "whether in pretense or in truth, Christ is proclaimed" (vs. 18).

His present rejoicing was, however, only a harbinger of what was to come: "and I shall rejoice." Paul had confidence in the community and the Spirit. Therefore he had hope. The interdependence of one member of the community with another, so graphically portrayed in Paul's image of the Body of Christ (I Cor. 12; Rom. 12:3–8), finds practical expression in verse 19. The prayers of the church and the Spirit of Jesus work together for Paul's deliverance. Deliverance from what? It is by no means certain that Paul means deliverance from the Roman executioner or from prison. That Paul contemplates the possibility of release is already implied by the last clause of verse 20. Yet the word translated "deliverance" in our English text also means "salvation," and Paul's use of this and related terms usually has a future, eschatological reference. From verse 21 we learn that Paul can regard death as well as life as the fulfillment of his hope for deliverance. Paul does not, however, allow himself to yearn for death—a not uncommon attitude in the ancient world. From verse 20 it is clear that he desires only to face either life or death with courage, so that Christ will be honored in his body. Here, moreover, is a good example of Paul's distinctive use of the Greek term *sōma*, body. In this context it surely does not mean merely the physical shape and substance, but

Paul's individual and personal presence in the world of men and events.

In verses 22–25 Paul lays out the relative advantages of living or dying and indicates what he means by "to die is gain." Life means labor (vs. 22), while death means being with Christ (vs. 23). Because of the continuing needs of the Philippians, Paul regards it as more urgent at the moment that he continue to live (vs. 24). This necessity is apparently the basis of his confidence that his life will now be spared so that he may visit the Philippians again (1:25 f.). Whether events proved him right in this expectation is a debatable question. If he was writing from Roman imprisonment, in all probability they did not. But the point is that Paul's eager expectation and hope of deliverance or salvation could by no means be disappointed, whatever the outcome of his situation, for he hoped in the God who raised Jesus Christ from the dead. This same Jesus Christ, in his humiliation, death, and resurrection life, was for Paul the pattern of Christian existence and the ground of Christian hope. So at what was very likely the end of his ministry, with the possibility of his own death looming before him, Paul had confidence, and not only confidence but joy (1:4, 18, 19). This was not, however, the first time Paul had faced death or mortal danger (cf. I Cor. 15:32; II Cor. 11:23 ff.).

In 1:27 ff. Paul makes an easy transition from encouragement to exhortation and in 2:1–11 (especially 5–11) offers a Christological model for Christian ethics. The pattern of humiliation, death, and exaltation mentioned above is explicitly derived from Christ and applied to the Christian. Paul may employ an earlier Christ-hymn in verses 6–11, but the ethical application is in all probability his own. This confession and its application are to be understood in conjunction with Romans 6. There Paul discusses Christian baptism as the analogue of Christ's death and resurrection and interprets it in terms of its ethical implications. In both cases Paul assumes that there is, or must be, an integral relation between Christ and the Christian. The characteristic Pauline phrase "in Christ" also implies such a relationship, as do the concepts "body" and "Body of Christ."

After 2:1–11 the remainder, and thus the greater part, of the letter to the Philippians consists of words of encouragement, a warning against heretics (especially in chap. 3), exhortation, personal reflections, and an expression of thanks. This last (4:14–20) may have provided the occasion for the entire letter, or at least for that segment (4:10–20) of which it is a part. The tone of the whole letter, with the possible exception of chapter 3, is consonant with this expression of thanks. Indeed, Philippians shows an ease and familiarity not found in Paul's other letters. Even chapter 3 implies no division between Paul and the church, but warns against outsiders and intruders, who quite possibly had not yet appeared in Philippi. More is implied in 4:14 ff. than perfunctory thanks; there exists a mutual sympathy and understanding between Paul and the first church he founded on the European continent.

After the problems of Galatians and the Corinthian letters, it is a refreshing change to find Paul in a more relaxed state of mind. It may even be that the preservation of his more controversial and polemical correspondence has produced a distorted picture of Paul as a man constantly agonized and agonizing. There is no question of his readiness to defend his understanding of the gospel and to attack those who endanger it; that is abundantly clear in the extant documents. What may be lacking is proportionate evidence of the Paul of Philippians, a man capable of genuine human affections and motivated by a profound faith and confidence that enabled him to face the possibility of death with tranquility and to overlook the machinations of his rivals when they did not affect the truth and advancement of the gospel.

HERESY (Col. 2:8–15)

What is the misunderstanding of Christ which Paul attacks?
How does this erroneous view affect the Christian's style of life?

NOTES ON COLOSSIANS

Whereas the Pauline authorship of Philippians is generally accepted, the same cannot be said of Colossians. The chief arguments against the authenticity of Colossians are: (1) differences in style from the undoubtedly Pauline epistles; (2) differences in development of theological thought; (3) the complex character of the "heresy" that Paul combats (could it have developed in Paul's lifetime?); (4) the close relation both in style and in thought to Ephesians, which is probably the work of a later Paulinist rather than of Paul himself. The above factors are undeniable; the problem is how to interpret them.

In the discussion that follows, the tradition of Pauline authorship is tentatively accepted, since: (1) there are variances in style among the uncontested Pauline epistles; (2) changes or developments in theological thought on the part of the same author are not inconceivable; (3) earliest Christianity was characterized by considerable doctrinal variety; (4) if, in fact, Ephesians is a pseudonymous work based on Colossians the author of Ephesians apparently took Colossians to be Pauline. Like Philippians, Colossians and Philemon were probably written during Paul's Roman imprisonment, which was of at least two years duration (Acts 28:30). Assuming Paul was the author of Colossians, the date and occasion of writing must have coincided very closely with Philemon, Paul's brief personal note on behalf of the slave Onesimus. The writing of Colossians was probably occasioned by the return of Epaphras from Colossae to Paul bearing news of the condition and problems of the church in that city (1:7; 4:12 f.).

Colossians is a difficult book. What is more, knowledge of the original language only multiplies the difficulties. The RSV translators have made passing good sense out of a number of quite obscure sentences whose meaning may never be surely known. Colossians appears to have been written to warn the church of Colossae against the dangers inherent in a certain aberrant form of Christianity, which, for want of a better term, we shall call the Colossian heresy:[15] Our knowledge of this heresy has to be gleaned from Paul's own statements. This heresy was, it seems at first glance, so far removed from our world and our ways of thought as to be scarcely worth the effort that genuine understanding might demand. Besides such obstacles, the problems of the uncertainties of the date and place of origin, or even of authorship, seem to pale by comparison. Yet difficult as it is, the problem of understanding may yield to persistent effort more readily than the other perplexities. No better test case can be found than the passage 2:8–15, for here Paul describes the Colossian heresy that he opposes. He characterizes it as "philosophy and empty deceit" having to do with "human tradition" and the "elemental spirits of the universe" and not with Christ (vs. 8.). There is a fundamental opposition between this, as Paul understands it, and the Christian gospel.

What is this philosophy that Paul denounces in so vigorous a way? The key term (vss. 8, 20) seems to be "elemental spirits of the universe" (Greek, *kosmos*). If we understood it fully we would understand the Colossian heresy. Paul uses the term elsewhere only in Galatians 4:3, 8 ff., where he apparently regards the observance of Jewish ceremonial law as submission to such spirits. This may also be the case in Colossians

---

[15] "Heresy" and "heretic" are somewhat anachronistic terms, since they presuppose a credal orthodoxy that did not, in fact, exist at the beginning of the development of Christian thought. Nevertheless, they are terms useful in describing Paul's Colossian opponents.

(2:20 ff.). But in Colossians at least it is clear that such observance is only an expression of a philosophy or world-view in which Christ has a subordinate place. We are probably here dealing with a quasi-philosophy of nature, permeated with mystical religious elements and motivations.[16] The elemental spirits of the universe may have been natural phenomena that were thought to sustain or determine life and therefore were endowed with a semireligious aura; for example, the heavenly bodies, which, like the sun, sustain life, or, like the stars, determine it. Within these natural phenomena the divine influences that work upon man were deemed to be active and accessible. Ritual demands and taboos and calendar observances accompanied this "philosophy" (2:16 ff., 20 ff.). For as the universe was filled with such numinous powers, it behooved man to propitiate them through appropriate rite and ritual.

What seems to have disturbed Paul most was not ritual observance per se, although he would have rejected any insistence upon that, but the heretics' apparent willingness to subsume Christ under the system of elemental spirits. Such religious syncretism was in the habit of absorbing strange deities, and Christ presented no special problem. The statement of verse 9 may counter the Colossian heretics' claim that the deity dwelt or subsisted in the elemental spirits of the universe. For Paul the whole fullness of deity dwells in Jesus Christ. The term "bodily" in this connection probably does not refer to the earthly body of Jesus, but to the dwelling of the deity in Christ understood as the body of the church or universe. For in Colossians both church (1:18) and the universe (1:15–17; 2:10) are described as the Body of Christ, or the body of which Christ is the head.

"Fullness of life" (vs. 10) may have been offered by the heretics through subservience to the elemental spirits of the universe. Against this contention Paul argues that fullness of life comes only from Jesus Christ. Far from being subordinate to these elemental spirits, he is the head of all rule and authority (vs. 10). Paul does not directly deny the existence of such beings, but only insists that they have been subordinated to Christ. Therefore there is no reason for the Christian to have any regard for them. In a different context Paul has already stated the same basic idea: "For although there are many so-called gods in heaven or on earth—as indeed there are many 'gods' and many 'lords'—yet for us there is one God, the Father, from whom are all things and for whom we exist, and one Lord, Jesus Christ, through whom are all things and through whom we exist" (I Cor. 8:5 f.).

Paul then reminds the Colossians, who may be about to succumb to this misleading teaching, of the real ground of their hope and confidence

---

[16] E. Lohmeyer, *Die Briefe an die Kolosser und an Philemon* ("Kritisch-exegetischer Kommentar über das Neue Testament," 9. Aufl.; Göttingen: Vandenhoeck & Ruprecht, 1961), pp. 102 f.

(vss. 11 ff.). The reference to "circumcision made without hands" (vs. 11) may imply that the Colossian heretics, like the so-called Judaizers of Galatia, demanded that Christians submit to circumcision in the flesh. Christian circumcision, replies Paul, is not "in the flesh" but has the effect of "putting off the body of flesh" (vs. 11). This does not mean leaving this mortal life, of course, but putting off the life that is determined by the flesh. (See the discussion of flesh and spirit, pp. 340 ff., and the reference to the "sensuous mind," literally "mind of the flesh" in 2:18.) The death of the body (and mind) of the flesh occurs in baptism, where the new believer is buried and rises with Christ in a kind of recapitulation of Christ's death and resurrection (vs. 12; cf. Rom. 6).[17] Typically, Paul does not claim that this dying and rising is an automatic or magical occurrence; rather it takes place "through [and under the auspices of] faith." Notice the close relation between sin and death, forgiveness and life (vs. 13), a pattern typical of Paul, who nevertheless usually speaks of righteousness or justification rather than forgiveness.

Although Paul here suggests his familiar interpretation of Christ as God's justifying grace, in verse 15 he introduces another interpretation of Christ's work, one better adapted to the situation in Colossae. Christ, he says, has decisively triumphed over the "principalities and powers." These are doubtless included among the elemental spirits of the universe, if not identical with them. His redemptive work means not only freedom from flesh, sin, death (vs. 13), and the law (vs. 14) but freedom from the oppressive powers of the universe that have held man under their dominion. For the Jew the law and sin working through the law were the chief oppressive forces in the human situation; but for many Gentiles the elemental spirits held essentially the same position and exercised the same function in Paul's view, as may also be inferred from Galatians 4:1 ff. For the baptized believer, however, subjection either to the law or to the worldly spirits, powers, or authorities was a thing of the past. As an individual, he had been freed from bondage to such powers. Yet this deliverance was not the ultimate extent of Christ's work, for the release that the believer enjoyed had its basis in the triumph of Christ over these powers. He was free because they had been conquered and rendered harmless or "disarmed."

Thus the event of Christ has its objective as well as its subjective side in the theology of Colossians. There are cosmological implications to be derived from the historical event of the life and death of Jesus. He is the universal or cosmic redeemer.

Paul now draws the ethical implications of his theological argument,

---

[17] Note that Paul here assumes that the baptized believer has not only died, but also risen with Christ (cf. 3:1). Significantly, in Romans 6 Paul does not speak of the Christian as already raised from the dead. In fact, a careful reading of that text reveals that Paul goes out of his way to say that the baptized believer participates in the newness of Christ's resurrection life—interpreted ethically—without saying that he has already risen from the dead.

and most of the remainder of the epistle (2:16–4:6) is concerned with them. In 2:16–23 he rejects the spurious asceticism of the Colossian heretics, which does not take account of Christ's lordship over the world, but is simply subservience to the things that Christ has already overcome (2:20). Such religiosity, ascetic though it may be, does not finally escape the lordship of the flesh (2:23; note especially the RSV's alternative reading). The believer, however, is not subject to the elemental spirits of the universe. He is instead in the realm of the resurrected Christ (3:1 ff.). With Christ and the believer now portrayed as sitting at the right hand of God, Paul seems on the verge of speculative fancy. But such resurrection life is interpreted as this-wordly existence free from the power of sin, death, and "earthly things" (vs. 2; Paul probably has in mind those elemental world spirits of which he has already spoken). To all these the Christian has died. His life is now secure with God (vs. 3), and he hopes to share in the eschatological glory of Christ (vs. 4).

These statements might be taken as encouraging moral complacency. Paul will not, however, allow this interpretation. Beginning in 3:5 and continuing throughout this long central section (3:1–4:6), he encourages the Colossians to greater and greater ethical sensitivity and effort. This characteristic paradox lies close to the heart of Pauline theology. What the man in Christ has as a gift, what he is assured of by God's grace, what he has guarded and preserved through the Holy Spirit—this must be continually received by faith and made real in life. The gospel of grace that Paul preaches could mean ethical complacency, and has in fact been reduced to that by some of Paul's successors. But for the apostle such complacency is entirely impossible. God's grace is not based on righteous works and is not their reward. Something like the opposite relationship holds: God's grace is the basis for righteous works. Because the Colossians have received God's grace they may be encouraged to obey him. This is what Paul elsewhere calls the obedience of faith (Rom. 1:5). It is the only valid obedience, because it is based on a God-given freedom, and not upon a legalism or a philosophy that is already under the sway of powers that predispose man toward evil.

Suggestions for Further Reading

The "Suggestions for Further Reading" at the end of the following chapter include works on Paul's theology. General treatments of Paul's letters and his career are to be found in the standard New Testament introductions and histories mentioned in the General Bibliography, IV.

A simple treatment by a reputable scholar is F. W. Beare, *St. Paul and His Letters* (New York: Abingdon, 1962). A. D. Nock, *St. Paul* (London:

Oxford, 1938), still serves as a valuable introduction to Paul. J. Knox gives an unorthodox interpretation of Paul's career and theology in *Chapters in a Life of Paul* (New York: Abingdon, 1950); he questions the historical value of the Acts framework of Paul's career and the possibility of reconciling its data with the apostle's letters. A recent reliable textbook on Paul is D. J. Selby, *Toward the Understanding of Paul* (Englewood Cliffs, N.J.: Prentice-Hall, 1962).

Paul's debt to his predecessors and to the earlier Christian tradition is the subject of a helpful book by A. M. Hunter, *Paul and his Predecessors* (rev. ed.; Philadelphia: Westminster, 1961). Paul's relation to the Jerusalem church has been treated by W. L. Knox, *St. Paul and the Church of Jerusalem* (Cambridge: Cambridge University Press, 1925). An eschatologically oriented interpretation of this relation and of Paul's whole career is offered by J. Munck, *Paul and the Salvation of Mankind*, trans. F. Clarke (Richmond, Va.: John Knox, 1959). See also W. Schmithals, *Paul and James*, trans. D. M. Barton (SBT, 46; Naperville, Ill.: Allenson, 1965). The collection that Paul made among his Gentile churches for the Jerusalem church has been studied of late by K. F. Nickle, *The Collection: A Study in Paul's Strategy* (SBT, 48; Naperville, Ill.: Allenson, 1966).

The most recent thorough investigation of the Corinthian situation is J. C. Hurd, *The Origins of I Corinthians* (New York: Seabury, 1965); he thinks the Corinthian controversies were in large measure the result of Paul's own changing position. A more popular book is W. Baird, *The Corinthian Church: A Biblical Approach to Urban Culture* (New York: Abingdon, 1964).

Up-to-date critical, but nontechnical, commentaries on Galatians, I Corinthians, and II Corinthians are regrettably scarce. The commentaries of R. T. Stamm, C. T. Craig, and F. V. Filson, *IB*, X (1950), are probably as good as any available. On Philippians there is F. W. Beare's worthwhile commentary in the Harper series (1959). Beare's commentary on Colossians, *IB*, XI (1955), is also useful. As this book went to press, there appeared C. K. Barrett's commentary on I Corinthians in the Harper series (1968).

8 Romans: Paul's Exposition of the Gospel

NOTES ON ROMANS

This most profoundly theological of all Paul's letters was probably written during, or shortly after, Paul's last visit to Corinth. It followed the resolution of the problems of the Galatian and Corinthian churches and the completion of the collection for Jerusalem (cf. Rom. 15:17–29; II Cor. 1:16; 8; 9; Acts 20:2 f.). Paul was clearly heading for Jerusalem when he wrote this letter (Rom. 15:26, 28, 30 f.). He regarded his work in the eastern part of the Mediterranean world as complete and was looking forward to a subsequent journey to Spain. Little did he realize that his plans were to be foreclosed by

318

his arrest and imprisonment. (Contrast Rom. 15:14 ff. and Acts 20:17 ff.; yet cf. Rom. 15:30–33). Romans is not addressed to a church lying within what had heretofore been Paul's missionary orbit. It is sent rather to a church that Paul expected to visit. For some reason Paul wished to present himself to the church or Christians at Rome. Perhaps he hoped to use Rome as the center for his future missionary endeavors in Spain,[1] although this admittedly cannot be proved from Romans or any of Paul's writings. The presentation that he gives says very little about his personal life or religious experience; instead he expounds the gospel.

Galatians, especially Paul's earlier conversation with Peter (Gal. 2:11 ff.), indicates that the seeds of Romans had already been planted in Paul's thought long before. Yet Paul was likely driven by experiences with his churches in Galatia and Corinth to formulate more carefully his understanding of the gospel. The basic theological themes set forth in Galatians receive more extensive and considered treatment in Romans, whereas some of the theological themes as well as the practical counsel of the Corinthian correspondence also appear here (for example, the Body of Christ in Rom. 12:3–8; love in 12:9 ff., 13:8 ff., and elsewhere; conscience and the weaker brother in chap. 14). One has the distinct impression that Romans embodies the relatively later and more considered reflection, a judgment borne out by other evidence for dating the letters.

Introduction: Righteousness by Faith (1:1–17)

How does the introduction of Romans compare with those of other Pauline letters?
What is the climax of the introduction?

The letter to the Romans opens with a long, formal salutation (1:1–7), containing a balanced confessional statement (vss. 2–4) alongside Paul's description of his apostolic office. The idea of the Davidic sonship of Jesus and such terms as "Spirit of holiness," both rare in Paul, suggest that the confessional statement may represent an earlier tradition. The customary thanksgiving extends from verses 8 through 15—perhaps through verse 17, for although verses 16 f. introduce the theme of the letter, they are integrally related to what precedes. Paul is effusive over the Romans' faith and gives elaborate assurances about his own prayers for them. Although such expressions were conventional in Hellenistic correspondence

---

[1] This thesis has been set forth by F. J. Leenhardt, *The Epistle to the Romans: A Commentary*, trans. H. Knight (London: Lutterworth, 1961), pp. 12–15, especially 13 f. Cf. Rom. 1:8–15; 15·14–33.

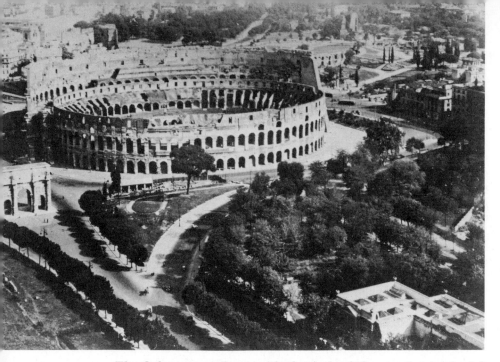

The Colosseum at Rome with the Arch of Constantine in the left foreground. Built by Vespasian and Titus about A.D. 80 as an amphitheater, it was used before Constantine for persecution of Christians. (Courtesy of Lufthansa German Airlines.)

of the time,[2] Paul is doing more than engaging in bare conventionalities, as is shown by the specific content of his prayers (vs. 10) and by the appropriate character of his praise for the Roman Christians.

The full meaning and import of verses 16 f. can only be seen in the light of the entire letter. Yet several crucial matters must be noted at once. Paul's disavowal of any shame (vs. 16) may be understood against the background of attacks upon him and his interpretation of the Christian gospel. Thus he sums it up here in a kind of technical theological shorthand: "the power of God for salvation," which implies God's grace, something freely given rather than earned. The pairing off of Jew and Greek is a further extension of the same line of thought. God gives his grace without regard for merit or national origin, without regard even for special religious distinction. It is universally bestowed among mankind. While "Jew" means for Paul "an Israelite according to the flesh," "Greek" is virtually a synonym for Gentile. The substance of Paul's gospel is spelled out more fully in verse 17. It is the revelation of the righteousness (*dikaiosynē*; see pp. 333 ff.) of God. By this Paul might mean a doctrine or fact about God, that he is righteous rather than unrighteous, which Paul would have by no means denied. But for Paul the term "righteous-

[2] Cf. A. S. Hunt and C. C. Edgar (eds. and trans.), *Select Papyri* ("The Loeb Classical Library"; London: Heinemann, 1932–34), I, 339, 369, for good examples of conventional thanksgivings.

ness of God" has a specific, dynamic meaning (cf. Rom. 3:26). It primarily refers to how God acts and relates to man and his history.

It may already be inferred from this brief but tightly packed utterance that the scope of the gospel is universal. The gospel is God's saving power for all humanity. At the same time the gospel shows forth and interprets God's righteousness, and it is this theme that Paul develops in Romans. His righteousness is made known to, and appropriated by faith; faith has now become a universal possibility. As we have already noticed in Galatians, emphasis on the importance and indispensability of faith is characteristic of Paul.[3] The theme of the righteousness of faith will be developed and refined in Romans.

God's Wrath: The Problem of Sin (1:18–3:20)

What is the condition of man in the light of God's revelation?
Are men responsible for their wickedness?
Are specific acts of wrong-doing ("sins") the cause or result of man's wickedness (or "sin")?

After having spoken of the revelation of God's righteousness in 1:17, Paul turns in 1:18 to the revelation of God's wrath. Both terms, "righteousness" and "wrath," are eschatological. That is, they speak of revelations expected in the last days of this world as signs that God is bringing human history to a climactic and perhaps catastrophic conclusion. Paul places God's righteousness and his wrath over against one another as if he believed that their presence already marked the final turning point of world history. Indeed, Paul can refer to Christians as those upon whom the end of the ages has come (I Cor. 10:11) and can advise against marriage or any other too close attachment to this world on the grounds that it is passing away (I Cor. 7:31). We may also recall the rather dramatic description of the return of Jesus in I Thessalonians 4:14 ff., which Paul evidently thought at one time that he might live to see.

Although the main tension in 1:17 f. is between God's righteousness and his wrath, Paul also introduces a secondary tension between the righteousness of God and the wickedness of man. This tension is somewhat obscured in the English translation, which cannot represent the Pauline

---

[3] Probably the RSV's alternative translation of the quotation from Habakkuk 2:4 in Romans 1:17 is preferable: "The righteous shall live *by faith*." This seems to be the meaning of the passage in the Hebrew text, the LXX, and the Targum (Aramaic translation), as well as the Habakkuk commentary of the Qumran sect. Moreover, this is surely what Paul intends in Galatians 3:11, where he quotes the same passage.

play upon the *dikaiosynē* ("righteousness") of God and the *adikia* ("wickedness") of men. With the setting up of these tensions or polarities the problem of Romans is posed, and the fundamental theological questions are raised. What is the relation between God's wrath and his righteousness? Moreover, how is it possible for man, characterized by *adikia*, lack of righteousness, to stand before a holy God, whose very essence is his righteousness?

At this point in Romans, Paul does not deal fully with these questions. He must first characterize mankind as the object and occasion of God's wrath (Rom. 1:18–3:20). Paul already (vs. 18) indicates that the characterization will not be favorable, even though he does not yet indicate the extent of the wickedness he here describes. Note that Paul speaks of a present outpouring of God's wrath, parallel with the revelation of his righteousness just mentioned. Thus Paul describes the condition of man from the standpoint of the revelation of God's righteousness and wrath in and through the gospel. He does not describe the human condition from the perspective of the neutral and strictly objective onlooker. Thus Paul could scarcely have expected everyone to subscribe to his characterization of mankind. The wrath of God against human wickedness accompanies the revelation of his righteousness, and only against the background of this norm—the righteousness of God in Jesus Christ—does the wickedness of man stand out in bold relief.

This wickedness or lack of righteousness (*adikia*)[4] is described first of all as suppression of the truth (vs. 18), the failure to recognize the truth about the creator implicit in the creation (vss. 19–20). It is not as if the world had no access to knowledge of God. In fact, precisely the opposite is true. Therefore Paul can say of men: "They are without excuse" (vs. 20). Not only do men have the possibility of knowing God and fail to exercise it; Paul goes so far as to attribute to men an actual knowledge of God (vs. 21). They lack, however, a proper *acknowledgment*: "They did not honor him as God or give thanks to him." Instead they became senseless and practiced disobedience—namely, idolatry (vss. 22 f.) —with the resulting defilement or dishonoring of their bodies (vs. 24). The grounds for the existing state of affairs lies in the fact that the values and loyalties of men have become perverted, even inverted, since they "exchanged the truth of God for a lie and worshipped and served the creature rather than the creator" (vs. 25).

Three important points emerge in this passage. First, Paul speaks of the wickedness or unrighteousness of man without yet saying that these characteristics are universal. Paul leaves open the option of extending the condemnation of human wickedness to include all men but does not yet

---

[4] The Greek word *adikia* means not just wickedness or unrighteousness, but the absence of righteousness. The initial *a* is the so-called alpha privative, which indicates the absence of the thing it qualifies. Compare the English *amoral*.

explicitly do so. Second, although Paul speaks initially of the present revelation of the wrath of God (vs. 18), he changes over to the past tense in describing the "history of sin" in the human race. Thus he indicates that the present situation, against which God's wrath is directed, did not come about in a day, but has a long and significant past. Third, that God gives men up to their lusts, an idea that occurs first in verse 24 and recurs in verses 26 and 28, does not mean that God is the cause of sin, but that God allows man to fall prey to the overt sinning that is already implicit in their misdirected loyalty and worship.

This inversion of the "natural order" (worship of the creator) concludes the first stage in the development of Paul's description of the human situation (vs. 25). The remainder of chapter 1 really elaborates and reiterates what has already been said. Nevertheless, verses 26–27 are especially interesting. Paul makes more explicit the nature of the impurity and dishonoring of the body already mentioned (vs. 24). Being a good Jew, Paul could not have considered sexual relations within marriage dishonorable, even though he himself was unmarried. He evidently had in mind in verse 24 the homosexuality he describes in verses 26 f.

Paul's singling out of homosexuality is hardly accidental. Of course, the Bible condemns homosexuality in the strictest terms (cf. Leviticus 18:22; 20:13), which in itself indicates it was not unheard of in Old Testament times (Genesis 19:4–8; Judges 19:22–26). Apparently, this practice was fairly prevalent in the Greco-Roman world as, for example, Plato's *Symposium* implies. Perhaps Paul simply speaks as a pious Jew enraged at what he regards as a most heinous violation of law and nature. But Paul has already argued that man's lack of righteousness results from his lack of a proper knowledge of God—a failing that bears its expected fruit in idolatry. For Paul idolatry, as a worshipping and serving of the creature rather than the creator (vs. 25), is literally a perversion, or as we have already suggested, the outward manifestation of the inverse of the natural order of things. The result of this reversal of the natural order—or, better, the created order—is the disordering and confusion of human life in general. Homosexual practices reverse the order in which sexual relations were obviously intended. Therefore not a puritanical disposition but Paul's understanding of man's fundamental wickedness (idolatry) suggests homosexuality as the best outward example of the depravity of human sinfulness. Sin is not merely the breaking of commandments or laws, although it certainly involves that; rather sin is a complete disorientation of life such that human existence and behavior become completely divorced and estranged from the ground of their being, the God who creates and orders all things.

Such disorientation does not stop with sexual aberrations, but extends to all life. "Improper conduct" (vs. 28) translates a Stoic expression meaning what is out of accord with the nature of man or of things. Moreover, "a base mind" translates *adokimon noun,* which plays upon the preceding assertion that men did not *edokimasan* ("See fit to acknowledge") God. One commentator aptly translates: "And as they did not see fit to take cognizance of God, God handed them over to an unfit mind."[5] The perversity of man in refusing to acknowledge God is thus manifest in homosexuality and no less strikingly in the general disordering of life, most especially of human relationships, for most of the catalogue of vices (vss. 29–31) pertains to human relationships. Paul describes men turned toward one another in animosity and suspicion rather than love. This is unnatural. It is a violation of the intended order of creation.

Paul has not yet explicitly extended his condemnations to include all of mankind. From the prominence given to homosexuality and the subsequent catalogue of vices, the Jewish reader would be justified in suspecting that Paul has in mind the Gentile and is making an exception of the Jew. After all, Paul was not above referring disparagingly to "Gentile sinners" (Gal. 2:15), as if the terms were practically synonymous. Probably Paul does have in mind here the sinful conduct of the Gentile. For the Jewish or Jewish Christian reader, what he has to say might seem quite convincing. In fact, in the apocryphal book of the Wisdom of Solomon one can find ideas akin to those that Paul sets forth here. For example, the author, in agreement with Paul, seems to assume that knowledge of God should be attainable from creation, although men by and large do not attain it (13:6–9). He gives a similar assessment of the relation between idolatry and immorality (14:12), and presents a catalogue of specific sins (14:22 ff.) not unlike that of Romans 1:29 ff.[6] So far in Romans there is little to make the Jewish reader uneasy. What Paul has written could pass as an eloquent condemnation of Gentile sin.

That Paul intends something more than this, however, is already clear from the first few verses of chapter 2. As Paul has the Gentile in the back of his mind in 1:18–32, so he seems here to be thinking of the Jew. That Paul would apply his hard words in 2:1–5 to any presumptuous and self-righteous human being need scarcely be denied, but that he specifically intends them for the Jew as well as the Greek becomes quite apparent (2:6 ff.). The idea that God shows no partiality (2:11) means that the Jew is brought to judgment on the same basis as the Gentile, as Paul in fact makes quite explicit (vss. 9–10). The naming of the Jew alongside the Gentile (vss. 9–10) probably indicates that the Jew has been in mind from the beginning of chapter 2.

[5] C. K. Barrett, *A Commentary on the Epistle to the Romans* ("Harper's New Testament Commentaries"; New York: Harper & Row, 1957), p. 32. *Adokimon* seems to mean "unfit" in the sense of "unapproved" or "disapproved," therefore "base" (RSV).

[6] The New Testament, and especially Paul's epistles, are full of these catalogues of vices (for example, Rom. 13:13; I Cor. 5:10 f.; 6:9 f; II Cor. 12:20 f.; Gal. 5:19 ff.; Eph. 4:31; 5:3 ff.; Col. 3:5, 8; I Tim. 1:9 f.; II Tim. 3:2–5).

What Paul has already stated in verses 9–11, he develops now by setting forth the basis for God's impartial judgment of Jew and Gentile (vss. 12–16). Interestingly, the law—and apparently Paul means here the Jewish law—is accepted as the definitive expression of the will of God, according to which he will judge mankind on the last day (vss. 12 ff.; but cf. vs. 16). Mere possession of the law has, however, no particular value. Therefore, if any Gentile fulfills the requirements of the law, perchance without even knowing it in its concrete form (vss. 14–15), his obedience is perfectly acceptable. The idea that God's election of Israel constitutes a special privilege and advantage even if Israel does not respond appropriately is already rejected (vss. 12 f.). In the two closing paragraphs (vss. 17–24 and 25–29) this point is driven home with the clear implication (especially in vss. 17–24) that the Jews by and large stand condemned. Despite their advantage as the recipients and bearers of God's law, they do not in fact do what the law commands. Thus their desire to instruct or reprove others is sheer presumption. Really to be a Jew is to obey God. Such obedience is not a matter of outward show, but "a matter of the heart, spiritual and not literal" (vs. 29). This, of course, does not mean that obedience has no visible form or tangible expression. It is, in fact, necessary to do the will of God. This true Judaism of which Paul speaks can be nothing less than obedience to God in the real world. It is not a specious and amorphous spirituality without concrete manifestations. Yet quite clearly being a real Jew is not to be identified with belonging to an institution or nation, or with fleshy marks of the same, such as circumcision.

Paul's following questions (3:1) are certainly well motivated, and from what Paul has so far said, we might expect a negative reply. In a sense this would be right, since the Jew has no advantage just because he is a Jew, and circumcision has no merit in and of itself.[7] Yet the Jewish possession of the scriptures (the "oracles of God," vs. 2) is in and of itself a great advantage. Paul mentions this as the first of what was apparently intended to be a series of items. But he immediately becomes side-tracked and does not mention the remaining advantages in this context (graphic proof of the more or less occasional character even of Romans). For the moment (vss. 3–8), Paul is obviously concerned with matters regarding which he has probably been challenged or even attacked. These verses (3, 5, and 7) raise a series of embarrassing questions, which Paul was probably not the first, nor the last, to ponder. (1) The unfaithfulness of the Jews constitutes a problem, since they do not now receive the promises vouchsafed to them (vs. 3): "Does their faithlessness nullify the faith-

---

[7] Paul seems to use the term *circumcision* in interesting ways. It may refer to the act or fact of removing the foreskin. It may also, however, imply belonging to the community of the circumcised as a whole—that is, Israel. Thus it can refer to the community of the circumcised.

fulness of God?" (2) To resolve this problem by blaming Israel rather than God so that God's righteousness is not impugned but rather established (vs. 4) raises the further problem of how God can justly condemn the transgressor when his wickedness really serves to vindicate God's righteousness (vs. 5). (3) In other words, "if through my falsehood God's truth abounds to his glory, why am I still being condemned as a sinner?" (vs. 7). Paul hardly answers these questions at this point. Indeed, he dismisses the questioner with a rather rude slap across the cheek (vs. 8). Yet as we shall see these questions are pivotal points in Paul's argument in Romans, and at length he returns to them in chapters 9–11.

In the next paragraph (3:9–20) Paul concludes the argument concerning the universality of sin which he has been developing since the introductory part of the letter. Uncertainty about the meaning of the particular form of a Greek verb makes it unclear whether in verse 9 Paul is asking whether the Jews are better or worse off. Whatever the question, however, Paul's basic contention is unaltered, as his positive statement shows (vs. 9). The Jews are actually no better off. To clinch his demonstration Paul characteristically calls upon the Hebrew scriptures (vss. 10–18). If there has been any doubt about what Paul is trying to prove, these verses should dispel it. Old Testament quotations from many different books (see the notes on the RSV text) have been skillfully woven together by Paul—if he did not find them already conjoined in an early Christian collection of Old Testament texts—to describe the general state of mankind (vss. 10–12) and to specify the details of that condition (vss. 13–18). Next comes an interpretative clarification (vs. 19) to remove any uncertainty as to the application of these Old Testament texts. They apply not only to Gentiles, but most particularly to those under the law—that is, Jews. Finally, Paul brings forth his own theological statement about what the law can and cannot do (vs. 20; see also 4:15; 5:20; 7:8, 10 f.). Clearly this long section extending from 1:18 to 3:20 is intended to show the universal sinfulness of man as the backdrop for the proclamation of the gospel (cf. 3:23), which reveals God's righteousness and also his wrath.

Is this lengthy prolegomenon a frightening diagnosis intended to induce the patient to accept the radical new cure? At first glance it may appear so. Yet Paul has already referred to the present, rather than the past, revelation of the wrath of God (1:18) precisely as proof that the revelation of God's righteousness is also taking place. For Paul the sinfulness of man becomes apparent only now with the revelation of the righteousness of God in Christ. Paul did not understand his own pre-Christian life as a period of disappointment over sinful humanity and disillusionment with his own sin.[8] His darker view of the predicament of man and his own past situation

8 Cf. Gal. 1:14 and Phil. 3:4–6. Romans 7 is the crucial text usually cited in support of Paul's alleged pre-Christian depression and discouragement, but it cannot be taken at its face value as either autobiographical or necessarily describing the prefaith state.

apparently arose only after his conversion to the Christian faith. Thus Paul does not think the hearer of the Christian preaching could be convinced of the seriousness of his plight apart from the message that the crucified one was the Christ.

On the other hand, we cannot maintain that nothing in this section (Rom. 1:18–3:20) could have been said by Paul except in the light of the Christian revelation and on the basis of Christian faith. His condemnation of the universal fact of Gentile sinfulness and his admission of the theoretical possibility of Gentile righteousness apart from the law are not unique to Paul the Christian. Probably he could have said as much before he became a Christian. Jewish condemnation of Gentile sin was not uncommon in New Testament times, and even in the New Testament itself (cf. Matt. 5:47; 6:7; Gal. 2:15). Really unusual are Paul's inclusion of the Jew under the same condemnation as the Gentile and his view that when the Jew and Gentile are judged on the same basis before God the Jew will have no particular advantage. And even this might not have seemed so offensive to his fellow Jew had Paul not gone on to say that the Jew actually falls short of fulfillment of the will of God and consequently with the Gentile stands condemned. In the light of the revelation of God's righteousness in the gospel of his Son, all men are sinners. Paul's affirmative answer to the question about the advantage of the Jew (3:1) scarcely seems convincing in the light of his wholesale condemnation of Jew and Gentile.

But is this condemnation really intelligible? Paul could scarcely argue that the unvarnished facts of human life support his position, unless he viewed mankind, Jew and Gentile, from a particular perspective, that of the revelation of God's righteousness and judgment in Jesus Christ. Yet even if we grant that Paul's condemnation (or, as he understands it, God's condemnation) of man's sinfulness is just, given his unique perspective, the origin of sin remains a mystery. Paul could have maintained that human nature in and of itself is evil. If so, what Paul calls wickedness, unrighteousness, or sin would be not a human possibility but a necessity. There would then be no such thing as meaningful human responsibility. Such a position with respect to a part of humanity may have been possible for some of Paul's contemporaries,[9] but this sort of determinism does not explain Paul's thought. On the one hand, the corruption of which he speaks extends to all humanity, not just a portion. On the other, Paul goes to great pains to maintain that mankind's plight is the result not of a corrupt

---

[9] Such a view is characteristic of Gnosticism; cf. R. M. Grant, *Gnosticism: A Sourcebook of Heretical Writings from the Early Christian Period* (New York: Harper & Row, 1961), esp. pp. 31, 133, 178–9, 194, 206–7. In a different form something of the same attitude finds expression in late Jewish apocalyptic; cf., for example, the War Scroll of the Qumran community. Although Gnosticism has theoretical grounds that exclude the possibility of salvation for some, apocalyptic thought regards only the enemies of God and of God's people as for all practical purposes irredeemable.

Christ acts as judge. Detail from the sixteenth-century Italian artist Michelangelo's "Last Judgment," on the ceiling of the Sistine Chapel at the Vatican in Rome. (Courtesy of Alinari-Art Reference Bureau.)

nature but of concrete sinning. Thus the point of verse 1:19 is, as we have seen, the establishment of man's responsibility for his own condition. God's giving man over to certain forms of wickedness (1:24, 26, 28) does not mean that God causes men to be evil, but that he allows them to be. Therefore Paul proclaims that man stands in a state of universal sinfulness because of his actual sinning. That specific acts of sinning carried with them ominous consequences for man's future and future generations is implied by verses 1:24, 26, 28, where Paul doubtless has more than one generation of mankind in view. Is sin some disease, perhaps, that has infected the human race at the outset and been passed on from one generation to the next? If so, then every man would be born with an inclination toward sin. Perhaps Paul would have agreed that this is the case. But he does not set out that venerable conception or original sin, according to which a sinful nature is inherited by each generation from its predecessor. That is a later development in the history of Christian doctrine.

On the other hand, Paul clearly does not regard sin as personal wickedness or individual transgression resulting from the ill will of single persons. Although he indicates that men are responsible for their sin and do not sin inevitably or by nature, he is quite aware of the suprapersonal character of evil among the human race. Specifically, he traces the origin of this evil or sin to Adam (Rom. 5:12–21; cf. I Cor. 15:45 ff.). Moreover, he can refer to the bondage of the creation to decay (8:21) or to the present evil age (Gal. 1:4) without ever mentioning Adam. Likewise without mentioning him, Paul speaks of sin as an external power that can enslave man (chap. 6) and describes its insidious attack upon man through the law (chap. 7). Yet in the light of his specific references to Adam we may maintain that his understanding of the corporate character of sin owes much to that strand of Jewish thought which laid responsibility for the corrupt state of humanity at Adam's doorstep (cf. especially IV Ezra 7:116–126 and II Baruch 54:15–19).

In summary, Paul's conception of sin has two foci, which remain in paradoxical and unresolved tension with one another. Man sins willingly, but inevitably. Paul can never speak of sin in such a way as to relieve mankind as a whole, and indeed the individual, of responsibility for it. Yet he would by no means subscribe to a purely personal or individual concept of sin. Like his predecessors among the ancient prophets of Israel, Paul was fully aware of both its individual and corporate dimensions. To this extent Paul's understanding of sin can be made fully intelligible.

Admittedly Paul's conceptual categories are foreign to us. We like to "explain" human evil in terms of historical cause and effect and environmental influence. Generally we do not describe our own situation, no matter how evil or dangerous, in terms of oppression by mythological demonic powers (Rom. 8:37). Yet the awareness of the awful depth and mystery of human evil, illumined but by no means exhausted by historical and sociological explanation, comes to expression in works of art, literature, and the theater. Man's rational efforts, significant as they may be, do not suffice to exorcise or even comprehend the demonic dimensions of our society and our world. Paul's awareness of being beset by mysterious, supernatural forces outside man's control, far from being utterly strange, corresponds to the character of contemporary existence. Moreover, his refusal to release humanity from responsibility for sin, paradoxical as it may appear, also characterizes our apprehension of life. We know that injustice, violence, and racism are our heritage, but also our responsibility.

God's Righteousness and the Response of Faith (3:21–4:25)

In what way is the preceding section (1:18–3:20) important for this part of Paul's argument?
How is God's righteousness manifested?
Are faith and works contradictory? Why?

God's wrath is not his only word. Although God has every reason to display righteous wrath against human perversity and rebelliousness, which ignores his long-suffering patience (2:4), he does not leave man to the condemnation that he deserves. Instead, he turns toward man in mercy and compassion, and, according to Paul, the evidence of this grace is Jesus Christ. The actual historic and public crucifixion of the expected Jewish Messiah reveals God's righteousness and his power for salvation (1:16). At a pivotal point of Romans, Paul announces this new manifestation in terms drawn largely from the Jewish sacrificial system (3:21–31). Probably the best point of departure for interpreting this passage is Paul's classic affirmation at the beginning of I Corinthians (1:18–25):

> For the word of the cross is folly to those who are perishing, but to us who are being saved it is the power of God. For it is written,
>
> > "I will destroy the wisdom of the wise, and the
> > cleverness of the clever I will thwart."
>
> Where is the wise man? Where is the scribe? Where is the debater of this age? Has not God made foolish the wisdom of the world? For since, in the wisdom of God, the world did not know God through wisdom, it pleased God through the folly of what we preach to save those who believe. For Jews demand signs and Greeks seek wisdom, but we preach Christ crucified, a stumbling block to Jews and folly to Gentiles, but to those who are called, both Jews and Greeks, Christ the power of God and the wisdom of God. For the foolishness of God is wiser than men, and the weakness of God is stronger than men.

Here Paul sets forth the word of the cross (that is, the preaching of Christ crucified) as God's saving power. Over against it he places all human wisdom. As the revelation of the foolishness and weakness of God in the face of this world's power the cross of Christ stands in judgment upon the power and wisdom of men. The cross therefore contradicts and negates man's trust in himself and what he regards as wisdom and power. Since the wisdom and power of this world crucified the Christ (cf. I Cor. 2:8), they thereby showed their true character and the gulf that separates them from the wisdom and power of God. The paradox and profundity of Paul's thinking about the cross of Christ, while not without its obscurities, has understandably provided a seedbed for the development of Christian theology, as well as for the literary and artistic portrayal of the cross as historical event and as symbol. The elements of surprise and reversal implicit in the cross are drawn out by Paul with far-reaching consequences for the understanding of the meaning of the revelation of God in Christ. In so manifesting himself within human history God stands ordinarily accepted values and standards on their head.

JUSTIFICATION BY FAITH (3:21-31)

As in Corinthians Paul radically revised notions of divine wisdom and power in the light of the cross, so in Romans he redefines God's righteousness. The situations are closely analogous. In Corinthians human wisdom and power are judged by the cross of Christ. In Romans human righteousness—that is, the righteousness based on works—is subjected to similar judgment. Thus the judgment of God against human self-assertion is extended to the realm of what today might be called religion and ethics, and the status of the person who considers himself upright before God is fundamentally challenged. For "now the righteousness of God has been manifested apart from the law, although the law and the prophets bear witness to it" (Rom. 3:21).

Paul is intrigued by paradox. The revelation of God's righteousness is attested in advance by the law and the prophets (that is, the Old Testament), although the revelation is apart from the law. That is, the appearance of God's righteousness, though predicted in the law, is not dependent or contingent upon the law. Neither is this righteousness gained through works of the law. Rather, it is contingent upon faith in Christ (vs. 22). Human wisdom, power, and righteousness all stand in opposition to the cross of Christ, because they represent man's attempt to establish his own life as secure apart from God (cf. 1:25). Faith, which is fundamentally acknowledgment of God's faithfulness to his promises in Christ (4:18–25), is the means by which man may find God's righteousness as his own salvation. That this is his only possibility of life is clearly spelled out by Paul in verses 22b–23, a summation of Paul's argument of 1:18–3:20. In verse 24, Paul specifies how God makes his righteousness accessible, that is, as a gift. This is in essence what "by his grace" means. This is the only fashion in which God could have imparted it, if faith as acceptance and acknowledgment were to be the proper stance of man before him (cf. Rom. 1:17). In the last half of verse 24, Paul refers to the historic event of Jesus Christ in which according to his gospel, this grace is bestowed.

The brief series of assertions in verses 24–26 is as difficult as it is important, for here, and especially in verse 25, Paul introduces unfamiliar terminology taken largely from Jewish sacrificial practice. The word *redemption* (vs. 24), however, means literally a buying back from slavery, although the specific meaning in this context is not certain. Redemption may simply have the general meaning of deliverance since in the next verse Paul drops this legal term and changes over to a sacrificial vocabulary. Thus in verse 25, he says that God put Christ forth as an expiation by his blood. The term *expiation* means a doing away with sin. The conviction that sin must be expiated is deeply imbedded in Old Testament religion and doubtless in the consciousness of Paul and the earliest Christian community.

That the expiation of the altar is in view is clear from Paul's reference to blood. The pattern for conceiving the significance of Christ's death is the sacrifice of the animal on the altar and the sprinkling of his blood. Paul, however, qualifies this idea of ritual sacrifice with the phrase "to be received by faith," showing that for him the effect of the sacrifice is dependent upon the manner of its reception. Christ is an expiation—but for faith alone.

Yet the power of sacrifice itself is not thereby dissipated. The event of Christ's death, understood as a sacrifice, shows God's righteousness (vs. 25). This righteousness needed to be demonstrated or vindicated, because God had not dealt with sin in the past (vs. 25b). This is apparently what is meant by his divine forbearance in passing over former sins. God exercises patience with sin, but not tolerance. In the face of human sin and evil, which has apparently been allowed to go unchecked and unpunished, God must act to demonstrate his righteousness (vs. 26). This could not have been done by a thunderbolt from the heavens, so to speak, but only by an event within human history. It is done in the cross of Christ, which God set forth as an expiation, literally, a means of dealing with sin.

Although Christ is cast in the sacrificial role, he does not offer himself to appease an angry God, nor is he offered by mankind in its own behalf. Rather God himself sets Christ forth as an expiation, and in so offering his own Son, contradicts ordinary notions of wisdom and power. The meaning of expiation in this context is, however, ambiguous. The Greek word *hilastērion*, here translated "expiation," can be used of the "mercy seat" or the covering of the Ark of the Covenant, which was kept in the holy of holies of the pre-exilic temple in Jerusalem (cf. Heb. 9:5). No one was allowed to enter the holy of holies except once a year, when the high priest entered on the Day of Atonement (Yom Kippur; the Hebrew word *kippur* is based on the same stem as the term *kapporeth*, which is translated into Greek as *hilastērion*). Once inside he sprinkled the covering of the Ark once and the Ark itself seven times with the blood of the sacrificial bull (Leviticus 16) to cover the pollution of the sins of the priests. This so-called mercy seat came to be thought of as a place of revelation, where God appeared to pronounce forgiveness upon his people. Paul may be suggesting that Christ, especially in his death, is the new mercy seat, the new place of forgiveness. Such a meaning would make good sense in the present context. The actual Ark, and with it the mercy seat, had of course, been destroyed in the conquest of Jerusalem by the Babylonians six centuries earlier. The way was thus open for the establishment of a new one, and the death of Christ would have provided the occasion for announcing the existence of a new place where God deals with sin.

Not only "expiation," but a number of other words and expressions found in verse 24 are rare in Paul. Even the term *redemption* (vs. 24) is not common in his letters. Moreover, Paul does not often speak of the blood of Christ, but of the cross, death, and body of Christ. The Greek word translated "show" (vs. 25) and "prove" (vs. 26) is otherwise rare in Paul, as is the term meaning "forbearance" and the Greek noun translated "he had passed over" (vs. 26). Also the word translated "put forward" (vs. 25) appears nowhere else in the Pauline corpus with this sense. Thus Paul has probably drawn upon traditional terms and concepts in this definitive statement of the nature and effect of the work of Christ. The source of his language may be the words of institution of the Lord's Supper (I Cor. 11:23–26; Matt. 26:26–28; Mark 14:22–24; Luke 22:17–19), where Jesus interpreted his own coming death as a sacrifice, or the primitive liturgy connected with it. Indeed, the belief that Christ's death was a sacrifice for sin is quite common in the New Testament (cf. I Cor. 15:3; John 1:29; I Peter 2:24; I John 2:2 and the theme of the entire Epistle to the Hebrews). Paul at least identifies his own view of the work of Christ with commonly accepted ideas about it (cf. also II Cor. 5:21; Gal. 3:13), if he is not drawing directly upon earlier credal or liturgical formulations. There is, of course, no reason to believe that he in any way questioned such traditional affirmations. In fact, Paul used sacrificial terminology elsewhere in Romans to describe the character of the Christian life (12:1 f.). Nevertheless, he was able to develop other interpretations of the significance of Christ's death independent of the sacrificial imagery (cf. Rom. 5:6–11; I Cor. 1:18–25; II Cor. 5:16 ff.). Already in the passage under consideration he places emphasis on faith (vs. 25). Although the first clause of verse 26 only reiterates what has been said in the previous verse, the second and concluding clause takes the thought further and in a decidedly Pauline direction. God shows himself to be righteous in justifying the man of faith.

The Greek verb translated "justify" (*dikaioō*) has exactly the same stem as the Greek noun translated "righteousness" (*dikaiosynē*). Therefore, according to the literal sense of the Greek word, "to justify" means "to make righteous." In Paul's thought, however, this process is not an infusing or a miraculous re-creation or transformation, but in the first instance a reckoning. As one can see (chap. 4), God reckons faith as righteousness and thus puts man in the right before him. To use the archaic English term, he *rightwises*[10] him. The model that Paul has in mind is the law court, with God the righteous judge. Rudolf Bultmann accurately and succinctly describes the concept of righteousness (*dikaiosynē*) in Paul as follows:

> When it denotes the condition for (or the essence of) salvation, *dikaiosynē* is a forensic term. It does not mean the ethical quality of a person. It does not mean any quality at all, but a relationship. That is,

[10] This term was first suggested and used by Kendrick Grobel in his translation of Rudolf Bultmann's *Theology of the New Testament*.

dikaiosynē is not something a person has on his own; rather it is something he has in the verdict of the "forum" (= law-court—the sense of "forum" from which forensic as here used is derived) to which he is accountable. He has it in the opinion adjudicated to him by another. . . . Specifically, the "righteous" one is that one in a legal action (. . . Rom. 3:4) who wins his case or is acquitted.[11]

That "righteousness" has this forensic meaning in Paul is plain in such passages as Romans 3:4, where Paul quotes Psalm 51:4 (here we find the verbal form translated "justified"), and 8:34, where the act of justifying or rightwising is set over against that of condemning in the context of a court scene when the judge pronounces a verdict. (Cf. Gal. 3:11 and Rom. 3:20, where the forensic meaning is also clear, and I Cor. 4:4, where the verb *dikaioun* is translated "acquitted.") The Old Testament precedent for this understanding of "righteousness" in the sense of "to pronounce righteous" can be seen in Isaiah 43:9:

> Let all the nations gather together, and let
> the peoples assemble . . .
> Let them bring their witnesses to *justify* them
>   [that is, show them righteous],
> and let them hear and say, It is true.[12]

Although this quotation shows a certain agreement between the Pauline and Old Testament understanding of righteousness, there is also an important difference with respect to the righteousness of God. For the Old Testament and Judaism generally it is self-evident that the *sinner* is not to be acquitted ("justified"), but the *righteous man* (Exodus 23:7; Proverbs 10:27 ff.; Psalm 1). Paul, on the other hand, maintains that God pronounces precisely the ungodly man righteous (Rom. 4:5) and that this is the marvel of the gospel.

Paul does not, however, envision God merely as a judge, much less as one who sits somewhere in heaven, aloof from human affairs, holding court and pronouncing verdicts. The righteous God is a saving God, and his righteousness and salvation are closely related. The background of this relationship can be seen in the Hebrew literary construction called synonymous parallelism found in the Old Testament:

> The Lord has made known his victory, he has revealed his vindication [Septaugint *dikaiosyne* = righteousness] in the sight of the nations (Psalm 98:2).

---

[11] *Ibid.*, I, p. 272.

[12] Cf. Isaiah 50:8 f.; 58:2. The terms used in the Septuagint are exactly those which Paul employs. This is particularly significant in view of the fact that when Paul quotes the Hebrew scriptures (Old Testament) he usually uses the Septuagint.

I bring near my deliverance [righteousness], it is not far off, and my salvation will not tarry (Isaiah 47:13).

My deliverance [righteousness] draws near speedily, my salvation has gone forth. . . . (Isaiah 51:5).

In such passages God's righteousness is understood as a saving act or event. Similarly, God *reveals* his righteousness in the gospel (Rom. 1:17), while at the same time manifesting his wrath against sin (1:18). Thus, for Paul God's righteousness is not primarily an abstract quality. Although a judgment, it is not a disinterested judicial pronouncement. It is an event in which God goes forth to judge and save—indeed, the climactic deed of salvation in the history of God's dealing with man.

The Christ event does not, of course, transport man into heavenly bliss. Yet it radically alters his status in the present world. That verdict of righteousness that the Jew expected or hoped for in the final judgment (cf. Rom. 2:12) has already been spoken in favor of mankind through Jesus Christ. Thus God does not simply sit back and wait until the end of history to pass judgment upon men, but in the manner known to the Old Testament goes forth to judge in favor of man and to save him. Although Paul believes that this salvation is only consummated at the day on which the Lord returns and gathers his own to his breast, he nevertheless maintains that the man who believes what God has done already finds himself in a decisively new situation.

ABRAHAM AND THE PROMISE TO FAITH (4:1-25)

Therefore, God's saving act in Jesus Christ is appropriated by faith rather than by works of the law (3:27 ff. and chap. 4). That this is no novel idea is shown by the example of Abraham, the father of Israel (chap. 4; cf. Gal. 3). Long before the law was given or even the requirement of circumcision established, Abraham "believed God and it was reckoned to him as righteousness." As Paul has already argued in the letter to the Galatians (see pages 291-297), a man is accounted righteous before God by faith, not by works. Man is pronounced righteous before God not on the basis of the character or quantity of his deeds—much less the accident of his birth—but on the basis of the fundamental conviction or allegiance determining his life. Now in view of Christ's crucifixion and resurrection this allegiance must focus upon a specific historical person and event. Paul sees Abraham's faith as a general prototype of specifically Christian faith and the righteousness reckoned to him as the model of that which the Christian receives by faith—that is, apart from works. Abraham, the father of Israel, shows that faith in God's promise has from the beginning of the story of salvation been man's proper attitude before God.

God's Grace and Man's Freedom (5:1–8:39)

How is the human situation changed by the coming of Christ (chap. 5)?
Why should men not sin in order to insure the supply of grace (chap. 6)?
What is the actual effect of the law upon man prior to faith (chap. 7)?
How does Paul distinguish between Spirit and flesh (chap. 8)?

Faith for Paul is not just believing a set of facts, much less adhering to a theory. Faith is the means of access to a new situation that God has created for man. After having shown the appropriateness and indispensability of faith by his argument based upon Abraham (chap. 4), Paul next turns to an avowal of the reality of this new situation (chap. 5). In fact, chapters 5 through 8 can profitably be viewed as Paul's effort to show that such a new situation actually exists, despite certain indications to the contrary.

THE NEW SITUATION (5:1–21)

In the solemn affirmation of this new reality (5:1–5), Paul's style suddenly changes. To this point he has set forth the revelation of God's wrath and righteousness in order to argue that the latter can be apprehended only in faith. Now he speaks from the standpoint of the community of faith—that is, in the first person plural. What he has previously sought to establish now becomes his working assumption: "Therefore, since we are justified by faith . . . ." On the basis of the new reality Paul can now speak of "this grace in which we stand." Having been put in the right through faith, the man of faith has peace with God—the cessation of hostility—and enjoys his grace. For Paul "grace" encompasses the entire Christ event and its effects. Grace is the mode of God's working and the resulting state in which man is placed. Grace is God's benevolent disposition and action on man's behalf, prior to and apart from man's own effort and accomplishment, the framework, so to speak, of faith.

Appropriately, the nature of grace is next spelled out (vss. 6–11). It is not an abstraction, but a real and specific event in human history, and recent history at that. Moreover, this event, the death of Christ, took place for the sake of sinful men (vss. 6–8). The pathos of this death is deeply felt by Paul himself, and reflected especially in verse 7. Interestingly enough, Paul does not reckon Christ's death as showing his own love for us, but God's (vs. 8). Paul thus emphasizes, not the personal motivation of the man Jesus as he went to the cross, but the underlying purpose and disposition of God. For God, even the cross is not wanton and meaningless violence; it is rather the means by which judgment and salvation are made known to and for sinful men.

That God justifies precisely the ungodly and unrighteous has already been affirmed in 4:3–8. There Paul first quotes Genesis 15:6—"Abraham believed God, and it was reckoned to him as righteousness." Then he interprets Genesis in the light of Psalm 32:1–2—"Blessed are those whose iniquities are forgiven . . . blessed is the man against whom the Lord will not reckon his sin." The man reckoned righteous by faith is the man whose iniquities are forgiven; God justifies the ungodly man who believes.

The distinction between salvation as future fulfillment and justification as the present assurance of this future reality comes to light in verse 9. "Blood" refers to the death of Christ, again alluding to the sacrificial system. Paul uses a form of the argument from the greater to the less in both verses 9 and 10. If *a* be true, then how much more is *b* also true. In both cases the point is that if God freely justifies even the ungodly, then we may safely infer that he will also preserve them from the wrath of judgment and grant them eternal life (cf. 2:7 for the Pauline use of "eternal life" as the destiny of the just). Because his future is no longer in jeopardy, but secure by virtue of the accomplished work of Christ, the man of faith already has grounds for rejoicing in God through the Lord Jesus Christ (vs. 11).

Between verses 9 and 10 a subtle shift of terminology occurs. Paul first speaks of being justified (vs. 9), the term he used in the key statement of 3:21–31 and in the discussion of Abraham in chapter 4. Now, however, the key word for the same state of affairs becomes "reconciled" and "reconciliation" (vss. 10 and 11). The work of Christ is no longer described in terms of the sacrificial cultus, but of the reorientation of the person. The man who was at odds with God is rightwised ("justified"). He is thereby at peace with God (5:1) and no longer stands under the dire threat of his wrath (1:18; 5:9). Paul thus maintains that the death of Christ directly affects the person. He is transformed from a state of hostility to one of reconciliation and peace. In a previous letter Paul spoke of the result of Christ's coming as reconciliation and described his own mission, or that of the Christian, as the ministry of reconciliation (II Cor. 5:18 ff.). Indeed, so radical was the transformation of the human situation that Paul declared the man in Christ to be a "new creature" or "new creation" (II Cor. 5:17).

In Roman 5:12–21 Paul completes the transition from the discussion of the righteousness of faith (3:21–4:25) to the exposition of the new life under God's power and grace which results from it. The passage is perplexing. The sentence structure and train of thought break off abruptly at the end of verse 12, but the basic idea is picked up again in verses 15–18. The digression of verses 13 f. is puzzling, because Paul's relatively simple earlier statements about Christ and Adam (I Cor. 15:21 f. and 45 ff.) seem needlessly complicated by the introduction of the ideas of sin and the law. Yet Paul introduces the complication because he is not satisfied to see the human problem as one of mortality and its solution as resurrection or the assurance of eternal life. The intrusion of sin and the law, which are integrally related to death (I Cor. 15:56), render the human problem more complex. Death for Paul is not simply the termination of all vital bodily functions. Instead death follows from man's sinfulness and ultimately negates and condemns human life; in turn, man's sin is accentuated rather than removed by the law (Rom. 3:20). Over against this knowledge of man's hopeless plight in oppression and bondage Paul places the assurance of God's all-sufficient grace in Jesus Christ. This power, effective for man in the righteous obedience of Jesus, frees him from the oppressive and enslaving bondage of sin, death, and law. Against the triumvirate of sin, death, and law are arrayed righteousness, life, and grace. As through one man, Adam, man was bound, so in one man, Jesus, man is set free. If condemnation and death could follow from one man's disobedience, then freedom and life can follow from one man's obedience.

The rather complicated juxtaposition of ideas in 5:12–21 results from Paul's recognition of death as the ultimate threat to human life, together with sin as the ultimate problem of human life, and his conviction that the two are interrelated. Man's problem is not just that he dies, but that he dies in a state of rebellion against his creator and in alienation from his fellow man. Thus his dying is death indeed. His plight is not helped, but worsened, by the law, which tells him what to do, but cannot give him the power to do it. Thus not only death but sin and dying in sin becomes man's fate, without God's ceasing to hold him responsible for his waywardness. Man is at the same time responsible for his existence and trapped in it. Paul may have thought that man's physical death was the result of Adam's sin, an idea that was current in his day; however, that death which enters human life through Adam's sin represents final condemnation before God. Similarly for Paul life is more than endless existence; life is that final blessedness whose essence is righteous—that is, being accounted as righteous before God.

Paul has just testified that the man who is accounted righteous by faith can live in grace with confidence about his ultimate destiny (5:1–11). Now he declares that those powers that oppressed man are overcome (5:12–21). Thus the rejoicing and reigning of the justified (see 5:2, 3, 11; 5:17) are not a fancy excess of the imagination, but a genuine, palpable reality. Whether this assertion can be maintained in the face of life's hard facts and whether conditions have actually changed so that the power of sin, law, and death are overcome is the fundamental question to which Paul next addresses himself (chaps. 6, 7, and 8).

This entire section (chaps. 5–8) is the center and heart of Romans, for here Paul sets forth and describes "this grace in which we stand" (5:2). Chapter 5 dealt with this new state in a more or less general way. Now chapters 6–8 take up specific problems and objections, phrased by Paul in the form of a battery of questions that punctuate these chapters: "Are we to continue in sin that grace may abound?" (6:1). "Are we to sin because we are not under the law but under grace?" (6:15). "Do you not know . . .

that the law is binding on a person only during his life?" (7:1). "What then shall we say? That the law is sin?" (7:7). "Did that which is good, then, bring death to me?" (7:13). "Wretched man that I am, who will deliver me from this body of death?" (7:24). "What shall we say to this? If God is for us, who is against us?" (8:31). "Who shall separate us from the love of Christ?" (8:35). From these questions the reader may correctly infer that chapter 6 deals with the new life under grace and the problem of sin; chapter 7 with the newly found freedom from the oppression of the law; and chapter 8 with freedom from death and the ground of the Christian's hope.

FREEDOM FROM SIN (6:1–23)

In chapter 6 Paul poses a problem that probably had already been raised by others. If the man in Christ receives grace in proportion to the sin that must be overcome (5:20 f.), why should he not go on sinning in order to increase the supply of grace? Paul understands the question, but not the motivation of the questioner (6:2 f.). The grace of God in Jesus Christ is indeed freedom (6:15 ff.; cf. Gal. 4–5), but freedom *from* sin, not freedom *for* sin. Paul understands sin as an oppressive and finally fatal enemy of mankind, a bondage and a burden. Therefore, he declares that baptism, understood as dying and rising with Christ, is a dying to sin and a rising to "newness of life." Paul thus takes the concept of dying and rising with the object of one's religious devotion—Christ—and interprets it ethically. It becomes the basis of the new and reformed life. Such dying and rising with the cult deity was a common and characteristic motif of the mystery religions. Paul, however, has radically reinterpreted this rite. He relates the cultic act to a concrete, recent historical event, the death of Jesus, and draws ethical implications from it.

A question repeatedly implied, if not explicitly stated (3:31) in Paul's discussion so far involves the place of the law. Yet Paul's statements about the law seem to contradict one another. On the one hand, he obviously takes the law (that is, the Jewish law as contained in the Old Testament) to be the definitive expression of God's will for the ordering of human life (Rom. 2; 3:31). On the other, he maintains that the law does not enable man to escape the sinful and death-oriented existence into which he casts and in which he finds himself (cf. 3:20; 4:15; 5:13, 20). Moreover, as we see in chapter 7, the law itself becomes an oppressive factor in man's plight.

FREEDOM FROM THE LAW (7:1–25)

Paul begins his extended discussion of the law by describing how death sets aside a former legal obligation (7:1–6). The marriage analogy that

Paul introduces in verses 1–3 is not completely appropriate for the point he wants to make and, therefore, must not be pressed. What Paul says here makes sense when we see that his argument is simply that a legal obligation is set aside by means of a death. Therefore, as the law binding a woman to a man is set aside by his death, so the law to which men formerly owed allegiance is set aside through dying with Christ (7:4).

The subsequent discussion of the law (vss. 7–25) ought to be understood in the light of the basic fact that death sets aside the law. Why should this fact be so important to Paul? This long excursus answering the question of whether the law is sin implies the prior question of why man must die to the law, or, conversely, why he may not be saved by it. Why does not life, in the pregnant sense of the word, result from keeping the law? The Jew believed that it did, and Paul himself had once believed it. Because his own view of law had been so radically reversed, however, he had a great deal at stake in showing that death cancels law. After having shown this (vss. 1–6), he could proceed to explain why the law cannot bring about the life it intends. This he does in verses 7–25. Paul's question (7:7) introduces this explanation. In order to maintain his position and avoid the charge of antinomianism, he must answer in such a way as to maintain the integrity of the law (3:31), but at the same time refuse to concede that the law in the present situation can rescue man from his predicament. Whether he successfully does this is a matter that the reader will have to decide, but in this connection a few points need elucidation.

The example of how the law makes sin known and stimulates it to action (7:7) is taken from the tenth commandment, "You shall not covet" (Exodus 20:17; Deuteronomy 5:21). In the Greek translation, which Paul quotes, the word "covet" also has the broader meaning of desire. So Paul's use of this commandment as an example is probably not accidental. He implies that the law inflames desire, a root cause of sin, rather than conquering it. Nevertheless, this is not the fault of the law, but of sin (7:8 ff.). Here again is the concept of sin as a power working upon and even in man from without. The medium and victim of sin's pernicious working is the flesh (vss. 14 ff.). One might think that by "flesh" Paul refers to the material side of man as contrasted with the spiritual (cf. 8:1–11 for the explicit contrast of flesh and spirit). Therefore, man would sin because he has a body, with all its instincts and urges. Yet this is not what Paul means. The matter is much more complex. Paul can speak of the mind or mind-set of the flesh (literal translation of 8:7; in Col. 2:18 "sensuous mind" is really "mind of the flesh") and living according to the flesh (8:12). Moreover, he baldly asserts that those who are in the flesh cannot please God (8:8). On the basis of the above interpretation this would suggest that one must die, and thus forsake this fleshly life, in order to please God. Yet on the heels of this Paul can tell his readers, who presumably are not ghosts, that they are not in the flesh (8:9) but in the

Spirit. For Paul flesh and spirit are not two parts of man, but two possibilities of existence. They are two realms, two dominions; a person may live in one or the other.[13] There is a sense in which one must "die" and thus forsake the flesh in order to please God. This dying is not, however, a physical death, but a dying with Christ to the enslavement of sin.

Looking back now to Paul's discussion of the law (7:7–25), we see that sin's perversion of the law takes place because man is under the power of sin which works in his flesh (7:14). Yet this flesh is not simply to be equated with the physical side of his being any more than is the body of death from which man yearns to be free (7:24). Sin has laid claim upon the intangible as well as the tangible aspects of man's life. When Paul says that "nothing good dwells within me, that is, in my flesh" (7:18), he is not qualifying the first assertion by the second (". . . that is, in my flesh"), but defining it. The "me" he speaks of here is fleshly man, man in Adam, as contrasted with man in Christ. This man knows that the law is good, but he cannot keep it. His life is a conflict between what he intends and what he actually accomplishes (7:13 ff., 21 ff.). Entrapped under sin and flesh, the law only adds to his torment, because in his very hearing of the law he disobeys it and is led further into sin. So, although the law continues to be holy and just and good (7:12), for the man "under the law" in the specifically Pauline sense it is fatal (vss. 11, 13).

But how does this perversion of the law by sin come about? In this regard 7:7–12 is of some help, especially if we are right in suggesting that Paul chose his example from the law (7:7) with deliberate forethought. Yet one aspect of Paul's thought regarding the relation of sin and the law is not made explicit here—the law, when misappropriated by sinful man, becomes the occasion for boasting. Faith in Christ, or what Paul calls the obedience of faith (literal translation of 1:5), is the antithesis of works of the law and boasting (3:27 ff. and chap. 4; cf. Rom. 9:30 ff.; 10:3 ff.; Phil. 3:4–11). The intrinsic character of the righteousness that seeks to establish itself by works is self-defeating. Such righteousness contradicts that submission to God that is the indispensable prerequisite to obedience, because, as Paul understands the matter, it is fundamentally self-seeking and therefore still rebellious. Paul never questions the goodness of the law itself. He does inveigh against "works of the law"—that is, the misuse of the law to the end of self-righteousness and boasting.

It may seem that the central problem of 7:7–25 has so far been ignored.

---

[13] Paul can also relegate religious acts and attitudes to the realm of the flesh, as in Philippians 3:4–6, where he refers to his own Jewish background as "reason for confidence in the flesh" (vs. 4). Moreover, the Judaizer's demand that the Galatian Christians accept circumcision is to be traced to their desire to make a show in the flesh (6:12 f.). Here the two-fold connotation of "flesh" is apparent: on the one hand, the physical substance of the body (II Cor. 12:7), on the other, a way of life (Gal. 3:3). "Flesh" can also be a way of referring to mankind, in the style of the Old Testament (cf. Rom. 3:20, where RSV's "no human being" translates what is literally "no flesh").

What about the fact that Paul everywhere speaks in the first person singular and even in the present tense? Is he, as we might at first think, recounting his own present experience, or does 7:9 indicate that he is speaking of his earlier life as a Jew under the law? Or, is it possible that by "I" Paul does not really refer to himself at all? In the language of Paul's time "I" did not necessarily mean the speaker or writer personally, but could mean man generally ("one," the German *man*; or the French *on*). Paul uses the first person pronoun in some such sense in I Corinthians 13, where the "I" includes himself but is not necessarily limited to Paul personally. Moreover, in spite of a long history of interpretation that sees Paul grappling with his own inadequacy and sin in 7:7–25, nothing in the context or in Paul's letters generally indicates that he had such a pessimistic view of his own possibilities *in Christ.* Quite the contrary. And it is far from clear that this is even a passing moment or phase of his consciousness. That the passage refers back to his conscious experience as a Jew is not borne out by Phillippians 3:4 ff. and other passages (especially Gal. 1:14) where Paul talks about his earlier life. At those points at which Paul is clearly talking about his past he does not indicate that he was anxious or depressed.[14]

LIFE IN THE SPIRIT (8:1–39)

If, however, we may understand Romans 7:7–25 as a description of the way sin works through the law, rather than an autobiographical confession or reminiscence, the problem of how to fit such despair (cf. especially 7:14) into Paul's personal experience disappears. Paul is analyzing law, sin, and existence under their dominion, rather than portraying his own state of mind. The opening verses of chapter 8 bear out this latter interpretation, for there the reverse of the situation described in chapter 7 is presented as typical of Paul and his brothers in Christ. For them a great revolution has occurred.

> For the law of the spirit of life in Christ Jesus has set me free from the law of sin and death. For God has done what the law, weakened by the flesh, could not do: sending his own son in the likeness of sinful flesh and for sin, he condemned sin in the flesh, in order that the just requirement of the law might be fulfilled in us, who walk, not according to the flesh but according to the Spirit (8:2–4).

[14] Romans 7:7–25 only seems to contradict this when read as an autobiographical account of *past* experience. Actually, verse 15a translated literally makes clear that Paul is not describing a conscious state of affairs: "I do not know what I am bringing about." The RSV translation of verse 15a, however, implies that the subject does know what he is bringing about, but cannot understand why he is doing it. Cf. R. Bultmann, "Romans 7 and the Anthropology of Paul," trans. S. M. Ogden, *Existence and Faith: Shorter Writings of Rudolf Bultmann* (New York: Meridian Press, 1960), pp. 147–57, especially p. 155.

Life is no longer dominated and defined by flesh, sin, law, and death—that is, by the old man Adam—but by Spirit, righteousness, grace, and life— that is, by the new man Christ. God himself has brought about this revolution in the human estate. The Spirit is God's Spirit. (Paul also speaks of the Spirit of Christ, and does not distinguish carefully between them; in verse 9 he refers in the same breath to the Spirit of God and the Spirit of Christ.) The conviction that God has acted decisively on man's behalf in the historical appearance of Jesus as the Christ leads Paul to encourage his fellow Christians. He speaks of the Spirit and its assuring role (vss. 16, 23, 26 f.), of the hope that lies ahead (vss. 18–25), and of the invincible plan and purpose of God (vss. 28–30), grounded in God's love (vss. 28, 35, 37, 39). With the magnificent peroration of verses 35–39, Paul ends this central section of his letter, having shown how the revelation of God's grace as righteousness in Christ has brought about a truly new situation in which the bondage of the old age has been broken and the promise of a new age is finding fulfillment.

Paul thinks it important that the knowledge of this new reality is given in and by the Spirit. He speaks frequently of the work of the Spirit, especially in Roman 8. The term itself translates the Greek *pneuma*, which like the Hebrew *ruach*, can also mean "wind" or "breath." Accordingly, in the Old Testament and earliest Christianity the appearance of the Spirit implied the advent of extraordinary divine power (cf. Acts 2 and the discussion in chapter 6 above; also I Cor. 14). Usually Paul means by "spirit" the Spirit of God or Christ, although he also uses the word in a somewhat more general sense of the human faculty (body, soul, and spirit), and it is sometimes difficult to know whether one should speak of spirit with a small or capital letter. For Paul the Lord is the Spirit (II Cor. 3:17); that is, he does not differentiate precisely between the risen Lord Jesus Christ and his Spirit. The Spirit is his and God's active and supporting presence in the individual believer and the whole community. As such, the Spirit is also the first fruits (Rom. 8:23) and guaranty (II Cor. 1:22; 5:5) of the salvation that lies just ahead. Early Christian thought took up the Jewish idea that the Spirit of God, absent since the cessation of Old Testament prophecy, would appear again in the last days (cf. Acts 2:16 ff.), and Paul's concept of the Spirit is based upon this traditional view. Probably Paul's own chief contribution to Christian thinking about the Spirit is his belief that the Spirit is both the life-giving power and the ethical norm of the believer's life (Gal. 5:25). Those who live in or by the Spirit live out of God's resources rather than their own and are able to break free from the power of the flesh, that is, the fate of human existence estranged from God ("the law of sin and death" of Rom. 8:2), and to attain life (Rom. 8:9–11). Paul's comprehensive view of the functioning of the Spirit allows him to understand the Christian's whole life in terms of the Spirit (Rom. 8:3–8) and its gifts (I Cor. 12–14, esp. 12:4–11; cf. Gal. 5:22 f.). Thus, he can also think of men's spirits as attuned to God's Spirit (Rom. 8:16) and of Christians as "spiritual" in this sense (Gal. 6:1). To sum up, with respect to the divine activity, the life of faith made possible by Christ can be thought of by Paul as the work of the Spirit.

God's Faithfulness (9:1–11:36)

Does God act arbitrarily in history?
Will the faithfulness of God embrace the people of Israel?

With the coming of the new age in Christ (cf. II Cor. 5:16–21) and the consequent fulfillment of God's promises in the new Christian community a serious question is raised about the promises of God to the old community, Israel. Paul never understands the Christian faith as a new religion founded by Jesus of Nazareth. Rather he sees the event of Christ's coming within the framework of a larger history of interaction between God and people which centers in Israel and is recorded in the Hebrew scriptures (Old Testament). For him the question now revolves about that history and those promises. Were they meaningless and are they now null and void?

Before Paul seriously tackles this question he makes clear by way of introduction (9:1–5) his abiding kinship with the Jewish people. He assumes, however, that the Jews have not, for the most part, accepted Jesus as the Messiah; thus they remain outside the circle of Christian faith (vss. 1–3). This situation is the crux of the problem with which Paul wrestles in Romans 9–11. Paul will not write off his kinsmen, nor will he concede that God has written them off. Although Paul discounts his own Jewish religious pedigree and accomplishments because of Christ (Phil. 3:7), he is not willing to discount the distinctive position of Israel as a people before God (9:4 f.; cf. 3:1 ff.). Apart from other considerations, Christ himself was by birth a Jew (9:5).

Yet not Paul's own feelings, nor his high esteem for the gifts God bestowed on Israel, nor even the fact that Jesus was a Jew are the primary considerations for Paul. His fundamental reason for regarding the given situation as a problem has to do with God, not Israel. For if the word of God has in fact failed, if God has simply cancelled out his promises, then everything that has been said by Paul up to this point is called into question, for God's righteousness is then jeopardized by his unfaithfulness (9:6). Paul will not countenance such blasphemy (cf. 3:3 ff.). If God were unjust (9:14), the note of supreme confidence struck in chapter 8 would be undermined. To put it bluntly, if God had reneged on his promises to Israel, how could the Christian be certain that He would not change his mind again? At stake is nothing less than the validity of the promises of God and by implication the character of God as righteous deliverer. For if the promises of God are revocable, then how can one have faith in his righteous judgment on man's behalf in Jesus Christ? Paul now turns to the questions of the faithfulness and righteousness of God in history (cf. Rom. 3:1–8). Romans 9–11 is not an appendix dealing with a question that, even to most of Paul's contemporaries, was peripheral. Rather, in order for the gospel to make sense, Paul must show that God's faithfulness vindicates itself in history.

Paul meets the implied charge that the word of God has failed in four different ways. In the first place, he argues that God's promise is based on the principle of election (9:5–26). Moreover, this election-based promise is not automatically passed down from one generation to the next, but is a dynamic process in history by which God continues to call and to choose (9:6b–13). From verse 18 it might appear that Paul thought God somewhat capricious in this respect. Indeed, in verse 19 ff. he seems to defend that capriciousness. Yet here Paul grounds election in a prior faith in God as Creator and Lord of creation (vss. 20 ff.), for what Paul ultimately has in view is not God's arbitrary rigor, but his mercy (vss. 22 ff.). Moreover, the rejection of large numbers of the sons of Israel is predicted by the prophets Hosea and Isaiah (vss. 25–29). Thus God himself has declared that it must occur.

In the second place, sufficient grounds for the rejection of Israel can be found in her own misguided effort to please God. In 9:30–10:4 Paul clarifies the concept of the righteousness of God. Because Israel has not understood that God's righteousness is to be received by faith (9:30 ff.), she has sought to establish her own by works (10:3). But Paul insists that God's righteousness is just that, God's. It cannot be earned. God pronounces man righteous and thus brings him into the right before himself through the cross of Jesus. Christ becomes "our righteousness" (I Cor. 1:30), and in the apostles' preaching the cross of Jesus is made known as the revelation of God's righteousness (1:16 f.; cf. I. Cor. 1:18 ff.). The effort to establish one's own righteousness means that man refuses the gift of God and seeks to promote his own piety or morality. If he is successful, or imagines that he is, the result is "boasting" (3:27), and what later Christian thought understood as that prideful self-seeking that lies at the root of sin. The right response to God's righteousness is faith, specifically faith in Jesus, who has come as the Messiah. But this faith is also the prerequisite for fulfillment of the law (cf. vss. 31 f.), for the law cannot be fulfilled by those who through it seek to establish their own righteousness. Christ is indeed the "end of the law" (vs. 4), but not in the sense that he simply sets it aside (3:31). Rather he is the one toward whom the law leads (Gal. 3:24). He terminates the law in that he brings to an end the effort of man to secure his own righteousness as a possession or quality through "works of the law." Thus he puts an end to the law as an occasion for boasting.

Israel thus brings reprobation upon herself (9:30–10:4; cf. 3:3 f.). To make clear that the responsibility rests fully upon Israel, not God, Paul contends that Israel has in fact heard the preaching of the gospel and rejected it (10:5–21, especially 14–21). He drives home this point, not by making specific references to the preaching of good news to the Jews, as he certainly could have, but by once again referring to scripture (10:18–20).

So far Paul has assumed the unbelief of Israel as the state of affairs calling for an explanation. Beginning with chapter 11, however, Paul's argument takes a new tack as he makes his third point. To the question of whether God has rejected his people Paul now says no. He himself is an Israelite (11:1). The example of Elijah (vss. 2–4) serves to show that Paul is not alone: "So too at the present time there is a remnant, chosen by grace" (vs. 5). Paul combines Isaiah's concept of the remnant with the idea of election already set forth in chapter 9 and his own understanding of the gospel as God's grace. Actually what Paul says here fits very well with the election doctrine of chapter 9. God's grace in Jesus Christ becomes the point at which the process of election in history takes another step forward, while the remnant from Israel provides continuity with the Old Testament people of God. So far, Paul's exposition of the way God works in history does not differ in principle from the Old Testament and Jewish understanding, or at least his interpretation of it. God elects not according to national, ethnic, or familial principles, however, but according to his own free choice. The only unhappy aspect of this doctrine is that God's election seems to work through a process of elimination, whereby the number of the elect becomes progressively fewer —not exactly a happy outcome except in view of the consideration that God could have elected to save no one at all.

But then the discussion takes another decisive and surprising turn (11:11). The outcome is not what we might have been led to expect, but decidedly more hopeful. Paul now expounds his expectation of God's continuing work in history for the salvation of mankind, Jew as well as Greek (vss. 11–32). The salvation of the Gentiles is to make the Jews jealous and thus to bring them back into the fold.

How seriously one can take this as a view of history is at least a legitimate question. For one thing, Paul did not anticipate an indefinite continuation of world history, even as late as the time of the composition of Romans (13:11 f.). He thought history was coming rapidly to a close. Furthermore, time has not produced the sequence of events that Paul anticipated. The conversion of the Gentiles does not seem to be complete—although "the full number of the Gentiles" (vs. 25) may not mean every Gentile. Moreover, there is not yet any indication of the conversion of

Israel. Paul's image of the olive tree (vss. 17–24; cf. Jeremiah 11:16) provides a graphic picture of his understanding of Gentile Christianity's relationship to contemporary Judaism, represented by the natural branches, and to the true Israel of God of the Old Testament, represented by the root of the tree. The olive tree itself is apparently the new universal people of God intended to comprise both Jew and Greek. Yet this picture ought not to be interpreted as Paul's attempt to predict the future; instead we have here an affirmation of the ultimate fulfillment of God's purposes among men.

Accordingly, Paul here gives expression to an important paradox of Christian faith, which he himself neatly summarizes: "For God has consigned all men to disobedience, that he may have mercy upon all" (11:32). This astounding statement is neither a passing thought nor a means of easing a difficult predicament into which Paul's argument has led him (cf. the occurrence of the same basic idea elsewhere, notably in 5:20 and Gal. 3:22). Even in the extremity of his severity, God's purpose, the end and goal of his activity, is mercy. This paradox is a

This wall is part of the original wall of Herod that enclosed the temple area. Known as the "Wailing Wall," it has become sacred to adherents of Judaism. (Courtesy of Israel Information Services.)

348 The Early Church and Paul

close corollary of Paul's proclamation of justification by grace alone. In the history of peoples, as of individuals, God's saving activity is grace, surpassing and contradicting human expectations and hopes, appearing where least expected and on behalf of the ungodly (4:5). For Paul, the ungodly are in the end all mankind, "for God has consigned all men to disobedience, that he might have mercy upon all."

The final paragraph of this chapter and of this section of Romans is a confession in almost hymnic form (vss. 33–36). The last verses (34–36) are not self-congratulatory. After having pointed out the mystery of the ways of God (vs. 33), Paul is not now letting the reader know how difficult they were to discover and, by implication, how unique and privileged is his knowledge of them. He intends, of course, to comment on the truly incredible character of God's mercy as its pattern has emerged in history. But over and above that Paul wishes to emphasize the continuing mystery, which his elaboration has only partly exhausted. Nevertheless, verse 32 implies Paul's conviction that he has received the key to God's dealing with men, not only in his own times, but in all times. The seeming triumph of iniquity in the human race is deceptive. The complete revelation, which is God's to give, is not yet completely disclosed. Because Paul understands the fundamental character, intention, and goal of God's working in history, he makes bold to suggest the theological significance of the acceptance of the gospel by the Gentiles while it is being rejected by the majority of his fellow Jews. Yet Paul's faith is not in his own theological exposition of history, but in the God who makes his mercy known in Christ: "For from him and through him and to him are all things. To him be glory forever. Amen."

The Obedience of Faith (12:1–15:13)

What are the practical, ethical implications of the gospel for Christians? Are there familiar elements in the ethical exhortations of chapters 12–15?

The final major division in the structure of Romans occurs after the hymn of praise (11:33–36) that concludes Paul's discussion of the destiny of Israel. With general exhortation (12:1–2) Paul then introduces a series of ethical instructions that concludes at 15:13. The character of this long "ethical" section and its relation to what precedes can best be grasped by looking closely at the introductory exhortation.

Addressing the Roman Christians as brethren, Paul bases his appeal on the "mercies of God." The most likely clue to the meaning of this term is to be found in the word "therefore," which suggests that Paul grounds what he now proposes to say in what has gone before. The extended theological discussion of chapters 1–11 might then be understood as an exposition of "the mercies of God," in the sense of the merciful activity of God on behalf of sinful and wayward man.[15] Paul is basing his ethical exhortations on the prior claim that God has on Christians by virtue of the grace shown them in Jesus Christ. The theological indicative ("what God has done for you") becomes the ground for the ethical imperative ("what you must do for God through your fellow man"), and this is altogether characteristic of Paul's thought (cf. esp. Rom. 6). This interpretation of the mercies of God also suggests that Paul is picking up in 12:1 the theme of mercy from 11:32: "For God has consigned all men to disobedience, that he may have mercy upon all." Admittedly, the Greek term in 12:1 is not identical with that in 11:32 (despite the English translation); nevertheless, the basic idea is the same.

The problem of the relation of 12:1–2 to what precedes does not seem as difficult as the interpretation of the text itself. "To present your bodies as a living sacrifice" and "spiritual worship" are difficult phrases. Here as previously (cf. 3:21 ff.), Paul appropriates the language of the sacrificial cultus at a crucial point of his exposition. Obviously, the sacrificial language cannot be taken literally, for it is quite clear that Paul is not talking about a material sacrifice when he speaks of "spiritual worship." Yet Paul is talking about a bodily commitment or offering to God in response to his mercy in Jesus Christ. By the sacrifice of the body Paul means the surrender of the self, most particularly that self that has heretofore been subjected to sin, flesh, and death (cf. 8:9–11; 7:21–25). Thus the sacrificial language is quite appropriate when understood in terms of "spiritual worship."

In verse 2 Paul introduces that tension between present and future which is characteristic of early Christian eschatology. The RSV's alternative translation, "Do not be conformed to this *age*," is almost surely more accurate than "this *world*," although Paul can speak of "this world" in an eschatological sense (I Cor. 7:31). The Greek word is best translated "age": "world" is a possible translation, but it is misleading here unless one understands that it means "this world which is passing away." The eschatological thrust of Paul's statement has been aptly summarized as follows:

> Since the life, death, and resurrection of Jesus, "this age" can no longer be the regulative principle of life for those who have died and been raised with Jesus (6:3 ff.). *In Christ* they have entered the new age; already they have received the first-fruits of the Spirit (8:23), and are under obligation not to the flesh but to the Spirit (8:12). In the present verse Paul expresses this truth in new terms.[16]

[15] Barrett, A *Commentary on the Epistle to the Romans*, p. 230.
[16] *Ibid.*, p. 232.

Paul warns his readers not to be schematized (the English cognate of the Greek word which Paul actually uses) according to the pattern of this old age, but to be metamorphosed (literally, changed in form or shape; again the English derivative of Paul's Greek) by the *renewal* of the mind. The mind here evidently means both man's knowing and willing faculties. "Prove" is to be understood in the sense of "try and approve" (Cf. Paul's use of the same term in 2:18 and 14:22, where it is translated "approve" and in I Cor. 3:13, where it is rendered "test.") "What is the will of God . . . good, acceptable and perfect" is to be tested and proved in the doing of the deed as well as in contemplating it. What is the will of God, of course, agrees perfectly with what is good and acceptable and perfect. For Paul, that goes without saying.

Thus 12:1–2 forms the connecting link between Paul's long theological discourse in chapters 1–11 and the ethical exhortations of chapters 12–15. These exhortations are of a general and more or less stereotyped nature, and do not necessarily reflect Paul's own first-hand knowledge of the situation among the Christians in Rome. Doubtless they indicate the state of Paul's own thinking and perhaps to a considerable degree the problems that he encountered in other churches. Probably also they contain certain pre-Pauline traditional materials.

The use of the image of the body to illumine the relation of Christians to one another and to Christ (12:3–8) recalls the earlier and more extensive elaboration of this image in I Corinthians 12. The paragraph 12:9–13 is simply a continuation of the preceding section. The general ethical injunctions of 12:14–21 recall the Old Testament, and verse 20 the words of Jesus (Matt. 5:44 and Luke 6:27). Yet in verse 20 Paul seems actually to be quoting directly from Proverbs 25:21 f. rather than giving Jesus' own words. This accounts for the inclusion of the "burning coals" clause, which is not found in Jesus' saying. The discussion of the governing authorities in 13:1–7 is strikingly similar to I Peter 2:13–17 and, if I Peter is not dependent upon Romans, probably indicates the existence of a common viewpoint and tradition regarding the relation of the church to worldly authority (cf. II Thess. 2:6, which may refer to the Roman government or the emperor; I Tim. 2:1–2; Tit. 3:1). In 13:7 we may see a dim reflection of the word of Jesus of Mark 12:17. But although this verse seems to summarize the teaching of the famous pericope of Mark 12:13–17, it is by no means certain that Paul had this story before him, or even in mind, when he wrote. Similarly, 13:8–10 evokes Mark 10:19 and especially 12:31, but without conforming closely enough to suggest any direct dependence. The eschatology of 13:11 ff. is quite Pauline (cf. I Cor. 7:31; I Thess. 4:13–18), as is the manner in which eschatology and ethics are combined (cf. 12:2). Chapter 14 continues the ethical reflections about the Christian's responsibility to his brother which we have already studied in I Corinthians 8 and 10. In 15:1–3, as he is bringing his exhortations to a close, Paul introduces the example of Christ himself (Phil. 2:5–11; cf. I Pet. 2:21; Mark 8:34; 10:38 ff.). The principle of Old Testament interpretation enunciated in verse 4 is stated more extensively in I Corinthians 9:8–10; 10:6, 11; and II Corinthians 3. In verses 5, 6, and 13 Paul's exhortation becomes almost a benediction or prayer. Paul introduces the subject of the Gentile mission by means of Old Testament quotations in 15:7–13, and is thus preparing the way for the exposition of his own missionary accomplishments and plan in 15:14–33. Chapter 16 is an appendix containing personal greetings, if it is not actually a separate letter that was added to the original, or to an early copy of Paul's letter, by an editor.

The hortatory chapters of Romans may seem somewhat anticlimactic after the theological and rhetorical pinnacle reached by Paul at the end of chapter 11. These chapters are not merely perfunctory admonitions, however, notwithstanding the fact that a concluding hortatory section is a stylistic characteristic of Paul's letters. Faith for Paul is not abandonment of moral responsibility, but the only real way of obedience to God (Rom. 1:6; 15:18). As he stresses again and again in Romans, faith in Christ does not overthrow the law, but rather upholds it. Paul has absolutely no tolerance for a Christianity that is morally lax or indifferent. Such a version of the faith would be as much "another gospel" or "no gospel" as the legalism of the Judaizers in Galatia. Thus the concrete ethical exhortations and advice in Romans 12:1–15:13 are entirely in accord with—in fact, the outgrowth of—Paul's fundamental theological stance. The gospel must elicit a faithful response that is obedience in God. Yet obedience in some vague or general sense is not enough. The obedience of faith must have specific relevance for the actual situations of life, otherwise it is vain and empty.

Throughout this chapter we have been endeavoring to understand Romans; now let us attempt to draw some threads together. The specific *historical occasion* of Romans can no longer be known with exactitude, although clearly it was written after the resolution of the Corinthian crisis and before Paul's subsequent arrest in Jerusalem. Paul himself indicates that he had in mind further missionary work in the West, beyond Rome (15:22 ff.). Evidently he sought at least the good wishes of the Roman church in this endeavor. To this end he wrote the letter to the Romans, preparing them for his forthcoming visit and further travels. The letter serves as a kind of theological introduction to Paul, and this is probably the purpose for which it was originally intended.

Perhaps in Romans more than in any other letter, Paul is in conversation and debate with his Jewish heritage and theological background. Not surprisingly then, Paul makes a concerted effort to do justice to his traditional roots, both Jewish and Jewish Christian. Thus we find a considerable amount of traditional material embedded in Romans, of which 1:2–4 and 3:24–26, as well as much of the hortatory materials of chapters 13–15, afford good examples. Yet one cannot make much headway separating *tradition* from *redaction* in Romans, for Paul is more likely to pick up traditional language and concepts than to use extended sources. Moreover, such traditional materials or concepts as he adopts have been well assimilated to his thought. It is more profitable simply to ask what Paul was thinking or what he intended. Although there are real difficulties of interpretation, the broad outlines of his thought are pretty clearly discernible from the structure and emphases of Romans.

The *structure* of Romans is more like a theological argument than any other book in the New Testament. It really has to be studied in its entirety to be understood, for one part relates to, or is built upon another. After a long introduction, in which the themes of the letter are set forth, Paul gives an extensive account of the human condition. He concludes that sin has pervaded the entire human race and left all men, Jews as well as Gentiles, in need of redemption (1:18–3:20). Paul then turns to the sacrificial and saving death of Jesus (3:21–26) and to the necessity of faith as the only way the benefits of that death can be gained. Abraham is brought forth as the prime example and the confirmation of the saving efficacy of faith: "Abraham believed God, and it was reckoned to him as righteousness" (Rom. 4:3; cf. Genesis 15:6).

The beginning of chapter 5 marks a turning point in the letter. Paul shifts from an argumentative to a confessional style, and from the second and third persons to the first. Chapters 5 through 8 are concerned with the question of whether and how the conditions under which man exists have been changed by Christ's coming. According to Paul, the Christian lives a new life in this old world, even before his salvation has fully arrived, and while the world continues to decay. He is able to overcome sin (chap 6); he is no longer under the law he cannot fulfill (chap 7); and he is full of the Spirit of life and free from death (chap. 8). Thus in chapters 5 through 8 Paul spells out the nature and effects of "this grace in which we stand" (5:2).

Chapters 9 through 11 are concerned with the question of God's faithfulness to his promises to Israel, which has been lurking in the background since 3:3 f. If there are present indications that the man of faith lives in a promising new situation, what is the prospect that the promise held out to him will in fact be realized? This is a pressing question, because on Paul's own terms Israel does not seem to be inheriting the promise. If God has been faithless with Israel, can he be counted on to be faithful to the Christian church? Yet it is not God, but Israel, who has defected on the terms of the promise. Moreover, Paul maintains that at length even a wayward Israel will return to God's favor and be saved.

As we have just seen, the final major section of the letter is devoted to spelling out the meaning of Christian faith for life's various circumstances (12:1–15:13). Paul scarcely strives for comprehensiveness, but rather lays down guidelines and directions, often relying on earlier and traditional formulations. Thereafter, Paul gives us an insight into his own view of his ground-breaking apostolic work, and sketches out his own plans to visit Rome and eventually to go to Spain (15:14–33). The letter ends with sundry words of personal greeting and a final general exhortation (chap. 16).

What are the principal *emphases* of Romans? These should already be apparent from our study of the text and its structure, but perhaps they can now be more succinctly stated. Romans concerns the meaning of the event of the Messiah's coming, particularly the fact of his death and the faith that he is risen. The Christ event sheds light backward, so to speak, to show the enormity of human sin, and forward to show the possible boundlessness of human freedom and life under grace. Paul carries on his discussion against the background of problems and assumptions arising out of his Jewish heritage. Thus the meaning of Christ is not discussed in abstraction, nor over against the problems of human existence in general, but with the history of Judaism and her understanding of God and man in view. The principal question arising out of that heritage in the light of the revelation of God's righteousness and wrath in Christ is how can sinful man be accounted righteous before God. Paul accepts this question as fundamental, but answers it in a new way. For Judaism the righteousness of God is to be attained or fulfilled by works of the law, good works. For Paul, the righteousness of God is revealed in Jesus Christ; it is an action and pronouncement of God. God bestows his righteousness upon man freely. Thus he shows himself to be a righteous and gracious God. Man, in turn, must show himself to be faithful. This means, first of all, that he must believe in what God has done—that is, believe in Jesus Christ. But this belief is not intellectual assent in the abstract. It must find expression in a new life. In a sense the possibility and power of the new life is already given. Still, it must be received and lived out. Paul not only speaks to his hearers in the indicative mood to tell them what God has done, he also appeals to them in the imperative mood to make their lives conform with this new reality.

Paul seems to be relatively little interested in the historical dimensions of Jesus' ministry as we see them in the Gospels. Why is this? Many reasons have been suggested, which need not be discussed here. The most obvious, and perhaps the most important, reason, however, is that Paul was principally concerned with the *meaning* of Christ's appearance, death, and resurrection. More particularly, he was interested in the significance of Christ for the proper understanding of God, man, and their relation, especially in view of the Jewish theological heritage, which was his own personal background. Thus Romans is a thoroughly theological book, not uninvolved with Jesus' history in principle, but not much concerned with its details. Although interpreters of Romans differ rather widely on some points, most would agree that the key to its understanding is a grasp and appreciation of Paul's theological intention.

Suggestions for Further Reading

A very distinctive treatment of Paul's theology is to be found in R. Bultmann, *Theology of the New Testament,** trans. K. Grobel (2 vols.; New York: Scribner's, 1951–55), I, 185–352. The most recent work in this area is V. P. Furnish, *Theology and Ethics in Paul* (New York: Abingdon, 1968); a helpful survey of modern interpretations of Paul's ethic is included. A general treatment of Paul's thought, organized under the doctrinal headings of traditional theology, is D. E. H. Whiteley, *The Theology of St. Paul* (Philadelphia: Fortress, 1964). J. A. Fitzmyer offers a concise interpretation of Paul's theology in *Pauline Theology: A Brief Sketch** (Englewood Cliffs, N.J.: Prentice-Hall, 1967). Two important scholarly works that view Paul against his contemporary Jewish background are W. D. Davies, *Paul and Rabbinic Judaism** (rev. ed.; London: S.P.C.K., 1955; paperback, Harper Torchbook) and H. J. Schoeps, *Paul: The Theology of the Apostle in the Light of Jewish Religious History,* trans. H. Knight (Philadelphia: Westminster, 1961).

On Romans, the commentary of C. K. Barrett in the Harper series (1957) deserves to be singled out as especially useful. Also worth noting are F. J. Leenhardt, *The Epistle to the Romans, A Commentary,* trans. H. Knight (London: Lutterworth, 1961); F. F. Bruce, *The Epistle of Paul to the Romans* ("The Tyndale New Testament Commentaries"; Grand Rapids, Mich.: Eerdmans, 1963); and the important works of A. Nygren, *Commentary on Romans,* trans. C. C. Rasmussen (Philadelphia: Muhlenberg, 1949), and K. Barth, *The Epistle to the Romans,* trans. E. C. Hoskyns (6th ed.; London: Oxford University Press, 1933).

9 The Post-
Pauline Letters

Whereas the Gospel is a distinctly Christian literary form, the other New Testament books simply adapt the forms and conventions of the day. The historical narrative (Acts) has classical and Hellenistic precedents. The apocalypse (Revelation) is a Jewish phenomenon. The letter, in that day as in ours, was universally popular and necessary, but there is no immediately obvious reason why it should have been so widely adopted as a mode of Christian communication. Of the twenty-seven New Testament books, twenty-one are called letters. Probably a number of these are not really letters at all, but for some reason have been cast in that form. Not only do we have the Pauline and later New Testament letters but the seven letters of the first three chapters of the Book of Revelation, and, outside the New Testament, a first century letter from Rome to Corinth and a whole collection of letters from Ignatius, bishop of Antioch, written at the beginning of the second century. There are also a number of later noncanonical letters, some of them obviously spurious documents attributed to Paul and even to Jesus.

These letters came into existence largely because of practical necessity. But this necessity scarcely accounts for the "letters" of Revelation or the imposition of epistolary form upon a document like Hebrews, which is

355

obviously not a letter in any ordinary sense. There may be theological reasons for the widespread adoption of the letter form. The New Testament gospel is first of all a message, and the letter is the most appropriate form for the delivery of news. The letter is also the literary means of direct and personal address, so appropriate to the gospel's character. Equally important, the letter form reflects the recognition of the need for communication among Christians and churches and thus testifies to the conviction that the Body of Christ, though scattered throughout the world, is in reality one. No part, individual, or group lives or dies to itself (Rom. 14:7). Yet real as they may be, such reasons were probably not consciously considered or thought out.

Another way of accounting for such widespread adoption of the letter form would be the example and precedent that Paul set. He is the letter writer par excellence. His influence as a letter writer is attested both in the collections of his own letters and in those pseudonymous letters of the New Testament which have been explicitly or traditionally attributed to him: Hebrews, I and II Timothy, Titus, probably Ephesians, and possibly Colossians and II Thessalonians. In addition, some letters not attributed to Paul show signs of his influence—for example, I and II Peter. Even the collection of Ignatius' letters and the "letters" of the book of Revelation may have been inspired by the existence of the Pauline corpus. One thing seems certain; within a half century of his death Paul had already become a literary influence,[1] something he doubtless never anticipated or intended. So to speak of the post-Pauline letters of the New Testament is to recognize the continuing influence of Paul in the latter writings of the New Testament.

It is customary and convenient to divide these documents into two groups: (1) the deutero-Pauline—those ascribed to Paul—and (2) the Catholic Epistles—those ascribed to various persons and directed to wide areas of Christendom or to the church in general. We have already mentioned the letters ascribed to Paul. The Catholic Epistles or letters are James, I and II Peter, I, II, and III John, and Jude. The latter letters differ widely in character and literary relationships. Thus the Johannine letters stand much closer to the Fourth Gospel than to the other Catholics, whereas II Peter is more closely related to Jude than to I Peter. In this book we have reserved consideration of I, II, and III John until the final chapter on the Johannine literature, and will deal with James, I Peter, and Hebrews alongside Ephesians and the Pastorals. The reasons for this plan should become more evident as we proceed.

---

[1] Cf. the work of A. E. Barnett, *Paul Becomes a Literary Influence* (Chicago: University of Chicago Press, 1941), who shows the extent of the literary dependence of the later New Testament and other early Christian writings on Paul. A significant study of the form and style of the New Testament letter is part of R. W. Funk's recent book, *Language, Hermeneutic, and Word of God* (New York: Harper & Row, 1966), pp. 250 ff.

The Establishment and Nature of the Church

After the initial expansion and enthusiasm of the apostolic age, the interest and attention of Christians underwent a certain transformation. Contrary to the expectations of many, the disciples died away, although Jesus had not returned (cf. Mark 9:1; John 21:23). Consequently, Christians prepared to live in the present world for an indefinite period of time. Under such circumstances, it was natural that they turned their attention increasingly to reflection upon the nature of the church and to its establishment as an institution.

CHRIST AND HIS CHURCH (Eph. 2:11–22)

What is the culmination of the work of Christ?
How does the perspective of Ephesians differ from that of Paul's letters?

NOTES ON EPHESIANS

Although Ephesians certainly purports to be a letter of Paul (1:1; 3:1; 4:1), it is probably the work of a disciple of the next generation. Several considerations govern this conclusion: (1) style and language differ from the other Paulines; (2) Ephesians seems to be directly dependent upon Colossians; (3) there are certain theological divergences from the other Pauline letters.[2] The style and language of Ephesians are markedly ceremonial and liturgical in comparison with the rest of Paul. Yet Ephesians appears also to draw upon words and phrases of the other letters, especially Colossians.[3] At the same time, the theological perspective of Ephesians differs in ways we shall observe. The fact that Ephesians seems to presuppose no specific situation or audience also has some bearing upon the question of authorship. (Note that the RSV text, following the better manuscripts, does not have "at Ephesus" in 1:1). The genuine letters seem to be addressed to specific churches and concrete problems.

If Ephesians was not written by Paul, why was it written in his name? It has been suggested that Ephesians was written by a devoted disciple of Paul as a covering letter for the Pauline corpus, which he himself had collected from the various churches to which Paul had written.[4] We note that although more than half of Acts is devoted to Paul's career, the author does not mention his

---

[2] Kümmel, *Introduction to the New Testament*, pp. 252 ff.

[3] The dependence of Ephesians upon Colossians has been shown by E. J. Goodspeed, *The Key to Ephesians* (Chicago: University of Chicago Press, 1956) and C. L. Mitton, *The Epistle to the Ephesians: Its Authorship, Origin and Purpose*, (Oxford: Clarendon Press, 1951), pp. 55–97. Cf. also John Knox, *Philemon Among the Letters of Paul: A New View of its Place and Importance* (rev. ed.; New York: Abingdon Press, 1959).

[4] Goodspeed sets forth this thesis in *The Meaning of Ephesians* (Chicago: University of Chicago Press, 1933). The above proposal regarding the origin of Ephesians is in the main a summation of Goodspeed's position.

writing letters. This may well mean that Acts was written before the Pauline letters were collected and circulated. A second generation disciple of Paul could have used Acts to trace down these letters, however, since the major churches that Paul founded are indicated there. Remarkably, all of the churches to which Paul's extant letters are addressed are mentioned in Acts, with one notable exception, Colossae, and Colossians is the one document upon which the author of Ephesians seems to have relied.

Perhaps then the hypothetical second generation disciple of Paul who composed Ephesians was already familiar with Colossians, as well as the book of Acts. Perhaps he himself was from Colossae, about one hundred miles from Ephesus. If with the help of Acts he set about to collect and publish the Pauline letters and then to write a covering letter, he would likely recover the letters from the churches mentioned in Acts and in his own composition make the greatest use of the one additional letter with which he had long been familiar. It would then be natural for his own letter to be regarded in later times as intended for the one great Pauline church (Ephesus) from which no genuine letter actually survives. This would explain the existence of manuscripts with "at Ephesus" in the salutation. Although hypothetical, this is a credible account of the circumstance under which Ephesians came to be written. It takes into consideration the probability that Paul was not the author together with the fact that, as far as we know, the genuine letters never circulated as a group without Ephesians. The same cannot be said for the Pastorals or Hebrews.

Ephesians does not possess a structure that is immediately obvious. Unlike Romans, it is not a theological argument that falls into several well-defined stages. Unlike I Corinthians it does not divide itself according to a series of specific problems and questions. Ephesians has a kind of flowing movement. At least three major parts of the letter, apart from the address (1:1–2) and conclusion (6:21–24) may be discerned and separated.

Outline of Ephesians
    Address (1:1–2)
        I. Thanksgiving and Praise of God and Christ (1:3–23)
        II. Christ's Work and Its Result (2:1–3:21)·
            A. Christ's Saving Work (2:1–10)
            B. The Founding of the Church (2:11–22)
            C. Paul's Ministry (3:1–13)
            D. Prayer for the Church (3:14–21)
        III. Ethical Instructions and Exhortations (4:1–6:20)
            A. Basis for Ethics in Christ and the Church (4:1–16)
            B. General Instructions for Christians (4:17–5:20)
            C. Instructions for Families (5:21–6:9)
            D. Final Summary Exhortation (6:10–20)
    Conclusion and Benediction (6:21–24)

Part I, a hymn of praise, takes up and elaborates the characteristic Pauline thanksgiving. Whereas the typical thanksgiving makes contact with the concrete situation of the church Paul is addressing, the Ephesian thanksgiving does not. It is long, solemn, and liturgical. The thanksgiving ends with chapter one, and the second major phase of the letter begins. It is a kind of declaration or address to the readers. The author starts speaking in the second person, but more than once slips over into the confessional first person plural (cf. 2:3–7; 10).

The section 2:1–10 is a statement of the character and result of God's saving act in Jesus Christ. The Pauline language and conceptuality is clearly visible. No single passage from Paul's epistles is the source or model of this passage, but many familiar Pauline themes appear. The relationship to Romans 6 or Colossians 2:11–15 is perhaps clearest. For obvious reasons, 2:8 f. is often quoted as the most succinct statement of Pauline theology in the New Testament, and perhaps it is, even though it was probably not written by Paul. This section is to be placed alongside others (Rom. 3:21–31; 5:1–11; I Cor. 1:18–25; II Cor. 5:16–21; and Gal. 2:14–21) as a classical summation of Pauline theology.

The same solemn tone that has so far dominated the letter continues into 2:11–22, but a subtle shift of emphasis occurs. Whereas 2:1–10 deals with the work of Christ on behalf of individuals, 2:11–22 has to do with the church. Of course, in 2:1–10 the church is already in view (cf. 1:22 f.), and the individual is not lost sight of in 2:11–22. Nevertheless, in a special sense the passage in question (2:11–22) focuses upon the church. Although the word "church" does not appear, emphasis falls upon the idea of community and the creation of this community through the death of Jesus.

From 2:11 we may infer that the author speaks to a church composed of Gentiles rather than Jews. Insofar as he speaks for Paul, he takes the position of the Jew, although he may have actually been a Gentile himself. Already in this verse we read of the existence of two groups, distinguished by their circumcision or lack of circumcision in the flesh. They are both communities in and of the flesh, which at best means they are ethnic communities. As far as the author is concerned, the circumcision made in the flesh by hands does not give the circumcised any particular advantage. Yet this does not mean that Israel as God's people has no theological significance. Here the author remains quite close to Paul's own thought. Israel as an ethnic group, as the circumcision, has no particular advantage, but the same may not be said of Israel as the inheritor of God's promises. The advantage of the Jew (cf. Rom. 3:1, 9) or of Israel in the latter sense is apparent in the statement that follows immediately (vs. 12). Even the phrase "separated from Christ" implies the advantage of the Jew over the Gentile, since the Messiah is promised to Israel. To be "alienated from the commonwealth of Israel" is also to be separated from the messianic hope, as is indicated by the phrase "strangers to the covenants of promise." Obviously what is meant are the covenant promises to Israel. Notice the way Gentiles are characterized: "separated," "alienated," "strangers." Their situation is one of being alone, cut off, lost in the most profound and far-reaching sense of the word. Moreover, they are hopeless and godless. Although the author does not grant any particular advantage or significance to fleshly circumcision per se, he ascribes the greatest significance to Israel as the object of God's redemption and the community of God's people. To be apart from Israel is to be without hope and without God in the world.

In verse 13 the work of Christ is interpreted as the recovery of the estranged. "In the blood of Christ" could as well be translated *"by* the blood of Christ." The reference is, of course, to Christ's death understood as a sacrifice on man's behalf. The concept of being "far off" can be understood in the light of what immediately precedes (vss. 11–12). But what is meant by "have been brought near"? Near to what or whom? The answer is doubtless to be found in verses 14–18. Naturally, one would suspect that since the estrangement was defined in terms of separation from Israel that reconciliation and salvation would be described as union or reunion with Israel. Thus "being brought near" would mean the Gentiles' association, or incorporation into, the covenant people. This is partly what is meant; however, Christ is peace for both Jew and Gentiles (vs. 14). He effects reconciliation (vs. 16) between them, making them one (vs. 14) by breaking down the "dividing wall of hostility."[5] Moreover, he sets aside the Jewish law, the commandments and ordinances (2:15). "Abolishing them in his flesh" may refer to Christ's fulfillment of the law in his life (Rom. 5:18 f.; Matt. 3:15), but more likely it points to his death (which is probably also the meaning of Rom. 5:18 f.; cf. Phil. 2:8). The author doubtless has in mind other similar Pauline statements (cf. Gal. 3:13; Rom. 7:4 and 8:3). Christ's death marks the end of the period in which the law holds sway (cf. Gal. 3:19). Thus Christ is the end of the law (Rom. 10:4). By bringing the law to naught Christ does away with the thing that separates Jew from Gentile, and thus becomes their peace. It is not simply a matter of Gentiles' becoming Jews, for the fundamental status of the Jew is also changed. Notice the author's careful qualification of the law as the "law of commandments and ordinances." This implies

[5] The translation of this passage is difficult. In the Greek "hostility" is actually a noun in the accusative case, which could stand in apposition to the law as well as to the dividing wall (as in RSV). Thus KJV translates: "Having abolished in his flesh the enmity (hostility), even the law of commandments . . ."

The breaking down of the middle wall of hostility (2:14), if indeed that is the correct translation, is often taken to be an allusion to the destruction of the wall of the Jerusalem temple which separated the court of the Gentiles from the inner court open only to Jews. This would allow those who were far off (the Gentiles) to be brought near (2:3). The destruction of Jerusalem in A.D. 70 and the consequent demolition of the temple walls may have suggested this way of describing the work of Christ. That this allusion to the temple is intended is suggested by the extensive use of temple imagery in verses 20–22.

that Christ sets aside the particular Jewish formulation of the law of God, not that he annuls any concrete expression of God's will and introduces an era of lawlessness. The result of the abolition of the distinction between Jew and Gentile is the creation of the "one new man" (vs. 15), the new humanity in Christ. The Greek word translated "man" is the generic term for the human species (*anthrōpos*, whence the English "anthropology"), not the word for an individual male (*anēr*). The creation of the new man is the prerequisite for peace, not only among men (vs. 15), but with God (vs. 16) as well.

At least three things stand out as important in verses 11–16. First, the recovery and reintegration of the Gentile is more than conversion to Judaism. For Christ does away with the law, the hallmark of Judaism as a religion. Furthermore, the new man, or mankind, is not Jewish any more than he is Gentile. As the new man he replaces the old (cf. 4:22 f.; "nature" is a free translation of *anthrōpos*), The Jew, as much as the Gentile, is in need of, and therefore the recipient of, reconciliation (vs. 16). Second, peace or reconciliation among men is not a purely human matter. There can be reconciliation among men only as there is reconciliation of men to God. Here again the author sets forth a genuine and fundamental theological conviction of Paul. Verse 16 recalls Paul's definitive statement of the work of Christ as reconciliation in II Corinthians 5:16–21. Indeed, the idea of the *creation* (vs. 15) of the new man in place of the old man probably intentionally recalls II Corinthians 5:17: "If anyone is in Christ, he is a new creation; the old has passed away, behold, the new has come." Third, while peace with God is necessary before there can be peace among men, reconciliation to God and peace with him necessarily means reconciliation and peace among men (2:14–16).

The idea that reconciliation comes through the cross of Christ is what we might have expected from a Paulinist (vs. 16). The term *body* (Greek *soma*) is thoroughly Pauline. In fact, Ephesians here combines different Pauline uses of the term *body*. Obviously the primary reference is to the crucified body of Jesus, who becomes a curse for us (Gal. 3:13), who becomes sin, or a sin offering, for our sake (II Cor. 5:21), who died for our sins (I Cor. 15:3), whose death is our reconciliation: "while we were enemies we were reconciled to God by the death of his Son" (Rom. 5:10). In addition, the peculiar wording of Ephesians 2:16, "in one body" implies an identification of those being reconciled with the reconciler. Again the union of the Christian with the crucified is a typical Pauline motif: "I have been crucified with Christ" (Gal. 2:20); "you have died to the law through the body of Christ" (Rom. 7:4). Moreover, the body is an important Pauline image signifying the unity of Christians in Christ—that is, the church (Eph. 1:22; I Cor. 12; Rom. 14:3–8). The initial theme of this passage was community, and the recitation of Christ's work has focused upon its effect in reconstituting unity or community between God and man and, especially, between man and man.

This emphasis on restored community is reiterated (vss. 17 f.). Those who are far off are doubtless Gentiles, and those who are near, Jews (vs. 17). It is surprising, however, to encounter here a reference to Christ's preaching. Up to this point his reconciling work has been understood to be primarily, if not exclusively, his death. It is unlikely that the writer harks back to a recollection or tradition of Jesus' preaching at this unexpected place. The explanation of this verse is more probably to be found in Isaiah 57:19. If, as seems to be the case, the author was recalling this passage and understood it to refer to Christ (note the occurrence of the word "Lord"), this would account for the unexpected reference to Jesus' preaching of peace.[6] Verse 18 describes the present status before God of both Jew and Gentile, now reconstituted as the one new man. Once again, the thought is a legitimate echo of Pauline theology. The idea of a new access to God through Jesus has appeared already (Rom. 5:2). That the mode of this access to God is the Spirit is a thought that pervades Paul's writings (cf., for example, I Cor. 12; Rom. 8). The Spirit assures the reality of the new condition enjoyed by the new man in Christ. The Spirit and Christ are not to be identified, but the Spirit is the means or mode of Christ's presence, and therefore of man's access to God.

Mention of the one Spirit leads to the theme of the unity of the new community (vss. 20–22) constituted by the new humanity. Again we have a Pauline web of ideas. For the new community is characterized by the possession of the Spirit, and the Spirit-possessed community is the Body of Christ (cf. vs. 16).

> For just as the body is one and has many members, and all the members of the body, though many, are one body, so it is with Christ. For by one Spirit we were all baptized into one body—Jews or Greeks, slaves or free—and all were made to drink of one Spirit (I Cor. 12:12 f.).

The idea of Spirit and body is not immediately developed, however. Instead, another typical Pauline image, that of the house or temple, is invoked, but with some uncharacteristic variations, as we shall soon see.

In verse 19 it is solemnly declared that the situation described in verses 11 and 12 is no more. The Gentiles have been incorporated into the reconstituted humanity which is the church. They are no longer "strangers" and "sojourners," no longer alienated from the commonwealth of Israel.

---

[6] Interestingly enough, traditional sayings in which Jesus speaks of introducing divisions, conflict, and upheaval seem to be more numerous than sayings in which he promises peace. The most famous of the latter is John 14:27, but this is in all probability a Johannine formulation. On the other side, one may cite such passages as Matthew 10:34–39; 10:21 f.; Mark 12:1–12; Luke 20:10–19; 12:49–53.

(The two terms are actually technical designations of foreign visitors and resident aliens.) They are now "fellow citizens with the saints"—that is, Israel. Yet as we have seen, "Israel" herself has been thoroughly redefined through Christ, who puts an end to the law and by implication to the "circumcision which is made in the flesh by hands" (2:11). "Saints" (vs. 19) now simply means "those consecrated to God," a common Pauline designation of Christians (I Cor. 1:2).

"Household of God" (vs. 19; literally "householders of God") evokes the temple imagery, which is developed in verses 20–22. The foundation of the building that is to be the temple is first described (vs. 20). The description given here is to be contrasted with I Corinthians 3:11, where Paul emphatically maintains that Jesus Christ alone is the foundation of the building which is the church. Although the sharpness of the disagreement is softened by the designation of Christ as the chief cornerstone (probably the keystone that holds the entire structure together, as in an arch; cf. vs. 21), there is still a considerable and important difference. This difference is heightened when the prophets and apostles are called "holy" (3:5). In contrast to Paul for whom every true member of the church is holy or a saint (the two words are the same in Greek), here the word is used to set apart the apostles and prophets as a special and superior group within the church—much in the manner in which the words are used in medieval and modern ecclesiastical parlance. The prophets and apostles appear to be elevated as a special group (vs. 20). True, in Paul's own thought the apostle plays a key role and the prophet is second only to him (I Cor. 12:28). Yet Paul goes out of his way in I Corinthians 12 to maintain that there are no fundamental distinctions among the members of Christ's body (12:13). Doubtless the author of Ephesians would not have denied this. Yet the idea of a special status of the apostolate slips into his understanding of the structure of the church.

Ephesians does not, however, consciously down-grade the role of Jesus Christ in favor of the apostles (cf. vs. 21). The church holds together in Christ and grows in him. Although being in Christ is a Pauline concept, there is a new twist here in that the church grows in Christ (vs. 21; 4:13, 15). Again, the Pauline imagery is developed further in Ephesians; moreover, in this passage, by a process of combining motifs. For actually the temple, not the body, is the explicit subject. Yet obviously the concept of growth relates to the body, as is made plain at other points in this letter (cf. especially 4:12, 16 where the building imagery also appears). Apparently the image of the body is in the background (cf. 1:22 f.; 2:16) and enriches the concept of the temple.

The Gentiles, who at one time were alienated and then were brought near and made fellow citizens, are now actually built into a new building or structure, which is to be a dwelling place of God in the Spirit (vs. 22). That God or His glory dwells in his temple is, of course, an Old Testament

The Dome of the Rock mosque presently stands where the Jerusalem temple was located. (Courtesy of Pan American Airways.)

and Jewish idea that was applied to the Jerusalem temple until its destruction. Although that temple had probably been destroyed by the time Ephesians was written,[7] making way for the designation of the church of Christ as the new temple, Paul had already anticipated this event by his use of the temple imagery in relation to the new community and its members (I Cor. 3:16 f.; 6:19 ff.; II Cor. 6:16). That God dwells in the church through his Spirit is, of course, an integral part of this

[7] See footnote 5 above.

complex of ideas, and of Paul's thought in general. Whereas the older view of God's dwelling in his temple envisioned his abiding in a building, in the new conception the "building" is the community of persons, the church. In I Peter 2:4 ff. the figure of the building or temple is taken yet a step further, and the individual Christians are described as "living stones."

The passage we have considered (2:11–22) is the culmination of the theological themes that the author has been developing. Formally, the theological section of the epistle continues to the benediction at the end of chapter three. But that chapter, with the possible exception of verses 9 and 10 (but cf. 1:22 f.), is basically a recapitulation of what has gone before with special reference to the role played by the apostle Paul.

Significantly, the drama of salvation narrated in 2:11–22 is in 3:4, 6 described as Paul's insight into the mystery of Christ, "that is, how the Gentiles are fellow heirs, members of the same body, and partakers of the promise in Christ Jesus through the gospel." Clearly the author regards this as the peculiarly Pauline understanding of the gospel. It is true that for Paul the gospel implies the church, and within the church abolishes the distinctions of an age that is already passing away. Moreover, the Old Testament prophecies are directed to men of faith, not to Israel according to the flesh. But Paul does not regard the incorporation of the Gentiles into the body of Christ as his *central* insight into the mystery of the gospel. The elements of the thought are Pauline, but somehow the focus has shifted. There has been a subtle change in the center of interest and emphasis in Ephesians from Christ to the church. This does not mean that the importance of Christ is lessened, but that the church as the result of Christ's work and the historical embodiment of Christ increasingly becomes the central subject of the author's theological concern.[8] Hence he takes Paul's central insight to be an ecclesiological one. He returns to the theme of the church again and again (1:22 f.; 2:11–22; 3:6, 10; 4:1–16; 5:21–33; 6:10–20, really a description of the proper posture of the church in this age). After chapter two what is not explicit discussion of the church is exhortation to the church. This exhortation, unlike Paul's, seems not to be directed to specific, individual problems and situations but to the church in general, "for the equipment of the saints, for the work of ministry, for building up the body of Christ, until we all attain to the unity of the faith and of the knowledge of the Son of God, to mature manhood, to the measure of the stature of the fullness of Christ" (4:12 f.).

Ephesians is apparently an exposition or re-exposition of Paul's thought in the light of a new situation, such a document as Paul himself might have written had he lived into the following generation. Its concentration

[8] Cf E. Käsemann, "Ephesians and Acts," *Studies in Luke-Acts*, p. 290.

of interest upon the church is not un-Pauline so much as it is a development on the basis of Paul. It is, moreover, a development in the light of a peculiar state of affairs that Paul did not anticipate and that, in a certain sense, makes us and the author of Ephesians closer to each other than to Paul. Paul anticipated the imminent return of Christ and the end of the age. No such urgent anticipation is reflected in Ephesians. The

*The "Pietà" by the Italian sculptor Michelangelo (1475–1564).
(Courtesy of Alinari-Art Reference Bureau.)*

church will have to exist as an institution in this world for quite a while. The solemn injunction to put on the whole armor of God indicates that the author expects a long fight. The author manifests no weakening of conviction or zeal, however, no attenuation of the faith. Rather he goes enthusiastically into battle, not knowing when the end will be, but knowing that the victory belongs to Christ and his church.

ORGANIZATION AND ORDER (I Tim. 4:1–16)

What are the problems facing the church?
What is the nature of church organization?

NOTES ON I TIMOTHY AND THE PASTORALS

I Timothy, II Timothy, and Titus constitute the Pastoral letters traditionally attributed to the apostle Paul. They are called "Pastoral" because they contain instructions for carrying out the pastoral or ministerial office of the church. These instructions are directed to two of Paul's associates, known from other letters. Timothy is also mentioned in Acts. According to the Pastorals Timothy is at Ephesus (I Tim. 1:3; II Tim. 1:15–18), Titus in Crete (1:5).

The Pastorals as a group present a number of distinct peculiarities, and problems:

(1) The first collection of Pauline letters for which we have concrete evidence, that of Marcion in the middle of the second century, did not contain the Pastorals. Although Marcion was condemned as a heretic, and his orthodox foe Tertullian accuses him of rejecting the Pastorals, the charge is probably inaccurate, because later Marcionite Christians seem to have included the Pastorals in their canon.[9] Probably he did not know them. An early (ca. A.D. 200) papyrus manuscript of the Greek New Testament (P 46) does not have, and perhaps never contained, the Pastorals. There seems to be no uncontestable attestation of the Pastorals as Pauline letters until the latter part of the second century.

(2) The style and especially the language of the Pastorals differ from that of the acknowledged letters as a whole by a factor of about two to three times the variation found in any one, or in any group, of the other letters. The Pastorals do not, however, differ from each other. They represent a single stylistic and linguistic group over against the other letters. Significantly, the Pastorals diverge from Pauline language in the direction of common Greek speech and, particularly, the vocabulary of the Apostolic Fathers and Apologists of the second Christian century.[10]

(3) The Pastorals presuppose a historical setting found in neither Acts nor the other letters.[11] They seem to presume a situation in which Paul had been released from his Roman imprisonment (Acts 28; cf. II Tim. 4:16 f.) for further work in the East. Apparently he was then arrested and imprisoned again, and it is implied that a second release was not to be expected (II Tim.

---

[9] J. C. Beker, "The Pastoral Letters," *IDB*, III, p. 670.

[10] The linguistic and stylistic evidence has been set forth by P. N. Harrison, *The Problem of the Pastoral Epistles* (Oxford: Humphrey Milford, 1921), pp. 18–86.

[11] A good brief statement of the difficulties may be found in Kümmel, *Introduction to the New Testament*, pp. 264–68.

4:6–18). The only tangible early evidence for this historical reconstruction, however, is the Pastorals themselves.

(4) The church situation is peculiar in two respects. First, the danger of heresy is now acute. Second, a regular ministry and system of ordination seems to exist (I Tim. 3:1–13; 4:14). Ministry and laity are now distinguished within the church. Both of these situations represent a development beyond what is found in the other letters of Paul.

(5) A certain theological difference is implied, especially by different uses of Pauline words. For example "faith" has now generally become "the faith" (I Tim. 3:9; 4:1; II Tim. 4:7); it is not primarily a relationship, but a body of doctrine.

It may be argued that all these facts taken individually mean nothing more than that Paul faced changing situations and times. But taken together, as they must be, they spell real difficulty for the tradition of Pauline authorship. In fact, they suggest that the letters were written fifty or so years after Paul by a man attempting to speak a genuine word of Paul to his own day. Evidence that is difficult to reconcile with the tradition of Pauline authorship illumines and supports the hypothesis of a later and different author. It is therefore not surprising that the weight of critical scholarly opinion now falls on the side of this hypothesis.

I Timothy and Titus are concerned with ecclesiastical organization, order, and doctrine, and somewhat secondarily with heresy, although the threat of false teaching may be a major motivation of the letters. II Timothy, on the other hand, is primarily concerned with the threat of false doctrine. In I Timothy injunction is piled on injunction and exhortation on exhortation, with a good share of traditional instructions and admonitions having to do with the conduct of church business and the behavior of church functionaries.

OUTLINE OF I TIMOTHY
  Address (1:1–2)
   I. Warning against Heresy and Heretics (1:3–20)
   II. Manual of Church Order (2:1–4:5)
    A. Worship (2:1–15)
    B. Qualifications and Duties of the Clergy (3:1–16)
    C. Appearance of Heresy (4:1–5)
   III. Manual for Ministers (4:6–6:19)
    A. Teaching in the Church (4:6–16)
    B. Dealing with Elders and Widows (5:1–22)
    C. Personal Advice (5:23–24)
    D. Advice to Slaves (6:1–2)
    E. Dangers of False Teachers and Teachings (6:3–10)
    F. Exhortation to Ministers (6:11–19)
  Conclusion (6:20–21)

The fourth chapter of I Timothy may not be a particularly noteworthy piece of prose. It is, however, a good cross section, revealing most of the distinguishing features of the Pastoral letters. The first five verses deal with heresy, false teaching, that has arisen within the Christian community. The remainder of the chapter is the opening of the section designated in the outline as a manual for ministers.

When the author says of the heretics against whom he struggles that they were to be anticipated (4:1), the edge is taken off the hard and discouraging fact that even within the community of faith error persists. This unhappy circumstance occurs only with the foreknowledge of God; the Spirit predicts it. The same motif appears elsewhere in the New Testament (Acts 20:28–30; Mark 13:5 f., 22 f.; Jude 18; II Peter 3:3; and I John 2:18). The common element in these texts is the fact that the church has been duly warned of the appearance of evil men within her midst. At an earlier period Paul recognized the existence and danger of such persons (Phil. 3:1 ff.) but said nothing about their having been predicted.

The attitude of our author is something less than tolerant, since the heretics have "departed from the faith" by attending to "deceitful spirits" and "demonic doctrines." Those responsible for this state of affairs, perhaps heretical teachers, are referred to in verse 2. There is no hesitancy at calling a spade a spade. The luxury of allowing each his own view in religious matters is impossible for the author. Individual tastes and preferences cannot be given free rein. The writer is a churchman concerned about the truth of the Christian message, the church's proper preservation of it, and the obedient ordering of church life in the light of the gospel. The false doctrine that he denounces and deplores has immediate practical ramifications; for the beliefs of the heretics lead inevitably to the wrong ordering of life (vss. 3–5).

The ascetic, world-denying character of their heresy is apparent (vs. 3). Their asceticism—avoidance of sex and certain foods—suggests that the opponents are closely related to, if not identical with, the Gnostic heretics denounced by the Christian Fathers in the second century. The earlier description of the false teachers (1:3–7) corresponds rather well with this aberrant form of Christianity. Confirmation is found in 6:20, where Timothy is advised to "avoid the godless chatter and contradictions of what is falsely called knowledge." The Greek word translated "knowledge" is none other than *gnōsis*, whence the name of this heresy, Gnosticism. The widespread appearance of this heretical version of the Christian gospel, which defined the Christian message as a program of escape from this evil world to a better one above, was probably the most important event in the development of second century Christianity. During this time it was by no means certain that Christian thought would move in the direction indicated in the New Testament books and the later creeds. The Gnostics were so numerous that in many places they constituted the majority of Christians. They, of course, did not consider themselves heretics. Consequently, the history of the development of Christian thought in the second and early third centuries is very largely the story of the exclusion of their point of view from the area of permissible Christian beliefs. Indeed, it was either Gnosticism or the "orthodox" form of Christianity that eventually had to emerge victorious, for Gnosticism was not a few doctrines added to or subtracted from Christianity, but a comprehensive, alternate understanding of Christian faith. I Timothy probably represents an early stage in the emergence, identification, and rejection of the Gnostic viewpoint. Perhaps an even earlier stage is to be found in Paul's own writings, possibly in the Corinthian correspondence, and almost certainly in Colossians. We cannot assume, however, that Gnosticism is the only heresy attacked in the Pastoral letters.

In opposition to this specious and harmful asceticism, "Paul" lays out the Christian position (vss. 4 f.). This view had already been adumbrated in verse 3 ("received with thanksgiving"; cf. the same phrase in vs. 4), where the phrase "by those who believe and *know the truth*" may be consciously formulated in opposition to the claims of the Gnostics. I Timothy (4:4 f.) vigorously reasserts the claim of the Old Testament (Gen. 1:29), Judaism, and Jesus himself that God's creation is fundamentally good. This view, though not denied by the earliest generation of Christians, was relegated to the periphery because of eager expectation of further revelations from the Lord and a correspondingly low estimate of the goods of this world. I Timothy clearly formulates what has become the classical Christian position. "Everything created by God is good, and nothing is to be rejected if it is received with thanksgiving." "Thanksgiving" involves consecration by the word of God and prayer (vss. 4 f.). It

A portion of the Isaiah Scroll of the Dead Sea Scrolls, housed in the Shrine of the Book in Jerusalem. (Courtesy of Israel Information Services.)

is not obvious what the "word of God" means in this context. Possibly it is a reference to prayer in Biblical terminology.

The author does not mean to say in verses 4 f. that "anything goes" because everything is created by God. No one could read the rest of his writings and imagine that. But he does express the fundamental conviction that there is nothing wrong with the well-ordered use and enjoyment of the things God has created. Probably he would have agreed with the more extensive statement of this position found in a document composed a couple of hundred years later.

> If any bishop, elder, or deacon or anyone of the clergy abstains from marriage, meat, or wine, not through self-discipline, but through abhorrence of them as evil in themselves, forgetting that "all things are very good" and the "God made man male and female," and thus blasphemously repudiating creation, either let him amend or be deposed and cast out of the church; likewise for a layman also.[12]

The next two paragraphs (vss. 6–10 and 11–16) instruct Timothy, and therefore the clergy, about the ministry and administration of the church. The section extending from 5:1 to 6:2 contains specific guidance for dealing with various groups in the church, especially widows, who were considered the responsibility of the community. We have then a kind of manual for the minister.

"These instructions" (vs. 6) may refer to all that has preceded in the letter or to what follows. Either makes good sense. The term *minister* (literally, "one who serves") here designates an office or class of offices in the church. In chapter 3 the qualifications for the ministry, the offices of bishop and deacon, have been outlined. "Timothy" is himself such a "minister" in the clerical, official sense. In fact, Timothy has been ordained to this ministry through the laying on of hands (vs. 14). The investment of the historical Timothy by a board of elders seems unlikely and does not agree with the account of Paul's enlistment of Timothy in Acts 16: 1–3. This section of the letter is intelligible, however, on the assumption that it was written for the benefit of the nascent official ministry of the church a generation or two after Paul.

The emphasis on right doctrine (vs. 6b) supports this assumption. "The words of the faith," an un-Pauline expression, refers to the right formulation of the confession of faith, as the immediately succeeding mention of "good doctrine" shows. For Paul, faith is belief, trust, obedience, an orientation of life, a relationship. Of course, faith for Paul has an object toward which it is directed and about which intelligible judgments can be made. Paul does, in fact, become quite exercised over dangerous and

---

[12] *Apostolic Constitutions*, VIII, 47, 51. Quoted by F. D. Gealy, "The Pastoral Epistles: Introduction and Exegesis," *IB*, 11 (1955), p. 498.

erroneous teaching. Thus much of his extant correspondence, especially the Corinthian and Galatian letters, is devoted to polemic, argument, and persuasion. Yet Paul does not emphasize the correct doctrinal formulation in the way the Pastorals do. Much less does he understand faith in the sense of "the faith"—the correct doctrinal formula.

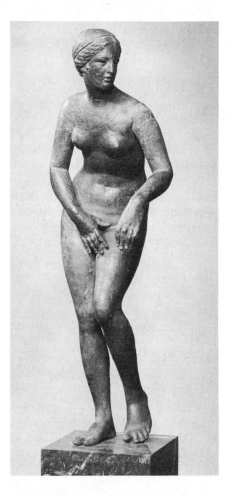

A classical Greek statue of Aphrodite, goddess of love and beauty (ca. fourth century B.C.). (Courtesy of Metropolitan Museum of Art, Rogers Fund, 1912.)

A major reason for the difference between Paul and the Pastorals appears in the reference to godless and silly myths (vs. 7). It has become necessary to emphasize the right content and formulation of the faith because anything and everything, but perhaps most especially Gnosticism, is trying to palm itself off as Christianity. Doubtless the rise of heresy leads to the emphasis upon right doctrine that we find in the Pastorals. The appearance of contradictory beliefs necessitates the definition of the true teaching. Now we may use the term *heresy* in its proper sense. The false teachers are now considered beyond the pale (cf. 4:1–5; 6:3 ff.). There is no question of discussion with them, much less of winning them back. They must be prevented from contaminating the church and pulling others down with them.

The author's attention next focuses (vss. 7b–10) upon the relative merits of physical training and training in godliness. The rather vague reference of verse 9 is apparently to verse 8. The Pastorals regularly underscore an important saying with some such assertion as "the saying is sure" (cf. 1:15; 3:1; II Tim. 2:11; Tit. 3:8). Probably this formula indicates a traditional saying. The KJV's "bodily exercise profiteth little" is closer to the Greek original than is the RSV; I Timothy wishes to contrast the little profit of bodily training with the great value of training in godliness—instead of wild speculations (vs. 7a), right doctrine and godliness. "Godliness" is a word found not at all in Paul, and quite rarely in the New Testament outside the Pastorals and II Peter. It is, in fact, a term at home in ancient Hellenistic piety rather than in specifically Biblical or Christian faith. "Piety" might be an equally good translation of the Greek word in question. The high value that the Pastorals plainly ascribe to this quality is significant. More light may be shed on the thought of the Pastorals at this point by further comparing their outlook with Paul's. For Paul the mode of Christian existence is faith, life in Christ or in the Spirit, and the term godliness or piety does not occur. In the Pastorals the mode of Christian existence is godliness and piety, and faith is the body of right doctrine. The concepts of "in Christ" and "in the Spirit" play little or no role in the Pastorals. We seem to have a contrast between Paul's vital faith, expressed in terms that convey the intimate relation of the believer to Christ and the Spirit, on the one hand, and an understanding of Christianity as institution, doctrine, and religious living on the other. Thus it is typical of the Pastorals that the promise for the present life and the life to come is not related directly to Christ and the Spirit but instead to "godliness" (vs. 8b).

To disparage the Pastorals as documents reflecting the degeneration of faith into institutionalism, dogmatism, and the practice of piety is unfair. The continuing vitality of the tradition that the author seeks to guard comes to light in verse 10. The toiling and striving of those whose exercise is godliness has as its end and goal the believers' hope in the living God and Savior. The anti-Gnostic character of the Pastorals' polemic probably appears again in this affirmation of God as the Savior of all men. Commonly in Gnosticism only an elect group of men with a disposition for and capability of possessing knowledge could attain salvation. Here God in intention is the Savior of all, not a special class. That God actually saves only those who believe is the probable meaning of the last clause (cf. 2:1–6). But I Timothy declares quite clearly that no man stands *a priori* outside the potential realm of God's redemption.

The specific referent of "these things" in the following exhortation is again unclear (vs. 11, cf. vs. 6). Does it refer to what precedes or what follows, or is it a general exhortation without any specific point of reference? The latter is more likely.[13] At any rate, what immediately follows (vss. 12–16) is not material that Timothy would command and teach, but advice to him personally. The injunction to Timothy to let no one despise his youth (vs. 12) and the indication that Paul plans a visit (vs. 13) lend a note of genuiness to the correspondence, but they are probably a part of the cloak of pseudonymity in which the letter is clad. The rest is general instruction to the pastor, like much of the Pastorals. We have already noted that verse 14 presupposes the existence of an ordained ministry. The word here translated "gift" is the Greek *charisma*, which implies a special spiritual endowment. Paul held that the *charismata*, "spiritual gifts," were distributed among all the members of the community, so that although there are varieties of gifts and services, all Christians are, so to speak, gifted (I Cor. 12). Here, however, the charismatic gift is limited, whether consciously or not, to the particular power and authority of ministerial office. It is granted by the laying on of hands as well as by prophetic utterance. "Prophetic utterance" is probably an allusion to the Spirit-inspired designation of men for certain tasks, which was characteristic of earliest Christianity (Acts 13:2). But in spite of the continuation of prophetic utterance, the dispensation of the Spirit is apparently tied to institutional office and ordination. What then of the free movement and authority of the Spirit in the community? Is spontaneity being sacrificed to the need for unity and order in the community? If so, is this necessary, or is the price too great to pay? The Pastorals do not represent the last period in the history of the church which has entertained such questions as these.

The other injunctions (vss. 12 f. and 15 f.) mirror the continuing life of the community, now a religious institution. The official leaders are to set the example in faith, conduct, and related matters (vs. 12), seeing after their duties of conducting public worship (vs. 13) and supervising the education of the people in sound doctrine (vss. 13–16), to the end that the ship of the church will safely make harbor, that both minister and people will be saved (vs. 16). The model of the church as a continuing community composed of leaders and followers, officers and men, clergy and laity, making its way through the world toward greater things that God has in store, is the legitimate legacy of the Pastoral epistles. Even more than Ephesians, the Pastorals stand closer to the present day church than to the apostle Paul, in whose name they were written.

[13] Cf. Gealy, *IB*, 11, pp. 428, 431.

Discipline and Doctrine

The documents now to be considered, though in some ways similar to Ephesians and the Pastorals, show certain significant differences in their focus and form of presentation. Ephesians and the Pastorals explicitly stand within the Pauline tradition. James, I Peter, and Hebrews do not. Although each of the latter books was probably influenced in some way by Paul, none is ascribed to him, not even Hebrews.[14] All are traditionally regarded as letters, but whereas Ephesians and the Pastorals possess a carefully worked out epistolary form, James has only a salutation with no conclusion; I Peter has both, but there is some suspicion that they are later additions to an original tract or homily; Hebrews has an epistolary conclusion but no salutation. Moreover, there is a perceptible difference of emphasis. Ephesians is interested in the theological understanding of the church and the Pastorals in its practical organization and administration, whereas James, I Peter, and Hebrews are more concerned with the inner life of the church, the conduct and conviction of its members.

FAITH AND ETHICS (Jas. 2:14–26)

What is the danger against which James is directed?
How are faith and works related?

NOTES ON THE LETTER OF JAMES

The very first verse of the letter of James presents several problems. Who is James? There are several possibilities: The brother of Jesus himself; one of the two disciples of Jesus bearing that name; or someone else. Who or what are the twelve tribes of the dispersion (1:1)? The reference is obviously to the twelve tribes of Israel dispersed around the Greco-Roman world, but James is not a letter to Jews (cf. 1:1; 2:1; 2:14–26). Apparently Christians could be referred to as the "disperson" also (I Pet. 1:1). The letter is addressed to Christians, but to no single Christian congregation. The conditions existing in a single congregation or in specific congregations are no more reflected in the letter as a whole than in the salutation. The conclusion tells us nothing; the "letter" stops quite abruptly.

Although tradition has ascribed the book to James, the brother of the Lord, it does not seem to have been known and quoted by other Christian writers until the early third century. The fourth century church historian Eusebius of Caesarea indicates that some Christians of his day doubted that it belonged in the New Testament at all. Martin Luther criticized the letter, calling it an "epistle of straw," and apparently did not regard it as the work of Jesus'

---

14 Although KJV gives the title of the document as the Epistle of St. Paul to the Hebrews, all reference to St. Paul has been dropped in RSV.

brother. In fact, the work itself nowhere makes this claim. Nor is the ascription of James to Jesus' brother supported by considerations of language and style. The style is that of the Greek diatribe, and the quality of the Greek is reasonably good. The content is nevertheless Jewish—so Jewish, in fact, that some scholars have proposed that James is really the product of a Christian editing and augmenting of a Jewish tract.[15] Whatever may be said for or against this thesis, it corresponds to the essentially Jewish, and especially Hellenistic Jewish, character of the book, its ethical emphasis, and content.

Plainly, little is known about the origin of James. All that we can safely say is that James represents a form of Jewish Christianity at the end of the first century or the beginning of the second. Its ethical exhortations reflect a knowledge and use of what had by then become an extensive ethical tradition—much of it drawn from Jewish and even pagan sources—in the expanding and consolidating Christian community. The best-known section (2:14–26) probably betrays a knowledge of the Pauline letters, especially Galatians and Romans.[16] If so, then the author very likely knew the collected Pauline corpus, which would date his writing no earlier than the end of the first century. On the other hand, Paul or the views of Paulinists are not above criticism (contrast II Pet. 3:15–17), making a much later date unlikely. Since the kind of Judaism that formed the background of James existed in many parts of the Hellenistic world, it is futile to try to locate the book's place of origin.

Despite the Jewish cast of James, references and quotations from the Old Testament are not frequent. There are a number of possible references or allusions to Jesus' sayings and teachings, however, especially in 5:1–6, 12. Whether these indicate a knowledge of any of our Gospels, or only of an independent tradition, is uncertain.

OUTLINE OF JAMES

    Address (1:1)
      I. Exhortation to Christian Practice (1:2–27)
     II. Faith and Ethics (2:1–26)
        A. Faith and the Poor (2:1–7)
        B. The Importance of the Law (2:8–13)
        C. Faith and Works (2:14–26)
     III. Teaching and Wisdom (3:1–18)
     IV. Condemnation of Pride and Passion (4:1–12)
     V. Concluding Exhortation (4:13–5:20)
        A. Warning against Boasting and Riches (4:13–5:6)
        B. Exhortation to Patience, Prayer, and the Restoration of the Sinner (5:7–20)

---

[15] For this view, B. S. Easton, "The Epistle of James: Introduction and Exegesis," *IB*, 12 (1957), pp. 3–74, especially 9–14. Easton cites the ground-breaking work of Spitta, Massebieau, and, especially, Arnold Meyer.

[16] A full collection of possible parallels between James and the Pauline letters may be found in Barnett, *Paul Becomes a Literary Influence*, pp. 186–96. Possible allusions to Paul are numerous, but there are no direct quotations. Barnett is cautious in drawing conclusions, but seems to agree with Goodspeed that the author knew Romans, I Corinthians, Galatians, and probably Ephesians (p. 196).

St. James on a plaque of a French altar frontal—second half of thirteenth century. (Courtesy of Metropolitan Museum of Art. Gift of J. Pierpont Morgan, 1917.)

The letter of James arose out of the specific needs of the expanding and consolidating Christian church, even though it is addressed to no specific congregation. Members of the newly formed churches needed concrete guidance about what to do in actual life situations in which ethical decisions were required. For the Christian converted from Judaism, the problem was less acute. For he brought with him the powerful and comprehensive tradition of the Jewish law. Even Paul, who emphatically rejected the law as a way of salvation, still appreciated and used the law as a way of life, although he himself probably did not continue to adhere to it in strict Pharisaic fashion. In addition, in certain circles of the early Christian church the teachings of Jesus were widely circulated and used for moral and spiritual guidance.[17] The existence of a substantial tradition of Jesus' teaching in the Gospels, especially Matthew and Luke, is ample testimony to this fact. The appropriation of the Jesus tradition in the

[17] The literature on this subject is immense. Perhaps most illuminating, is Dibelius' *From Tradition to Gospel*, especially pp. 9–132.

377

Gospels and the incorporation of all four Gospels into the canon of the church naturally resulted in the increasing availability and use of the tradition of Jesus' ethical teaching as a norm and guide for Christian life. Already in James we see the beginning of this development in those passages that seem to reflect a saying of Jesus known from the Synoptic Gospels.

But why was this ethical instruction necessary? From Paul's letters we can already see that there were various ideas about what it meant to be Christian, just as there are today. The character of Christian existence had to be defined, and for the individual this definition by and large took place after, not before the experience of conversion. "The apostles went out into the highways and hedges and compelled men to come in—and the post-apostolic church had to contend with the result. . . . Great numbers of men and women had not learned the first elements of morality and were in pressing need of instruction and discipline."[18]

James helps define Christian life in terms of concrete advice and admonition. The contact with the tradition of Jesus' sayings has just been observed. Even more impressive is the prevalent hortatory style, the stringing together of one injunction after another, which was a common early Christian literary and traditional form, with roots in the pagan and Jewish culture of the day. The ethical exhortations of James have much in common with those of other Christian documents, such as the Pauline epistles (cf. I Thess. 4:1–12; Col. 3:5–4:5); Ephesians (4:25–6:20); I John (3:11–18); Hebrews (13:1–8); the postapostolic Letter of Barnabas; and the Didache.

Perhaps the ethical interest and character of James is most graphically portrayed at the point where the author takes up the cudgels against a dangerous form of Christianity, which evidently holds that man is justified before God by faith alone (2:14–26). The initial hypothetical situation (described in vss. 14–17) and the moral lesson drawn from it appeal immediately to pious, practical Christian people. For the man, ancient or modern, for whom theological subtleties are either incomprehensible or irrelevant James' point of view seems refreshingly plain and obviously right. No doubt his point well deserves making, especially over against all forms of orthodoxy or piety that exclude moral considerations or push them to the periphery. On the other hand, a quite narrow understanding of faith is presupposed; for James, faith equals belief (vs. 19). This view of faith, similar to that of the Pastorals, takes faith to be primarily the content of belief. It is remote from Paul, for whom faith is the *act of believing* and the *relationship* between the believer and the one believed.

The antinomy between faith and works reminds the reader of Paul's

[18] B. S. Easton, quoting B. W. Bacon, in *The Pastoral Epistles: Introduction, Translation, Commentary and Word Studies* (New York: Charles Scribner's Sons, 1947), pp. 23 f.

intense theological discussion of this very subject. In fact, James' arguments may even be directed against the position of Paul. Paul would have surely agreed with the intention of verses 18 and 20. Yet the use of the example of Abraham (vss. 21 ff.) and the citation of the same Old Testament passage (Gen. 15:6) that Paul used to prove a quite different point (Rom. 4 and Gal. 3) suggest some sort of contact and disagreement with Paul or an interpretation of him. The disagreement concerns the relationship of faith and works and the place of works in the economy of salvation (vss. 21–24).

We have already noted the discrepancy between James' and Paul's view of faith. We must now ask how James understands works and whether he regards them as necessary for salvation. Paul, of course, espouses justification by faith and excludes "works of the law," deeds done in fulfillment of the law and thought to be meritorious, as a viable alternative. James, on the other hand, does not oppose justification by works to justification by faith. He does not accept Paul's posing of the alternatives. Rather, he regards the performance of "works of the law," along with faith, as indispensable for justification (2:24). Yet he does not intend to espouse the kind of legalism that Paul condemned. He refers to the law more than once as the "law of liberty" and in 2:8 brings forth the Old Testament passage (Leviticus 19:18) with which both Jesus (Matt. 22:34–40; Mark 12:28–31; Luke 25:28) and Paul (Rom. 12:8–10; Gal. 5:14) sum up the law. That he opposes a crass legalism may be inferred also from 2:12 f. Still, Paul and James really differ on the question of justification. Whether James would have expressed himself in this fashion had he accepted Paul's understanding of faith or faced Paul's situation in the controversy with Jewish Christians is a moot question. There is, however, a kind of practical agreement between them. James says (vs. 24) that belief alone is not enough, that pure religion, as he styles it (vs. 25), involves faith and ethics. Paul would have quite agreed: "For in Christ Jesus neither circumcision nor uncircumcision is of any avail, but faith working through love" (Gal. 5:6). James insists on works as the proof of faith (vs. 18); faith without works is dead. Paul would prefer to say that faith without works is less than genuine faith.

We cannot determine whether James intends to oppose Paul directly. He seems to be fighting a misunderstood Paulinism that separates faith from life. Quite possibly this is his own misunderstanding. Or such a misunderstanding of Paul's thought may have been prevalent in the church of his day (cf. II Pet. 3:15–17). Paul encountered in Corinth among his own converts those who thought that their faith, knowledge, and possession of the Spirit put them beyond any paltry considerations of right and wrong, sin and righteousness. They separated faith or piety from this-worldly ethical questions. Thus Paul had to exhort the Corinthian Christians to abstain from, or give up, immoral practices. It would therefore not be surprising if the subtleties of Paul's theological and ethical reflection, his relating of the indicative and the imperative, of grace, faith and obedience, were lost on later generations of Christians. After all, Paul is not widely understood in church circles today, which is why some people prefer the less demanding, and less profound, common sense view of James.

But is the simple paralleling of faith and works in James an adequate solution to the problem of man's orientation to God and to his fellow man? The answer depends on how one understands the human situation and what one takes man and his essential problem in life to be. If man is free to do and to believe according to his own choice and without any predisposition to good or evil, then James certainly does make more sense than Paul. On the other hand, if man's present existence in the world is to be understood in terms of oppressive bondage to sin, as alienation and rebellion, then the simple gospel of James does not suffice, at least not as a theological analysis of the state of man in the world and the manner of· his redemption. But James is a manual for Christian behavior, not a fundamental theological treatise. James may display a certain theological shallowness alongside a Paul or John, but in its own way his book had, and has, its usefulness and function within the Christian community.

CHRIST AND THE CHRISTIAN

The theme of the relation of Jesus Christ and the Christian is developed most extensively in the Gospels and the pre-Gospel tradition. In fact, even in Paul, the crucified and resurrected Christ, but apparently not Jesus as an historical individual, is used as a model for the ethical behavior of the Christian (Phil. 2:6–11; Rom. 6). Naturally, his metaphor of the Body of Christ also reflects a consciousness of the close relationship. I Peter and Hebrews mark a further stage in the use of the figure of the earthly Jesus in theological and ethical reflection. Here we find for the first time outside the Gospels the explicit recognition of the conviction that the life of the Christian has an indispensable connection with the historic life of Jesus. In I Peter this relationship is expounded for the sake of its ethical implications, whereas in Hebrews, not the exemplary but the theological significance of the relationship is primary.

The Suffering Servant (I Pet. 2:11–25)
How does the Christian conduct himself in the face of persecution?

NOTES ON I PETER

I Peter presents itself as the work of the great apostle; no grounds for doubting this claim were advanced until modern times. Yet there are at least three reasons for questioning the tradition:

(1) The Greek of I Peter is very good. Could a Galilean fisherman have written it? Aramaic, Peter's native tongue, differs from Greek more than Greek differs from English.

(2) I Peter contains many Pauline motifs and ideas, especially the concept of Jesus' death atoning for sin and effecting righteousness (1:18 f.; 2:24). The Pauline expression "in Christ" also occurs in I Peter (3:16; 5:10, 14), and there is a striking similarity between the view expressed in 2:14 ff. and the attitude toward the state commended by Paul in Romans 13:1–7. Did the author of I Peter know Romans? The Pauline letters? If he knew the collected Pauline letters, this would imply that I Peter was written perhaps a generation later and could not be the work of Peter, who is supposed to have died in the 60's in Rome. Yet the possibility that Peter could have known only Romans cannot be excluded.

(3) I Peter contains no indication of acquaintanceship with the historical Jesus of the sort we would expect from the man who in many ways was closest to him. The claim to be a witness of the suffering of Christ (5:1) does not necessarily mean an eyewitness. According to the Gospels, Peter fled Jesus on the night he was betrayed and presumably did not see the crucifixion. Moreover, the passage that deals with Christ's suffering and death (2:22 ff.) seems to be based on the suffering servant passages of Isaiah rather than on historical observation. Although this does not disprove Peter's authorship, the text can scarcely be taken as evidence for it.

Modern defenders of Petrine authorship acknowledge the weight of at least the first and second arguments and offer the explanation that these factors are due to Silvanus (5:12), a coworker of Paul (I and II Thess. 1:1), who as secretary actually composed the letter in its present form. But if Silvanus is the same as the Silas of Acts, as is usually supposed, he too was originally an Aramaic-speaking Palestinian (Acts 15:22, 27); therefore the first difficulty would not be removed.

If the letter is by Peter, it must date from about A.D. 60, give or take a few years. The suffering of Christians to which the letter refers would be under the persecution of the Emperor Nero. Yet in that case the warnings and admonitions would seem pointless, for Nero's persecution took place in Rome (the probable place of origin; "Babylon," 5:13; cf. Rev. 18), not in Asia Minor, to which the letter is addressed. If the letter is not Petrine, the period of the Emperor Domitian's persecution would be indicated as the time of composition. This would date I Peter in the last decade of the first century and also make knowledge of the Pauline letters a possibility. Whatever the conclusion concerning the origin of I Peter, the purpose of the author was to encourage early Christians in their faith.

Structurally, I Peter presents some peculiarities. Salutation (1:1–2) and epistolary conclusion (5:12–14) fall easily away. At 4:11 there is a conclusion of sorts and 4:12 makes a new beginning. The fact that in 4:12 ff. persecution seems an imminent possibility, whereas in the preceding part of the letter it is more remote, has led to speculation that the different parts were written at different times. The hortatory and even homiletical character of much of the letter suggests that its basis may be a baptismal sermon (cf. 3:21), with the epistolary form a later editorial addition.

Madonna and child enthroned with Saints Catherine, Peter, Cecilia, Paul, and the infant Saint John the Baptist. Altarpiece painted for the Convent of St. Anthony of Padua, Perguia, Italy, by Raphael (1483–1520). (Courtesy of Metropolitan Museum of Art. Gift of J. Pierpont Morgan, 1916.)

OUTLINE OF I PETER

Address (1:1–2)

  I. The Hope of Salvation (1:3–12)

  II. The Holiness of the Christian (1:13–2:10)

  III. Instructions and Appeal for Good Conduct (2:11–4:11)

    A. Honoring Public Opinion and Institutions (2:11–17)

    B. Proper Household Relationships (2:18–3:7)

      1. Servants (2:18–25)

      2. Wives and Husbands (3:1–7)

    C. Christian Conduct before the World (3:8–4:6)

I Peter is one of the choice writings of the early Christian period and of the New Testament, whether or not one reckons it to be the work of the apostle Peter. It is written with good taste and restraint, and it bespeaks a wholesome, if critical, understanding of the world. I Peter calls the Christian to obedient work and witness in the world without surrendering himself to the world's standards and demands.

The interests of I Peter might be characterized as primarily ethical and secondarily theological. We have seen that the main body of the document falls into four sections, the last three having to do with Christian conduct. The first of these (1:13–2:10) is more explicitly theological, dealing with the basis of the ethical demand of the gospel, and culminating in the hortatory use of the image of building or temple (2:4–10), an image already noted in Ephesians and I Corinthians. The second (2:11–4:11) is specific and practical, without losing contact with its theological roots or becoming banal or trivial. Throughout this section the theme of submissiveness occurs repeatedly (2:13, 18; 3:1). Yet quite obviously this submission is no cowardly grovelling before worldly power, but an acceptance of the divinely ordained structures of order and authority in the world. The Christian submits without capitulating and without surrendering his conscience. That he may have to suffer on account of his faith is a real possibility reflected throughout the letter. The final section (4:12–5:11) deals specifically with conduct in the face of persecution. The potential hostility between the church and the world, stated so succinctly in the Gospel and epistles of John and so extravagantly in Revelation, is here recognized without becoming the central point. The central point is that the Christian should be obedient to God, conduct himself in a manner beyond reproach, and endure with patience and courage the evil that unrighteous men may nevertheless inflict upon him.

The author expresses himself clearly and impressively in 2:11–25. The first paragraph (vss. 11–12) is a general introductory exhortation. "Aliens and exiles" possibly alludes to Genesis 23:4 (LXX), where Abraham calls himself an alien and exile (cf. also Heb. 11:13 and Psalms 39:12 [LXX, 38:13]). The Christian church is a pilgrim people, as was the Old Testament people of God. Here, as at many points, the language and conceptuality applied to Israel in the Old Testament is adopted for the Christian community, which regards itself as heir to the ancient promises of God. The urgent appeal to abstain from the passions of the flesh which war against the soul probably owes something, but not everything, to

Pauline usage. Uncharacteristic of Paul is the flesh-soul dualism, which is typically Greek. Yet despite the adoption of this conceptuality Peter apparently does not mean to condemn the physical aspect of man's being and exalt the psychic. For insofar as we can discern the nature of these fleshly passions, they are not primarily sexual or related lusts, but the "natural" desires of the unredeemed life. Thus although the playing off of flesh against soul is not Pauline, the actual understanding of the term "fleshly" seems to be.

The author's main interest (cf. vs. 12) is that the Christian's behavior before the world should be above reproach. Obviously he anticipates that Christians will be denounced by the Gentiles. "Gentiles" here seems to mean non-Christian rather than non-Jew, an indication that the church regards itself either as a "third race" over against both Jew and Gentile or as the true Israel, and that, in any case, the church exists against the horizon of a largely Gentile culture. All of this bespeaks a second rather than first generation origin for I Peter. "The day of visitation" refers to the eschatological event, called in traditional terminology the Last Judgment, an event anticipated in the near future (4:7). It is implied that there may be some hope for those Gentiles who have previously maligned Christians if in the end they are led by their good works to an acknowledgment of God as God (which seems to be the meaning of "glorify"). Such a humane and hopeful view would accord with I Peter's doctrine of Christ's preaching to the dead (that is, "the spirits in prison"; cf. 3:19; 4:6).

In view of the kind of conduct expected of Christians in this world, the

Emperor Otto I (962–973) offering a model of Magdeburg Cathedral to Christ in majesty (second half of tenth century). (Courtesy of Metropolitan Museum of Art. Gift of George Blumenthal, 1941.)

author urges subjection to and support of civil authority (2:13–17). This passage finds a close parallel in Romans (13:1–7). If the author of I Peter did not actually use Romans, the similarity may rest on a common tradition concerning church and state reflected also in I Timothy (2:1 f.) and perhaps going back to Jesus himself (Mark 12:17). In any event, I Peter declares that Christianity is not a this-worldly revolutionary movement. Perhaps influenced by the expectation of the near end of worldly authority with the coming of Christ (cf. 1:5, 7, 13, 20, and *passim*), I Peter deliberately and thoroughly acknowledges the right of the state to exercise its authority. The government is ordained by God for the enforcement of order and justice (1:14; cf. Rom. 13:1–5). Whereas Paul assumed that the civil authority would carry out this function, this is not quite so clear in I Peter. Nevertheless, fundamental confidence in the emperor is affirmed (vss. 13, 17).

Obedience is not urged for the sake of sheer conformity, however, and is therefore not fundamentally self-serving. First of all, it is intended to silence the calumnies against the church and against Christians that must already have been breaking out. Moreover, its ultimate end is not the complete docility of Christians and their enslavement to whatever worldly order exists at any given time or place. The two-fold injunction of verse 16, "Live as free men . . . live as servants of God," makes this very clear. These admonitions at least credit the civil order with the intention of being just. Yet clearly I Peter intends to prepare Christians for blameless behavior in the world so that charges brought against them from any quarter may be shown to be palpably false. The author does not blandly assume that all will be well in this world for Christians whose conduct is unexceptionable. The prospect of unmerited punishment and suffering is for him and for his church already a real one (1:6; 4:12 ff.; 5:9 f.). The Christian is to *respect* the secular ruler, along with men in their places; but he is to *fear* only God and to *love* the brotherhood, meaning his fellow Christians in the church (2:17).

The following paragraph (vss. 18–25) is directed specifically to servants, but has far-reaching implications for other Christians. The term translated "servants" (vs. 18) is literally "house-servants," almost surely to be understood in the sense of "slaves of the household" (cf. vs. 20). Verse 19 expresses a fundamental conviction, a point that the author makes in various ways and with respect to various situations. Within the established order the Christian conforms to the legitimate demands that are placed upon him. Even if illegitimate demands and punishment be forthcoming, he accepts his lot without rebelling. The person who has done wrong and suffers has nothing of which to boast. Rather, the righteous man who suffers unjustly has God's special approval (vss. 19, 20). The warrant for such an assertion is the example of Jesus Christ (vss. 21–25). Because

Christ has suffered for him, the man of faith follows in his steps by suffering willingly also.

The mention of Christ's suffering launches the author into a series of descriptive and theological statements about the suffering of Christ (vss. 22 ff.). These statements are probably constructed out of the Septuagint version of the servant songs of Isaiah. Their intrinsic appropriateness should not disguise the fact that they are not historical descriptions. If they seem appropriate when applied to the suffering and death of Jesus, it is partly because from I Peter on—and perhaps earlier—these Isaiah passages have been used in describing and interpreting Jesus' death. We have in I Peter the *locus classicus* for the interpretation of the death of Jesus in terms of suffering. Indeed, in relating Christ and the Christian this passage marks an important point in the development of Christological thought and its ethical implications—the recognition that Jesus' historical life and death is the norm and model for the Christian's own conduct. That the descriptive material is taken from Isaiah rather than historical observation does not alter this fact.

The author's immediate purpose was to speak a redeeming and comforting word, a word of encouragement. To do this he points to the real and meaningful relation between the slave who is perhaps unjustly beaten and Christ, who was also unjustly punished, but by whose wounds the same slaves are healed. As they are united with him in suffering, so they will be united in his glory (1:3–9; 5:10). The relevance of the suffering of Christ is not, however, limited to slaves who are being unjustly punished. Any man of faith who suffers evil unjustly for righteousness' sake will be blessed (3:14), for it is better to suffer for doing right than for doing wrong (3:17). Such a one, if he suffers according to God's will, is comparable to Christ himself (3:18). Indeed, he may be said to share in the sufferings of Christ (4:13).

The question of what historical circumstance evoked this emphasis on suffering (cf. also 1:6) has been touched upon in the notes. In all probability I Peter anticipates the harassment, if not the systematic persecution, of the readers *as Christians*. It is uncertain, however, whether the author expects a general state-sponsored persecution of Christians as such. The references to suffering as a Christian (4:14, 16) and the coming "fiery ordeal" (4:12) suggest as much. Yet the positive attitude to Roman authority expressed in 2:13–17 implies that the authority of the state is not behind the persecution of Christians, or at least is not recognized as hostile. The tenor of I Peter suggests a time, probably around the end of the first century, when the state's hostility to the church had not yet been unequivocally manifested, but was anticipated as a real possibility. The reigns of Domitian (81–96) or Trajan (98–117) are therefore likely periods.[19]

---

[19] It is possible that I Peter reflects a situation similar to that described in the cor-

Mocking and flagellation of Christ from French painted enamels by Pierre Reymond (sixteenth century). (Courtesy of Metropolitan Museum of Art. Fletcher Fund, 1945.)

Although the possible persecution, punishment, and harassment of Christians were very much on the author's mind, the situation was apparently not so acute that he was preoccupied with this problem. Most of the letter concerns the normal day-to-day business and behavior of individuals and church congregations. Thus we find in I Peter something already seen in James, Ephesians, and Colossians: the more or less stereotyped and probably traditional ethical exhortation directed to various persons or groups. In fact, despite its originality in appealing to the suffering of Christ, 2:18–25 is just such an exhortation addressed specifically to slaves. Similar exhortations to wives (3:1–6), husbands (3:7), and the whole congregation (3:8–12) follow. Possibly also the exhortations to patience, courage, and steadfastness in the face of suffering are of a traditional nature.[20] The

respondence between Pliny and the Roman Emperor Trajan (*ca.* A.D. 112). Pliny writes Trajan asking for instructions on handling the problem presented by Christians, and especially accusations made against Christians, and Trajan responds. Although Pliny and Trajan are not disposed to let Christians go unpunished, neither do they want to hunt them out. The motivating force in the persecution is apparently not Roman officialdom, but the hostility of citizens who denounce Christians to the government. Yet though Pliny and Trajan display an admirable desire to act fairly, it must be also noted that they preside over the execution of Christians who refuse to recant. Does this policy and procedure admit of the kind of approbation found in I Peter 2:13–17? (The correspondence between Pliny and Trajan is available in English translation in Henry Bettenson, *Documents of the Christian Church.* [New York: Oxford University Press, 1947], pp. 5–7.)

[20] So E. G. Selwyn, *The First Epistle of Peter: The Greek Text with Introduction, Notes and Essays* (2nd ed.; New York: Macmillan Co., 1947), pp. 439–58.

author may be an original thinker or writer, but he is also a churchman steeped in what has already become a significant body of Christian tradition. In and by tradition the church is guided and through the passing generations maintains countinuity with the past.

The Superior High Priest (Heb. 4:14–5:10)
Why is Jesus' priesthood unique and superior?

NOTES ON THE LETTER TO THE HEBREWS

Hebrews has been traditionally ascribed to the apostle Paul, but as some theologians and scholars of the ancient church suspected, it is certainly not his work. Neither the letter itself nor the ancient superscriptions claim Pauline authorship. Even less than the Pastorals, and far less than Ephesians, does it express typically Pauline ideas and interests. For example, whereas in the Pastorals faith has become belief in doctrine about Jesus instead of a vital relationship to Christ, in Hebrews faith is simply steadfastness. It does not necessarily express the relationship of the Christians to Christ at all.

Along with Pauline authorship, the document's literary character has also been questioned. Is it a letter at all? Despite the lack of an epistolary salutation, Hebrews concludes as if it were a letter (cf. 13:22–25). Yet without chapter 13 Hebrews would probably be taken for a tract or perhaps a sermon. Extensive hortatory passages or exhortations are scattered throughout the book. Hebrews differs from many other New Testament books, however, in that such passages are integrally related to the author's theological thought. They do not appear to be traditional or conventional bits of ethical wisdom and admonition joined, so to speak, end to end.

The thought of Hebrews is complex, subtle, and sophisticated. The author, whoever he may have been, was no amateur in the use of the Greek language and the methods of Biblical interpretation of his day. We should not expect to grasp the full range and complexity of Hebrews on first reading. A few questions might well be borne in mind at the outset lest the reading of the book lose direction and become confusing. What was the character of the life of the church (or churches) to which Hebrews was addressed? Were its problems similar to those Paul encountered in Galatia or Corinth? Does the character of the church and its people—for example, their seeming lassitude—indicate anything about the times in which Hebrews was written? Is any practical purpose or goal reflected in the author's subtle treatment of Old Testament themes?

The exact date, author, intended readers, place of origin, and geographic destination of Hebrews are uncertain. The situation and mood of the intended readers and the kind of ethical exhortations suggest second generation Christianity, perhaps ca. A.D. 80–90. Yet the author does not mention the destruction of the Jerusalem temple (A.D. 70) in the course of his argument concerning the new priesthood in Jesus Christ. Perhaps he is concerned with the Old Testament tabernacle and not with the contemporary temple.

The author himself is unknown. Apollos, coworker with Paul (Acts 18:24; I Cor. 1:12; 3:4 ff.), has been suggested by some, including Martin Luther in the sixteenth century. The suggestion is reasonable but can scarcely be either proven or disproven. The readers suggested by the title must be Jewish Christians, not Jews. The title is probably a later addition, however, and the author's argument does not necessarily suppose a Jewish background for his readers, only a Christian one. The reference to those from Italy sending greetings (13:24) suggests that Rome may have been the destination of Hebrews, as does its use in the late first century letter of Clement of Rome. Because of the similarities in biblical exegesis and thought patterns between Hebrews and Philo of Alexandria, it is often conjectured that the document was composed in or near Alexandria in Egypt.

OUTLINE OF HEBREWS
>Prologue: God's Final Word to Man (1:1–2)
>I. Argument: Jesus as Son and High Priest (1:3–10:18)
>>A. The Person of the Son (1:3–4:13)
>>>1. His Superiority to Angels (1:3–2:18)
>>>2. His Superiority to Moses (3:1–6)
>>>3. Warning and Admonition (3:7–4:13)
>>B. The Son as High Priest (4:14–10:18)
>>>1. Jesus' Qualifications as High Priest (4:14–5:10)
>>>2. Exhortation to Maturity (5:11–6:20)
>>>3. The Superiority of Christ's Priesthood (7:1–28)
>>>4. The High Priestly Work of Jesus (8:1–10:18)
>II. Application: the Necessity of Faithfulness (10:19–12:39)
>>A. The Response of Faith (10:19–39)
>>B. Forerunners in Faithfulness (11:1–12:11)
>>>1. The Examples of Israel (11:1–40)
>>>2. The Example of Jesus (12:1–11)
>>C. Exhortation and Warning (12:12–29)
>Conclusion: Final Exhortation, Personal Matters, and Benediction (13:1–25)

The author of Hebrews has been described as one of the three theologians of the New Testament, the others being Paul and John.[21] Our somewhat limited treatment does not reflect a low estimate of his value in relation to Paul and John. Nevertheless, Paul, by virtue of his incisiveness and insight into the human situation, and John, because of his mystical appeal and masterly portrayal of Jesus as the Christ, make contact more readily with interests of later generations than the author of Hebrews, whose central image is Jesus the great High Priest. Nevertheless, Hebrews is an important example of the depth and range of early Christian thought.

The Christological statement of the first two chapters expounds the

[21] Edwyn Hoskyns and Noel Davey, *The Riddle of the New Testament*, pp. 146 ff.

exaltation of Jesus to heaven (cf. 1:3 f.). There as the Son of God he reigns above all the angels (1:4 ff.), that is, above all heavenly and earthly powers. This exaltation of Christ is grounded in his pre-existence and his role in creation (1:2; cf. I. Cor. 8:6; John 1:1 ff.). Already the Christological confession contains a word of warning and admonition to the reader (2:1–4). Moreover, not just the heavenly exaltation of the Son, but also his earthly ministry comes into view (2:5–9), and the essential aspects of that ministry are emphasized.[22] The example of Christ's faithfulness (3:1–6) leads to an extended exhortation to faithfulness (3:6–4:13). As the careful reader perceives, this section is not just a series of exhortations strung together; Hebrews represents a careful and elaborate argument in which the church's situation is compared with that of Israel in its forty years of wandering in the wilderness. On the basis of the Old Testament scriptures, the author strenuously contends that there is a "sabbath rest for the people of God," into which his readers, or the church, must strive to enter. They, like ancient Israel, are a people on the way, although their goal is not the attainment of an earthly territory or kingdom, but one which is future and heavenly. The author conceives the church as the wandering people of God.[23] While this conception is based upon an interpetation of the Old Testament, it is also related to the actual situation of the church to which the author wrote. Plainly in need of challenge, and in danger of losing faith and never reaching the promised rest (already in 2:3 and 2:12–14; but note especially 5:11–6:12 and 10:19–12:29), the church faced the danger of weariness after the enthusiasm and hope of the earliest days had faded—perhaps when the first apostles had died. (Compare the problem found here with the excess of enthusiasm that Paul faced in Corinth, or the zeal for the observance of the law which became a problem in the Galatian churches.) The road ahead was long, and many were tempted to abandon the journey. Perhaps, there was a danger that they would fall back into Judaism, although the malaise may have been of a more general nature.

The author's method of paralleling the Christian church with the Old

---

[22] The usually reliable RSV translators, along with many commentators, translate 2:8b "in putting everything in subjection to man." But this translation introduces a strange thought into the text and is not supported by the Greek. Some such translation as "in putting everything in subjection to him," with "him" being the Son of Man (Jesus Christ), would probably be better. The fact that Hebrews does not elsewhere use the term Son of Man is no serious objection, since the author is here using traditional Old Testament material. Moreover, this rendering fits in perfectly with the development of the author's thought. The most reliable German commentators, Otto Michel, Der Brief an die Hebräer ("Kritisch-exegetischer Kommentar," 13. Abt., 11. Aufl.; Göttingen: Vandenhoeck & Ruprecht, 1960), p. 71, and Hans Windisch, Der Hebräerbrief ("Handbuch zum Neuen Testament," 14, 2. Aufl.; Tübingen: Mohr, 1931), p. 20, understand the text in this way.

[23] E. Käsemann, Das wandernde Gottesvolk: Eine Untersuchung zum Hebräerbrief (2. Aufl.: FRLANT, 55; Göttingen: Vandenhoeck & Ruprecht, 1957).

Testament is called typology or typological exegesis. An Old Testament figure is understood as the type or prototype of some aspect of Christian revelation. Yet the moving force of his appeal is not the Old Testament. The ground upon which the author stands, and upon which he urges his readers to stand, is the reality of Jesus Christ as the basis of hope and faith. Nevertheless, faith is mentioned quite apart from Jesus (cf. chap. 11), and in the long section 3:6–4:3 faith is not related to Jesus in the way we would expect in the light of Acts, Paul, the Gospels, and even James. For Hebrews faith is steadfastness or persistence in hope; this is clear here as well as in the famous faith chapter (11). It is not specifically faith in Jesus Christ.[24]

Yet the ultimate ground of faith is Jesus Christ. Clearly the "holding fast" of faith (4:14 ff.) would be pointless apart from him. Central to the author's understanding of Jesus is the concept of the "great high priest who has passed through the heavens." He is the guarantor of the salvation that is promised. The description of the heavenly enthronement of Jesus as the Son (chaps. 1 and 2) precedes an extended discussion of the heavenly high priestly activity of the enthroned Christ. The explanation and exposition of his high priestly ministry is the subject of much of the remainder of the letter, especially chapters 7–10.[25] Hebrews seeks to show in detail how Jesus' heavenly high priesthood directly affects the church and the Christian. It is the surety supporting the Christian's life in the world and sustaining his hope. With such encouragement he can "hold fast our confession" (4:14), which is doubtless the church's expression of faith and hope in God, through Jesus Christ.

That the high priestly ministry of Jesus is the basis for renewal of confidence and hope is succinctly stated in verses 4:15 f. In fact, the Christology of Hebrews is well summarized in 4:14–16, especially in the two very different assertions about Jesus in verses 14 and 15—namely, that he is the great heavenly high priest (vs. 14), and at the same time the "one who in every respect has been tempted as we are, yet without sinning" (vs. 15). It is not sufficient to ground the church's confidence in the heavenly ministry of Jesus. This alone could have no effect, no relevance,

---

24 A recent full-scale treatment of the subject of faith in Hebrews has established the reasons for this remarkable fact: cf. E. Grässer, *Der Glaube im Hebräerbrief* ("Marburger theologische Studien," 2; Marburg: Elwert, 1965).

25 The author could assume his readers' familiarity with the concept of a priest as a mediator between God and man, especially in matters of sin and purification. In the Jewish tradition sacrifices were, of course, made at the Jerusalem temple, over which the priesthood, headed by the high priest, presided. The function of the priest was to maintain an open channel of communication with the divine and, by offering sacrifice for sin and abolishing impurity, to insure the divine favor. Ordinary priests had continually to offer sacrifice to insure this favor. Thus the effectiveness of their work was always open to question. According to Hebrews, however, Jesus sacrificed himself in obedience to God and became the eternal sacrifice and High Priest, a sure and permanent mediator of divine favor.

for men on earth. Already the author's logic impresses itself upon the reader. Christ could not act for men unless he sympathized with them and he could not sympathize with men unless he had really shared human nature and experience (cf. 2:14). The heavenly, high priesthood of Jesus is relevant to mankind because it is the high priesthood of a man. Hebrews perhaps contains the earliest clear, straightforward New Testament statement of what in later years became the classical Christian understanding of the incarnation—that is, God's presence in Jesus of Nazareth. God is present in Jesus, in his earthly and in his heavenly ministry, but not in such a way that Jesus ceases to be a man and becomes by this fact a heavenly supernatural being, unbelievable or irrelevant to men.

Nevertheless, in spite of Jesus' full participation in human life, he is not overcome by its temptation; he does not sin. It would be a mistake to think that the author of Hebrews had such intimate historical knowledge as to know that Jesus at every moment of his earthly existence was free from sin. On the other hand, it would be equally wrong to suppose that by sin the author meant some kind of personal impurity. "Without sinning" means that Jesus did not succumb to the fundamental temptation to abandon God in faithlessness—that is, in weakness, cowardice, lack of persistent steadfastness. This is the sin against which the author warns his readers.

This two-fold Christological assertion (vss. 14 f.) lays the basis for the following exhortation and invitation (vs. 16). The term "throne of grace" implies the presence of Christ the high priest at the right hand of God (1:3). The understanding of the gospel as God's grace is, of course, a thoroughly and typically Pauline thought. The fact that the concept of grace was from the first recognized as Pauline is shown by its presence not only in the genuine Pauline letters, but also in the Pastorals, Ephesians and Acts, especially the chapters dealing with Paul. The use of "grace" in I Peter and Hebrews may indicate that these documents also belong within

A Byzantine medallion with Christ enamelled on gold (eleventh century). (Courtesy of Metropolitan Museum of Art. Gift of J. Pierpont Morgan, 1917.)

the Pauline sphere of influence, for elsewhere in the New Testament the term is surprisingly infrequent.[26] Although in Hebrews "grace" is not the object of theological discussion, it seems to have Pauline roots. It is God's graciousness, his love freely given. As in the case of faith, however, grace in Hebrews does not appear to be clearly and explicitly tied to the event of Christ's coming. Yet the concept of grace is important to the author in that he wishes to emphasize the God-givenness as well as the dependability of the ground of the Christian hope. For all his urgings, he does not ask that the church become what it is not, but only that it be what it already is—a people whose status and assurance is grounded in a merciful God (vs. 16; 6:13–20). Confidence is expected to lead not to complacency, but to further striving. No one is asked to act, to get busy and do something, because he is in desperate circumstances. On the contrary, his welfare is assured, if only he will persist in faith and not grow weary.

The people of God must not lose its will or its way; therefore, the people must be reminded of the sure hope of reaching the goal. Although the general theme of the wandering people of God gives continuity to the entire book, the climactic theological moments have to do with Christ himself, the heavenly high priest.[27] An extensive statement of Jesus' qualifications for the high priesthood appears in 5:1–10. It falls into two distinct parts—first, a general statement of the qualifications for the high priesthood (5:1–4); second, a declaration of the way in which Jesus corresponds to these qualifications (5:5–10).

The model of the high priestly ministry (5:1–4) is the Jewish priesthood, which administered the temple cult in Jerusalem until the siege and ultimate destruction of the city and the temple in the Roman war.[28] No other priesthood comes into consideration except insofar as the Jewish priesthood bore certain resemblances to that of other religions. This priesthood provides the pattern for Jesus' own ministry. The succinct, clear definition of the high priest's office and function (vs. 1) could equally apply to the entire Levitical priesthood. Although the high priest had a special office, he could effectively exercise this office only because of his common lot with the people (vs. 2). This is, in effect, the first qualification of the priest. In the case of the ordinary priest, and in distinction from Jesus, there was nothing particularly commendable about this, since what he shared with the people led him to sin. He had to offer sacrifice on his own

---

[26] The Greek *charis*, grace, occurs not at all in Matthew and Mark, a few times in Luke (but more often than not without theological meaning), only in the prologue of John, twice in one verse and nowhere else in James, twice each in II and III John and Jude, but not at all in I John. By contrast *charis* occurs in every Pauline and deutero-Pauline letter, including the brief note to Philemon, and is quite frequent—for example, 22 occurrences in Romans and 18 in II Corinthians.

[27] Käsemann, *Das wandernde Gottesvolk*, p. 156.

[28] On the meaning of sacrifice see the discussion of Romans 3:21 ff., pages 331 ff.

behalf (vs. 4). Christ, on the other hand, although subject to human temptation, was without sin (4:15). The second qualification (vs. 4) speaks for itself.

In showing that Christ fulfills both qualifications for the high priesthood (vss. 5–10), the author begins with the second. He affirms with the New Testament generally that the significance, honor, and glory of Christ are not things he claims for himself. They are based neither upon fantastic egoism nor self-esteem. Quite the contrary, Jesus' own life is one of self-giving service, not arrogance. His peculiar dignity has no human basis, but stems from the call and appointment of God. As proof the author turns once again to the Old Testament, which he regards as the definitive expression of the will and purpose of God, when rightly understood and interpreted. Psalm 2:7, quoted in 5:5, appears also in 1:5 and in Acts 13:33 and seems to have been an important Christain proof-text. However, the quotation from Psalm 110:4 (Heb. 5:6) is even more important for the author's argument. For the theological exposition from this point through chapter 10 (as distinguished from the exhortations) will be devoted to the theme of Jesus as high priest after the order of Melchizedek.

The larger part of the next paragraph (vss. 7–9) deals with Jesus' fulfill-ment of the first qualification of the high priest (cf. vs. 2). Here the author takes up and develops ideas already set forth (2:9, 11, 14, 17 f.). There is little doubt that verse 7 is a conscious reference to the agony of Jesus in the Garden of Gethsemane (Mark 14:32–42 parr.), although the details do not correspond to the Synoptics and the meaning of the last clause is not clear. Jesus apparently was not heard, since God did not save him from death, unless we suppose that the author has the resurrection in view. This is a possible conclusion, although the more appropriate understanding of the text is that such prayer does not necessarily remove suffering, even when God hears it. God heard Jesus, but did not spare him from the cross.

The attitude of those to whom the author speaks is almost the opposite of that of a modern religious humanism that easily sees in Jesus the social reformer but balks at statements implying his divinity. That Christ was the exalted Lord was the assumption of both the reader and the author. But Hebrews emphasizes the real humanity of the Son, so that he can claim Jesus' own experience as a relevant example for the church of his day. That church, like Jesus, must learn obedience through suffering (vs. 8); it must actualize obedience in the willing acceptance of suffering.

The perfection of which the author speaks (vs. 9) comes about then through suffering. Not only is this implied by the context, but it is explicitly stated in 2:10 that Jesus, the "pioneer of salvation," was made perfect through suffering. It is not a matter of one who was morally imperfect being made perfect, since Jesus was already without sin. Rather, it is perfecting in the sense of completing and fulfilling the qualifications of the high priest, who as one of the people leads them before God. The term "pioneer" (2:10) is well chosen, for the author looks upon Jesus not only as the heavenly high priest above and beyond the people, but as the one who leads them to salvation, undergoing the same experience as they (cf. again 2:10; also 2:14 ff.). The wandering people of God have Jesus as their pioneer. Through suffering he has been made perfect. Thus he has already arrived at the heavenly goal. His people follow, enabled to do so because he has both led them and arrived ahead of them. He now lives and works at God's right hand as the superior high priest after the order of Melchizedek (5:10). So the Christian can affirm:

> We have this as a sure and steadfast anchor of the soul, a hope that enters into the inner shrine behind the curtain, where Jesus has gone as a forerunner on our behalf, having become a high priest forever after the order of Melchizedek (6:19–20).

To say that Jesus is the great Melchizedekian high priest does not seem to be a very helpful way of explaining who he is. Yet about four chapters of Hebrews (7–10) are devoted to this theme. Why should the author attempt to explain the relatively better known, Jesus, by means of the lesser known, Melchizedek (cf. Genesis 14:17–20; Psalm 110:4)?

The author proposes to demonstrate that the Old Testament Jewish priesthood is but a prototype and a shadow of the true priesthood and that this true priesthood is to be found in Jesus Christ. The key to his procedure is concealed in the quotation from Psalm 110:4 (cf. Heb. 5:6). When this Psalm is read in its entirety, the reason for the author's peculiar preoccupation with Melchizedek comes to light. The Psalm is addressed to the king, the Lord's anointed (the Messiah), and he is called a priest forever after the order of Melchizedek in verse 4. Since Jesus was the Messiah, the Christ, what is said of the Messiah in the Old Testament is said of him; and since Psalm 110 is about the Messiah, the Melchizedek title is a messianic designation applying to Jesus. Genesis 14:17–20, the brief Old Testament story of Melchizedek, then serves to demonstrate that the Melchizedekian high priesthood is superior to the Levitical (cf. Heb. 7:1–10). It is the true, real and effective priesthood. This point is elaborated and supported by additional Old Testament evidence and other arguments, which comprise the greater part of chapters 7–10. The author does not wish to say anything about Melchizedek per se, but the concept of his priesthood provides a means of showing from scripture that the Levitical priesthood and sanctuary are only a shadow and prototype of the one great High Priest in his heavenly sanctuary (9:24).

The central fact is the eternal validity and effectiveness of the ministry of Jesus, the exalted Lord, as heavenly High Priest (8:1 ff.). The discussion of the nature of the Old Testament Levitical high priesthood serves indirectly to illumine it. That high priesthood was not wrong or unnecessary, but it was, nevertheless, ultimately ineffectual. Because both it and all that pertained to it were a shadow and a copy (8:5) of Jesus' heavenly high priesthood, it had to be replaced by him. The author seeks to make the death and heavenly ministry of Christ intelligible through the Biblical descriptions of the purpose and practice of the Levitical high priesthood. The sacrifical system then becomes a means of understanding and interpreting what Christ accomplished and accomplishes. What other priests did over and over again in a vain attempt to deal with sin, Christ has done once and for all (9:25 ff.).

Hebrews grounds the call to follow, to be steadfast, to have faith, in the reality of this true High Priest, qualified by virtue of his human experience, validated by Old Testament prophecy, and now at the right hand of God. Having successfully run the course himself, he is not only the great example, but as heavenly High Priest, the source of encouragement and consolation for those who have grown weak or faithless along the way.

Suggestions for Further Reading

In addition to the commentaries in the General Bibliography, note B. Reicke, *The Epistles of James, Peter, and Jude* ("The Anchor Bible," 37; Garden City, N.Y.: Doubleday, 1964). The development of the church, particularly its ministry, during the period of these later letters is dealt with by B. H. Streeter, *The Primitive Church* (London: Macmillan, 1929). E. Schweizer has analyzed the understanding of the structure of the church explicit or implicit in the various New Testament books; his *Church Order in the New Testament* (SBT, 32; Naperville, Ill.: Allenson, 1961) will be particularly helpful for the later New Testament books. A good summary of these books and their meaning is found in J. C. Beker, *The Church Faces the World* (Philadelphia: Westminster, 1960).

Ephesians. Perhaps the best commentary on the English text is F. W. Beare, *IB,* X (1953). E. J. Goodspeed, *The Meaning of Ephesians* (Chicago: University of Chicago Press, 1933), sets forth his position regarding the letter's origin; the work is technical. Goodspeed's view is essentially confirmed by C. L. Mitton, *The Epistle to the Ephesians: Its Authorship, Origin, and Purpose* (Oxford: Clarendon Press, 1951). Both works are helpful in understanding Ephesians as the work of a later disciple of Paul. The position of Goodspeed on the origin of Ephesians is developed by J. Knox, *Philemon among the Letters of Paul* (rev. ed.; New York: Abingdon, 1959).

Pastorals. B. S. Easton, *The Pastoral Epistles* (New York: Scribner's, 1947), is a good commentary. Also valuable is F. D. Gealy, *IB,* XI (1955).

P. N. Harrison, *The Problem of the Pastoral Epistles* (Oxford: Humphrey Milford, 1921), demonstrates why the Pastorals in their present form can scarcely be considered the writings of Paul.

James. There is a recent extensive commentary by C. L. Mitton, *The Epistle of James* (Grand Rapids, Mich.: Eerdmans, 1966).

I Peter. The discussion of authorship and related problems in F. W. Beare, *The First Epistle of Peter: The Greek Text with Introduction and Notes* (rev. ed.; Oxford: Blackwell, 1958), will be of service to the student who knows no Greek. On the historical figure of Peter, see O. Cullmann, *Peter: Disciple—Apostle—Martyr*, trans. F. V. Filson (rev. ed.; Philadelphia: Westminster, 1962).

Hebrews. F. F. Bruce, *The Epistle to the Hebrews*, ("The New International Commentary on the New Testament"; Grand Rapids, Mich.: Eerdmans, 1964) offers perhaps the most substantial commentary on the English text of Hebrews. Also worthwhile is the commentary of Montefiore in the Harper series (1964). A general treatment of Hebrews is W. Manson, *The Epistle to the Hebrews: An Historical and Theological Reconsideration* (London: Hodder & Stoughton, 1951). Most recently there has appeared F. V. Filson, *Yesterday: A Study of Hebrews in the Light of Chapter 13* (*SBT*, n.s. 4: London: SCM, 1967).

Conclusion

10 The

Johannine

Literature

So far, we have dealt with the background of the New Testament, the Synoptic Gospels and Jesus, and the early church and Paul. All the major parts of the New Testament except one have thus been considered.[1] That one remaining part is the so-called Johannine literature. The Johannine books in the order in which they appear in the New Testament are the Gospel of John, the three letters of John, and the Revelation to John.

[1] Although II Corinthians and II Thessalonians have not been treated, I Corinthians and I Thessalonians have. II Timothy and Titus have not been treated directly, but we have dealt with the Pastorals generally and I Timothy in particular. Thus only II Peter and Jude are omitted. They illustrate the further development in early Christianity of themes that have already been observed: the growth of orthodoxy and church order and the fight against heresy. The two documents are similar in other ways. Probably both, and certainly II Peter, are pseudonymous. Both are probably late, written in the second century. Moreover, Jude is the earlier, for the author of II Peter evidently had the little letter before him when he wrote.

"Christ in Glory," a tapestry in the Coventry Cathedral, England, designed by Graham Sutherland. It is 78 feet long, 38 feet wide, and weighs nearly a ton. (Courtesy of Thompson-Art Reference Bureau.)

From ancient times these five have been considered the work of the apostle John, the son of Zebedee, who with his brother James and Peter was one of the inner circle of Jesus' twelve disciples. The Johannine literature stands with Paul's letters and Luke-Acts as one of the three major groups of New Testament books ascribed to one author.

The question of the authorship of the books ascribed to John is quite difficult. Whereas, for example, we certainly have four genuine letters of Paul (Roman, I and II Corinthians, and Galatians), probably have at least seven (adding I Thessalonians, Philippians, and Philemon), and possibly have as many as ten (with Ephesians, Colossians, and II Thessalonians), it is by no means even probable that any of the Johannine books were written by the apostle John. None of the five books explicitly claims to have been written by him. The most important textual evidence is the ascription of Revelation to someone named John (1:1, 4, 9; 22:8), who never calls himself an apostle, but rather a brother, a servant of Jesus Christ, and a prophet. I John is completely anonymous. II and III John are written by a mysterious figure who refers to himself only as the elder. In the Gospel the author is finally identified as the Beloved Disciple (21:24), an unnamed follower of Jesus who plays an important role in the book. Yet the whole of chapter 21 is almost surely a later addition and its testimony therefore somewhat questionable. Although the Beloved Disciple has for centuries been identified with John, the son of Zebedee, this identification cannot be proved from the Gospel itself.

We may well ask by what right we speak of the "Johannine literature" at all. The tradition ascribing the books to the apostle John, the son of Zebedee, cannot be traced back to a time earlier than the latter part of the second Christian century. On the other hand, important reasons for considering all except one of these books as a group were set forth as early as the third century by Dionysius, the scholarly bishop of Alexandria in Egypt. He clearly saw the close relation in language, style, and thought between the Gospel and the First Letter of John. In addition, he pointed out how greatly Revelation differs in speech and thought from the Gospel and I John, concluding that Revelation could not be the work of the same author.[2] (The very brief II and III John were rather slow in being recognized as canonical books, although they too have close affinities with the Gospel and with I John.[3]) With the general acceptance of Revelation into the New Testament, Dionysius' misgivings were forgotten and the book was ascribed to the apostle along with the other Johannine writings. Occasionally, however, a dissenting voice was raised—for example, Martin Luther's in the sixteenth century. When in the modern period the New Testament was subjected to literary and historical criticism, Dionysius'

---

[2] See Eusebius, *EH*, VII, xxv, 1–24.

[3] See R. H. Charles, *A Critical and Exegetical Commentary on the Revelation of St. John* (*ICC*; Edinburgh: Clark, 1920), I, xxiv ff., xlii f.

objections to the unity of authorship were rediscovered. Since that time there has been a consensus of critical opinion against the ascription of Revelation to the same author as the Gospel and Epistles, although some scholars have refused to grant that Revelation and the Gospel could not have been written by the same man. R. H. Charles, who has written the most extensive English treatment of Revelation, denies the traditional claim of common authorship, but adduces striking evidence of a real and tangible relationship between the Gospel and Revelation.[4] Thus although the Johannine literature probably cannot be considered the work of one man, apostle or other, the Gospel and Epistles are closely related, and some as yet undefined relation may very well exist between them and Revelation.

The Johannine literature as traditionally defined comprehends the range of literary forms to be found in the New Testament. There is, in the first place, that most ancient form of Christian writing, the letter, represented by II and III John, if not by I John. Possibly an editorial revision has attempted to make a letter out of I John, which may have originally been a homily or tractate. (Such a combination of literary forms already finds precedent in the New Testament in such books as Hebrews, I Peter, and James.) The Revelation to John represents another ancient form of Christian as well as Jewish literature, the apocalypse. As a form of Christian expression, the apocalypse is older than the Gospel; our oldest Gospel, Mark, incorporates a still older apocalyptic document in chapter 13. Finally, we have the Gospel of John, sufficiently different from the other Gospels to set it apart as a special case, sufficiently similar to leave no doubt that it belongs to the same general category.

Corresponding to the variety of literary forms is a variety of theological and other interests also closely paralleling the rest of the New Testament. The ethical exhortations that fill the Pauline and especially the deutero-Pauline books are frequent in I John. The concern with church organization and orthodoxy which we have seen in other later New Testament documents appears in all three letters. The Synoptic and Pauline expectation of the end time and the return of Jesus becomes the chief subject of Revelation. The Gospel of John has the same general purpose as the Synoptic Gospels, which is aptly summarized in the original conclusion of the book: "these things are written that you may believe that Jesus is the Christ, the Son of God, and that believing you may have life in his name" (20:21). That many differences appear when one begins to define more precisely the purposes and character of each Gospel is beyond

---

[4] For the arguments against common authorship, *ibid.* I, xxix–xxxii; for evidence supporting a relationship, xxxii ff. Also note C. K. Barrett, *The Gospel According to St. John: An Introduction with Commentary and Notes on the Greek Text* (London: SPCK, 1956), pp. 113 f., for an interesting attempt to account for this relationship by the hypothesis of a Johannine circle or school. Most recently a similar suggestion of a Johannine school has been put forward by R. E. Brown, *The Gospel According to John (I-XII)* ("The Anchor Bible," 29; Garden City, N.Y.: Doubleday & Co., 1966).

doubt, but such differences also appear among the Synoptic Gospels alone. The Johannine literature is a distinct and separate witness to the reality of the Christ event, embracing the central interests and concerns, as well as the literary forms, of the other New Testament books.

The Gospel According to John: The Glory of Jesus

NOTES ON THE GOSPEL ACCORDING TO JOHN

Of all the books of the New Testament, John's Gospel is perhaps at once the most intriguing and perplexing—intriguing because of its contents and the questions it raises, perplexing because of the seemingly insoluble nature of some of these same questions. We shall here deal briefly with only the most important problems.

(1) The most obvious problem is the relation of John to the Synoptics. The Gospel of John differs widely from the other Gospels in a number of very specific ways. In John the geographical locus of Jesus' ministry is mainly Judea rather than Galilee; Jesus travels to Jerusalem more frequently; his ministry apparently takes place over a longer period; there are fewer, but more impressive miracle stories; and Jesus speaks in long discourses about himself and his mission. Besides this, many events of the Synoptic accounts are missing in John. The most notable omissions are Jesus' temptation, the confession of Peter, the institution of the Lord's Supper, and the agony in Gethsemane. Conversely, much of what is found in John does not appear in the other Gospels—for example, the wine miracle at Cana, the long controversies with the Jews, the raising of Lazarus, and the extended farewell discourse and prayer with the disciples. In reading John after having studied the Synoptics one can quickly grasp the extent and nature of these differences and discover others. How are they to be explained? Did John know the other Gospels and attempt to supplement, correct, or replace them with his own? Or, did he not know them, either because he lived in a remote place, or because he wrote before the other evangelists—at least before he was able to see and digest their works?

(2) A related question has to do with the identity of the author and the date and place of composition.[5] According to the ancient and generally accepted tradition of the church, dating at least as far back as the end of the second century, the Fourth Gospel is the work of the apostle John (presumably the son of Zebedee, although this is not always clearly stated in the early sources), who lived to a ripe old age in the city of Ephesus and composed the Gospel while residing there. But there are reasons for taking a skeptical attitude toward this tradition. First, our earliest sources are silent about any Ephesian residence of the apostle John. For example, in writing to the Ephesians at the beginning of the second century, Ignatius makes a great deal of Paul's connection with

---

[5] For a fuller treatment of these matters see Barrett, *The Gospel According to St. John*, pp. 83–119, and Brown, *The Gospel According to John*, pp. lxxxvii–civ.

Ephesus, but says nothing about John's having lived there. Yet if the tradition is right, John lived in Ephesus much longer and later than Paul, and the memory of him should have been much fresher. Second, John is not widely quoted by orthodox Christian writers until the end of the second century. This suggests that the acceptance of John's Gospel as canonical was not immediate. Moreover, we know that the Fourth Gospel was rejected completely in some quarters of the church. In the third place, traces of evidence indicate that John, the son of Zebedee, may have been martyred, perhaps at the same time as his brother James (Acts 12:2). How seriously one takes this evidence is likely to depend on whether he understands Mark 10:39 as a positive indication of the martyrdom of John as well as James. It is argued, with some force, that this saying of Jesus would not have been preserved had it not been fulfilled by the death of both James and John. Fourth and finally, the Gospel of John itself does not name the Son of Zebedee as its author. It is often argued that the Gospel points unerringly in this direction. If, however, the ancient tradition of the church did not name John as the author, it is doubtful that one would think of him in connection with this Gospel. Some would say that John presents himself under the guise of the Beloved Disciple. But if this is so he presents himself incognito, for nowhere is the Beloved Disciple identified with John, not even in 21:24, where he is named the author of the Gospel. Furthermore, at least this verse, and probably all of chapter 21, is a later editorial addition to the original Gospel.

(3) Over and above these reasons for questioning the traditional view of Johannine authorship, there is the further question posed by the character of the Gospel itself. Does it represent an eyewitness report of Jesus' ministry? Probably not. If we take the Synoptic Gospels, especially the Synoptic tradition of Jesus' preaching, as a reliable guide to the way Jesus spoke and taught, then it is difficult to accept the Johannine picture of Jesus as historical in the strictest sense. The words of John's Jesus have a different aura about them. Thus even those who defend Johannine authorship usually acknowledge that the evangelist has by no means presented a verbatim account of Jesus' words and deeds, but has exercised a free hand in reinterpreting what Jesus actually said and did.[6]

Although the date and place of composition must remain uncertain, especially if the tradition of Johannine authorship is doubtful, we are not completely at a loss in fixing the origin of the Gospel. The earliest certain evidence of its use (that is, commentaries, papyrus fragments, and the like) stems from Egypt. However, those scholars who do not accept the traditional locus of Ephesus tend to favor a Near Eastern, especially Syrian, origin. Although it can no longer be assumed that the Fourth Gospel is dependent on one or all of the other three, and is thus necessarily later, the situation of the church and the development of Christian thought that it reflects combine to indicate a date no earlier than about the last decade of the first century.[7]

(4) Another problem that further complicates the picture is the religious and cultural background of the Fourth Gospel. From what milieu does it stem

---

[6] Brown, *The Gospel According to John*, pp. xcix–c.

[7] *Ibid.*, pp. lxxx–lxxxvi, especially lxxiv.

and to what sort of audience is it addressed? If the Gospel stems directly or indirectly from John, the son of Zebedee, a Palestinian background must be presupposed. The many differences from the Synoptics and the apparently Hellenistic language and thought of the Fourth Gospel once made a Palestinian origin appear impossible. The discovery of the Dead Sea Scrolls and the recognition that Palestinian Judaism of the first century took several forms and was not simply the prototype of rabbinic Judaism have meant that a Palestinian origin of the Johannine tradition no longer appears out of the question. At present the problem of the origin and background of the Fourth Gospel is vigorously debated.

(5) The question of the intended audience of the Gospel is no less contested. Is the Gospel addressed to Jews, Jewish Christians, Christians in general, or the unconverted pagan world? It may well be that the evangelist envisions more than one, or all, of these groups. Efforts to pinpoint the intended audience in terms of one specific cultural or religious group have not been successful; at least no one proposal has produced anything resembling a consensus of opinion. Of course, the key statement in the Gospel is the closing words: "These are written that you may believe that Jesus is the Christ, the Son of God, and that believing you may have life in his name" (20:31).

(6) Uncertainty exists as to whether the canonical text of John has been partially rearranged and edited. Probably at least chapter 21 is a later addition. Nevertheless, we shall take as a starting point the Gospel in the form in which it lies before us in all Greek manuscripts and versions. The basic organization is rather simple:

OUTLINE OF THE GOSPEL ACCORDING TO JOHN

Introduction (1:1–51)
- A. The Prologue: Jesus Christ as the Word (1:1–18)
- B. The Baptist's Witness and the Gathering of Disciples (1:19–51)

I. The Revelation of Christ's Glory Before the World (2:1–12:50)
- A. Jesus Before the Institutions and Representatives of Judaism (2:1–4:54)
- B. Jesus and the Jewish Authorities (5:1–11:53): The Healing of the Man Born Blind (9:1–41)
- C. The Conclusion of Jesus' Public Ministry (11:54–12:50)

II. The Revelation of the Glory of Christ Before the Community (13:1–20:31)
- A. The Last Supper (13:1–38)
- B. Jesus' Farewell Discourses with His Disciples (14:1–16:33)
- C. Jesus' Last Will: The Prayer of Consecration (17:1–26)
- D. The Arrest and Trial (18:1–19:16)
- E. The Crucifixion and Burial (19:17–42)
- F. The Empty Tomb and the Resurrection Appearances (20:1–31)

Appendix (21:1–25; probably a later addition)

THE PROLOGUE: JESUS CHRIST AS THE WORD (1:1–18)

Why is the term "Word" used in the prologue and to whom is it applied?
What does the prologue say about Jesus' origin and mission?
What is the purpose of the recurring references to John the Baptist?

The prologue of John is the traditional Gospel reading for Christmas Day, for the church has discerned that it expresses more fully than the birth stories of Matthew and Luke the import of the coming of the Christ into the world.

Plaque from a tenth-century German or north Italian book cover. Agnus Dei displayed on a cross between emblems of the four evangelists—Matthew, the man; Mark, the lion; Luke, the ox; and John, the eagle. (Courtesy of Metropolitan Museum of Art. Gift of J. Pierpont Morgan, 1917.)

The rhythmic, poetic character of the prologue can best be perceived in Greek, especially when the text is printed in strophic form. But even the English translation conveys something of the solemn and portentous character of the prologue's language and style. There is, for example, a peculiar chain-like progression in the repetition of key words in verses 1–5 and 9–12. A recent translation admirably preserves both the strophic form and this chain-like sequence:

> In the beginning was the *Word;*
> the *Word* was in God's presence,
> and the *Word* was *God.*
> He was present with *God* in the beginning.
> Through him all things *came into being,*
> and apart from him not a thing *came to be.*
> That which had *come to be* in him was *life,*
> and this *life* was the *light* of men.
> The *light* shines on in the *darkness,*
> for the *darkness* did not overcome it.[8]

Although the sequence is not perfect, it is too pronounced to be coincidental and unintentional. The poetic structure of the prologue is, however, sharply broken by 1:6–8 and 15 (set off in RSV by a separate paragraph in the one case and by parentheses in the other), which refer not to the Word, the subject of the rest of the prologue, but to John the Baptist. In addition, several other verses (for example, 13, 17–18) are probably not a part of the basic poetic structure.

Probably we are here dealing with an early Christian hymn that the evangelist has annotated and incorporated into his Gospel. (Cf. Phil. 2:6–11; Col. 1:15–20; and I Tim. 3:16 for other such hymns.) The hymn might possibly be pre-Christian, but more likely the evangelist adopted a Christian hymn used by his own church. When the probable additions and annotations are stripped away, its language, style, and theology are still "Johannine"; the basic hymn and the Gospel appear to share a common perspective and vocabulary.[9]

The RSV paragraphing offers an initial clue to the character and content of the prologue. As we can see, verses 1–5 are a literary unit, the first part of the prologue or hymn; verses 6–8 are a prosaic interpolation. Then comes the second section of the hymn, verses 9–12(13), followed by the third and concluding section, verses 14–18 (less vs. 15, another prosaic interpolation). These divisions correspond roughly to the thematic divisions of the prologue. In verses 1–5 the theme is God, creation, and the Word;

---

[8] Brown, *The Gospel According to John,* p. 3.

[9] Quite aside from its importance in the Gospel, this hymn is significant for another reason. Along with other similar passages in the New Testament, it shows that the earliest church had a lively and enthusiastic service of worship in prayer and song. The study of the thought of the New Testament writers is bound to lead us to emphasize the literary and theological aspects of early Christianity and its missionary vigor. Yet if we wish to understand primitive Christianity, which gave birth to the New Testament, we must not lose sight of the vitality of the congregational life, especially as it was expressed in the praise of God and Christ. The Johannine prologue hymn is a noteworthy reminder of this.

in verses 6–8, John the Baptist; in verses 9–13, the Word in the world; and verses 14–18, the community's confession of the Word.

This structure, however, only raises the basic questions of the meaning of the prologue and its relation to the rest of the Gospel. An answer to these questions probably has to proceed initially by way of an analysis of the key term "Word" (Greek, *logos*). Who or what is the Word? In the first place, the Word is Jesus Christ. When this is said, however, several related questions are cast into sharp relief. In verses 1–5 does the author speak of the man Jesus of Nazareth, of the pre-existent Christ, or of a Christ principle? He can hardly mean that Jesus of Nazareth was with God before all creation and that he was the mediator of all creation. Where, moreover, does this concept of the "Word" originate? It is perhaps to be understood against the background of Greek philosophy, in which the term and concept of *logos* were quite important. Or it might be seen against the background of the Old Testament and Jewish concept of the word of the Lord. It is clear that the Word *denotes* Jesus Christ; what more it *connotes* remains to be determined.

The Greek philosophical meaning of *logos* is probably not related to John's use of the term. The Stoic understanding of *logos* as the world principle has little or nothing to do with the Word which is Jesus Christ. Nevertheless, the fact that the Greek term *logos* comprehends such varied meanings as explanation, argument, principle, thought or reason, language, speech, and divine utterance is relevant. So is the use of the term in late Jewish and pagan religious texts to designate God's agent in creation and world government. This last usage occurs especially in Jewish texts influenced by Greek thought, where word is sometimes identified with wisdom (Greek, *sophia*) as God's agency of communication with the world. It is clear enough that the *logos* of John is God's speech, his self-disclosure to the world, and, as the text makes plain, the means through which God creates. This range of meaning is the background of the author's usage.

But what of the Old Testament and Jewish concept of the word of God? That the word of God which spoke through the prophets was now incarnate in Jesus Christ is a proposition to which John would doubtless have assented. But nothing in the text indicates that precisely this thought was at the center of his attention when he wrote. Probably the most obvious and immediate background of the concept of the Word is the creation story of Genesis 1, which also opens with the phrase "in the beginning." Like Genesis, John speaks of the creation. Although Genesis does not say that God created all things by the Word, it does portray each stage of creation as resulting from God's speaking. "And God said, 'Let there be light'; and there was light" (Genesis 1:3). The fact that in Genesis God first creates light is paralleled by John's emphasis on light throughout the prologue. Moreover, the motifs of darkness and light appear together in both places. In Genesis God speaks and there is light where darkness had heretofore prevailed; and God separates the light from the darkness (1:3–5). This then leads to an account of the beginning of night and day. In John's prologue, however, the distinction between light and darkness develops into a sharply defined dualism, which is characteristic of the Gospel as a whole. The similarity between John and Genesis reveals the common ground on which they stand. But the strikingly different dualism of John is equally significant, for it shows that John belongs in the first-century religious world. This sharp distinction between the forces of light and darkness, truth and falsehood, God and Satan, and so on, was common not only to Zoroastrianism, Gnosticism, and late Platonism, but also to certain forms of Judaism. That such a dualistic world view could arise even within the bounds of first-century Palestinian Judaism has been shown by the discovery of the Qumran scrolls. In these documents is to be found a dualistic view of the world, men, and events very similar to that of the Gospel of John.

Nevertheless, it would be wrong to leave the impression that understanding the prologue first requires understanding the Greek use of *logos*, the Old Testament creation story, or first-century sectarian Judaism. All of these are helpful, but John speaks clearly and directly apart from those contexts. Perhaps this is why John has always been a popular Gospel for Christians, most of whom had not the faintest conception of its historical background.

The major reason why John speaks plainly is that he intends to speak only about Jesus Christ. His choice of terminology and use of motifs from the Genesis creation story turn upon his purpose of setting forth the meaning and significance of Jesus. This is true even though the name Jesus does not occur until the end (vs. 17). Of course, any Christian would know that the Word was Jesus Christ before he read further in the Gospel. Yet the name of Jesus is not called until the prologue has moved from the cosmic or the metaphysical plane to the historical.

The movement from the rather abstract, if dramatic and impressive, talk about the *logos* to the level of historical events takes place by stages. Verses 1 and 2 deal with the relation of the Word to God, which is defined in the closest possible terms without John's saying that *logos* and God are simply equivalents. The statement, "And the Word was God," is immediately qualified by "He was in the beginning with God." In addition, the Greek of the former statement lacks the definite article (*ho* = "*the*") before "God," which indicates something less than a total identification of the word with God. Still, in verses 3 and 4 the most exalted status and functions are attributed to the Word.

At this point we can scarcely avoid asking whether the evangelist actually thought that Jesus created the world. He does not explicitly say this. Yet that he thinks of the pre-existence of Jesus, not merely of the Word of God, is clear from 17:5. So we cannot deny that he could have entertained this idea. Yet certain things must be borne in mind in interpreting this text. This is a line from a hymn, not a piece of philosophical or theological prose. (The statement of 17:5 also occurs in the context of a prayer, whose formulation may have been influenced by the way early Christians actually prayed.) The early prayers and hymns of the New Testament frequently speak of the pre-existent Christ (cf. Phil. 2:6 f. and Col. 1:15 f. for example), and in I Corinthians 8:6 Paul in a liturgical or semiliturgical formula refers to "one Lord, Jesus Christ, through whom are all things and through whom we exist," as if Jesus Christ were God's instrument in creation (cf. also Heb. 1:2 f.). So the idea of Christ's playing a role in creation is not distinctively Johannine, but is characteristic of New Testament faith. Moreover, such affirmations tend to occur in solemn, if not liturgical, formulations.

That the *man* Jesus was the agent by whom God created the world is a very strange idea. For New Testament faith, however, Jesus Christ is not simply to be equated with the historical man Jesus of Nazareth, although he is inseparable from him. He is the Son of God, the Word of God, the Christ, the Son of Man. In him God reveals himself to man and acts on behalf of man in a decisive way, and the terms and categories that we find appropriate to describe historical persons and events can no longer quite comprehend him. In him the God who creates the world now saves it from its evil and folly. God's action in creation and redemption are one. Over against any purely otherworldly spirituality John affirms that the Word by which God creates the world is the same Word by which he redeems it. This Word can be identified with a special historical person and event, Jesus, whom John will name before the prologue is complete. To ask whether John, or any other New Testament writer, conceives of the man Jesus as working alongside God in creation is really to ask a question that leads away from, rather than toward, the essential theological point about the unity of creation, revelation, and redemption in Christ. The God who creates through his Word also reveals himself and saves through the same Word. Since the coming of Jesus Christ, this Word cannot be conceived in abstraction from him.

Whether verse 5 refers to the Word present in creation at the beginning and throughout history or to the Word revealed in Christ is the next question.[10] Interpreters have never agreed. Probably John intends the statement to apply to Jesus Christ as the Word become flesh. Yet the prologue could be read down to verse 14 under the assumption that the author is speaking of God's activity through his Word first in creation (vss. 1-4) and then in revelation—that is, the word of the Lord to the

[10] It is possible that the Greek *katelaben* (RSV, "overcome") in verse 5 should be translated "comprehended," in the sense of "understood." This would make the verse closely parallel to verses 10 and 11. It is not impossible that the author realizes the ambiguity of the term and intentionally uses it to convey both meanings.

Old Testament prophets and seers. In verses 10–13, however, it becomes increasingly clear that the evangelist must have had Jesus Christ already in view, although the non-Christian reader of the Gospel might not have realized this. This contention is supported by the position of the passage dealing with the Baptist (vss. 6–8). The Baptist comes before Jesus, preparing his way. Thus it would be natural to suppose the mention of the Baptist leads directly to the first explicit reference to Jesus' coming (vss. 9 ff.); or, conversely, that the first suggestion of Jesus' presence in the world, if that is to be found in verse 5, evokes the recollection of John the Baptist.

The treatment of John (vss. 6–8) is most interesting. He is a man sent from God and a witness sent beforehand that all men, or at least all Israel, might believe. The place of John as forerunner is already fixed by the earlier tradition, and it is here accepted in principle. Yet the evangelist also finds it necessary to say that the Baptist is not the light (vs. 8), probably indicating that already (vs. 5) he understands the light to be Jesus himself. This and subsequent negative statements about the Baptist in which he denies he is the Christ may represent a subtle polemic against certain of his disciples. That there were disciples of the Baptist is clear enough from the Gospels (cf. also Acts 18:25). John's Gospel affords the most tangible evidence that there was an actual rivalry between the early church and the Baptist sect.[11] Probably such a rivalry existed, extending back all the way to the period of Jesus' ministry, but the New Testament evidence permits few firm conclusions as to the nature of the Baptist sect or of that rivalry. In any event, the evangelist wishes to emphasize the singular importance of Jesus by asserting his superiority to any possible rival. The witness of John the Baptist appears again in verse 15 (cf. vs. 30). The fact that John should be introduced somewhat awkwardly at this point in order to make his witness indicates that verse 15, like verses 6–8, is probably an interpolation. Moreover, we observe the same polemical interest at work here. John bears witness as much against himself as for Jesus.

At verse 9, John shifts back into the poetic style and returns to the themes of the first five verses, as he thinks of the coming of Jesus Christ into the world (vss. 9–13). In verse 10, the "world" is used in two different senses—creation ("the world was made through him"), and the world of men ("the world knew him not"). Of the two the second is most characteristic of the Fourth Gospel and I John, where it implies the world in alienation from God. His own people is Israel, the Jews (vs. 11). The ways in which they reject him are put forth in the first half of the Gospel (chaps. 2–12), especially the closing verses of chapter 12. By their rejection of Jesus, the Jews become the prime representatives of the world. In the last half of the Gospel, the world, whether Jew or Gentile, forms the

---

[11] Such a rivalry may also be implied by such passages as Luke 7:18–35 and 11:1, although their tone is by no means so clearly polemical as John's.

hostile background against which Jesus gathers together his community of disciples, the church.

Now (vss. 12 f.) the evangelist speaks of those who receive Jesus—that is, "believe in his name." As in the Old Testament, "name" indicates more than just the verbal designation. It signifies the reality and importance of the person himself. To believe in Jesus' name is, therefore, not merely to confess him verbally, but to have faith in who and what he is. To all who so believe Jesus gives power or authority (Greek, *exousia*) to become children of God. Such children of God are born through no human agency, but through the will of God. The story of Nicodemus (chap. 3) takes up this theme of rebirth. In John those who are begotten by God are begotten by faith. Those who believe, however, may ground the certainty of their faith and of their Christian existence in the knowledge that they are children of God, his offspring. Thus through faith man acquires a certain status that nourishes and sustains him in it. Yet no one who professes to believe is told that he cannot belong to the circle of Jesus' disciples because he is not begotten of God. For John, faith is the decisive thing.

After John 3:16, 1:14 is probably the most cited passage in the Fourth Gospel. In the history of theology, it has proven to be extremely suggestive. It is the prime scriptural basis for belief in the incarnation, the Christian doctrine that in Jesus God became man. Against any Gnostic or docetic watering down of the full humanity of the Word, John 1:14 stands as an impregnable bulwark. In contrast to the modern state of mind that looks with skepticism upon any claims of manifestations of God in human life and history, ancient man was, by and large, willing and able to entertain a variety of such claims. Thus the idea that God had in some form dwelt among men was not so likely to give offense. What would be novel and potentially offensive both to Jew and to Greek was the claim that God, or at least the Word, had become flesh—that is, real, mortal man. Therefore the claim that the one who fully reveals God is nevertheless a man whose origins can be accounted for quite naturally (cf. 1:45 f.; 7:15, 41, 52; 8:48) is a constant source of consternation and offense throughout the first half of the Fourth Gospel. John's statement that the Word became flesh is unique in the New Testament. Nevertheless, it does not stand out as a strange or foreign body. If anything, the reverse is true; John 1:14 has been taken to be a kind of summation of the New Testament view of Christ, and in a real sense it is. The interpretation of the meaning and significance of Jesus as presented in the whole range of New Testament teaching is aptly epitomized in John's statement that the Word became flesh.

The Word not only became flesh or man, Jesus as a man was "full of grace and truth." Here a distinctively Pauline term, "grace," is combined with the distinctively Johannine "truth." By the time John wrote, "grace" was probably a part of the standard Christian vocabulary, a brief but meaningful way of referring to all God had done in Jesus. Although the word "truth" was certainly not strange to Christian ears, John is noteworthy for the way in which he applies the term to Jesus himself. It becomes a virtual synonym for Jesus in his solemn manifestation as the Christ. "I am the way, the truth, and the life," says Jesus to Thomas and the other disciples in the farewell discourses (14:6). Jesus is truth. In John this does not mean he is the right in contrast to the wrong, or the correct in contrast to the erroneous, not even the true in contrast to the false in the usual sense. Rather, he is the real, the genuine, the trustworthy, in contrast to everybody and everything that is false and deceptive. In short, he is the one upon whom man can depend, and who will not let him down, in contrast to all the false supports and securities of life.

Preoccupation with the doctrine of the incarnation has nevertheless meant that the rest of this verse (vs. 14) has not received the attention it deserves. The fact of Jesus Christ's coming is not introduced, but summarized, in the statement that the Word became flesh. Although the significance of this statement as a concise summation of Christian belief about Jesus is clear, the latter half of the verse is important in the development of the Gospel. Not only has this gracious and true man dwelt among men, but they—or at least some of them—have really seen him. That is, they have seen him for who he is. Thus, "We have beheld his glory. . . ." His glory is the presence and activity of God in him. In Judaism "glory" is the shining radiance of God's presence, once thought to dwell in the temple. The verb "dwell" in this same verse has the more specific meaning of "to pitch a tent," "to tabernacle." According to Jewish tradition God dwelt in his temple as in a tabernacle or tent. Indeed, the ancient predecessor of the Jerusalem temple was a tabernacle or tent, and according to the Old Testament, God's glory, name, or presence dwelt there. Thus the dwelling of the Word among us and the beholding of the glory are ideas with a prior relationship in Jewish thought. Against this background the thrust of the evangelist's statements becomes even clearer. Jesus is the new temple or tabernacle, the new place where God manifests himself to man, where his glory is beheld (cf. 2:19–22). The description of this glory, "as of the only Son from the Father," is typically Johannine. In John, Jesus is the Son and God is his Father in a special sense.

Where or how is this glory to be manifest? Only the Gospel proper can answer this question. The first half of the Gospel provides a partial answer. The glory is manifest in the word and deeds of Jesus, which are called signs. Chapters 2–12 relate these manifestations of the glory (cf. 2:11). The use of miracles as signs of Jesus' glory in John sets that Gospel in sharp contrast to the Synoptics, for in the latter Jesus refuses to do miracles as signs in this sense. Yet Jesus' glory is not simply his miraculous power. The supreme manifestation of his glory is his death on the cross (cf. especially 12:23 ff.).

When John writes, "We have beheld his glory," he refers to the apos-

tolic "we" (cf. I John 1:1 ff.). The authoritative witness in the church
attests the glory of Christ. The "we have beheld" is founded upon the
apostolic eyewitness of Jesus Christ, but is not limited to it. The physical
seeing of Jesus is not disparaged by the author, but in itself it is of no
particular advantage. Faith has direct access to Jesus. At the end of the
Gospel, Jesus says to "doubting Thomas," who has just received physical
evidence of his resurrection, "Have you believed because you have seen
me? Blessed are those who have not seen and yet believe" (20:29). Moreover, genuine seeing is not confined to physical sight, but involves true
perception of the nature of a person or thing (cf. chaps. 9 and 14). "We
have beheld his glory," therefore, does not simply vouch for the apostolic-
ity or authenticity of an eyewitness standing behind the Gospel. The "we"
who speak are not necessarily first-generation Christians or the disciples
of the historical Jesus, but all those who have rightly perceived the Word of
God in Jesus Christ and have thereby beheld his glory.

After the Baptist interpolation (vs. 15), the theme of the incarnate
glory is again taken up (vs. 16). The fact that here the "we" so obviously
means the Christian community supports our contention that the whole
church is included in the "we" of verse 14. The fullness (vs. 16) is presumably the fullness of grace and truth in the Word become flesh (vs. 14). This
is confirmed by the concluding phrase "grace upon grace," which probably
ought to be understood in the sense of "grace abounding." Jesus and Moses
are then set over against one another in almost Pauline fashion, with
Moses representing the law and grace and truth again associated with
Jesus Christ (vs. 17). Only now is Jesus actually named, and his identity
with the Word put beyond question. In a skillful way the prologue leads
the reader up to the point at which Jesus' name is called, although almost
from the beginning the Christan reader would have recognized who was
in view. The dramatic sense, demonstrated throughout the Gospel, appears
at the outset as the evangelist builds toward the climax of the prologue.
Although the polarity between Moses as law-giver and Jesus as the source
of grace and truth occupies an important place in the prologue, it is not
prominent in the rest of the Gospel. The central problem for Paul, the
relation of law and grace, has apparently become for John a thing of the
past. Later he calls the law "your law," clearly indicating that the law as
such is now considered only an aspect or institution of the Jewish religion
(8:17).

The concluding verse (18) presents a textual problem because all the
ancient manuscripts do not agree. Probably the reading "God" (RSV,
footnote) is to be preferred over "Son," even though "only Son" accords
somewhat better with John's usage elsewhere.[12] Then we would have to

[12] Both the manuscript evidence and the logic of textual criticism ("Prefer the harder
reading or the one which best explains the others") argue in favor of this reading. Its
existence in a very early papyrus manuscript (P66) indicates that it could not have been
introduced to combat the later Arian heresy.

read "only begotten God," or the like. Jesus as only begotten God would not, however, be an impossible concept for John, particularly in view of his understanding of him as the creating and revealing Word. The point is clear enough. That no one had ever seen God would have been a commonplace to the educated Jew or the sophisticated Greek, and it is surely not the author's principal purpose to enlighten his reader on this point. Instead he points once again to the definitive character of the revelation of God in Christ: "he has made him known." In a real sense, verse 18 reiterates the burden of the message of verses 14–17. The glory of God is manifest for the salvation of man in Jesus. Possibly it is significant that the evangelist maintains that no one has seen God and does not claim that now in Jesus he is seen. Jesus does say, "He who has seen me has seen the Father" (14:9); however, this statement occurs after extensive exposition on the theme of the subordinate relation of Christ to God. It is made to the disciples and presupposes the Johannine notion of seeing as truly preceiving. Moreover, it is clear from the immediate context that it does not imply a one-to-one identity of Jesus and the Father.

As verse 14 points forward to the revelation of the glory in Jesus' public ministry and finally his death, verses 16–18 point to the revelation of the glory of God in a fuller, more immediate way to the Christian church, the community of Jesus' disciples. For if the end of Jesus' public ministry is his rejection (12:37–43) and death, the end of his more intimate concluding revelations to his disciples is their believing, seeing, and knowing (chap. 17). Yet John knows that this fuller knowledge did not actually occur during Jesus' earthly life. Both the farewell discourses and certain sayings in the first part of the Gospel (2:22; 7:39; 12:16) point foward to Jesus' death and the period thereafter. The time of the resurrection, the Spirit, and the church is the time when the meaning and significance of his life and death is to be more fully understood and appreciated by his own followers.

THE HEALING OF THE MAN BORN BLIND (9:1–41)

What is the purpose of the miracle stories in the Fourth Gospel?
What is emphasized in the account of the healing of the blind man?

The miracle stories of the Fourth Gospel are distinctive. They are significantly fewer than in the Synoptic Gospels, but nevertheless more important, for they are signs manifesting Jesus' glory. The sheerly miraculous element seems heightened in John, yet the acts themselves are no more sensational than in the other Gospels. After all, Jesus appears as quite a miracle worker in Mark. But by and large John develops each story more fully by showing Jesus talking with bystanders and opponents about the miracle. He also employs a somewhat different set of narratives. The transformation of water into wine at Cana (2:1–12) has no parallel in the Synoptics; nor do the stories of the Samaritan woman (chap. 4— Jesus' knowledge of her past is miraculous), the man at the sheep gate pool (chap. 5), the man born blind (chap. 9), and the raising of Lazarus (chap. 11). Jesus' foreknowledge of Nathanael (1:45–51) may also be miraculous, in which case it also has no parallel. On the other hand, the bread miracle (6:1–14), the walking on the water (6:16–21), and the healing of the ruler's son (4:46–54) have definite Synoptic parallels (cf. Mark 6:32–44, 6:45–51, and Matt. 8:5–10, respectively). Other incidents— including the passion—have clear Synoptic parallels but are not miraculous (cf. 2:13–22; 12:1–11; 12:12–19; 13:21–30). Of the miracle stories found only in John, those of chapters 5 and 9 are similar to several Synoptic stories. The changing of water into wine, however, is a feat unparalleled in the Synoptics, where Jesus' miracles are characteristically healings or demon exorcisms. Of the latter there is not one in John. Although Jesus raises the dead in the Synoptics, there is nothing like the elaborate story of the raising of Lazarus anywhere else in the New Testament. Among the non-miraculous narratives, the story of the Samaritan woman and the parallel account of Jesus' conversation with Nicodemus (3:1–21) are without precedent in the Synoptics.

Some significance has to be attached to the arrangement of the miracle stories in John. Although there is no systematic progression from one to another, most are especially suited for their positions in the Gospel. The miracle of the new wine symbolically introduces Jesus' public ministry. The story of Jesus' revelation to the Samaritan woman (chap. 4) stands directly over against the inability of Nicodemus, the teacher of Israel, to grasp his meaning (chap. 3). The miracles of chapter 5 and 6 are integrally related to the long dialogues which follow them. The most artfully constructed and theologically pregnant of the miracle stories (chaps. 9 and 11) appear last. In the one, Jesus restores the gift of sight (light), and in the other, life. The raising of Lazarus from the dead (chap. 11) gives concreteness to Jesus' claim that "as the Father raises the dead and gives them life, so also the Son gives life to whom he will" (5:21). Thus this miracle graphically portrays the character of his mission and work. Moreover, it leads directly to Jesus' own death, which, paradoxically, is the source of life to all who believe.

Because of its distinctly Johannine character, the story of the restoration of sight to the blind man (chap. 9) merits further attention. In both style and content it is typical of the Fourth Gospel. The first paragraph (9:1–12) is in many respects similar to the Synoptic miracle stories. The story is introduced in a fairly nondescript way, with only the vaguest kind of connection with the preceding scene. Such an introduction is common in the Synoptics. The idea that sickness or deformity is punishment for sin (vss. 2 f.) is an ancient one, and dies hard (cf. Luke 13:1–5). Although Jesus rejects it (vs. 3), his own interpretation of the man's blindness is scarcely more acceptable to modern humanitarianism. Here we have one of two remarkable parallels to chapter 11, where the sickness of Lazarus is said to be for the glory of God and of the Son (11:4). The point, however, is not that God deforms people in order to show his own power, but that in and through such misfortune the power of God vindicates itself (cf. Genesis 50:20). The second parallel (vss. 4 f.) corresponds to 11:9 f. Here, and probably also in 11:9 f., we are dealing with a subtle allusion to the coming death of Jesus. Already its inevitability has been indicated by passing references of the evangelist (2:22; 7:39) and by the attitude of the Jews in controversy with Jesus (5:18; 8:37, 40, 59). Now as the public ministry begins to draw toward a close, Jesus' last acts of healing are placed under the shadow of the cross. That Jesus calls himself the light of the world (vs. 5) shows the close connection between the prologue and the Gospel proper.

The miracle itself is described briefly and with restraint (vss. 6 f.). In Mark also Jesus is said to heal with spittle (8:23); once in Luke (17:12–15) the healing likewise takes place after Jesus has sent the persons involved away. The pool of Siloam, where Jesus sent the man, has actually been located in modern times. For the evangelist, however, the significant thing

The pool of Siloam of Jesus' time is still in use in Jerusalem today. (Courtesy of Arab Information Center.)

about the pool was the meaning of its name, "sent." Throughout the Gospel Jesus is described as the one sent by God. The man's obedience to Jesus and the results are described as succinctly as possible. In fact, the basic miracle story is much less elaborate and detailed than many similar stories in the Synoptic tradition. This may indicate that John possessed a primitive miracle story in simple form. At least it shows that in this instance he was not interested in the details of the miracle (but contrast 11:38–44).

We have already seen (vss. 4 f.; possibly vs. 3), examples of the evangelist's own additions to this simple story. From verse 8 onward we lose track of the older story almost completely. We have now a dialogue, mostly in Johannine style and principally concerned with questions fundamental to Johannine theology. At most, the Synoptic miracle stories concisely report the reaction to Jesus' miracles. By contrast, John's main interest is quite obviously in the theological issues that arise as a consequence of the miracle. His emphasis is reflected in the literary form; a traditional story forms the basis of, and affords the springboard for, a developed dialogue. The dialogue, unlike anything in the Synoptics, is quite typical of John. Much the same pattern of event plus interpretation may be observed in chapters 5 and 6, and a variation upon it in chapter 11, where a traditional miracle story has apparently been interlaced with Johannine dialogue and discourse. In fact, something of the same style appears also in chapters 3 (Nicodemus) and 4 (the Samaritan woman). In both instances a meeting between Jesus and another person leads into a dialogue or a dialogue and discourse, and in each case the conversation develops just those themes that the evangelist wishes to emphasize. On a smaller scale this occurs in connection with the cleansing of the temple (2:13–22). On a considerably larger scale chapters 13 through 17 may be interpreted as conforming to this pattern. There the events of the Last Supper, especially the washing of the disciples' feet and the identification of Judas as the betrayer of Jesus, lead into an extensive dialogue and discourse. Something of the same phenomenon occurs in the trial scene, where the arraignment before Pilate, recounted in the Synoptics, provides the occasion for a uniquely Johannine account of the conversation between Jesus and the Roman procurator. Even in the resurrection story (chap. 20) the evangelist does not end the Gospel with an account of the empty tomb (Mark) or a vision of the risen Lord and a commission (Matthew and Luke). Instead, the risen Jesus engages in dialogue with Thomas, and his last word—virtually the last word of the Gospel—is his response to him (20:29). Even in the appendix (chap. 21) the same pattern appears, with Peter and Jesus engaged in conversation and Jesus' final word addressed to him.

In the Synoptic Gospels the emphasis is usually implicit in the choice, structure, and editing of the material. In John, however, such points become explicit and even tend to occupy the center of the stage. The evangelist wishes to make the issues clear and at the same time show that they are rooted in the words and work of the historical Jesus.

After the account of the healing, there are several interrogations of the blind man (9:8–12, 13–17, 18–23, 24–34). First the man's neighbors question him (vss. 8 ff.), then the Pharisees (vss. 13–17). Then the man's parents are questioned by the Jews (vss. 18–23). Finally, the Jews return to question the man himself a second time (vss. 24–34). Probably no distinction is to be drawn between Pharisees and Jews in this instance. John's characteristic designation of those who oppose Jesus and his work is simply "the Jews." When he does mention a particular sect of Judaism it is generally the Pharisees. The reason for this is not obvious. If, however, John was written after the Roman war (A.D. 70), the main Jewish opponents of Christianity would have been Pharisees. The other principal sects, Sadducees, Zealots, and Essenes, had been either dissolved or sharply reduced in size and influence as a result of that conflict. Therefore, John's reference to the Pharisees is probably an indication that they were the group most actively competing with or opposing Christianity at the end of the first century. We shall see some indication that this is the case before the end of this chapter. By contrast, the Synoptic material still views Jesus' ministry from the standpoint of Palestinian Judaism before the destruction of the temple, despite the fact that the evangelists themselves reflect a later time and far distant places.

A brief narrative (vss. 8–12) allows us to learn something more of the healed man's background and conveys the astonishment and even disbelief of his neighbors (vss. 8 f.). The man calmly and certainly identifies himself as the blind beggar whom they have known, and describes how and by whom he has been healed. As the story progresses, this man's modest but unwavering certainty becomes one of its noteworthy features. Here, as elsewhere, he possesses no theoretical or other knowledge about his benefactor except that the man called Jesus has healed him.

When brought before the Pharisees (vss. 13–17), the man's certainty and simplicity are impressive (vs. 15). For the first time we learn that the healing had been performed on the sabbath day (vs. 14), a common feature of the Synoptic tradition, where Jesus is more than once accused of illegally performing healings—and therefore working—on the sabbath (cf. also John 5). The division among the Pharisees (vs. 16) is typical of the division that Jesus causes among men. Some reject him out of hand, because he violates their preconceptions of what a holy or righteous man must be. "He does not keep the sabbath." Others are at least open to the testimony of his works, to see them as "signs," signifying who Jesus is. The question is then put to the blind man: "What do you say about him, since he has opened your eyes?" Earlier the man has simply spoken of "the man called Jesus." Now he says that he is a prophet. Probably the significance of the term "prophet" is to indicate that Jesus is not a sinner, as his detractors contend, but a man sent from God.

The Jews' mounting opposition to Jesus next takes the form of refusal to believe that the man had actually been born blind (vs. 18), so his parents are called to testify (vss. 18–23). The parents are obviously not anxious to involve themselves, but they do give a minimally truthful testimony. The man who claims to have been healed by Jesus the prophet is, in fact, their son who was born blind (vs. 20). This, however, is as far as they are willing to go. For all questions about how or by whom he was healed, the parents refer their questioners back to their son (vs. 21). The evangelist now interjects an explanation of the reticence of the parents (vss. 22 f.). This explanation does not really fit the time of Jesus, but rather the end of the first Christian century, when after the destruction of Jerusalem and the Jewish Council of Jamnia people were actually being forced to leave the synagogue for professing Christ.[13] The theme of being cast out of the synagogue occurs more than once in John (12:42; 16:2; cf. Luke 6:22). Despite the timidity of the parents, the attempt to discredit the claims of the man, and indirectly to discredit Jesus, comes to grief on the hard fact that a change has occurred in him. He was born blind, but is so no longer.

The same hearing continues and the man is called a second time (vss. 24 ff.). The opening statement scarcely encourages any hope that the Jews will function as an impartial tribunal. Despite the lack of conclusive evidence against Jesus, the opposition to him has now hardened (vs. 24). The serenity of the man healed contrasts with the obviously hostile jury (vs. 25). Rather than entering into a debate with his questioners, he simply recites what he knows on the basis of what he has experienced. This most effective and infuriating response (especially in view of the failure to show that the man was not blind in the first place) drives the questioners now to take a new tack (vs. 26). This apparent attempt to get at the facts may hide a suspicion that Jesus has used spittle in the act of healing and is therefore guilty of adopting the tricks of an illegal sorcerer. At this point the man shows the first signs of irritation (vs. 27). His reply is intentionally cutting and draws a bitter retort (vss. 28 f.). Of course, the Jews' claim to be the true disciples of Moses would not have been accepted by the evangelist (5:45–47). That the man is Jesus' disciple has not heretofore been suggested. Nevertheless, before the end it turns out to be true.

In verse 29, as throughout chapters 2–12, rejection of Jesus is based upon a religious certainty that refuses to question itself, a harking back

[13] Brown, *The Gospel According to John*, pp. lxxxv, 374, 379 f. Cf. now also J. L. Martyn, *History and Theology in the Fourth Gospel* (New York: Harper & Row, 1968), especially pp. 3–41.

to an earlier revelation that is now viewed as immutable law, admitting of no further clarification, alteration, or argument. That the Jews or Jesus' opponents do not know the origin of Jesus is altogether typical of John's thought. To know Jesus' true origin is to know that he is sent by God. The Jews ironically do not know the tragic truth of their observation that they are ignorant of Jesus' origin.[14] The man's response to the statement of the Jews, who have set themselves up as religious authorities (vs. 30), is a classic reflection upon the capacity of the self-styled judges to judge Jesus. The didactic elaboration of the brusque retort (vss. 31–33) strikes home, because it is based on presuppositions that the questioners turned accusers also share. The response of the man healed is so devastating that the Jews can only lash out in frustrated anger and vent their rage upon him. They cast him out—possibly out of the hearing room, but more probably out of the synagogue or the Jewish community (cf. vss. 22 f.).

The latter interpretation is in accord with the remainder of the account (vss. 35 ff.). After the man healed has been ejected from the Jewish community because of his refusal to repudiate Jesus, Jesus himself returns to him. At this point the man still has no special theological knowledge about Jesus. In vs. 35 we find one of the fairly numerous instances of the term "Son of Man" in John's Gospel. As in the Synoptics it appears on the lips of Jesus himself, presumably as a self-designation. Although in John it has lost much of its apocalyptic coloration (cf. Daniel 7), it is still a term of dignity, not of humiliation. The man's answer to Jesus' question is typically guileless (vs. 36). Only now does Jesus reveal his full and true identity (vs. 37). The man's response (vs. 38) indicates that he understands Son of Man to be a messianic title. How we should understand "Lord" in vs. 38 is a question. In the Synoptics the word can appear as only a polite form of address, "Milord," or "Sir," but here the meaning almost certainly goes beyond that. "Lord, I believe" is a Christological confession, as is made plain by the statement that at this point the man worshipped Jesus. The final words of Jesus (vss. 39 ff.), now addressed not so much to the man as to the total situation, are a commentary on his whole mission.[15]

What are we to make of the strange statement that Jesus has come in

---

[14] On the motif of Jesus' origin and background in the Fourth Gospel, note several earlier passages: 1:46; 3:31 ff.; 6:42; 7:15, 27, 41 f., 52; 8:23, 41 f., 57 f.

[15] There is an apparent anomaly in this statement of Jesus. For elsewhere it is explicitly said that he does not come in order to judge (3:17 f., where the word "condemn" translates the same Greek word *krinō*, "to judge"; also 12:47). From 5:22 ff, however, it is clear that the son does judge. The difficulty is resolved if we see that the ultimate purpose of Jesus' coming is not judgment but salvation (3:16 ff.). Yet from this judgment inevitably results, since some reject with great hostility the salvation that is offered and persist in evil (3:19 ff.). This negative statement of Jesus' purpose is doubtless influenced by the context, as it follows a narrative in which hostility toward Jesus and his work has been vigorously expressed.

order that those who do not see may see and in order that those who
see may become blind (vs. 39)? The traces of Jewish-Christian polemic
at the end of the first century already noted in this chapter lead us to
suspect that the same situation is in view here. Those who do not see are
not the physically blind, or the import of Jesus' statement would be that
as he goes about giving sight to the blind, so he also puts out the eyes of
those who see. Obviously this is absurd. The blindness and sight referred
to here are of a different order. Jesus said at the first of this story (vs.
5) that he is the light of the world (cf. also 1:4 ff.; 8:12; 12:46). He gives
sight to those in darkness, but those who try to walk by their own light are
blinded. To receive sight, to see the true light, one must recognize his
condition of blindness. The Jews, who insist upon their prior revelatory
knowledge ("we see") and their right to judge Jesus, become blind because
of this pretension. Their rejection of Jesus proves their blindness, whereas
their insistence that they see confirms their guilt (9:41). From here it is
only a step—perhaps the evangelist has already taken that step, but at
least he lays the basis for it—to the application of this principle to mankind at large. The pretension that one already sees prevents that self-
knowledge and recognition of one's true condition that is the first step to
genuine sight. So the effect of Jesus' appearance is to blind such people
(vs. 39), at least until they are ready to recognize their actual state.

On the basis of these observations we are in a position to make some
generalization about this chapter and its relation to the Gospel as a whole.
The chapter is a kind of paradigm of Jesus' public ministry, portraying in
dramatic form the statement of the prologue (vs. 5) that the light shines
in darkness and the darkness has not comprehended (or "overcome") it.
Moreover, verses 9–13 of the prologue take on concreteness in the light of
this story. At the same time it represents a movement or progression in
Jesus' ministry. The hostility that has become evident already (cf. chaps.
7 and 8) could not be made plainer than here. Also, this portrayal of
Jesus as the giver of sight and, by implication, of light, prepares the way for
the final manifestation of Jesus as the giver of life (chap. 11). The principal point of the story does not lie in its contribution to historical knowledge of Jesus' ministry. The questions addressed arise not out of Jesus' own
time, but out of encounters between Christianity and Judaism or Christianity and the world. That this is no "spiritualizing" interpretation of the
text, but represents the genuine intention of the author, seems clear from
the concluding word of Jesus (vss. 39 ff.); in the terms of the narrative
he succinctly characterizes his whole mission.

In the background of this chapter stands John's distinctive view of Jesus
as the light and life of mankind. The miracle itself is indispensable in that
it manifests the fact that Jesus really changes men. The stubborn insistence
of the healed man upon the fact of his healing bears eloquent testimony
to this. He grounds his relation to Jesus on what has actually happened

to him, even though he cannot give this experience adequate expression until Jesus reveals himself to him, and he acknowledges and worships the Christ whose reality and activity on his behalf he has already felt. Although the Johannine Christology is here in evidence, it is more or less in the background. In the foreground is soteriology (the concept of salvation and its effect)—not so much who Jesus is, but what he does. In fact, who he is becomes known through, and is grounded upon, what he does. As Jesus here manifests himself as the light of the world by giving sight to the blind, so in chapter 11 he appears as the resurrection and the life by raising the dead.

The fact that the specific doctrine of Christ and Jesus himself remain somewhat in the background suggests another observation. There is a sense in which the real hero of the story is the nameless man who is healed. This is true of this particular miracle story as of no other in John. Certainly not the restored man of chapter 5, nor even Lazarus in chapter 11, emerges as a hero. The ruler of 4:46–54 comes off well, as in the Synoptic parallels, but his character is not displayed and developed in the same way. However, if Jesus did not reappear at the end of chapter 9 to confirm the man in his new found faith and to pronounce a final interpretative word over the whole affair, we would have to say that after the brief account of the miracle Jesus simply fades out of the picture, except as he is present in his embryonic disciple.

Although there is no exact parallel to this in a Johannine miracle story, the account does bring to light an important Johannine characteristic—namely, the author's interest in the various types of people who confront Jesus. Whatever one thinks about the historical basis of the stories of John, clearly many of the characters who encounter Jesus are typical and perhaps symbolic. There is Nathanael, the true Israelite in whom there is no guile (1:47 ff.). There is Nicodemus, the teacher of Israel, who at first cannot comprehend Jesus and yet later defends him and finally returns to help bury him (3:1 ff.; 7:50; 19:39). In contrast to Nicodemus is the nameless Samaritan woman, the representative of a heterodox Judaism (4:7 ff.). Yet if the characters are symbolic, they are also lifelike. In chapter 11 Mary and Martha, along with the wily Caiaphas, stand out as real people. And even Pontius Pilate shows a touch of humanity in the passion narrative (18:28 ff.). Although the disciples do not appear in the farewell discourses except to ask questions, their questions are understandable in view of the total picture that John has painted. Thus Thomas' question (14:5) contributes to the traditional portrayal of him as "doubting Thomas." With the exception of Peter, and perhaps James and John, the other disciples are shadowy characters in the Synoptics. By contrast, in John some of these other disciples play significant roles (for example, Philip, Thomas, Lazarus, and Nathanael), but James and John are not mentioned by name.

Pre-eminent among the disciples in the Fourth Gospel is, of course, the unnamed Beloved Disciple, certainly an exemplary figure among Jesus' circle of disciples. We have seen that there is no firm basis in the Gospel for the traditional identification of this disciple with John, the son of Zebedee. Alternatively, the Beloved Disciple has been identified with Lazarus by some interpreters, while others have insisted that he is a composite, ideal figure, and not any single historical person. The objection that John would not have invented such a person is met by the rejoinder that we cannot prove that John did not invent any number of the characters in the Gospel, about whom we know nothing either from the Synoptics or from any other source. Here as at so many points, John alternately mystifies and tantalizes the reader and defies the historical investigator.

The story of the healing of the blind man mirrors both the characteristics and the perplexities of the Fourth Gospel. We find here a true-to-life picture of how people react when older orthodoxies are confronted by new claims and a remarkably lifelike and sympathetic picture of the man whom Jesus healed. In and behind this scene there appears John's understanding of the nature and work of Jesus Christ. Yet for all that the portrait of Jesus lacks the humanity of the other characters. This is all the more surprising in view of the intensely human—if authoritative—Jesus who emerges at many points in the Synoptic account. The Johannine Jesus, however, behaves strangely by human standards (2:4; 7:2–10; 11:6). This state of affairs is enough to· set us on our guard against reading John as a historical book. It is finally less so than any of the other Gospels. John's portrayal of Jesus is not designed to represent his humanity for the benefit of our curiosity and to make him personally more familiar. Rather, as in the prologue he speaks of Jesus as the Word or revelation of God, so in the body of the Gospel he speaks of the Word of God under the form of Jesus of Nazareth. Although he does not deny that Jesus was really man, his primary interest and emphasis is focused upon his conviction that through him God is speaking to man. The single-mindedness of this theological concept is etched sharply against the background of John's perceptive presentation of humanity in all its color and concreteness. At this he is a master, and it is nowhere more apparent than in the story of the man blind from birth.

JESUS' LAST WILL: THE PRAYER OF CONSECRATION (17:1–26)

To whom is the prayer really addressed?
What are the major themes of the prayer?

From the end of the first half of the Gospel when he withdraws from the world (chap. 12) until the moment of his arrest (18:1 ff.), Jesus is

"The Last Supper" by German artist Emil Nolde (1909). (Courtesy of Alinari-Art Reference Bureau.)

continually with his disciples.[16] In this period fall the Last Supper (chap. 13), the farewell discourses (chaps. 14–16), and the prayer of consecration (chap. 17). There is a certain rough conformity with the Synoptics, in which Jesus first gives his eschatological discourse (Mark 13), then eats the Last Supper with his disciples (Mark 14:12–25), and finally, after they have all gone out from the supper, prays (Mark 14:32–42).[17] The similarity does not, however, extend far. The basic character of the various events is different. In the Synoptic account the supper is a passover meal, at which Jesus institutes the sacrament of the Lord's Supper. In John the meal is not a Passover celebration and Jesus, instead of instituting the sacrament of the Lord's Supper, washes the disciples' feet. The Johannine discourses have to do with Jesus' death and reunion with his disciples, the Synoptic with the cataclysmic events leading up to the end of the world. Jesus' last

---

[16] The disciples have usually been taken to mean the twelve, although this is nowhere made explicit in the text. In 6:66 ff. all the disciples except the twelve seem to be drawing back from Jesus. Yet immediately thereafter (7:3) it appears that Jesus has disciples other than the twelve. Therefore one ought not to assume that "disciples" (after 6:66) always implies the twelve.

[17] Also, in both John and the Synoptics, Jesus concludes the meal on the solemn note of the disciples' desertion and Judas' betrayal. Mark 14:26–31 is paralleled by John 13:36–38 (at the end of the supper proper) and 16:32 (at the end of the discourses).

prayer in John is a carefully wrought exposition of his legacy to his disciples. His own death is mentioned, but in its peculiarly Johannine significance as the glorification and consecration of the Son of God. In the Synoptics Jesus prays in Gethsemane his famous "Abba, Father, all things are possible to thee; remove this cup from me; yet not what I will, but what thou wilt" (Mark 14:36). Undoubtedly the Synoptic account is closer to the actual historical situation of Jesus than the more abstractly theological, polished petitions of the Johannine prayer. Yet the Johannine prayer is important, especially in illuminating the Fourth Gospel.

The first verse establishes the fact that this is, in form at least, a prayer; the simple, direct way of addressing God is typical of Jesus (Mark 14:36; cf. Luke 11:2). With the announcement that the hour has come (17:1; cf. 12:23), Jesus signals the imminence of the crucifixion, which is also the hour of his glorification. The glorifying of the Son is now to take place in his death and exaltation to heaven. Especially in John crucifixion, resurrection, and exaltation are tied closely together. God glorifies Jesus by turning his death into victory, and the glory that Jesus thereby shares is nothing less than the glory of God, his imposing power and nature as he makes it known to men. Already the Word's becoming flesh and dwelling among men has been subtly compared with God's glory dwelling in the temple (1:14; cf. also 2:19 ff. and 4:20: ff.). Now the close connection between the Father and Jesus allows the evangelist to assert that Jesus shares in the Father's glory (cf. especially vs. 5).

Because Jesus' authority or power to give eternal life (vs. 2) can be fully exercised only after he is glorified, he calls upon the Father to glorify him (vs. 1). At this point the Johannine predestination comes to light (cf. vs. 6). Jesus has authority over all flesh (all men), but gives life only to those God gives him (vs. 2). As in Paul, emphasis in John falls upon the security of the elect (those God has given Jesus) in God, not on the exclusion of others. The fundamental Johannine theological premise is that God loves the world and sent the Son to save it (3:16 ff.; 12:47; 17:20 ff.). Jesus has been given authority over all humanity. He is not related only to the elect. Whatever else it may be, John's concept of election is a way of explaining how Christ could be sent to save men, and yet not all men are saved (cf. 12:37–43). Their loss could not occur apart from the divine will and purpose. Neither God nor Christ could fail. The predestination may also be a product of the Johannine dualism of which we have already spoken. Where such dualism occurs in either Gnosticism or apocalypticism, different as they may be, the doctrine of predestination often appears also. Still, John's unwillingness to be bound by such a dualistic world-view is reflected in his insistence that God loves the world and that the Word became flesh in Jesus.

The definition of eternal life (vs. 3) shows the distance between John and any apocalyptic world-view. Eternal life is an eschatological concept, and in chapter 3 it appears in conjunction with the term kingdom of God, so familiar from the Synoptic Gospels. The phrase "eternal life" also occurs in the Synoptics themselves (cf. Mark 10:17; "Good Teacher, what must I do to inherit eternal life?"). There it is understood to refer to the life of the age to come (Mark 10:30). Although in John eternal life is not robbed of its future dimension (14:1–7; 17:24), the evangelist emphasizes its present reality (vs. 3).

The Son glorifies the Father—that is, renders the praise and service due him—by obediently doing his work (vs. 4). Now he prays, "Father, glorify thou me" (vs. 5; cf. vs. 1). The new element in this petition is the reference to Christ's pre-existence, his being with the Father before creation. There is thus a close connection between this passage and the prologue (1:1; see pages 407 ff.). The meaning of God's glorifying Jesus is that he fully affirms and accepts his work.

Since verse 5 harks back to verse 1 and brings to a conclusion the theme of the glory of Christ, we may regard verses 1–5 as the introduction of the prayer (cf. RSV paragraphing). The remainder and greater part of the chapter contains Jesus' petition for the church, although the term *church* itself is never used. This longer section falls into three parts (vss. 6–19, 20–23, 24–26), but the division between them is not sharp. There is some justification for viewing verses 6–8 as the continuation of the first part, or as a transitional section, because in these verses (as perhaps in vss. 12 and 14) the ministry of the earthly Jesus as it touches upon the disciples is still in view. One might suggest that verse 4 refers to Jesus' ministry before the world (chaps. 2–12), whereas verses 6–8 (cf. vss. 12, 14) focus upon his special work among his disciples.

The name of God (vs. 6), an Old Testament expression, indicates the very reality of God himself, and Jesus reveals nothing less to his disciples. "Thy word" is simply another way of referring to God's self-disclosure in Jesus, approximately the equivalent of "thy name." Alongside men Jesus stands out as the man in whom God is incarnate; however, over against the Father he is not a rival or second God. His subordination to the Father is emphasized throughout the Gospel (for example, 5:19–24, 30–46, *passim*) and is reflected in the fact that those who believe in him have been given him by the Father (vss. 2, 6). They are not his personally, but his in so far as they are God's. Both verses 7 and 8 underscore Jesus' subordination to the Father. Jesus says nothing of his own accord (vs. 7). His word is the word of God, and in so far as he says anything about himself he says that he is from God, the one whom God has sent. To believe in Jesus is first of all to believe that God has sent him.

It is somewhat strange that Jesus speaks of himself in verses 1–5 in the third person and even refers to himself as "Jesus Christ" (vs. 3), a name which never appears on his lips in the Synoptic Gospels. In fact, through verse 8 the prayer contains no genuine petitions, with the possible exceptions of verses 1 and 5. Instead, Jesus tells the Father what he has done (vs. 4), what authority he has (vs. 2), and the nature of eternal life (vs. 3). We can scarcely think that God does not already know these things and needs Jesus to tell him, for everything Jesus says and does comes from God. Probably the author of the Gospel had the reader in mind in the composition of this prayer. Thus in the opening verses he provides the proper setting and gives the reader a clear orientation by having Jesus expound the character and meaning of his ministry. As the hour tolls and he goes to the cross (vs. 1), he does so in the full knowledge that in both life and death he glorifies God by accomplishing his work. The success of that work can be seen in the faithful disciples, whom he has called out of the world and instructed in the most intimate communion with himself (chaps. 13–16). The prayer occurs only after the Last Supper and Jesus' extensive discourses and conversations with the disciples. Only then is the groundwork laid for such statements about the disciples as we find in this prayer. Having now secured the disciples to himself, Jesus turns with them to God.

Throughout the farewell discourses the disciples remain full of misunderstandings and uncertainties. Jesus' own piercing retort (16:31 f.) reveals the inadequacy of their final solemn affirmation (16:29 f.). The evangelist knows well that the disciples' awareness of Jesus and his work remains incomplete until after his death (cf. 2:22; 7:39; 12:16; 13:7; 16:7–15; 16:31 f.). In the discourses Jesus tells his disciples things they cannot fully understand until he has departed from them. Yet Jesus has guarded them and they have kept his word, despite the fact that in his own lifetime they have not understood it. With his departure, however, his word and work take on new meaning. Now in the prayer Jesus already views his disciples as if they had moved into this deeper understanding. In fact, one might say that in the farewell discourses the Christ speaks to his earthly disciples from the perspective of his resurrection, whereas their perspective is limited because they stand on this side of Jesus' departure and return. In the prayer, however, the postresurrection church comes into view, and the statements that Jesus now makes about his disciples are made not on the basis of their behavior during his earthly ministry but of their postresurrection faith, which is about to become a reality.

In verse 10 the unity of the Father and the Son is again the theme. The glory of the Son manifests itself in this world in Jesus' disciples: "and I am glorified in them." But the situation of the disciples in the world is contrasted with that of Jesus, who now returns to the Father (vs. 11). As he returns to his heavenly glory, he prays for his disciples: "Keep them in thy name." This means "keep them in closest communion with thee." For the first time in the prayer the motif of the unity of the disciples emerges (vs. 11); it will be developed further (vss. 20 ff.). Those who are given to Jesus come into closest unity with him and thereby with God and also with each other. In praying the Father to keep the disciples in his name, Jesus only asks that the work that he has done be continued (cf. vs. 12). He has already promised his disciples (cf. chaps. 14–16) that it will be. The only one lost is Judas, and his loss is in fulfillment of scripture (cf. Matt. 27:9 f.; Acts 1:15–26).

The somewhat repetitious style of the prayer and of the Johannine discourses in general now becomes apparent (vs. 13). The last part of the verse is of interest for two reasons. First, Jesus now indicates that his words are not primarily for the benefit of the Father, but of the disciples, who are listening ("these things I speak in the world . . ."). The author probably has in view not only the disciples of the historical Jesus, but any Christian who may read this book. If so, this says something about the purpose and character of this chapter. It is more a "last will and testament" than a prayer in the usual sense. Second, the theme of the disciples' rejoicing, which has already come into prominence in the farewell discourses (15:11; especially 16:20, 24; cf. also 16:33), is introduced here for the first time. A fundamental characteristic of the disciples' existence in the world is joy. This joy does not include the assurance of peace, security, and worldly pleasure. The disciples will experience tension and hostility vis-à-vis the world (vs. 14). Far from being comfortably at home in the world, they are not of the world. So their peace and joy is of another order, as Jesus himself has already said (14:27; cf. 16:33); it is the quality of their life in fellowship with God through Christ.

Despite their alienation from the world (vss. 14 and 16), Jesus does not ask that his disciples be taken out of the world (vs. 15; cf. I Cor. 5:9 ff.). This important petition, occurring in the midst of repeated assertions that the disciples, like Jesus, are not of this world, excludes any Gnostic or otherworldly piety that rejects the world. The Johannine position is not otherworldly or Gnostic. In fact, it may be explicitly and pointedly anti-Gnostic. "World" in John is not identical with creation, but is man's world, or the world man creates in alienation from God. Therefore, rejection of this world is not the rejection of the created order or of things material. Moreover, God loves the world, even in its alienation from him. This petition (vs. 15) means that the Christian is not to be prematurely removed even from this sinful world. His separation from the world is separation from the world's sin. He is protected from the Evil One, that is, Satan. He is therefore sanctified (made holy) in or by the truth (vs. 17). As the one who reveals the only true God (17:3), Jesus is the personification of truth. He signifies what is finally real, dependable, and trustworthy, over against all that is only appearance or sham. So the Christian is made holy in the truth which is Jesus, consecrated to God, and separated from the world. Yet even as the disciples are inwardly separate from the world, they are also sent out into the world.

They are sent as Jesus himself was sent. "The holiness of the community is therefore not something purely negative, but includes a positive task. . . . As the sending of the Son into the world is not only his fate, but also his task, so it is with the sending of the community through the Son."[18] The church is not a community living in seclusion, for it lives for the world.

As Jesus makes his disciples holy, so also he makes himself holy (vs. 19; the same Greek word, *hagiadzo*, is translated in vs. 17 "sanctify" and in vs. 19 "consecrate") for their sake. Jesus' consecration of himself culminates in his death. Taken out of context this statement would not necessarily inply a reference to Jesus' death; however, the long discussion of his death and its meaning in the farewell discourses warrants such an interpretation. The prayer is a culmination and capstone of these discourses. Furthermore, it stands immediately before the passion narrative and in a real sense introduces it. For the evangelist does not wish to tell the traditional passion story until he has made clear to his reader exactly who is dying, what is to be accomplished by his death, and for whom it is being accomplished.

After the long petition for the disciples (vss. 6–19, or at least 9–19), Jesus prays for "those who are to believe in me through their word" (vss. 20 ff.). This can only be the later church. We should not think, however, that now Jesus ceases to pray for his disciples and begins to pray for the church. Instead John extends the scope of the entire prayer to include not only those who believe through actual contact with Jesus, but also those who believe the apostolic witness. The latter have equal access to the truth of Jesus Christ (20:29).

Jesus' prays for the unity of the church (vs. 21; cf. vs. 11). But in what does this unity consist? It is grounded upon the unity of Jesus and the Father. It is an incorporation of the believers into that unity ("that they may be in us"). The unity of the church is therefore no purely social or organizational phenomenon. Neither is it a matter of agreement on doctrinal or other matters. Unity involves what the philosopher might call ontological union, a union of beings in the One Being. Yet John has to be interpreted carefully on this point, and his understanding probably ought to be distinguished from various forms of Oriental and other mysticism. He does not speak of the absorption of souls into the One Soul or of the obliteration of individuals. Individual personal identity is maintained within this union. And except for 10:34, an Old Testament proof text used in a debate about messiahship, there is no talk of the deification

---

[18] R. Bultmann, *Das Evangelium des Johannes* ("Kritisch-exegetischer Kommentar über das Neue Testament," 2. Abt., 15 Aufl.; Göttingen: Vandenhoeck & Ruprecht, 1957), pp. 390 f. We wish to acknowledge indebtedness here as elsewhere in the interpretation of John's Gospel to Bultmann's commentary, unfortunately still unavailable in English.

of believers in John. Nevertheless, in this union the Christian attains a new status, if not a new being.

The end in view is not, however, the self-glorification of the disciple. Jesus is glorified in accomplishing his mission in the world and among men. His glory is manifest in the crucifixion. The follower of Jesus is sent into the world on the same mission (vs. 18). The unity of the church serves the purpose of that mission (vs. 21). The church's glory in this world is the accomplishment of that mission—that the world may know. Thus Jesus can say (vs. 22) that he gives to the disciples the glory that God has given him. Such glory is no heavenly radiance having nothing to do with this world or its needs. It is indeed a heavenly glory, which only God may give, but it is given only in conjunction with the fulfillment of God's work in the world. Unity in glory means unity in mission. Through the sharing of this glory the church becomes one with itself—an integral unity—and one with its Lord. Such unity is also unity with God (vs. 23). Again, the purpose of this unity is said to be "that the world may know." In vs. 23 this knowledge has to do not only with God's sending of the Son, and therefore the Son's status and mission, but with the practical meaning of that sending. In it God's love for Christ, and also for his disciples, is made manifest. The unity of the church thus bears witness to God's sending of the Son and to the right interpretation of that sending as the expression of his love.

To speak abstractly of the union of God, Christ, and the believers, and of the believers with one another leaves unanswered the question of how this unity achieves tangible form. Such visible expression is found in the love of the brethren for one another. The one explicit command of Jesus (13:34 f.) is that his disciples love one another. This is the indispensable outward mark of discipleship. In the long allegory of the vine (15:1 ff.) it became apparent that the key to abiding in the vine is obedience to the love commandment (cf. 15:6–17). The crucial importance of the commandment to love is also underscored by I John (cf. 3:11 ff.). The argument of the First Letter that God in Christ has shown his love toward the community, and that the brethren ought therefore to love one another (especially 4:7–21), or otherwise their religious confession is a delusion, is mirrored in the Gospel. If we take with proper seriousness the repeated statement of I John that God is love (4:8, 16), and give due weight to the assertion that the coming of the Son is the expression of God's love (3:16 ff.; I John 4:9 f.), we are not surprised to learn that the unity of the church is a unity of love. Nor should we make a rigid distinction between an ontological unity of the believers in God and Christ and a practical unity in love. God's being as he reveals it to man is in fact his being favorable toward man; it is his love. The church's unity in love is the communal expression of the reality of God's love. At the same time this love is no illusion, nor is it some sort of invisible spiritual reality that no one can touch or see. Just as I John insists on the tangible expression of love (3:15–18), the Gospel defines love as the willingness to wash the guests' feet (13:1–17) or to lay down one's life for one's friends (15:13). Jesus himself exemplifies this love by his death on the cross.

The prayer now ends (vss. 24–26). Jesus looks beyond the disciples' present existence in this world to the heavenly glory (vs. 24). This glory is not their own, however, but a beholding of Christ's original heavenly glory (cf. vs. 5). Thus heaven is where Christ is; and, insofar as it can be conceived at all, it is the beholding of Christ. In a concluding summary certain motifs of the whole prayer are taken up and reiterated (vss. 25 f.). The world's rejection of God is contrasted with Jesus' and his church's acknowledgment of him (vs. 25). Jesus then bids farewell with a promise (vs. 26). Pointing to his earlier revelation of God's name (vss. 6, 12), he promises to continue to make it known to his people, to the end that God's love for him, and Jesus himself, may be in them. The prayer thus concludes on a note that calls attention to the distinction between church and world. Christ and his church stand over against the world, yet not for the sake of the world's condemnation but for its salvation. A positive outlook on the world's possibility of salvation is basic to Johannine thought.

That the Gospel does not end after this magnificent prayer is a sure indication that for the evangelist Christianity is life and event as well as meditation and prayer. The death that we have been prepared to witness and to understand must now take place. So Jesus moves into the garden, where Judas betrays him, and thence to the court of the high priest, to Pilate's judgment seat, and to Calvary. Christ does not ascend from the cross, as in some Gnostic accounts, leaving Jesus behind. Jesus dies a real death and is buried, and, according to John's firm conviction is really raised from the dead.

Yet the risen Christ does not add anything essentially new to the historical Jesus as John portrayed him in the Gospel. For in a sense that Jesus already is the risen Christ, the exalted one. But until his hour arrives he cannot be recognized as such. Not even his disciples, who believe in him, can comprehend the full import of his mission and message. Only in the light of his death and exaltation does his true nature become manifest to his own disciples, who are then able to see the real meaning and import of his earthly ministry. Whoever the author of the Gospel may have been, he was certainly such a disciple, and his portrayal of Jesus takes into account the fuller knowledge of him that is only possible after his death.

If we knew more about the *historical circumstances* under which the Fourth Gospel was written, or if we were in a better position to *separate tradition* from *redaction*, we could interpret the Gospel with greater accuracy and assurance. As it is, the historical background and origin of the Gospel, as well as its literary history, are the subjects of much scholarly effort and debate, but little agreement. We do not know exactly when or why the Fourth Gospel was written, nor can we be certain of the formative influences that shaped it. Similarly, the sources from which the author drew, whether written or oral, are either lost or obscured from view. We may make conjectures in both areas, but it is necessary to be cautious in attaching weight to them.

Still, it is possible to understand the Gospel of John even today. The structure and emphases of the Gospel are clear enough. Although there may be some doubts as to exactly what the author meant in certain places or by certain terms, the subject and movement of his thought are not unclear. As to the *structure*, he tells the story of Jesus' ministry, and although his version is quite different from the Synoptics it is recognizably the same story. The prologue, unique to John, identifies Jesus in relation to the creative and redemptive activities of God. Then follows an account of the Baptist and of the calling of Jesus' disciples. This in turn followed by a narrative of Jesus' public ministry, at least part of which is Galilee. Finally, Jesus enters Jerusalem to face his opponents and his ultimate fate. After having instructed his disciples and eaten a last meal with them, he is arrested, put on trial, and executed. The broad outline of the Gospel is similar to the Synoptics.

Nevertheless, there are peculiarly Johannine features of this outline that cannot be dismissed as mere minor differences. Jesus' public ministry is even more sharply distinguished from his last days in Jerusalem than in the Synoptics. After the conclusion of the public ministry (chap. 12), Jesus has nothing more to do with the Jews or this world. To be sure, he goes to his death at their hands, but they are only agents of the divine plan, of which he seems to be fully aware. This sharp division in the structure of the Fourth Gospel corresponds to the Johannine dualism, in which the forces aligned with evil are drawn up against those aligned with Christ. Indeed, the division is reflected in the prologue's statements regarding the reception of Jesus' mission (1:10–12). As in the other Gospels, the crucifixion is a public event, but its real significance is only understood by the faithful, who view it in the light of the glorification.

The character of Jesus' public ministry differs markedly from the Synoptics, in which the setting is Galilee. In John, Jesus goes repeatedly to Jerusalem, and most of the action takes place there. He appears repeatedly at Jewish festivals, where he can be contrasted with the sources of revelation in the old Israel and where he can engage the Jewish authorities in debate. Moreover, the patterns of his speech and action differ in ways we have already noted.

The *emphases* of the evangelist are mirrored in the structure of his Gospel. Jesus reveals himself to the world through signs and words (chaps. 2–12), after which he reveals himself fully to his disciples in a most intimate interchange in seclusion from that world (chaps. 13–17). What he reveals is God. We often read of the glory or the glorifying of Christ in the Fourth Gospel. This glory is not a personal quality, but Jesus' transparency to the will and work of God. Jesus glorifies God in that he lets God's glory shine through him by doing the work—that is, carrying out the mission that God has given him (John 5:36; 9:4; 17:4). God glorifies Jesus by revealing himself as God in and through his works. God's glory is already seen in Jesus' public ministry in a preliminary way. His miracles are signs of the glory. But finally and most importantly the glory is seen in the crucifixion (12:23); which is the culmination and completion of the manifestation of the glory. According to John, the last word of Jesus is, "It is finished" (19:30). His work has been accomplished.

In his death Jesus transcends the limitations of his earthly existence so that the glory of God in him becomes visible to all who will believe, whether or not they have seen or known him (20:29). The resurrection for John can then only be the divine Yes to what is already present in Jesus' life and death. Jesus performs preliminary signs indicating who he is, but in his self-giving death he becomes a model or symbol of God's self-giving love.

Quite obviously John's emphasis falls heavily upon the questions of who Jesus is and what his appearance means, not only in the signs and passion narratives, but in the words of Jesus himself. In the Fourth Gospel Jesus talks at length about himself and his mission. He talks about Christology. This way of talking stands in contrast to the Synoptic Gospels, where the Christological question is more implicit than explicit. For John, however, it was imperative that Christology should be put on Jesus' own lips, for he wished to maintain that the Christian affirmations about Jesus of Nazareth were inseparable from the historical figure, and, conversely, that such affirmations were the only adequate explanations of who he really was.

In many ways the Gospel represents the most advanced development of New Testament thought. As we have seen, Christianity was born amidst enthusiastic expectation of the imminent return of Jesus and the establishment of God's kingdom. Probably there was at first little thought for such things as ecclesiastical organization and the theological expression of the faith, for institutional self-preservation and self-explanation. Although in Paul the church had its first, and in some ways its greatest, seminal theological mind, his insights were left largely undeveloped for a generation after him. Meanwhile, the Gospels were composed as the church felt the need for ordering its life in accord with Jesus' way of life and explaining its own existence by reference to his. Certain authors developed particular theological and practical themes as the needs arose. The author of Ephesians presented a compendium of Pauline theology geared to the situation of his day. Luke incorporated the time of the church into the primitive Christian understanding of salvation-history by writing the first church history. The unknown author of Hebrews interpreted the church's existence in this age as a journey in which the whole entourage moves both forward, in conformity with the Jewish historical consciousness, and upward toward a heavenly goal conceived in Gnostic or Hellenistic terms. At its head is Jesus, the pioneer and perfecter of faith, whose status and function is described in a most significant way.

It remained, however, for John to reinterpret definitively the primitive faith at a time when eschatological expectation had waned and the church was growing as an institution. Significantly, he wrote not a church history, not a manual of discipline, not an apocalypse, not a treatise, but a Gospel narrative. Thus, with considerable literary skill and theological acumen he reminded his readers that faith is not finally a matter of future expectation or contemporary institutional life, whether conceived sacramentally or hierarchically. Faith is knowing Jesus and being sustained by the food and drink that he gives to those who hunger and thirst. It is walking by the light of Christ. It is dependence on the source of life, the only true God and Jesus Christ whom he has sent. According to John, the fundamental question to which faith must answer is the question posed by Jesus Christ. Who is he? It is the measure of John's importance that he identified this question and out of his own conviction gave a decisive theological answer. In both respects he helped determine the direction and shape of Christian thought for many centuries to come.

The Letters of John: The Spirit of Jesus as Love (I John 4:1–21)

What criteria may be used to test the spirits?
Why is it not possible to possess faith or the Spirit without love?

NOTES ON THE JOHANNINE LETTERS

As we have noted, II and III John seem to be genuine letters, whereas it is not clear that I John was originally conceived as a letter. It lacks the customary epistolary introduction as well as a conclusion. In fact I John seems to end in mid-air with no conclusion at all. Nevertheless, the text more than once indicates that the author is writing to someone (2:12 ff., 26; 5:13), thus the document has at least the appearance of a letter.

Significant similarities of I John to the Gospel will be pointed out in the discussion of the text. They are both formal and substantial, or to put it another way, stylistic and theological. Although there are also some differences, the close relation of the Gospel and letters cannot be denied.

The place and date of origin as well as the author of the Johannine letters are uncertain. Tradition holds that they, like the Gospel, were written in Ephesus by the apostle John. But most of the same reservations cited in connection with the tradition of the Gospel's authorship apply also to the letters. There was a prominent Asian churchman called the Elder John who lived at the end of the first century or the beginning of the second and was actually confused with the apostle John in ancient times (Eusebius, EH, III, xxxix). It is tempting to suggest that he is the "John" who wrote the Gospel and letters, as the author of the brief second and third letters identifies himself as "the Elder." Perhaps, but this is slim evidence for identifying the author of II and III John with this ancient and largely unknown man.

II and III John are so brief as to yield little data about their origin. Their obvious similarity to I John makes it probable that they were written by the same author. Although II John seems to presuppose and resist the same heretical views opposed by I John, this problem is not discussed in III John. Rather, some question of ecclesiastical politics seems to be the center of attention. Possibly Diotrephes (vs. 9) is trying to establish himself as a sort of ruling bishop in a particular church and thus to resist the spiritual authority of the Elder.[19] Unlike the Gospel and Revelation, I John has little distinct structure or pattern. The following major thematic units may assist the reader as he makes his way through the book:

OUTLINE OF I JOHN
      Prologue: Christian Fellowship (1:1–4)
        I. The Nature and Essence of Christianity (1:5–2:29)
       II. The Marks of True Life in the Community (3:1–24)
     III. Criteria for Certainty and Assurance among the Faithful
           (4:1–5:12): The Spirit of Jesus as Love (4:1–21)
      Postscript: Sin and Forgiveness (5:13–21)

There is no logical progression of thought in I John. After the introductory prologue, which is not unlike that of the Fourth Gospel, the author treats two basic themes, one ethical and the other Christological— that is, the Christian life and the Christian faith. He defines the Christian faith so as to exclude certain erroneous views, including the notion that it is possible to have faith without its taking concrete, bodily form in one's manner of life.

The passage selected for more intensive examination (chap. 4) is actually not a complete literary unit according to most analyses of I John, including our own. But because the structure of the document is at best indefinite, and at any rate indecisive for interpretation, this is of little

---

[19] E. Käsemann, "Ketzer und Zeuge," *Exegetische Versuche und Besinnungen,* I (Göttingen: Vandenhoeck & Ruprecht, 1960), pp. 168–87.

consequence. In fact, by taking a segment of this length from virtually any point in the book one could obtain a fair idea of its nature and content, since the major themes are intertwined and repeated throughout.

Chapter 4 begins with a warning to test the spirits (vss. 1–6). Apparently the spirits are ultimately only two, the spirit of truth and the spirit of error (vs. 6). The spirit of error manifests itself in false prophets (vs. 1). This is the spirit of the antichrist, whose coming was predicted (vs. 3; cf. I Tim. 4:1 and p. 369). It is now in the world, and those who obey it are of the world (vss. 4 f.), whereas the intended readers are of God (vs. 6). The opposition of world and God in I John is well-nigh irreconcilable (cf. 2:15–17).

A fuller understanding of this passage entails some knowledge of the phenomenon of prophecy in the early church. The role of the Christian prophet has probably been underestimated, because none of the New Testament books except Revelation seems to have been written by a man who was primarily a prophet. Yet Paul ranks prophets immediately after apostles in importance (I Cor. 12:28). When the author of Ephesians speaks of the church's being built upon the foundation of the prophets and the apostles, he probably means not Old Testament but Christian prophets (2:20). Although prophets were doubtless important figures (cf. also Acts 11:27 ff.; 21:10 ff.), they constituted a potential problem. For their claim to speak inspired words of Christ or the Spirit (cf. Rev. 1:1–3; 22:18 f.) might result in confusion, especially if divinely inspired prophets disagreed. Thus, the early Christians saw the necessity of distinguishing among the spirits—"test the spirits" (4:1). The idea of discerning among the spirits, or among the prophets claiming to speak in the Spirit, is already present in Paul (I Thess. 5:19–22), who laid down some fundamental rules for distinguishing the inspiration of the Holy Spirit in I Corinthians 12:3, and went on to outline procedures for regulating Spirit-inspired prophecy (I Cor. 14). A half century or so later the author of the Didache was to suggest that prophets who stayed in one place for longer than a brief period, sponging off the community, were very likely false prophets—not to mention those who, while purporting to speak in prophetic ecstasy, ordered a meal or demanded money.[20]

John's criterion for distinguishing the Spirit of God from that of the antichrist (4:2 f.) reveals a great deal about the understanding of Christianity which he opposed. John's own positive affirmation or confession appears in verse 2: the man inspired by the Spirit of God confesses that Jesus Christ has come in the flesh. The contrary confession would then deny that he had come in the flesh but would maintain instead that he was actually a spirit or matterless manifestation that had only appeared

---

[20] xi, 7–12; xii–xiii. Yet, "Every true prophet who wishes to settle among you is worthy of his food" (xiii, 1).

to take on an actual human body. In the apocryphal New Testament literature of the second century one may clearly see the burgeoning of this "docetic" view ("docetic" from the Greek word meaning "to seem or appear"; that is, Christ only seems to be human). It was characteristic of Gnostic Christianity and went hand in hand with the abhorrence of this world and all things material (cf. I Tim. 4:3–5; pp. 369 ff.). John castigates this docetic Christology as the work of the antichrist. Not confessing Jesus means to deny the genuinely human dimension of the Christ event. An important textual variant at this point reads "divides Jesus" instead of "does not confess Jesus." It was understood by the interpreters of the ancient church to refer to the Gnosticizing division between Jesus and the Christ. Although this reading is probably not original, it may be accurate commentary on our text. These heretics apparently distinguished between "Jesus" and "the Christ" and denied that God had really revealed himself in a man, that "the Word had become flesh" (John 1:14).

The antichrist (vs. 3), whose spirit speaks through the false prophets, is the antithesis of God's revelation in Christ. Therefore the typically Johannine dualism or polarity of God and world can be used in describing him and his adherents (vss. 4 ff.). The world in this sense is not the good creation of God but the bad creation of man. The world represents human society organized and operating without reference to, or concern for, the existence and will of God. World and Christ, world and church, are placed sharply over against one another. We have observed that in the Fourth Gospel this world is nevertheless described as the object of God's love (3:16 ff.); I John is not so explicit, yet even here Jesus is called "the Savior of the world" (4:14).

The antichrist is an apocalyptic figure, whose traces appear elsewhere in the New Testament. Although the actual term "antichrist" is found only in the Johannine letters, the idea of an individual or collective opponent of God's purposes, especially of his messiah, appearing as a prelude to the winding up of world history, is not uncommon in Jewish and early Christian apocalyptic (cf. Mark 13, II Thess. 2, and Revelation). I and II John (cf. I John 2:18–25; II John 7) apparently presuppose a tradition concerning the appearance of the antichrist at the last hour. This concept, however, is significantly altered. Instead of seeing the antichrist as a purely supernatural, apocalyptic being, the author now equates him with the emergence of false teachers (2:18) or false teaching—that is, with an historical event. That teaching which denies the humanity of the Son of God, and in effect denies Jesus, is the spirit of the antichrist, or if we may coin a term, of "antichristology."

In the face of this powerful movement, which is "of the world" (vs. 5), the Christian may be of good courage. He has overcome (vs. 4), for as the author elsewhere says, "the darkness is passing away, and the true light is already shining" (2:8). The effective power of the new life which God gives through Christ is already present and available to the Christian. With Christ he has already overcome the power of the world (cf. John 16:33). Notice how the concept of the world develops in verses 3 ff. From the simple statement that the antichrist is in the world, and a neutral concept of "world," we move to an idea of the indwelling of the antichrist, or perhaps of Satan, in the world analogous to God's dwelling in the believer (vs. 4). Now the world becomes the hostile entity of which we have already spoken. Thus it can be said that those heretics who have

Virgin and Child from the first half of the fourteenth century in France. (Courtesy of Metropolitan Museum of Art. The Cloisters Collection. Purchase, 1937.)

the spirit of the antichrist are "of the world" in the negative sense so characteristic of John's understanding of the term. As they are of the world, so the Christian is of God (vs. 6). Those who do not listen to us, but presumably listen to the heretics instead (that is, those who do not accept the orthodox teaching about Christ), thereby show themselves to be not of God, but of the world.

The next section (4:7–12) introduces a major new motif. Being born of God is brought into closest relation to the exhortation to love. The act of love determines one's relationship to God. Who is born of God and knows God? He who loves. The possibility of knowing God in lovelessness is absolutely excluded (vs. 8): "God is love." The very character of love is to be understood with reference to the way in which God has loved by sending his Son as the expiation for sin (vs. 9; cf. John 3:16 ff. and Rom. 3:25). Love is not a quality by which God is to be defined. Rather, God is the active subject by which love is to be defined. Therefore, the question of human love toward God is secondary (vs. 10). Yet human love is certainly not a matter of indifference. Because God loves us we ought to love one another, says John (vs. 11). Man's primary responses to God's love are faith in Jesus, as God's revelation in the flesh, and love for his brother. The real Christian, as distinguished from the pretender, is the one who believes in Jesus and practices love. Through such human love God and his love become real and accessible to man, despite the fact that man cannot and does not see God (vs. 12; cf. John 1:18).

The assurance that God abides in the believer and the believer in God is the Spirit (vs. 13). Obviously, it is not possible to possess the Spirit without love. What is more, neither love nor Spirit are abstract, "spiritual" concepts hanging in the air. They are grounded upon a particular confession of Jesus Christ, restated in verses 14 and 15. The confession of Jesus, and of God's action toward the world in Jesus (vss. 15 and 14 respectively), is the basis for the Christian's understanding of both love and the Spirit. Of course, no one can truly claim the Spirit who does not believe in Jesus and live in love. The Spirit gives the Christian assurance (vs. 13), but not in abstraction from faith and love. Those who lack faith and love can only be possessed of the spirit of the antichrist (4:1, 3).

The meaning of verse 17 is less than clear. John refers again to the ground of the Christian's confidence, which is ultimately confidence before the God who judges, and therefore confidence in the day of judgment. Presumably, the perfecting of love of which he speaks is based upon a relation to Jesus ("he," translates the Greek *ekeinos*, "that one," a common designation of Jesus found in John). As Jesus is in this world, so is the Christian; his pattern of life is modeled after Christ's (cf. John 13:12–17). In verse 18 the thought of confidence is carried a step forward by the introduction of a new idea, the incompatibility of love and fear. The perfecting of love means confidence in the day of judgment, because love excludes fear. One could, of course, think that perfect love casts out fear because it does away with the danger of judgment. Yet the author's initial statement, "there is no fear in love," indicates that he wished to assert an intrinsic incompatibility between fear and love. "Perfect love casts out fear," because the one who loves is born of God and knows him (vs. 7), and because love is the negation of that concern for self that breeds anxiety. Therefore, the presence of fear means that one is not perfected in love. Here the terms "perfect" and "perfected" are based on a Greek stem meaning complete in the sense of finished. In the person who is perfected, love has reached its desired fulfillment; it determines his life.

John returns to the theme of God's prior love and the way it motivates men to love in verse 19. The chapter ends with a simple but pointed statement on the relationship of love of God and love of brother (vss. 20 f.), as the author puts matters succinctly and pungently. The commandment (vs. 21) cannot be exactly identified as to origin. One thinks, however, of Jesus' "new commandment" of John 13:34 or his "great commandment" of Mark 12:28–31 and parallels. In any event the commandment concisely conveys the burden of Jesus' teaching. At the same time it effectively reiterates a central conviction of the author, that faith and obedience, religion and ethics, the vertical and horizontal dimensions of man's existence, can on no account be separated from one another but always belong together.

The similarities of I John 4 to the Gospel of John are numerous. Some have already been noted, but in conclusion it may be helpful to call attention to the most prominent. The concept of the Spirit (I John 4:1 ff.) plays a prominent role in the Gospel. "Spirit of Truth" (I John 4:6) occurs several times in the farewell discourses (John 14–16), although it is not set over against the spirit of error or the antichrist as in I John. The idea of Jesus' coming in the flesh (I John 4:2) is reminiscent of John 1:14. The negative valuation of the world (I John 4:5) is altogether typical of the Fourth Gospel (John 1:10), as is the emphasis upon knowing God or Christ (I John 4:6; cf. especially John 17). The idea of birth (I John 4:7) as regeneration also appears in John (especially chap. 3). We have already noted the importance of the theme of love (I John 4:7 ff.) in the Fourth Gospel. Most remarkably, I John 4:9 reflects the basic motifs and even the language of John 3:16. That no man has ever seen God (I John 4:12) is also an affirmation of the prologue of the Gospel (1:8). The concept of abiding in Christ (I John 4:13, 15 f.) and the themes of seeing and testifying or witnessing (4:14) are commonplace in John, and the possible connection of "this commandment" (I John 4:21) and the "new commandment" of the Fourth Gospel has already been noted. Furthermore, the Greek text reveals many common stylistic traits that cannot be easily reproduced or explained in English.

Still, the Fourth Gospel does center upon the past, that is, the glory of the crucified and resurrected Jesus, while I John stresses the present necessity of love among the brethren. The final Johannine writing, the book of Revelation, looks to the future.

The Revelation to John: The Vision of the Prophet on Patmos (1:1–20)

What is the source of the seer's inspiration to write?
Is the threat of persecution evident?
What is the author's view of history?

NOTES ON REVELATION

Revelation was written during a period of crisis in the church brought about by the active opposition of the Roman government. It is a message of resistance and hope in times of hardship and persecution. A problem arises, however, when we attempt to identify the Roman emperors alluded to in chapters 13 and 17 and thus to date the book. The beast is presumably the Empire and the seven heads seven emperors (cf. 17:9 ff.). Which emperors are represented? Julius Caesar was the first emperor, so Claudius would be the fifth and Nero the sixth. The sixth, according to 17:10, is currently reigning. It is true that Nero (A.D. 57–68) put to death a number of Christians in Rome after the burning of that city, but he conducted no systematic persecution of Christians throughout the empire such as Revelation presupposes (1:9; 2:10; 2:13; 6:9–11; 14:12 f.; 17:6; and so on). Nero also did not attempt to force Christians to worship him as a god. Domitian (A.D. 81–96), however, demanded divine honors for himself and put to death Christians who refused to worship him (cf. 13:4–10, 12, 15). A date during Domitian's reign also corresponds to the earliest Christian tradition and to the postapostolic character of the book. The problem of identifying the emperors represented by the horns, which becomes difficult if the composition of the book is placed in Domitian's reign, may be resolved by regarding the statement of 17:10 (and perhaps much related material) as coming from a source dating from the time of Nero.

The emperor Domitian (A.D. 81–96), on a Roman coin. (Courtesy of American Numismatic Society.)

As to the place and conditions of writing and the identification of those addressed, there is no reason to doubt the statements of chapter 1. Nor is there any reason to doubt what the author says about himself in the same chapter. He is clearly an important church figure of Asia, a prophet, whose name is John.

The traditional identification with John, the son of Zebedee, is not impossible, but nothing in the book itself either demands or indicates this. This John does not call himself an apostle, and he refers to the apostles as revered figures of the past (18:20; 21:14). He gives no indication of having accompanied Jesus or having known those who did. The suggestion that the author is the church-man known from second-century sources as the Elder John is plausible, but sufficient evidence is lacking either to confirm or deny it.

Revelation is unique in that it is the only thoroughly apocalyptic book in the New Testament, although apocalyptic materials and themes appear in the letters of Paul and in the Gospels. The Apocalypse, as it is sometimes called, deals with "what must soon take place" (1:1; 22:6)—that is, the winding up of worldly history and the events leading thereto. This series of cataclysmic events is described with a wealth of symbols and images, many of which are quite strange to us. Understanding Revelation is further complicated by the fact that John purports to be relating things he has seen in visions. To what extent the "visions" are a mere literary device is unclear, since visions were a stock in trade of the authors of Old Testament, Jewish, and Christian apocalyptic. The visionary material contains numerous Old Testament allusions, references, and quotations, but this in itself proves nothing concerning its authenticity or origin. The author was doubtless saturated with the language and imagery of the Old Testament. He could have dreamed in these terms. Even if the visions are to some extent literary devices, this does not necessarily mean that the book that lies before us does not have its origin and roots in the visionary experiences of the author. The visionary origin of the material in Revelation may account for some of the many obscurities. In order to become more familiar with the nature of apocalyptic literature, the student would do well to read in the Old Testament Ezekiel 37–39; Isaiah 24–27; Joel, Zechariah, Zephaniah, Obadiah 15 ff. or Daniel 7–12. The intertestamental books and the literature of Qumran also illustrate the flourishing of apocalyptic writing in the period before, during, and after the time of Jesus and the earliest Christian church.

The structure of Revelation is complex, and there is reason to suspect that the original order has at some points been disrupted or augmented in a confusing way. The following outline is developed in terms of a simple time-scheme.

OUTLINE OF REVELATION
>Introduction: The Vision of the Prophet on Patmos (1:1–20)
>>I. The Present Time of the Church Struggle: The Letters to the Seven Churches (2:1–3:22)
>>II. The Time between the Present and the End (4:1–18:24)
>>>A. The Vision of Heaven (4:1–5:14)
>>>B. The Opening of the Seven Seals (6:1–8:1)
>>>C. The Blowing of the Seven Trumpets (8:2–11:19)
>>>D. Apocalyptic Vision of Happenings on Earth (12:1–13:18)
>>>E. Preparatory Vision of the End (14:1–20)
>>>F. The Pouring Out of the Seven Bowls of Wrath (15:1–18:24)

III. The End: Judgment, the Return of Christ, and the Coming of
the New World (19:1–22:5)
    A. The Judgment and Christ's Return (19:1–20:15)
    B. The New World (21:1–22:5)
Conclusion: Present Time with the Prophet on Patmos (22:6–21)

Chapter 1 is not altogether typical of Revelation, but it affords a springboard for understanding the entire book, since it contains hints and indications of what is to come.

The preface (1:1–3) is of a piece with the epilogue or conclusion (22:6 ff.). From beginning to end this is an apocalyptic work, a revelation. (The Greek word *apokalypsis* simply means an "uncovering" or a "revelation," so the term *apocalyptic* means "revelatory.") *Apocalyptic* is used in a specialized sense of religious books, especially intertestamental Jewish and early Christian books, in which the secrets of the last times are revealed. Thus John declares that his book will show the servants of God what must soon take place (vs. 1). The author of the revelation is God, who apparently gives it to Jesus Christ, who gives it to his angel, who in turn delivers it to John (cf. 22: 6, 8, 16). John has "borne witness" (1:2), doubtless a reference to the writing of this book, and the object of this witness is the word of God and the testimony of Jesus Christ— that is, the revelation (cf. vs. 1), as is clear from the explanatory phrase "even to all that he saw." A blessing is pronounced on anyone who reads aloud, hears, and keeps (gives heed to) this prophecy about the future (vs. 3), and the imminence of what is to be narrated is again emphasized.

Several important characteristics of Revelation may be observed in this brief paragraph. The author's own title, "the revelation of Jesus Christ," reveals the apocalyptic character of the book. This is indicated also in several other ways: the content is to be revealed only to the faithful ("his servants"); it has to do with things that are soon to take place; the mediator between the divine realm (represented by God and Christ) and the human (represented by John and the other servants of God) is an angel; what the angel communicates John somehow "sees," presumably as a vision. All these traits are typical of the Jewish-Christian apocalyptic tradition. Furthermore, in the apocalyptic understanding of history, events unfold according to the plan and purpose of God ("*must* soon take place"). John sees a pre-enactment of the unfolding culmination of world history. In keeping with the apocalyptic character of the book, "Jesus Christ" (vs. 1) is primarily the heavenly Christ, who later appears in great splendor (1:12 ff.), and is to return from heaven at the end of the age (22:20).

John next addresses himself to· the seven churches of Asia (vss. 4 ff.;

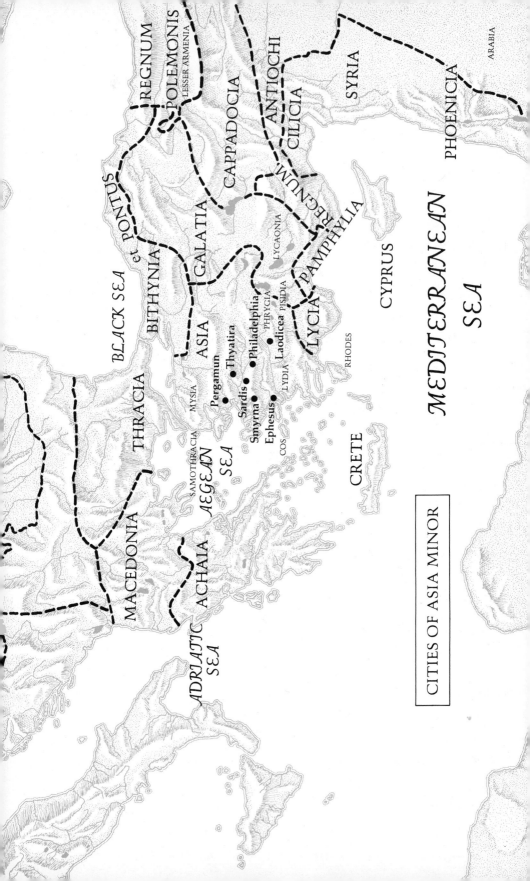

CITIES OF ASIA MINOR

cf. 1:11 and see map) with an epistolary salutation. This mixing of apocalyptic and epistolary form, is not unprecedented.[21] It is unusual, however, that John writes in his own name, in sharp contrast to the authors of late Jewish apocalyptic, who almost always adopted the name of a famous person out of Israel's past. Jewish apocalyptic writers used such pseudonyms because they were generally in agreement that the era of prophetic interpretation lay in the past. No book avowedly written in post-prophetic times could command or hope for authoritative rank and general acceptance. Moreover, by adopting the stance of a figure of five hundred or a thousand years back, the writer could "predict" the intervening events, thus lending credence to his predictions of the actual future. John, however, writes confidently under his own name and from the standpoint of his own time to the churches of Asia. Although probably an authoritative figure, his confidence lies not in his own name, but rather in his conviction that prophetic inspiration has been reborn in the church. He seems to have been one of the Christian prophets of whom the letters of Paul, Ephesians, and the Didache speak. As the Lord of Israel spoke through prophets in ancient times, so the Lord Jesus Christ speaks through prophets to the church and to the world. Although the prophet is addressed through angels, this mediation does not dilute his awareness of the powerful presence of the Lord in his own experience.

The greeting "grace and peace" (vs. 4) is typical of the New Testament, especially of Paul. "Who is and who was and who is to come" is God. Judaism and the pagan world, as well as Christianity, afford examples of such speaking of God in the past, present, and future tenses. As for the seven spirits, they are probably the author's unique way of referring to the Holy Spirit. The number seven may be suggested by the seven churches to which John addresses the letters of chapters 2–3. But this is doubtful, since elsewhere (4:5, 5:6) he can speak of seven spirits, where the context excludes any reference or even allusion to the churches. Could the odd term be explained on the basis of John's fondness for the number seven? We might well consider again the outline of the book and remember the seven seals, trumpets, and bowls—and, for that matter, the seven churches. Revelation may even be divided into seven scenes or acts as well (II, A through F, and III in the above outline).

The description of Jesus as a faithful witness (vs. 5) recalls 1:2 (the "testimony" or "witness" of Jesus). "Witness" (Greek, *martyr*) is the term used of a person who bears witness or testimony in the sense of witnessing an event or witnessing on behalf of someone. In early Christian usage, however, it soon took on a specific connotation. For example, in

---

21 II Baruch 76–87, although apocalyptic, is also in the form of a letter. Note also the probable imposition of the epistolary form upon other documents in the Catholic Epistles of the New Testament.

Revelation 2:13, 11:3–7, and 17:6 it is clear that the witness has died as a result of his witnessing. In fact, this is so obviously the case in 17:6 that the RSV translators have simply transliterated the Greek term *"martyr."* (The extent to which the idea of dying became integral to the term itself because of the early Christian experience is indicated by the meaning of the word "martyr" in English.) Jesus Christ is the archetypal witness and martyr, the one who gives his life as his testimony, and others follow in his footsteps. Therefore, the historical death of Jesus is crucial for John. His martyrdom is not, of course, just the end of a great and good man. As the first-born from the dead (Col. 1:18) he is the exalted Messiah, the ruler of earthly kings. As in I Corinthians 15, his resurrection is related to the resurrection of the believer. The believer, especially the man whose faith and testimony have led to his own death, is to share Christ's glory. In Revelation this triumph is often referred to simply as "conquering" (cf. 2:26, and *passim*). It is not, however, an immortality easily gained. The resurrection life is attained through "conquest" of the power of this world, especially by means of martyrdom at the hands of the world (cf. John 16:33). It is then a hidden conquest, at least for the time being.

Christ's present rule over the kings on earth (vs. 5) is as hidden as is his martyr's conquest. Yet it is nonetheless real. And in the one case as in the other, what is already real in the eyes of God will be made manifest before the eyes of man. In words made famous by Handel's *Messiah*, "the Lord God omnipotent reigneth" (19:6 KJV). His reign is exercised through his Christ, who, although crucified, dead, and buried, nevertheless now lives and rules. That God through Christ actually does reign, and that his reign will be made manifest to bring all men into subjection, whether for their weal or woe, may be said to be the basic theme of Revelation. Of course, this is either the hope or the assumption of almost every book in the New Testament. The uniqueness of Revelation, however, is that in one way or the other this theme is constantly in the foreground and is always presented in apocalyptic imagery.

The remainder of the Christological confession (vss. 5b–7) appears to be traditional (cf. vs. 5b with Rom. 3:23 ff.; 8:35 ff.; Gal. 2:20; and vs. 6 to I Peter 2:9.). That Christians in some sense already possess the good things promised is typical of the realized or partially realized eschatology of other parts of the New Testament. Yet the future-oriented apocalyptic point of view, more characteristic of our author, appears again in verse 7. Jesus' return to earth as conqueror "coming with the clouds" is not a new idea (cf. Daniel 7:13; Mark 13:26; 14:62; Matt. 24:30; 25:31). That every eye shall see him forecasts the future universal recognition of the lordship of Christ (cf. I Cor. 15:24 ff. and Phil. 2:10 f.). The references to piercing and wailing allude to the crucifixion (cf. Zechariah 12:12 and John 19:37) and the judgment of the nations which it implies.

The end of the epistolary salutation is indicated by the "Even so. Amen," a liturgical formula. The prophetic word of verse 8 has no obvious connection with what precedes or follows. In a sense the verse is related to the prediction of the parousia of Jesus in verse 7, since it affirms that God is the sure ground of this hope. The first and the last parts of the statement, the word of the Lord God ("I am the Alpha and the Omega") and the description of him in terms of past, present, and future, are more closely related than may initially appear. Alpha and omega are the first and last letters of the Greek alphabet, the equivalent of the English expression "from A to Z." God is the first and the last (cf. 22:13, where this explanation is given), the one who was and is and is to come. Thus he is the Lord of history at its beginning, at its end, and in the interim. The apocalyptic character of the book and its abuse by ancient and modern enthusiasts have obscured the indispensable link with the past and the significance of the present as real and important aspects of the author's thought. In connection with verses 4–7 we have already observed the significance of the past: church tradition, the historical Jesus, and the Old Testament. As for the present, the author's message for the contemporary churches of Asia appears in chapters 2–3. Although chapters 19 ff. plainly have to do with the future return of Christ and the end of world history, the long central section (chaps. 4–18) does not deal solely with the end time. Although the end is constantly in view, the author is also concerned with his own period. For example, the material of chapters 11, 12, and 13 is almost surely to be understood as John's apocalyptic interpretation of past and present historical events—that is, the destruction of Jerusalem (chap. 11), the destiny of the Messiah and the church in the world (chap. 12), and the depredations of the Roman Empire (chap. 13). All of history is under the sign of the alpha and the omega, the lordship of the God who was and is and is to come; nothing falls outside the scope of Revelation.

John's own involvement in that history becomes clearer in the following paragraph (1:9–11), and the reader learns that this involvement includes participation in the events of the world as well as in the life of the church. This section marks the beginning of the book proper, for it serves to introduce the author's visionary experiences, which comprise chapters 2 and 3 (cf. vs. 11) as well as the rest of his work. The so-called letters to the seven churches are no less visions than the sighting of the New Jerusalem (chap. 21). Yet the naming of the locations of the churches (vs. 11) makes graphic and concrete the this-worldly dimension of Revelation.

Verse 9 is crucial for grasping John's situation as he writes, and therefore for understanding his book. John's statement that he was on Patmos "on account of the word of God and the testimony of Jesus" is subject to several interpretations. Probably, however, he means that he is on Patmos as punishment for preaching the word of God and testifying to Jesus; this is especially likely in view of his use of these same terms in connection with martyrdom (cf. 6:9 and 20:4). John speaks of sharing not only the kingdom, but the tribulation and the patient endurance. "Tribulation" is perhaps a technical eschatological term referring to the woes just preceding the last days (7:14). The persecutions perpetrated against God's people are a part of these woes. They call for "steadfast endurance." Hebrews also mentioned the need for endurance with the possibility of persecution already in view (10:34 f.; 12:4). In Revelation persecution is the predominant reality. Moreover, we know that Patmos was used as a penal colony, a place of banishment, by the Romans. Ancient church tradition also understood John to have been in prison because of his Christian preaching.[22] We are justified in accepting this tradition as an accurate interpretation of Revelation 1:9.

Not surprisingly, John receives his revelations "in the Spirit" (vs. 10); the association of the Spirit with visions and ecstatic utterances is common to primitive Christianity. The speaking in tongues that Paul discusses in I Corinthians 14 is called the utterance of mysteries in the Spirit (cf. Acts 2:1 ff.). By "the Lord's day" John evidently means Sunday. He was in the Spirit on Sunday. This is probably the earliest reference to Sunday, the Lord's day, as the distinctly Christian holy day. "The sabbath" in the New Testament as in the Old always means the Jewish sabbath, that is, Saturday. Now, however, Sunday has appropriately replaced Saturday as the Christian day of celebration, for according to tradition it was on Sunday (the third day after, and including, Friday) that Jesus rose from the dead. The voice like a trumpet which John hears is probably that of the Son of Man (vs. 13), the heavenly Christ.

John writes not of his own accord, but by command (vs. 11), and by command he sends what he writes to the seven churches of Asia. The command is to "write what you see," rather than what you hear. The mode of the communication of revelation is not verbal, as is usual in the earlier Old Testament prophets, but visual, as in the tradition of Ezekiel, the later, postexilic prophets and, above all, the Jewish apocalyptic writers. Despite the bizarre character of what John sees and writes, this vision is not meant to remain his own personal experience or the property of certain esoteric circles. The whole book, visions, predictions, warnings, condemnations, and commendations, is a communication to the church. During this time of crisis John delivers to the church a revelation containing dire warnings along with profound encouragement.

With verse 12 the visionary scenes begin, and we encounter for the first time the problem of how to interpret them. On the one hand, the narrations of the visions are carefully constructed literary works, replete with allusions to and quotations from the Old Testament. (Note the footnotes

---

[22] Charles, *The Revelation of St. John*, I, 23, cites the relevant passages from Pliny, Tertullian, Clement of Alexandria, and Origen.

in the RSV here and throughout the book.) On the other hand, we cannot arbitrarily exclude ecstatic or visionary experience as the germinal basis for what the author has written. Evidence of the genuineness of the attested experiences is the absence of certain conventionalities of literary form that appear in most late Jewish apocalyptic. As we have observed, John is not pseudonymous and does not utilize the fiction of prophecy written in an earlier era. In other words, he does not find it necessary to accredit his message by concealing himself, nor does he attempt to gain credence for his prophecy of things to come by dressing out as predictions the recitation of generally known historical facts.

Verse 12 means only that John turned to see who was speaking to him, not that he expected to *see* a voice. The seven lampstands recall the seven-branched candelabrum (Hebrew, *menorah*) that was said to stand outside the second veil of the Israelite tabernacle (Exodus 25:31–40; cf. Zechariah 4). In all probability the allusion is intentional despite the fact we here seem to be dealing with seven separate stands, not one. The presence of the lampstands indicates an approach to the holy place.[23] However, the explicit interpretation of John is that the seven lampstands represent the seven churches to be addressed in chapters 2 and 3. The appearance of the Christ (vs. 13) evokes Daniel 7:13, "one like a son of man." We are not yet told that he is the Christ, and John does not favor "Son of Man" as a messianic title (but cf. 14:14), yet 1:17 ff. makes this identification certain. The clothing of this still mysterious figure (vs. 13) may have been suggested by Ezekiel 9:2 and 11, and Daniel 10:5. The remainder of the description is for the most part derived from the appearance of the one that was Ancient of Days (Dan. 7:9 f.), although the comparison of his voice to the sound of many waters probably comes from Ezekiel 1:24 and 43:2.

Obviously John's mind was steeped in the language and imagery of the Old Testament. He regards the words of the Old Testament and its prophecies as applying to the coming of Jesus Christ, to the church and the times in which it lives, and to the course of world history up to and including its completion. This view of the Old Testament fits perfectly with the author's understanding of the lordship of God over history. God directs history and makes known its secrets to his prophets, principally through the gift of rightly understanding the Old Testament.

The seven stars (vs. 16) are interpreted in verse 20. The sharp two-edged sword recalls Genesis 3:24 (cf. Ezekiel 21:9–10) and especially Hebrews 4:12. In the latter passage, as apparently here, the sword symbolizes the word of God. Christ's shining face indicates nearness to, if not possession of, the glory of God himself (cf. II Cor. 3:7–18; 4:6). With verse 16 the

---

[23] Furthermore, the connection of the *menorah* with the appearance of the Christ may have been suggested to the author by the *menorah* in Zechariah 4, a passage dealing with the messianic hope of Israel.

description of the vision of the Son of Man is complete. John's reaction and Christ's response in identifying himself and explaining the vision to John follow (vss. 17–20).

John's physical reaction to his vision (vs. 17) is not only understandable, but also liturgically appropriate. Daniel 10:7–10 is evidently the immediate background if not the direct inspiration of this verse. Christ reaches out, however, restores John (vs. 17), and identifies himself to him (vss. 17b–18). That Christ is the first and the last implies that like God, and with him, he exercises lordship over history from beginning to end. From verse 18 it is apparent that the speaker is Christ. "Living one" and "alive forevermore" in conjunction with the statement "I died" refer unmistakably to the crucifixion and resurrection. The power of the keys, in Matthew 16:19 given to Peter, is here reserved for Christ. This means that as a result of his own death and resurrection Christ assumes power over death and Hades. "Death no longer has dominion over him" (Rom. 6:9 f.). Rather Christ has dominion over death and Hades. His resurrection is no mere resuscitation, but exaltation to supreme power and authority. The divine ascriptions and prerogatives applied to Christ mean that man's ultimate destiny depends upon and is assured by him. The statement of 1:18 may also imply the primitive Christian concept of Christ's descent into hell and his freeing of the captives there (I Pet. 3:18–22; 4:6; cf. Eph. 4:8–10).

Ancient tomb at Bethshearim with the seven-branched menorah. (Courtesy of Israel Government Tourist Office.)

Attention turns once again to the prophet's task (vs. 19). Revelation is written in response to command. It concerns not only the unfolding of the future, but also the interpretation of present events: "what is" as well as "what is to take place hereafter." Christ interprets the seven stars and seven lampstands (vs. 20). The notion that nations, communities, or even individuals had guardian angels was not uncommon in the ancient world (cf. Tobit 5:21). At any rate, John assumes that each church has its angel, who serves it as a medium of revelation or communication with the divine. The letters to the seven churches (chaps. 2 and 3) are then directed to them through these guardian angels.

The seven letters are no ordinary letters at all, but are as much supernatural in their source and delivery as the rest of the book. Nevertheless, they again show the author's concern, not only with heavenly things and things to come, but with the this-worldly life and problems of the churches. This concern is directed toward both the inner life of the church and its witness to a hostile world. Naturally, the two are related, for no church with chinks in its moral armor would be strong enough to stand before such a world and resist the demand that it worship the gods of that world.

Chapters 4 and 5 picture the heavenly court. The seer describes the throne of God Himself and the momentous events taking place there, particularly the designation of the Lamb who had been slain to open the scroll. The Lamb is, of course, Christ. The opening of six of these seals is described in chapter 6. Heavenly events and realities have their earthly counterparts and consequences. With the opening of the seals catastrophes break out across the earth. Then there follows an interlude (chap. 7). The first part (7:1–8) shows the gathering of the elect from the four corners of the earth and the latter (vss. 9–17) their appearance in heaven. At the beginning of chapter 8 we have the opening of the seventh seal—and silence. After about one-half hour of silence, the sounding of the seven trumpets begins (chaps. 8 and 9; 11:15–19) with disasters erupting upon the earth.

Chapters 10–13 deal with contemporary events or those of the recent past. The prophet's own experience (chap. 10) is like that of the prophet Ezekiel (Ezekiel 2:8–3:3). Since Ezekiel's word of the Lord had to do with lamentations and woes, especially against Jerusalem (cf., for example, Ezekiel 4:1 ff.), not surprisingly Revelation 11 reflects the devastation of that same city. The birth and persecution of the Messiah and of his church are envisioned in chapters 12 and 13. In chapter 12 the heavenly dimension of the conflict is paramount, whereas in 13 attention focuses on Rome, described under the apocalyptic symbol of the beast. The sounding of the seventh trumpet is delayed by intervening scenes, just as the opening of the seventh seal was delayed. The seventh and final stage of each sequence has a peculiar significance, for apparently it stands symbolically at the borderline between the apocalyptic and catastrophic dissolution of this world and the coming of God's kingdom. The events following upon the sounding of the trumpets recapitulate those following the opening of the seven seals. Yet there may also be a progression. After the seventh seal there is only silence, but after the seventh trumpet we get a preview of the glory that is to come (11:15–19).

From chapter 14 onward we no longer have apocalyptic interpretations of the immediate past or present. Again the seer has a vision of heaven (14:1–5), this time followed by a series of warnings from angels flying in heaven and the command that the heavenly Christ reap the harvest of the earth (14:14–20). Chapters 15 and 18 describe in appropriately symbolic terms the final upheavals to be wrought on earth by the outpouring of the bowls of divine wrath.

The seer's prophecy about the remainder of world history is completed with the outpouring of the seventh bowl of wrath and the destruction of Babylon, which is, of course, Rome (chaps. 17 and 18). Yet we can actually discern no clear distinction between world history as we understand it and the last days. John understands his own time to be the last days. He does not conceive the present as a period of secular history where everything is governed by natural, social, or psychological laws of cause and effect. There is for him no secular history, for all time is ultimately under the lordship of God. Nevertheless, immense powers of evil, with other-worldly origins and dimensions (for example, the beast, the dragon or serpent, who is called the Devil and Satan, 12:9), seem to hold sway in the world. Their lordship is, however, unreal and ephemeral. God's wrath is directed against them and they are overthrown. But victory does not occur easily or without vast repercussions. Chaos and disaster break out upon earth as the power of God overwhelms the forces of evil. Even the advent of Christ, traditionally called the second coming, does not put an end to the struggle once and for all (chap. 19). After the thousand year reign of Christ, the millennium (after the Latin word for thousand), there is still another outbreak of evil, led by Satan himself (chap. 20), before God finally brings everything into subjection (21:1–22:5). Yet the substance of the seer's message is not that the end is a long way off, but that the night is already far spent, the day is at hand (Rom. 13:12). The apocalyptic drama is underway and moves inexorably toward its conclusion. "Surely I am coming soon. Amen. Come, Lord Jesus!"

Christians of John's day were willing to resist at the risk of their lives the demand that they worship the Roman emperor, the incarnation of worldly order and power, the epitome of man's deification of himself. Why did they dare to do so? Such worship seems little more than a perfunctory gesture, although it was a significant token of subjection to the power and authority of this world. These Christians resisted because they believed in an authority that so thoroughly transcends this world that it could be

"The Vision of St. John the Divine" by the Spanish artist El Greco (1541–1614). (Courtesy of Metropolitan Museum of Art, Rogers Fund, 1956.)

revealed in the death of a man upon the cross and in the conviction that God had raised him from the dead to his own right hand. They refused to worship the deities of this world, preferring to obey God rather than men. Yet the book of Revelation shows that for many, if not most of them, this conviction and the refusal to fall down and worship the beast were set in the context of a lively future hope, not primarily for their own personal survival of physical death, but for the manifestation of God's authority and rule before all men. God's Christ and his saints were to be vindicated before the eyes of a skeptical and evil world.

This study began with a consideration of history, the historical background of the New Testament in Judaism, the Greco-Roman world, and early Christianity. It concludes with another and different consideration of history, the history of God's coming lordship over men and nations depicted in Revelation. We have, in the one case, a modern perspective on the historical problem of origins, and in the other case, an apocalyptic preview of the end of history.

The two perspectives may seem to have little in common and the purposes of each may be quite different, but in both cases there is an effort to comprehend the mystery of the relation of men and events in time and space. This alone reveals something of the character of early Christianity and the New Testament. In a variety of ways our study of the New Testament has led to a consideration of history, even though our primary interest has not been that of establishing the so-called historical facts. From a concern for historical background we have moved to an investigation of the Synoptic Gospels, which reflect both the church's existence as a historical community and its interest in the historical Jesus. Next we constructed an historical portrait of Jesus based upon these Gospels. Interpretation of Acts, the Pauline letters, and the later New Testament books necessitated an understanding of the historical circumstances of the church in which they arose. Such concern with history has a most ancient precedent, for the earliest Christian theologian, Paul, was profoundly concerned with the meaning of the process and end of history (cf. Rom. 9–11 and I Cor. 15). The Gospel of John grounded Christian belief in the historical Jesus, whereas Revelation set forth the meaning of contemporary events for the ultimate purposes of God in history. In so doing, the seer visualized in a highly symbolic way the unfolding of the remainder of history up to, and including, its final consummation.

Thus Revelation gives testimony to faith in the lordship of God over history. The author is convinced that the apparent confusion of events does in fact lead somewhere. It is not meaningless. Yet this meaning is not apparent in individual events, for it can only be grasped when history is viewed in its entirety—that is, from the standpoint of its expected end. Christ is the light by which all history is illuminated for John. The Old Testament provides the imagery by means of which he portrays the end. Of course, Revelation is not unprecedented in the New Testament in its interest in the final days. Already Paul's correspondence testifies to his conviction that the projected end provides the key to understanding the present. The various apocalyptic discourses of the Gospels (Mark 13, parr.) disclose the existence of widespread early Christian concern about the end-time, its signs and warnings. For the early church and the writers of the New Testament, faith meant not only looking upward to God and Christ, but backward to the manifestations of God's reality in the past and forward in expectation to his further and final revelations in the future.

The look backward fixed first and foremost upon Jesus of Nazareth, a real historical person whose mission and message inaugurated the expected kingdom of God. The look forward anticipated the end of history as it was known and the completion of God's kingdom with the return of Christ. All the while the Christian lived by faith in the reality of God's presence through the Spirit in the church.

Although somewhat trite, it is nonetheless true that Christianity is a historical religion. Moreover, this historical orientation is an important aspect of the anatomy of the New Testament. In the broadest sense, the literature and faith of the New Testament are structured in historical terms and center upon what transpires between man and man and between God and man. But for the New Testament authors, the evangelists and Paul, as well as the seer of Revelation, the concept of history as we understand it is foreign. For the modern mind history is man's story, told by man, and based upon the assumption that man is the creator, prime mover, and judge. For the New Testament, however, God is the creator, prime mover, and judge. In the New Testament literature the panorama of men and events is finally under God's guiding care. As religious literature the New Testament is primarily concerned with what God has done, is doing, and will do.

We are likely to regard the history of Jesus, of Paul, or the early church, insofar as these can be reconstructed and depicted by the modern historian, as real; but the history of Jesus in the Gospel of John or the future projections of history in Revelation may seem less real, the products of dogmatic interests or fanciful imagination. Such a judgment reveals the gulf separating modern ways of thinking from the New Testament. The evangelist and the seer would not have considered their writings to be further from historical reality than, for example, the Synoptic tradition of Jesus' words or the history of the book of Acts—much less the works of modern historians. Mark did not view the miracles or the "little apocalypse" (chap. 13) as less real than the story of Jesus' baptism. For the New Testament, reality consists not merely in what is recordable or provable. The total reality with which the authors in various ways deal includes the Spirit-led perception in faith of what actually happened, happens, and is going to happen. The reality upon which the faith centers cannot be separated from the eyes of faith.[24]

The twentieth century may no longer share many of the assumptions of first-century man. Some of his important presuppositions do indeed belong to the past. Nevertheless, it is possible to appreciate the convictions and aspirations of the men of the New Testament and at the same time to

[24] Cf. P. S. Minear, *Eyes of Faith: A Study in the Biblical Point of View* (Philadelphia: Westminster Press, 1946), for a stimulating attempt to recover the perspective of the Biblical writers.

understand that they could not avoid the influence of the times and circumstances in which they wrote. Basic to those convictions and aspirations was faith in the fundamental, final goodness of God. The crucial insight into God's character and disposition stemmed from their belief in Jesus as the Christ, God's man. This faith and insight implied or assumed that God's reality, now veiled from mortal sight, nevertheless is, and was, and is to come (Rev. 1:8)—that he is, was, and would be the sovereign, controlling power in each man's life and in the history of men and nations. For New Testament Christianity God was no abstract idea or principle, but the key to understanding the past, existing in the present, and hoping in the future. To such a faith Revelation in its own way gives impressive testimony. It points the reader to the future and invites him to hope and to be steadfast. Its author never imagined that his book would conclude the New Testament. But the later church, in putting it at the end of its canon of scripture, nevertheless understood and honored his basic intention. The fathers of the early church thereby revealed their own understanding of the anatomy of the New Testament message.

Suggestions for Further Reading

The amount of literature on the Johannine documents, excluding Revelation, is immense. On the interpretation of this material R. Bultmann, *Theology of the New Testament*,* 2 vols., trans. K. Grobel (New York: Scribner's, 1951–55), II, 3–92, is outstanding, although controversial. Somewhat more conservative is W. F. Howard, *Christianity according to St. John* (London: Duckworth, 1943).

The Gospel According to John. In addition to the commentaries in the series mentioned, there are several noteworthy commentaries on the Fourth Gospel. Older, somewhat obscure at points, but nevertheless still stimulating is E. C. Hoskyns, *The Fourth Gospel*, ed. F. N. Davey (rev. ed.; London: Faber and Faber, 1947). A reliable commentary is R. H. Lightfoot, *St. John's Gospel*,* ed. C. F. Evans (London: Oxford University Press, 1956). Probably the two-volume work of R. E. Brown will be the best commentary on John's Gospel and letters available in English. Only the first volume has been published, however, as this book goes to press: *The Gospel according to John (i–xii)* ("The Anchor Bible," 29; New York: Doubleday, 1966).

Other noteworthy works on John are the two scholarly studies by C. H. Dodd, *The Interpretation of the Fourth Gospel** (Cambridge: Cambridge University Press, 1953), and *Historical Tradition in the Fourth Gospel* (Cambridge: Cambridge University Press, 1963). O. Cullmann, *Early*

Christian Worship, trans. A. S. Todd and J. B. Torrance (*SBT*, 10; Naperville, Ill.: Allenson, 1953), interprets the Fourth Gospel against the background of the sacraments. J. L. Martyn, *History and Theology in the Fourth Gospel* (New York: Harper, 1968), suggests that the Fourth Gospel arose out of an acute controversy between the early church and Judaism.

The Johannine Letters. The Commentary of C. H. Dodd in the Moffatt series (1946) merits special mention. The general works suggested under Chapter 9 also deal with the Johannine letters.

The Revelation to John. Old, but extensive and useful, is the commentary of I. T. Beckwith, *The Apocalypse of John* (New York: Macmillan, 1922; reissued by Baker Book House). The most recent commentary is that of G. B. Caird in the Harper series (1966; cf. General Bibliography, III). Another recent work on Revelation is M. Rissi, *Time and History*, trans. G. C. Winsor (Richmond, Va.: John Knox, 1966). On apocalyptic literature see D. S. Russell, *The Method and Message of Jewish Apocalyptic: 200 B.C.–A.D. 100* (Philadelphia: Westminster, 1964).

Revelation raises the questions of church-state relations, persecution, and martyrdom. In this area note O. Cullmann, *The State in the New Testament** (rev. ed.; London: SCM, 1963); R. M. Grant, *The Sword and the Cross* (New York: Macmillan, 1955); and W. H. C. Frend, *Martyrdom and Persecution in the Early Church** (Oxford: Blackwell, 1965; paperback, Anchor Books), an extensive scholarly work.

Glossary

Abba: the intimate, familiar Aramaic word for father. In the normal piety of first-century Judaism this form of address was too intimate to be used of God. But Jesus (Mark 14:36) and the early Christians (Rom. 8:15, Gal. 4:6) used it in this way.

A.D.: abbreviation of the Latin *Anno Domini*, which means "in the year of our Lord." In the western world the birth of Christ is customarily the point of reference for dating events. Events occurring before the birth of Jesus are indicated by the abbreviation B.C., "before Christ."

Agrapha: literally, unwritten words or sayings. The term refers to words and sayings of Jesus not contained in the canonical Gospels.

Allegory: a story whose details or actions illustrate or tell about something quite different. Each element of an allegory possesses its own distinct meaning, which is determined by something outside the story, e.g., the Christian faith in the case of Bunyan's *Pilgrim's Progress.*

Amen: the transliteration of a Greek word that in turn transliterates a Hebrew word. In common usage "amen" is either a solemn confirmation of what has been said or a response of assent to words of another.

Antichrist: an apocalyptic figure, the arch enemy of Christ who will appear shortly before the parousia to wage war against the friends of Christ. (*See* Parousia.)

Antinomianism: the belief that the Christian who has been freed by Christ has no ethical or moral obligations at all. (*See* Grace.)

Antitheses: the six contrasts with Moses' teaching that Jesus proclaims in the Sermon on the Mount (Matt. 5:21–48) in the antithetical form, "You have heard . . . . But I say to you. . . ."

Apocalyptic: an uncovering or a revelation. The term is applied to a type of literature that is pessimistic of man's possibilities and hence discloses God's plan for the last days (e.g., the Apocalypse or Revelation of John). Although related to prophecy and eschatology, apocalyptic thought stresses more precisely and forcefully the future intervention of God in the end time.

Apocrypha: the fourteen books of the Septuagint Bible not found in the Hebrew Bible; it is a part of the Roman Catholic Bible but not the Protestant Bible. More generally the term means "hidden or spurious" and is also applied to early Christian writings not admitted to the New Testament.

Apostle: a term meaning "one who is sent" specifically applied to the twelve disciples who were close to Jesus (see Mark 3:14 ff.). Paul also appropriates

461

this designation for himself because of the risen Christ's appearance to him (see I Cor. 15:1 ff.).

Apostolic Fathers: a collection of second century noncanonical writings supposedly written by personal followers of the apostles.

Aramaic: the language of Palestine during the time of Jesus and the early church. A Semitic tongue, it is closely related to Hebrew.

Archaeology: the scientific study of ancient cultures on the basis of their remains, such as fossil relics, artifacts, monuments, pottery, and buildings.

Ascension: traditionally the visible departure of Jesus into heaven forty days after his resurrection (see Acts 1:9).

Baptism: the act or sacrament by which a person was received into the early Christian Church. The Greek term means "to dip" or "immerse."

B.C.: the abbreviation of "before Christ." (*See* A.D.)

Beatitudes: the nine blessings that stand at the beginning of Jesus' Sermon on the Mount (see Matt. 5:3–12).

Canon: a term originally applied to a reed used for measuring. It was later used of those books or writings that became standard or authoritative for the early Christians. By the close of the fourth century the Christian canon was largely fixed. (*See* Apocrypha; Pseudepigrapha.)

Catholic: universal, affecting mankind as a whole; an adjective used by the early church to refer to whatever was universally shared among the various churches.

Catholic Epistles: James; I and II Peter; I, II, and III John; and Jude. These seven letters are supposedly "general" in destination and in character and hence Catholic.

Charisma: "free gift." The term came to be used in the early church for the various gifts of the Spirit, such as wisdom, knowledge, faith, healing, and speaking in tongues (see I Cor. 12).

Christ: (*See* Messiah.)

Christology: that aspect of Christian thought specifically concerned with the revelation of God in Jesus the Christ.

Church: the community of believers in Jesus Christ. The term is used of individual congregations and of the entire fellowship of Christians.

Council of Jamnia: the group of rabbinical scholars who settled in Jamnia shortly before the fall of Jerusalem in A.D. 70 and helped standardize the Jewish religion. They are usually credited with having fixed the Hebrew canon of the Old Testament, now followed by Protestants.

Covenant: a solemn agreement that binds two parties together. The Old Testament (Covenant) depicts the agreement by which God and the people of Israel were bound together, and the New Testament (Covenant) tells the story of the new agreement effected by God with the new Israel through Jesus the Christ. Ordinarily in Biblical usage a covenant is sealed in blood.

Crucifixion: a Roman form of execution in which the victim was nailed or bound to a wooden cross and left to die.

Dead Sea Scrolls: ancient Jewish documents from the period of Christian origins, found near the Dead Sea. (*See* Essenes; Qumran.)

Decalogue or Ten Commandments: the name given to the words Moses received, according to tradition, from God on Mt. Sinai (see Exodus 20:1–17 and Deuteronomy 5:6–21).

Diaspora or dispersion: the Jewish community scattered (dispersed) outside the holy land of Palestine.

Didache or "Teaching of the Twelve Apostles": an anonymous second-century Christian manual for church life.

Docetism (derived from the Greek meaning "to seem"): an early Christian heresy according to which Jesus Christ only seemed to suffer and die. A divine being, it was thought, could not suffer.

Epistle: a letter of a formal or didactic nature; the term used to be regularly applied to the New Testament letters.

Eschatology: discourse about the last things or the end of the age (Greek *eschatos* meaning "last"). Traditionally the term is used of Christian thought concerning all the events and actions associated with both the end of history and the end of human life. (*See* Apocalyptic; Parousia.)

Essenes: an ascetic, Jewish religious group existing at the time of the New Testament. They stressed radical obedience to the Jewish law. (*See* Qumran.)

Ethics: a broad term applied to such related matters as moral codes and practices, theories of value, and the imperatives of Christian faith as they pertain to relations between man and man (not God and man).

Eucharist: the sacrament of the Lord's Supper in which bread and wine are consecrated and distributed to the faithful Christians. (*See* Lord's Supper; Sacrament.)

Exegesis: the critical interpretation of a text. Literally the term means "to lead out" the meaning from the text.

Exile: specifically the removal of defeated Israelites by the Babylonians in 586 B.C.

Exodus: a going out; used specifically of Israel's departure from Egypt under the leadership of Moses about the thirteenth century B.C.

Expiation: "making right" by means of some act or rite the offense done by one party to another, especially man's expiation for his sin before God. (*See* Propitiation; Sacrifice.)

Form Criticism: the classification of the "forms" in which the tradition, esp. the Gospel tradition, circulated before being written down and the attempt to determine the "setting in life" of the church which they reflect. (*See* Redactor.)

Gentile: A non-Jew.

Gnosticism: a religious movement-or attitude widespread about the time of the emergence of the Christian faith. Believers possessed a secret knowledge (*gnosis*) and sought to escape the ephemeral earthly world for the eternal heavenly world.

Gospel: originally the message of good news that God has revealed Himself as gracious in the event of Jesus Christ. The term later came to designate also the literary form in which the good news of Jesus' life, death, and resurrection is narrated; e.g., the Gospel according to Matthew.

Hasmonean: another name for the Maccabees, leaders of the Jewish revolt against Syria.

Hellenization: the process or result of the spread of Greek language and culture in the Mediterranean world after Alexander the Great (died 323 B.C.).

Holy: that which has to do with God or the divine power and majesty.

Immanence: the nearness or involvement of God in the world. (*See* Transcendence.)

Incarnation: literally means "becoming flesh"; the embodiment of the . divine in the man Jesus of Nazareth.

Justification: the act or process by which God brings man into proper relationship with himself. In Paul the justification or righteousness of God is to be received by faith. (*See* Righteousness.)

Kerygma (literally "proclamation"): the early Christian preaching about Jesus as the Christ intended to elicit the decision of faith.

Kingdom of God or rule of God: God's Lordship over mankind and the world. The kingdom is the center of Jesus' message in the Synoptic Gospels.

Koinē ("common" in Greek): the everyday Greek speech used throughout the Hellenistic world during the period of early Christianity. The New Testament books are written in *koinē* Greek.

Law: in the New Testament generally the revelation of God through Moses to the people of Israel embodied in the cultic, ritual, and moral commandments of the Old Testament. (*See* Gospel; Torah.)

Lord's Supper: the church's continuing re-enactment of the last supper of Jesus with his disciples. (*See* Eucharist.)

Maccabees: the priestly family who successfully led a revolt against Hellenistic Syrian rule beginning in 167 b.c. They ruled over Palestine from 142 b.c. to 63 b.c. (*See* Hasmonean.)

Manuscripts: handwritten documents, especially the ancient New Testament documents from which our present text is determined. The earliest complete manuscripts come from the fourth century, although there are sizeable fragments of earlier date.

Messiah: from the Hebrew term meaning "anointed one." "Messiah" was used of the Davidic king, whose restoration was expected in Jesus' day. Its Greek equivalent is *Christos* (Christ), the basic designation of Jesus in the New Testament. He was believed to be the expected Messiah of Israel.

Miracle: an extraordinary event, a manifestation of the activity of God.

Myth: the result of man's effort to communicate his faith in transcendent reality by means of story and symbol. This technical use of the term should be distinguished from the popular meaning of a fantastic or untrue story.

Oral Tradition: any teaching or similar material transmitted from person to person or generation to generation by word of mouth rather than by use of writing; also the process of such transmission.

Parable: a brief story that makes its point by the unusual development or imagery of the narrative. The various details do not function as allegory but are significant for the story itself. Although the parable was already known to the Jewish religious tradition, Jesus made especial use of it. (*See* Allegory.)

Paraclete: helper, comforter, or mediator. The term is used in the Fourth Gospel of the Holy Spirit as the Christian community's helper after the death of Jesus (see John 14:16, 15:26, 16:7).

Parousia (literally "coming" or "presence"): the early Christian belief in the second coming of Christ, a glorious advent in power and judgment at the end of the age. (*See* Eschatology; Son of Man.)

Passion: suffering, particularly the suffering of Jesus during the last week of his life in Jerusalem and especially the suffering leading to his death.

Passover: the annual Jewish celebration of the deliverance from slavery in Egypt under the leadership of Moses. Jesus was crucified at the time of the Passover. (*See* Exodus.)

Pastoral Epistles: I and II Timothy and Titus. These letters give advice to the church leader or pastor concerning matters of church government and discipline.

Patriarch: the father of a people, especially the three great ancestors of the people of Israel (Abraham, Isaac, and Jacob). The period of Israel's history before the Exodus out of Egypt is frequently called the patriarchal period.

Pericope: a "cutting around" or section. The term is used of the individual, complete units of tradition about Jesus that circulated separately in the early church and were ultimately joined together to form the Gospels. (*See* Form Criticism; Redactor.)

Pharisees: the dominant Jewish religious group at the time of Jesus, who practiced strict observance of both the written and oral law of Judaism. The name probably comes from a Semitic term meaning "separated." (*See* Sadducees.)

Pre-existence: the term used to designate the New Testament belief that Jesus of Nazareth in some way existed with God before his earthly advent (see John 1:1–18).

Priest: a holy man authorized to perform ritual and cultic acts whereby man and God are enabled to commune with one another. (*See* Holy; Sacrifice.)

Procurator: an official of the Roman empire, responsible to the emperor, exercising administrative authority in a province or district.

Prophet: someone who speaks or acts for the divine, transcendent reality. In general, the prophet not only predicted God's action but also pled with men to respond to God's will. Prophets existed in the early church, as well as in ancient Israel.

Propitiation: a placating or pacifying of the deity; a sacrifice that induces God to be favorable or beneficent to the sacrificer. (*See* Expiation.)

Pseudepigrapha: literally "false writings," particularly a group of late Jewish writings claiming Old Testament figures as their authors. They reflect Jewish religious thought in the intertestamental period. (*See* Apocrypha.)

Q Source: the hypothetical source, consisting primarily of sayings of Jesus, used by both Matthew and Luke in the writing of their respective Gospels.

Qumran: the site on the northeast shore of the Dead Sea where a Jewish sect lived in strict obedience to the law of its covenant community until approximately A.D. 70. Near this site the library of the community or the Dead Sea Scrolls was discovered. (*See* Essenes.)

Rabbi: "master," a Jewish religious leader especially trained and qualified to expound and apply the law of Moses.

Redactor: one who edits, revises, or shapes the literary sources that he has at hand. The separation of tradition and redaction is the primary task of form criticism. (*See* Form Criticism.)

Redemption: literally "to buy" or "take back," particularly the act or process of God's taking back sinful or rebellious man by means of the event of Jesus Christ.

Resurrection or rising from the dead: a central hope in the New Testament based upon the early Christians' belief that Jesus was raised from the dead by God. In general the New Testament view of resurrection of the body or person should be distinguished from the widely held notion of the immortality of the soul.

Revelation (translated from the Greek word *apokalypsis*): an uncovering, revealing, or laying bare. It refers to the uncovering of the transcendent God in human events, particularly the event of Christ in the Christian tradition.

Righteousness: primarily the quality and action of God; hence man's righteousness proceeds from God's initiative in Christ and is based upon a relation with God as revealed in Christ. "Righteousness" and "justification" translate the same Greek noun in the New Testament. (*See* Justification.)

Sacrament: a sacred rite, "an outward and visible sign of an inward and spiritual grace," namely the presence of the transcendent God. The term "sacrament" per se does not occur in the New Testament, but it is commonly used to refer to the acts of baptism and the Lord's Supper, which are reported there. (*See* Baptism; Eucharist.)

Sacrifice: the act of offering something held valuable to the deity. By the act of sacrifice communion with the divine is initiated, reestablished, or continued. (*See* Priest.)

Sadducees: a religious group of the intertestamental period who represented the priestly aristocracy of Jewish life. In distinction from the Pharisees, they held only to the written Mosaic law and did not believe in the resurrection.

Salvation: the state of complete liberation from sin, brokenness, and estrangement between man and God. In general the New Testament locates salvation in the future, although its inauguration is already effected in Christ.

Sanctification: the process of being made holy. The term refers to the life of the Christian under the guidance of the Spirit as the effects of Christ's work, especially the love of God and of man, become more and more manifest.

Scribes: a title applied to learned men in post-exilic Judaism who studied and copied the law and exercised judgment in matters pertaining to the law. (*See* Pharisees.)

Second Coming: *See* Parousia.

Septuagint (usually designated LXX): the Greek translation of the Hebrew Old Testament for Diaspora Jews which originated before the rise of Christianity. (*See* Apocrypha.)

Sin: generally any act, whether in thought or deed, which violates the law or will of God. In the New Testament particularly, it denotes the broken or estranged relation between man and God. (*See* Righteousness.)

Son of God: in Hebraic thought someone especially selected or anointed by God for a task, such as the king of Israel, a prophet, or the people of Israel. In Hellenistic religious thought the term refers frequently to a male offspring of the gods. In the New Testament Jesus functions as the Son of God primarily in the Hebraic sense.

Son of Man: an apocalyptic Jewish figure who was to come at the end of the ages to serve as judge between the righteous and the wicked. (*See* Apocalyptic; Parousia.)

Soteriology: discourse about salvation. Soteriology refers to the New Testament understanding of the righteousness of God, the sin of man, the work of Christ, man's response of faith, and the work of the Spirit in sanctification.

Soul: a spiritual entity within each person that survives death. The concept of the soul plays little role in Hebraic or New Testament thought. Its prominence in Christian thought derives from later Greek influence.

Source Criticism: the work of identifying the written sources that were used in the composition of any given document, such as one of the Gospels.

Spirit: the dynamic power and activity of God directed toward the world, especially active in the history of Israel, the life of Jesus, and the early church; in the Christian tradition usually referred to as the Holy Spirit.

Synoptic Problem: the problem of understanding the relationship between the Synoptic Gospels (Matthew, Mark, and Luke), taking account of their great similarities as well as their distinct differences. The generally accepted solution is that both Matthew and Luke used Mark, the Q source consisting largely of Jesus' sayings, and distinct material to which each had access separately.

Talmud (meaning instruction or study): the authoritative body of Jewish tradition that developed several centuries immediately preceding and following the beginning of the Christian era. It exists in Palestinian (early fifth century) and Babylonian (late fifth century) forms.

Theology: discourse on God; the study of or reflection upon the nature of God and the nature of God's relationship to man.

Torah: the Hebrew term meaning law or teaching, especially law as divine revelation. (*See* Law.)

Transcendence: in theology God's distance from the world; alternatively, God's holiness or "otherness" as distinct from the secular or profane. (*See* Immanence.)

Trinity: the Christian doctrine that God exists in three persons: the Father, Jesus Christ as the Son, and the Holy Spirit. The developed doctrine is not found in the New Testament although Father, Son, and Spirit are spoken of frequently.

Virgin Birth: the miraculous birth of Jesus to Mary, his mother, without the participation of a human father in the conception.

Witness: in the New Testament includes both observation and testimony, especially to the life, death, and resurrection of Jesus. In one sense, martyrdom is an especially appropriate witness to Jesus. The English term "martyr" is a transliteration of the Greek word for "a witness."

Word: a technical, literary designation of a complete saying, especially a saying of Jesus. In the Johannine literature Jesus himself is called the Word (John 1:1–18).

Word of God: frequently a designation for the Holy Bible. In the New Testament, however, it is used in close connection with the event of Jesus Christ, especially the preaching about that event. (*See* Kerygma.)

Works or works of the law: the attempt to earn righteousness before God instead of acknowledging sin and relying on His grace. (*See* Justification.)

Zealots: members of a fanatical, Jewish sect who sought to overthrow Roman rule of Palestine by means of violent revolution.

General
Bibliography

Books available in paperback are marked by an asterisk (*). Paperback publishers are indicated only when they differ from the original publisher. Subtitles and series titles have often been omitted to conserve space.

I. BIBLICAL TEXTS

The Revised Standard Version has become the English version most widely used in America, and justly so, for it is a good and reliable translation. The New Testament of a comparable official translation made in Great Britain, *The New English Bible* (Oxford University Press and Cambridge University Press, 1961), has already appeared and the Old Testament will be forthcoming. Other modern translations such as J. Moffatt, *A New Translation of the Bible* (rev. and final ed.; New York: Harper, 1935), and *The Complete Bible: An American Translation* (Chicago: University of Chicago Press, 1948) are worth consulting. The Authorized, or King James, Version is a monument of the English language, but contains numerous archaic expressions and is based on late and unreliable Hebrew and Greek originals. Earlier revisions of this most famous English Bible, the English Revised Version and the American Standard Version, are accurate literal translations, but not very readable.

A good and accessible edition of the Synoptic Gospels arranged in parallel columns for easy study and comparison is B. Throckmorton, Jr., ed., *Gospel Parallels: A Synopsis of the First Three Gospels* (New York: Nelson, 1957), which is based on the RSV.

A brief outline of the history of the English Bible may be found in H. M. Buck, *People of the Lord* (New York: Macmillan, 1966), pp. 613–18, 633 f. More extensive are I. M. Price, *The Ancestry of Our English Bible*

(3rd rev. ed. by W. A. Irwin and A. P. Wikgren; New York: Harper, 1956), and S. L. Greenslade (ed.), *The Cambridge History of the Bible: The West, from the Reformation to the Present Day* (Cambridge: Cambridge University Press, 1963).

II. TOOLS FOR NEW TESTAMENT STUDY

Because relatively few students will likely know or learn New Testament Greek, we shall include under II and III such aids as may be employed by the student who uses only English.

Concordances, which cite the occurrences of every significant word in the Bible, are often very helpful in determining what that word means in the New Testament or in a particular book or author. For accuracy a Greek concordance must be used, since one Greek word may be translated by several English words, while a single English word may translate more than one Greek term. A concordance of the English Bible that breaks down each English entry under the several Greek words (or Hebrew in the case of the Old Testament) translated is Robert Young, *Analytical Concordance to the Bible* (New York: Funk & Wagnalls, n.d.). Shorter and less expensive is *Cruden's Complete Concordance to the Old and New Testaments** (Philadelphia: Winston, 1949; paperback, Zondervan, *Cruden's Handy Concordance*, 1949). Alexander Cruden compiled this work some two hundred years ago, but it is still the most serviceable shorter concordance. *Nelson's Complete Concordance of the Revised Standard Version Bible*, ed. J. W. Ellison (New York: Nelson, 1957), is valuable because it is based on the standard modern translation in common use in America.

The most up-to-date dictionary of Biblical terms, names, places, etc., is *The Interpreter's Bible Dictionary*, 4 vols. (New York: Abingdon, 1962). There are several one-volume Bible dictionaries of quality, such as J. Hastings (ed.), *Dictionary of the Bible*, rev. ed. F. C. Grant and H. H. Rowley ed. (New York: Scribner's, 1963); M. S. and J. L. Miller, *Harper's Bible Dictionary* (New York: Harper, 1952); and *The Westminster Dictionary of the Bible* (Philadelphia: Westminster, 1944), originally compiled by J. D. Davis and later rewritten and revised by H. S. Gehman. For the meaning of theological terms, see A. Richardson, *A Theological Word Book of the Bible** (London: SCM, 1950; paperback, Macmillan). There are also many good Bible atlases. G. E. Wright, *The Westminster Historical Atlas to the Bible* (rev. ed.; Philadelphia: Westminster, 1956), is very widely used. Inexpensive and reliable is *The Oxford Bible Atlas,** ed. H. G. May (New York: Oxford, 1962). F. van der Meer and C. Mohrman, *Atlas of the Early Christian World*, trans. and ed. M. F. Hedlund and H. H. Rowley (New York: Nelson, 1958), provides detailed maps and information of New Testament and later times. Note also G. E. Wright, *Biblical Archaeology** (rev. ed.; Philadelphia: Westminster, 1962); the paperback version is abridged. A recent and valuable atlas is that of Y. Aharoni and M. Aui-Yonah, *The Macmillan Bible Atlas* (New York: Macmillan Co., 1968).

III. COMMENTARIES

Among the tools for New Testament study none is more important than a reliable commentary on the text. Several good commentary series should be noted. *The Interpreter's Bible*, 12 vols. (Nashville: Abingdon, 1952–57) provides reliable comment ("exegesis") on the Old and New Testaments, as well as a number of good articles. The "exposition," however, is of no value to the general reader. *Harper's* (or *Black's*) *New Testament Commentaries* (New York: Harper) is a serious but nontechnical work of recent vintage. A somewhat older commentary series of comparable format is *The Moffatt New Testament Commentary*, based upon Moffatt's translation of the New Testament (New York: Harper). *The Cambridge Bible Commentary** (Cambridge: University Press), another recent series, is based on the *New English Bible* and provides guidance for the general reader. New volumes in the comparable *New Clarendon Bible* will also be based on this translation. *The Layman's Bible Commentary* (Richmond: John Knox) is simple, but reliable. Perhaps the best one-volume commentary on the Bible is *Peake's Commentary on the Bible*, ed. M. Black and H. H. Rowley (New York: Nelson, 1962). There are modern editions of the Bible which provide brief introductory articles and notes on the text. Two of the best of these are *The Jerusalem Bible*, ed. A. Jones *et al.* (Garden City, N.Y.: Doubleday, 1966), and *The Oxford Annotated Bible*, ed. H. G. May and B. M. Metzger (New York: Oxford, 1962). The former is a new translation by Roman Catholic scholars, the latter is based on the RSV.

IV. INTRODUCTIONS

There are a number of introductions to the New Testament and similar works, many of which are quite good. Perhaps the most recent and complete technical introduction is W. G. Kümmel's revision of the Feine–Behm *Introduction to the New Testament*, trans. A. J. Mattill, Jr. (New York: Abingdon, 1966). A rewriting of an older work, it is for all practical purposes a new book. Also quite important is the extensive *Introduction to the New Testament*, ed. A. Robert and A. Feuillet and trans. P. W. Skehan *et al.* (New York: Desclee, 1965). The Kümmel book is a work of

Protestant scholarship, whereas the Robert and Feuillet volume was compiled by Roman Catholic scholars.

Among recent less technical introductions, two are particularly worth noting: R. H. Fuller, *A Critical Introduction to the New Testament* (London: Duckworth, 1966), and Willi Marxsen, *Introduction to the New Testament: An Approach to its Problems,* trans. G. Buswell (Oxford: Blackwell, 1968). Marxsen's book is designed to point up questions crucial for interpretation. An older book by M. S. Enslin, *Christian Beginnings** (New York: Harper, 1938), is still worth reading.

Several other introductory books, which are not introductions in the strict sense of the word, are also useful. H. C. Kee, F. W. Young, and K. Froelich, *Understanding the New Testament* (2d rev. ed.; Englewood Cliffs, N.J.: Prentice-Hall, 1965), and J. L. Price, *Interpreting the New Testament* (New York: Holt, Rinehart & Winston, 1961), are standard works of this sort. Also noteworthy is W. D. Davies, *Invitation to the New Testament* (Garden City, N.Y.: Doubleday, 1966), which concentrates on the Synoptic Gospels, Paul, and the Fourth Gospel.

Of the histories of earliest Christianity, the most recent is F. V. Filson, *A New Testament History* (Philadelphia: Westminster, 1964). Two important older works are H. Lietzmann, *The Beginnings of the Christian Church,** trans. B. L. Woolf (3rd ed.; London: Lutterworth, 1953; paperback, Meridan Books), and J. Weiss, *Earliest Christianity,** 2 vols., trans. F. C. Grant *et al.* (New York: Harper Torchbook, 1959). Both the Lietzmann volume and Weiss's work were originally published in English translation in 1937.

On the text and canon of the New Testament the best compact treatment is probably A. Souter, *The Text and Canon of the New Testament,* rev. C. S. C. Williams (London: Duckworth, 1954). A longer treatment of textual history and criticism is provided by B. M. Metzger, *The Text of the New Testament* (New York: Oxford, 1964).

V. NEW TESTAMENT THEOLOGY

The outstanding work on New Testament theology is still R. Bultmann, *Theology of the New Testament,** 2 vols., trans. K. Grobel (New York: Scribner's, 1951–55), which is especially notable for its treatment of the theologies of Paul and John. Of more limited scope and different perspective is O. Cullmann, *The Christology of the New Testament,* trans. S. C. Guthrie and C. A. M. Hall (rev. ed.; Philadelphia: Westminster, 1964). A valuable guide to contemporary views and works in the field of New Testament theology has been provided by R. Schnackenburg, *New Testament Theology Today,* trans. D. Askew (New York: Herder & Herder,

1963). C. H. Dodd's brief but important treatment of *The Apostolic Preaching and Its Developments* [New York: Harper, 1951 (orig. 1936)] has not lost its significance as an investigation of the earliest stages of Christian proclamation. More up-to-date and complex is R. H. Fuller, *The Foundations of New Testament Christology* (New York: Scribner's 1965), which also deals with the earliest period.

VI. HISTORY OF CRITICISM AND INTERPRETATION

For an overall view of the modern era the most convenient work is S. Neill, *The Interpretation of the New Testament, 1861–1961** (London: Oxford, 1964). For more recent research see A. M. Hunter, *Interpreting the New Testament, 1900–50* (London: SCM, 1951), and R. H. Fuller, *The New Testament in Current Study** (New York: Scribner's, 1962). A survey of the history of Biblical interpretation from earliest times is provided by R. M. Grant, *The Bible in the Church: A Short History of Interpretation** (New York: Macmillan, 1958; paperback title, *Short History of the Interpretation of the Bible*).

VII. BIBLIOGRAPHY

Since the resources for Biblical study are immense, there is a problem in selecting worthwhile and helpful works. The introductions of Robert and Feuillet and Kümmel provide extensive and reliable guidance. The journal *New Testament Abstracts*, published at Weston College, Weston. Massachusetts, catalogues and summarizes articles and important books in New Testament as they appear. J. C. Hurd, Jr., has published *A Bibliography of New Testament Bibliographies** (New York: Seabury Press, 1966), which will be of great value for the student doing a thorough piece of research. Also indispensable for such research are the bibliographical volumes on Paul, Christ and the Gospels, and the Acts of the Apostles published as volumes I (1966), VI (1966), and VII (1966) in the series "New Testament Tools and Studies," ed. B. M. Metzger (Leiden: Brill). Probably more relevant to the needs of the majority of students is F. W. Danker, *Multipurpose Tools for Bible Study* (Saint Louis: Concordia, 1960), some of which is intended to aid the student who knows the Biblical languages. Much of the discussion, however, should be helpful to the student limited to the English language.

Name and Subject Index

Biblical Index